Family Therapy

History, Theory, and Practice

Second Edition

Samuel T. Gladding

Wake Forest University

Merrill,
an imprint of Prentice Hall

Upper Saddle River, New Jersey   Columbus, Ohio

Library of Congress Cataloging-in-Publication Data

Gladding, Samuel T.
    Family therapy : history, theory, and practice/Samuel T. Gladding.—2nd ed.
      p. cm.
    Includes bibliographical references and index.
    ISBN 0-13-836396-X
    1. Family psychotherapy.   I. Title.
RC488.5.G535   1998
616.898156—dc21

96-39579
CIP

Cover art: Diana Ong/Super Stock
Editor: Kevin M. Davis
Production Editor: Stephen C. Robb
Photo Coordinator: Anthony Magnacca
Design Coordinator: Julia Zonneveld Van Hook
Text Designer: STELLARViSIONs
Cover Designer: Raymond Hummons
Production Manager: Patricia A. Tonneman
Electronic Text Management: Marilyn Wilson Phelps, Matthew Williams, Karen L.
    Bretz, Tracey B. Ward
Director of Marketing: Kevin Flanagan
Advertising/Marketing Coordinator: Julia Shough

This book was set in Century Schoolbook and Zapf Humanist 601 by Prentice Hall and was printed and bound by Quebecor Printing/Book Press. The cover was printed by Phoenix Color Corp.

© 1998, 1995 by Prentice-Hall, Inc.
Simon & Schuster/A Viacom Company
Upper Saddle River, New Jersey 07458

Photo credits: Scott Cunningham/Merrill, pp. 2, 30, 60, 90, 118, 150, 178, 208, 230, 280, 308, 338, 368, 398, 428; Anthony Magnacca/Merrill, p. 254.

Printed in the United States of America

10 9 8 7 6 5 4 3 2

ISBN: 0-13-836396-X

Prentice-Hall International (UK) Limited, *London*
Prentice-Hall of Australia Pty. Limited, *Sydney*
Prentice-Hall of Canada, Inc., *Toronto*
Prentice-Hall Hispanoamericana, S. A., *Mexico*
Prentice-Hall of India Private Limited, *New Delhi*
Prentice-Hall of Japan, Inc., *Tokyo*
Simon & Schuster Asia Pte. Ltd., *Singapore*
Editora Prentice-Hall do Brasil, Ltda., *Rio de Janeiro*

To my family,
especially my parents
Gertrude Barnes Templeman Gladding
and
Russell Burton Gladding
who taught me by example
how to handle adversity,
give love,
and work for the greater good.

Preface

Therapeutic work with families is a recent scientific phenomenon but an ancient art. Throughout human history, designated persons in all cultures have helped couples and families cope, adjust, and grow. In the United States, the interest in assisting families within a healing context is a twentieth century movement. Family life has always been of interest, but because of economic, social, political, and spiritual values, little direct intervention was made by outsiders into ways of helping family functioning until the 1920s. Now, there are literally thousands of professionals who focus their attention and skills on improving family dynamics and relationships.

In examining how professionals work to assist families, it must be remembered that there are as many ways of offering help as there are families. However, the most widely recognized methods are counseling, therapy, educational enrichment, and prevention. The general umbrella term for remediation work with families is *family therapy*. This concept includes the type of work done by professionals who identify themselves as family therapists, family counselors, and family psychologists.

Family therapy is not a perfect term; politically it gets bantered about by a number of professional associations such as the American Association for Marriage and Family Therapy (AAMFT), the American Counseling Association (ACA), the American Psychological Association (APA), and the National Association of Clinical Social Works (ASCSW). Physicians who treat families also debate this term, as well as whether as doctors they are "family therapists" or engaged in the practice of medicine and therefore "family medical specialists." For purposes of this book, the generic term *family therapy* is used because of its wide acceptance among the publics and professionals who engage in the practice of helping families. Within this term, some aspects of educational enrichment and prevention are included.

As a comprehensive text, this book focuses on multiple aspects of family therapy. Part I introduces the reader to the various ways that families develop and the characteristics of healthy and dysfunctional families. Part II examines the rationale and history of family therapy, its general processes, and the main theoretical approaches to therapeutically working with families: psychoanalytic, Bowen, experiential, behavioral and cognitive-behavioral, structural, strategic, systemic (Milan), solution-focused, and narrative. Each theoretical chapter emphasizes the major theorists of the approach, premises, techniques, process/outcome, and unique aspects of the theory. A case illustration is provided also.

Part III examines issues and dynamics in working with special family forms—single-parent families, remarried families, and culturally diverse families—as well as the different therapeutic approaches used, according to family type and background. Finally, Part IV discusses ethical, legal, and professional issues in being a family therapist. It also explores research and assessment and current trends in family therapy, including issues clinicians can expect to confront in their practice.

In undertaking the writing of this work, I have been informed not only by massive amounts of reading in the rapidly growing field of family therapy but also by my own experiences over the past 20 years of therapeutically working with families. Both my family of origin and current family of procreation have influenced me as well. In addition, because I belong to the American Association of Marriage and Family Therapists (AAMFT), the International Association for Marriage and Family Counseling (IAMFC), and Division 43 (Family Psychology) of the American Psychological Association (APA), I have tried to view families and family therapy from the broadest base possible. Readers should find information within this work that will help them gain a clear perspective on the field of family therapy and those involved with it.

Like the authors of most books, I truly hope you as a reader enjoy the contents of this text. I have learned in the process of writing. It is my wish that when you complete your reading you will have gained a greater knowledge of family therapy, including aspects of therapy that affect you personally as well as professionally. If such is the case, then you will have benefited and possibly changed, and I, as an author, will have accomplished the task I set out to do.

Acknowledgments

I am grateful to the reviewers who spent many hours critiquing the first edition of this book: James Bitter, California State University at Fullerton; Donald Bubenzer, Kent State University; Harper Gaushell, Northeast Louisiana University; J. Scott Hinkle, University of North Carolina at Greensboro; Gloria Lewis, Loyola University of Chicago; Donald Mattson, University of South Dakota; Eugene Moan, Northern Arizona University; and Tom Russo, University of Wisconsin, River Falls.

I also gratefully acknowledge the contributions of time and insightful suggestions from reviewers for the second edition: Charles P. Barnard, University of Wisconsin—Stout; Peter Emerson, Southeastern Louisiana University; and Eugene R. Moan, Northern Arizona University.

I especially thank Virginia Perry and my graduate assistant, Michele Kielty, both of Wake Forest University, for their constructive suggestions and positive input. I am also indebted to my editor at Merrill/Prentice Hall, Kevin Davis, for his tireless effort and assistance on my behalf.

This text is dedicated to my family, especially my parents. My father died in April of 1994, at the age of 84, shortly after I completed the first edition of this text. My mother is now 86. Although she has slowed down considerably, her love and courage, along with that of my father's, have affected me positively. I know I am most fortunate.

Finally, I am grateful for the support and comfort of my wife, Claire, who has insisted throughout this effort that we talk and build our marriage. She has employed all of her communication skills, including a generous dose of humor, to help me. She has also been throughout these years my partner, friend, and lover in the raising of our three children: Benjamin, Nathaniel, and Timothy.

Samuel T. Gladding

Contents

P A R T   T W O

Therapeutic Approaches to Working with Families   59

P A R T   T H R E E

Special Populations in Family Therapy   279

16 Current Trends in Family Therapy   429

UNDERSTANDING FAMILIES

Individual and Family Life Cycles

He was as nervous as a cat
in a room full of rockers
stiffly dressed in formal black
uptight, and afraid of moving quickly
least he break a button or the mood from the organ music.

She was serene
as if living a dream from childhood
dressed in layers of white with a lilac bouquet
unable to conceal her contentment
she remained poised amid the quiet
of assembled excitement.

Together they exchanged formal wedding vows,
homemade bands, and brief, expectant glances.

Then numbed, as if by novocaine,
they slowly greeted guests and themselves anew
As they whispered good-bye to innocence
and hello to the opening of a marriage.

Gladding, 1993

F amilies have historically played an important part in the life and development of people and nations. The origin of families "dates back to prehistoric times when our hominid ancestors developed the original family unit. Although the family has evolved, it has maintained many of its original functions. It produces and socializes children, acts as a unit of economic cooperation, gives us significant roles as children, husbands, wives, and parents, and provides a source of intimacy" (Strong & DeVault, 1986, p. 4). Furthermore, it provides some of the deepest and most satisfactory emotional experiences of life, such as love, devotion, attachment, belonging, fun, and joy (Framo, 1996).

The early Egyptians considered the royal family so important that they encouraged marriages among kin. In Chinese dynasties, family life was crucial to the survival of power and empires; consequently, marriages were arranged. In medieval Europe, powerful families interwed in order to rule and maintain wealth. As a result, certain families, such as the Hapsburgs, enjoyed great success in accumulating wealth and power.

Throughout time, social and economic factors have forced modifications in the customs governing family life. New rules have been established and/or abandoned as a result of societal changes resulting from such events as revolutions, economic turmoil, or natural disasters. For example, in the late 1800s the United States made a major transition from an agricultural to an industrial society. This socioeconomic change altered the lives of American families. "Industrial workers of agricultural backgrounds exchanged their rural 'freedom' of flexible schedules, lack of control over environmental uncertainties on their work effort, and social isolation of rural living for regimented time schedules, lack of control over extreme and tedious work conditions, and city living. . . . In large measure, this shift resulted in an exchange of independence and economic self-reliance for social and economic dependence within families" (Orthner, Bowen, & Beare, 1990, p. 18).

In examining families and how to work with them, a professional must explore historical, societal, economic, and governmental factors that have had an impact on family life over time. This knowledge includes seeing the systemic interaction of personalities, communities, and events. It involves an appreciation for the tension that is within the structure of families for dealing with outside environmental forces and internal relationship difficulties. After all, "families do not dance alone or in isolation" (Stevenson, 1994, p. 39). Take, for example, the following case.

CASE ILLUSTRATION

THE HARDY FAMILY

The Hardy family requested family therapy because of a promiscuous and defiant teenage daughter. Upon further investigation, the therapist found that the father lost his job 2 years ago, and since then the family has been strapped for money. Currently, they are receiving food stamps and live in public housing. In addition, the family has moved from a small town to a large city, where they know very few people. The mother's health has declined to the point that she is now almost an invalid. In addition, the younger brother of the identified patient has taken on a star student role and is the antithesis of his sister, who is being teased by her classmates in high school about her looks, poor dress, and lack of ability.

If the family therapist makes the mistake of ignoring the economic, social, health, and historical factors the Hardy family bring into therapy, he or she probably may not be able to offer them any meaningful help. It is only when the therapist takes all the interactive variables the family brings into account and looks at how each member influences others and the family as a whole that a useful intervention can be designed and delivered. Basically, individuals and families are like a mobile—the movement of each part has an impact on the entire structure. This type of systemic interrelatedness governed by rules, sequences, and feedback is known as cybernetics. The term *cybernetics* was introduced as a concept to family therapy by Gregory Bateson (1971). It is artificial to try to isolate individual and family life cycles from one another or to separate interactions in a "freeze frame" fashion.

In essence, understanding the various developmental and systemic nuances of family life is the first step in the process of becoming a family therapist. The second step involves becoming knowledgeable about the dynamics of individual and family life cycles. Families share universal and unique functions. Universally, they provide a structure for sexual, reproductive, economic, and educational endeavors (Cavan, 1969). Defining and appreciating the global and essential components of families, such as their **subsystems** (i.e., parents, children) and behavior patterns, in various contexts is essential. Families attend to the specific needs of all or some of their members for better or worse.

This chapter tackles the task of exploring how a family's form and context play a part in its well-being. Life cycles are examined from both a developmental and a systems perspective. An attempt is made to interconnect aspects of growth and interaction among family members.

What Is a Family?

Ideas about what a family is and how it should be structured vary across cultures and are constantly changing (Gullotta, Adams, & Alexander, 1986). In America, "families have been changing since the first settlers arrived on the shores of the new world" (Bird & Sporakowski, 1992, p. xiv). For some, the family is blood-related kin. For others it is anyone who is psychologically connected. For yet others, the family is composed of people living in the same house or neighborhood. In essence, the definition of a family is not clear. It varies according to cultural groups. Getting a consensus of what constitutes a family is difficult at best.

In formulating a definition of a family, there are inclusive as well as exclusive elements to consider. The U.S. Bureau of the Census defines a **family** as "a group of two or more persons related by birth, marriage, or adoption and residing together in a household" (U.S. Bureau of the Census, 1991, p. 5). This broad definition includes people who never marry, those who marry and never have children, those whose marriages end in divorce or death, and a variety of nontraditional family arrangements, such as the estimated "3.4 million children in America . . . growing up in households headed by one or more grandparents" (Copeland, 1995, p. 275). This definition of *family* is the one used in this book. It allows for maximum flexibility and fosters an understanding of the different forms of family life available, without describing each in great detail. This definition also engenders an appreciation of persons within family units, as well as the systems of governance under which families operate.

Overall, families are characterized by economic, physical, social, and emotional functions. There is a dual emphasis on fostering the development of individuals within families while simultaneously offering family members stability, protection, and preservation of the family unit structure (Burr, Hill, Nye, & Reiss, 1979; Strong & DeVault, 1995). An example of these emphases and what they foster can be seen in the Temple family. The Temple family is composed of a stepfather, a biological mother, and two daughters, ages 11 and 9. Both the mother and stepfather work outside the home to provide economic and physical support for themselves and the children. In addition, the mother makes sure the daughters behave properly by monitoring the time and people with whom she allows them to socialize. She listens and reflects with them as well and has enrolled them in gymnastics and music classes. The family routine of supper, homework, and television is run by the clock and strictly monitored. However, the parents take a night out once a week to bowl and enjoy themselves as a couple. Although there are disagreements in the family, there is also balance.

The **nuclear family** (a core unit of husband, wife, and their children) has traditionally been seen as the main provider of socialization for the young and as a preserver of cultural traditions (Scanzoni & Scanzoni, 1988). This family type has also been viewed as the social grouping in which society sanctions sexual relationships. However, the traditional nuclear family household is shrinking as a percentage of family types in the United States and, in 1993, comprised 28% of all families (U.S. Bureau of the Census, 1993). Of the more than 67 million families in the United States, only a fraction over 19 million of them are biologically intact families (i.e., nuclear families with original parents and children).

Many alternative family life styles have emerged and are now competing for recognition as legitimate and healthy life styles. "It no longer makes sense to refer to what is 'typical' when speaking of American family life. More accurately, we need to consider varying types of families—with diverse organizational patterns, styles of living, and living arrangements" (Goldenberg & Goldenberg, 1994, p. 6). Consequently, in discussing the term *family,* an appreciation of differences works best. Among the many family forms outside the nuclear model, the following are referred to most often: (1) single parent, (2) remarried (i.e., blended, step), (3) dual career, (4) extended (three generational), and (5) childless. Family life is part and parcel of most people who have wed, never married, or who are living in alternative family arrangements.

Individual and Family Development

Development is a powerful factor in individuals and in families. The process is often uneven, with alternating times of growth and regression. In examining the concept of development, the factors of time and stages must be addressed. In the broadest sense, development is a "life course." As such, it refers to three different time dimensions in human life: individual time, social time, and historical time (Elder, 1975). **Individual time** is defined as the span of life between one's birth and death. Notable individual achievements are often highlighted in this perspective, for example, being recognized as "teacher of the year." **Social time** is characterized by landmark social events such as marriage, parenthood, and retirement. Family milestones are a central focus here. **Historical time** is the era in which people live. It consists of forces that affect and shape humanity at a particular point in time, such as during economic depression or war. For example, a Vietnam veteran may still be angry about government decisions involving the Vietnam War, and a survivor of the Great Depression may still hoard money and be distrustful of banks. In both cases, memories of time influence present life styles (see Figure 1.1).

Everyone is influenced by the three dimensions of time, both concurrent[l]y and sequentially. The term *life cycle* is used in this text, instead of *life cou* to describe life events. Life cycle presents an active way to conceptually p·

Figure 1.1
Three different time dimensions in human life.

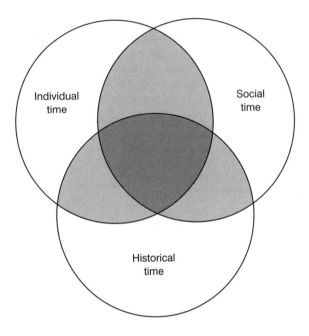

Individual time

Social time

Historical time

time in human development. It denotes the continuous development of people over time.

Life cycles have been formulated for both individuals and families. Neither people nor families develop or interact in isolation from each other. Rather, their life cycles often juxtapose and intertwine. Interactions with family members, both living and dead, influence the course of one's life (Bowen, 1978; Okun, 1984). For example, the choice of career and professional development is frequently connected with one's family life and history. Take the case of a 39-year-old single woman who was named after her maiden aunt, a former school teacher. This woman has always valued education. She turned down dates in college in order to devote more time to her studies, and now her primary focus has paid off: She has been promoted to a full professor at a major university. Her life up to this point parallels her aunt's. In examining her life after her latest academic achievement, she continues to take her cues from the life of her namesake. She may wonder about marriage or adopting a child. If she were to elect either of these routes, she would deviate from the life pattern she set in motion. Such a change would not be impossible but would require more effort because she has no family role model to follow.

Individual Life Cycle Development

Up until the 1970s, the word *development* usually referred to an individual. Part of the reason is attributable to the popularization of Erik Erikson's (1950,

1959, 1968) theory on human growth and development. Erikson was a pioneer in describing human life in terms of "stages," sequential developmental occurrences. Following Erikson's lead, Daniel Levinson (1978), Roger Gould (1972, 1978), and Gail Sheehy (1977, 1981) proposed adult developmental stages that focus on the individual. Indirectly reinforcing this personal emphasis has been the concentration in the helping professions on counseling individuals. With the exceptions of social work and marriage and family therapy, most helpers work on a one-to-one basis (Gladding, 1996).

From an individual point of view, people face predictable **developmental crises** (i.e., times of turmoil and opportunity) throughout their life spans. These times involve such events as aging, retirement, birth, and marriage. It is important to recognize how people handle and adjust to these events. The early and later phases of life and the tasks that are faced during these times result in either failure or success on many levels. Erikson's (1950, 1959, 1968) first five stages specifically focus on the formation of the person into a competent individual with adequate skills and identity. These stages are sequential, with individuals having to achieve a percentage of accomplishment in one stage before they can proceed to take on the goals of the next (Allen, 1990). The stages and their tasks are as follows:

Stage	Age	Task
1. Trust vs. mistrust	1st year	Emphasis on satisfying basic physical and emotional needs
2. Autonomy vs. shame/doubt	2 to 3 years	Emphasis on exploration and developing self-reliance
3. Initiative vs. guilt	4 to 5 years	Emphasis on achieving a sense of competence and initiative
4. Industry vs. inferiority	6 to 12 years	Emphasis on setting and attaining personal goals
5. Identity vs. role confusion	12 to 18 years	Emphasis on testing limits, achieving a self-identity

The last three stages of Erikson's eight-part developmental scheme are more interpersonally based. They have not been elaborated on much until recently. The processes involved in these final stages are intimacy, generativity, and wisdom. They are tied to and dovetail with family life processes. The satisfaction people receive from intimate relationships goes a long way in influencing what they will do in helping prepare the way for the next generation. Intimacy and generativity consequently relate to the total quality of life and how persons integrate overall life experiences in a healthy or unhealthy manner (Allen, 1990). Briefly, these stages can be described as follows:

Stage	Age	Task
6. Intimacy vs. isolation	18 to 35 years	Emphasis on achieving intimate interpersonal relationships
7. Generativity vs. stagnation	35 to 65 years	Emphasis on helping next generation, being productive
8. Integrity vs. despair	65+ years	Emphasis on integration of life activities, feeling worthwhile

According to Erikson (1968), there are other factors, in addition to the initial achievement of identity, that are important to the formation of a family. These factors, which typically increase as a person matures, are intimacy, productivity, and integration. As individuals grow into adulthood, they are challenged and tested "by new conflicts that must be mastered" (Lorton & Lorton, 1984, p. 454). These conflicts come in the form of interactions with others in leisure and work settings.

Family Life Development

The *family life cycle* is generally the term used to describe developmental trends within the family over time (Carter & McGoldrick, 1988). This model includes all dimensions of the individual life course but emphasizes the family as a whole. Inherent in this model is tension between the person as an individual and the family as a system. Like other views, the family life cycle emphasizes some stages and aspects of life more than others. It should be stressed that what is considered an appropriate family life cycle is a social/cultural variable. Therefore, the family life cycle of many families in the United States that is outlined here is not universally accepted.

The initial version of the family life cycle was proposed by Evelyn Duvall (1977) in 1956. This model has lost some of its potency over the years as the traditional nuclear families exemplified in it have decreased in number and influence. New models have replaced Duvall's original concept and are more relevant for conceptualizing family life today. Among these are the life cycle of the intact middle-class, nuclear family; the life cycle of the single parent family; and the life cycle of the blended family. The life cycle of the intact middle-class, nuclear family is highlighted here. (The life cycles of single parent families and blended families are discussed in later chapters.)

Carter and McGoldrick (1988) outline a six-stage cycle of the intact middle-class, nuclear family, which begins with the unattached adult and continues through retirement: (1) single young adults—leaving home; (2) the new couple; (3) families with young children; (4) families with adolescents; (5) families launching children and moving on; and (6) families in later life. Each of the stages of this life cycle involve key adjustments, tasks, and changes that must be accomplished if the individual, family as a whole, and specific family members are going to survive and thrive. Not all intact nuclear families go through all of the stages in this model. Yet for those who do, the crucial aspects of their lives can be conceptualized as follows.

Single Young Adults—Leaving Home

The first stage is one that individual and family life cycle theorists both emphasize. A major task of this period is to disconnect and reconnect with one's family on a different level while simultaneously establishing one's self as a person (Haley, 1980). Developing such an identity—what Murray Bowen (1978) calls "a 'solid self' (i.e., a sense of one's own beliefs and convictions that are not simply adaptive to others)"—is difficult at best and requires emotional maturity (Gerson, 1995, p. 96).

Being single requires a person to strike a balance between a career and/or marriage ambitions and a desire for personal autonomy. However, being single is now a more accepted status than it was in the past, and its popularity as a life style appears to be growing (Corey & Corey, 1997). For example, in 1990 the number of single adults over the age of 18 in the United States population, when compared with 1970, increased for women from 32% to 40% and for men from 22% to 36%, creating a total single population of 22 million (Holland, 1992; U.S. Bureau of the Census, 1991). At the same time only 61% of adult Americans were married compared with a record high of 74% in 1960 (Usdansky, 1992). In 1995, over 24 million Americans lived alone, and the number is expected to increase to 31 million by 2010 (Carey & Bryant, 1996).

Singlehood is a viable alternative to marriage. "Indeed, singles are usually the second-happiest group (married couples being the happiest), ranking above homosexual couples, unmarried couples, and others. . . . Singlehood can be as fulfilling as marriage, depending on the needs and interests of the individual" (Gullotta et al, 1986, p. 172). Being single and mentally healthy requires that individuals establish social networks, find meaning in their work or avocations, and live a balanced life physically and psychologically. Singles must also develop coping strategies so as not to become distressed (Kleinke, 1991). Living a healthy single life in the United States requires making adjustments to cultural demands and realizing that culture is a phenomenon to which one must accommodate.

A major challenge for singles is overcoming internal and external pressures to marry. They must also find ways to deal with loneliness. On the other hand, the personal freedom to choose one's actions is a major attraction and benefit to this style of life.

Issues that are likely to prompt singles to seek family therapy are those connected with:

- a weak personal sense of self
- the inability to emotionally and/or physically separate from one's family of origin
- a lack of social skills to establish significant relationships with others

The New Couple

The new-couple relationship begins with courtship, the period when individuals test their compatibility with others through dating. This process may involve a number of partners before one becomes committed to marriage. Secure men tend to become involved with secure women, and anxious women tend to become involved with less committed and more disengaged men (Lopez, 1995). Generally, individuals tend "to be most comfortable with others who are at the same or similar developmental level" (Lorton & Lorton, 1984, p. 456). That is one reason why relationships between dissimilar people rarely last. Environmental, psychological, and situational factors can also hinder people's adjustment to marriage (see Figure 1.2).

In marriage, men seem to benefit the most; their mental health generally improves. However, for women the reverse may occur. Single women, as a rule, have better mental and physical health than their counterparts (Apter, 1985). The reason is related to a number of variables including the fact that some women who are emotionally unstable may marry, a phenomenon that is not as likely to occur with emotionally unstable men. In addition, newly married women may cater to the wishes of their husbands at the expense of meeting their own needs.

Figure 1.2

Factors that negatively influence marriage.

From *The Changing Family Life Cycle: A Framework for Family Therapy* (2nd ed.) by Betty Carter and Monica McGoldrick, 1988. Copyright Allyn & Bacon. Reprinted by permission.

1. The couple meets or marries shortly after a significant loss.
2. One or both partners wish to distance from family of origin.
3. The family backgrounds of each spouse are significantly different (religion, education, social class, ethnicity, age, etc.).
4. The couple has incompatible sibling constellations.
5. The couple resides either extremely close to or at a great distance from either family of origin.
6. The couple is dependent on either extended family financially, physically, or emotionally.
7. The couple marries before age 20 or after age 30.
8. The couple marries after an acquaintanceship of less than 6 months or after more than 3 years of engagement.
9. The wedding occurs without family or friends present.
10. The wife becomes pregnant before or within the first year of marriage.
11. Either spouse has a poor relationship with his or her siblings or parents.
12. Either spouse considers his or her childhood or adolescence as an unhappy time.
13. Marital patterns in either extended family were unstable.

In general, the early stages of a couple relationship are characterized by idealization. Both men and women in marriage initially idealize each other and relate accordingly. This phenomenon is likely to dissipate naturally to some degree over the course of a marriage, although there is some evidence that individuals who report a high level of marital satisfaction also maintain a high level of idealistic distortion about their marriages and spouses—that is, they report them to be better than they actually are (Fowers, Lyons, & Montel, 1996).

Overall, the new-couple stage of the family life cycle is one of adjustment and adaptation. For example, new couples must learn how to share space, meals, and work, leisure, and sleep activities. They must accommodate to each other's wishes, requests, and fantasies. This process takes time, energy, good will, and the ability to compromise. For example, Will must understand that his new wife, Jane, takes longer to get dressed than he does. At the same time, Jane must take into consideration that Will is more carefree about taking responsibility for the upkeep of the house than she is.

It is not surprising that this stage of marriage is one of the most likely times for couples to divorce due to an inability of individuals to resolve differences. It is also often seen as a time of life when couples experience the greatest amount of satisfaction, especially if they later have children (Glenn & McLanahan, 1982). The new couple is free to experiment with life and to engage freely in a wide variety of activities. Financial and time constraints are the two main limitations for couples at this time.

Issues that are likely to prompt new couples to seek family therapy are those connected with:

- the inability to adjust to living as a couple instead of as an individual
- difficulty with relatives, either family of origin or in-laws
- the inability to work through interpersonal issues, such as developing adequate or optimal communication patterns

Families with Young Children
Becoming a parent is a physical, psychological, and social event that alters a couple's life style dramatically. The arrival of a child has an impact on a couple's lifestyle (e.g., place of residence), marital relationship (e.g., sexual contact), and paternal/maternal stress (e.g., new demands) (Hughes & Noppe, 1991). When a newborn enters a family, the family becomes unbalanced, at least temporarily. Couples have to adjust the time they spend working outside the house, socializing with friends, and engaging in recreational activities. They also have to arrange between themselves who will take responsibility for the child, as well as when, where, and how this responsibility will be met. A crucial task in caring for an infant is ensuring an enduring attachment bond occurs (Bowlby, 1988). In the process of caregiving, a rebalancing occurs between husbands and wives in regard to their investment of time, energy, and focus (Bradt, 1988).

After attachment is achieved, other important tasks families in this stage must accomplish are those connected with meeting the physical and psychological demands involved in having preschool children. This challenge becomes especially great when both partners within a marriage are working outside the home, which is the case with over 55% of the couples in the United States with children under the age of 6 (Bradt, 1988). In such arrangements, husbands are more involved in child care than the norm, but it is women who still carry the burden of being the primary caregivers (Darling-Fisher & Tiedje, 1990).

Other aspects of family life where adjustments must be made include relationships with extended family, demands of work, use of leisure, and finances. Often there are strains and tension in one or more of these areas. "The strength of the marital bond (i.e., marital satisfaction) goes a long way toward mediating stress and time constraints associated with the presence of children and work" (Giblin, 1994, p. 50). Overall, marital satisfaction tends to go down with each child that is added to a family (see Figure 1.3) (Mattessich & Hill, 1987).

Issues that are likely to prompt families with young children to seek family therapy are those connected with:

- "the fallout that accompanies the necessary reorganization of relationships and activities" of the married couple
- "the establishment of controls" for a young child (Minuchin, 1995, p. 115)

Families with Adolescents

Couples who have adolescents must take care of themselves, their relationship, their teenagers, and often their aging parents (Hughes & Noppe, 1991). Because of the squeeze they may be in psychologically and physically, they are sometimes referred to as the **sandwich generation**. This is one of the most active and exciting times in the family life cycle. It is filled with turbulence that varies across

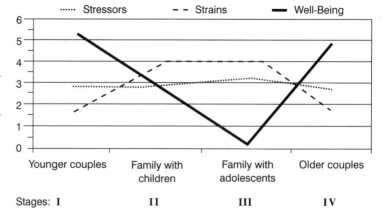

Figure 1.3

Stressors, strains, and well-being across the family life cycle.

From "Life Cycle and Family Development" by P. Mattessich and R. Hill, in *Handbook of Marriage and the Family* (p. 447), edited by M. Sussman and S. K. Steinmetz, 1987, New York: Plenum. Copyright Plenum Press. Reprinted by permission.

families (Ellis, 1986). Some families may have trouble in setting limits, defining relationships, and taking adequate care of one another. Others do just fine.

The most obvious sign of stress in families with adolescents is seen in the number and kinds of disagreements between parents and teens. Increased family conflict and tension often occur during the time adolescents are in the family (Worden, 1992). The reasons for this increased conflict and tension are numerous. For one, "in families with adolescents, there seems to be a difficulty on the part of parents to make a distinction between what they want for their youngsters and what their youngsters want for themselves. This leads to parents' unwillingness to let youngsters make decisions for themselves even if they are good decisions" (Dickerson & Zimmerman, 1992, p. 341).

A second reason for the rise of tension in these families is related to the process of adolescence itself. At this time of life, young adults express more of a desire and an assertiveness to be autonomous and independent (Collins, Newman, & McKenry, 1995; Fishman, 1988). Peer groups and siblings become more important for them, and parental influence decreases while conflicts with parents increase. Yet, because adolescents are limited in experience, "they are restrained from seeing the multitude of possibilities available to them and are vulnerable to others' ideas . . . [which they] fight against" (Dickerson & Zimmerman, 1992, p. 344). In response to this situation, families "must establish qualitatively different boundaries . . . Parents can no longer maintain complete authority" (McGoldrick & Carter, 1982, p. 183). Families with adolescents also need to facilitate the recognition and acceptance of differences of family members (Worden, 1992).

If all goes well during this time in the family life cycle, adolescents develop what is known as a "planful competence," which entails having a reasonably realistic understanding of their intellectual abilities, social skills, and personal emotional responses in interrelationship with others (Clausen, 1993). No environmental influence in the preadolescent years is as important to the development of adolescent planful competence as parenting. "Significant influences include parents paying attention to the child, providing intellectual stimulation, being supportive rather than abusive, involving the child in decision making, and conducting consistent disciplining" (Nurse, 1994, p. 36). Fathers who are as involved with their adolescents as mothers help raise psychologically healthier children who have less delinquent behavior and who obtain more education (Elias, 1996).

Yet, parenting may change during this stage as the couple relationship changes. "In the early afternoon of life—the forties, usually—many couples' relationships undergo a kind of sea change. [Either] the partners start to move closer, in ways that were not possible earlier in the marriage, or a huge amount of emotional distance begins to develop" (Scarf, 1992, p. 53). This change is related to the aging process and heightened feelings of vulnerability, "hers, about her desirability and attractiveness; his, about his virility and about physical survival itself" (Scarf, 1992, p. 53). If the couple treat each other with tenderness, empathy, and understanding, they become stronger partners and comfort each other. If, on the other hand, the couple misread each other and do not understand the physiological changes occurring, they are likely to be rejecting and hostile toward each other.

Issues that are likely to prompt families with adolescents to seek family therapy are those connected with:

- conflict between parents and their teenage offspring, such as the setting of limits and the expression of opinions
- detachment or anger over the couple relationship as partners age developmentally and psychologically and realize dreams and opportunities are slipping away
- stress related to the care of aging parents and/or the demands of work and family life

Launching Children and Moving On

As children leave home for college, careers, marriage, or other options, parents face the so-called **empty nest**—life for couples without childrearing responsibilities. The percentage of empty nesters is increasing in the United States and will include 59% of all families by 2010, with the aging Baby Boomer generation fueling the trend (Carey & Rechin, 1996). This time is ideal for couples to rediscover each other and have fun together. It is also a stage of vulnerability where couples may split up.

Most middle-aged women at this stage "are likely to be energetically attending to their own interests and thankful for the freedom to pursue them at last" (Scanzoni & Scanzoni, 1988, p. 535). For some women, who have mainly defined themselves as mothers and invested heavily in their children, the empty nest can be a time of sadness. In such situations, depression, despondency, and divorce may occur (Strong & DeVault, 1992).

For men, the empty nest usually corresponds to midlife. At this time, men may focus on "their physical bodies, marriages, and occupational aspirations," as well as the new changes in the behaviors of their wives (Scanzoni & Scanzoni, 1988, p. 540). Because few studies have focused on men and the empty nest period, there is little data to report in regard to how these men feel about the launching of their children. However, factors that correlate negatively for the happiness of men at the time of launching children are having few children, being older at the time of their children's leaving, experiencing unsatisfactory marriages, and being nurturant as fathers (Lewis, Freneau, & Roberts, 1979).

In recent years, there has been a trend for children to remain with their families of origin for longer periods of time. This failure to leave is usually due to financial problems, unemployment, or an inability or reluctance to grow up (Clemens & Axelson, 1985). When children do not leave home, the result is often increased tension between parents and the young adult. Overall, as pointed out by Haley (1973), pathological behaviors tend to surface at points in the family life cycle when the process of disengagement of one generation from another is prevented or held up.

Issues that are likely to prompt empty nesters to seek family therapy are those connected with:

- a sense of loss in regard to oneself, a marriage, or the moving out of a child
- a sense of conflict with a child who is not becoming independent enough
- a sense of frustration or anger in regard to one's marriage or career ambitions

Families in Later Life

The family in later life is usually composed of a couple who are in the final years of employment or who are in early retirement. The age range is from about 65 years and up. This stage of family life can cover a span of 20 or 30 years depending on the health of those involved. Within this group are three groups—"the **young old** (65–74), the **old old** (75–84), and the **oldest old** (85 and after)" (Anderson, 1988, p. 19).

A major concern of some members of this group is finances. Elderly couples often worry about whether they will have enough money to take care of their needs. This concern is heightened when retirement occurs. It may be especially crucial to men who stop working.

A second equally important concern of elderly couples involves health and the loss of a spouse. "Only about half of the men and women over sixty-five are married; most of the others are widowed" (Strong & DeVault, 1986, p. 301). Recovering from the loss of a spouse is a difficult and prolonged process. It is one that women are more likely to face than men. The absence or presence of extended family at such times can make a difference in how one adjusts. The preservation of a coherent sense of self in the midst of loss is the best predictor of psychological and physiological resilience for the elderly (Kaufman, 1986).

A third concern of the aging and their families is mental illness. "The incidence of psychopathology increases with age, particularly organic brain disease and functional disorders such as depression, anxiety, and paranoid states. Suicide also rises with age, with the highest rate among elderly white men" (Walsh, 1988, p. 312). Keeping mentally healthy, as well as physically healthy, is a major task of this group.

The aging family also has advantages. One of them is being a grandparent. Interacting with their children's children heightens the sensitivity of many aging couples and helps them become more aware of the need for caring (Mead, 1972). The ability to do what one wants at one's pace is another advantage of this family stage. Finally, the aging family can experience the enjoyment of having lived and participated in a number of important life cycle events. This is a time when couples can reflect on the activities they were too busy with previously.

Issues that are likely to prompt families in later life to seek family therapy are those connected with:

Table 1.1

Family Life Cycle Phases, Stages, and Crises

Phases	Family life cycle stage	Practical challenges	Emotional challenges	Relational challenges	Potential crises
Coupling	Unattached young adult	Financial independence Caretaking of self	Secure sense of self Feelings of competency	Differentiation of self from family of origin	Failure to grow up
	Family formation through coupling	Finding potential mate Economic partnership Domestic cooperation Compatibility of interests	Commitment Balancing needs and expectations of self and partner	Form stable marital unit Shifting allegiances from family of origin to new family	Failure to find a mate or commit End of "honeymoon" In-law conflict
Expansion	Family with young children	Financial obligations Organizing household for raising children	Accepting new members Nurturance Parental responsibilities	Maintaining marital unit Integrating grandparents and other relatives	Marital dissatisfaction School and behavior problems
	Family with adolescents	Less predictable routines and schedules Adolescent unavailability	Flexibility with change Sense of irrelevance Loss of control	Maintaining contact between parents and adolescent Caring for elderly parents	Adolescent rebellion
Contraction	Launching children and moving on	Financial burdens (college, weddings, etc.) New financial resources Refocus on work	Loss of family life with children Aging and death of parents	Reestablishing primacy of marriage Adult relationship with children	"Empty nest" Children returning home
	Family in later life	Uncertainties of old age: economic insecurities Medical care	Coping with loss Maintaining dignity despite decline	Maintaining adequate support systems Reconciliation	Retirement Illness and death

From "The Family Life Cycle: Phases, Stages, and Crises" by Randy Gerson, in *Integrating Family Therapy* (p. 96), edited by R. H. Mikesell, D. D. Lusterman, and S. H. McDaniel, 1995, Washington, DC: American Psychological Association. Copyright © 1995 by the American Psychological Association. Reprinted with permission.

- a lack of meaning or enjoyment related to the loss of actively working or caring for children or the death of a spouse

- a concern over adjustments in aging, such as diminished energy or facing one's own mortality

- an inability to establish good relationships with children, in-laws, or grandchildren

A summary of family life cycle phases, stages, and crises can be seen in Table 1.1.

Unifying Individual and Family Life Cycles

At first glance it would appear difficult to unite individual and family life cycles in more than a superficial way. The reason is that, outwardly, stages in the individual life cycle do not always parallel and complement those within a family's development (e.g., Erikson 1959; Gilligan, 1982; Levinson, 1978, 1986; Sheehy, 1977). The two life cycle concepts are unique because of the number of people involved in them, the diversity of tasks required in each, and gender distinctions. Yet, the differences in these ways of viewing life may not be as sharp or contrasting as they first appear.

One unifying emphasis of both the individual and family life cycle is the focus within each on growth and development. In most types of growth there is "change in the direction of greater awareness, competence, and authenticity" (Jourard & Landsman, 1980, p. 238). Within individuals and families, growth can be a conscious process that involves "courage," that is, the ability to take calculated risks without knowing the exact consequences. When planned strategies and activities are outlined and accomplished as a part of growth, persons understand the past more thoroughly, live actively and fully in the present, and envision possibilities of the future more clearly.

A second unifier of individual and family life cycles is that they can both be viewed from a systemic perspective. *Systems theory* focuses on the interconnectedness of elements within all living organisms. It is based on the work of Ludwig von Bertalanffy (1968), a biologist, who proposed that to fully understand how a living creature operates, it is necessary to see the interfunctioning of the entire unit. A person and a family are more than the separate parts that compose them. They are a whole—a system that expresses itself through an organization, rules, and repetitive patterns.

Therefore, in working with individuals and families, therapists must emphasize **circular causality,** the idea that actions are a part of "a causal chain, each influencing and being influenced by the other" (Goldenberg & Goldenberg, 1994, p. 39-40). For instance, a mother overprotects her awkward and shy daughter, who stays awkward and shy due to a lack of opportunities to do otherwise, which leads to continued overprotection, which results in more awkwardness and shyness, and so forth. This idea is the opposite of **linear causality,** in which forces are seen as moving in one direction with each action causing another. In linear causality, a mother's overprotection would be targeted as the cause of her daughter's awkwardness and shyness.

A third unifying aspect of the individual and family life cycles is that they are complementary and competitive (McGoldrick & Gerson, 1985). People within each cycle go through experiences for which they are usually developmentally ready. For example, children enter school at age 5 or 6. Most couples become parents in their late 20s or early 30s. Likewise, from interacting with their environments, the majority of individuals and families become aware of their skills and abilities. For example, from his play with peers, an adolescent may realize he is not as gifted an athlete as he previously thought. Similarly, family members may appreciate each other more from having survived a natural trauma, such as an earthquake, a hurricane, or a fire (Figley, 1989).

In the competitive realm, the needs and desires of individuals within the family and the needs of the family to sustain itself often differ. For example, a young couple might want to visit friends or relatives, but are distracted by the demands of their toddler who might prefer running around their host's house. A second area of conflict involves launching young people into the world. Sometimes these individuals are hesitant to go and resist leaving home (Haley, 1980). Both the family and the young adults suffer in the struggle that ensues.

Implications of Life Cycles for Family Therapy

Life cycles have a number of implications regarding family therapy. Some are more subtle than others, but all are important.

Match of Life Cycles Between Family and Therapist

The "fit" between a family's and a therapist's life cycles plays a major role in the process of helping a family change. Fit is an ever changing variable that fluctuates according to the ages and stages of all involved in the therapeutic process. Basically, the "life cycles of therapist and family can combine in three major ways: (1) the therapist has not yet experienced the family's stage; (2) the therapist is currently experiencing the same stage of the life cycle as the family; and (3) the therapist has already been through that stage of the life cycle. Each situation has its special flavor" (Simon, 1988, p. 108).

Empathy, understanding, and rapport may be difficult to build in cases where the therapist has not yet experienced the family's stage of development. Contempt, anxiety, or jealousy may interfere with therapists whose life cycles parallel families with whom they work. On the other hand, "fit with families gets a little easier" as therapists get older and past crucial life stages (Simon, 1988, p. 110). In such circumstances, families may feel that therapists recognize and understand their problems better. However, on the downside, therapists who are beyond the life stage of their client families may have difficulties in regard to acting too knowledgeable, dealing with ghosts of their own pasts, and being "distant, cynical, or patronizing" (Simon, 1988, p. 111).

To compensate for a lack of fit between themselves and the families they are working with, therapists of all ages can do several things. First, they can work on increasing their sensitivity to particular families. Each family differs, and therapists, regardless of age, can usually be helpful if they are attuned to the specific issues of a family. Second, therapists who do not ideally fit certain families can have their work supervised. Often, through peers and supervisors, family therapists learn ways to overcome their deficits. Finally, a lack of fit can be addressed by continuing education programs that give the therapist greater knowledge and skill in dealing with specific types of families.

Ethnicity and Life Cycle

The ethnic background of families influences their concept of life cycles and their behaviors in regard to life events. "It is important for clinicians to evaluate families in relation to their ethnic background" and to not judge them from a limited cultural perspective (McGoldrick, 1988a, p. 75). For example, different ethnic groups place more value on certain events and rituals, such as funerals, weddings, and transitions from childhood to adulthood. Types of interaction dominant in a majority culture, such as among white Americans of European descent, may not be considered appropriate in a minority culture, such as among African Americans or Asian Americans.

In therapeutic situations, families become more attuned to their ethnic backgrounds and values. In family therapy it is "important to encourage families to use their life cycle transitions to strengthen individual, family, and cultural identities" (McGoldrick, 1988a, p. 89). Through such a process, families and their members gain a greater appreciation of and sensitivity to their heritage and the role of the past in present day life.

Family therapists, regardless of their cultural backgrounds, can work with a variety of families if they attune themselves to learning about the culture and the circumstances from whence these families came. Therapists must acquire special skills as well, through both formal training and continuing education. Finally, therapists must realize that, regardless of their best efforts, gender and ethnicity differences between themselves and their clients may enhance or detract from the therapeutic experience, at least initially (Gregory & Leslie, 1996).

Illness and Life Cycles

The onset of an illness in a family member can disrupt life cycles temporarily or permanently. If the illness is acute and of short duration, the person and family may suffer only a mild setback. However, if the illness is more severe, the family and its members may be severely affected. Therefore, in examining illness and life cycles, therapists must examine the onset of the disorder, its course, the outcome, and its degree of incapacitation, if any (Rolland, 1988). For example, a progressive and chronic disease, such as Alzheimer's, can put a major strain on caretakers within a family and the family as a whole. The result may be the delay of life cycle transitions, such as marriage, and the blockage of unfinished business.

Therapeutically, it is imperative that those who work with families help them assess present ways of functioning in relationships as compared with past coping strategies (Rolland, 1988). For example, a therapist may explore with family members how they previously dealt with a family illness. Thus, therapists may better understand present family behaviors and the individuals within them. Therapists may also assist families in resolving the developmental disruptions that occur in dealing with diseases. There is a growing movement in family therapy to focus on mental and physical issues in families (Wynne, Shields, & Sirkin, 1992). To work best in this domain, family therapists must prepare themselves through direct educational and supervisory experiences.

Alcoholism, Substance Abuse, and Life Cycles

Alcoholism is a family disease. It affects "every member of the family—for years, for decades, and perhaps, for generations" (Stanton & Heath, 1995, p. 329). The disease "may be transmitted from one generation to the next. If one generation has an alcoholic, the chances increase that the next generation will also have an alcoholic. Nonalcoholic sons or daughters of alcoholics frequently marry an alcoholic and keep the intergenerational cycle functioning" (Fenell & Weinhold, 1996, p. 4).

Regardless, the abuse of alcohol and other drugs has a profound affect on life cycles. Developmental stages are altered significantly. Family members often fail to define themselves outside of the context of alcohol. In fact, families often organize themselves around alcoholism in a systemic way and enable family members to drink excessively (Bateson, 1971; Steinglass, 1979).

Similarly, families of addicts are often stuck in a life style that promotes dependency of the young and a false sense of identity known as **pseudo-individuation**. Young people in such circumstances lack basic coping skills and fail to achieve real identity. As a result, they become "competent within a framework of incompetence" (Stanton et al., 1982, p. 19).

Families with alcoholic members are frequently treated with family therapy (Edwards & Steinglass, 1995). In such treatment, alcoholism is considered a disease that the family shares for a variety of reasons, for example, as a way of coping with stress. In any case, rehabilitation involves dealing with physical, emotional, social, and vocational impairments (Fenell & Weinhold, 1996). Clinicians who realize the dysfunctional impact of alcohol and drug misuse in families can work to help family members deal with feelings (e.g., anger) and defense mechanisms (e.g., denial), once abusive drinking has stopped and the alcoholic member of the family has "dried out." Therapists can also help the family as a whole take responsibility for behaviors (Krestan & Bepko, 1988). In essence, they can help the family get back on track as a functional system by getting "involved in the treatment process" and "helping the abusing member overcome . . . addiction, rather than serving as a force that maintains it" (Van Deusen, Stanton, Scott, Todd, & Mowatt, 1982, p. 39). In the process, families are assisted in regard to developmental issues as well.

Poverty, Professionalism, and Life Cycles

As indicated throughout this chapter, individuals and families are affected by economic as well as social factors. Dual-career professional families and low-income families do not go through life cycle stages in the same way or at the same rate as other families. There is an "extreme elongation of the process of forming the family in the professional class and an extreme acceleration in the lower class" (Fulmer, 1988, p. 548).

Poverty and professionalism have several implications for family therapy. One of the most obvious is for therapists to realize that the structure of these two types of families differ. *Families in poverty* are generally larger, more dependent on kin, and maternal. Continuing poverty pushes fathers away from their children and families because these men are often working two or three jobs and are simply not available (Elias, 1996). In contrast, *families of professionals* are generally smaller, dependent on hired help, and often more individual or career focused. They can afford to buy services and engage in a number of enriching activities.

In addition to structural differences, symptom formation differs, with symptoms in poor families often connected with sudden shifts and changes in life cycle events and symptoms in professional families often connected with delays in reaching developmental milestones. The comparison of family life stages for these two types of families from ages 12 to 35 is shown in Table 1.2, as outlined by Fulmer (1988). Therapists must acquaint themselves with the issues of both types of families. To be of assistance to each, they must cognitively and psychologically learn to address their unique problems and possibilities.

Summary and Conclusion

This chapter examined different models of individual and family life cycles. Erik Erikson first popularized the idea of a life cycle through his research and writings on the eight stages of life. His work has been praised for its innovation but criticized for its limited focus on males. In recent years, other researchers, such as

Table 1.2

Comparison of Family Life Cycle Stages

Age	Professional Families	Low-Income Families
12–17	a. Prevent pregnancy b. Graduate from high school c. Parents continue support while permitting child to achieve greater independence	a. First pregnancy b. Attempt to graduate from high school c. Parent attempts strict control before pregnancy; after pregnancy, relaxation of controls and continued support of new mother and infant
18–21	a. Prevent pregnancy b. Leave parental household for college c. Adapt to parent-child separation	a. Second pregnancy b. No further education c. Young mother acquires adult status in parental household
22–25	a. Prevent pregnancy b. Develop professional identity in graduate school c. Maintain separation from parental household; begin living in serious relationship	a. Third pregnancy b. Marriage—leave parental household to establish stepfamily c. Maintain connection with kinship network
26–30	a. Prevent pregnancy b. Marriage—develop nuclear couple as separate from parents c. Intense work involvement as career begins	a. Separate from husband b. Mother becomes head of own household within kinship network
31–35	a. First pregnancy b. Renew contact with parents as grandparents c. Differentiate career and child-rearing roles between husband and wife	a. First grandchild b. Mother becomes grandmother and cares for daughter and infant

From "Lower-Income and Professional Families: A Comparison of Structure and Life Cycle Process" by R. H. Fulmer, in *The Changing Family Life Cycle* (2nd ed., p. 551), edited by B. Carter and M. McGoldrick, 1988, New York: Gardner. Reprinted by permission of the publisher.

Roger Gould, Daniel Levinson, Gail Sheehy, and Carole Gilligan, have proposed either modifications to Erikson's work or new conceptual models of development.

The idea of a family life cycle was first popularized by Evelyn Duvall in 1956, only a few years after Erikson's model was introduced. Duvall's model was based on the nuclear family of the 1950s, and most of the stage transitions are linked to the maturity of the oldest child, from infancy to young adulthood. In more recent years, as families in the United States have become more diverse, varied models of family life cycles have been proposed. The cycles of Carter and McGoldrick (1988), which cover many different forms of family life, are among the most useful. This chapter presented the six-stage model of the intact, middle-class nuclear family. This model is used for comparison with other life cycle models, including Erikson's individual life cycle model.

Individual and family life cycles intertwine at times. Events in one impact those in the other. Individual and family life cycles are similar in their emphasis on growth, development, and systemic interaction. However, they often differ in emphasis, with individual life cycles focused more narrowly and family life cycles focused more systemically. Family therapists must be aware of individual issues, as well as family issues, that are brought before them.

As a rule, family therapists should be aware of how their own individual and family life stages compare with those of their clients. They must also be sensitive to health, ethnic/cultural, and socioeconomic issues as they relate to families. A general systems perspective of individuals and families allows for such a broad-based view. It permits therapists to observe dynamics within the system of the person and family without blaming or focusing on unimportant micro-issues. Family therapists can study and receive supervision to overcome deficits they may have in regard to issues surrounding a particular type of family. Overall, the family life cycle and the variables that compose it are exciting to study and complex entities with which to work.

SUMMARY TABLE

Individual and Family Life Cycles

Families date back to prehistoric times and have played an important part in the development of persons and nations.

Social and economic forces, wars, national policies, and natural disasters have modified the structure and governance of families.

Families must be worked with from a developmental, systemic, and historical perspective. The dynamics of external and internal pressures and interactions should be taken into consideration.

What Is A Family?

The definition of a family varies across cultural settings and often changes.

The U.S. Bureau of the Census (1991, p. 5) gives a broad definition of a family as "a group of two or more persons related by birth, marriage, or adoption and residing together in a household."

Overall, families are characterized by economic, physical, social, and emotional functions. They foster development and offer stability.

Among the different types of families are nuclear, single parent, remarried, dual career, extended, and childless.

Individual and Family Development

Development is an uneven and powerful factor in families.

Three different time dimensions affect personal and family life: individual time, social time, and historical time.

The term *life cycle* is used to describe personal and family life development. These two life cycles intertwine and are interactional. It is artificial to try to isolate them.

The term *cybernetics* is used to describe the systemic interrelatedness of systems, such as life cycles, that are governed by rules and feedback.

Individual life cycle development has been popularized in the work of Erikson and others who describe human life in terms of stages. People face developmental crises in each of these stages.

The first five stages Erikson describes deal with the formation of a person as a competent individual. His final three stages are more interpersonally based.

Developmental theories have focused mainly on men, but are slowly being formulated for women as well.

The family life cycle is a social/cultural phenomenon that was first proposed by Duvall in 1956. It has been modified over the years, and there are now life cycles describing many types of families.

A family life cycle for middle-class, nuclear families proposed by Carter and McGoldrick outlines the following six stages:

1. Single young adults—tasks: to develop personal autonomy, leave home, establish a career, and develop a support group
2. The new couple—tasks: to adjust and adapt, and learn to share with partner
3. Families with young children—tasks: to adjust time, energy, and personal schedules to take care of child[ren], self, and other relationships
4. Families with adolescents—tasks: to physically and psychologically take care of self, couple relationship, child[ren], and aging parents, and successfully handle increased family tension and conflict
5. Families launching children and moving on—tasks: to rediscover each other as a couple, deal with midlife events, and let child go
6. Families in later life—tasks: to adjust to aging, loss of a spouse, and decreased energy

Unifying Individual and Family Life Cycles

Individual and family life cycles are characterized by:

- growth and development
- systemic interconnectedness of people
- complementary and competitive experiences

Implications of Life Cycles for Family Therapy

Life cycles impact family therapy through:

- the matching or fitting of the therapist's life stage(s) with that of the family
- the understanding, or lack thereof, between the therapist's ethnic background and that of the family

- the influence of the unexpected, like illness, on the stage development of the family/individual
- the negative systemic function of alcohol and drug abuse on the development of the family/individual
- the uniqueness of poverty or professionalism on the rate of recovery and the resources of the family as therapy progresses

Family therapists can overcome developmental or systemic handicaps in regard to families through education, supervision, consultation, and experience.

References

Allen, B. P. (1990). *Personal adjustment*. Pacific Grove, CA: Brooks/Cole.

Anderson, D. (1988, July/August). The quest for a meaningful old age. *Family Therapy Networker, 12,* 16–22, 72–75.

Apter, T. (1985). *Why women don't have wives*. New York: Schocken.

Bateson, G. (1971). The cybernetics of 'self': A theory of alcoholism. *Psychiatry, 34,* 1–18.

Bertalanffy, L. von (1968). *General systems theory: Foundation, development, and application*. New York: Braziller.

Bird, G., & Sporakowski, M. J. (1992). Introduction. In G. Bird & M. J. Sporakowski (Eds.), *Taking sides: Clashing views on controversial issues in family and personal relationships* (pp. x–xv). Guilford, CT: Dushkin Publishing.

Bowen, M. (1978). *Family therapy in clinical practice*. New York: Jason Aronson.

Bowlby, J. (1988). *A secure base: Parent-child attachment and healthy human development*. New York: Basic Books.

Bradt, J. O. (1988). Becoming parents: Families with young children. In B. Carter & M. McGoldrick (Eds.), *The changing family life cycle* (2nd ed., pp. 235–254). New York: Gardner.

Burr, W. R., Hill, R., Nye, F. I., & Reiss, I. L. (1979). *Contemporary theories about the family*. New York: The Free Press.

Carey, A. R., & Bryant, W. (1996, June 25). Living alone. *USA Today*, A1.

Carey, A. R., & Rechin, K. (1996, July 5–7). Nation of 'empty nests.' *USA Today*, A1.

Carter, B., & McGoldrick, M. (1988). *The changing family life cycle* (2nd ed.). New York: Gardner.

Cavan, R. S. (1969). *The American family* (4th ed.). New York: Thomas Y. Crowell Co.

Clausen, J. A. (1993). *American lives*. New York: Free Press.

Clemens, A., & Axelson, L. (1985). The not-so-empty-nest: The return of the fledgling adult. *Family Relations, 34,* 259–264.

Collins, W. E., Newman, B. M., & McKenry, P. C. (1995). Intrapsychic and interpersonal factors related to adolescent psychological well-being in stepmother and stepfather families. *Journal of Family Psychology, 9,* 433–445.

Copeland, C. C. (1995). The family: Grandparents raising grandchildren. In B. Evraiff (Ed.), *Proceedings of Counseling in the 21st Century: Fifth International Conference* (pp. 275–280). Hong Kong.

Corey, G., & Corey, M. S. (1997). *I never knew I had a choice* (6th ed.). Pacific Grove, CA: Brooks/Cole.

Darling-Fisher, C. S., & Tiedje, L. B. (1990). The impact of maternal employment characteristics on fathers' participation in child care. *Family Relations, 39,* 20–26.

Dickerson, V. C., & Zimmerman, J. (1992). Families with adolescents: Escaping problem lifestyles. *Family Process, 31,* 341–353.

Duvall, E. (1977). *Marriage and family development* (5th ed.). Philadelphia: Lippincott.

Edwards, M. E., & Steinglass, P. (1995). Family therapy treatment outcomes for alcoholism. *Journal of Marital and Family Therapy, 4,* 475–509.

Elder, G. H., Jr. (1975). Age differentiation and the life course. *Annual Review of Sociology, 1,* 165–190.

Elias, M. (1996, August 22). Teens do better when dads are more involved. *USA Today,* D1.

Ellis, G. F. (1986). Societal and parental predictors of parent-adolescent conflict. In G. K. Leigh & G. W. Peterson (Eds.), *Adolescents in families* (pp. 155–178). Cincinnati: South-Western Publishing.

Erikson, E. H. (1950). *Childhood and society.* New York: Norton.

Erikson, E. H. (1959). *Identity and the life cycle: Psychological issues.* New York: International Universities Press.

Erikson, E. H. (1968). *Identity: Youth and crisis.* New York: Norton.

Fenell, D. L., & Weinhold, B. K. (1996, March). Treating families with special needs. *Counseling and Human Development, 28,* 1–12.

Figley, C. R. (1989). *Helping traumatized families.* San Francisco: Jossey-Bass.

Fishman, H. (1988). *Treating troubled adolescents.* New York: Basic Books.

Fowers, B. J., Lyons, E. M., & Montel, K. H. (1996). Positive marital illusions: Self-enhancement or relationship enhancement? *Journal of Family Psychology, 10,* 192–208.

Framo, J. L. (1996). A personal retrospective of the family therapy field: Then and now. *Journal of Marital and Family Therapy, 22,* 289–316.

Fulmer, R. H. (1988). Lower-income and professional families: A comparison of structure and life cycle process. In B. Carter & M. McGoldrick (Eds.), *The changing family life cycle* (2nd ed., pp. 545–578). New York: Gardner.

Gerson, R. (1995). The family life cycle: Phases, stages, and crises. In R. H. Mikesell, D. Lusterman, & S. H. McDaniel (Eds.), *Integrating family therapy* (pp. 91–112). Washington, DC: American Psychological Association.

Giblin, P. (1994). Marital satisfaction. *The Family Journal, 2,* 48–50.

Gilligan, C. (1982). *In a different voice: Psychological theory and women's development.* Cambridge, MA: Harvard University Press.

Gladding, S. T. (1996). *Counseling: A comprehensive profession* (3rd ed.). Englewood Cliffs, NJ: Prentice Hall.

Gladding, S. T. (1993). *Nervous beginnings.* Unpublished manuscript.

Glenn, N., & McLanahan, S. (1982). Children and marital happiness: A further specification of the relationship. *Journal of Marriage and the Family, 43,* 63–72.

Goldenberg, H., & Goldenberg, I. (1994). *Counseling today's families* (2nd ed.). Pacific Grove, CA: Brooks/Cole.

Gould, R. L. (1972). The phases of adult life: A study in developmental psychology. *American Journal of Psychiatry, 129,* 521–531.

Gould, R. L. (1978). *Transformations,* New York: Simon and Schuster.

Gregory, M. A., & Leslie, L. A. (1996). Different lenses: Variations in clients' perception of family therapy by race and gender. *Journal of Marital and Family Therapy, 22,* 239–251.

Gullotta, T., Adams, G., & Alexander, S. (1986). *Today's marriages and families.* Pacific Grove, CA: Brooks/Cole.

Haley, J. (1973). *Uncommon therapy: The psychiatric techniques of Milton Erickson, M.D.* New York: Norton.

Haley, J. (1980). *Leaving home.* New York: McGraw-Hill.

Holland, B. (1992, July/August). One's company. *Family Therapy Networker, 16,* 45–49.

Hughes, F. P., & Noppe, L. D. (1991). *Human development across the life span.* New York: Macmillan.

Jourard, S. M., & Landsman, T. (1980). *Healthy personality* (4th ed.). New York: Macmillan.

Kaufman, S. R. (1986). *The ageless self: Sources of meaning in later life.* Madison, WI: University of Wisconsin Press.

Kleinke, C. L. (1991). *Coping with life challenges.* Pacific Grove, CA: Brooks/Cole.

Krestan, J., & Bepko, C. (1988). Alcohol problems and the family life cycle. In B. Carter & M. McGoldrick (Eds.), *The changing family life cycle* (2nd ed., pp. 483–511). New York: Gardner.

Levinson, D. J. (1978). *The seasons of a man's life.* New York: Knopf.

Levinson, D. J. (1986). A conception of adult development. *American Psychologist, 41,* 3–13.

Lewis, R., Freneau, P., & Roberts, C. (1979). Fathers and the postparental transition. *Family Coordinator, 28,* 514–520.

Lopez, F. G. (1995). Attachment theory as an integrative framework for family counseling. *The Family Journal, 3,* 11–17.

Lorton, J. W., & Lorton, E. L. (1984). *Human development through the lifespan*. Pacific Grove, CA: Brooks/Cole.

Mattessich, P., & Hill, R. (1987). Life cycle and family development. In M. B. Sussman & S. K. Steinmetz (Eds.), *Handbook of marriage and the family* (p. 447). New York: Plenum.

McGoldrick, M. (1988a). Ethnicity and the family life cycle. In B. Carter & M. McGoldrick (Ed.), *The changing family life cycle* (2nd ed., pp. 69–90). New York: Gardner.

McGoldrick, M., & Carter, E. A. (1982). The family life cycle. In F. Walsh (Ed.), *Normal family processes* (pp. 167–195). New York: Guilford.

McGoldrick, M., & Gerson, R. (1985). *Genograms in family assessment*. New York: Norton.

Mead, M. (1972). *Blackberry winter*. New York: Morrow.

Minuchin, P. (1995). Children and family therapy: Mainstream approaches and the special care of the multicrisis poor. In R. H. Mikesell, D. Lusterman, & S. H. McDaniel (Eds.), *Integrating family therapy* (pp. 113–140). Washington, DC: American Psychological Association.

Nurse, A. R. (1994, Spring). A 60-year study of normals through time: Implications for practice. *The Family Psychologist, 10*, 35–36, 38.

Okun, B. F. (1984). *Working with adults: Individual, family, and career development*. Pacific Grove, CA: Brooks/Cole.

Orthner, D. K., Bowen, G. L., & Beare, V. G. (1990). The organization family: A question of work and family boundaries. *Marriage and family review, 15*, 15–36.

Rolland, J. S. (1988). Chronic illness and the family life cycle. In B. Carter & M. McGoldrick (Eds), *The changing family life cycle* (2nd ed., pp. 433–456). New York: Gardner.

Scanzoni, L. D., & Scanzoni, J. (1988). *Men, women, and change* (3rd ed.). New York: McGraw-Hill.

Scarf, M. (1992, July/August). The middle of the journey. *Family Therapy Networker, 16*, 51–55.

Sheehy, G. (1977). *Passages*. New York: Bantam.

Sheehy, G. (1981). *Pathfinders*. New York: Bantam.

Simon, R. M. (1988). Family life cycle issues in the therapy system. In B. Carter & M. McGoldrick (Eds.), *The changing family life cycle* (2nd ed., pp. 107–117). New York: Gardner.

Stanton, M. D., & Heath, A. W. (1995). Family treatment of alcohol and drug abuse. In R. H. Mikesell, D. D. Lusterman, & S. H. McDaniel (Eds.), *Integrating family therapy* (pp. 529–544). Washington, DC: American Psychological Association.

Stanton, M. D., Todd, T. C., Heard, D. B., Kirschner, S., Kleiman, J. I., Mowatt, D. T., Riley, P, Scott, S. M., & Van Deusen, J. M. (1982). A conceptual model. In M. D. Stanton, T. C. Todd, & Associates (Eds.), *The family therapy of drug abuse and addiction* (pp. 7–30). New York: Guilford.

Steinglass, P. (1979). Family therapy with alcoholics: A review. In E. Kaufman & P. N. Kaufman (Eds.), *Family therapy of drug and alcohol abuse* (pp. 147–186). New York: Gardner.

Stevenson, H. C. (1994, Spring). Research on African-American family life: Learning to interpret the dance. *The Family Psychologist, 10*, 38–40, 46.

Strong, B., & DeVault, C. (1986). *The marriage and family experience* (3rd ed.). St. Paul: West Publishing.

Strong, B., & DeVault, C. (1992). *The marriage and family experience* (5th ed.). St. Paul: West Publishing.

Usdansky, M. L. (1992, July 17). Wedded to the single life. *USA Today*, 8A.

U.S. Bureau of the Census. (1991). *Statistical abstracts of the United States 1991* (111th ed.). Washington, DC: U.S. Government Printing Office.

U.S. Bureau of the Census. (1993). *Statistical abstract of the United States, 1993* (113th ed.). Washington, DC: U.S. Government Printing Office.

Van Deusen, J. M., Stanton, M. D., Scott, S. M., Todd, T. C., & Mowatt, D. T. (1982). Getting the addict to agree to involve his family of origin: The initial contact. In M. D. Stanton, T. C. Todd, & Associates (Eds.), *The family therapy of drug abuse and addiction* (pp. 39–59). New York: Guilford.

Walsh, F. (1988). The family in later life. In B. Carter & M. McGoldrick (Eds.), *The changing family life cycle* (pp. 311–332). New York: Gardner.

Wynne, L. C., Shields, C. G., & Sirkin, M. I. (1992). Illness, family theory, and family therapy: I. Conceptual issues. *Family Process, 31*, 3–18.

Worden, M. (1992). *Adolescents and their families*. New York: Haworth Press.

Healthy and Dysfunctional Characteristics of Families

Amid the white sterility of intensive care
and the cries of incubated newborns
I watch your parents struggle in the quiet realization
that your life hangs by a thread too thin to sustain it.

Tenuously you fight to hold onto every breath
until peacefully, in your father's arms,
you give up in exhaustion
and with a final release, almost like a whisper,
air leaves your lungs forever.

Your mother has said her gentle good-byes
only hours after your birth
with her dreams turning into nightmares
as she contemplates her loss in the thought
of going home to silence.

Life, like faith, is sometimes fragile
best personified in newness and simple acts of courage.

Gladding, 1992

The health of families varies over the lifespan. The fact that a family is healthy at one stage of life is no guarantee that it will remain that way (Carlson & Fullmer, 1992; Carter & McGoldrick, 1988). In fact, achieving and maintaining health demands constant work for members of a family unit as well as the family as a whole.

Numerous events can throw families into new or unexpected ways of functioning. When such events occur, family relationships are altered and the family as a whole is shaken up. "Destabilizing events create stress to which family systems can react in different ways. Some systems respond by transforming the rules under which they operate, thereby allowing new, more functional behaviors. In other systems, rather than changing shape, a medical or psychological symptom emerges" (Fishman, 1988, p. 15). Healthy families reorganize their structure to accommodate to new circumstances (Nichols & Schwartz, 1995). This type of readjustment keeps most families from becoming chaotic (Cuber & Harroff, 1966).

This chapter examines the patterns of healthy and dysfunctional families. First, the qualities of healthy families are explored. Next family stressors, both expected and unexpected, are looked at in regard to their impact. Third, the influence of family structure on functionality is considered. Then, the coping strategies for dealing with family stress are highlighted. Finally, the implications of health (especially mental health) in working with families are featured.

Qualities of Healthy Families

Healthy families are both an ideal and a reality. Such families have been written about theoretically and studied empirically (Smith & Stevens-Smith, 1992). Yet, there is still disagreement as to the qualities of ideal families. Even more fundamental is a disagreement about what the word *health* means. **Health** is more than the absence of pathology. Rather, it is an interactive process associated with positive relationships and outcomes (Wilcoxon, 1985). Health in the family involves ethical accountability. Good relationships exist in families when there is a balance of give and take among members (Boszormenyi-Nagy & Ulrich, 1981). Several studies have estimated that a large percentage of "American families can be classified as dysfunctional" at one time or another (Hurn, 1993, p. 63). Although these findings need to be examined in context, the point is that most families experience times of both healthy and unhealthy interactions during the family life cycle.

Thus, it cannot be assumed that healthy individuals necessarily come from continuously healthy families (Wolin & Wolin, 1993). In fact, highly resilient individuals who successfully overcome adversities do best in life (Walsh, 1995). However, being in a healthy environment is more helpful than not.

Healthy families have a number of characteristics in common. Some of their most salient qualities have been compiled in various lists. Although there is disagreement about these qualities, a number of overlapping aspects seem to distinguish healthy families from those who function less well (McCoy, 1996). For example, Becvar & Becvar (1982, p. 74) state that healthy families have a majority of the following characteristics:

- a legitimate source of authority, established and supported over time
- a stable rule system established and consistently acted upon
- stable and consistent shares of nurturing behavior
- effective and stable childrearing and marriage-maintenance practices
- a set of goals toward which the family and each individual works
- sufficient flexibility and adaptability to accommodate normal developmental challenges as well as unexpected crises

Families that are most successful, happy, and strong are balanced in a number of ways. For example, they seem to know what issues to address and how to address them. Furthermore, they do not operate from either an extreme cognitive or emotional framework. They exert the right amount of energy in dealing with the matters before them, and they make realistic plans. Overall, in families with a sense of well-being, multiple forces and factors interact in complex but positive ways. One of the most vital of these factors is "the strength of the marital unit" (Beavers, 1985; Lavee, McCubbin, & Olson, 1987). "A healthy marriage is able, flexibly and even synergistically, to adapt to the individual growth of each partner" (Goldenberg & Goldenberg, 1994, p. 14). If couples get along and work at keeping the marriage exciting and open, chances are greatly improved that the family will be well and do well.

According to research (Krysan, Moore, & Zill, 1990; Stinnett & DeFrain, 1985), healthy families also include the following characteristics:

- commitment to the family and its individuals
- appreciation for each other (i.e., a social connection)
- willingness to spend time together
- effective communication patterns

- a high degree of religious/spiritual orientation
- ability to deal with crisis in a positive manner (i.e., adaptability)
- encouragement of individuals
- clear roles

The following sections address these characteristics, along with the importance of structure and development within families.

Commitment

At the core of healthy family functioning is the idea of commitment. "In strong families, members are devoted not only to the welfare of the family but also to the growth of each of the members" (Thomas, 1992, p. 62). A commitment to the family is the basis for family members giving their time and energy to family-related activities.

Commitment involves staying loyal to the family and its members through both good and adverse life events. It is based on both emotion and intentionality. Couples and individuals who have not thought through their commitment to one another or who are ambivalent about how committed they are have difficulty in staying in a marriage and working with each other. The result is often infidelity (Pittman, 1989).

Appreciation

The commitment that family members have toward one another is strengthened when they verbally or physically express their appreciation. In healthy families, "the marital partners tend to build the self-esteem of their mates by mutual love, respect, [and] compliments" (Thomas, 1992, p. 64). In dysfunctional families, there is considerable conflict in the form of personal attacks by members on each other (Wills, Weiss, & Patterson, 1974). Taken to an extreme, members of dysfunctional families engage in violence toward one another (Mathias, 1986). Domestic violence in the United States, where it is estimated that a spouse (usually a woman) is assaulted and battered every 15 to 18 seconds, is an example of such extreme family dysfunction (Copeland, 1994).

Willingness to Spend Time Together

Healthy families spend both quantitative and qualitative time together. "The time they spend together needs to be good time; no one enjoys hours of bickering, arguing, pouting, or bullying. Time also needs to be sufficient; quality interaction isn't likely to develop in a few minutes together" (Stinnett & DeFrain, 1985, pp. 83-84).

Events that encompass both qualitative and quantitative time abound. They range from family picnics, to overnight campouts, to vacations, to special nights out that involve entertainment such as a play, ball game, or concert. They also encompass rituals and traditions such as celebrating birthdays and anniversaries, family interactions at mealtimes, and observing rites of passage together such as graduations, weddings, and funerals (Giblin, 1995). The idea behind spending time together is sharing thoughts, feelings, and identities. In the process, family members come to think of themselves as a cohesive unit and not just a random group of individuals.

Effective Communication Patterns

"Communication is concerned with the delivery and reception of verbal and nonverbal information between family members. It includes skills in exchanging patterns of information within the family system" (Brock & Barnard, 1992, p. 25). When families are healthy, members attend to the messages from one another and pick up on subtle as well as obvious points. Within these families there is support, understanding, and empathy (Giblin, 1994). In dysfunctional families, there is often competition for "air time" or silence. Messages are sent but seldom received in a sensitive or caring manner. "Distressed families exhibit a greater frequency of aversive communications and blaming statements than nondistressed families" (Melidonis & Bry, 1995, p. 451).

Brock and Barnard (1992, p. 25) have delineated characteristics of *optimal family communication situations*. They state that in the best of circumstances, communication within families is of a high volume and includes seeking and sharing patterns. The messages between family members are clear and congruent. In addition, healthy families deal with a wide range of topics and are open to talking rather than remaining silent. When there is conflict, these families seek to work it out through discussion. Family members seek to problem solve. They are more likely than not to communicate in a positive tone.

Religious/Spiritual Orientation

A religious/spiritual orientation to life is a characteristic of "the vast majority of the world's families" (Prest & Keller, 1993, p. 137). Involvement in the religious/spiritual dimension of life also correlates with an overall sense of marital and family health and well-being. According to research, religion and spirituality have traditionally played an important part in the lives of some groups more than others. For example, collective faith has been the cornerstone by which African Americans were supported and sustained from the "oppression of slavery" to the "civil rights movement" (Hampson, Beavers, & Hulgus, 1990, p. 308).

In the 1990s, there is still an orientation toward the religious/spiritual in regard to both organized and unorganized efforts. The elderly and adolescent, to say nothing of those in middle age, are frequently involved in life matters that can best be described as religious/spiritual (Campbell & Moyers, 1988). In addition, members of families often deal as a group with religious/spiritual questions during certain events, for example, deaths, births, and marriages. Couples who share a common faith or orientation toward religious matters and who are intrinsically motivated in their religious orientation report more satisfaction in their relationships than those who are divided on these issues (Anthony, 1993). Persons whose spouse and/or family are of a different religious/spiritual persuasion report lower levels of satisfaction in their marriages and family relations (Ortega, Whitt, & Williams, 1988; Shehan, Bock, & Lee, 1990).

Ability to Deal with Crisis in a Positive Manner

A number of different types of crises affect families over the life span. One type of crisis is an *expected event*. An expected event takes several forms, including **nonevents** and *active events* (Schlossberg, 1984). An example of a nonevent is the failure of a couple to have children or to have the number of children they had planned. In such circumstances, healthy families deal with the situation by expressing their emotions and supporting one another. Unhealthy families, on the other hand, blame and attack persons within the family structure.

An **expected crisis** characterized as an active event is one that is predictable and actually occurs. For example, leaving one's family of origin to make a life for oneself is a crisis for most young people (Haley, 1980). Similarly, getting married or having a baby are also viewed as expected crises. In these situations the general nature of the event is known but the specifics are always unique. Families that function well use such coping strategies as negotiating, seeking advice from those who are more experienced, rehearsing, using humor, and expressing emotions to deal with such transitions (Schlossberg, 1984).

Encouragement of Individuals

Because families work as systems, they are only as strong as their weakest members. Therefore, it behooves families to encourage the development of talents and abilities within their individual members. Such a process is generally done systemically and is carried out over the family life cycle (Carter & McGoldrick, 1988).

Encouragement is especially important at certain times in the life cycle. Among the most crucial times encouragement is needed are with school-age children as they engage in the educational process, with adolescents as they cope with physical changes and peer groups, and with young adults as they move from their parents houses into their own psychological and physical spaces filled with dreams and possibilities (Lambie & Daniels-Mohring, 1993).

Clear Roles

Roles are prescribed and repetitive behaviors involving a set of reciprocal activities with other family members (Steinhauser, Santa-Barbara, & Skinner, 1984). Roles in healthy families are clear, appropriate, suitably allocated, mutually agreed upon, integrated, and enacted (Minuchin, 1974). Some roles are necessary, such as the provision of material resources. Others are unique and/or unnecessary, such as the acquiring of coins for a coin collection.

The exact roles within families are determined by such factors as age, culture, and tradition. "Symptoms often develop in family members who are cast, because of the nature of the family system, into idiosyncratic roles" (Barker, 1986, p. 162). Consequently, healthy families strive to make roles as interchangeable and flexible as possible.

Growth-Producing Structure and Development Patterns

Healthy families are organized in a clear, appropriate, and growth-producing way (Lewis, Beavers, Gossett, & Phillips, 1976; McGoldrick & Gerson, 1985; Napier & Whitaker, 1978). There are no intergenerational **coalitions** (e.g., mother and daughter against everyone else in the family) or conflictual **triangles** (e.g., mother and father arguing over and interacting with their rebellious son) as the basis for keeping the family together. Instead, parents are in charge (or, in the case of single-parent families, the single parent is in charge). **Subsystems,** such as those composed of family members logically grouped together because of age or function (e.g., parents), carry out needed tasks (e.g., parenting). Because the structure is clear, the **boundaries** (physical and psychological) are, too, and growth can take place. When a family member steps out of bounds, family pressure brings him or her back into line. This process takes place through **homeostasis**—the tendency to resist change and keep things as they are. For instance, if a teenager violates a curfew, the parents may "ground" the young person for a week or until responsibility is taken for coming home on time.

Other salient features of healthy families that center around structure are those connected with the formation and display of symptoms (Barker, 1986). Some individual dysfunctions, such as depression (Lopez, 1986), career indecisiveness (Kinnier, Brigman, & Noble, 1990), and substance abuse (West, Hosie, & Zarski, 1987), are related to family structure. In these situations, families are usually too tightly or too loosely organized, a matter that is discussed more fully later in this chapter.

Family Life Stressors

Stress is a part of every family's life. As with individuals, families attempt to keep stressful events from becoming distressful (Selye, 1976). They do this through a variety of means, some of which are more healthy (such as planning ahead) than others. Sometimes families cope with stressors according to whether they are prepared to deal with the situations or not.

Carter and McGoldrick (1988) have placed family stressors into two categories: vertical and horizontal (see Figure 2.1). Among the **vertical stressors** are those dealing with family patterns, myths, secrets, and legacies. These stressors are historical and inherited from previous generations. **Horizontal stressors** are those related to the present. Some horizontal stressors are developmental, such as life cycle transitions (e.g., the transition from being a new couple to being a couple with a new child). Others are unpredictable, such as having an accident or winning the lottery.

In addition, the occurrence and impact of some developmental stressors can be predicted for the future. For example, as society progresses into the twenty-first century, the structure of the family and its vertical and horizontal stressors will shift. This transition will occur in several ways, but one prevalent way will be with the addition of an extra generation to the life of the family (e.g., having aging parents come and live with their grown children). Such a change will tilt

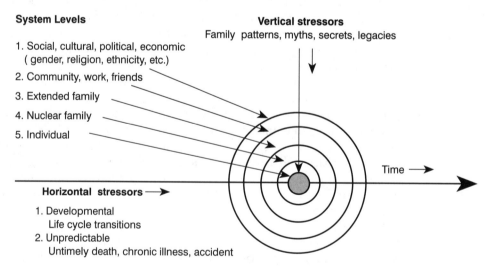

Figure 2.1

Horizontal and vertical stressors.

From *The Changing Family Life Cycle* (2nd ed., p. 9) by Betty Carter and Monica McGoldrick, 1988. Copyright Allen & Bacon. Reprinted by permission.

the family as a whole from a more horizontal to a more vertical emphasis. Likewise, if couples in the United States continue to have fewer children, "individuals in upcoming generations will have fewer siblings and cousins (horizontal dimension) and more relatives in the older generations (vertical dimension). . . . Divorces and remarriages by children may multiply the vertical lines of the family," too (Shields, King, & Wynne, 1995, p. 141).

Overall, the Carter and McGoldrick model of family life stressors is systemic and in line with how most family therapists view families. However, families are unique in their timing of transition events. For example, families plan for their children to grow up, leave home, and start families, but British-American families usually expect a much faster shift in these events than Italian-American families. Anticipating when events may happen helps family members prepare mentally and physically for changes. Sometimes family life stages and individual life stages complement each other (Bowen, 1978); however, at other times, families and individuals may become distressed and dysfunctional.

Expected Life Stressors

Families can expect a number of stressors regardless of their level of functioning. As indicated, some are *developmental stressors* (i.e., age and life-stage related), and others are *situational stressors* (i.e., interpersonal, such as dealing with feelings) (Figley, 1989). Some stressors are related to present events such as work, school, and social functions (Kaslow, 1991). Others are more historical in nature (i.e., they have family life heritage).

When surveyed, family members frequently cite prevalent stressors in their families as those associated with (1) economics and finances, (2) children's behaviors, (3) insufficient couple time, (4) communicating with children, (5) insufficient personal time, and (6) insufficient family play time (Curran, 1985). Clearly, some of these everyday stressors deal with deficiencies, such as not having enough time. In these types of stress situations families can resolve problems through planning ahead, lowering their expectations, or both. They are then better able to cope. The flip side of this solution-based stress relief is that families and their members may experience stress from not accomplishing enough of what they planned and from overscheduling family calendars.

Unexpected Life Stressors

Some family-life situations take family members by surprise or are beyond their control. If life events come too soon, are delayed, or fail to materialize, the health, happiness, and well-being of all involved may be affected (Schlossberg, 1984). Intensified emotionality and/or behavioral disorganization in families and their members are likely to occur as a result (Roberto, 1991).

Timing is crucial to the functioning of families and their members, especially in dealing with the unexpected. Struggle results if timing is off, or families are "off-time" (Neugarten, 1979). For example, if a first wedding is either relatively early or late in one's life (e.g., before age 20 or after age 40, respectively), the difficulty of accepting or dealing with the circumstances surrounding the event, such as interacting with the new spouse, is increased for both the persons marrying and their families (Carter & McGoldrick, 1988). Also, if grandparents assume the task of raising their grandchildren because of unexpected circumstances, such as the incarceration of the biological parents, greater risks for all are involved (Pinson-Milburn, Fabian, Schlossberg, & Pyle, 1996). Risks for the grandparents include increased psychological stress, financial difficulties, and health problems. Children in such circumstances are likely to suffer from a lack of consistent parenting and discipline and thus may do less well academically and socially.

Another crucial variable in dealing with the unexpected is **family development and environmental fit** (Eccles et al., 1993). Some environments are conducive to helping families develop and resolve unexpected crises. Others are not. For example, despite its best effort, a family living in an impoverished environment that experiences the loss of its major wage earner may not recover to its previous level of functioning. Such would probably not be the case with a family experiencing the same circumstance but living in a more affluent and supportive environment.

In addition to the situations just cited, families may have special difficulty in handling the following unexpected events in their life cycles (McCubbin & Figley, 1983):

1. *Happenstance and chance.*   One unpredictable in the life cycle is happenstance and chance (Bandura, 1982; Seligman, 1981). It is impossible to gauge when a person or an event may have a major impact on an individual or family that alters the style and substance of their existence. For example, members of a family on vacation may become friends with members of another family because they were housed in adjoining motel rooms. The results may be a marriage of their children, a business deal that produces wealth/frustration, or extended visits to each other's home. Another chance event that may have a major impact on a family is the birth of a disabled child. Such a child may strain the psychological and financial resources of a family and increase stress and, at the same time, reduce pleasant interactions and communications within the family (Seligman & Darling, 1989). It may also draw the family closer together physically and emotionally.

2. *Physical/psychological trauma.*   People can be traumatized by experiencing natural events such as hurricanes, earthquakes, or fires, as well as by experiencing violent crime and physical abuse. These events may happen singularly or collectively. They share in common the fact that they are "sudden, overwhelming, and often dangerous, either to one's self or significant other.

These experiences are usually horrific in nature" (C. Lee & C. Figley, personal communication, November 18, 1992).

Regardless of the form or circumstances, traumatic experiences have an impact on families. "Traumatized families are those who are attempting to cope with an extraordinary stressor that has disrupted their normal life routine in unwanted ways" (Figley, 1989, p. 5). Trauma can upset the family's organizational ability and adaptability. The greater the distress of the victim(s), the greater the distress within the family as a whole (Figley, 1989). For instance, an adolescent girl may find it impossible to have a relationship with the brother who raped her. Similarly, a mother and children may be unable to reorganize themselves into a functional family unit after the untimely death of the husband/father. Symptoms displayed by families in these circumstances include role reversals, somatization of experiences, interruption of normal developmental life cycles, alienation, and inappropriate attempts at control, such as emotional withdrawal.

3. *Success and failure.*   In his poem "If," Rudyard Kipling describes success and failure as "impostors" that should be treated just the same. Indeed, success and failure are both unsettling events for individuals and families. For example, a family that wins a lottery or sweepstake may find its members disagreeing over how the monies will be spent. Family members may also find themselves besieged with solicitations. In another example, a family that acquires fame and notoriety may become isolated from routine interactions with friends or colleagues, thereby cutting off a social system of support and comfort.

The results of success or failure can leave people who experience them with mixed and volatile feelings ranging from depression to elation. The outcome may be progression or regression. Consequently, emotions and behaviors may be directed at increasing intimacy, physical or psychological distancing, or the adoption of a new set of values. In any such scenarios, life styles and life cycle events are altered.

When anyone or anything either enters or leaves the family system, members within the family become unsettled. This point is seen graphically in the Social Readjustment Rating Scale (Holmes & Rahe, 1967). Of the 43 life-stress situations listed in the scale, 10 of the top 14 involve gaining or losing a family member.

In general, events such as illness, loss of a job, or inheriting a substantial amount of money are unpredictable and stressful. These occurrences add tension to the family system because of their newness, demands, and the changes they require of family members (Carter & McGoldrick, 1988). "Dysfunctional family behaviors develop when unexpected crises unbalance the system beyond its natural ability to recover" (Burgess & Hinkle, 1993, p. 134). Even in the best circumstances, certain events can cause families to behave in dysfunctional ways.

Family Structure and Functionality

In addition to stress, another factor that contributes to the health or dysfunctionality of families is structure/organization. A variety of family forms are present in society (Bubenzer, West, & Boughner, 1994). Some work better than others in handling life events. For example, a family that is rigidly structured may respond best in a crisis situation, and one that is loosely organized may do best in recreational circumstances. The roles family members enact make a difference in regard to family health. For instance, "organized cohesiveness, sex role traditionalism, role flexibility, and shared roles" are correlated with husbands' health, and "organized cohesiveness and differentiated sharing" are correlated with wives' health, in middle-class families (Fisher, Ransom, Terry, & Burge, 1992, p. 399). Three common family organizational forms are (1) symmetry/complementary, (2) centripetal/centrifugal, and (3) cohesive/adaptable.

Symmetry/Complementary

In western society, families vary in the way they function. Although some are mainly symmetrical and others are mainly complementary, most successful couples show an ability to use both styles of interaction (Main & Oliver, 1988). In symmetrical families the relationship is based on similarity of behavior. At its worse, family members—especially the couple subsystem members—act alike. For example, if she screams, he screams back. At its best, a **symmetrical relationship** is one where each partner tries to become competent in doing necessary or needed tasks (Watzlawick, Beavin, & Jackson, 1967). Members within these units are versatile. For example, either a man or a woman can work outside the home or take care of children. The major time of difficulty in a symmetrical relationship is when partners do not minimize differences and instead compete with each other or when one member of the relationship is not skilled in performing a necessary task (Sauber, L'Abate, & Weeks, 1985).

In **complementary relationships,** family member roles are defined more rigidly and differences are maximized. For example, one is either dominant or submissive, logical or emotional. If members fail to do their tasks, such as make decisions or nurture children, other members of the family are adversely affected. As long as the prescribed roles in these relationships dovetail with each other and there is no change in the status quo, complementary families do fine.

Overall, both symmetrical and complementary forms of family life will work as long as at least two conditions are met. First, members in the relationships must be satisfied with and competent in their roles. Second, there must be a sufficient interrelationship of roles so that necessary tasks are accomplished. In these cases, harmony results and the family functions adequately. However, it is not always possible to meet these two conditions, and thus families, especially the couples in them, do best if they practice **parallel relationships** (Main & Oliver, 1988). In parallel relationships, both complementary and symmetrical exchanges occur as appropriate.

Centripetal/Centrifugal Families

The term ***centripetal*** (directed toward a center) is used to describe a tendency to move toward family closeness. The term ***centrifugal*** (directed away from a center) is used to describe the tendency to move away from the family (i.e., family disengagement). In all families, there are periods of both closeness and distance over the individual and family life cycles. Some of these periods "coincide with oscillation between family development tasks that require intense bonding or high levels of family cohesion, like early child rearing, and tasks that emphasize personal identity and autonomy, like adolescence" (Rolland, 1988, p. 447).

One of the strongest models that outlines the natural tendencies of three-generational families to be close to or distant from each other has been formulated by Lee Combrinck-Graham (1985) (see Figure 2.2). It relates strength and health to the developmental state of the family and its individuals. It also stresses the importance of working through transitions in the family.

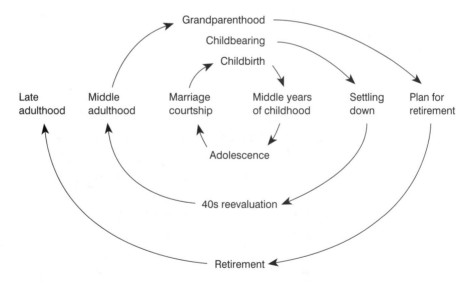

Figure 2.2

Density of the family over time.

From "A Developmental Model for Family Systems" by L. Combrinck-Graham, 1985, *Family Process, 24,* p. 142. Reprinted by permission of the publisher.

The work of Robert Beavers and associates at the Timberlawn Psychiatric Center in Dallas, Texas, shows that extremes in either a centripetal or centrifugal style of family interaction as a life style is likely to produce poor family functioning (Lewis et al., 1976). Figure 2.3 describes the relationship between family interaction style and family health. Families with a centripetal style have members who "view their relationship satisfactions as coming from inside the family" (Nichols & Everett, 1986, p. 77). They tend to produce children who are too tightly held by the family and who are prone to be antisocial, irresponsible, and egocentric. "Certain types of symptoms in teenagers, such as eating disorders and schizophrenia, indicate centripetal forces at work in the family"

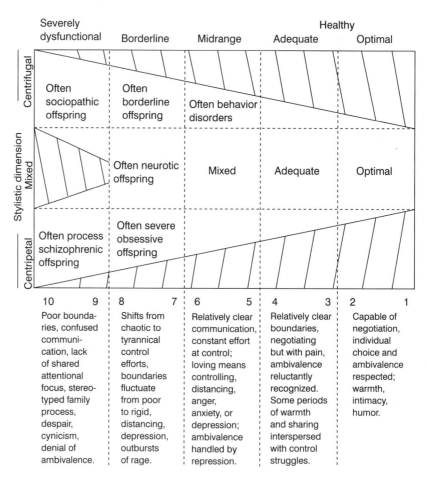

Figure 2.3

Beavers's concept of family health.

From *Successful Marriage, A Family Systems Approach to Couples Therapy* by W. Robert Beavers, M.D., 1985. Copyright 1985 by W. Robert Beavers. Reprinted by permission of W. W. Norton & Company, Inc.

(Thomas, 1992, p. 105). Also, young adults who are unable or unwilling to leave home are the products of such families (Haley, 1980).

Families with a centrifugal style "are characterized by the tendency to expel members and view their relationship satisfactions as coming from outside the family" (Nichols & Everett, 1986, p. 77). They are likely to produce children who become socially isolated, disorganized, or withdrawn. "Adolescents who run away from home after enduring rejection or neglect and who remain on the street as casual, prematurely independent runaways would come from families in which centrifugal forces are dominant" (Thomas, 1992, p. 105).

Cohesion/Adaptability

Regardless of timing, all families have to deal with family cohesion (i.e., emotional bonding) and family adaptability (i.e., the ability to be flexible and change) (Olson, 1986; Strong & DeVault, 1992). In the Circumplex Model of Marital and Family Systems shown in Figure 2.4, cohesion and adaptability are highlighted. These two dimensions each have four levels (Olson, 1986). Adaptability ranges from a low to high dimension on the categories characterized as (1) rigid, (2) structured, (3) flexible, and (4) chaotic. The structured and flexible categories are the two most moderate levels of functioning. Cohesion ranges from low to high on these four levels: (1) disengaged, (2) separated, (3) connected, and (4) enmeshed. It is hypothesized that high levels of enmeshment or low levels of cohesion in the form of disengagement may be problematic for families. For example, a lack of family cohesion, along with poor discipline, appears to raise the risk for serious delinquency in adolescents (Gorman-Smith, Tolan, Zelli, & Huesmann, 1996). Overall, the two dimensions of adaptability and cohesion are curvilinear. "Families that apparently are very high or very low on both dimensions seem dysfunctional, whereas families that are balanced seem to function more adequately" (Maynard & Olson, 1987, p. 502).

As previously seen from the Combrinck-Graham diagram (1985) (Figure 2.2) and as recently acknowledged by Olson, the degree of adaptability and cohesion within families is dependent on their life cycle stage and their cultural background. Therefore, caution must be exercised in stressing these two dimensions of family life in isolation from other factors.

Coping Strategies of Families

The coping strategies of healthy and dysfunctional families vary both quantitatively and qualitatively. According to Figley and McCubbin (1983), families that are generally able to cope with stress have most of the following characteristics (p. 18):

Low ——— COHESION ——— High

	DISENGAGED	SEPARATED	CONNECTED	ENMESHED

High
F
L
E
X
I   CHAOTIC
B
I
L
I   FLEXIBLE
T
Y
    STRUCTURED

    RIGID
Low

LEVELS OF FLEXIBILTY

CHAOTIC
- Lack of leadership
- Dramatic role shifts
- Erractic discipline
- Too much change

FLEXIBLE
- Shared leadership
- Democratic discipline
- Role sharing change
- Change when necessary

STRUCTURED
- Leadership sometimes shared
- Somewhat democratic discipline
- Roles stable
- Change when demanded

RIGID
- Authoritarian leadership
- Strict discipline
- Roles seldom to change
- Too little change

Circle diagram (CHAOTIC / FLEXIBLE / STRUCTURED / RIGID rows × DISENGAGED / SEPARATED / CONNECTED / ENMESHED columns):

	DISENGAGED	SEPARATED	CONNECTED	ENMESHED
CHAOTIC	CHAOTICALLY DISENGAGED	CHAOTICALLY SEPARATED	CHAOTICALLY CONNECTED	CHAOTICALLY ENMESHED
FLEXIBLE	FLEXIBLY DISENGAGED	FLEXIBLY SEPARATED	FLEXIBLY CONNECTED	FLEXIBLY ENMESHED
STRUCTURED	STRUCTURALLY DISENGAGED	STRUCTURALLY SEPARATED	STRUCTURALLY CONNECTED	STRUCTURALLY ENMESHED
RIGID	RIGIDLY DISENGAGED	RIGIDLY SEPARATED	RIGIDLY CONNECTED	RIGIDLY ENMESHED

○ BALANCED   ◐ MIDRANGE   ■ UNBALANCED

LEVELS OF COHESION:	DISENGAGED	SEPARATED	CONNECTED	ENMESHED
I-We Balance:	I	I-we	I-We	I-We
Closeness:	Little Closeness	Low-moderate	Moderate-high	Very high closeness
Loyalty:	Little loyalty	Some loyalty	High loyalty	Very high loyalty
Independence/ Dependence:	High independence	Interdependent (More independence than dependence)	Interdependent (More dependence than independence)	High dependence

Figure 2.4

Circumplex Model of Family Systems.

From "Circumplex Model of Family Systems: Integrating Ethnic Diversity and Other Social Systems" by Dean M. Gorall and David H. Olson, in *Integrating Family Therapy* (p. 219) edited by R. H. Mikesell, D-D. Lusterman, and S. H. McDaniel, 1995, Washington, DC: American Psychological Association. Reprinted by permission.

- ability to identify the stressor
- ability to view the situation as a family problem, rather than a problem of one member
- solution-oriented approach rather than blame
- tolerance for other family members
- clear expression of commitment to and affection for other family members
- open and clear communication among members
- evidence of high family cohesion
- evidence of considerable role flexibility
- appropriate utilization of resources inside and outside the family
- lack of physical violence
- lack of substance abuse

The appropriate utilization of resources inside and outside the family is simply illustrated in Hill's (1949) ABCX diagram (see Figure 2.5), sometimes referred to as the "checkmark diagram." In this diagram, "A" is the level of functioning before a crisis, "B" is the period of disorganization, and "C" is the angle of recovery. All depend on "X," the utilization of internal and external resources by the family. Families that make the most of resources and/or have resources available are more likely to recover.

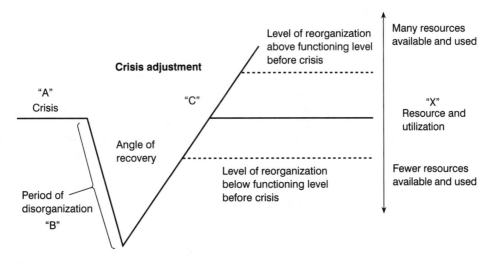

Figure 2.5

Checkmark or ABCX model of family's reaction to crisis.

From *Families Under Stress: Adjustment to the Crisis of War, Separation, and Reunion* by R. Hill, 1949, Westport, CT: Greenwood Press.

The process whereby families that are unable to adjust to new circumstances and try the same solutions over and over again (Watzlawick, 1978) or intensify nonproductive behaviors is referred to as **first-order change** (Watzlawick, Weakland, & Fisch, 1974). Such solutions often lead to exacerbation of the symptoms (Burgess & Hinkle, 1993). For example, a husband, concerned about his wife's weight, may tease or criticize her in an attempt to have her lose pounds. If this strategy does not work, he may tease or criticize her more or he may yell at her. These behaviors ultimately result in hurt feelings, resentment, anger, frustration, and a lack of effort to change.

The opposite of first-order change is **second-order change**. The dynamics surrounding second-order change are those that result in a metachange, that is, a changing of rules sometimes referred to as a *change of change* (Watzlawick et al., 1974). In this process, a new set of rules and behaviors are introduced into the existing behavioral repertoire, often in an abrupt way (Burgess & Hinkle, 1993). The outcome is that a qualitatively new type of behavior appears.

In the previous example, a second-order change would occur if the husband suggested to his wife that she gain more weight because she could then look back and be happy with her present weight. This type of response, if conveyed sincerely, might appear puzzling to the wife. However, in making such a statement, the husband would reframe the problem and in the process give up his attempt to modify or change a situation he could not control. The wife and the husband would then have more options from which to choose. In this respect the situation would be like a client feeling empowered to take charge of his or her life, instead of being dependent on the suggestions and feedback from others (Burgess & Hinkle, 1993). In such a process, better communications are fostered because power struggles are no longer a part of the agenda, and divisive arguments are thereby prevented.

A study of 78 French-Canadian couples who had been living together an average of 13 years further illustrates the difference between first- and second-order change. According to the result of this investigation, "when compared to nondistressed spouses, distressed spouses showed less problem solving confidence, a tendency to avoid different problem solving activities, and poor strategies to control their behavior" (Sabourin, Laporte, & Wright, 1990, p. 89). In other words, first-order change spouses were stuck in repetitive, nonproductive behaviors, but their counterparts engaged in new, productive behaviors.

Other dysfunctional patterns in families, such as sexual abuse of children, also show first-order change patterns. In families where there is incest, for instance, the family is "typically a closed, undifferentiated and rigid system primarily characterized by sexualized dependency" (Maddock, 1989, p. 134). In these families the same pattern of abuse is repeated because the family unit is "insulated from critical social feedback that might influence their behavior" (Maddock, 1989, p. 134).

Other coping strategies that relieve stress in well-functioning families include:

- recognizing that stress may be positive and lead to change
- realizing that stress is usually temporary
- focusing on working together to find solutions
- realizing that stress is a normal part of life
- changing the rules to deal with stress and celebrating victories over events that led to stress (Curran, 1985)

Implications of Health in Working with Families

Studying healthy families is a complicated process (Smith & Stevens-Smith, 1992). It requires that researchers invest considerable time and effort in observing and calculating the multiple impact of numerous interactions that occur in families, such as speech and relationship patterns. In addition, to study the health of families, researchers must overcome "the individually oriented, linear causation thinking of psychopathology" as represented in the *Diagnostic and Statistical Manual of Mental Disorders* of the American Psychiatric Association (Huber, 1993, p. 70). Family therapists have "typically worked with clients experiencing stress and crisis in relationships, a viewpoint indicating transient dysfunctioning" (Sporakowski, 1995, p. 61). Both the complexity of families and the bias toward researching individuals inhibits many clinicians from carefully investigating families. Yet, knowledge about the health of families can assist family therapists in a number of ways.

First, through studying the literature on family health, therapists can appreciate the multidimensional aspects of family life and how members influence each other systemically (Wilcoxon, 1985). This knowledge and awareness can be useful to practitioners as they interact with families experiencing difficulties. For instance, if a family member abuses alcohol, estimated by Treadway (1987) to be a factor in possibly half of the cases treated, the therapist can work to identify the problem and break the dysfunctional pattern of secrecy and silence by working in a confrontive but caring way.

A second benefit for therapists in examining healthy families is the realization that even dysfunctional families have areas of adequate or above average performance. Because novice therapists tend to "overpathologize" client families, knowledge of healthy families is essential in gaining a balanced perspective (Barnhill, 1979). A knowledge of healthy families can be useful because it, for example, provides insight into the developmental aspects of enmeshment and disengagement that occur over the family life cycle (Combrinck-Graham, 1985). This type of information can help therapists become aware of what is normal and healthy behavior and thereby focus in on situations that are not normal and healthy.

A third advantage of exploring characteristics of healthy families is the realization that health and pathology are developmental (Wilcoxon, 1985). For example, in midlife, couples may grow together and function with less conflict and stress as they launch their children (McCullough & Rutenberg, 1988). Similarly, couples that maintain positive interactions during this time may be less susceptible to premature death from such disorders as hypertension, stroke, and coronary heart disease (Lynch, 1977). This type of knowledge helps clinicians realize more fully that change is possible and probable if proper therapeutic interventions are made.

A fourth implication of studying healthy families is that through such a focus, therapists can delineate areas of deficiency and strength (Huber, 1993). Healthy families have weaknesses and dysfunctional families have strengths. Secrets, conflict, jealousy, guilt, and scapegoating, as well as openness, cooperation, admiration, understanding, and accepting of responsibility, may occur on occasions in almost any family (Framo, 1996). Realizing the range and extent of behaviors in families gives therapists an awareness of how to potentially deal in an effective way with severely stressed families as well as understand how healthy families develop.

Tomm (1989) has conceptualized how transitions lead to pathology or wellness. His model provides a basis for helping family therapists realize the dynamics of family situations and plan constructive and effective interventions. In this wellness and dysfunctionality cycle, there are acronyms that stand for patterns of functioning among family members and in the family itself. These acronym patterns are characterized as follows:

PIPS = Pathologizing Interpersonal Patterns (such as failure to speak or communicate effectively)

HIPS = Healing Interpersonal Patterns (such as support or understanding)

TIPS = Transforming Interpersonal Patterns (such as using psychological resources or material resources)

Slips = Events that trigger HIPS back to PIPS (such as cutting oneself off from the family physically or psychologically)

DIPS = Deteriorating Interpersonal Patterns (such as accidentally or intentionally avoiding a member of the family)

WIPS = Wellness Interpersonal Patterns (such as honest and open communication)

Altogether Tomm's cyclical model of transition looks like the following:

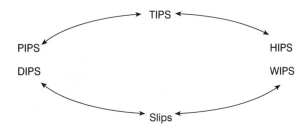

For example, in the case of the marriage of a new couple, a wife might feel verbally misunderstood by her husband (Slip) after a pattern of open communication (WIP) had been established. The result on her part would be sullenness and silence (DIP), followed by avoidance (PIP). If the husband were to ask her to help him understand her behavior and after her reply to understand and seek to rectify the situation (TIP), a new trusting environment might be created in which each member of the couple system would understand the other one better (HIP). In such an atmosphere, the couple might work even harder on being effective communicators (WIP).

Another example of the Tomm system is a situation in which a parent deviates from her general understanding behavior (WIP) and yells (Slip) at an adolescent for telling the truth about getting into trouble, resulting in the adolescent hiding facts from his parent the next time (DIP) and continuing to do so on future occasions (PIP). If the parent were to apologize for yelling (TIP), the adolescent might feel psychologically closer to the parent (HIP) and reestablish trust and understanding with her (WIP).

Tomm's model is useful as a way of understanding how systems, such as families, change with time, events, and circumstances. Expected events and unusual circumstances may become more or less stressful depending on how family members and families as a whole react to them.

A final implication for studying healthy families is educational. An awareness of potential stressors in life can help therapists prepare a family and its members to deal with situations in advance. For instance, "those struggling to recover from traumatic events appear to need to resolve five fundamental questions: (1) What happened? (2) Why did it happen? (3) Why did I and others act as we did then? (4) Why did I and others act as we did since then? (5) If something like this happened again, would I be able to cope more effectively?" (Figley, 1989, p. 14). Only by directly addressing these questions can a person or a family realize to the greatest extent possible the effect of a trauma on them and their life cycle development.

Education concerning healthy families also emphasizes the values of previously tried solutions (O'Hanlon & Weiner-Davis, 1989). Families and their members sometimes do not deal appropriately with events because they fail to examine strategies they could employ or have utilized at exceptional times for reaching successful resolutions. By focusing on universal or unique strategies that enable them to deal with stress, families may become healthier and more satisfied with themselves and their environments.

Knowledge is not a guarantee that families will handle changes in their life cycles without turmoil and crisis. However, through educating themselves and the families they work with about potential difficulties, family therapists and families are given a choice as to what they do and when.

Summary and Conclusion

Exploring aspects of healthy families is important from a conceptual and treatment basis. Clinicians must be aware of the ramifications of the dynamics they encounter in families and whether to make interventions at certain times. One aspect of family life that stands out is that families go through periods of transition and develop according to general and specific milestones in their lives. The life cycle of the family influences what are appropriate and inappropriate actions. Within their life cycles, families are influenced in their interactions for better or worse by expected and unexpected events. Families that work best are those that plan and use their time in setting up and implementing positive activities (Becvar & Becvar, 1996).

This chapter examined several aspects of family health. First, the nature of healthy families was explored. Healthy families are in a cycle that when unbalanced eventually changes in order to accommodate new situations. Family stressors were also discussed. Stressors come in many forms, such as vertical and horizontal, present and past. Handling expected stressful situations, through such techniques as time management, is difficult for many families. More troublesome is the management and recovery from unexpected life stressors, such as traumas from natural disasters such as a hurricane.

A third area explored was family structure. There are many ways families organize. However, families that are primarily symmetrical, versus those that are predominantly complementary, will vary in their ability to achieve tasks. Parallel family structure, which depends on flexibility and appropriateness of couples, seems to be most successful. Centripetal and centrifugal families differ in the way they address family matters. Centripetal families depend more on other members for help, and centrifugal families focus outwardly. Both are appropriate ways for families to be structured at different times in the life cycle. A final characteristic of structure is cohesion and adaptability. Again, both of these qualities differ in families depending on their cultural background and stage of life. The point is that family therapists need to realize that there are preferred family structures at various times in the family life cycle. Therapists also need to know how family structure influences family system dynamics.

The final two sections of this chapter dealt with coping strategies of families and the implication of understanding health as it pertains to family therapy. Generally, families cope the best they can. Families that are able to make second-order changes, that is, try totally new responses, do a better job in marshalling their resources than those who repeat old patterns or make incremental changes regardless of the situation (first-order changes). By studying healthy families, family therapists educate themselves to the complexity of family life and change. They also become sophisticated in realizing the developmental aspects of health and dysfunctionality. Therefore, they tend to be appropriately cautious in their assessment and treatment procedures. This type of knowledge gives therapists and the families they work with more choice in regard to what they do and how, thereby empowering all concerned in the process of change. With such information, family therapists "can take a leadership role in helping society come to terms with what is needed to create strong [and healthy] families" (Arnold & Allen, 1996, p. 84).

SUMMARY TABLE

Healthy and Dysfunctional Characteristics of Families

The health of families varies over the lifespan.
Healthy families readjust their rules and structure in dealing with crises and change. Dysfunctional families become rigid or chaotic.

Qualities of Healthy Families
Healthy families interact in a productive manner.
Healthy families are characterized by:

- a legitimate source of authority
- stable and consistent rules
- nurturing and appreciative behavior
- productive goals for individuals and the family
- flexibility and adaptability
- commitment of family members
- spending of qualitative and quantitative time together
- effective communication patterns
- a religious/spiritual orientation to life
- dealing with crises in a positive and effective manner
- clear roles and encouragement of members
- an appropriate structure and organization

Family Life Stressors

Stress is a part of family life. It may be vertical (i.e., historical) or horizontal (i.e. current), predictable (e.g., aging) or unexpected (e.g., death).

Expected life stressors are developmental and situational. They revolve around issues associated with economics, children, time, and behavior.

Unexpected life stressors are beyond a family's control and include happenstance and chance, physical/psychological trauma, and success/failure. Timing and environmental fit are crucial factors in dealing with unexpected stress.

Stress events initially unbalance the family.

Family Structure and Functionality

The way a family is structured affects its ability to respond.

Three common ways families organize are:

- symmetry/complementary
- centripetal/centrifugal
- cohesive/adaptable

Coping Strategies of Families

The ability of families to cope is both a qualitative and quantitative process.

Coping is characterized by:

- an ability to identify a stressor
- viewing a problem from a family perspective
- adopting a solution-oriented approach
- showing tolerance for other family members
- establishing clear communication patterns
- high family cohesion and role flexibility
- appropriate utilization of resources
- lack of physical violence and substance abuse
- use of second-order change strategies
- recognizing that stress is normal and may lead to change
- celebrating victories over events that led to stress

Implications of Health in Working with Families

Studying family health helps family therapists:

- appreciate the complexity of families
- realize that health is developmental and situational
- be less prone to pathologize families
- be aware of families' strengths and deficits
- be more educational in assisting families with problems

References

Anthony, M. (1993). The relationship between marital satisfaction and religious maturity. *Religious Education, 88,* 97–108.

Arnold, M. S., & Allen, N. P. (1996). Andrew Billingsley: The legacy of African American families. *The Family Journal, 3,* 77–85.

Bandura, A. (1982). The psychology of chance encounters and life paths. *American Psychologist, 37,* 747–755.

Barker, P. (1986). *Basic family therapy* (2nd ed.). New York: Oxford University Press.

Barnhill, L. R. (1979). Healthy family systems. *Family Coordinator, 28,* 94–100.

Beavers, W. R. (1985). *Successful marriage.* New York: Norton.

Becvar, D. S., & Becvar, R. J. (1996). *Family therapy: A systemic integration* (3rd ed.). Boston: Allyn & Bacon.

Becvar, R. J., & Becvar, D. S. (1982). *Systems theory and family therapy: A primer.* Washington, DC: University Press of America.

Boszormenyi-Nagy, I., & Ulrich, D. N. (1981). Contextual family therapy. In A. S. Gurman & D. P. Kniskern (Eds.), *Handbook of family therapy* (pp. 159–186). New York: Brunner/Mazel.

Bowen, M. (1978). *Family therapy in clinical practice.* New York: Jason Aronson.

Brock, G. W., & Barnard, C. P. (1992). *Procedures in marriage and family therapy* (2nd ed.). Boston: Allyn & Bacon.

Bubenzer, D. L., West, J. D., & Boughner, S. R. (1994). Michael White and the narrative perspective in therapy. *The Family Journal, 2,* 71–83.

Burgess, T. A., & Hinkle, J. S. (1993). Strategic family therapy of avoidance behavior. *Journal of Mental Health Counseling, 15,* 132–140.

Campbell, J., & Moyers, B. (1988). *The power of myth.* New York: Doubleday.

Carlson, J., & Fullmer, D. (1992). Family counseling: Principles for growth. In R. L. Smith & P. Stevens-Smith (Eds.), *Family counseling and therapy* (pp. 27–52). Ann Arbor, MI: ERIC/CAPS.

Carter, B., & McGoldrick, M. (1988). *The changing family life cycle* (2nd ed.). New York: Gardner.

Combrinck-Graham, L. (1985). A developmental model for family systems. *Family Process, 24,* 139–150.

Copeland, C. C. (1994). Out of the shadows: Domestic violence in the 20th century. In B. Evraiff (Ed.), *Proceeding of Fourth International Conference—Counseling in the 21st Century* (pp. 237–242). Vancouver, British Columbia, Canada.

Cuber, J., & Harroff, P. (1966). *Sex and the significant Americans.* Baltimore: Penguin.

Curran, D. (1985). *Stress and the healthy family.* San Francisco: Harper & Row.

Eccles, J. S., Midgley, C., Wigfield, A., Buchanan, C. M., Reuman, D., Flanagan, C., & MacIver, D. (1993). Development during adolescence: The impact of stage-environment fit on young adolescents' experiences in schools and families. *American Psychologist, 48,* 90–101.

Figley, C. R. (1989). *Helping traumatized families.* San Francisco, CA: Jossey-Bass.

Figley, C. R., & McCubbin, H. (1983). *Stress and the family: Vol. 2: Coping with catastrophe.* New York: Brunner/Mazel.

Fishman, C, H. (1988). *Treating troubled adolescents.* New York: Basic Books.

Fisher, L., Ransom, D., Terry, H. E., & Burge, S. (1992). The California family health project: IV. Family structure/organization and adult health. *Family Process, 31,* 399–419.

Framo, J. L. (1996). A personal retrospective of the family therapy field: Then and now. *Journal of Marital and Family Therapy, 22,* 289–316.

Giblin, P. (1994). Marital satisfaction. *The Family Journal, 2,* 48–50.

Giblin, P. (1995). Identity, change, and family rituals. *The Family Journal, 3,* 37–41.

Giblin, P. (1996). Spirituality, marriage, and family. *The Family Journal, 4,* 46–52.

Gladding, S. T. (1992). *On the death of Paul.* Unpublished manuscript.

Goldenberg, H., & Goldenberg, I. (1994). *Counseling today's families* (2nd ed.). Pacific Grove, CA: Brooks/Cole.

Gorman-Smith, D., Tolan, P. H., Zelli, A., & Huesmann, L. R. (1996). The relation of family functioning to violence among inner-city minority youth. *Journal of Family Psychology, 10,* 115–129.

Haley, J. (1980). *Leaving home: The therapy of disturbed young people.* New York: McGraw-Hill.

Hampson, R. B., Beavers, W. R., & Hulgus, Y. (1990). Cross-ethnic family differences: Interactional assessment of white, black, and Mexican-American families. *Journal of Marital and Family Therapy, 16,* 307–319.

Hill, R. (1949). *Families under stress: Adjustment to the crisis of war, separation, and reunion.* Westport, CT: Greenwood.

Holmes, T. H., & Rahe, R. H. (1967). The social readjustment rating scale. *Journal of Psychosomatic Research, 2,* 213–228.

Huber, C. H. (1993). Balancing family health and illness. *The Family Journal: Counseling and Therapy for Couples and Families, 1,* 69–71.

Hurn, J. J. (1993). Functional dysfunctions. In T. S. Nelson & T. S. Trepper (Eds.), *101 interventions in family therapy* (pp. 63–65). New York: Haworth Press.

Kaslow, F. W. (1991). The art and science of family psychology. *American Psychologist, 46,* 621–626.

Kinnier, R. T., Brigman, S. L., & Noble, F. C. (1990). Career indecision and family enmeshment. *Journal of Counseling and Development, 68,* 309–312.

Krysan, M., Moore, K. A., & Zill, N. (1990). *Identifying successful families: An overview of constructs and selected measures.* Washington, DC: Child Trends.

Lambie, R., & Daniels-Mohring, D. (1993). *Family systems within educational contexts.* Denver, CO: Love.

Lavee, Y., McCubbin, H. I., & Olson, D. H. (1987). The effects of stressful life events and transitions on family functioning and well-being. *Journal of Marriage and the Family, 49,* 857–873.

Lewis, J. M., Beavers, W. R., Gossett, J. T., & Phillips, V. A. (1976). *No single thread: Psychological health in family systems.* New York: Brunner/Mazel.

Lopez, F. G. (1986). Family structure and depression: Implications for the counseling of depressed college students. *Journal of Counseling and Development, 64,* 508–511.

Lynch, J. J. (1977). *The broken heart: The medical consequences of loneliness.* New York: Basic Books.

Maddock, J. W. (1989). Healthy family sexuality: Positive principles for educators and clinicians. *Family Relations, 38,* 130–136.

Main, F., & Oliver, R. (1988). Complementary, symmetrical and parallel personality priorities as indicators of marital adjustment. *Journal of Individual Psychology, 44,* 324–332.

Mathias, B. (1986, May/June). Lifting the shade on family violence. *Family Therapy Networker, 10,* 20–29.

Maynard, P. E., & Olson, D. H. (1987). Circumplex model of family systems: A treatment tool in family counseling. *Journal of Counseling and Development, 65,* 502–504.

McCoy, C. W. (1996). Reexamining models of healthy families. *Contemporary Family Therapy, 18,* 243–256.

McCubbin, H. I., & Figley, C. R. (1983). Bridging normative and catastrophic family stress. In H. I. McCubbin & C. R. Figley (Eds.), *Stress and the family.* New York: Brunner/Mazel.

McCullough, P. G., & Rutenberg, S. K. (1988). Launching children and moving on. In B. Carter & M. McGoldrick (Eds.), *The changing family life cycle* (2nd ed., pp. 285–309). New York: Gardner.

McGoldrick, M., & Gerson, R. (1985). *Genograms in family assessment.* New York: Norton.

Melidonis, G. G., & Bry, B. H. (1995). Effects of therapist exception questions on blaming and positive statements in families with adolescent behavior problems. *Journal of Family Psychology, 9,* 451–457.

Minuchin, S. (1974). *Families and family therapy.* Cambridge, MA: Harvard University Press.

Napier, A. Y., & Whitaker, C. A. (1978). *The family crucible.* New York: Harper & Row.

Neugarten, B. L. (1979). Time, age, and the life cycle. *American Journal of Psychiatry, 136,* 887–894.

Nichols, M. P., & Schwartz, R. C. (1995). *Family therapy: Concepts and methods* (3rd ed.). Boston: Allyn & Bacon.

Nichols, W. C., & Everett, C. A. (1986). *Systemic family therapy.* New York: Guilford.

O'Hanlon, W. H., & Weiner-Davis, M. (1989). *In search of solutions: A new direction in psychotherapy.* New York: Norton.

Olson, D. H. (1986). Circumplex model VII: Validation studies and FACES III. *Family Process, 25,* 337–351.

Ortega, S. T., Whitt, H. P., & Williams, J. A., Jr. (1988). Religious homogamy and marital happiness. *Journal of Family Issues, 9,* 224–239.

Pinson-Milburn, N. M., Fabian, E. S., Schlossberg, N. K., & Pyle, M. (1996). Grandparents raising grandchildren. *Journal of Counseling & Development, 74,* 548–554.

Pittman, F. (1989). *Private lies.* New York: Norton.

Prest, L. A., & Keller, J. F. (1993). Spirituality and family therapy: Spiritual beliefs, myths, and metaphors. *Journal of Marital and Family Therapy, 19,* 137–148.

Roberto, L. A. (1991). Symbolic-experiential family therapy. In A. S. Gurman & D. P. Kniskern (Eds.), *Handbook of family therapy, Vol. II,* (pp. 444–476). New York: Brunner/Mazel.

Rolland, J. S. (1988). Chronic illness and the family life cycle. In B. Carter & M. McGoldrick (Eds.), *The changing family life cycle* (2nd ed., pp. 433–456). New York: Gardner.

Sabourin, S., Laporte, L., & Wright, J. (1990). Problem solving self-appraisal and coping efforts in distressed and nondistressed couples. *Journal of Marital and Family Therapy, 16,* 89–97.

Sauber, S. R., L'Abate, L., & Weeks, G. R. (1985). *Family therapy: Basic concepts and terms.* Rockville, MD: Aspen.

Schlossberg, N. K. (1984). *Counseling adults in transition: Linking practice with theory.* New York: Springer.

Seligman, D. (1981, November 16). Luck and careers. *Fortune,* 60–75.

Seligman, M., & Darling, R. B. (1989). *Ordinary families, special children.* New York: Guilford.

Selye, H. (1976). *The stress of life* (2nd ed.). New York: McGraw-Hill.

Shehan, C. L., Bock, E. W., & Lee, G. R. (1990). Religious heterogamy, religiosity, and marital happiness: The case of Catholics. *Journal of Marriage and the Family, 52,* 73–79.

Shields, C. G., King, D. A., & Wynne, L. C. (1995). Interventions with later life families. In R. H. Mikesell, D. Lusterman, & S. H. McDaniel (Eds.), *Integrating family therapy* (pp. 141–160). Washington, DC: American Psychological Association.

Smith, R. L., & Stevens-Smith, P. (1992). A critique of healthy family functioning. In R. L. Smith & P. Stevens-Smith (Eds.), *Family counseling and therapy* (pp. 3–13). Ann Arbor, MI: ERIC/CAPS.

Sporakowski, M. J. (1995). Assessment and diagnosis in marriage and family counseling. *Journal of Counseling & Development, 74,* 60–64.

Steinhauser, P. D., Santa-Barbara, J., & Skinner, H. (1984). The process model of family functioning. *Canadian Journal of Psychiatry, 29,* 77–88.

Stinnett, N., & DeFrain, J. (1985). *Secrets of strong families.* Boston: Little, Brown.

Strong, B., & DeVault, C. (1986). *The marriage and family experience* (3rd ed.). St. Paul, MN: West Publishing.

Thomas, M. B. (1992). *An introduction to marital and family therapy: Counseling toward healthier family systems across the life span.* New York: Macmillan.

Tomm, K. (1989). *PIPS, TIPS, HIPS, and Slips: A heuristic alternative to DSM-III?* Paper presented at the AAMFT annual conference, San Francisco.

Treadway, D. (1987, July/August). The ties that bind. *Family Therapy Networker, 11,* 16–23.

Walsh, F. (1995). From family damage to family challenge. In R. H. Mikesell, D-D. Lusterman, & S. H. McDaniel (Eds.), *Integrating family therapy* (pp. 587–606). Washington, DC: American Psychological Association.

Watzlawick, P. (1978). *The language of change.* New York: Basic Books.

Watzlawick, P., Beavin, J. H., & Jackson, D. D. (1967). *Pragmatics of human communication.* New York: Norton.

Watzlawick, P., Weakland, J. H., & Fisch, R. (1974). *Change: Principles of problem formation and problem resolution.* New York: W. W. Norton.

West, G. D., Hosie, T. W., & Zarski, J. J. (1987). Family dynamics and substance abuse: A preliminary study. *Journal of Counseling and Development, 65,* 487–490.

Wilcoxon, S. A. (1985). Healthy family functioning: The other side of family pathology. *Journal of Counseling and Development, 63,* 495–499.

Wills, T. A., Weiss, R. L., & Patterson, G. R. (1974). A behavioral analysis of the determinants of marital satisfaction. *Journal of Consulting and Clinical Psychology, 42,* 802–811.

Wolin, S., & Wolin, S. (1993). *The resilient self: How survivors of troubled families rise above adversity.* New York: Villard.

PART TWO

THERAPEUTIC APPROACHES TO WORKING WITH FAMILIES

Rationale and History of Family Therapy

In the lighting of candles and exchanging of vows
we are united as husband and wife.

In the holiday periods of non-stop visits
we are linked again briefly to our roots.

Out of crises and the mundane
we celebrate life
appreciating the novel
and accepting the routine
as we meet each other anew
amid ancestral histories and current reflections.

Families are a weaver's dream
as unique threads from the past
are intertwined with the present
to form a colorful tapestry
of relationships in time.

Gladding, 1991

The profession of family therapy is relatively new. Its formal theoretical beginnings are traced to the 1940s, 1950s, and 1960s. Its real growth as a legitimate form of therapy occurred in the 1970s, 1980s, and 1990s (Foley, 1989; Kaslow, 1991). Family therapy differs from individual and group counseling both in its emphasis and in its clientele (Hines, 1988; Trotzer, 1988). Family therapy concentrates on making changes in total life systems; individual and group counseling focus on select intrapersonal and interpersonal changes.

The rise of family therapy closely followed dramatic changes in the form, composition, and structure of the American family. These variations were a result of the family's shift from a primarily nuclear unit to a complex and varied institution, for example, single parents, blended families, and dual-career families (Goldenberg & Goldenberg, 1994; Pickens, 1997). Family therapy has also been connected to the influence of creative, innovative, and assertive mental health practitioners who devised and advocated new ways of providing services to their clients (Nichols, 1993).

Although some of the theories and methods employed in family therapy are similar to those used in other settings, many differ. This chapter examines the genesis and development of family therapy. The emphasis is on the people, events, and interactional processes that most contributed to the formation of the field. Before examining these historical events, the rationale for working with families is highlighted.

The Rationale for Family Therapy

One reason for conducting family therapy is the belief that most life difficulties arise and can best be addressed within families (Carter & McGoldrick, 1988). In this view, families are seen as powerful forces that work for either the good or the detriment of their members. Because an interconnectedness exists among family members, the actions of the members affect the health or dysfunctionality of each individual and the family as a whole. This systemic viewpoint, that families are interconnected systems, is explained in the next section of this chapter.

Another reason for working therapeutically with families is the proven effectiveness of such treatment. In a landmark issue of the *Journal of Marital and*

Family Therapy edited by William Pinsof and Lyman Wynne, a meta-analysis was conducted on more than 250 studies. The results showed that various forms of family therapy worked at least as strong as other forms of psychotherapy. In addition, family and marital therapy was particularly effective in treating such disorders as adult schizophrenia, adult alcoholism and drug abuse, depression in women, adult hypertension, elderly dementia, adult obesity, adolescent drug abuse, anorexia in young adult women, child conduct disorders, aggression and noncompliance in children with attention deficit disorders, childhood autism, chronic physical illnesses in adults and children, and couple distress and conflict.

A final rationale for family therapy concerns client satisfaction. In a national survey of family therapists and their clients, Doherty and Simmons (1996) found that over 97% of clients were satisfied with the services they received from marriage and family therapists and rated these services good to excellent. In addition, an equally large percentage of clients reported that the services they received from marriage and family therapists helped them deal more effectively with their problems. They got the help they wanted.

In summary, given the nature and origin of family troubles, as well as the effectiveness and satisfaction with forms of family therapy, it is little wonder that this form of treatment has gained and is continuing to achieve recognition and status in the mental health field.

The Family as a System

The concept of a family as a system is based on the work of the biologist Ludwig von Bertalanffy (1934). Bertalanffy "saw the essential phenomena of life as individual entities called 'organisms'" (Okun & Rappaport, 1980, p. 6). He defined an **organism** as a form of life "composed of mutually dependent parts and processes standing in mutual interaction" (Bertalanffy, 1968, p. 33). As such, an organism was primarily motivated behaviorally by internal mechanisms. From Bertalanffy's work, social scientists conceptualized that all living systems, including families, operate on a similar set of principles, that is, they are internally interdependent.

Therefore, in a family, members are constantly interacting and mutually affecting one another (Bertalanffy, 1968). When change or movement occurs in any of the members or circumstances that make up the *family system,* all aspects of the family are affected. In essence, a family system is a living organism. Its well-being and ability to function are influenced by the health of all of its members. Overall, in the family as a system, "the focus is upon the relationship between elements rather than on the elements themselves" (Sauber, L'Abate, & Weeks, 1985, p. 164).

From a systems perspective, families are continuously changing and reconstituting themselves. They are open and self-regulating. They are also interactive within larger social systems. The family stabilizes and changes by using negative **feedback** loops (morphostasis) (see Figure 3.1). These loops, like a thermostat in a home heating system, allow family expansion and contraction within the limits of a range of behaviors. If for some reason the negative feedback loops do not work, the family gets out of control. Times of stability and homeostasis are temporary, and a major task for families is to maintain a balance between change and stability. If there is too much of either, the family and those within it suffer.

"Viewing families as systems involves recognizing that the relationships formed among family members are extremely powerful and account for a considerable amount of human behavior, emotion, values, and attitudes. Moreover, like strands of a spiderweb, each family relationship, as well as each family member, influences all other family relationships and all other members" (Figley, 1989, p. 4).

Systemic Versus Individual Therapeutic Approaches

As a result of taking a systemic counseling approach, family therapists make interventions differently than helping professionals, who primarily focus on individuals. For instance, the philosophy underlying individual counseling is **linear**

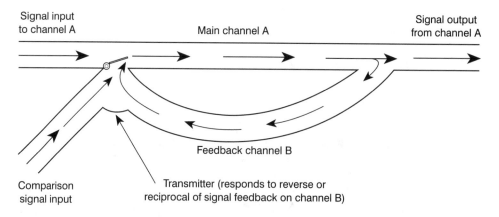

Signal input to channel A

Main channel A

Signal output from channel A

Feedback channel B

Comparison signal input

Transmitter (responds to reverse or reciprocal of signal feedback on channel B)

In this illustration of negative feedback, part of a system's output is reintroduced into the system as information about the output, thus governing and correcting the process. A negative signal from channel A, fed back to the sender through channel B, alters the signal in A. Feedback loops characterize all interpersonal relationships.

Figure 3.1

Negative feedback loops.

From "The Nature of Living Systems" by J. G. Miller, 1971, *Behavioral Science, 16,* p. 293. Reprinted by permission.

Figure 3.2
Linear versus circular thinking.

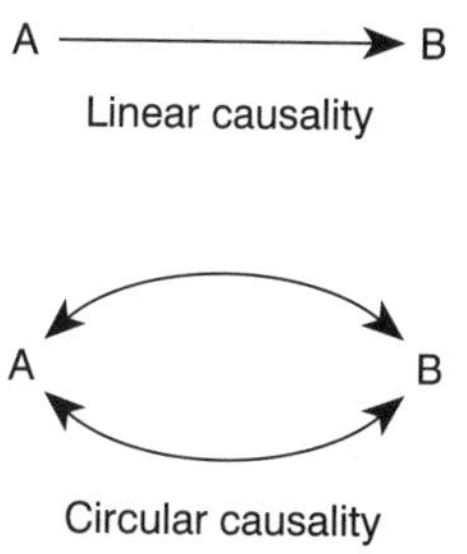

causality (i.e., A causes B). In contrast, family therapy is based on a **circular causality** (i.e., A and B influence each others' behaviors) (see Figure 3.2).

In addition, individual counseling focuses primarily on "why" (e.g., Why did Johnny do that?). In contrast, family therapy focuses on "how" and "what" (e.g., How does a certain behavior help the family? and What needs to be different?). These different types of questions yield different answers and, consequently, different interventions. For example, a father may not know why he did not set firm boundaries with his children, but he can usually talk about what he did and how he did it in relationship to them. Through understanding events and the reasoning behind them, changes can be made.

A third area separating family and individual approaches concerns process versus content. Family therapy focuses considerable attention on exploring interactive dynamics. However, individual counseling focuses attention on the specific content of the material being related. The contrast is between that of dealing with a whole picture versus that of working with various pieces of the picture.

Finally, family therapy deals primarily with here and now material, with the focus, in most cases, on bringing about immediate change. In contrast, individual counseling looks at historical data (Juhnke, 1993). Historical facts are relevant to situations where analysis of this material results in reconstructing one's personality.

Reasons for Working with Families

In addition to those already mentioned, there are other advantages to working with entire families as a unit rather than just the individuals within them. First, family therapy allows practitioners to "see causation as circular as well as, at times, linear" (Fishman, 1988, p. 5). This type of view enables clinicians to examine events broadly and in light of their complexity. It keeps therapists from being overly simplistic in offering help to those with whom they work. For example, a circular view of the problem of anorexia nervosa considers the friction within the whole family, especially the couple relationship. With this perspective, the inward and outward social pressures of the young person displaying obvious symptoms are examined, but in a much broader interactive context. Some dysfunctional behaviors, such as those involved in eating, can be addressed from a linear viewpoint—for example, a daughter does not put food in her mouth. Other behaviors, such as relationship dynamics are circular—for example, when parents fight, a daughter becomes depressed and frightened and refuses to eat, which results in her losing weight, which results in parents paying more attention to her, which results in less fighting, and so forth.

Second, family therapy involves real, significant individuals as a part of the process. As in individual therapy, there are no surrogate substitutes who may or may not act as significant people in a client's life. Instead, therapists deal directly with the persons involved. In other words, most family therapy does not depend on role plays or simulations. Therefore, if a young man is having difficulty with his parents or siblings, he is able to address them and strive toward resolution in person. This type of emphasis cuts through to the reality of a situation more quickly and more efficiently than indirect methods.

Third, in family therapy, all members of a family are given the same message simultaneously. Thus, they are challenged to work on issues together. This approach eliminates "secrets" and essentially makes the covert overt. The result is an increase in openness and communication. For example, if a couple is fighting, the issues over which there is tension are discussed within the family context. In this setting, family members become aware of what is involved in the situation. They deal with conflict directly. They also have the opportunity to generate ideas on what might be most helpful in bringing their situation to a successful resolution.

Fourth, family therapy usually takes less time than individual counseling. Many family therapists report that the length of time they are engaged in their work with a family can literally be as brief as a few sessions (Fishman, 1988). In fact, some family therapy approaches, notably those connected with brief and strategic family therapy, emphasize contracting with client families for limited amounts of time (usually no more than 10 sessions). The stress on time is motivational for therapists and families in maximizing their energy and innovation in creating resolutions.

Fifth, the approaches utilized in working with families focus on interpersonal instead of just intrapersonal relationships. This type of difference is comparable with seeing the forest instead of just the trees. The larger scope by which family therapy examines problematic behavior enables practitioners to find unique ways to address difficulties.

Finally, in family therapy, there is documented evidence that some approaches within it work under certain circumstances (Gurman, Kniskern, & Pinsof, 1986). Within the past two decades, a plethora of research has shown how family therapy has fostered changes in individuals and systems for the good of all. This type of efficiency is something that not all forms of therapy or counseling can claim.

Having examined the rationale for using family therapy, it is important to understand how it developed. The following sections trace the development of family therapy over time.

Family Therapy Through the Decades

Family therapy is an extension of the attempt by people throughout history to cure emotional suffering. "Over 2,000 years ago the first written accounts of an integrative system of treating mental illness were recorded" (Kottler, 1991, p. 34). Prehistorical records indicate that systematic attempts at helping were prevalent even before that time. Family members throughout history have tried to be of assistance to each other. This help initially took two forms:

1. Elders gave younger members of family clans and tribes advice on interpersonal relationships.
2. Adult members of these social units took care of the very young and the very old (Strong & DeVault, 1992).

Despite this history of care, family therapy is one of the newer methods of professional helping, with its roots in the twentieth century.

Even though it is relatively recent in its formal development, multiple events have influenced and shaped the profession of family therapy. Although all of the facts and personalities mentioned here had some impact on the growth of the field, some were more pivotal than others. The exact importance of particulars sometimes changes according to who is recounting events. The order in which these developments occurred, however, can be charted chronologically, and some historical facts and figures stand out regardless of one's historical orientation.

Family Therapy: Before 1940

Inhibitors of the Development of Family Therapy

Prior to the 1940s, family therapy in the United States was almost a nonentity. Three social influences contributed to this phenomenon. The first involved myth and perception. The myth of rugged individualism was the predominant deterrent to the genesis of family therapy. Healthy people were seen as adequate to handle their own problems. Rugged individualism stemmed from the settling of the United States, especially the American West. Individuals were expected to solve their own problems if they were to survive. Intertwined with this myth was the perception handed down from the Puritans and other religious groups that those who prospered were ordained by God (Strong &

DeVault, 1995). To admit one had difficulties, either inside or outside of a family context, was to also admit that one was not among the elect.

A second social factor that deterred the development of family therapy was tradition. Historically, people usually confided "with clergy, lawyers, and doctors, rather than with mental-health professionals," when they discussed their marital and family concerns (Brown & Christensen, 1986, p. 4). These professionals knew the families in question well because they usually lived with them in a shared community over many years. Seeking advice and counsel from these individuals was different from talking to a professional family specialist.

A third factor that prevented family therapy from evolving before the 1940s was the theoretical emphases of the times. The major psychological theories in the United States at the early part of the twentieth century were psychoanalysis and behaviorism. Both were philosophically and pragmatically opposed to dealing with more than individual concerns. Proponents of psychoanalysis, for instance, believed that dealing with more than one person at a time in therapy would disrupt the transference process and prevent depth analysis from occurring. Likewise, behaviorists stressed straightforward work with clients, usually in the form of conditioning and counterconditioning. The social and political climate for family therapy to develop and grow was almost nonexistent.

Catalysts for the Growth of Family Therapy

Despite this inhospitable environment, four factors combined to make family therapy accepted and eventually popular. The first was the growth of the number of women enrolled in colleges and their demand for courses in family life education (Broderick & Schrader, 1981). Educators from a number of disciplines responded to this need. Among the most noteworthy was Ernest Groves, who taught courses on parenting and family living at Boston University and the University of North Carolina. Groves later became instrumental in founding the American Association for Marriage Counselors (AAMC) in 1942 (Broderick & Schrader, 1991).

The second event that set the stage for the development of family therapy was the initial establishment of marriage counseling. In New York City, Abraham and Hannah Stone were among the leading advocates for and practitioners of marriage counseling in the late 1920s and 1930s. Emily Mudd began the Marriage Council of Philadelphia in 1932, which was devoted to a similar endeavor. Meanwhile, in California, Paul Popenoe established the American Institute of Family Relations, which was in essence his private practice. Popenoe introduced the term *marriage counseling* into the English language. He popularized the profession of marriage counseling by writing a monthly article, "Can this Marriage Be Saved?" in the *Ladies Home Journal*—a practice that began in 1945 and continues today (Broderick & Schrader, 1991).

A third impetus to the genesis of family counseling was the founding of the National Council on Family Relations in 1938 and the establishment of its journal, *Marriage and Family Living,* in 1939. This association promoted research-based knowledge about family life throughout the United States. Through its pioneer efforts, and those of the American Home Economics Association, information about aspects of family life were observed, recorded, and presented.

The fourth favorable event that helped launch family therapy as a profession was the work of county home extension agents. These agents began working with families educationally in the 1920s and 1930s and helped those they encountered to better understand the dynamics of their family situations. Some of the ideas and advice offered by agents were advocated by Alfred Adler, who developed a practical approach for working with families that became widespread in the United States in the 1930s (Dinkmeyer, Dinkmeyer, & Sperry, 1987).

Family Therapy: 1940 to 1949

Several important events took place in the 1940s that had a lasting impact on the field of family therapy. One of the most important was the establishment of an association for professionals working with couples. The American Association for Marriage Counselors (AAMC) was formed in 1942. Its purpose was to help professionals network with one another in regard to the theory and practice of marriage counseling. It also devised standards for the practice of this specialty.

A second landmark event of the 1940s was the publication of the first account of concurrent marital therapy by Bela Mittleman (1948) of the New York Psychoanalytic Institute. Mittleman's position stressed the importance of object relations in couple relationships. It was a radical departure from the previously held intrapsychic point of view.

A third significant focus during the 1940s was the study of families of schizophrenics. One of the early pioneers in this area was Theodore Lidz, who published a survey of fifty families. He found that the majority of schizophrenics came from broken homes and/or had seriously disturbed family relationships (Lidz & Lidz, 1949). Lidz later introduced into the family therapy literature "the concepts of '**schism,**' the division of the family into two antagonistic and competing groups, and '**skew,**' whereby one partner in the marriage dominates the family to a striking degree, as a result of serious personality disorder in at least one of the partners" (Barker, 1986, p. 4).

The final factor that influenced family counseling in the 1940s was World War II and its aftermath. The events of the war brought considerable stress to millions of families in the United States. Many men were separated from their families because of war duty. Numerous women went to work in factories. Deaths and disabilities of loved ones added further pain and suffering. A need to work with families suffering trauma and change became apparent. To help meet mental health needs, the National Mental Health Act of 1946 was passed by Congress. "This legislation authorized funds for research, demonstration, training, and assistance to states in the use of the most effective methods of prevention, diagnosis, and treatment of mental health disorders" (Hershenson & Power, 1987, p. 11). Mental health work with families would eventually be funded under this act.

Family Therapy: 1950 to 1959

Some family therapy historians consider the 1950s to be the genesis of the movement (Guerin, 1976). Landmark events in the development of family therapy in the 1950s centered more on people than on organizations, because of the difficulty of launching this therapeutic approach in the face of well-established opposition groups, such as psychiatrists.

Important Personalities in Family Therapy in the 1950s

A number of professionals contributed to the interdisciplinary underpinnings of family therapy in the 1950s (Shields, Wynne, McDaniel, & Gawinski, 1994). Each, in his or her own way, contributed to the conceptual and clinical vitality as well as the growth of the field.

Nathan Ackerman was one of the most significant personalities of the decade. Although he advocated treating the family from a systems perspective as early as the 1930s (Ackerman, 1938), it was not until the 1950s that Ackerman became well known and prominent. His strong belief in working with families and his persistently high energy influenced leading psychoanalytically trained psychiatrists to explore the area of family therapy. An example of this impact can be seen in Ackerman's book *The Psychodynamics of Family Life* (1958), in which he urged psychiatrists to go beyond understanding the role of family dynamics in the ethology of mental illness and to begin treating client mental disorders in light of family process dynamics. To show that his revolutionary ideas were workable, he set up a practice in New York City.

Another influential figure of the time was Gregory Bateson, in Palo Alto, California. Bateson, like many researchers of the 1950s, was interested in communication patterns in families of schizophrenics. He obtained several government grants for study and, with Jay Haley, John Weakland, and eventually Don Jackson, Bateson formulated a novel, controversial, and influential theory of dysfunctional communication called the **double-bind** (Bateson, Jackson, Haley, & Weakland, 1956). This theory states that two seemingly contradictory messages may exist on different levels and lead to confusion, if not schizophrenic behavior, on the part of some individuals. For example, a person may receive the message to "sin boldly and be careful." Such communication leads to ignoring one message and obeying the other or to a type of stressful behavioral paralysis where one does nothing because it is unclear which message to follow and how.

Bateson left the field of family research in the early 1960s, and the Bateson group disbanded in 1962. However, much of the work of this original group was expanded upon by the Mental Research Institute (MRI), which Don Jackson created in Palo Alto in 1959 (Barker, 1986). Among the later luminaries to join MRI were Virginia Satir and Paul Watzlawick. A unique feature of this group was the treatment of families, which was resisted by Bateson. In fact, the MRI established **brief therapy,** an elaboration of the work of Milton Erickson and one of the first new approaches to family therapy (Haley, 1976).

A third leading professional in the 1950s was Carl Whitaker. Whitaker "risked violating the conventions of traditional psychotherapy," during this time, by including spouses and children in therapy (Broderick & Schrader, 1991, p. 26). As chief of psychiatry at Emory University in Atlanta, Whitaker (1958) published the results of his work in **dual therapy (conjoint couple therapy)**. He also set up the first conference on family therapy at Sea Island, Georgia, in 1955.

A fourth key figure of the 1950s was Murray Bowen. Beginning in the mid-1950s, under the sponsorship of the National Institute of Mental Health, Bowen began holding therapy sessions with all family members present, as part of a research project with schizophrenics (Guerin, 1976). Although he was not initially successful in helping family members constructively talk to each other and resolve difficulties, Bowen gained experience that would later help him formulate an elaborate theory on the influence of previous generations on the mental health of families.

Other key figures in family therapy who began their careers in the 1950s were Ivan Boszormenyi-Nagy, at the Eastern Pennsylvania Psychiatric Institute (EPPI), and his associates, including James Framo and Gerald Zuk. The work of this group eventually resulted in the development of Nagy's contextual therapy. "At the heart of this approach is the healing of human relationships through trust and commitment, done primarily by developing loyalty, fairness, and reciprocity" (Anderson, Anderson, & Hovestadt, 1993, p. 3).

Family Therapy: 1960 to 1969

The decade of the 1960s was an era of rapid growth in family therapy. During this time, the idea of working with families was embraced by more professionals, a number of whom were quite charismatic. Four of the most prominent of these figures were Jay Haley, Salvador Minuchin, Virginia Satir, and Carl Whitaker. Other family therapists who began in the 1950s, such as Nathan Ackerman, John Bell, and Murray Bowen, continued contributing to the concepts and theories in the field. Another factor that made an impact at this time was the widespread introduction of systems theory. Finally, in the 1960s, training centers and academic programs in family therapy were either started, strengthened, or proposed.

Major Family Therapists of the 1960s

Numerous family therapists emerged in the 1960s. They came from many interdisciplinary backgrounds, and like their predecessors of the 1950s, most were considered "mavericks" (Framo, 1996). The following therapists are discussed here because of their significant impact in shaping the direction of family therapy.

Jay Haley was probably the most important figure in family therapy in the 1960s. During this time, Haley had connections with most of the important figures in the field, and through his writings and travels, he kept professionals linked and informed. Also during this time, he began to formulate what would become his own version of strategic family therapy. Haley relied most on expanding and elaborating on the work of Milton Erickson (Haley, 1963). He shared with Erickson an emphasis on gaining and maintaining power during treatment. Like Erickson, Haley often gave client families permission to do what they would have done naturally (e.g., to withhold information). Furthermore, Haley used directives, as Erickson had, to get client families to do more within therapy than merely gain insight.

From 1961 to 1969, Jay Haley edited *Family Process,* the first journal in the field of family therapy. Through it, he helped shape an emerging profession. In the late 1960s, Haley moved from Palo Alto to Philadelphia to join the Child Guidance Clinic, which was under the direction of Salvador Minuchin. His move brought two creative minds together and helped generate new ideas in the minds of both men and the people with whom they worked and trained.

Salvador Minuchin, the psychiatrist with whom Haley collaborated in 1967, first began his work with families at the Wiltwyck School for Boys in New York State in the early 1960s. He used his own form of family therapy with urban slum families he encountered because it reduced the recidivism rate for the delinquents who comprised the population of the school. The publication of his account of this work, *Families of the Slums* (Minuchin, Montalvo, Guerney, Rosman, & Schumer, 1967), received much recognition and led to his appointment as director of the Philadelphia Child Guidance Clinic and to the formulation of a new and influential theory of family therapy: structural family therapy.

Like most pioneers in the field of family therapy (e.g., Whitaker, Haley), Minuchin did not have formal training in how to treat families. However, he did have an idea of what healthy families should look like in regard to a hierarchy, and he used this mental map as a basis on which to construct his approach to helping families change. Another innovative idea he initiated at the end of the 1960s was the training of "indigenous members of the local black community as paraprofessional family therapists. The reason for this special effort is that cultural differences often make it very difficult for white middle-class therapists to understand and relate successfully to urban blacks and hispanics" (Nichols & Schwartz, 1995, p. 53-54). Overall, Minuchin began transforming the Philadelphia Child Guidance Clinic from a second-rate and poor facility to the leading center for the training of family therapists on the East Coast of the United States.

Virginia Satir was the most entertaining and exciting family therapist to emerge in the 1960s. Satir, as a social worker in private practice in Chicago, started seeing family members as a group for treatment in the 1950s (Broderick & Schrader, 1991). However, she gained prominence as a family therapist at the Mental Research Institute. There she collaborated with her colleagues and branched out on her own. Satir was unique in being the only woman among the pioneers of family therapy. She had "unbounded optimism about people . . . and her empathic abilities were unmatched" (Framo, 1996, p. 311). While her male counterparts concentrated on problems and building conceptual frameworks for theories and power, she "touched and nurtured her clients" and "spoke of the importance of self-esteem, compassion, and congruent expression of feelings." (Nichols & Schwartz, 1995, p. 100).

Satir gained national recognition with the publication of her book *Conjoint Family Therapy* (1964). In this text, she described the importance of seeing both members of a couple together at the same time, and she detailed how such a process could and should occur. Her clear style of writing made this book influential. Overall, "Satir's ability to synthesize ideas, combined with her creative development of teaching techniques and general personal charisma, gave her a central position in the field" of family therapy (Guerin, 1976).

Carl Whitaker can be described in many ways. He dared to be different and at his best was creative as well as wise (Framo, 1996). He was never "conventional." Whitaker, a psychiatrist, became interested in working with families in the 1940s. As already mentioned, he was chair of the psychiatry department of Emory University in the early 1950s. In 1955, he resigned to begin a private practice.

His main influence and renown in the field, however, came following his move to become a professor of psychiatry at the University of Wisconsin in 1965. It was at Wisconsin that Whitaker was able to write and lecture extensively. Beginning in 1965, his affectively based interventions, which were usually spontaneous and sometimes appeared outrageous, gained notoriety in the field of family therapy. In the 1960s, Whitaker also nurtured the field of family therapy by connecting professionals with similar interests.

Continuing Leaders in Family Therapy During the 1960s

Nathan Ackerman "continued to be a leader of the family therapy movement throughout the 1960s. In 1961, with (Don) Jackson, he cofounded *Family Process,* the first journal to be devoted to family therapy, and one which is still pre-eminent in the field" (Barker, 1986, p. 10). One of Ackerman's most significant books during this decade was *Treating the Troubled Family* (1966). In this text, he elaborated on how to intervene with families and "tickle the family's defenses" through being involved with them, being confrontive, and bringing covert issues out into the open.

John Bell, like Carl Whitaker, began treating families long before he was recognized as a leader in the field of family therapy. Bell's work began in the 1950s when he started using group therapy as a basis for working with families (Kaslow, 1980). He published his ideas about **family group therapy** a decade later (Bell, 1961) and proposed a structured program of treatment that conceptualized family members as strangers. Members become known to each other in stages similar to those found in groups.

Bell taught his natural family group approach at the University of California, Berkeley, in 1963 in one of the first graduate courses on family therapy ever offered in the United States. From 1968 to 1973, he directed the Mental Research Institute in Palo Alto. It was Bell's belief that "all children 9 years or older and all other adult family members living in the home should be included in family therapy and should be present for all sessions" (Nichols & Everett,

1986, p. 43). Bell's ideas were unique and received considerable criticism, thus generating a good deal of discussion about family therapy (Hines, 1988).

Murray Bowen gained considerable insight into the dynamics and treatment of families during the 1960s. Part of the reason was that he was able to successfully deal with problems within his own family of origin. Another reason was that he began to see a connectedness between working with families that had a schizophrenic member and working with families that had other problems (Barker, 1986).

One of his most significant discoveries was the "emotional reactivity" of many troubled families when brought together to solve problems (Nichols & Schwartz, 1995). In these situations, family members had difficulty in maintaining their identities and their actions. They would often resemble what Bowen (1961) called an **undifferentiated family ego mass**. In working with these families, Bowen found that by being cognitive and detached, he could help them establish appropriate relationship boundaries and avoid projecting (or **triangulating**) interpersonal dyadic difficulties onto a third person or object (i.e., a **scapegoat**).

General Systems Theory

With the emergence of new ideas came a novel theoretical perspective on which to center these concepts: **general systems theory.** This view of life originated among many theorists but was refined and developed by Ludwig von Bertalanffy (1968), a biologist. General systems theory attempts to explain how organisms thrive or die in accordance with their openness or closedness to their environments. (Although general systems theory has been briefly described previously, it will be elaborated on here to put it in an historical context).

In general systems theory, a **system** is "a set of elements standing in interaction" (Nichols & Everett, 1986, p. 69). Each element in the system is affected by whatever happens to any other element. Thus, the system is only as strong as its weakest part. Likewise, the system is greater than the sum of its parts. Whether the system is a human body or a family, it is organized in a particular manner with boundaries that are more or less open (i.e., permeable) depending on the amount and type of feedback received.

By viewing the family in this manner, clinicians in the 1960s focused away from **linear causality** (direct cause and effect) and more on **circular causality** (the idea that events are related through a series of interacting loops or repeating cycles) (Nichols & Schwartz, 1995). Subsequently, family therapists began to claim their role as specialists within therapy. This position was reinforced in 1963, when the first state licensure law regulating family counselors was passed in California. This legislation was just the beginning of family therapy's increasing prominence.

Institutes and Training Centers

In addition to the rise of personalities and general systems theory, in the decade of the 1960s, training institutes and centers also came into prominence. In California, the Mental Research Institute in Palo Alto flourished even after Jay

Haley's departure for Philadelphia in 1967 and Don Jackson's death in 1968. Likewise, the Family Institute of New York (headed by Ackerman) thrived during this time, as did the Albert Einstein College of Medicine in New York City and the affiliated Bronx State Hospital (Broderick & Schrader, 1991).

In Philadelphia, the Philadelphia Child Guidance Clinic opened its facilities to surrounding neighborhoods and to aspiring family therapists. Innovative techniques, such as the "bug in the ear" form of communication, were devised at the clinic during this time. In 1964, the Family Institute of Philadelphia emerged. This institute was a merger of the EPPI and the Philadelphia Psychiatric Center and fostered such notable practitioner/theorists as Gerald Zuk and Ross Speck (Broderick & Schrader, 1991).

Meanwhile, in Boston, the Boston Family Institute was established in 1969 under the direction of Fred Duhl and David Kantor (Duhl, 1983). This institute focused on expressive and dramatic interventions and originated the technique of family sculpting.

Overseas, the Institute for Family Studies in Milan was formed in 1967. This institute was based on the MRI model and came into prominence in the 1970s with many innovative, short-term approaches to working with families (Selvini Palazzoli, Boscolo, Cecchin, & Prata, 1978).

Family Therapy: 1970 to 1979

The 1970s were marked by several nodal events in regard to family therapy. These events centered around many activities, including a major membership increase in the American Association for Marriage and Family Therapy (AAMFT), the founding of the American Family Therapy Association (AFTA), the refinement of theories, the influence of foreign therapies and therapists (especially the Milan Group), the growth of family enrichment, and the introduction of feminism into the family therapy field.

Membership in the American Association
for Marriage and Family Therapy (AAMFT)

In 1970, the membership of the AAMFT stood at 973. By 1979, membership had increased over 777% to 7,565 (Gurman & Kniskern, 1981). The dynamic growth of the association can be explained in many ways including that it was recognized by the Department of Health, Education, and Welfare in 1977 as an accrediting body for programs granting degrees in marriage and family therapy. Also, at about the same time, the association changed its name from the American Association for Marriage and Family Counseling to the American Association for Marriage and Family Therapy (AAMFT).

In addition, more focus was placed on families and therapeutic ways of working with them as a result of the upheavals in family life in the 1960s. Furthermore, many of the pioneers of the family therapy movement, such as Virginia Satir, James Framo, Carl Whitaker, Salvador Minuchin, Jay Haley, and Florence

Kaslow, began making a greater impact on therapists across the nation with their workshop presentations and writings. To add to this impact, in 1974, the AAMFT began publishing its own professional periodical, the *Journal of Marital and Family Therapy,* with William C. Nichols, Jr., as the first editor, and made plans late in the decade to move its headquarters from Claremont, California, to Washington, D.C. (an event that actually transpired in 1982).

Establishment of the American Family Therapy Association (AFTA)

The AFTA was founded in 1977 by a small group of mental health professionals who were active during the early years when the field of family therapy was emerging. Initially, it strove to represent "the interests of systemic family therapists as distinct from psychodynamic marriage counselors" (Sauber et al., 1985, p. 180). Leaders of the AFTA included Murray Bowen and James Framo. As a "think tank," the AFTA's annual meeting brings together professionals to address a variety of clinical, research, and teaching topics.

In 1981, a joint liaison committee of the AAMFT and the AFTA representatives was formed to address the respective roles of the two organizations within the profession. The AFTA was identified as an academy of advanced professionals interested in the exchange of ideas; the AAMFT retained government recognition for its role in providing credentials to marriage and family therapists (Nichols & Schwartz, 1995).

Refinement of Family Therapy Theories

The 1970s marked the growth and refinement of family therapy theories outside the psychoanalytical tradition. It is ironic and symbolic that Nathan Ackerman, who carried the banner of psychoanalytical family therapy, died in 1971 (Bloch & Simon, 1982). It is also interesting to note that the works of Salvador Minuchin (structural family therapy), Gerald Patterson (behavioral family therapy), Carl Whitaker (experiential family therapy), and Jay Haley (strategic family therapy) increased in frequency, scope, and influence during this decade. The newness of ideas generated in the 1960s bore fruit in the 1970s.

One major example of this phenomenon was the work of Salvador Minuchin. In a clearly articulated book, *Families and Family Therapy,* Minuchin (1974) outlined a practical guide for conducting structural family therapy. He followed this publication, later in the decade, with a complementary coauthored text entitled *Psychosomatic Families: Anorexia Nervosa in Context* (Minuchin, Rosman, & Baker, 1978), which showcased in a dramatic way the power of the therapy he had created. These writings, combined with his well-staffed training center in Philadelphia, made structural family therapy a major theoretical force in family therapy circles in a relatively brief period of time.

Influence of Foreign Therapies and Therapists

In Europe, in the late 60s and early 70s, the development of family therapy grew rapidly. By the mid-70s, theories and theorists, especially in Italy and Great Britain, became influential in the United States. The influx of foreign family therapists' ideas led many American professionals to question "particular ethnocentric values about what is good and true for families" (Broderick & Schrader, 1991, p. 35).

Particularly influential was the Milan (Italy) Group headed by Mara Selvini Palazzoli and staffed by three other psychoanalytically trained psychiatrists: Gianfrano Cecchin, Giulana Prata, and Luigi Boscolo. Their book, *Paradox and Counterparadox* (1978), was influenced by the work of Bateson and Watzlawick in Palo Alto; but it was original in its emphasis on **circular questioning** (asking questions that highlight differences among family members) and **triadic questioning** (asking a third family member how two others members of the family relate). The Milan approach emphasized developing an hypothesis about the family before their arrival. Furthermore, it prescribed homework assignments that were often ritualistic and difficult (Barker, 1986; Nichols & Schwartz, 1995).

Two British leaders in the helping profession who influenced the development of family therapy in the United States were R. D. Laing and Robin Skynner. Laing (1965) coined the term ***mystification*** to describe how some families mask what is going on between family members by giving conflicting and contradictory explanations of events. His complicated but interesting book, *Knots* (1970), further enhanced his status as an original thinker in understanding universal family dynamics in dysfunctional families. Skynner (1981) developed a brief version of psychoanalytic family therapy in the 1970s that helped complement and enrich the work done by Ackerman and Boszormenyi-Nagy.

Growth of Marriage/Family Enrichment
The exact date of the launching of preventative programs for family enhancement is difficult to trace, but credit is often given to David and Vera Mace. The Maces were pioneers of marriage counseling in England. After they moved to the United States in the early 1960s, they began leading retreats for couples and developing enrichment programs (Mace, 1983). On their 40th wedding anniversary, in July 1973, they established the Association of Couples for Marriage Enrichment (ACME).

At about the same time as the Maces were initiating their efforts in marriage enrichment, a Catholic priest, Father Gabriel Calvo, began leading retreats for married couples in Barcelona, Spain. His efforts later evolved into the Marriage Encounter Movement.

Other pioneers in marriage/family enrichment were Bernard G. Guerney, Jr., (1977) and his four-basic-skill Relationship Enhancement approach, and the staffs of the Family and Children's Service in Minneapolis and the University of Minnesota Family Study Center, who developed the Couples Communication Programs (Miller, Nunnally, & Wackman, 1977, 1979).

Feminist Theory and Family Therapy
"Feminist thinking explicitly entered the family therapy field in the 1970s and has increasingly influenced the theory and practice of family therapy" (Framo, 1996, p. 303). The challenge to family therapy by feminist theory began in 1978,

when an article by Rachel Hare-Mustin entitled "A feminist approach to family therapy" was published in *Family Process*. Hare-Mustin took the position that family therapy discriminated against women because it basically promoted the status quo that women were unequal in regard to their duties and roles within families.

Hare-Mustin's publication was the start of a number of other pieces on the adequacy of family therapy from a systemic perspective. Among the most consistently voiced views, from feminist therapists' perspectives, is that historic sexism and structural inequalities cannot be corrected through improving relationships among family members or creating a new family hierarchy. Rather, the goals of working with a family are "to facilitate the growth of a strong, competent woman who has enhanced control over resources" and "to increase the ability of women to work together politically to change society and its institutions" (Libow, Raskin, & Caust, 1982, p. 8).

Although feminist family therapists "represent a wide range of theoretical orientations," they are "drawn together by their recognition that sexism limits the psychological well-being of women and men, by their advocacy of equality in relationships and society, and by their refusal to use any counseling methods or explanatory concepts that promote bias" (Enns, 1992, p. 338). The future of family therapy is tied to whether historical systems theory and feminist theory can be reconciled.

Family Therapy: 1980 to 1989

Several important events marked the emergence of family therapy in the 1980s. One was the retirement or death of some of the leading pioneers in the movement and the emergence of new leaders. A second was the growth in the number of individuals and associations devoted to family therapy. A third was an increase in research in family therapy (Miller, 1986) and an explosion in publications devoted to family therapy. And finally, further recognition of marriage and family therapy came about on a national level.

Change in Family Therapy Leadership

In the 1980s, new leadership began to emerge in family therapy circles. One reason was the aging of the initial pioneers in the field. Another reason was the maturity of clinicians who studied in the 1960s and 1970s with the founders of the movement. The second and third generations of family therapists had new ideas and abundant energy (Kaslow, 1990). They basically preserved the best of the founders while forging out in different directions. Some of the more established leaders in the field, such as Jay Haley, switched emphases at this time and maintained their leadership roles.

Within the growth of this movement, many women came to the forefront. Among them were Monica McGoldrick, Rachel Hare-Mustin, Carolyn Attneave, Peggy Papp, Peggy Penn, Cloe Madanes, Fromma Walsh, and Betty Carter. These women began to create novel theories and to challenge older ones. Cloe Madanes was especially prolific and creative during the last part of the 1980s. Overall, the work of new women leaders in family therapy contributed much to the profession. Their presence and prominence altered the view that a professional panel of family therapists consisted of four men and Virginia Satir.

Growth in the Profession of Family Therapy

Family therapy grew significantly as a profession in the 1980s. The membership of the American Association for Marriage and Family Therapy, for instance, almost doubled to a total of 14,000 members. At the same time, two new associations devoted to the study and practice of family therapy were formed. The first was the Division of Family Psychology, which was established within the American Psychological Association (APA) in 1984. The division was established because of the desire by some family practitioners to maintain their identity as psychologists (Kaslow, 1990). Such noted individuals as James Alexander, Alan Gurman, Florence Kaslow, Luciano L'Abate, Rachel Hare-Mustin, Duncan Stanton, and Gerald Zuk were among those who became affiliated with this division.

The second new professional association formed in the 1980s was the International Association for Marriage and Family Counselors (IAMFC), which was established initially as an interest group within the American Counseling Association (ACA) in 1986. The IAMFC grew from an initial membership of 143 in 1986 to over 7,000 in 1993. In 1990, IAMFC became a division of ACA.

The initial goals and purposes of the IAMFC were to enhance marriage and the family through providing educational programs, conducting research, sponsoring conferences, and establishing interprofessional contacts, and by examining and removing conditions that create barriers to marriages and families. Since its formation, the IAMFC has broadened its vision to include work in promoting ethical practices, setting high quality training standards, helping families and couples cope successfully, and using counseling knowledge and systemic methods to ameliorate the problems confronting marriages and families (Maynard & Olson, 1987).

Development of Research Techniques in Family Therapy

Until the 1980s, research techniques and solid research in family therapy were scarce. It was implicitly assumed that other research methodologies could be translated to the family therapy field or that case study reports were sufficient in validating the impact of family therapy. In the 1980s, however, this changed.

A forewarning of the increased emphasis on family research came when a 1982 edition of the *Journal of Marriage and the Family* devoted an entire issue to family research methodologies. A parallel event occurred in the *Journal of Family Issues* in 1984 (Miller, 1986). In addition, a research methods book by Adams and Schvaneveldt (1985) was among the first to use examples involving families.

Since the 1980s, research in family therapy has become increasingly sophisticated in terms of the questions posed and the methods used to address these questions (Nichols & Schwartz, 1995). Research indicates that family therapy is clearly effective as a form of treatment. Research further verifies that both behavioral and systems approaches to working with families are effective (Gurman et al., 1986).

Publications in Family Therapy

The growth in the number of individuals and associations involved in family therapy was paralleled by an increase in publications in this area. Some major publishing houses, such as Guilford Press and Brunner/Mazel, began to specialize in books on family therapy. Almost all publishers of texts in counseling, psychology, and social work added books on marriage and family therapy. In addition, new periodicals were established, and older ones grew in circulation.

Family Therapy Networker, a periodical with a subscription list of over 50,000, was the success story of the 1980s. The success of the *Networker* is attributable to its timely and interesting articles and its journalistic (as opposed to scholarly) form of writing. Its magazine format and featured information on professional conferences across the country are undoubtedly additional factors in its success.

National Recognition of Family Therapy

The main national event for family therapy in the 1980s was the listing of the profession as one of the four core mental health professions eligible for mental health traineeships (Shields et al., 1994). This action occurred as a part of the Public Health Service Act, Title III, Section 303 (d) (1). It basically placed the profession, in the eyes of the federal government, on a par with other professions vying for federal training grants, such as psychology and psychiatry.

Family Therapy: the 1990s

The 1990s continue to be an exciting time in the field of family therapy. One reason is that new theories and specialty areas have emerged. Another reason is that the number of professionals who primarily identify themselves as family therapists continues to grow. Still another reason is that academic curriculums and experiential components in family therapy are being continually refined. The term *family therapist* is now definable in regard to course work, competencies, and clinical experience. Furthermore, there are now a number of well-respected and researched theories practitioners can claim (Piercy & Sprenkle, 1986). The issues of the 1990s concern professional affiliation, accreditation, and licensure, that is, matters related to power and influence. They also involve identification and influence specifically regarding whether family therapy will continue to be interdisciplinary or if it will be "marginalized" (Shields et al., 1994).

New Theories and Specialties within Family Therapy

The 1990s have seen a number of new theories of family therapy either emerge or gain added attention. Solution-focused and narrative theories developed in the Midwest by Steve deShazer (1988) and Bill O'Hanlon (O'Hanlon & Weiner-Davis,

1989) and in Australia and New Zealand by Michael White and David Epston (1990), respectively, have received the most publicity. These theories are characterized by their brevity and creativity and are covered in chapter 10 of this text.

Other emerging theories of the 1990s that have promise for the treatment of families in the twenty-first century are:

- the reflecting team approach of Tom Andersen (1991)
- the therapeutic conversations model of Harlene Anderson and Harry Goolishian (Anderson, 1994)
- the improvisational therapy model of Bradford Keeney (1990)
- the psychoeducational model of Carol Anderson (1988)
- the internal family systems model of Richard Schwartz (1994)

Of these new family theories, some are radically different from their forerunners because they are based on **social constructionism,** a philosophy that states our experiences are a function of how we think about them instead of objective entities. This viewpoint is opposed to systemic assumptions and has caused many family therapists to reexamine their basic assumptions (Piercy & Sprenkle, 1990).

Equally pervasive in the 1990s has been the redirection of the family therapy education field from a focus on producing narrowly trained theory-specific clinicians to a focus on training practitioners who know how to work with special types of families (Broderick & Schrader, 1991). This shift has produced a plethora of new books and an emphasis on distinct types of family problems and families (Nichols & Schwartz, 1995). For instance, there are books and specialized courses on working with families comprised of individuals who abuse drugs, alcohol, food, or other family members. In addition, literature and academic offerings are available in treating single-parent families, remarried families, aging families, and families with young children, adolescents, or disabled members. Further, there are opportunities for reading about or studying culturally diverse families as well as gay and lesbian families. "As opposed to the 1960s and 1970s, during which the followers of a particular model read little but what came out of that school . . . this recent trend toward specialization by content area rather than by model [or theories] has decreased factionalism and increased communication" in the family therapy field (Nichols & Schwartz, 1995, p. 144).

Growth in Number of Family Therapists

The major professional associations for family therapists (i.e., AAMFT, IAMFC, AFTA, and Division 43 of APA) continue to attract members in the 1990s. The largest (over 20,000) and most organized during this time is the AAMFT. The second largest association, the IAMFC, grew from a membership of approximately 4,000 members in 1990 to over 7,000 by 1997. It had the distinction during this time of being the fastest growing association for family therapists. The third association, Division 43 (Family Psychology), increasingly brings psychologists into working with family systems but at a rate slower than the first two groups because of its APA membership requirement. Likewise, the AFTA, with its strict experiential requirement, has grown more slowly (1,000 members in 1994).

Whether these associations will try to undermine each other or cooperate in areas of mutual interest is yet to be decided. It appears that there will be competition for status and recognition on a state-by-state level. However, under the regulations published in the Federal Register (Vol. 57, No. 14), marriage and family therapists have officially become the fifth "core" mental health profession, along with psychiatrists, psychologists, social workers, and psychiatric nurses (Shields et al., 1994). Therefore, the number of family therapists will most likely continue to grow.

Accreditation and Licensure of Family Therapists

There are now two associations that accredit programs in family therapy: AAMFT and IAMFC. Both do so under accrediting commissions that operate independently from their associations. The AAMFT standards are drawn up and administered by the Commission on Accreditation for Marriage and Family Therapy (CAMFT). Those for IAMFT are similarly handled through the Council for Accreditation of Counseling and Related Educational Programs (CACREP) (Hollis, 1996). A minimum of a masters degree is required as the credential for entering this specialty, although there is debate over the exact content and sequencing of courses.

Both the AAMFT and IAMFC have been working hard to increase the number of programs they accredit. Making these programs more rigorous has also been a goal for these associations. The health reform agenda of the decade will influence educational programs and the work of family therapists regardless of their professional setting. Being recognized as a core mental health provider will be crucial to the well-being of educational programs in family therapy and the profession as a whole.

In regard to licensure and recognition, 37 states either license or certify family therapy professionals. The number of states that will continue to regulate family therapy in this way will likely increase into the twenty-first century. Such a practice is designed to protect the public from unscrupulous and unqualified practitioners. The costs are minimal because regulating boards are self-governing. Overall, the future of family therapy looks bright.

Summary and Conclusion

This chapter examined the rationale for conducting family therapy. It also gave a brief history of family therapy. Both the reasons for working with families and the traditions and methods employed with such groups have expanded with time.

The rationale for conducting family therapy is based on a systems viewpoint of personality disorders. From a systems perspective, people's mental health and difficulties are based more on interpersonal dynamics than on an intrapersonal struggle. Because families, like other living organisms, are only as healthy as their weakest members, it makes logical and empirical sense to treat individuals within a family context, so that the power and resources of families and their members can be supportively maximized. This is a macro, as opposed to a micro, viewpoint of dysfunctionality and one that has an increasing amount of research support.

Parallel to the rationale for family therapy is the history of this movement, primarily seen in this chapter from the perspective of its development within the United States. Notable events in the life of family therapy have been traced through the decades. Before the 1940s, this form of treatment was virtually nonexistent, because of prevailing beliefs within the culture of the United States that stressed the importance of the individual. A further factor prohibiting the development of family therapy was historic tradition. Individuals in need of assistance in their relationships consulted first with other family members, then with clergy and physicians.

Family therapy grew, however, due to a number of events such as the growth of the number of women in higher education and increased demand for more courses in family life. Likewise, the founding of associations (e.g., the National Council of Family Relations), the pioneer work in marriage counseling, the growth in the role of county home extension agents, and World War II influenced the formation of the profession.

The 1940s saw the formation of the American Association for Marriage Counselors (AAMC) and initial treatment of schizophrenics through treating their families. The 1950s was a decade that saw the emergence of strong personalities who advocated for family therapy, such as Nathan Ackerman, Gregory Bateson, Don Jackson, Carl Whitaker, and Murray Bowen. Their work was expanded on in the 1960s, and new important figures that became pioneers at this time were Jay Haley, Salvador Minuchin, Virginia Satir, and John Bell. In retrospect, all of these professionals began their therapeutic journeys in the 1950s, but some came into prominence before others.

In the 1970s, family therapy became more respectable, and the American Association for Marriage and Family Therapy (AAMFT) grew rapidly and was recognized by government agencies. New journals and books appeared on a range of family therapy topics. In addition, established family therapies were refined, and foreign practitioners from Great Britain and Italy began to have greater influence. Complementing these developments was an emerging emphasis on marriage and family enrichment, the rise of feminist theory influence in family therapy, and the development of assessment techniques geared to families.

In the 1980s and 1990s, there has been an increase in the number of professionals involved in working with couples and families. Two new associations were established in the mid-1980s: Division 43 (Family Psychology) of the American Psychological Association (APA) and the International Association for Marriage and Family Counselors (IAMFC), an affiliate of the American Counseling Association (ACA). Amidst the excitement, growth and continuing governmental recognition of family therapy, turf wars between associations regarding recognition and accreditation have begun.

Family therapy appears to be basically healthy. More women have emerged as leaders, and feminist theory has grown in its influence and impact to make the entire field reexamine itself anew. As in the 1970s, the proliferation of publications in family therapy has increased, with the most widely read periodical being the *Family Therapy Networker*. New theoretical approaches, such as solution-focused and narrative family therapies, are also making an impact. Licensure efforts are growing. Health care reform has become an issue. Yet, considering everything, the outlook for family therapy is promising.

SUMMARY TABLE

History of Family Therapy

Before 1940
Culture beliefs stress the individual, the use of community resources, and psychoanalytic theory.

Ernest Groves, Alfred Adler, and county home extension agents teach family living/parenting skills.

Abraham and Hannah Stone, Emily Mudd, and Paul Popenoe begin marriage counseling.

National Council on Family Relations is founded (1938).

1940 to 1949
The American Association for Marriage Counselors (AAMC) is established (1942).

Milton Erickson develops therapeutic methods that will later be adopted by family therapy.

First account of concurrent marital therapy is published by Bela Mittleman (1948).

Theodore Lidz and Lyman Wynne study schizophrenic families.

World War II brings stress to families.

Mental Health Act of 1946 is passed by Congress.

1950 to 1959
Nathan Ackerman develops a psychoanalytical approach to working with families.

Gregory Bateson group begins studying patterns of communication in families.

Don Jackson creates the Mental Research Institute (1959).

Carl Whitaker sets up the first conference on family therapy at Sea Island, Georgia (1955).

Murray Bowen begins National Institute of Mental Health (NIMH) project of studying families with schizophrenics.

Ivan Boszormenyi-Nagy begins work on contextual therapy.

1960 to 1969

Jay Haley refines and advocates therapeutic approaches of Milton Erickson. He moves from Palo Alto to join the Philadelphia Child Guidance Clinic (1967).

Family Process, the first journal in family therapy, is cofounded by Nathan Ackerman and Don Jackson (1961).

Salvador Minuchin begins development of structural family therapy at Wiltwyck School and continues at the Philadelphia Child Guidance Clinic. He coauthors *Families of the Slums.*

John Bell publishes the first ideas about family group therapy (1961).

Virginia Satir publishes *Conjoint Family Therapy* (1964). She gains a national following.

Legislation authorizing community mental health centers is passed by Congress (1963).

First state licensure law regulating family counselors is passed in California (1963).

Nathan Ackerman publishes *Treating the Troubled Family* (1966).

Carl Whitaker moves to the University of Wisconsin. He begins to write and lecture extensively.

General systems theory, formulated by Ludwig von Bertalanffy (1934/1968), becomes the basis for most family therapy.

Murray Bowen begins to formulate his own theory.

Training centers and institutes for family therapy are established in New York, Philadelphia, and Boston.

1970 to 1979

Membership in the American Association for Marriage and Family Counseling (AAMFC) grows by 777% to 7,565 members.

Nathan Ackerman dies (1971).

Association of Couples for Marriage Enrichment is established by David and Vera Mace (1973). The marriage/family enrichment movement grows.

The *Journal of Marital and Family Therapy* is founded (1974).

Families and Family Therapy and *Psychosomatic Families* are published by Salvador Minuchin and associates.

The *Family Therapy Networker* is created (1976).

The American Association for Marriage and Family Counseling (AAMFC) becomes the American Association for Marriage and Family Therapy (AAMFT) (1979). Its degree granting programs are recognized by the Department of Health, Education, and Welfare.

The American Family Therapy Association (AFTA) is created (1977).

Paradox and Counterparadox is published by the Milan group (1978). Foreign family therapists become influential in the United States.

Feminist theorists, led by Rachel Hare-Mustin, begin questioning the premises of family therapy.

Jay Haley publishes *Uncommon Therapy* (1973) and *Problem Solving Therapy* (1976).

1980 to 1989

Membership in the AAMFT grows to 14,000.

Division 43 (Family Psychology) in the American Psychological Association (APA) is established (1984).

The International Association for Marriage and Family Counselors (IAMFC) in the American Counseling Association (ACA) is established (1986).

New leaders in family therapy emerge.

Research procedures in family therapy are developed and refined.

Publications in family therapy increase. *Family Therapy Networker* reaches a circulation of 50,000.

Virginia Satir dies (1988).

1990 to the Present

Solution-focused family therapies of deShazer and O'Hanlon become popular. Narrative approach of White and Epston is introduced.

Other new theories are developed, including constructionist theories, challenging systems thinking.

The integration and merger of family therapy theories occurs, with less emphasis on specialization.

Professional membership grows in AAMFT, IAMFC, AFTA, and Division 43 of APA.

Accreditation of programs and licensure efforts at state level increase.

Health care reform and mental health care provider status become increasingly important.

Tension between professional associations in family therapy develops.

References

Ackerman, N. (1938). The unity of the family. *Archives of Pediatrics, 55,* 51–62.

Ackerman, N. (1958). *The psychodynamics of family life.* New York: Basic Books.

Ackerman, N. (1966). *Treating the troubled family.* New York: Basic Books.

Adams, G. R., & Schvaneveldt, J. D. (1985). *Understanding research methods.* New York: Longman.

Andersen, T. (1991). *The reflecting team: Dialogues and dialogues about dialogues.* New York: W. W. Norton.

Anderson, C. M. (1988). Psychoeducational model different than paradigm. *Family Therapy News, 19,* 10–12.

Anderson, H. (1994). Rethinking family therapy: A delicate balance. *Journal of Marital & Family Therapy, 20,* 145–149.

Anderson, R., Anderson, W., & Hovestadt, A. J. (1993, May/June). Family of origin work in family therapy: A practical approach. *Family Counseling and Therapy, 1,* 1–13.

Barker, P. (1986). *Basic family therapy* (2nd ed.). New York: Oxford University Press.

Bateson, G., Jackson, D. D., Haley, J., & Weakland, J. (1956). Toward a theory of schizophrenia. *Behavioral Science, 1,* 251–264.

Bell, J. E. (1961). *Family group therapy.* Public Health Monograph #64. Washington, DC: U.S. Government Printing Office.

Bertalanffy, L. (1934). *Modern theories of development: An introduction to theoretical biology.* London: Oxford University Press.

Bertalanffy, L. (1968). *General systems theory.* New York: George Braziller.

Bloch, D., & Simon, R. (1982). *The strength of family therapy: Selected papers of Nathan W. Ackerman.* New York: Brunner/Mazel.

Bowen, M. (1961). Family psychotherapy. *American Journal of Orthopsychiatry, 31,* 40–60.

Broderick, C. B., & Schrader, S. S. (1981). The history of professional marriage and family therapy. In A. S. Gurman & O. P. Kniskern (Eds.), *Handbook of family therapy* (pp. 5–38). New York: Brunner/Mazel.

Broderick, C. B., & Schrader, S. S. (1991). The history of professional marriage and family therapy (pp. 3–40).

In A. S. Gurman & O. P. Kniskern (Eds.), *Handbook of family therapy, II.* New York: Brunner/Mazel.

Brown, J. H., & Christensen, D. N. (1986). *Family therapy.* Pacific Grove, CA: Brooks/Cole.

Carter, B., & McGoldrick, M. (1988). *The changing family life cycle* (2nd ed.). New York: Gardner.

deShazer, S. (1988). *Clues: Investigating solutions in brief therapy.* New York: Norton.

Dinkmeyer, D. C., Dinkmeyer, D. C., Jr., & Sperry, L. (1987). *Adlerian counseling and psychotherapy* (2nd ed.). Columbus, OH: Merrill.

Doherty, W. J., & Simmons, D. S. (1996). Clinical practice patterns of marriage and family therapists: A national survey of therapists and their clients. *Journal of Marital and Family Therapy, 22,* 9–25.

Duhl, B. S. (1983). *From the inside out and other metaphors.* New York: Brunner/Mazel.

Enns, C. Z. (1992). Dilemmas of power and equality in marital and family counseling: Proposals for a feminist perspective. In R. L. Smith & P. Stevens-Smith (Eds.), *Family counseling and therapy* (pp. 338–357). Ann Arbor, MI: ERIC/CAPS.

Figley, C. R. (1989). *Helping traumatized families.* San Francisco: Jossey-Bass.

Fishman, C. H. (1988). *Treating troubled adolescents.* New York: Basic Books.

Foley, V. D. (1989). Family therapy. In R. J. Corsini & D. Wedding (Eds.), *Current psychotherapies* (4th ed., pp. 455–502). Itasca, IL: F. E. Peacock.

Framo, J. L. (1996). A personal retrospective of the family therapy field: Then and now. *Journal of Marital and Family Therapy, 22,* 289–316.

Gladding, S. T. (1991). *Present vows and memories.* Unpublished manuscript.

Goldenberg, H., & Goldenberg, I. (1994). *Counseling today's families.* Pacific Grove, CA: Brooks/Cole.

Guerin, P. J., Jr. (1976). Family therapy: The first twenty-five years. In P. J. Guerin, Jr. (Ed.). *Family therapy: Theory and practice* (pp. 2–22). New York: Gardner.

Guerney, B. G., Jr. (1977). *Relationship enhancement.* San Francisco: Jossey-Bass.

Gurman, A. S., & Kniskern, D. P. (1981). Preface. In A. S. Gurman & D. P. Kniskern (Eds.), *Handbook of family therapy* (pp. xiii–xviii). New York: Brunner/Mazel.

Gurman, A. S., Kniskern, D. P., & Pinsof, W. (1986). Research on the process and outcome of marital and family therapy. In S. L. Garfield & A. E. Bergin (Eds.), *Handbook of psychotherapy and behavior change* (3rd ed.). New York: Wiley.

Haley, J. (1963). *Strategies of psychotherapy.* New York: Grune & Stratton.

Haley, J. (1976). Development of a theory: A history of a research project. In C. E. Sluzki & D. C. Ransom (Eds.), *Double-bind: The foundation of the communication approach to the family.* New York: Grune & Stratton.

Hare-Mustin, R. T. (1978). A feminist approach to family therapy. *Family Process, 17,* 181–194.

Hershenson, D. B., & Power, P. W. (1987). *Mental health counseling: Theory and practice.* New York: Pergamon Press.

Hines, M. (1988). Similarities and differences in group and family therapy. *Journal for Specialists in Group Work, 13,* 173–179.

Hoffman, L. (1981). *Foundations of family therapy: A conceptual framework for systems change.* New York: Basic Books.

Hollis, J. W. (1996). *Counselor preparation 1996–1998.* Bristol, PA: Taylor & Francis.

Juhnke, G. A. (1993). *Effective family counseling: Applications for school counselors.* Paper presented at the 66th annual convention of the North Carolina Counseling Association, Raleigh, NC.

Kaslow, F. W. (1980). History of family therapy in the United States: A kaleidoscopic overview. *Marriage and Family Review, 3,* 77–111.

Kaslow, F. (1990). *Voices in family psychology.* Newbury Park, CA: Sage.

Kaslow, F. W. (1991). The art and science of family psychology. *American Psychologist, 46,* 621–626.

Keeney, B. (1990). *Improvisational therapy.* St. Paul, MN: Systemic Therapy Press.

Kottler, J. A. (1991). *The compleat therapist.* San Francisco: Jossey-Bass.

Laing, R. D. (1965). Mystification, confusion, and conflict. In I. Boszormenyi-Nagy & J. L. Framo (Eds.), *Intensive family therapy: Theoretical and practical aspects.* New York: Harper & Row.

Lang, R. D. (1970). *Knots.* New York: Pantheon.

Libow, J. A., Raskin, P. A., & Caust, B. L. (1982). Feminist and family systems therapy: Are they irreconcilable? *American Journal of Family Therapy, 10,* 3–12.

Lidz, R. W., & Lidz, T. (1949). The family environment of schizophrenic patients. *American Journal of Psychiatry, 106,* 332–345.

Mace, D. (1983). *Prevention in family services.* Beverly Hills, CA: Sage.

Maynard, P. E., & Olson, D. H. (1987). Circumplex model of family systems: A treatment tool in family counseling. *Journal of Counseling and Development, 65,* 502–504.

Miller, B. C. (1986). *Family research methods.* Beverly Hills, CA: Sage.

Miller, S., Nunnally, E., & Wackman, D. B. (1977). *Couple communication instructor's manual.* Littleton, CO: Interpersonal Communication Programs.

Miller, S., Nunnally, E. W., & Wackman, D. B. (1979). *Couple communication: Talking together.* Littleton, CO: Interpersonal Communication Programs.

Minuchin, S. (1974). *Families and family therapy.* Cambridge, MA: Harvard University Press.

Minuchin, S., Montalvo, B., Guerney, B. G., Rosman, B. L., & Schumer, F. (1967). *Families of the slums.* New York: Basic Books.

Minuchin, S., Rosman, B. L., & Baker, L. (1978). *Psychosomatic families: Anorexia nervosa in context.* Cambridge, MA: Harvard University Press.

Mittleman, B. (1948). The concurrent analysis of married couples. *Psychoanalytic Quarterly, 17,* 182–197.

Nichols, M. & R. C. Schwartz (1995). *Family therapy: Concepts and methods* (3rd ed.). Boston: Allyn & Bacon.

Nichols, W. C. (1993). *The AAMFT: 50 years of marital and family therapy.* Washington, DC: AAMFT.

Nichols, W. C., & Everett, C. A. (1986). *Systemic family therapy: An integrated approach.* New York: Guilford.

O'Hanlon, W., & Weiner-Davis, M. (1989). *In search of solutions: A new direction in psychotherapies.* New York: Norton.

Okun, B. F., & Rappaport, L. J. (1980). *Working with families: An introduction to family therapy.* North Scituate, MA: Duxbury Press.

Pickens, M. E. (1997, January). Evolving family structures: Implications for Counseling. *Counseling and Family Development, 29,* 1–8.

Piercy, F. P., & Sprenkle, D. H. (1986). *Family therapy sourcebook.* New York: Guilford.

Piercy, F. P., & Sprenkle, D. H. (1990). Marriage and family therapy: A decade review. *Journal of Marriage and the Family, 52,* 1116–1126.

Satir, V. (1964). *Conjoint family therapy.* Palo Alto, CA: Science and Behavior Books.

Sauber, S. R., L'Abate, L., & Weeks, G. R. (1985). *Family therapy: Basic concepts and terms.* Rockville, MD: Aspen.

Schwartz, R. (1994). *Internal family systems therapy.* New York: Guilford.

Selvini Palazzoli, M., Boscolo, L., Cecchin, G., & Prata, G. (1978). *Paradox and counterparadox.* New York: Jason Aronson.

Shields, C. G., Wynne, L. C., McDaniel, S. H., & Gawinski, B. A. (1994). The marginalization of family therapy: A historical and continuing problem. *Journal of Marital and Family Therapy, 20,* 117–138

Skynner, A. C. R. (1981). An open-systems, group-analytic approach to family therapy. In A. S. Gurman & D. P. Kniskern (Eds.), *Handbook of family therapy* (pp. 39–84). New York: Brunner/Mazel.

Strong, B., & DeVault, C. (1992). *The marriage and family experience* (5th ed.). St. Paul, MN: West.

Trotzer, J. P. (1988). Family theory as a group resource. *Journal for Specialists in Group Work, 13,* 180–185.

Whitaker, C. A. (1958). Psychotherapy with couples. *American Journal of Psychotherapy, 12,* 18–23.

White, M., & Epston, D. (1990). *Narrative means to therapeutic ends.* New York: Norton.

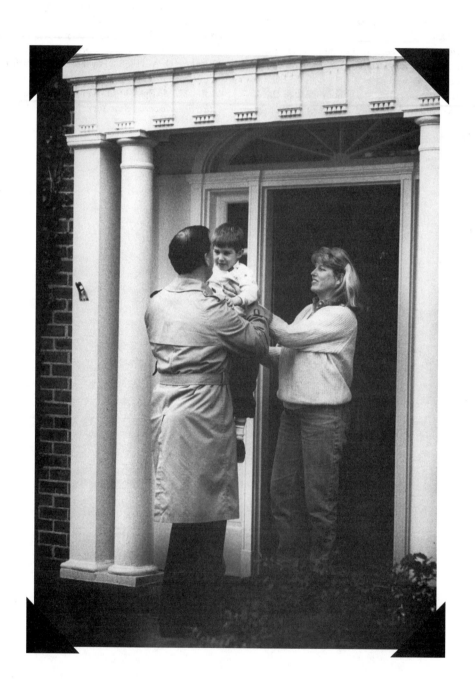

CHAPTER 4

The Process of Family Therapy

My son, Benjamin, rolls over in his crib
to the applause of his mother and delight of himself
while I catch an afternoon flight to Saint Paul
to conduct a counseling seminar.

These are milestones in our lives
marking steps in family development
as we reach out to touch
and are changed through our behaviors.

At 33,000 feet, I drift in and out of sleep,
aware that in the process, but on a different level,
my wife and child do the same.

In the construct of images and depth of thought
we attempt in special ways
to bridge the gap of distance.

Gladding, 1988

There is a predictable process in conducting family therapy, regardless of one's theoretical approach. "All schools of family therapy have a theoretical commitment to working with the process of family interaction" (Nichols & Schwartz, 1995, p. 487). Despite outward appearances, different systems of family therapy are more alike in practice than their theories would suggest. For example, family therapists of all persuasions are concerned with processes involved in clarifying communications among family members, overcoming resistance, and rectifying dysfunctional behaviors. Consequently, family therapists have many common concerns and procedures that transcend their different theoretical emphases. In fact, surveys indicate that the predominant theoretical orientation to family therapy is eclectic (e.g., Rait, 1988).

Therefore, it is important for family therapists to be aware of the universal methods of working with families. By being so attuned, they are better able to communicate with a variety of professionals. They are also better able to realize the uniqueness of the theories under which they work. Such knowledge gives them a flexibility and common bond to others in the helping professions.

This chapter covers potential problems encountered by inexperienced family therapists. Along with this material are guidelines concerning appropriate process and expected procedures for the main stages of family therapy. Although this material is targeted toward new family therapists, it is also applicable to experienced therapists.

Common Problems of Beginning Family Therapists

Several problems are germane to family therapists in general. These common concerns must be addressed if the therapeutic process is to have a significant impact. Some therapists' downfalls are a result of a failure to act, while others are the result of overaction.

Failure to Act

Failure to act can be as bad as *overaction*. By failing to make an intervention at a strategic time, a therapist might subtly suggest that the family's interaction is adequate when, in fact, nothing could be further from the truth. Failure to act takes several forms. Among the most prominent are the following.

Failure to Establish Structure

If family therapy is to achieve a positive outcome, it helps to start properly. The struggle to establish the parameters under which therapy is conducted is referred to as the **battle for structure** (Napier & Whitaker, 1978). This battle must be won by the therapist, otherwise the family members could attempt to run the therapy sessions in the same nonproductive manner they conduct their family life.

A key component in winning the battle for structure is the therapist delineating the conditions under which treatment will occur. "Clients have both a right and a need to know about fees and payment schedules, your theoretical framework and treatment approach, rules about appointments, how and when they are allowed to contact you, rules about confidentiality, and your educational background and training" (Kaplan & Culkin, 1995, p. 33). Much of this information can be provided to families through a **professional self-disclosure statement** (see Figure 4.1) (Gladding, 1996).

In addition to setting guidelines, the therapist must also physically structure the room so that therapeutic interactions can take place. This includes arranging the furniture so that family members can talk directly with each other. It also requires that the structure be flexible, so the therapist can move family members closer to or farther away from each other.

Failure to Show Care and Concern

Most families enter counseling with some trepidation. Their anxiety might be increased if family members think they are being treated as objects and not persons, or if they perceive the therapist as rigid and distant. Effective family therapists follow the guidelines of other helping professionals; they are caring, open, sensitive, and concerned; and they are empathetic and show it.

Family therapists can convey this professional care by demonstrating the skills in the acronym *SOLER* (Egan, 1990). The *S* stands for facing the client or family squarely, either in a metaphorical or literal manner. The *O* is a reminder to adopt an open posture that is nondefensive, such as avoiding crossing one's arms or legs. The *L* indicates that the therapist should lean forward toward the client family to show interest. A therapist can overdo this procedure and must gauge what is appropriate for each family. The *E* represents good eye contact. One way of letting family members know they are cared about is by looking at them. Finally, *R* stands for relaxation. Working with families is an intense process, but therapists need to feel comfortable.

```
Professional Disclosure Statement
Dr. Jane Smith
205 Healy Building
Philadelphia, Pennsylvania 16006
814–777–6257
```

The Nature of Family Therapy

There are many approaches to family therapy, and different clinicians utilize a number of theories and techniques in their practice. Some work only with the individual or couple, while others insist that the whole family be seen. I have prepared this brief professional self-disclosure form to inform you how I conduct sessions.

My Qualifications

I am a graduate of Purdue University's marriage and family therapy doctoral program. I have been in practice for the past 10 years in the Philadelphia area. I am licensed as a marriage and family therapist by the state of Pennsylvania. I am a clinical member of the American Association for Marriage and Family Therapists. I also belong to the International Association of Marriage and Family Counseling and Division 43 (Family Psychology) of the American Psychological Association.

I have done extensive work with families under supervision at the Philadelphia Child Guidance Clinic. I am not a physician and cannot prescribe medicine. However, if medical treatment seems warranted, I consult with a psychiatrist and can make a referral.

Family Therapy as a Process

Family therapy is a process that requires a considerable investment of time. I prefer to work with the entire family, and I realize that this style may make one or more of you uncomfortable. Although each family is unique, there are some common stages you can expect.

The first stage is the beginning session(s) where we will work to clarify your concerns and difficulties. This process will require observation on my part and verbalization/behavior on your parts. My belief is that there is no one single cause of or cure for a family's problems.

The second stage is the working sessions in which we will concentrate on helping you make changes that will work for you and make your relationships and family life better. During this time, I will ask you to be active as problem solvers.

The final stage is termination, in which we will complete the process of change and end our sessions. It is at this time when you may wish to be most reflective.

Length of Family Therapy and Fees

Family therapy sessions are 50 minutes in length once a week. They begin on the hour. The fee is $75 per session and payment is expected at the end of each session. I will work to help you file insurance, if you wish. Although no one can guarantee how many sessions a particular family may need, I have found the range to be between 10 and 30.

Your Rights

As a consumer of therapeutic services, you have a right to be treated with dignity, respect, and in a professional manner. You have the right to ask me questions about your therapeutic concerns at any time.

Emergency

There is someone from the office on call 24 hours a day. Although you will probably not need this service, the number for emergencies is 814–275–8309.

Figure 4.1

Sample professional disclosure statement.

Effective family therapists also make brief disclosure statements (when appropriate). For example, in response to a parent who reports having been previously married, a therapist might briefly reveal that he or she is also a stepparent. Therapists might also show concern by using self-effacing humor that indicates to family members their awareness of the difficulties families encounter (Piercy & Lobenz, 1994). For instance, a therapist might briefly recount a time in his or her own family when the family struggled in a futile but serious way—such as trying to make it to church on time the day after daylight savings time ended, with family members waking up late and having to rush, only to find they were hassled, haggled, irreverent, and an hour early!

Failure to Engage Family Members in the Therapeutic Process

Engaging family members in therapy includes attending to each one personally. For example, shaking hands or establishing eye contact are two ways this connection can be made (Olkin, 1993). If a family member feels slighted, chances are increased that this person will overtly refuse to participate or will sabotage the therapeutic process in some subtle manner. Although personally soliciting the participation of all family members takes times, it pays off in the long run.

When therapists meet new families and their members, it is crucial that they spend some time with each person. They should concentrate on the interests and dislikes of each individual for a few moments. For example, therapists might talk to children about school and to parents about different aspects of work and family life. In so doing, therapists help build rapport and create an atmosphere of cooperation through acknowledging each person's importance to the family.

Failure to Let the Family Work on Its Problems

Just as the family therapist must win the **battle for structure,** the family must win the **battle for initiative** (Napier & Whitaker, 1978). This battle centers around the family becoming motivated to make changes. A family that does not see any benefit in altering its behaviors is likely to either drop out of therapy or simply go through the motions. On the opposite side is the effect of initiative on family therapists. When families are not working or working well, some family therapists mentally take these families home, much to their own distress (Guy, 1987).

Families can be assisted in winning the battle for initiative if therapists help them envision how their lives can become healthier collectively and individually. Such a process means that therapists must be enterprising and sell the family a set of possibilities (Holland, 1973). For example, the therapist might say to a family that is constantly fighting: How would it be for you to be able to live in peace with one another? or Think for a moment what you really want from this family? Can you envision some ways that you could settle your differences and get on with your lives?

Failure to Attend to Nonverbal Family Dynamics

Nonverbal messages are a major part of any therapeutic process (Egan, 1990). These messages include eye glances, hands folded across one's body, and even the distancing of people through the arrangement or rearrangement of chairs. The most frequent nonverbal cues are facial. However, facial and other body movements often are combined. For example, "when clients are describing feelings about an object or event, there may be increased animation of the face and hands" (Cormier & Hackney, 1993, p. 150).

Family therapists who do not pay attention to the *nonverbal aspects of family dynamics* will only partially decipher what is being conveyed among family members (Brock & Barnard, 1992). The result might be that crucial issues within the family are not addressed and change is limited. For instance, if a daughter tells her father she loves him but does so in a trembling voice and with a look of fear, the therapist would be wise to pursue what the relationship between these two family members is really like.

Overaction

Family therapists can overreact and try to do too much. The following are some common ways overaction is expressed.

Overemphasis on Details

Two primary components of family therapy are content and process. "When families come for treatment, they are usually focused on a content issue: a husband wants a divorce, a child refuses to go to school, a wife is depressed, and so on" (Nichols & Schwartz, 1995, p. 487). **Content** involves details and facts. **Process** focuses on how information is dealt with. Sometimes content is essential. Knowledge of past patterns and the sequencing of family interaction are helpful in breaking up dysfunctional forms of relating. At other times, facts get in the way of helping families make necessary changes. In such cases, the therapist might concentrate on the trees instead of the forest. For example, if a family therapist says to a wife, "Tell me about every time your husband has hit you," the therapist might be focusing too closely on a specific behavior and not enough on the significance of the behavior. In such a circumstance, the family therapy is limited.

A good rule of thumb to follow in dealing with facts is to ask "how" questions along with "what," "where," and "when" queries. For example, "How does your son's behavior affect your ability to relate to him?" Such a question helps get to the heart of the relationship between the individuals involved.

Overemphasis on Making Everyone Happy

Sometimes family therapists become concerned or overconcerned when families leave their offices in a state of tension. The reason for their disturbance is an illogical belief, the essence of which is that if they were competent, the family would be able to resolve its difficulties. While therapists can do a great deal to help families, friction is sometimes unavoidable. Furthermore, friction can be productive. It can motivate individuals to try new behaviors and break out of old patterns.

When clients leave a session in turmoil, the therapist can paradoxically ask them to stay that way until next session or instruct the family to "go slow" in coming to a resolution of the difficulty. The end result in either case is usually that the family resolves the conflict fairly quickly after a counseling session and either returns to a previous homeostatic balance or moves on to a more functional set of behaviors. Regardless of whether the family resolves the issue or not, the therapist can use the next session to ask each member of the family what the family tried in response to their discomfort. Using this information, the family and the therapist will gain a clearer perspective on the processes the family employs in creating strategies. Then new or varied themes can be explored.

Overemphasis on Verbal Expression

Well-chosen words can have a therapeutic effect on families. For example, if the therapist can verbally assure the family that what they have been through and the strategies they have tried in the past are normal, the family might be open to new ways of working on their present situation. However, in most cases, the exact words said by a therapist are not remembered. A helpful way of understanding the limited impact of the therapist's words is to think about what words or advice you most remember in your life. For the majority of people, the list of such remarks and the people involved are few.

Therapists must work with families in a number of ways. They must instruct, comment, and inquire; but they must also model behavior, use role plays, and assign homework. In other words, they must recognize and utilize teachable moments (Brock & Barnard, 1992). It is what the family and therapist do and when, as well as what is said, that makes a difference. For example, a therapist could use hand signals like a traffic officer at a crucial time in a family's therapy to indicate who may talk. Although the family might not remember all of what was said, the use of the therapist's nonverbal directions can leave a lasting impression and message about the art of effective communication.

Overemphasis on Coming to Too Early or Too Easy Resolutions

There is a tendency in therapy for families to "fly into health." After a couple of sessions, for example, a family might report that they are doing better and are ready to terminate therapy. Although such circumstances are true for a few families, most who report feeling better quickly are experiencing the euphoria that often comes out of discussing a situation rather than actually changing it. Therefore, flights into health and early or easy resolutions of family problems seldom succeed. Families involved in such processes rarely examine the dynamics in their problems.

From all theoretical perspectives, the conducting of family therapy is an ongoing process. Consequently, families need to be initially advised of how long the process of therapy generally takes and what will be expected from them. For example, a brief theory therapist might say: "We will be working together on your situation for ten sessions. It is crucial that you define what you wish to change as soon and as concretely as possible."

Overemphasis on Dealing with One Member of the Family

When family therapists concentrate on just one member of a family, they fall into the same trap that has caused the family difficulty—that is, they **scapegoat** (select one person as the cause of difficulties). Family problems are not linear in nature, and one person does not cause a family to be dysfunctional. It is crucial that beginning family therapists recognize the dynamics within families and the power of homeostasis in keeping families operating at a certain level, even if it is dysfunctional. Only when therapists consider the relationships between everyone in the family can meaningful interventions be made. It is imperative that family therapists periodically remind themselves and their client families about the importance of examining interpersonal dynamics in regard to dysfunctionality.

In working with a couple who bring their adolescent in for breaking curfew, the therapist might say: "While Jane's behavior is of concern, in our sessions we will look at the behaviors of everyone. I have found that when one person in a family is having difficulties, others usually are as well." By alerting the family to this systemic view of family relations, the therapist makes it easier for everyone to become more aware of their actions and how they personally contribute to the family's well-being or lack thereof.

Appropriate Process

The process of family therapy can be conducted in a variety of ways, but some vital aspects of it must be included. If therapists do not plan properly, they are likely to fail. *Proper planning in family therapy* includes careful consideration of how to conduct sessions based on one's impression of a family and one's clinical skills (Rickert, 1989).

Pre-Session Planning and Tasks

Family therapy "begins the moment of the first interaction" between the family and therapist (Olkin, 1993, p. 32). Initial contact is generally made by a family members' telephone call to a therapist. Also, the individuals who initiate the phone calls are usually "the most interested in change and may be the most open to engaging in therapy" (Weber & Levine, 1995, p. 54). Some calls are handled by an intermediary (e.g., a secretary); but the family and the therapist are better served if calls are directed to and handled by the therapist (Brock & Barnard, 1992). One reason is that the therapist can directly answer questions about who should attend the sessions and how the sessions will be structured. A second reason is that through the phone conversation, the therapist gains an opportunity to establish rapport and a cooperative alliance with the family member (Weber, McKeever, & McDaniel, 1992). Finally, in answering calls, therapists have an opportunity to demonstrate their own competency and credibility.

Regardless of who answers calls, it is essential during this first contact to obtain certain information and establish a professional but cordial atmosphere (Snider, 1992). Essential information to be gathered includes the name, address, and phone number of the caller. A concise statement of the problem to be addressed is also helpful, even if it is modified or changed later. Other information that is useful includes the referral source, history of previous treatment, and preferred method of payment (if relevant).

The tone and type of speech used by the secretary or therapist can either help or hinder the decision of the family to engage in the treatment process. If the receiver of the call is supportive, caring, and talks in a manner that conveys respect and receptivity, an appointment is more likely to be made and kept. Whenever possible, the initial appointment should be made within 48 hours of the call. The reason is that most families who call for help are ready to begin the process. Delaying an appointment can cause some members to reconsider their decision to attend or to resist coming.

When evaluating intake information, hypotheses about dynamics within the family should be made, especially if the therapist is operating from a problem-oriented position (Weber et al., 1992). One source to consider in making such speculations is the family life cycle (Duvall, 1977; Carter & McGoldrick, 1988). Therapists need to ask themselves what issues are to be expected from a family in a certain stage of life. Some transitional difficulties are natural and some are not. The ethnic/cultural background of the family is also a consideration. In some traditional Italian families, for example, an unmarried daughter leaving home might bring about a crisis that would not develop in a traditional British family.

A final pre-session task is to form a preliminary diagnosis of what is happening within the family (Rickert, 1989). For example, in a family where an adolescent male is becoming a delinquent, the therapist might hypothesize that the boy and his father are **disengaged** and cutoff from each other physically as well as psychologically. Similarly, in the case of child who refuses to attend school, the therapist might hypothesize that the child and the family are enmeshed and that the child's actions are somehow being reinforced or supported.

Engaging in this diagnostic exercise, which is a hallmark of the Milan approach, requires that the therapist spend time thinking about possible linkages within the family and the development of persons and systems. The payoff for this investment in time is that the therapist can hone in on issues more quickly and effectively. Through diagnostic procedures, therapists are more likely to "work within the limits of their training and experience" (Carlson, Hinkle, & Sperry, 1993, p. 309). The therapist is also in a good position to formulate a treatment plan that is communicable to other mental health professionals (Barker, 1986). Finally, diagnosis is a way for family therapists to comprehend more thoroughly what is happening with family members as well as with the family as a whole (Carlson et al., 1993).

Initial Session(s)

During the initial session(s), in order to be successful with the family, the therapist must achieve a number of crucial tasks. Some of the goals of the initial session(s) must be accomplished simultaneously and others sequentially. As with other stages of family therapy, "timing is everything." Some of the most important tasks in the first session are as follows.

Join the Family: Establishing Rapport

The first step in helping a family during the initial session(s) is for therapists to establish a sense of trust between themselves and the members of the family. This stage is referred to as **joining** (Haley, 1976; Minuchin, 1974). It is a crucial component of family therapy and requires therapists to meet, greet, and form a bond with family members in a rapid but relaxed and authentic way. Therapists must make the family comfortable through social exchange with each member.

If a therapist fails to join with a family, its most disengaged members, or the family as a whole, could leave treatment either physically or psychologically. It is usually the least involved member of a family who has the most power in deciding whether the family stays in therapy or not (Mark Worden, personal communication, 1982). A weak alliance with family members is a frequently cited reason for treatment not working (Coleman, 1985).

Inquire About Members' Perceptions of the Family

In making inquiries from family members, it is essential that family therapists challenge old perceptions. Individuals within families usually have a problem, person, or situation framed in a certain manner. A **frame,** a concept originated by Bateson (1955), is a perception or opinion that organizes one's interactions so that "at any given time certain events are more likely to occur and certain interpretations of what is going on are more likely to be made" (Coyne, 1985, p. 338).

By challenging the perception (or frame), therapists can get family members to define problems, persons, or situations differently, as well as "look for different solutions" (Olkin, 1993, p. 33). Such a change sets up the opportunity for success.

Observe Family Patterns

Families, like individuals, have unique personalities. They come into therapy and display these personalities both in a verbal and nonverbal manner, a phenomenon referred to as the **family dance** (Napier & Whitaker, 1978). Some systematic ways of observing family interactions are helpful for novice and experienced therapists. The following questions are among those that Resnikoff (1981) advised family therapists to ask themselves in regard to how a family functions:

- "What is the outward appearance of the family?" (p. 135). For example, how far do members sit from each other and who sits next to whom?

- "What is the cognitive functioning in the family?" (p. 136). For example, how specifically and straightforwardly do family members communicate? Is there much give and take in the communication patterns?

- "What repetitive, non-productive sequences do you notice?" (p. 136). For instance, do parents scold or praise their children in certain ways after special behaviors?

- "What is the basic feeling state in the family and who carries it?" (p. 136). All families have a variety of feelings, but often one member conveys the overall affect of the family. For example, a depressed child might indicate a depressed family.

- "What individual roles reinforce family resistances and what are the most prevalent family defenses?" (p. 136). Individuals and families sometimes have characteristic responses to stress, such as anger or denial. It is crucial to recognize these responses and to be sensitive and innovative in responding to them.

- "What subsystems are operative in this family?" (p. 137). Almost all families have **subsystems,** that is, members who because of age or function are logically grouped together, such as parents or siblings. It is important to identify these subsystems and how they function. Some work well, but others end up with someone being scapegoated or triangulated (i.e., focused on as a way of relieving tension between two other family members). It is crucial for the therapists to recognize and work through subsystems so that families can relate in a more open and healthy manner.

- "Who carries the power in the family?" (p.137). Persons who have power in families make the rules and decisions. They might act in a benign manner, but what they say or do is adhered to by others. For instance, a mother who acts as the family spokesperson probably has considerable power. Families that operate in a functional way have flexibility in regard to rules and the balance of power.

- "How are the family members differentiated from each other and what are the subgroup boundaries?" (p. 137). In some families there is **enmeshment** (overinvolvement either physically and/or psychologically), and in others there is **distancing** (isolated separateness, either physically and/or psychologically). In healthy families, a balance exists between these two extremes. Therapists need to be aware of family member's degree of separation and individuation.

- "What part of the family life cycle is the family experiencing and are the problem-solving methods stage appropriate?" (p. 138). For example, is a family treating its 18-year-old like an 8-year-old? Family therapists need to check on how well a family deals with current developmental reality.

- "What are the evaluator's own reactions to the family?" (p. 138). Reactions to families are made on both an emotional and cognitive level. Sometimes, the therapist might see the family in light of his or her own family of origin and confuses the issues to be worked on. Such a perception is not in the service of the family or the therapist. To truly be helpful to a family, a therapist must be aware of the root of his or her reaction, and must know how to respond appropriately.

Assess What Needs to Be Done

The family therapist needs to assess what changes should be made or can be made in order to help the family function better (L'Abate & Bagarozzi, 1993). This assessment can mean the employment of specific diagnostic instruments (West, 1988). In most cases, however, this procedure can also be conducted more informally, such as through observation.

Engender Hope for Change and Overcome Resistance

Many family members need assurance that their situations can become better. Hope motivates them to work and make difficult changes and choices. Essential elements of hope can be given in direct or indirect ways. For instance, a family therapist might say: "Your situation did not get this way overnight, and it will not change overnight. But, I think if you work hard it will change." This type of comment directly addresses the family's plight and possibilities. Other less formal statements, such as "I think you might be able to do something more productive," can also be encouraging and foster a positive attitude in family members.

Further, family therapists can engender hope that change can take place within families by helping them identify their assets and strengths (Nichols & Everett, 1986). Most families know their liabilities. However, discovering strengths, such as that they live in a supportive neighborhood, helps families recognize they have more potential than they might have previously thought.

Regardless of the therapist's words of encouragement or the identified family strengths, almost all families exhibit some form of **resistance** to treatment (Anderson & Stewart, 1983). Resistance comes in many forms, such as "members attempting to control sessions, absent or silent members, refusal of family members to talk to each other in sessions, hostility, and failure to do homework" (Olkin, 1993, p. 33). Other forms of resistance include lateness, denying reality, rationalization, insisting that one family member is the problem, and challenging the therapist's competence. If treatment is to be successful, family therapists have to understand the nature of resistance and overcome it without alienating family members. "When therapists . . . intervene, their choice of a type of intervention, and whether to attempt to overcome, avoid, or use resistance to produce change, will be based on their theoretical orientation and their understanding of where on the compliance/defiance continuum a family or family member is at any given time" (Anderson & Stewart, 1983, p. 38).

One way to overcome resistance is to create **boundaries** for the family (Jaffe, 1991). For instance, all family members must be present for a session to occur, or there will be no name calling in or outside the therapy sessions. Through the use of boundaries, members and the family as a whole can feel safe and begin opening up to one another. Another strategy is to interpret positively the actions associated with resistance as ways the family copes or protects itself. This is a type of **reframing:** "the art of attributing different meaning to behavior so the behavior will be seen differently by the family" (Constantine, Stone Fish, & Piercy, 1984). Thus, a therapist might commend family members who refuse to participate in a session for being "rightfully cautious" about opening themselves or the family up to new situations. A final way to deal with this phenomenon is to endorse it. For example, the therapist might say, "Go slow." This strategy is called a **paradox,** or a form of treatment in which therapists give families permission to do what they were going to do anyway. This type of directive allows a family to be more flexible in their responses and to deal with matters in a more open manner.

Make a Return Appointment and Give Assignments

At the end of a first session, some beginning therapists make the mistake of waiting to see if a family wishes to make another appointment. Although it is appropriate to let the family make a decision regarding future sessions, it is equally important that the therapist offer to see the family again. For instance, the therapist can propose that the family come for a set number of additional sessions (e.g., four). After the additional sessions have taken place, the family can evaluate them and decide what progress has been made. This approach relieves the therapist and the family of the burden of dealing with the question of future sessions after each appointment. However, regardless of whether the number of sessions are agreed upon ahead of time or session-by-session, the therapist needs to take the lead in giving the family options.

If future sessions are agreed upon, then the next step in the process is to assign the family **homework** (i.e., tasks to do outside the therapy session), if theoretically appropriate. For example, in structural, strategic, Bowen, and behavioral family therapy there is an emphasis on working between sessions. According to Haley (1987), there are three reasons for giving homework. First, it helps families behave and feel differently. Many families need practice in order to be comfortable with new or prescribed ways of interacting. Second, homework assignments intensify the relationship between the therapist and the family. Finally, homework gives the therapist an opportunity to see how family members relate to each other. Therefore, homework or directives can be a way to help families help themselves and assist the therapist in deciding what course of action to take next.

In assigning homework, family therapists should make it clear to their families the specifics of what they are to do, as well as when and how often they are to do it (Schilson, 1991). A "trial run" should be conducted in the therapist's office, if time allows. For some families, a time should be scheduled to talk over and process what they did; for others, simple action is enough. An example of a homework assignment would be for family members to practice listening to one another, and then for each member to paraphrase what another family member said before making a statement of his or her own.

Record Impressions of Family Session Immediately

Impressions of particular families are fleeting, especially if therapists are busy. The result is that information about a family or a session can become unintentionally distorted over time (Gorden, 1992). Thus, it is crucial that those who work with families record their impressions in the form of *clinical notes* as soon as possible after sessions. "Historically, clinical notes have been more content oriented than process oriented" (Brock & Barnard, 1992, p. 139). However, family therapists have a choice as to what they record and how they do so. A balance between noting the process and the content of sessions probably works best.

In writing clinical notes, therapists accomplish three vital tasks. First, clinical notes can be studied over time in regard to patterns or processes that may evolve. This type of "paper trail" is invaluable because it helps therapists remember nonverbal interactions and occurrences. Clinical notes lend themselves to future use (Gorden, 1992).

Second, clinical notes give therapists the opportunity to be reflective and objective, and to pull away from the seductive power of becoming a family member (Mark Worden, personal communication, 1982). Families are powerful and can easily engulf outsiders into their ways of thinking.

Finally, clinical notes can help therapists probe in a specific way by reminding them of what has been previously said or dealt with. Many families are theme oriented and talk about behaviors and events in some detail. By referring to notes, therapists can avoid going over the same material twice (Gorden, 1992).

A unique way of recording clinical notes, used by Michael White and other narrative family therapists, is through the practice of writing a letter to the family about what occurred during the session. The letters then become the clinical record—that is, the clinical notes.

The Middle Phase of Treatment

If rapport, structure, and initiative have been fostered in the initial sessions of family therapy, the middle phase of treatment can begin. During this phase, family therapists push family members and the family as a whole to make changes and breakthroughs. To do so, the therapist should employ the following procedures.

Involve Peripheral Family Members

A family is only as productive as its least-involved member. Therefore, in most orientations to family therapy, the middle phase of treatment emphasizes making sure that all family members are committed to and working toward a common goal. If a family member is not involved in the process of therapy, the therapist can invite him or her in one or more of three ways (Barker, 1986).

The first way is to invite the uninvolved family member to be an observer of the family. In this role, he or she begins to participate by giving the family feedback on what has transpired in their interaction. He or she acts as a reporter, summarizing what has occurred, at the end of a session.

The second way to get the uninvolved family member to participate is through the Milan therapy technique of **circular questioning**. In this procedure, the detached family member is asked to give his or her impressions about the different interactions of other family members. For example, the therapist might ask: "How does your father act when *that* happens? How does your mother respond?" The process, in itself, elicits involvement and helps the family recognize the uniqueness of the individuals within it. Circular questioning "can and does trigger therapeutic change" (Tomm, 1987, p. 5).

The third way to entice an uninvolved family member is to use the power of the family group as a whole. This could mean that the uninvolved person is literally carried into the session. However, most often it involves physical reassurance and verbal insistence that the reluctant member be present for the session.

Seek to Connect Family Members Together

A second goal of the middle phase of family therapy is to link members of the family together in an appropriate manner. This objective is especially noticeable in structural family therapy in which boundaries are emphasized (Minuchin & Fishman, 1981). However, the proper joining and separating of family members from one another is not owned by any theoretical position. Making sure of linkage between individuals (e.g., siblings) whose generational interests and concerns are common is crucial at this time. Similarly, breaking up inappropriate intergenerational coalitions is a must (e.g., a parent and child functioning as two parents).

Establish Contracts and Promote Quid Pro Quo Relations

A third dimension of the middle phase of family therapy is to foster "payoffs" in relationships, especially in newly formed connections. This procedure can be done through the use of contracts, a type of **quid pro quo** (something for something) relationship in which family members begin to benefit from their involvement with each other. For instance, in return for doing chores on Saturday morning, parents make Saturday dinner "pizza time." In such a circumstance, household tasks are completed more easily (a benefit for the parents), and the children enjoy a special treat while also taking on appropriate responsibilities.

Emphasize Some Change within the Family System

The process of change is difficult for most individuals, let alone families. In helping families consider change, therapists must assist families in understanding what is currently happening in their lives, what options are available, what the consequences are for change, and what new skills they will have to acquire if they change (Snider, 1992). Sometimes change is best approached in small steps. Using this strategy, families can begin to get used to behaving differently. For example, suppose family members have difficulty clearly communicating with one another in the morning because they are so rushed. A small change might be to start getting up 15 minutes earlier and then moving the clock back in 5-minute-segments each day until the family arises 30 minutes earlier than before. A similar small change might be a husband and wife who agree to concentrate on listening to each other exclusively for 15 minutes each day.

Emphasizing contracts and small changes is helpful because these procedures are relatively nonthreatening. In addition, they help everyone envision future happenings in a concrete way.

Reinforce Family Members for Trying New Behaviors

Family members and the family as a whole need to be reinforced when they take risks and attempt new behaviors. Such a policy encourages families to try different ways of interacting. For example, when children ask parents if they can have candy instead of just taking it, they should be rewarded (possibly with candy). Similarly, if a man appropriately asks his estranged spouse if she would sit and talk with him about their relationship, he should be rewarded.

Family therapists can use many different means to reinforce family members, but probably the most simple and effective, in most cases, is a brief verbal acknowledgement of what has been done (Brock & Barnard, 1992). For example, therapists can say "good" or "nice work" to clients immediately following or learning about the risks they have taken. The goal of this procedure is for the therapist's role of giving awards to gradually be taken over by the family members or for the process of reward to become internalized by the family.

Stay Active as a Therapist

Being a family therapist means being mentally, verbally, and behaviorally active (Friedlander, Wildman, Heatherington, & Skowron, 1994). Few approaches to working with families are passive. Therapists are expected to be involved; otherwise, they will probably fail. On the importance of being active, Haley (1969) offers "the Five B's, which guarantee dynamic failure" (p. 61):

- Be Passive
- Be Inactive
- Be Reflective
- Be Silent
- Beware

The case for focusing on behavior and action in family therapy "is based on the observation that people often do not change even though they understand why and how they should. The truth of this is familiar to anyone who has ever tried but failed to lose weight, stop smoking, or spend time with the kids" (Nichols & Schwartz, 1995, p. 508). Promoting insight in people may help them understand themselves better and freely act in their own best interest; but family therapists do not, as a rule, count on this happening. Instead, the therapist invests a great deal in bringing about change in families and does not wait for insight or spontaneous remission of symptoms.

Link Family with Appropriate Outside Systems
Family therapy is limited in time and scope. It is important that families and their members learn to link up with outside groups whenever possible. For example, when families are working to overcome problems related to alcohol abuse, it is crucial that members connect with Alcoholics Anonymous (AA) and Al-Anon. By so doing, they can receive the additional necessary support and knowledge they need in order to cope and change.

Linkage between families and agencies should be made during the middle phase of family therapy. Consequently, family therapists avoid making hasty and often ineffective referrals to outside agencies at the end of treatment. The importance of outside groups to the health and well-being of families is highlighted in the writings of Boszormenyi-Nagy (1987), who stresses that healing and growth for families take place best when the total context in which families operate is included in treatment.

Focus on Process
Family therapy is a continuous process, and when changes are made in families, it is usually because therapists have focused on the process instead of the content. Those who practice family therapy must realize that just as "one swallow does not a summer make," one change or even several within the family does not indicate that the family is ready to be discharged from treatment. Rather, changes occur over time and tend to be affective, behavioral, and cognitive, with affective changes among family members being especially significant (Friedlander et al., 1994).

In many cases, family members make their easiest adjustments first. Consequently, family therapists must keep unbalancing, or disturbing, the family when it resists dealing with difficulties or focuses on one person instead of on systemic changes. This requires that the therapist engage the family continuously in a therapeutic alliance of collaboration (Friedlander et al., 1994).

Introject Humor When Appropriate
Many families enter therapy with the perception that life is a tragedy. As a result, they struggle, suffer profoundly, and feel alone and unable to change. Although some events and circumstances in life are tragic, most families who seek therapy are not in such a state. Therefore, it is appropriate at times, espe-

cially in the middle phase of family therapy, to help families become more aware of and even enjoy the folly of their existence. In doing so, families might see how they have painted themselves into corners or acted in absurd ways.

Caution must be taken to not make fun of families but rather to let them have fun and simultaneously gain insight. As Frank Pittman (1995) says: "In my therapy, I don't eschew laughter, but the patients have most of the funny lines" (p. 39). For example, if a mother is obsessed with the fact that her 12-year-old daughter will not pick up her clothes, the therapist might have the mother project the concern into future years and events. In this exercise the mother might imagine her daughter getting married and never being able to have romantic times with her spouse because of her inability to wade through the sea of clothes she has habitually tossed on the floor. Although such an example is absurd, it helps illustrate a point and aids the mother and daughter in sharing a moment of levity. Again, as Pittman (1995) says: "We can bear far more in comedy than in tragedy, because in comedy we don't have to be perfect, we are not alone in our suffering, and we get to change in time to not die from our hopeless emotional position. If we are fully embedded in our comic perspective then we can bear all the reality life has to offer" (p. 40).

Look for Evidence of Change in the Family

If therapy is going well, it will become evident. Therefore, therapists need to closely observe the family system to see if it is accommodating "to new experiences/data from therapy" (Nichols & Everett, 1986, p. 255). There are usually many subtle and many blatant signs that changes are occurring. For example, family members might appear to be more relaxed with one another and to talk more directly with one another; or conflict and defensiveness might lessen, and humor and good will might increase.

When family therapists discover these changes along with families, it then becomes evident that the work of the middle phase of therapy is winding down. In such cases, families and clinicians move their focus and efforts to termination.

Termination

"Progress in family therapy moves in a circular direction. The potential for reaching new goals depends on the growth that has occurred previously. If one understands systems to be open and changing, it is hard to define the conclusion of family therapy simply in terms of accomplished goals, for the goals themselves may change over the course of therapy" (Nichols & Everett, 1986, p. 266). Nevertheless, family therapy reaches a point in which either the family or the therapist or both agree that it is time to end. The family and the therapist are more likely to benefit if termination is handled in a planned and systematic way, rather than in an abrupt manner.

The termination process has four steps: (1) orientation, (2) summarization, (3) discussion of long-term goals, and (4) follow-up (Epstein & Bishop, 1981).

1. *Orientation.* Just as with other therapeutic processes, the subject of termination is best raised before it is actually implemented. This is accomplished in the orientation step of termination. Orientation commences when therapists realize that families have reached their goals or will be concluding their contracted sessions.

2. *Summarization.* After the family has become oriented to the fact that therapy will be ending, the therapist goes over with the family what has occurred during their sessions together. This process can replace the therapist as chief spokesperson, or it can involve both the therapist and family taking equal responsibility for summarizing their time and experiences together.

3. *Discussion of Long-Term Goals.* The discussion of long-term goals is a means by which families can be helped during termination to anticipate, avoid, or modify potential troublesome situations. For example, a therapist may ask a family how they are going to avoid yelling at each other when they get tired. In raising such an issue, the therapist and family have an opportunity to identify resources both within and outside the family system that may be helpful to them in the future (Barker, 1986).

4. *Follow-up.* The idea behind follow-up is that family therapy is a never-ending process; it continues long after the therapist and family have finished their formal work. Such a premise considers therapy and termination "open-ended," that is, the family may need to return (Nichols & Everett, 1986, p. 266). It also acknowledges that some families do better over time when they know someone will check up on their progress. In essence, follow-up is a paradox. It is the last step in family therapy, but it can lead to more family therapy.

As far as mechanics go, one of the simplest ways to achieve termination is to reduce the frequency of sessions. This may be implemented informally or formally, over a number of months. One suggestion for bringing family therapy to a close is through a *three-session termination process*—that is, setting the date, a next-to-the-last session, and the final farewell session (Thomas, 1992). The use of rituals and tasks can be especially meaningful during termination and can remind family members of what they have achieved and of behaviors they need to continue (Imber-Black, Roberts, & Whiting, 1989). For example, in a final session, members of a family can give each other wishes for the future in a written form that can be revisited later. The family can also plan a celebration of who they have become and symbolically lay to rest in a mock funeral the family that originally entered therapy.

Overall, the process of termination, like the therapeutic process itself, is more complicated than it seems (Lebow, 1995). If conducted over time and with sensitivity, it can help families and family members recognize their growth and development during treatment. It can also help families and their members recognize and accept their feelings, thoughts, behaviors, failures, and accomplishments. Unfortunately, termination is often premature, and about 40% to 60% of families who begin treatment drop out before therapy is finished (Kazdin, Stolar, & Marciano, 1995). The result is a loss of benefits for families and a lost opportunity for family therapists to work with those in need of mental health services.

Therefore, careful attention must always be paid to all aspects of the therapeutic process. Termination should not be treated as the highlight of the therapeutic experience, but it should certainly be a goal (Hackney & Cormier, 1994). Although termination can help bring the therapeutic process to a logical and positive conclusion, it is only one part of the entire system of family therapy. If possible, termination should take into account the family's progress in therapy, including skills they have learned that can be applied later (Lebow, 1995).

Adlerian Family Therapy: An Example of Appropriate Process

Although there are a number of family therapies that could be used to illustrate appropriate process, Adler's model is used here for two reasons. First, it is one of the oldest forms of family therapy. Second, it is not easily categorized, and therefore, can be employed in a variety of settings.

Background of Adlerian Theory

Adlerian family therapy is an offshoot of the socially oriented and pragmatically focused treatment approach developed by Alfred Adler (1870-1937). It has been perpetuated in the United States by individuals such as Rudolph Driekurs, Don Dinkmeyer, Robert Sherman, Roy Kern, and Thomas Sweeney; organizations such as the Alfred Adler Institute of Chicago and the North American Society of Adlerian Psychology; and journals such as *Individual Psychology* and the *Journal of Individual Psychology*.

A major premise of Adlerian theory is that "individuals and social systems are holistic and indivisible in nature, that behavior is purposeful and interactive, and that the individual seeks significance by belonging within a social system" (Walsh & McGraw, 1996, p. 103). The family is seen as the prototype of a social system.

Another premise of this theory is that perception is subjective, and individuals create their own meaning from experiences. Meaning may be influenced by the family atmosphere in which one grows up. A family that is nurturing and democratic may help produce a child with a positive self-concept whose behaviors are purposeful and goal directed. On the other hand, a family that is authoritarian is more likely to foster a feeling of inferiority in a child that leads to unproductive or even destructive behaviors.

Birth order, sibling rivalry, and gender roles are also important. A child's ordinal position (i.e., first, second, middle, youngest, or only) may impact the way that child responds to his or her family and society in general. For instance, firstborn are often achievement oriented, and youngest are often socially oriented. Sibling rivalry, such as that between firstborn and second-born children, can also make a difference, with second-born children seeking to pursue roles taken by firstborns and firstborns striving to avoid being "dethroned." In addition, gender roles and the expectations associated with them may either enhance behaviors within a family or lead to conflict.

These underlying assumptions are considered by Adlerian family therapists in the preplanning stage of family therapy, because theory is the basis for therapy. Inattention to one or more of these basic assumptions can lead to actions that are incongruent with therapeutic purposes.

Initial Session(s)

Unlike Adlerian family counseling, which focuses on parent education and prevention, Adlerian family therapy is directed toward changing family interactions (Walsh & McGraw, 1996). Therefore, it requires that entire families be present in sessions.

Within initial sessions, joining and establishing rapport with a family is accomplished by making contact with each family member and listening to his or her concerns. Family dynamics are directly observed, especially in regard to **power** (i.e., decision making, manipulation, negotiation), **boundaries** (i.e., physical and emotional closeness), **coalitions** (i.e., two or more people joined together for support), **roles** (i.e., behaviors members expect from one another), **rules** (i.e., implicit or explicit guidelines that determine behaviors of family members), and patterns of communication (i.e., double messages, withholding information, and overgeneralizing).

In addition to viewing family patterns, an Adlerian family therapist might ask family members to give self-reports about how the family functions. One way of doing this is for family members to talk about a typical day in the life of their family. Inventories and assessment techniques, such as the recalling by family members of their earliest recollections, are also employed.

With this material in hand, Adlerian family therapists can engender hope that change can take place within the family by reframing problems to have more positive connotations and working with the family to formulate appropriate goals. Resistance may be dealt with by renegotiating goals, confronting the family with the fact that it is resisting and thus making them aware of their behaviors, assigning a positive connotation to the resistance to avoid a power struggle, and joining the resistance and even exaggerating it so that to resist, the family has to be more cooperative (Walsh & McGraw, 1996).

Middle Phase of Treatment

In the middle phase of treatment, an Adlerian therapist would concentrate on helping family members become more aware of their behaviors and to reorient (i.e., change what they are doing). Awareness is increased through such processes as examining individual versus family goals, exploring life styles and types of communication between family members, and making explicit the needs and wants of the family as a whole, as well as of its individual members. Through such an understanding, families may become more motivated to want to try new behaviors and ways of interacting.

Reorientation and change can take place by simultaneously addressing several areas of difficulty (Sherman & Dinkmeyer, 1987). Among the most important of these areas are:

- changes in perceptions, beliefs, values and goals
- changes in the structure and organization of the family
- changes in the skills and social behavior of the family through teaching
- changes in the way direct and indirect power is employed in the family

Termination

Termination is initiated in Adlerian family therapy when a family and a therapist agree that change has occurred and that the family is making progress or has made the type of progress initially agreed upon. Measuring progress comes through observation of family interactions, self-reports, and various assessment techniques. In initiating termination, the Adlerian family therapist reinforces newly learned skills or ways of behaving. Because Adlerian theory has a strong teleological (i.e., futuristic) component, a family during termination is encouraged to project ahead to problems that might arise and discuss how they would handle such difficulties.

Finally, during termination, a family's strengths and abilities to continue their success are reiterated by the Adlerian family therapist. The family is then followed-up through a variety of means at a predetermined time. At follow-up, the family is again reinforced by the therapist in regard to competencies and ability to maintain or continue change.

Summary and Conclusion

This chapter concentrated on universal aspects in the process of conducting family therapy. Specific topics that were addressed include the initial session(s), the middle phase of therapy, and termination. Within each of these three topics numerous points were discussed.

During the initial session(s) the task of the therapist is to create a structure in which change can take place. This "battle for structure" process begins on the phone and/or in studying background material. Through such involvement, the family therapist establishes rapport and structure. He or she also hypothesizes what is happening within the family (i.e., makes a diagnosis) from a developmental and systemic frame of reference. It is hoped that during the initial session(s), families will become more motivated and win what has been defined as the "battle for initiative." It is important that families win this battle because the best success in any clinical setting comes when families are motivated to accomplish goals.

During the middle phase of family therapy, most of the work of therapy takes place. If family therapy is like a play, then the middle phase contains the most action. It is crucial in this phase that clinicians pay more attention to the processes within families more than the content. It is also important that families be helped or encouraged to make links to support groups and resources within their communities. It is during the middle phase that family therapists are extremely involved in helping families overcome natural and artificial barriers that keep them from achieving their goals.

Finally, the process of termination is the last part of the therapeutic cycle. Termination works best when client families are prepared for it. The results are usually better when it is agreed to by both the therapist and family. Termination is not the highlight of therapy, but if conducted properly, it can help families reflect on what they have accomplished and learned. It can motivate families and their members to continue new behaviors, especially if follow-up is included.

At the conclusion of the chapter, Adlerian family therapy was introduced as an example of how a theory is implemented in the process of working with a family. The Adlerian approach is one of the oldest in the field of family therapy and is socially and pragmatically based. Like other forms of therapy, the Adlerian approach is driven by its theoretical presuppositions about how families function. From the theory, Adlerian family therapists focus on certain aspects of the family as shaping a treatment process that includes initial sessions, a middle or working phase, and then, finally, termination and follow-up.

SUMMARY TABLE

Process of Family Therapy

Common Problems of Beginning Family Therapists
Failures to Act

Beginning therapist can fail to establish structure (use of self-disclosure statements can avoid this problem).

They can fail to show care and concern.

They can fail to engage family members in the therapeutic process

They can fail to let the family work on its problems, that is, win the battle for initiative

They can fail to attend to nonverbal family dynamics.

Overaction

Beginning therapists can overemphasize details.

They can overemphasize making everyone happy.

They can overemphasize verbal expression.

They can overemphasize coming to early or easy resolutions.

They can overemphasize dealing with one member of the family.

Proper Process

Pre-Session Planning and Tasks

Establish initial professional relationship with referral source/person.

Collect essential information about the family.

Make arrangements to see the family (within 48 hours if possible).

Hypothesize about dynamics within the family (from family life cycle literature).

Form a preliminary diagnosis (e.g., distancing, cutoffs, enmeshment, disengagement, friction, denial, enabling, unresolved grief).

First Session

Make the family comfortable through social exchange with each member, that is, establish rapport and join with the family.

Inquire from each member a perception of the family.

Observe family patterns, that is, the "family dance" (who speaks to whom and how, what is the outward appearance of family, what is the family mood, etc.).

Assess what needs to be done (e.g., treatment, referral, testing, and so forth).

Engender hope for change and overcome resistance.

Break dysfunctional patterns through words and actions congruent with one's theoretical perspective (if appropriate).

Make a return appointment and assignments.

Write impressions of family and session immediately after the session ends.

Middle Phase of Treatment

Involve peripheral family members in the therapeutic process, (e.g., use circular questioning).

Seek to connect together family members with appropriate generational interests and concerns (i.e., break up intergenerational coalitions).

Promote quid pro quo (something for something) relationships so that family members begin to think they are benefiting from the therapeutic process.

Emphasize progress or change within family system however small.

Reinforce family members for taking risks and trying new behaviors.

Stay active as a therapist by continuing to probe, direct, and suggest.

Link family members with appropriate outside support systems if needed.

Focus on process.

Look for evidence of change in the family (i.e., utilize all of the techniques within your approach that are germane to the family with whom you are working).

Termination

Plan with the family for a mutually agreed upon termination.

Consider termination "open-ended" (i.e., the family may need to return).

Reduce the frequency of sessions.

Follow the four-step termination process: a) orientation, b) summarization, c) discussion of long-term goals, and d) follow-up.

Formally bring family therapy to a close (i.e.,discuss what was learned and achieved during family therapy).

Celebrate and/or resolve grief.

Adlerian Family Therapy: An Example of Appropriate Process

Background of Adlerian Theory

The theory was created by Alfred Adler (1870–1937).

Theory is socially oriented and pragmatically focused.

Social systems are indivisible and holistic; a family is a prototype of a social system.

Perception is subjective; individuals create their own meaning from experiences.

A family atmosphere either promotes or inhibits positive social behaviors.

Birth order, sibling rivalry, and gender roles either enhance or detract from behaviors in families and societies.

Therapists must consider these underlying assumptions of Adlerian theory in the preplanning stage.

Initial Session(s)

The whole family is seen in therapy.

After joining and initial rapport building, the therapist observes family dynamics related to power, boundaries, coalitions, roles, rules, and patterns of communication. Also, self-reports are received.

Adlerian family therapists engender hope for change, reframe problems, and work with family to formulate appropriate goals.

Resistance is dealt with in a number of ways, including confrontation and joining.

Middle Phase of Treatment

Therapist helps families become more aware of their behaviors and to reorient (i.e., make changes).

Individual and family goals are compared and contrasted.

Several areas of change may be addressed at once, for example, perceptions, beliefs, social skills, family structure, and power.

Termination

Termination is initiated when the therapist and family mutually agree concerning progress and goals.

New skills and ways of behaving are reinforced.

Potential future problems are addressed.

Family strengths are reinforced.

A time of follow-up is planned.

References

Anderson, C. M., & Stewart, S. (1983). *Mastering resistance: A practical guide to family therapy*. New York: Guilford.

Barker, P. (1986). *Basic family therapy* (2nd ed.). New York: Oxford.

Bateson, G. (1955). A theory of play and fantasy. *Psychiatric Reports, 2,* 177–193.

Boszormenyi-Nagy, I. (1987). *Foundations of contextual therapy*. New York: Brunner/Mazel.

Brock, G. W., & Barnard, C. P. (1992). *Procedures in marriage and family therapy* (2nd ed.). Boston: Allyn & Bacon.

Carlson, J., Hinkle, J. S., & Sperry, L. (1993). Using diagnosis and DSM-III-R and IV in marriage and family counseling and therapy: Increasing treatment outcomes without losing heart and soul. *The Family Journal, 1,* 308–312.

Carter, B., & McGoldrick, M. (1988). *The changing family life cycle* (2nd ed.). New York: Gardner.

Cormier, L. S., & Hackney, H. (1993). *The professional counselor: A process guide to helping*. Boston: Allyn & Bacon.

Coleman, S, (1985). *Failures in family therapy*. New York: Guilford.

Constantine, J. A., Stone Fish, L. S., & Piercy, F. P. (1984). A systematic procedure for teaching positive connotation. *Journal of Marital and Family Therapy, 10,* 313–316.

Coyne, J. C. (1985). Toward a theory of frames and reframing: The social nature of frames. *Journal of Marital and Family Therapy, 11,* 337–344.

Duvall, E. (1977). *Marriage and family development* (5th ed.). Philadelphia: Lippincott.

Egan, G. (1990). *The skilled helper* (4th ed.). Pacific Grove, CA: Brooks/Cole.

Epstein, N. B., & Bishop, D. S. (1981). Problem centered systems therapy of the family. *Journal of Marital and Family Therapy, 7,* 23–31.

Friedlander, M. L., Wildman, J., Heatherington, L., & Skowron, E. A. (1994). What we do and don't know about the process of family therapy. *Journal of Family Psychology, 8,* 390–416.

Gladding, S. T. (1988). *Milestones*. Unpublished manuscript. Winston-Salem, NC.

Gladding, S. T. (1996). *Counseling: A comprehensive profession* (3rd ed.). Englewood Cliffs, NJ: Prentice-Hall.

Gorden, R. (1992). *Basic interviewing skills*. Itasca, IL: F. E. Peacock.

Guy, J. D. (1987). *The personal life of the psychotherapist*. New York: Wiley.

Hackney, H., & Cormier, L. S. (1994). *Counseling strategies and interventions* (4th ed.). Boston: Allyn & Bacon.

Haley, J. (1969). *The power tactics of Jesus Christ and other essays*. New York: Grossman.

Haley, J. (1976). *Problem-solving therapy*. San Francisco, CA: Jossey-Bass.

Haley, J. (1987). *Problem solving therapy* (2nd ed.). San Francisco: Jossey-Bass.

Holland, J. L. (1973). *Making vocational choices: A theory of careers*. Englewood Cliffs, NJ: Prentice-Hall.

Imber-Black, E., Roberts, J., & Whiting, R. (1989). *Rituals in families and in family therapy*. New York: Norton.

Jaffe, D. T. (1991). *Working with the ones you love*. Berkeley, CA: Conari Press.

Kaplan, D., & Culkin, M. (1995). Family ethics: Lessons learned. *The Family Journal, 3,* 335–338.

Kazdin, A. E., Stolar, M. J., & Marciano, P. L. (1995). Risk factors for dropping out of treatment among white and black families. *Journal of Family Psychology, 9,* 402–417.

L'Abate, L., & Bagarozzi, D. (1993). *Sourcebook of marriage and family evaluation*. New York: Brunner/Mazel.

Lebow, J. (1995). Open-ended therapy: Termination in marital and family therapy (pp. 73–86). In R. H. Mikesell, D-D. Lusterman, & S. H. McDaniel (Eds.), *Integrating family therapy*. Washington, DC: American Psychological Association.

Minuchin, S. (1974). *Families and family therapy*. Boston: Harvard.

Minuchin, S., & Fishman, H. C. (1981). *Family therapy techniques*. Boston: Harvard.

Napier, A. Y., & Whitaker, C. (1978). *The family crucible*. New York: Bantam Books.

Nichols, M. P., & Schwartz, R. C. (1995). *Family therapy: Concepts and methods* (3rd ed.). Boston: Allyn & Bacon.

Nichols, W. C., & Everett, C. (1986). *Systemic family therapy: An integrative approach*. New York: Guilford.

Olkin, R. (1993, Winter). Teaching family therapy to graduate students: What do we teach and when do we teach it? *Family Psychologist, 9,* 31–34.

Piercy, F. P., & Lobenz, N. M. (1994). *Stop marital fights before they start*. New York: Berkeley Press.

Pittman, F. (1995, November/December). Turning tragedy into comedy. *Family Therapy Networker, 19,* 36–40.

Rait, D. (1988). Survey results. *Family Therapy Networker, 12,* 52–56.

Resnikoff, R. O. (1981). Teaching family therapy: Ten key questions for understanding the family as patient. *Journal of Marital and Family Therapy, 7,* 135–142.

Rickert, V. (1989). *The initial family interview*. Presentation at the annual convention of the American Association for Marriage and Family Therapy, San Francisco, CA.

Schilson, E. A. (1991). Strategic therapy. In A. M. Horne & J. L. Passmore (Eds.), *Family counseling and therapy* (2nd ed.) (pp. 141–178). Itasca, IL: F. E. Peacock.

Sherman, R., & Dinkmeyer, D. (1987). *Systems of family therapy: An Adlerian integration*. New York: Brunner/Mazel.

Snider, M. (1992). *Process family therapy*. Boston: Allyn & Bacon.

Thomas, M. B. (1992). *An introduction to marital and family therapy*. New York: Macmillan.

Tomm, K. (1987). Interventive interviewing: Part 1. Strategizing as a fourth guideline for the therapist. *Family Process, 26,* 3–13.

Walsh, W. M., & McGraw, J. A. (1996). *Essentials of family therapy*. Denver, CO: Love.

Weber, T., & Levine, F. (1995). Engaging the family: An integrative approach. In R. H. Mikesell, D-D. Lusterman, & S. H. McDaniel (Eds.), *Integrating family therapy* (pp. 45–71). Washington, DC: American Psychological Association.

Weber, T., McKeever, J. E., & McDaniel, S. H. (1992). A beginner's guide to the problem-oriented first family interview. In R. L. Smith & P. Stevens-Smith (Eds.). *Family counseling and therapy* (pp. 202–212). Ann Arbor, MI: ERIC/CAPS.

West, J. D. (1988). Marriage and family therapy assessment. *Counselor Education and Supervision, 28,* 169–180.

CHAPTER 5

Psychoanalytic and Bowen Family Therapies

I walk thoughtfully down Beecher Road
at the end of a summer of too little growth,
the autumn wind stirring around me
orange remnants of once green leaves.

I am the son of a fourth-grade teacher
and a man who dabbled in business,
a descendant of Virginia farmers
and open-minded Baptists,
the husband of a Connecticut woman,
the father of preschoolers.

Youngest of three, I am a trinity:
counselor,
teacher,
writer.

Amid the cold, I approach home,
midlife is full of surprises.

Gladding, 1993

P
sychoanalytic and Bowen family therapies began developing in the
1950s. Their founders, Nathan Ackerman in New York and Murray
Bowen in Washington, D.C., were both known for their strong personalities and
loyal followings. They originally were educated to utilize Freud's (1940) psychoanalytic theory with individual clients. Indeed, the tenets of psychoanalysis are
a shared source from which psychoanalytic and Bowen family therapies sprang.
However, Ackerman and Bowen, because of their interests and circumstances,
took liberties to apply Freud's theory to families and stressed the development
of interpersonal as well as intrapersonal relationships.

This chapter examines the main aspects of psychoanalytic and Bowen family
therapies. In identifying themselves as either psychoanalytic or Bowen family
therapists, clinicians are distinct in emphasizing specific theoretical techniques
and factors associated with each theory (e.g., who is worked with, as well as
how and when treatment occurs). At the heart of treatment, from both viewpoints, is a belief that changes in families and their members occur best when
the family is examined in the context of its history and development. Conscious
and unconscious processes are collectively and individually the focus of therapeutic interventions.

Common Characteristics of Psychoanalytic and Bowen Theories

On the surface, psychoanalytic and Bowen family therapies have much in common. This is particularly true in regard to numerous premises and beliefs. For
instance, psychoanalytic and Bowen family treatments are based on conceptual
models that are comprehensive in scope. They also have applied techniques
that have developed from both research and practice (e.g., Papero, 1990; Titelman, 1987).

Another unifying feature that psychoanalytic and Bowen family therapies
share is the belief that in family therapy an emphasis should be placed on the
fact that "the past is active in the present" (Smith, 1991, p. 24). These two
approaches stress the importance of social and historical data in the lives of

families. For example, early childhood experiences (ie., the past), whether consciously maintained or not, can have an impact on an individual and a family now (i.e., the present) and for years to come. Initial experiences associated with bonding and connectedness are particularly relevant. The memories and patterns of interaction established during these moments continue to influence present levels of functioning in multiple ways (Gibson & Donigian, 1993). For example, a couple's struggle over emotional and physical closeness might be a renewal of difficulties each had in forming relationships early in life.

A further common denominator of these theories is their focus on how intrapersonal and interpersonal aspects of life impact on each other. Basically, the way people relate to themselves influences how they interact with others. Similarly, the way in which people have been reacted to by others in the past affects how they perceive and treat themselves. For instance, an 11-year-old girl who withdraws from social activities may be expressing her feelings about her inadequacy in a family and minimizing her risk of being ridiculed.

Those associated with psychoanalytic and Bowen family therapies have created their own specific descriptors of interactions as well. A number of phrases from each theory characterize family dynamics. Psychoanalytic theorists, for instance, have coined terms such as ***marital schism, marital skew*** (Lidz, Cornelison, Fleck, & Terry, 1957), and ***pseudomutuality*** (Wynne, Ryckoff, Day, & Hirsh, 1958) to describe dysfunctional relationships within families. Bowen family therapists have invented other words or phrases such as ***differentiation, fusion,*** and ***emotionally cutoff*** (Kerr & Bowen, 1988).

A final premise these two theories share is their view that change is usually gradual and requires hard work with a heavy investment of time and resources. Bowen and Ackerman, as psychoanalytically trained psychiatrists, did not let their theories stray far from an in-depth treatment perspective. Although Bowen family therapy may sometimes achieve good results in as few as 5 or 10 sessions, families using either of these two approaches generally require 20 to 40 sessions (Bowen, 1975). Members within families usually examine their relationships in regard to themselves and others before they risk trying new patterns of behavior.

Psychoanalytic Family Therapy

Major Psychoanalytic Family Therapy Theorists

The most prominent professionals associated with psychoanalytic family therapy are Nathan Ackerman, Ivan Boszormenyi-Nagy, James Framo, Theodore Lidz, Norman Paul, Donald Williamson, Robin Skynner, and Lyman Wynne. However, Ackerman is generally credited as the founder of psychoanalytic family therapy.

Nathan Ackerman

Nathan Ackerman (1908–1971) became a family therapist over an extended period of time. Initially, he was educated as a child psychiatrist and followed the traditional psychoanalytic approach of seeing one patient at a time. However, in the 1930s Ackerman became interested in families and their influence on mental health/illness (Ackerman, 1937). This interest was sparked by his observations about the effect of unemployment on men and their families in a mining town in western Pennsylvania and about how families seemed to change more rapidly when all members were interviewed together (Broderick & Schrader, 1991). In his initial clinical work at the Menninger Clinic in Topeka, Kansas, he began treating whole families and sending his staff on home visits (Guerin, 1976). He was especially interested in the psychosocial dynamics of family life and in applying psychoanalytical principles to family units.

In the 1950s and 60s, Ackerman was even more heavily involved in his work with families and, consequently, became the leading family therapist on the East Coast (Nichols & Schwartz, 1995). He opened the Family Mental Health Clinic at Jewish Family Services in New York in 1957 and established the Family Institute in New York in 1960. In 1961, he became the cofounder of *Family Process,* the first journal in family therapy. This publication, along with Ackerman's earlier landmark text, *The Psychodynamics of Family Life* (1958), gave credibility and credence to the field of family therapy. Ackerman remained staunchly psychodynamic in outlook throughout his professional career.

Two of the most notable contributions of Ackerman to the field of family therapy were his strong, charismatic personality, which helped attract interest in what he was doing, and his overall success as a therapist (Bloch & Simon, 1982). He was also an excellent theorist who made unique contributions to the literature in the field of family therapy through his writings and practice. His arguments were based on principles and filled with passion. Ackerman was a fighter for what he believed in. "Innumerable minor skirmishes and border wars" that Ackerman engaged in "were never chronicled but clung to the man's reputation like the leathery scars of an old warrior chief" (Block & Simon, 1982, pp. xv-xvi). He has been described as feisty, brilliant, charming, and a gadfly. Regardless, he was hardworking and responsible.

Ackerman influenced many psychoanalytically-oriented practitioners, as well as other professionals, to treat individuals and families together as a system. He helped open the field of psychoanalysis to nonmedical specialists by establishing the American Academy of Psychoanalysis in 1955.

Ackerman defined the difference between family psychotherapy and psychoanalysis (Ackerman, 1962). His conceptualizations of families and presentations about them were noteworthy and creative. For instance, Ackerman published transcripts of family therapy sessions with interpretive comments in the margins, such as "Therapist contrasts father's quiet way with Alice's noisy aggressiveness" (Ackerman, Beatman, & Sherman, 1961, p. 139). Ackerman is recognized as being the initiator of and/or the one who emphasized such concepts as scapegoating, tickling of defenses, complementarity, focus on strengths, interlocking pathology, and live history.

Overall, Nathan Ackerman was a leading pioneer in family therapy. His early death, at the age of 63, deprived the field of a crusader and innovative thinker.

Premises of Psychoanalytical Family Theory

Psychoanalytical family therapy is based on the classic work of Sigmund Freud, as interpreted, modified, and applied to family life. Freud viewed human nature as one based on drives (e.g., sexuality and aggression). Mental conflict arises when children learn, and mislearn, that expressing these basic impulses will lead to punishment. Conflict is signaled by unpleasant affect: anxiety or depression" (Nichols & Schwartz, 1995, p. 247). In other words, to resolve conflict one of two actions must occur: There must be a strengthening of defenses against a conflicted wish, or defenses must be relaxed sufficiently to permit some gratification.

In addition to Ackerman, several other theorists and practitioners helped apply Freud's individually focused approach to families, including Heinz Kohut (1977), James Framo (1981), and Ivan Boszormenyi-Nagy (1987). However, Ackerman took the lead by setting up a training and treatment center for this purpose, the Family Institute (now known as the Ackerman Institute). This facility provided a place where professionals could come and observe his work. He also wrote prolifically on the diagnosis and treatment of families (e.g., Ackerman, 1958). As a psychoanalytically-oriented therapist, he initiated a new way of thinking about individuals and families and advocated that an accurate understanding of an individual's unconscious requires an understanding of its context. One of the primary contexts is the reality of family interactions. The importance of context in the treatment of families has continued to be stressed by Boszormenyi-Nagy (1987).

Ackerman (1956) clearly articulated the concept of **interlocking pathology** to explain how families and certain of their members stay dysfunctional. In an interlocking pathology there is an unconscious process that takes place between family members that keeps them together. If members violate the unwritten family rules, then the members either make a conscious decision to leave the family and become healthier or they are drawn back into the familiar family pattern by other members and continue to function in a less than ideal manner. For example, a young adult who has not adequately separated from his parents may move into an apartment. If the young adult gets an adequate job and makes new friends in his or her age group, he or she may avoid being pulled back into the family and may begin to establish a new identity and way of life.

A more recent focus of psychoanalytical theory is **object relations theory** (Kohut, 1977; Scharff, 1989; Slipp, 1988). Object relations theory is the bridge between classical Freudian theory, with its emphasis on individual drives, and family therapy, with its emphasis on social relationships (Nichols & Schwartz,

1995). An **object** is something that is loved, usually a person. Therefore, the term *object relations* means "relations between persons involved in ardent emotional attachments. These attachments can exist in the outer world of reality or as residues of the past—that is, inner presences, often unconscious, that remain vigorous and very much alive within us" (Scarf, 1995, p. xxxvii).

Through object relations theory, relationships across generations can be explained. According to this theory, human beings have a fundamental motivation to seek objects, that is, people in relationships, starting at birth (Fairbairn, 1954; Klein, 1948). In this case, an object is a significant other (e.g., a mother during infancy) with whom children form an interactional, emotional bond. As they grow, children will often internalize (interject) good and bad characteristics of these objects within themselves. Over time, these interjects form the basis for how individuals interact and evaluate their interpersonal relationships with others, especially those with whom they are close.

This process of evaluation occurs at its lowest level through an unconscious procedure known as **splitting** (Kernberg, 1976). In splitting, object representations are either all good or all bad. The result is a projection of good and bad qualities onto persons within one's environment. Through splitting, people are able to control their anxiety and even the objects (i.e., persons, within their environment) by making them predictable. However, the drawback to splitting is that it distorts reality. When splitting occurs, children (and later their adult counterparts) fail to integrate their feelings about an object (a person) into a realistic view (Hafner, 1986). For example, in a couple relationship, each spouse might project unrealistic patterns of behavior onto the other. In addition to distorting the relationship, this type of projection causes conflict and confusion. Individuals who operate in this way have trouble dealing with the complexity of human relationships and may be immature in their interactions (Kernberg, 1976; Kohut, 1971).

The importance of object relations theory in family therapy is that it provides a way for psychoanalytic clinicians to explain reasons for marital choices and family interactional patterns (Dicks, 1963). It stresses the value of working with unconscious forces in individuals and families beyond Freud's metaphorical concepts of id, ego, and superego. Unconscious and unresolved early object relations that adults may bring into their marriage relationships can result in the development of dysfunctional patterns in which persons cling to each other desperately and dependently (Ackerman, 1956; Napier & Whitaker, 1978). These patterns keep repeating themselves until one or both spouses (or in some cases their children) become more aware, take actions to differentiate themselves from past objects, and in the process, learn to act in new and productive ways.

Psychoanalytical Treatment Techniques

In psychoanalytic family therapy, there is considerable emphasis on the unconscious, early memories, and object relations. The therapeutic techniques used include transference, dream and daydream analysis, confrontation, focusing on strengths, life history, and complementarity.

Transference

Transference is the projection onto a therapist of feelings, attitudes, or desires. This technique is employed in individual analysis to help clients work through their feelings by viewing the therapist as a significant other with whom relationships are unresolved (Ellis, 1991). Transference is utilized in family therapy in order to understand dominant feelings within a family unit and delineate which emotions are being directed toward what people.

In cases where transference occurs, clients in the family form a bond with the therapist and act toward the therapist as they would toward people with whom they are having difficulties. Thus, they benefit through the expression of pent-up emotion (i.e., catharsis) and through self-discovery, insight, and the learning of new ways to interact. For example, family members who are angry with each other and frustrated with social service agencies might say to the family therapists such words as:

- "I don't see what good you are going to do us."
- "What's the use of talking to you."
- "I'm really mad that this family is going down the tubes and all we are doing is talking to you. When are we going to get some real help?"

By treating these sentences in a nondefensive and understanding way, the family therapist can help a family get through dealing with unproductive emotions and get on to working on important issues in their lives.

Dream and Daydream Analysis

The objective of having family members discuss their dreams or daydreams is to analyze what needs within the family are not being met. For example, if a father has a recurring dream of being abandoned, he may be expressing a need for greater affiliation with family members. Strategies are then developed to meet members' deficits. For instance, in the case of the father, family outings or dinners could be planned to help tie the father closer to other members in a pleasant way.

Overall, dream analysis may be quite useful for some families in helping them see areas that need attention. However, dream analysis can become problematic if the number of family members participating is large.

Confrontation

In **confrontation** procedures, the therapist points out to families how their behaviors contradict or conflict with their expressed wishes (Ackerman, 1966). For example, a father who protests that he wishes to spend more time with his wife and children, yet who continues to work late at his office on a consistent basis, may be confronted by the therapist as follows:

> George, I see you voluntarily working at your business all hours of the night and day. Yet, I hear you want to spend more time with your family. Help me understand what you are doing to get what you say you want.

The idea behind confrontation is to help family members become more aware of what they are doing and to change their strategies for coping and becoming functional.

Focusing on Strengths

As with other therapeutic endeavors, psychoanalytical family therapists are aware that most families come to treatment because they are focused on perceiving and dealing with weaknesses in themselves and their families. By concentrating on strengths, family therapists help change the family's focus. For instance, the therapist may point out to a family that they all seem quite willing and capable of breaking past patterns of interaction by saying:

> I have heard from each of you how you would like for your family to work. Bill, I am impressed with your strong commitment to doing whatever it takes. Sue, I am equally struck by the fact that you have stated you are willing to make any sacrifice necessary for the family to run more smoothly. Likewise, Chip, even though you are only 14-years-old, I am aware that you are mature and willing to work with your parents to bring about needed changes.

As a consequence of focusing on strengths, structured activities can be designed to promote cooperation and break dysfunctional patterns of behaving. For instance, a family can be asked to plan an event that will utilize the abilities of all family members.

Life history

By taking and assessing a family's life history, psychoanalytical family therapists can report present and past patterns of interaction within the family. This process also affirms to family members that they are valued and accepted regardless of their backgrounds. Taking a family life history promotes trust in the therapist and also provides family members with insight. The history can be written in a narrative or an abbreviated form.

Complementarity

Complementarity is the degree of harmony in the meshing of family roles. For example, if a husband and wife agree that her role should be planning the family budget and his should be balancing the checkbook, they have established a complementarity relationship in regard to financial roles. When roles dovetail, as in the previous example, family life is likely to be satisfactory. One task of the therapist is to help family members provide and receive satisfaction from their relationships. It may mean asking members what they want and what they are willing to do in return.

Role of the Psychoanalytic Family Therapist

In psychoanalytic treatment, the therapist plays several roles. One is that of a teacher. It is crucial that family members understand how influences in their past, especially those that were unconscious, have an impact on them now. Therefore, it is essential that family members learn basic psychoanalytic terms and how these terms apply on a personal and interpersonal basis.

A second role the therapist might play is that of a **good enough mother** (Winnicott, 1965). A good enough mother is one whose infant feels loved and cared for and, thus, is able to develop trust and a true sense of self. This role might call for the therapist to actually nurture the family member by providing encouraging behaviors that were absent at earlier developmental stages. In this role, the therapist might involve family members in interactions with one another that help them make up for past deficits. This behavior could take the form of anything from pats on the back to the giving of compliments.

A final role the psychoanalytic therapist might play is that of a catalyst who moves into the "living space" of the family and stirs up interactions. Ackerman (1966) was a master of engaging families in this manner. The result was that families in treatment would often have a meaningful emotional exchange. In the role of a catalyst, the therapist activates, challenges, confronts, sometimes interprets, and helps integrate family processes. Such a role requires high energy and stamina.

In fulfilling any of these roles, but especially the last one, the therapist must be careful to emphasize family as well as individual interactions. It is crucial that family members have extensive and free-flowing interchanges and that the therapist not become overly involved or central in the process. Such a stance is easier to describe than to implement.

Process and Outcome of Psychoanalytic Family Therapy

A major goal of psychoanalytical family therapy is to free family members of *unconscious restrictions*. This outcome is sometimes achieved through the therapist's interpretation of events and insight on the part of family members regarding events. Interpretation is best offered by the therapist on a *preconscious level,* that is, on material that family members are almost aware of. When insights are achieved in such an endeavor, they must be *worked through,* that is, "translated into new and more productive ways of behaving and interacting" (Nichols & Schwartz, 1995, p. 267).

Once unconscious restrictions are worked through, family members are able to interact with one another as whole, healthy persons on the basis of current realities rather than unconscious images of the past. When this goal is achieved, the results are usually manifested in changes that are described by the term *differentiation*. The idea behind **differentiation** is that individuals have reached a level of maturity in which they can balance their rational and emotional selves. When this dynamic occurs, family members can interact thoughtfully as persons. They can participate in the family fully and can also be themselves. Furthermore, they do not get caught up in dysfunctional interactions with other family members.

Sometimes the achievement of differentiation is not possible. In such cases, professionals often opt for *crisis resolution,* which is similar to that of other treatment modalities and basically involves a reduction in symptoms. Therapists in these circumstances "focus more on supporting defenses and clarifying communication than on analyzing defenses and uncovering repressed needs and impulses" (Nichols & Schwartz, 1995, p. 264).

Unique Aspects of Psychoanalytic Family Therapy

As with other therapeutic approaches, psychoanalytic family therapy has some original dimensions. These qualities help others understand the strengths and limitations of the approach in regard to what is emphasized compared with other theories.

Emphases of Psychoanalytic Family Therapy

A major emphasis of psychoanalytic family therapy is that it concentrates on the *potency of the unconscious* in influencing human behavior. How the unconscious influences interpersonal and intrapersonal relationships, such as those found in marital and family living, is a focus. This method of treatment can increase family members' awareness of how forces within themselves and others, such as **invisible loyalties** to their parents, either bring them closer to each other or influence their distancing (Boszormenyi-Nagy & Spark, 1973).

The psychoanalytic approach examines *basic defense mechanisms* and the part they play in family relationships. This is a unique contribution to the literature on family dynamics and helps make interactions among some family members more understandable (Skynner, 1981). For example, abused children who stay loyal to their parents may be seen from this perspective as employing the Freudian defense mechanism of identification with the aggressor (see Table 5.1).

A third novel aspect of psychoanalytic family therapy is its emphasis on historical origins of dysfunctionality and the treatment of persons and families so affected. By working with a family or an individual, therapists get to the roots of problems formulated in childhood. They are then able to help families resolve troublesome issues by exploring past ways the family, as a unit, acted during troublesome times.

Finally, psychoanalytic family theory, especially object relations, helps explain how persons form *attachments* and how family members function as a result. This emphasis on the genesis of family relationships is something no other approach to working with families explores in as much depth.

Table 5.1
Basic Psychoanalytic Defense Mechanisms

Repression	The most basic of the defense mechanisms, repression is the unconscious exclusion of distressing or painful thoughts and memories. All other defense mechanisms make some use of repression.
Denial	In this process, a person refuses to see or accept any problem or troublesome aspect of life. Denial operates at the preconscious or conscious level.
Regression	When individuals are under stress, they often return to a less mature way of behaving.
Projection	Instead of stating what a person really thinks or feels, he or she attributes an unacceptable thought, feeling, or motive onto another.
Rationalization	This defense mechanism involves giving an "intellectual reason" to justify doing a certain action. The reason and the action are only connected in the person's mind after the behavior has been completed.
Reaction Formation	When an individual behaves in a manner that is just the opposite of how he or she feels, it is known as a "reaction formation." This type of behavior is usually quite exaggerated, such as acting especially nice to someone whom one dislikes intensely.
Displacement	This defense is a redirection of an emotional response onto a "safe target." The substitute person or object receives the feeling instead of the person directly connected with it.

From *Group Work: A Counseling Specialty* (2nd ed., p. 297) by S. T. Gladding, 1995, Englewood Cliffs, NJ: Prentice. Hall.

Comparison of Psychoanalytic Family Therapy with Other Theories

As opposed to most family therapies, psychoanalytic family therapy is linear, that is, it focuses on cause and effect interactions. This quality of the theory has resulted in criticism. For example, Thomas (1992) has stated: "One of the main limitations of psychoanalytically oriented approaches to family therapy is the emphasis on an analytic linear model" (p. 254). Although Ackerman and others attempted to make psychoanalytic theory applicable to family systems, they only partially succeeded. Too often this type of treatment is either limited to an individual or not broadened to family life (Perosa, 1996).

A second comparison of psychoanalytic family therapy to other approaches is its expense in regard to financial and time commitments. Psychoanalytically based approaches are demanding in the investment they require of their participants. Individuals and families must be prepared to explore the roots of their difficulties, including early childhood/parent interactions. Most cannot afford to take the time or afford the price of the sessions.

A third comparison that can be made between psychoanalytic family therapy and other approaches is that psychoanalytic treatment generally requires higher than average intellectual ability. Psychoanalytic theory may not be appropriate for families that are concrete in handling situations or become impatient with the abstract. These families want immediate results and cannot cope well with abstract concepts, such as the unconscious.

Finally, compared with most family therapy approaches, especially recently developed ones, psychoanalytic treatment lacks empirical research (Shields, Wynne, McDaniel, & Gawinski, 1994). Instead, psychoanalysis has a strong preference for nonempirical and nonquantitative studies. Such an emphasis "has contributed to the near demise of psychoanalysis as a recommended therapy" (Shields et al., 1994, p. 121).

CASE ILLUSTRATION

THE CASA FAMILY

Maria Casa is a 39-year-old single parent with a 13-year-old daughter, Gloria, and an 11-year-old son, Juan. She has been divorced for 5 years, but before her divorce was married for 10 years. Her husband, Roberto, kept in touch with the children for about 2 years after the divorce, but then moved to a distant city, and last year quietly remarried. The children hear from him only at Christmas, when he sends them each a present and a card.

Maria works as an executive assistant to a vice president of a major local employer. Earlier, she had been on the company assembly line, so she appreciates her position because of its greater benefits and flexibility. Yet, she resents having to dress well for the job and to occasionally stay late at the office to finish reports. She feels she is losing touch with her children because of her work responsibilities.

Recently, Juan has started using profanity and being disrespectful to his mother and sister. He does a poor job on family chores, such as cutting the grass. In addition, he has begun to hang out after school with a group of boys Maria considers undesirable. Gloria, on the other hand, is making good grades in school and working especially hard to please her mother by doing extra tasks Maria does not have time for, such as sweeping the walk. Maria is angry at Juan and proud of Gloria. She is worried that both children may get stuck in patterns that will ultimately not benefit them. She is particularly concerned about Juan.

Conceptualization of Family: Psychodynamic Perspective

On an unconscious level, this family appears to be enacting roles that are noncomplementary. Maria and Gloria are acting out heroine roles; Juan is the rebel. Underneath all of their public behaviors are feelings, most likely anger, about their life condition and the desertion of their father, Roberto. Juan is playing the role of the scapegoat to bring the family into treatment. Interestingly, all members of the family are seeking some social interaction—either with other family members (e.g., Gloria and Maria) or with a group, (e.g., Juan and his gang). Defense mechanisms, such as sublimation by Gloria, are also evident.

Process of Treatment: Psychodynamic Family Therapy

To help the family, a psychodynamic therapist need not bring all members of the present family into treatment. However, to understand the family thoroughly, it would be beneficial to have all members present, including Roberto if he would agree to come. After taking time to join with the family, a therapist should take a history of the family up to and after the time of the mother–father divorce. Nodal points in the family's history before and after that time should be assessed. In taking the family history, the therapist should observe the similarities and discrepancies voiced by the members of the family and the feelings associated with particular events, people, and times.

From this point on, a psychoanalytic therapist has several choices. First, the therapist can try to get family members to engage in **transference** and ventilate their feelings about their situation and themselves. Through such a collective process, catharsis could be promoted. Second, the therapist can look for and utilize opportunities to confront family members in regard to their present behaviors and the behaviors they claim they want. This type of confrontation may be especially helpful to Juan because of the nature of his aggressive actions. Such a confrontation starts with the therapist saying: "Juan, I hear you really want to be close to others, such as your mother and sister. Yet, I notice you are cursing at them and staying away from them. Help me understand how what you are doing is helping you."

A third option for the therapist is to examine cultural and unique family/individual patterns related to the current crisis. Psychoanalytic theory is not culturally specific, but a therapist should view a family in light of its cultural background regardless of the theory being utilized. The Casas are Hispanic/Latino, and as pointed out in a later chapter, there are general cultural influences that impact on family life from this tradition.

A fourth option that may come up immediately, later, or concurrently through treatment is exploring the unconscious. It is the task of a psychoanalytically oriented family therapist to help family members delve into themselves intrapersonally as well as interpersonally. Unconscious material may surface and can be handled through dream analysis or through dealing with memories. The idea is that through handling aspects of the unconscious, family members will get insight into themselves and others. They can then use this knowledge to change their behavior.

Overall, a psychoanalytic therapist's work with families, such as the Casas, is to identify and utilize individual and family unit strengths. It is hoped that through the therapeutic process, unconscious aspects of family life that keep members apart will surface and be resolved.

Bowen Family Therapy

Major Bowen Family Therapy Theorists

Murray Bowen and Michael Kerr have been the chief architects and advocates of Bowen family therapy. However, the major originator of this approach was Murray Bowen. Bowen formulated the ideas that resulted in a distinct theory of family therapy. The theory and its techniques were popularized by authors such as Monica McGoldrick and Randy Gerson (1985) (*Genograms in Family Assessment*) and Edwin Friedman (1985) (*Generation to Generation: Family Process in Church and Synagogue*).

Murray Bowen

The oldest of five children, Murray Bowen (1913–1990) grew up in a tightly knit family that for several generations resided in a small town in Pennsylvania. After growing up, Bowen moved away and kept a formal distance from his parents. He maintained family relations on a comfortable but superficial level. Bowen, like Nathan Ackerman, was a psychiatrist who became interested in working with families while employed at the Menninger Clinic. As early as 1951, he began to require that mothers of disturbed children live in the same hospital setting as their offspring (Guerin, 1976). From this experience, he became interested in studying "mother-patient symbiosis," that is, the intense bond that develops between a parent and child that does not allow for either to differentiate themselves from the other (Bowen, 1960, 1961).

In 1954, Bowen moved to join Lyman Wynne at the National Institute of Mental Health (NIMH), where he continued to be involved in studying the dynamics of families with schizophrenic children. As a part of the treatment, Bowen worked with the research team at NIMH on a pilot project to hospitalize and treat all members of such families. He recognized during this time "that the characteristics exhibited by a schizophrenic family were similar to symptoms in many dysfunctional families" (Fenell & Weinhold, 1989, p. 104). A few years later he moved to Georgetown University, where he researched family dynamics and developed his therapeutic approach until his death.

During his years at Georgetown, especially in the 1970s, Bowen completed his most productive personal and professional work. Personally, he detriangulated himself from his parents by returning home and reacting cognitively and neutrally to a number of emotional issues family members presented to him (Anonymous, 1972). Professionally, he clarified his theory (Bowen, 1978); began the Georgetown Family Center Symposium; expanded the Georgetown Family Center to new, off-campus quarters; and initiated the founding of the American Family Therapy Association (AFTA), "in order to restore a serious research effort in family therapy" (Wylie, 1991, p. 77).

Premises of Bowen Family Therapy

For Bowen, therapy and theory are part of the same fabric and cannot be separated without doing a disservice to each. Bowen preferred to think of himself as a theorist. He saw himself as one who stood alone in conceptualizing "the family as a natural system . . . which could only be fully understood in terms of the fluid but predictable processes between members" (Wylie, 1991, p. 26). Bowen was a scientist in search of universal truths. "Bowen theory constantly strives to make continuous what other theories dichotomize" (e.g., nature/nurture, male/female, and physical illness/emotional illness) (Friedman, 1991, p. 136).

Bowen's life, especially his difficulties with his own family of origin, had a major impact on what he proposed. He was influenced by events in his own life history (Anonymous, 1972; Papero, 1991). Basically, Bowen stated that unless individuals examine and rectify patterns passed down from previous generations, they are likely to repeat these behaviors in their own families (Kerr, 1988). The possibility of repeating certain behaviors in interpersonal relations is particularly likely if family members, especially between the generations, are characteristically either **emotionally overinvolved** (i.e., fused) with each other or **emotionally cutoff** (psychologically or physically) from each other. Bowen concerned himself with the family's emotional system.

A key element of Bowen family therapy is "that there is a *chronic anxiety* in all of life that comes with the territory of living" (Friedman, 1991, p. 139). This anxiety is both emotional and physical and is shared by all protoplasm. Some individuals are more affected than others by this anxiety "because of the way previous generations in their families have channeled the transmission" of it to them (Friedman, 1991, p. 140).

If anxiety remains low, few problems exist for people or families. In such cases, the *family emotional system* is undisturbed. However, in the midst of anxiety, some predictable patterns occur. According to Greene, Hamilton, and Rolling (1986, p. 189):

> Lower scale [undifferentiated] people are vulnerable to stress and are much more prone to illness, including physical and social illness, and their dysfunction is more likely to become chronic when it does occur. Higher scale people can recover emotional equilibrium quickly after the stress passes.

To address chronic anxiety and emotional processes in families and society, Bowen emphasized *eight basic concepts*. Through understanding these concepts, a therapist understands and successfully treats a family. These basic concepts are (Bowen, 1978; Kerr, 1981):

- Differentiation
- Emotional system
- Multigenerational transmission process

- Nuclear family emotional system
- Family projection process
- Triangles
- Sibling position
- Societal regression

Differentiation refers to the ability of persons to distinguish themselves from their family of origin on an emotional and intellectual level. There are two counterbalancing life forces: togetherness and individuality. People vary as to the level of self-differentiation that they achieve at any one time, and the concept itself denotes a process (Bowen, 1965). The level of differentiation is on a continuum, from autonomy at one end (which signals an ability to think through a situation clearly) to *undifferentiated* on the other end (which implies an emotional dependency on one's family members, even if living away from them). In such cases, the relationship is described as being *fused* or as an **undifferentiated family ego mass** (Bowen, 1965). It is through the process of differentiation that families and the individuals in them change (see Figure 5.1).

Coping strategies and patterns of coping with stress tend to be passed on from generation to generation, a phenomenon known as the **multigenerational transmission process.** Families who present a problem have had the forces of several generations shaping and carrying the symptom. In marriage, people tend to select partners at their own level of differentiation (Bowen, 1976). In these unions, a *nuclear family emotional system evolves.* Spouses with equally high levels of identity are able to establish and maintain clear individuality "and at the same time to have an intense, mature, nonthreatening, emotional closeness" (Bowen, 1965, p. 220). On the other hand, spouses with

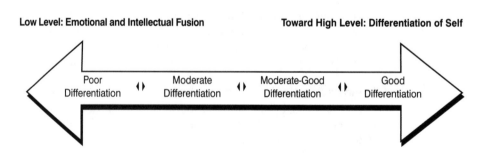

Figure 5.1

Bowen's Continuum of Self-Differentiation

From *Working With Families* (p. 116) by B. F. Okun and L. J. Rappaport, 1980, Pacific Grove, CA: Brooks/Cole. Reprinted by permission.

equally low levels of differentiation have difficulty establishing intimacy because they have developed only **pseudo selves,** that is, "pretend" selves (Kerr, 1988, p. 43). The pseudo selves fluctuate according to situations and usually result in the fusion of these selves into a *"common self* with obliteration of ego boundaries between them and loss of individuality to the common self" (Bowen, 1965, p. 221). Couples tend to produce offspring at the same level of differentiation as themselves, a process Bowen describes as "family projection" (Kilpatrick, 1980).

To rid themselves of anxiety, spouses who are low on differentiation of self keep an emotional distance from each other. When anxiety becomes too great, it is frequently manifested in one of four ways: (1) marital conflict, (2) physical or emotional illness in one spouse, (3) projection of the problem to the children, or (4) a combination of these (David, 1979).

Bowen family therapists look for **triangles** when working with couples. Triangles can occur between people or between people and things. They consist of a state of calm between a comfortable twosome and an outsider (Anonymous, 1972). A triangle is "the basic building block of any emotional system and the smallest stable relationship system" (Kilpatrick, 1980, p. 168). Some triangles are healthy, others are not. In the latter case, triangles are a frequent way of dealing with anxiety in which tension between two persons is projected onto another object. The original triangle is between a child and parents. In stressful situations, anxiety spreads from one central triangle within the family to *interlocking triangles* outside the family, especially in work and social systems (Kerr, 1988).

Given this background, it is understandable why Bowen family therapists work to help people, especially couples, separate their feelings from their intellect and in the process **detriangulate**. They do this through asking questions about thoughts and constructing a type of family tree (which is explained later) called a *multigenerational genogram* (McGoldrick & Gerson, 1985). They also give homework assignments that require individuals to visit their families in order to learn through questioning (Bowen, 1976). Furthermore, Bowen therapists examine sibling positions; people can develop fixed personality characteristics based on their functional birth order in the family (Toman, 1961). The more closely a marriage replicates a couples' *sibling positions* in the family of origin, the better the chance for success. For example, if a youngest son marries an oldest daughter, both have much to gain from the arrangement because the youngest son will most likely enjoy "being taken care of," and the oldest daughter will probably enjoy "taking care of" someone.

By examining the processes just mentioned, family members gain insight and understanding into the past and are freed to choose how they will behave in the present. Similarly, they gain a perspective on how well society as a whole is doing. If a society is under too much stress (e.g., population growth, economic decline), **societal regression** will occur, because of too many toxic forces countering the tendency to achieve differentiation.

Bowen Treatment Techniques

Bowen family therapy focuses on the promotion of differentiation (in regard to self/family and intellect/emotion). This approach is not technique oriented, because of the tendency to get caught up and overpowered by particular techniques at particular times. However, among those techniques most often employed are genograms, going home again, detriangulation, person-to-person relationships, differentiation of self, and asking questions.

Genograms

A **genogram** is a visual representation of a person's family tree depicted in geometric figures, lines, and words (Sherman, 1993) (see Figure 5.2). Genograms include information related to a family's employment, health, marriage, and so forth, and members' relationships with each other over at least three generations. A genogram helps people within the family see and understand patterns in the context of historic and contemporary events (McGoldrick & Gerson, 1985). The tangibility and nonthreatening nature of this process helps family clinicians gather a large amount of information in a relatively short period of time. Furthermore, genograms can increase "mutual trust and tolerance" among all involved in their construction (Sherman, 1993, p. 91).

Bowen family therapy "advises people to go 'back, back, back; and up, up, up' their family tree to look for patterns, 'recycling,' getting not just information but a feel for the context and milieu that existed during each person's formative years" (White, 1978, p. 25-26). This process promotes the shift from emotional reactivity to clear cognitions. Data in a genogram is scanned for (1) "repetitive patterns," such as triangles, cutoffs, and coalitions; (2) "coincidences of dates," such as the death of members or the age of symptom onset; and (3) "the impact of change and untimely life cycle transitions," such as "off-schedule" events (e.g., marriage, death, and the birth of children) (McGoldrick & Gerson, 1985, p. 38).

Going Home Again

In **Going Home Again,** the family therapist instructs the individual client or family members to return home in order to better get to know their family of origin (Bowen, 1976). The idea behind this technique is that with this type of information, individuals can differentiate themselves more clearly. Such a process allows persons to operate more fully within all family contexts of which they are a part. Before returning home, clients may need to practice learning how to remain calm (Bowen, 1976).

Detriangulation

The concept of **detriangulation** involves "the process of being in contact and emotionally separate" (Kerr, 1988, p. 55). It operates on at least two levels. On one level, a person resolves his or her anxiety over family situations and does not project feelings on to another. At a second level, Bowen therapists help individuals separate themselves from becoming a focus when tension or anxiety

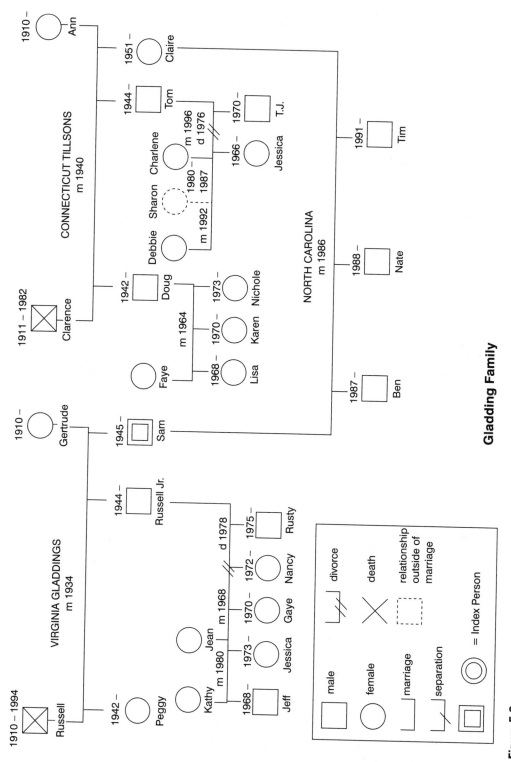

Figure 5.2
A family genogram.

arises in the family. In this procedure, persons do not become targets or scapegoats for others who may be overcome with anxiety. For example, if a usually triaded person stays rational during times of emotional stress, he/she will seldom become the attention of two other people (Bowen, 1972). On both levels, families and their individuals are free to voice their concerns and try out new ways of acting (Piercy & Sprenkle, 1986; Thomas, 1992).

Person-to-Person Relationships

In the person-to-person relationships, two family members "relate personally to each other about each other; that is, they do not talk about others (**triangling**) and do not talk about impersonal issues" (Piercy & Sprenkle, 1986, p. 11). For instance, a father may say to his son: "Your actions remind me of myself when I was your age." In return the son may say: "I really don't know much about you when you were a boy. Please tell me about what you did and how you felt when you were my age." Such a process helps promote individuation (autonomy) and intimacy.

Differentiation of Self

"**Differentiation of self** has to do with the degree to which a person is able to distinguish between the subjective feeling process and the more objective intellectual (thinking) process" (Gibson & Donigian, 1993, p. 28). This procedure may involve all of the preceding techniques plus some confrontation between family members and the therapist. A failure to differentiate results in fusion in which "people are dominated by their automatic emotional system." In such circumstances, they have "less flexibility, less adaptability, and are more emotionally dependent on those around them" (Sauber, L'Abate, & Weeks, 1985, p. 43). Over generations, children most involved in family fusion move toward a lower level of differentiation of self (Bowen, 1972).

Asking Questions

In each of the techniques in Bowen family theory, an underlying aspect is to ask questions. In fact, from this perspective, asking questions is deemed the "magic bullet" and is a main tool of Bowen therapists. Nodal events such as deaths, births, and marriages have an impact on families. For instance, death of family members disturbs the equilibrium of a family, and "emotional shock waves" can be expected as a result (Bowen, 1976). By asking questions, people involved in Bowen family therapy learn to understand the reactions of those in their families better.

Role of the Bowen Family Therapist

In the Bowen model, the *differentiation of the therapist* is crucial. The Bowen family therapist must maintain a calm presence and be differentiated from his/her family of origin (Friedman, 1991). Objectivity and neutrality are important behavioral characteristics for therapists to display. To be able to work with families, the therapist must first undergo an emotional change (Kerr, 1981). The idea is that if those who do treatment do not first undergo changes important in family therapy, those they work with will not experience healthy shifts either.

As someone who has personally resolved family of origin concerns, the Bowen therapist is usually involved in coaching and teaching. These activities occur on more cognitive levels, initially with family members, primarily individuals or couples, talking to the therapist or to one another through the therapist so that emotional issues do not cloud communication messages. "According to Bowen, therapists should not encourage people to wallow in emotionalism and confusion, but teach them to transcend it by setting examples as reasonable, neutral, self-controlled adults. Therapy should be, in fact, just like a Socratic dialogue, with the teacher or 'coach' calmly asking questions, until the student learns to think for him- or herself" (Wylie, 1991, p. 27).

In the process of therapy, there is concern with boundary and differentiation issues from an historical perspective. The therapist instructs individuals to search for "clues" as to where the various pressures on the family have been expressed and how effectively the family has adapted to stress since its inception. One way of obtaining this information is for individuals to draw a genogram or to visit their family of origin. Through examining the dynamics in these experiences, therapists become interpreters with their clients in assessing and working through multigenerational patterns of fusion and cutoffs. Unresolved areas of difficulty become resolved.

Process and Outcome of Bowen Family Therapy

One of the primary outcomes of successful treatment with families from a Bowen standpoint is that family members will understand intergenerational patterns and gain insight into historical circumstances that have influenced the ways they currently interact (Learner, 1983). Furthermore, it is expected that accompanying this knowledge is a focus on changing "intergenerational inferences operating with the current family" (Smith, 1991, p. 25). Changes such as these occur when therapists help family members differentiate from each other and become more diverse and fluid in their interactions (Bowen, 1978). At the end of treatment, issues related to fusion and unconscious relationship patterns should be cleared up. Individuals should be able to relate on an autonomous, cognitive level, and projective patterns of blame should be changed (Kerr & Bowen, 1988). There should be a greater self-differentiation among nuclear family members.

In Bowen family therapy, the chief focus and place where change is emphasized is the individual or couple. The whole family is usually not seen. Instead, individuals are often targeted for treatment even though the emphasis in this approach is systemic. "A theoretical system that thinks in terms of family, with a therapeutic method that works toward improvement of the family system, is 'family' regardless of the number of people in the sessions" (Kerr, 1981, p. 232). There-fore, by changing one person, a family may be directly influenced for the better.

"Since the two spouses are the two family members most involved in the family ego mass, the most rapid family change occurs when the spouses are able to work as a team in family psychotherapy" (Bowen, 1965, p. 220). The family can improve its functioning when spouses become more cognitively based, although in this process, the therapist may work "with all involved family mem-bers present, with any combination of family members present, or with only one family member present" (Bowen, 1965, p. 220).

Unique Aspects of Bowen Family Therapy Approach

Emphases of Bowen Family Therapy

Bowen theory calls attention to family history and the importance of noticing and dealing with past patterns in order to avoid repeating these behaviors in interpersonal relationships. The use of the genogram in plotting historical link-ages is a specific tool developed for this purpose. The genogram is increasingly being used by theorists of all persuasions in assessing their client families.

The theory and the therapy of Murray Bowen are extensive, complex, and intertwined. The theory is a blueprint for therapy. Therefore, therapy is consis-tent with and inseparable from theory. Family therapists are indebted to Bowen for intertwining these two aspects of his approach. He was also insightful and detailed in suggesting the course of working with families. The Georgetown Family Center, which he established for educating practitioners in his method, ensures the Bowen approach will continue to be learned and used.

Bowen family therapy is systemic in nature, controlled in focus, and cognitive in practice, thereby giving clinicians and their clients a way of concretely evalu-ating progress (Bowen, 1975). Unlike many other systemic family approaches, Bowen family therapy can be used extensively with individuals or couples.

Comparison of Bowen Family Therapy with Other Theories

Bowen's stress on the importance of the past encourages some families or fam-ily members to examine their history rather than deal immediately with pre-sent circumstances. Such a process promotes insight before action. Client fami-lies in which there is severe dysfunctioning or low differentiation of self benefit most from this emphasis.

Another aspect of Bowen family therapy that makes it unique compared with other approaches is that the theory underlying the approach is its own paradigm (Friedman, 1991). Thus, setting up research questions to refute or verify this way of working with families is a challenging task of the highest order. One way theoretical research is being conducted is by exploring the significance of family of origin experiences (Hovestadt, Anderson, Piercy, Cochran, & Fine, 1985).

A final unique angle in regard to Bowen family therapy is the time and, conse-quently, the money it requires of its clients. Most people cannot afford to invest as heavily in this process as is necessary. As with psychoanalytically oriented therapy, the number of people who can benefit from this approach is limited.

CASE ILLUSTRATION

THE COBB FAMILY

The Cobb family is a three-generational family composed of the father, David, age 45; mother, Juanita, age 42; son, James, age 16; daughter, Anita, age 12; and maternal grandmother, Lilly, age 65. The maternal grandfather, John, a farmer, died 3 years ago of a heart attack. The paternal grandparents, Dan, a retired banker, age 70, and Ruth, a homemaker, age 68, live in a nearby city. The couple, David and Juanita, have been married for 20 years. Like his father, David, is emotionally withdrawn from his family and overinvolved with his job.

In terms of family background, David comes from a middle-class background. He had an older sister, Daisy, who was 3 years his senior. His father has a history of high blood pressure, but his mother is in good health. Juanita was an only child. After 20 years of marriage, her mother, Lilly, almost divorced her father, when Juanita was 13-years-old. Juanita and her mother have had a close but conflictual relationship since that time, with Lilly coming to live with her daughter after the death of John. At present, Juanita and Lilly take care of the house and children, and David works as a salesperson for a cleaning supply company.

The problem that the Cobb family has requested help for centers around James. Instead of doing well academically and socially, James is failing all his subjects and staying out late at night. He has been arrested once for vagrancy, and David and Juanita suspect he is drinking alcohol and doing drugs. Money from Juanita's purse has been stolen twice in recent weeks. Lilly has written James off as a delinquent. Interestingly enough, he has the same first name as her former lover who almost ended her marriage. Anita simply ignores James whenever possible. Although she is a good student, her relationship with her mother is conflictual.

Conceptualization of Family: Bowen Perspective

The Cobb family is notable from a Bowen family perspective for several reasons. For one, there is a repeated pattern of mother/daughter conflict over the generations. For another, there is a tendency for men in the family to be emotionally cutoff from other family members through withdrawing or rebelling. It is also striking that James has the same name as his maternal grandmother's lover, who almost broke up her marriage of 20 years when Juanita was 13-years-old. It appears to be more than coincidental that during the 20th year of Juanita's marriage, another James has created turmoil in the family's life.

Process of Treatment: Bowen Family Therapy

Treatment of any family from a Bowen Family Therapy perspective usually involves either an individual or a couple. In the case of the Cobbs, initially, the therapist might help the marital unit make a genogram (see Figure 5.3). The genogram would then be examined by the therapist and the family to denote patterns such as those mentioned previously.

After analysis of family life patterns, the therapist might concentrate with the couple on issues involving detriangulation. For instance, there is a triangle between Lilly, Juanita, and James that works in a dysfunctional way. Likewise, the issue of emotional disengagement would be addressed, such as the ones Dan and David have exemplified. Their lack of involvement in the family has created a parenting void. It is most likely associated with James' present rebellious behavior. Therefore, parenting skills and ways of interacting in parent/child relationships might be stressed, especially as they relate to previous family-of-origin patterns.

To help the Cobb family break out of its present condition, the therapist could have the couple engage in person-to-person conversations on a dyadic basis. This might begin with David and Juanita talking to each

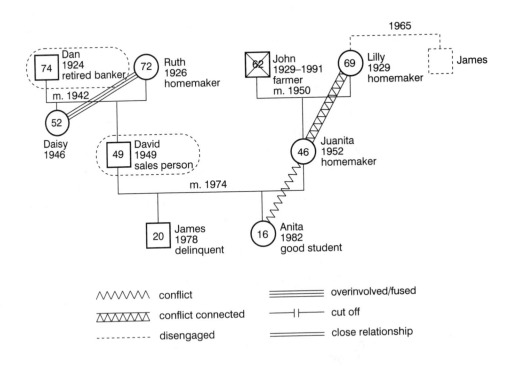

Figure 5.3
Cobb family genogram.

other about their marriage. Other person-to-person relationships might be conducted outside of the treatment sessions, with James and Juanita, or Lilly and Juanita, talking with each other. In these exchanges, the asking of cognitively-based questions would be encouraged, especially about topics not discussed previously, such as Lilly's affair.

Overall, through these procedures, the family would begin to engage in new behaviors that were less blaming, conflictual, or withdrawn. Appropriate ways of interrelating could then be set in motion, with family members interacting from a position of differentiation.

Summary and Conclusion

Psychoanalytic and Bowen family therapies are two of the most established approaches to working with families. Psychoanalytic family therapy was first developed by Nathan Ackerman, who applied the principles of individual psychoanalysis to families. In doing so, he made the treatment of families more respectable and prevalent among psychiatrists. Murray Bowen, a psychoanalytically trained psychiatrist, devised his own approach to working with families, especially couples, based in part on his life experiences and in part on psychoanalytic theory.

Both psychoanalytic theory and Bowen theory emphasize the importance of unconscious forces in family life. Psychoanalytically oriented family therapy, however, is an eclectic mix of psychoanalysis and systems concepts that sometimes make it more linear in its stress on working with individuals in families. Bowen theory is systemic, although its primary clients are individuals and couples. It emphasizes the importance of looking at historical intergenerational patterns. The Bowen approach uses a cognitive strategy to help couples and family members differentiate; psychoanalytic family therapy is insight oriented. In both approaches, the therapist acts as a coach, a teacher, and a catalyst, although the content and unit of treatment, as well as final end results, differ.

Overall, both approaches are in-depth and concentrate on long-term results. They emphasize the unconscious and require a considerable investment of time and resources. Bowen theory is concrete in outcome and gives its clients a way to recognize dysfunctional patterns transmitted across generations (i.e., a genogram). On the other hand, psychoanalytic theory provides its recipients a way of working through issues that frees them from relying on defense mechanisms. Each theory can be beneficially utilized by some client families/individuals.

SUMMARY TABLE

Psychoanalytic Family Therapy

Major Theorists
Sigmund Freud
Nathan Ackerman
Ivan Boszormenyi-Nagy
James Framo
Theodore Lidz
Norman Paul
A. C. Robin Skynner
Donald Williamson
Lyman Wynne

Underlying Premises
Unconscious processes link family members together and influence individuals in the decisions about who they marry. Objects—significant others in one's life—are identified with or rejected.

Unconscious forces must be worked through and "interlocking pathologies" must be broken up.

Role of the Therapist
The therapist is the teacher (especially of terms), "good enough mother" [or "parent"], and interpreter of experience.

Unit of Treatment
The individual or the individuals within a family are the units of treatment.

Goals of Treatment
The goals of treatment are:
- to break dysfunctional interactions within the family based on unconscious processes
- to resolve individual dysfunctionality

Therapeutic Techniques
The therapeutic techniques include:
- Transference
- Dream analysis
- Confrontation
- Focusing on strengths
- Life history

Unique Aspects of the Approach
The psychoanalytic approach emphasizes:

- the potency of the unconscious in influencing human behavior
- defense mechanisms and the part they play in family relations
- an in-depth historical perspective on the development of problems and a treatment of dysfunctionality that is thorough
- an attachment of people to objects (i.e., other people)

Comparisons with Other Approaches
Compared with other approaches, psychoanalytic therapy:

- offers a treatment that is primarily linear and limited more to individuals than families
- offers a treatment that is expensive in regard to both time and money
- is not appropriate for concrete-thinkers or those who want immediate results
- lacks traditional empirical research and is reliant on case history reports

Bowen Family Therapy

Major Theorists
Murray Bowen
Michael Kerr

Underlying Premises
Theory and therapy are the same.
Family patterns are likely to repeat.
It is important to differentiate oneself from one's family-of-origin.
Uncontrolled anxiety results in family dysfunctionality.
The formation of triangles are a key manifestation of uncontrolled anxiety.

Role of the Therapist
The therapist is a differentiated person who acts as a coach and teacher and concentrates on boundary and differentiation issues.

Unit of Treatment
The individual or the couple are the units of treatment.

Goals of Treatment
The goals of treatment are:

- to prevent triangulation and help couples and individuals relate more on a cognitive, as opposed to an emotional level
- to stop dysfunctional, repetitive, intergenerational patterns of family relations

Therapeutic Techniques
The therapeutic techniques include:
- Genograms
- Going home again
- Detriangulation
- Person-to-person relationships
- Differentiation of self

Unique Aspects of the Approach
The Bowen approach emphasizes:
- intergenerational relationships and the nature of repeating patterns
- an in-depth theory of family relationships
- a systemic and cognitive theory that provides a concrete evaluation of progress

Comparison with Other Approaches
Compared with other approaches, Bowen therapy:
- stresses the importance of the past, thereby encouraging some families or family members to examine history and not deal with present circumstances
- is difficult to research
- requires a high degree of investment in time and money

Similarities Between Psychoanalytic and Bowen Family Therapies
Both theories are conceptual and comprehensive. They emphasize the importance of historical, social, and childhood experiences and stress the significance of unconscious forces in the lives of families.

The founders of the two approaches were trained as psychoanalytical therapists.

Each theory has developed its own terminology.

Both treatments may be long term (over 20 sessions).

References

Ackerman, N. (1937). The family as a social and emotional unit. *Bulletin of the Kansas Mental Hygiene Society*, 12.

Ackerman, N. (1956). Interlocking pathology in family relations. In S. Rado & G. Daniels (Eds.), *Changing concepts of psychoanalytic medicine* (pp. 135–150). New York: Grune & Stratton.

Ackerman, N. (1958). *The psychodynamics of family life*. New York: Basic Books.

Ackerman, N. (1962). Family psychotherapy and psychoanalysis: The implications of difference. *Family Process, 1,* 30–43.

Ackerman, N. (1966). *Treating the troubled family*. New York: Basic Books.

Ackerman, N. W., Beatman, F. L., & Sherman, S. N. (1961). *Exploring the base of family therapy*. New York: Family Service Association of America.

Anonymous. (1972). Differentiation of self in one's family. In J. L. Framo (Ed.), *Family interaction*. New York: Springer.

Bloch, D. A., & Simon, R. (Eds.). (1982). *The strength of family therapy: Selected papers of Nathan W. Ackerman*. New York: Brunner/Mazel.

Boszormenyi-Nagy, I. (1987). *Foundations of contextual therapy: Collected papers of Ivan Boszormenyi-Nagy*. New York: Brunner/Mazel.

Boszormenyi-Nagy, I., & Spark, G. M. (1973). *Invisible loyalties: Reciprocity in intergenerational family therapy*. New York: Brunner/Mazel.

Bowen, M. (1960). A family concept of schizophrenia. In D. Jackson (Ed.), *The etiology of schizophrenia*. New York: Basic Books.

Bowen, M. (1961). Family psychotherapy. *American Journal of Orthopsychiatry, 31*, 40–60.

Bowen, M. (1965). Family psychotherapy with schizophrenia in the hospital and in private practice. In I. Boszormenyi-Nagy & J. T. Framo (Eds.), *Intensive family therapy* (pp. 213–243). Hagerstown, MD: Harper & Row.

Bowen, M. (1965). Family psychotherapy with schizophrenia in the hospital and in private practice. In I. Boszormenyi-Nagy & J. T. Framo (Eds.), *Intensive family therapy* (pp. 213–243). Hagerstown, MD: Harper & Row.

Bowen, M. (1972). Toward the differentiation of self in one's family of origin. In F. D. Andres & J. P. Lorio (Eds.), *Georgetown Family Symposia* (pp. 70–86). Washington, DC: Georgetown University.

Bowen, M. (1975). Family therapy after twenty years. In S. Arieti, D. X. Freedman, & J. E. Dyrud (Eds.), *American handbook of psychiatry V: Treatment* (2nd ed.). New York: Basic Books.

Bowen, M. (1976). Theory in the practice of psychotherapy. In P. J. Guerin (Ed.), *Family therapy: Theory and practice* (pp. 42–90). New York: Gardner Press.

Bowen, M. (1978). *Family therapy in clinical practice*. New York: Jason Aronson.

Broderick, C. B., & Schrader, S. S. (1991). The history of professional marriage and family therapy. In A. S. Gurman & D. P. Kniskern (Eds.), *Handbook of family therapy* (Vol. II, pp. 3–40). New York: Brunner/Mazel.

David, J. R. (1979). The theology of Murray Bowen or the marital triangle. *Journal of Psychology and Theology, 7*, 259–262.

Dicks, H. V. (1963). Object relations theory and marital studies. *British Journal of Medical Psychology, 36*, 125–129.

Ellis, A. (1991). Rational-emotive family therapy. In A. M. Horne & J. L. Passmore (Eds.), *Family counseling and therapy* (2nd ed.) (pp. 403–434). Itasca, IL: F. E. Peacock.

Fairbairn, W. R. (1954). *An object-relations theory of personality*. New York: Basic Books.

Fenell, D. L., & Weinhold, B. K. (1989). *Counseling families*. Denver, CO: Love.

Framo, J. L. (1981). The integration of marital therapy with sessions with family of origin. In A. S. Gurman & D. P. Kniskern (Eds.), *Handbook of family therapy*. New York: Brunner/Mazel.

Freud, S. (1940). An outline of psychoanalysis. In *The standard edition of the complete psychological works of Sigmund Freud* (Vol. 23, pp. 139–171). London: Hogarth Press.

Friedman, E. H. (1985). *Generation to generation: Family process in church and synagogue*. New York: Guilford.

Friedman, E. H. (1991). Bowen theory and therapy. In A. S. Gurman & D. P. Kniskern (Eds.), *Handbook of family therapy* (Vol. II, pp. 134–170). New York: Brunner/Mazel.

Gibson, J. M., & Donigian, J. (1993). Use of Bowen theory. *Journal of Addictions and Offender Counseling, 14*, 25–35.

Gladding, S. T. (1993). *Beecher Road*. Unpublished manuscript.

Greene, G. J., Hamilton, N., & Rolling, M. (1986). Differentiation of self and psychiatric diagnosis: An empirical study. *Family Therapy, 8*, 187–194.

Guerin, P. J. (1976). Family therapy: The first twenty-five years. In P. J. Guerin (Ed.), *Family therapy: Theory and practice* (pp. 2–22). New York: Gardner.

Hafner, R. J. (1986). *Marriage & mental illness*. New York: Guilford.

Hovestadt, A. J., Anderson, W. T., Piercy, F. P., Cochran, S. W., & Fine, M. (1985). A family of origin scale. *Journal of Marital and Family Therapy, 11*, 287–297.

Kernberg, O. F. (1976). *Object-relations theory and clinical psychoanalysis*. New York: Jason Aronson.

Kerr, M. (1981). Family systems theory and therapy. In A. S. Gurman & D. P. Kniskern (Eds.), *Handbook of family therapy*. New York: Brunner/Mazel.

Kerr, M. E. (1988). Chronic anxiety and defining a self. *The Atlantic Monthly, 262,* 35–37, 40–44, 46–58.

Kerr, M. E., & Bowen, M. (1988). *Family evaluation: An approach based on Bowen theory.* New York: W. W. Norton.

Kilpatrick, A. C. (1980). The Bowen family intervention theory: An analysis for social workers. *Family Therapy, 7,* 167–178.

Klein, M. (1948). *Contributions to psychoanalysis, 1921–1945.* London: Hogarth Press.

Kohut, H. (1971). *The analysis of self.* New York: International Universities Press.

Kohut, H. (1977). *The restoration of the self.* New York: International Universities Press.

Learner, S. (1983). *Constructing the multigenerational family genogram: Exploring a problem in context* (videotape). Topeka, KS: Menninger Video Productions.

Lidz, T., Cornelison, A., Fleck, S., & Terry, D. (1957). The intrafamilial environment of schizophrenic patients. II: Marital schism and martial skew. *American Journal of Psychiatry, 114,* 241–248.

McGoldrick, M., & Gerson, R. (1985). *Genograms in family assessment.* New York: W. W. Norton.

Napier, A., & Whitaker, C. A. (1978). *The family crucible.* New York: Bantam.

Nichols, M. P., & Schwartz, R. C. (1995). *Family therapy* (3rd ed.). Boston: Allyn & Bacon.

Papero, D. V. (1990). *Bowen family systems theory.* Boston: Allyn & Bacon.

Papero, D. V. (1991). The Bowen theory. In A. M. Horne & J. L. Passmore (Eds.), *Family counseling and theory* (2nd ed., pp. 47–76). Itasca, IL: F. E. Peacock.

Perosa, L. (1996). Relations between Minuchin's structural family model and Kohut's self-psychology constructs. *Journal of Counseling & Development, 74,* 385–392.

Piercy, F. P., & Sprenkle, D. H. (1986). *Family therapy sourcebook.* New York: Guilford.

Sauber, S. R., L'Abate, L., & Weeks, G. R. (1985). *Family therapy: Basic concepts and terms.* Rockville, MD: Aspen.

Scarf, M. (1995). *Intimate worlds: Life inside the family.* New York: Random House.

Scharff, J. (Ed.). (1989). *The foundations of object relations family therapy.* New York: Jason Aronson.

Sherman, R. (1993). The intimacy genogram. *The Family Journal, 1,* 91–93.

Shields, C. G., Wynne, L. C., McDaniel, S. H., & Gawinski, B. A. (1994). The marginalization of family therapy: A historical and continuing problem. *Journal of Marital and Family Therapy, 20,* 117–138.

Skynner, A. C. R. (1981). An open-systems, group analytic approach to family therapy. In A. S. Gurman & D. P. Kniskern (Eds.), *Handbook of family therapy.* New York: Brunner/Mazel.

Slipp, S. (1988). *The technique and practice of object relations family therapy.* New York: Aronson.

Smith, R. L. (1991). Marriage and family therapy: Direction, theory, and practice. In J. Carlson & J. Lewis (Eds.), *Family counseling* (pp. 13–34). Denver, CO: Love Publishing.

Thomas, M. B. (1992). *An introduction to marital and family therapy.* New York: Macmillan.

Titelman, P. (1987). *The therapist's own family: Toward the differentiation of self.* Northvale, NJ: Jason Aronson.

Toman, W. (1961). *Family constellation: Its effects on personality and social behavior.* New York: Springer.

White, H. (1978). Exercises in understanding your family. In *Your family is good for you.* New York: Random House.

Winnicott, D. W. (1965). *The maturational processes and the facilitation of environment.* London: Hogarth Press.

Wylie, M. S. (1991, March/April). Family therapy's neglected prophet. *Family Therapy Networker, 15,* 24–37, 77.

Wynne, L., Ryckoff, I., Day, J., & Hirsh, S. (1958). Pseudomutuality in the family relations of schizophrenics. *Psychiatry, 21,* 205–220.

Experiential Family Therapy

My father tells me
my mother is slowing down.

He talks deliberately and with deep feelings
as stoop-shouldered he walks to his garden
behind the garage.

My mother informs me
about my father's failing health.

"Not as robust as before," she explains,
"Lower energy than in his 50s."

Her concerns arise as she kneads dough for biscuits.

Both express their fears to me
as we view the present from the past.

In love, and with measured anxiety,
I move with them into new patterns.

Gladding, 1992

T he experiential branch of family therapy emerged out of the humanistic-existential psychology movement of the 1960s. It was most popular when the field of family therapy was new. Some of its proponents and creators drew heavily from Gestalt therapy, psychodrama, client-centered therapy, and the encounter group movement of the time. The emphasis has been on immediate, here-and-now experience as opposed to historical information. Therefore, concepts such as encounter, process, growth, spontaneity, and action are emphasized. Theory and abstract factors are avoided. The quality of ongoing experiences in the family is the criterion for measuring psychological health and for deciding whether to make therapeutic interventions.

Experiential family therapy emphasizes *affect,* that is, emotions. Awareness and expression of feelings are considered the means to both personal and family fulfillment. Professionals who operate from this perspective consider the expression of affect to be a universal medium in which all can share. Therefore, the expression of feelings in a clear and effective way is encouraged (Kane, 1994). A healthy family is a family that openly experiences life with each other in a lively manner. Such a family supports and encourages a wide range of emotions and personal encounters. In contrast, dysfunctional families resist taking affective risks and are rigid in their interactions.

Major Theorists

A number of professionals have contributed significantly to the development of experiential family therapy. Among the most notable are David Kantor, Fred Duhl, Bunny Duhl, Virginia Satir, Carl Whitaker, Walter Kempler, August Napier, David Keith, Leslie Greenberg, and Susan Johnson. Virginia Satir and Carl Whitaker are examined here as representatives of this approach.

Satir conducted much of her work using structured experiential exercises (Woods & Martin, 1984). Whitaker is the embodiment of an unstructured and a theoretical clinician (Whitaker, 1976). Since 1988 his approach has been called "symbolic-experiential family therapy."

Virginia Satir

Virginia Satir (1916–1988) was born and raised on a farm in Wisconsin. She was extraordinarily different from others even at an early age. At three, she had learned to read, and "by the time she was 11, she had reached her adult height of nearly six feet" (Simon, 1989, p. 37). Although she was sickly and missed a lot of school, she was a good student and began her college experience after only 7½ years of formal education. Her initial goal, which she achieved, was to become a school teacher. "Growing up a big, awkward, sickly child, Satir drew from her experience of being an outsider" an acute sensitivity for others (Simon, 1989, p. 37). This quality eventually led her from the classroom to social work with families.

Satir entered private practice as a social worker in 1951 in Chicago. This venture came after 6 years of teaching school and 9 years of clinical work in an agency. Her unique approach to working with families evolved from her treatment of a schizophrenic young woman whose mother threatened to sue her when the young woman improved. Instead of becoming defensive, Satir invited the mother to join the therapy and worked with them until they reached communication congruence (Satir, 1986). She then invited the father and oldest son into treatment until the family had achieved a balance.

Satir was influenced by Murray Bowen's and Don Jackson's work with schizophrenic families, and in 1959 she was invited by Jackson and his colleagues to help set up the Mental Research Institute (MRI) in Palo Alto, California. From her clinical work and interaction with other professionals there, she refined her approach to working with families, which was simultaneously folksy and complex. "Satir was the prototypical nurturing therapist in a field enamored with experience-distant concepts and tricky strategic maneuvers. Her warmth and genuineness gave her a tremendous appeal and impact . . . " (Nichols & Schwartz, 1995, pp. 289–290). At the core of Satir's approach was "her unshakable conviction about people's potential for growth and the respectful role helpers need to assume in the process of change" (Simon, 1989, p. 38).

Satir gained international attention in 1964 with the publication of her first book, *Conjoint Family Therapy*. The clarity of her writing made the text a classic and put Satir in demand as a workshop presenter. She continued to write and demonstrate her "process model of therapy" (Satir, 1982) until her death. Among her many contributions were a strong, charismatic leadership (Beels & Ferber, 1969); a simple but eloquent view of effective and ineffective communication patterns (Satir, 1972; Satir & Baldwin, 1983); and a humanistic concern about building self-worth and self-esteem in all people. Satir is often described as a master of communication and even as an originator of family **communications theory** (an approach that focuses on clarifying transactions among family members).

Carl Whitaker

Carl Whitaker (1912–1995) grew up on a dairy farm in upstate New York. With few exceptions, his nuclear family was his "entire social existence" (Simon, 1985, p. 32). He was shy, and when his family moved to Syracuse in 1925, he felt awkward and out of place. He attributed his ability to stay sane and adjust to two "cotherapists"—two fellow students with whom he made friends, one the smartest and the other the most popular in the school (Whitaker, 1989).

Whitaker entered medical school in 1932, penniless but with a sound work ethic and a bent toward public service. He had originally planned to specialize in obstetrics and gynecology, but a tragic operation on a patient who died even though his surgery was perfect proved to be a turning point in Whitaker's life. It influenced him to switch to psychiatry during the last year of his residency and to concentrate his attention on working with schizophrenics. Toward the end of his medical training in 1937, Whitaker married and later fathered six children.

Whitaker developed the essence of his approach to therapy while assigned to Oak Ridge, Tennessee, during World War II (Whitaker, 1990). There he saw as many as 12 patients a day in half-hour sessions. He did not have any mentors and basically taught himself psychiatric procedures. From his experience, he realized he needed a cotherapist in order to be effective. He also experimented during this time with the technique of using the spontaneous unconscious in therapy (Whitaker & Keith, 1981).

"The turning point in Whitaker's career came in 1946 when he was named chairman of the Department of Psychiatry at Emory University" at age 34 (Simon, 1985, p. 33). It was at Emory that Whitaker hired supportive colleagues, increased his work with schizophrenic patients, and began developing his own free-wheeling style. He was dismissed from Emory in 1956 and went into private practice with his colleagues in Atlanta. In 1965, he accepted a faculty position at the University of Wisconsin's Department of Psychiatry, where he stayed until his retirement in 1982. During the Wisconsin years, Whitaker devoted his efforts almost entirely to families and served as a mentor to young practitioners, such as Augustus Napier, who coauthored with him one of the best selling books in the field of family therapy, *The Family Crucible* (1978). Also during this time, Whitaker traveled extensively, giving workshops on family therapy.

"More than with most well-known therapists, it is difficult to separate Whitaker's therapeutic approach from his personality" (Simon, 1985, p. 34). As a family therapist, Whitaker was quite intuitive. His surname, derived from *Witakarlege* (meaning a wizard or witch) has prompted at least one writer (Keith, 1987) to put Whitaker in a class of his own. Yet, Whitaker focused on some therapeutic elements that are universal. His main contribution to family therapy was in the uninhibited and emotional way he worked with families by teasing them "to be in contact with their absurdity" (Simon, 1984, p. 28). He used the term ***absurdity*** to refer to half-truthful statements that are silly if followed out to their natural conclusion (Whitaker, 1975). He likened the use of *absurdity* to the Leaning Tower of Pisa, which if built up high enough would crash.

Whitaker accomplished his tasks in family therapy by being spontaneous, especially in dealing with the unconscious, and by highlighting the absurd. He influenced family members to interact with each other in unique and new ways. For example, Whitaker once encouraged a boy and his father, who were having a dispute over who had the most control in the family, to arm wrestle, with the winner of the match becoming the winner of the argument. Obviously, the flaw in such a method, that is, its absurdity, was crucial to Whitaker in helping the family gain insight and tolerance.

Regardless of what he suggested on the spur of the moment, Whitaker refused to become involved in giving families overt directives for bringing about change. He was a "Don Quixote" who challenged people to examine their own view of reality and the idea that they can be in control of their lives apart from others in the family (Simon, 1984, p. 28).

Overall, Whitaker (1989) emphasized uncovering and utilizing the unconscious life of the family. In this respect, he related to some of the psychoanalytic dimensions of other family therapy pioneers. However, in contrast to this connection, Whitaker focused on helping the family live more fully in the present. As mentioned earlier, Whitaker's approach has been labeled **experiential symbolic family therapy**. In this position, he assumed that

> experience, not education . . . changes families. The main function of the cerebral cortex is inhibition. Thus, most of our experience goes on outside of our consciousness. We gain best access to it symbolically. For us "symbolic" implies that some thing or some process has more than one meaning. While education can be immensely helpful, the covert process of the family is the one that contains the most power for potential changing (Keith & Whitaker, 1982, p. 43).

Whitaker died at the age of 83 on April 21, 1995, after an illness of 2 years (Andolfi, 1996).

Premises of the Theory

The underlying premise of the experiential approach is that individuals in families are not aware of their emotions, or if they are aware of their emotions, they suppress them. Because of this tendency not to feel or express feelings, a climate of **emotional deadness** is created that results in the expression of symptoms within one or more family members. In this type of atmosphere, family members avoid each other and occupy themselves with work and other nonfamily activities (Satir, 1972). These types of behaviors perpetuate the dysfunctionality of the family further in a downward spiral.

The resolution to this situation is to emphasize sensitivity and feeling-expression among family members and within the family itself. This type of expression can come verbally, but often it is expressed in a nonverbal manner through liberating impulses and affect. For instance, family members may represent the distance they wish to maintain between themselves and other family members by using role play, mime, or even arranging physical objects such as furniture in a particular way. Regardless of how relationships are enacted or represented, it is crucial that emphasis be placed on the present. Overall, the experiential family therapy approach concentrates on increasing self-awareness among family members "through action in the here-and-now" (Costa, 1991, p. 122). The theoretical roots of this treatment are humanistic and phenomenological in origin. Theory is always secondary to process in attempts to bring about change.

Treatment Techniques

Experiential family therapists "can be divided into two groups in regard to therapeutic techniques" (Costa, 1991, p. 121). Some therapists (e.g., Virginia Satir, Peggy Papp, Fred Duhl, and Bunny Duhl) employ highly structured activities, such as sculpting and choreography. Others (e.g., Carl Whitaker) rely more "on their own personality, spontaneity, and creativity" (Costa, 1991, p. 121). It is probably safe to say that most experiential family therapists take a middle road between these two positions. They use techniques that are most often extensions of their personalities. In such cases, the effectiveness of experiential family therapy depends on the personhood of the therapist (Brown & Christensen, 1986; Kempler, 1968).

Experiential family therapists employ many different processes. Even therapists who do not consider techniques important may advocate at least a few of these processes. For instance, according to Whitaker (Keith & Whitaker, 1982), seven different interventions aid the therapeutic process:

1. *Redefining symptoms as efforts for growth.* By viewing symptoms in this way, therapists help families see previously unproductive behaviors as meaningful. Families and therapists are able to evaluate symptoms as ways families have tried to more fully develop.

2. *Modeling fantasy alternatives to real-life stress.* Sometimes change is fostered by going outside the realm of the expected or conventional. Modeling fantasy alternatives is one way of assessing whether client families' ideas will work. The modeling may be done through role play by either therapists or families.

3. *Separating interpersonal stress and intrapersonal stress.* Interpersonal stress is generated between two or more family members. Intrapersonal stress is developed from within an individual. Both types of stresses may be present in families, but it is important to distinguish between them because there are often different ways of resolving them (e.g., face-to-face interactions versus muscle relaxation exercises).

4. *Adding practical bits of intervention.* Sometimes family members need practical or concrete information to make needed changes. For example, adolescents may find it beneficial to know that their fathers struggled in achieving their own identity. Such information helps teenagers who are confused feel more "normal." They may be further assisted through finding that there are career tests they can take to help them sort out their preferences.

5. *Augmenting the despair of a family member.* Augmenting the despair of a family member means to enlarge or magnify his or her feelings so that other family members, and the family as a whole, understand them better. When families have difficulties, they often deny that any of their members are in pain. In addition, family members may suppress their feelings. Augmenting despair prevents the occurrence of such denial or suppression.

6. *Affective confrontation.* As mentioned earlier, a major premise of the experiential approach and those associated with it is its emphasis on the *primacy of emotion.* Therefore, in confronting, therapists will often direct family members to examine their feelings before exploring their behaviors.

7. *Treating children like children and not like peers.* A major emphasis of the experiential approach is to play with children and treat them in an age appropriate manner. Therefore, although children are valued as a part of the therapeutic process, they are treated differently from the rest of a family.

Among the most widely used structured therapeutic responses are the employment of questions, empathic responses, humor, games, clarification, directives, and modeling of effective communication procedures (Satir, Stachowiak, & Taschman, 1975). Family sculpting and choreography are also frequently employed in order to increase family members' awareness and thereby alter their relationships (Duhl, Kantor, & Duhl, 1973; Jefferson, 1978). In addition, techniques of experiential family therapists include family drawing (Bing, 1970) and family puppet interviews (Duhl et al., 1973).

A discussion follows of some of the most widely used technical procedures employed by experiential family therapy.

Modeling of Effective Communication Using "I" Messages

In dysfunctional families, members often speak in the third person plural (i.e., "we"); give unclear and nonspecific messages; and tend to respond to others with monologues (Stoltz-Loike, 1992). For example, in response to her daughter, a mother might drone on about her daughter's behavior by saying: "Someone is going to get angry unless you do something good quickly."

To combat such ineffective and indirect communication patterns, experiential family therapists insist that family members take "I" positions in expressing their feelings. For example, in response to the situation just given, a mother might say to her daughter: "I feel discouraged when you do not respond to my requests."

"I" statements involve the expression of feelings in a personal and responsible way and encourage others to express their opinions. This type of communication also promotes **leveling** or congruent communication, in which straight, genuine, and real expression of one's feelings and wishes are made in an appropriate context. When leveling and congruence occur, there is an increase in communication, a lack of stereotyping, and an improvement of self-esteem and self-worth (Satir, 1972). When leveling does not occur, Satir states that people adopt four other roles: blamer, placater, distractor, and computer (or rational analyzer). These four roles are used by most individuals at one time or another. They can be helpful in some situations, but when they become a consistent way of interacting, they become problematic and dysfunctional.

Blamer

A **blamer** is one who attempts to place the focus on others and not take responsibility for what is happening. This style of communication is often done from a self-righteous stance. A blamer's statement might be: "Now, see what you made me do!" or "It's your fault." In blaming, a person may also point his or her finger in a scolding and lecturing position.

Placater

A **placater** is one who avoids conflict at the cost of his or her integrity. This type of stance is one that originates out of timidity and an eagerness to please. For example, a placater might say in response to something in which he or she disagrees: "That's fine," or "It's ok."

Distractor

A **distractor** is one who says and does irrelevant things. This type of person does not seem to be in contact with anything that is going on. For instance, when a family is talking about the importance of saving money and being thrifty, a distractor might try to tell a joke, say something flippant, or even walk around looking out the windows and calling the family over to look at a stray cat or a passing car.

Computer (or Rational Aanalyzer)

A **computer** (or **rational analyzer**) is one who interacts only on a cognitive or intellectual level. This type of person avoids becoming emotional and stays detached. In a situation where the person playing this role is asked how he or she feels, the response might be: "Different people have different feelings about this circumstance. I think it is difficult to say how one feels without first looking at what one's thoughts are."

To help family members level and become congruent, Satir (1988) sometimes incorporated a technique known as the **communication stance.** In this procedure, family members are asked to exaggerate the physical positions of their perspective roles. For example, a blamer may be asked to make an angry face, bend over as in scolding, and point a finger at the person he or she is attacking. This process promotes an increase in awareness of what is being done and how it is being conveyed. Feelings may surface in the process. The result may be a conversation on alternative ways of interacting, which may lead to practicing new ways of opening up.

Sculpting

In **sculpting,** "family members are molded during the therapy session into positions symbolizing their actual relationships as seen by one or more members of the family" (Sauber, L'Abate, & Weeks, 1985, p. 147). In this process, past events and patterns that affect the family now are perceptually set up. The idea is to expose outgrown family rules and clarify early misconceptions so that family members and the family can get on with life. For example, an historic scene of a father's involvement with a television program and his neglect of his son might be shown through having the father sit close to an imaginary television and the son sit isolated in a corner. The point is that in this "still life portrait of time," family members and the therapist gain a clearer view of family relationships. Often the therapist plays the part of the person setting up the scene. Sculpting consists of four steps and their accompanying roles (Duhl et al., 1973; Moreno & Elefthery, 1975):

1. *Setting the scene.* The therapist helps the sculptor identify a scene to explore.

2. *Choosing role players.* Individuals are chosen to portray family members.

3. *Creating a sculpture.* The sculptor places each person in a specific metaphorical position spatially.

4. *Processing the sculpture.* The sculptor and other participants derole and debrief about experiences and insights acquired through engaging in this exercise.

Choreography

In **choreography,** family members are asked to symbolically enact a pattern or a sequence in their relationship to one another. This process is similar to mime or a "silent movie." Through it, family members come to see and feel alliances and distances that are not obvious through merely discussing problem situations (Papp, 1976).

For instance, in a family with an overinvolved mother and an underinvolved father, members may be asked to act out a typical scene showing this dynamic at a certain time of the day, for example, breakfast. Each family member then takes a turn positioning other family members in certain spatial relationships to one another. In such a scenario, a daughter might have her father turn the pages of a newspaper and sit away from her while her mother heaps cereal into the daughter's bowl and/or straightens the daughter's hair or dress while the daughter leans toward her father and pushes away her mother.

Such scenes should be reenacted three or four times so that family members get a good feeling for what certain experiences are like from the perspectives of other family members. Then, the family and the therapist can sit down and discuss what has occurred and what family members would like to have happen. In many cases, new scenes are created and acted out (Papp, 1976).

Humor

Creating humor within a family therapy session is a risky proposition. If successful, humor will reduce tension and promote insight. Laughter and the confusion that goes with it create an open environment for change to take place (Whitaker & Keith, 1981). If unsuccessful, attempts at humor may alienate the family or some of its members. Therefore, creating humor is an art form that is carefully employed by some experiential family therapists.

Humor is often initiated with families by pointing out the absurdity of their rigid positions or relabeling a situation to make it seem less serious (Carter & McGoldrick-Orfanidis, 1976). In regard to absurdity, a mother might say to a therapist, for example, that she "will die" if her daughter is late for curfew again. A humorous response by the family therapist might be: "Take it easy on your mother. Just paralyze her arm next time."

If the therapist is really into acting out the absurdity, he or she might then ask the daughter to show how she would go about paralyzing her mother's arm. In the interaction following such a strange request, the therapist would probably even engage the mother to help her daughter in such a process. The idea behind this request is to help everyone recognize the distorted power given up by the mother to her daughter. If such insight into this absurdity is developed, a more functional mother/daughter relationship can be formed.

Touch

Satir, Whitaker, and Kempler are among the most prominent of experiential therapists to use touch to communicate in family therapy sessions. Touch may be putting one's arms around another, patting a person on the shoulder, shaking hands, or even, in an extreme case, wrestling (Napier & Whitaker, 1978). In using touch, experiential family therapists are careful not to violate the personal boundaries of their clients. Physical touch is representative of caring and concern. It loses its potency if it is employed inappropriately or if it is overused.

Props

Satir used props, such as ropes and blindfolds, in her work with families (Satir & Baldwin, 1983). These props are metaphorical in nature. For instance, a rope may represent how family members are connected to each other. In her work with the family, Satir sometimes literally tied ends of the rope around all members' waists and selectively asked them to move. In this way, the entire family could experience being tied to one other. They also got a feel for how the movement of one family member influenced the rest of the family.

After the props are used, the therapist might ask the family to process the experience and then relate how the experience is similar to and/or different from the dynamics in their present family relationship.

Family Reconstruction

Family reconstruction is a therapeutic innovation developed by Satir in the late 1960s. The purpose of family reconstruction is to help family members discover dysfunctional patterns in their lives stemming from their families of origin. It concentrates on (1) revealing to family members the sources of their old learning, (2) enabling family members to develop a more realistic picture of who their parents are as persons, and (3) setting up ways for family members to discover their own personhood.

Family reconstruction begins with a "**star**," or "**explorer**," (i.e., a central character) who maps his or her family of origin in visually representative ways (Nerin, 1986; Satir, Bitter, & Krestensen, 1988). A **guide** (usually the therapist) can help the star or explorer chart a chronological account of significant family events from paternal, maternal, and family-of-origin histories. The process of family reconstruction attempts to uncover facts about the origin of distorted learning, about parents as people, and about the person as a separate self. "Family maps, the family life fact chronology, and the wheel of influence (Satir & Baldwin, 1983) are the points of entry, the tools, for a family reconstruction" (Satir et al., 1988, p. 202).

1. *Family map.*   As shown in Figure 6.1, a **family map** is "a visual representation of the structure of three generations of the star's family" (Satir et al., 1988, p. 202), with adjectives to describe each family member's personality. Circles represent people on the map and lines suggest relationships within the family.

2. *Family Life Fact Chronology.*   The **family life fact chronology** is the next tool employed in family reconstruction (see Figure 6.2). "The star creates the chronology by listing all significant events in his or her life and that of the extended family. Chronologies begin with the births of each set of grandparents. All events having an impact on the people in the family, all significant comings and goings, are then listed in order. The family life fact chronology includes the demographic information already on the family map as well as noting illnesses, geographical moves from one place to another, a father going off to war, a sister's teenage pregnancy, or the long-term alcoholism of a family member. When appropriate, historical events associated with given dates are noted to ground the event in time and place" (Satir et al., 1988, p. 203).

3. *Wheel or Circle of Influence.*   A **wheel or circle of influence** representing those who have been important to the star or explorer is the final tool employed in family reconstruction (see Figure 6.3). The star is shown in the

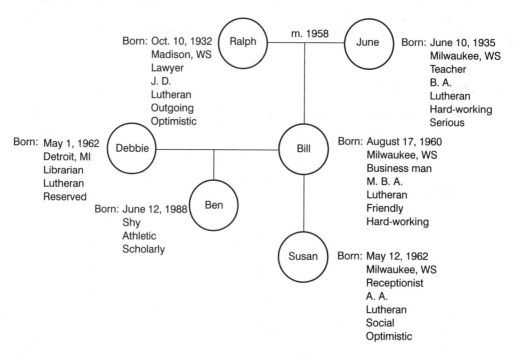

Figure 6.1
Basic family map of a star.

Date	Event	Relation	Location
Paternal			
1-1-1918	John S. born	Star's paternal grandfather	Hastings, MN
2-27-1921	Martha R. born to rich family	Star's paternal grandmother	Minneapolis, MN
1941	John S. is 4F	Star's paternal grandfather	Minnesota draft board
1944?	John S. courts & wins rich man's daughter; married Martha R.	Star's paternal grandparents	Minneapolis, MN war in Europe
8-8-1946	Thomas born	Star's father	Minneapolis, MN
10-1-1946	John S. goes to work for father-in-law	Star's paternal grandfather	Minneapolis, MN
4-18-1949	Sam S. born	Star's paternal uncle	Minneapolis, MN
Maternal			
12-4-1918	Hugh G. born	Star's maternal grandfather	Homer, NY
10-9-1930	Emma B. born	Star's maternal grandmother	Oshkosh, WI
1943	Hugh seriously wounded in war and returns home	Star's maternal grandfather	Homer, NY
12-1-1947	Janice born out of wedlock	Star's mother	Milwaukee, WI
5-1-1948	Hugh moves to start sales job; meets Emma 1st day	Star's maternal grandfather	Oshkosh, WI
9-9-1948	Hugh marries Emma	Star's maternal grandparents	Milwaukee, WI
1949?	Hugh, Emma, & Janice move to escape gossip	Star's mother's family	Saint Paul, MN
Family of Origin			
9-22-1961	Thomas & Jan meet and fall in love	Star's parents	Minneapolis, MN
9-22-1968	Thomas & Jan marry	Star's parents	Minneapolis, MN
3-9-1970	Annie is born	Star	Mankato, MN
2-3-1979	Thomas & Jan divorce	Star's parents	Mankato, MN
1-1-1982	Thomas dies of sudden heart attack	Star's father	Mankato, MN
9-5-1987	Annie enters college; lives at home with mom	Star	Mankato, MN

Figure 6.2

Reconstruction of the star's family.

From "Family Reconstruction: The Family Within—A Group Experience" by V. Satir, J. R. Bitter, and K. K. Krestensen, 1988, *Journal for Specialists in Group Work, 13*, p. 204. Reprinted with permission. No further reproduction authorized without written permission of the American Counseling Association.

Figure 6.3
Wheel of influence.

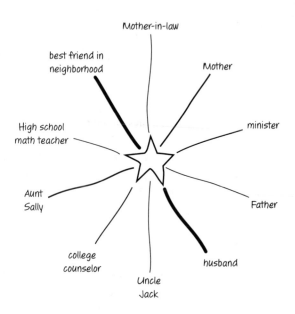

middle of those who have had either positive or negative impacts on him or her. A spoke is drawn for every relationship important to the star. The thicker the line, the more important or closer the relationship. "When completed, the wheel of influence displays the star's internalized strengths and weaknesses, the resources on which he or she may rely for new and, it is hoped, more effective ways of coping" (Satir et al., 1988, p. 205).

The final aspect of family reconstruction is to have the star or explorer give life to the events he or she has discovered. This is done by working with a group of at least 10 people, aided by a leader guide (i.e., a therapist), to enact important family scenes. Members of the group play key figures in the star's life or the life of his or her family. The idea behind this procedure is to help the star or explorer gain a new perspective on family characteristics and patterns. "It is a time when significant questions can receive straight answers, when old, distorted messages can be cleared up, and when understanding can replace judgment and blame" (Satir et al., 1988, p. 207).

Family Drawings

There are several variations on the technique of family drawings that experiential family therapists employ. One is the **joint family scribble** in which each family member makes a brief scribble. After these scribbles have been made, the whole family incorporates their scribbles collectively into a unified picture (Kwiatkowska, 1967). In this procedure, family members get a feel for what it is to work both individually and together. The advantages and disadvantages of each can be talked about, as well as what was produced in each case.

Another drawing approach is known as the **conjoint family drawing**. In this procedure, families are given the instruction to "draw a picture as you see yourself as a family" (Bing, 1970). Each member of the family makes such a drawing and then shares through discussion the perceptions that emerge. For example, a younger son might see his older brother as being closer to their parents. His drawing would reflect this spatial difference. On the other hand, a parent in the same family might see all the family members as being equally close to one another and portray that perception in his or her drawing.

Still another type of family drawing is the **symbolic drawing of family life space** (Geddes & Medway, 1977). In this projective technique, the therapist draws a large circle and instructs family members to include within the circle everything that represents the family and to place outside of the circle those people and institutions that are not a part of the family. After this series of drawings, the family is asked to symbolically arrange themselves, through drawing, within a large circle, according to how they relate to one another. An example of symbolic drawing of family life space is shown in Figure 6.4.

Discussion should follow all of these types of drawing techniques. Family members can discuss what was drawn and why, as well as the dynamics of their life as seen from the perspective of the individual members and the family as a whole. In addition, different ways of interacting can be explored with the therapist and illustrated in another drawing.

Figure 6.4
Symbolic drawing of family life space.

Puppet Interviews

In this procedure, the therapist asks one of the family members to make up a story using puppets (Irwin & Malloy, 1975). The idea is that family difficulties can be displayed in the story and the therapist can gain valuable insight in an indirect manner. In the case, for example, of a 4-year-old girl who is having nightmares, the story might be one of a child who is taken by a witch to a land of dragons, where she is constantly threatened and helpless. Actual circumstances could relate, for example, to the child's day care arrangement in which personnel are scaring children into behaving. Through acting out the scene with puppets, the child can begin to feel safe enough to talk about what is happening in real life.

Family therapists who utilize this process need to be sure they have a variety of puppets for family members to use. In actual practice, this technique is limited. Adults may resist expressing themselves through puppets because they prefer verbal interaction. Children may make up stories that have little or no relationship to what is occurring in their actual lives. However, a puppet technique may be employed effectively in situations in which there are young children, shy children, or selectively mute children who would not or could not relate much about family dynamics in other ways.

Role of the Therapist

The role of the experiential family therapist from the Satir tradition is best described as that of being a *facilitator* and *resource person*. In these roles, therapists help family members understand themselves and others better. Furthermore, they help families discover their innate abilities and help promote clear communication. The therapist makes use of him- or herself in interacting with the family and, thus, "the therapist enters into relationship with each of the family members, uses his or her feelings as guides toward intervention, and models effective interactional styles" (Kane, 1994, p. 256).

From the Whitaker tradition, a family therapist assumes the role of *active participant,* a whole person—not a director or teacher. To be effective in this capacity, the therapist can use a *cotherapist.* According to Whitaker and other symbolic-experiential therapists, the presence of a cotherapist allows greater utilization of intuition (Napier & Whitaker, 1978). Feedback and supervision can also be utilized beneficially in this process.

Generally, experiential therapists try to assist family members in discovering their individuality and in finding fulfilling roles for themselves. They do this by establishing an environment that communicates warmth, acceptance, respect, hope, and an orientation toward improvement and change (Woods & Martin, 1984). A warm environment promotes a willingness to take risks and open up.

In such a setting, therapists help families take the first step toward change by **verbalizing presuppositions** of hope that the family has. They also help family members to clarify their goals and to use their natural abilities.

In addition to setting an atmosphere that encourages change, experiential family therapists promote growth through *stimulating experiences* that provide opportunities for personal existential encounters. Through these encounters, it is hoped that awareness and authenticity will increase and lead "to a reintegration of repressed or disowned parts of the self" (Costa, 1991, p. 122). Experiential family therapists who follow Whitaker's lead at times engage in spontaneous and absurd activities, such as falling asleep in a therapy session or having a dream about a family and reporting back to the family what they dreamed. This use of the absurd can result in raised emotions, anxiety, and, often, insight (Keeney, 1986). It can also break down rational defenses.

Some experiential family therapists, most noticeably those who emulate Virginia Satir, use props, such as ropes, to metaphorically represent distances and interaction patterns between people in families (Satir & Baldwin, 1983). Experiential therapists who follow the tradition of Satir concentrate on being a *model of effective communication* (Simon, 1989).

Overall, experiential family therapists are likely to behave as real, authentic people. In contrast to psychoanalytic therapists, they do not encourage projection or act as blank screens for their families. The more involved, energetic, and creative experiential family therapists are, the greater chance they have of making a major impact on the families with whom they work. Experiential family therapy is an approach to working with families that helps both the families and the therapists gain self-awareness and growth. It requires not only commitment but also *active risk taking* to be an effective experiential family therapist. For instance, experiential family therapists must ask their client families to try new ways of interacting without knowing the ultimate effect of these behaviors.

Process and Outcome

During experiential family therapy, family members should become more aware of their own needs and feelings. They should share these impressions with each other. This illustrates the *inside out process of change* promoted by experiential therapists (Duhl, 1983). Through therapy, family members become more attuned to their emotions and more capable of autonomy and real intimacy. "Treatment is generally designed to help individual family members find fulfilling roles for themselves, without an overriding concern for the needs of the family as a whole" (Nichols & Schwartz, 1995, p. 293).

Many experiential family therapists concentrate on whoever comes to therapy. However, others insist on having the whole family in treatment. In fact, they request that three generations be present during each session (Whitaker,

1976). Even though the entire family is present, experiential family therapists usually do not treat the family as a systematic unit. Rather, the emphasis is on the impact of what the therapist and other members of the family do in the sessions. It is thought that this knowledge is more powerful when shared with everyone present than when it is conveyed to others in the family indirectly.

The process of family therapy differs for each experiential family therapist. Whitaker described family therapy as a process that "begins with a blind date and ends with an empty nest" (Whitaker & Bumberry, 1988, p. 53). For Whitaker, therapy occurred in three phases: (1) engagement, (2) involvement, and (3) disentanglement. During these phases, the therapist increases, in a caring way, the family's anxiety. The idea is to escalate pressure in order to produce a breakdown and breakthrough, both among family members and in the functioning of the family itself. *Therapists use themselves,* as well as planned and spontaneous actions, to intensify the sane and crazy elements within the family (Whitaker & Keith, 1981). Through these means, they get the family to move toward change.

Engagement consists of therapists becoming personally involved with their families through the sharing of feelings, fantasies, and personal stories. During this time, therapists encourage families to become invested in making needed changes within a structured environment. If all goes smoothly, therapists are able to demonstrate their care to client families. Next, during the involvement stage, therapists concentrate on helping families try new ways of relating through the use of playfulness, humor, and confrontation. The emphasis in this stage is on families' broadening their horizons and trying new behaviors. Once constructive action is taken and roles/rules are modified, therapists disengage from families and become their consultants.

Similarly, Satir's approach has three phases of intervention. In Satir's Human Validation Process Model, the three stages are (1) making contact, (2) chaos, and (3) integration. These phases are present in each interview and in the therapy as a whole. In the first stage, Satir would shake each person's hand and focus her attention on that person, in an attempt to raise the level of the person's self-esteem and self-worth. Satir (1988) compared self-worth with a pot. When "the pot of self-worth is high," people are vitally alive and have faith in themselves. The opposite is true when the "pot of self-worth is low." The establishment of trust and hope takes place during this first 45- to 60-minute nonjudgmental session as well. Family members would be asked what they hoped would come out of the therapy. Then through active techniques, Satir would begin to make interventions.

During the second stage, chaos and disorder among family members is prevalent. Individuals are engaged in tasks, take risks, and share their hurt and pain. This stage is unpredictable, as family members open up and work on issues in a random order.

In the last stage, integration and closure are worked on in regard to issues raised in the second stage. Often the third stage is quite emotional. However, Satir would interject cognitive information at this time to help members understand themselves and issues more thoroughly. For example, she might have said to a man grieving the loss of his father with whom he was always distant: "You now understand through your hurt how your father kept all people, including you, from getting close to him."

The family is terminated when transactions can be completed and when family members can see themselves as others do. It is vital that family members be able to share with each other honestly. It is a positive sign when members can argue and disagree and make choices by taking responsibility for outcomes. The sending and receiving of clear communication is a further indicator that the family is ready to end treatment (Satir, 1964). For example, if family members can tell each other that they would rather go somewhere different on vacation than back to the same beach they visited last year, progress has been made.

Regardless of the techniques employed in the experiential approach, the primary goal of therapy is growth, especially in the areas of sensitivity and the sharing of feelings. Therapists and families focus on growing. Growth is usually accomplished through the therapist winning the "**battle for structure**" and client families winning the "**battle for initiative**" (Napier & Whitaker, 1978). In the battle for structure, the therapist sets up the conditions (e.g., the length of sessions and/or the order of speaking) under which the family will proceed. In the battle for initiative, the family becomes actively involved and responsible for making changes that help them as individuals and as a family (e.g., several family members express a desire to work out or work through a disagreement that has continued to keep them angry and apart). If the battle for structure is won, chances are improved that the battle for initiative will go well. An ideal outcome for experiential family therapists is to help individuals gain congruence between their inner experiences and outward behaviors.

Unique Aspects of Experiential Family Therapy

Emphases

The unique qualities of the experiential approach are found on several levels that involve both people and processes. A major uniqueness developed by Virginia Satir is the training program set up to educate others in this process. The **Avanta Network** (139 Forest Avenue, Palo Alto, California, 94301) now carries on the interdisciplinary work of training therapists in Satir's methods. This program holds promise for keeping the therapeutic contributions of Satir alive and developing.

A second novel element of the experiential approach relates to research. Although Satir gave consent for only her model and methods to be used in one research project, this study (Winter, 1989), which compared her work with Bowen and Haley, produced very favorable results on both a multiple-family group level and with individual family units. Their results, plus her own demonstration of work before large audiences of professionals, have given her approach, and the experiential school of therapy in general, credibility, with the possibility that more will be gained in the future through the generation of data (Satir & Bitter, 1991).

Whitaker, on the other hand, has been unique in his stance that empirical research, just like theory, can get in the way of helping a family. Whitaker reported numerous examples of how he conducted family therapy. However, he insisted that because each family is different, each treatment plan should be different and, therefore, cannot really be used for research. In essence, Whitaker is impossible to imitate, as are his therapeutic sessions (Framo, 1996).

The length of treatment and the focus of experiential family therapists is a third unique aspect of it. Experiential family therapy focuses on immediate experiences and the uniqueness of every family. Treatment tends to be of shorter duration and often more direct than with historical-based approaches.

A fourth quality of experiential family therapy is that it calls attention to emphasizing people as well as structures within the change process. As a theory, experiential family therapy places a great deal of attention on persons within families. It emphasizes that families are composed of individuals. For family systems to change, those who are a part of them must alter their behaviors (Duhl, 1983).

Comparison with Other Theories

Experiential family therapy is often seen as hard to conceptualize and, therefore, hard to compare with other approaches. However, experiential approaches can be contrast to other types of family therapy both directly and indirectly.

One comparative aspect of many of the experiential approaches is their dependence on sensitive and charismatic therapists. Virginia Satir and Carl Whitaker, pioneers in the family therapy movement, both fit this profile. Additionally, they were both rather large-framed. They encouraged family members to physically participate in activities, for example, by using props, in the case of Satir, and by using their person (e.g., as in arm wrestling contests), in the case of Whitaker. Both had a spontaneous theatrical style that was uniquely their own and made them difficult to emulate. Whitaker especially has been hard to model, partly because of his encouragement of intuitive action by a therapist and partly because of the need for a therapist to do an apprenticeship with him in order to really learn his approach (Sugarman, 1987).

Unlike other forms of family treatment, experiential family therapies focus on the present rather than on the past. Such an emphasis can keep therapists and families from dealing with historical patterns or events. By neglecting historical information, therapists could miss data that sheds light on patterns, which if properly understood can be altered and thereby help alleviate problems. In this last respect, however, experiential and strategic therapies are the same.

Further, experiential family therapies promote individual growth and intrapersonal change as opposed to family growth and interpersonal change. Although personal development is an admirable and noteworthy goal, it may not be sufficient to help families alter their dysfunctional behaviors. For instance, individual members who have become healthier during treatment may leave the family, or if the family stays together, more dysfunctional family members may work hard to return the family to the way it was before therapy.

Finally, experiential approaches emphasize dealing with feelings in the here and now rather than concentrating on guidance for now and the future. Some theorists criticize making therapeutic interventions without offering family members education about how to help themselves in the future. This critique of the experiential therapies, however, has not altered the overall emphasis of the approach (Duhl & Duhl, 1981).

CASE ILLUSTRATION

THE SMITH FAMILY

When Fred first bumped into Heather, it was literally in a car. The accident was minor, but the mutual interest between the divorced man and the widow soon grew. In 6 months, Fred had proposed, and the wedding took place on the anniversary of their collision. Fred's 16-year-old son, Stan, was reluctantly his father's best man; and Heather's 8- and 9-year-old daughters, Ann and Mary, respectively, were her bridesmaids.

Heather's daughters quickly accepted Fred as their new father. (Their biological father had died of cancer when they were 4 and 5). Stan was not as accepting, and told Heather prior to the wedding ceremony that he already had a mother, Judy. Judy and his father divorced in an nasty civil suit 2 years previously.

Although Stan has been disrespectful to Heather in subtle ways since, Heather worries more about her daughters' behavior in regard to Fred. They frequently manipulate him into buying them clothes and toys that the family budget cannot afford. Fred reassures Heather that his behavior with respect to the girls is temporary, but she thinks otherwise. Fred is 40, the oldest in his family of origin, which was composed of him, his 8 year younger sister, Emily, and his parents, both hardworking school teachers. Heather thinks he should be wiser and more appropriate in his interactions with her daughters. Lately, Heather has started scolding Fred and then withdrawing into silence. According to Fred, she is acting more like a 3-year-old than like the 33-year-old woman that she is.

Conceptualization of Family: Experiential Perspective

As a remarried family, the Smiths are encountering difficulties in becoming a functioning unit. Some of it is on a conscious, overt level; and some of it appears unconscious and covert. Stan is openly withdrawn from his stepmother and Heather has begun an emotional withdrawal from Fred. At the same time, Fred is being drawn into a relationship with Heather's daughters, who are manipulating him into buying them things they want. Fred is treating them well on the surface, but it is difficult to tell whether he has anything more than a superficial interaction with them. Furthermore, it is interesting to note that Fred has continued his behavior with Heather's daughters despite her disapproval.

There is stress in the marital unit, as well as between the generations. It appears individual members of the family are having problems, too. Clear communication is lacking. In fact, family members seem to hurt themselves and others when they try to make a point (e.g., by giving one another the "cold shoulder").

Process of Treatment: Experiential Family Therapy

To help the Smiths become a more functional family, an experiential family therapist would go through three phases of treatment, and most likely would use a number of procedures. If the therapist followed Whitaker's symbolic-experiential approach, he or she might initially show care and concern for the family through expressing feelings about individual family members. In this process, the therapist would address remarks to one member of the family at a time. However, it is the manner in which the therapist's remarks are conveyed that establishes trust among all members.

The therapist following Satir's model would likewise focus initially on making contact with family members on a personal level. In such a scenario, the therapist would use "I" statements, for example, "Heather, I really hear that you are feeling hurt and angry about Fred's behavior." The emphasis in such a first session would be on making sure family members felt validated and affirmed as members of the family unit.

After this preliminary engagement/contact, the therapist would move the family into involvement. For a therapist following Whitaker's symbolic-experiential approach, involvement is getting the family to win the "battle for initiative" by working on problematic areas. In the case of the Smiths, these behaviors range from the proper expression of affection to the expression of anger. To make the family more aware of the importance of the issues involved, a symbolic-experiential therapist might do something absurd, such as sharing a daydream with the family about their situation. Through such a process, some unconscious aspects of the family's life would become more obvious. In most cases, the therapist would also try to get individuals talking to one another about their feelings and how they have handled them previous to this family situation. An opportunity would then be given for family members to try new behaviors.

In the Satir model, the middle part of the therapeutic process might involve chaos, out of which would come clarity. This middle phase would involve such procedures as sculpting, choreography, or art, in which members would get an opportunity to express their feelings in direct and indirect ways. Props might be used in these situations to enhance the quality of the affect that is generated. There would be an emphasis at this stage on exploring, through activities, concerns such as individual self-worth and/or their family life together (Satir, 1972).

In the final stage of the experiential process, a symbolic-experiential therapist would disengage from the Smith family by encouraging family members to speak more to each other. Likewise, in the Satir model, the therapist would help the Smith family integrate what they learned through their enactments and come to closure. A more cognitive focus would eventually be emphasized by Satir, after emotions concerning the therapeutic experience were expressed.

Summary and Conclusion

Experiential family therapy grew out of the humanistic-existential psychology movement of the 1960s. Its original founders were involved with experimental and experiential forms of treatment. They concentrated on immediate personal interactions and sometimes conducted their family sessions like a group by treating all members of the family as equals. Above all, they stressed the importance of taking risks and expressing emotions.

Some of the founders of this approach, such as Virginia Satir and Peggy Papp, developed highly structured treatment methods, such as using "I" messages, sculpting, and family reconstruction. Other practitioners within this theoretical camp, such as Carl Whitaker, relied more on their personality, creativity, and spontaneity to help them make timely and effective interventions. Most clinicians who favor this approach today lean toward the former method of treatment just described rather than the latter.

Some of the major roles of experimental family therapists are to act as facilitators and resource persons. Therapists encourage change and set up a warm and accepting environment in which such a process is possible. Experiential family therapists use a wide variety of techniques that are both concrete and metaphorical. They act as models of clear communication in the hope of promoting intimacy and autonomy. It is assumed that if individuals within families find proper roles for themselves, the family as a whole will function well.

Some of the pioneers of family therapy, such as Virginia Satir and Carl Whitaker, are among the best-known experiential family therapists. Although the therapy they helped develop is valued for its emphasis on stressing the importance of affect in families, it is perceived as weak from a traditional research perspective. Furthermore, focusing on persons within the family, instead of the family as a whole, could make systemic change difficult. Complicating the matter still further is the emphasis from the experiential perspective of concentrating on the here and now at the expense of teaching families how to work better in the future. Overall, experiential family therapy is seen as less viable in the 1990s than previously because of the accountability that is linked with therapeutic treatment. However, it continues to be an attractive approach for many practitioners.

SUMMARY TABLE

Experiential Family Therapy

Major Theorists
Virginia Satir
Carl Whitaker
Fred Duhl
Bunny Duhl
Walter Kempler
Augustus Napier
David Keith
Leslie Greenberg
Susan Johnson
Peggy Papp

Underlying Premises
Family problems are rooted in suppression of feelings, rigidity, denial of impulses, lack of awareness, emotional deadness, and overuse of defense mechanisms.

Role of the Therapist
Therapists use their own personalities.

Therapists must be open, spontaneous, empathic, sensitive, and demonstrate caring and acceptance.

They must be willing to share and risk, be genuine, and increase stress within the family and its members.

They must deal with regression therapeutically and teach family members new skills in clearly communicating their feelings.

Unit of Treatment
The focus is on individuals and couple dyads, except for Whitaker, who concentrated on three generational families. It is assumed that families will benefit if the individuals within them receive help.

Goals of Treatment
The goals of treatment are:

- to promote growth, change, creativity, flexibility, spontaneity, and play-fulness
- to make the covert overt
- to increase emotional closeness of spouses and disrupt rigidity
- to unlock defenses, enhance self-esteem, and recover potential for experiencing

Therapeutic Techniques
Therapeutic techniques of the experiential approach include:

- Sculpting
- Choreography
- Modeling and teaching clear communication skills
- Humor
- Puppet interviews
- Art therapy
- Role playing
- Reconstruction
- Disregarding theory and emphasizing intuitive spontaneity
- Sharing feelings and creating an emotionally intense atmosphere
- Having the therapist win the battle for structure and the family win the battle for initiative
- Making suggestions and giving directives

Unique Aspects of the Approach
Experiential family therapy emphasizes:

- creativity and spontaneity in families
- changing roles and increased understanding of self and others
- treating all members of the family as equal in status
- increased awareness of feelings within and among family members
- the breakdown of defenses within the family and among family members through structured exercises
- growth

Comparison with Other Theories
In experiential family therapy, there is little interest in research or data on results of using the theory.

Much of the practice of experiential family therapy is not systems oriented.

The experiential approach can overemphasize emotion.

Experiential family therapy may be too advice-oriented and individualistic.

Experiential family therapists use a lot of borrowed techniques that have not been empirically tested.

Much of the effectiveness of experiential family therapy depends on the spontaneity, creativity, and timing of the therapist.

References

Andolfi, M. (1996). Let it flow: Carl Whitaker's philosophy of becoming. *Journal of Marital and Family Therapy, 22,* 317–319.

Beels, C., & Ferber, A. (1969). Family therapy: A view. *Family Process, 8,* 280–332.

Bing, E. (1970). The conjoint family drawing. *Family Process, 9,* 173–194.

Brown, J. H., & Christensen, P. N. (1986). *Family therapy: Theory and practice.* Pacific Grove, CA: Brooks/Cole.

Carter, E. A., & McGoldrick-Orfanidis, M. (1976). Family therapy with one person and the family therapist's own family. In P. J. Guerin, Jr. (Ed.), *Family therapy* (pp. 119–219). New York: Gardner.

Costa, L. (1991). Family sculpting in the training of marriage and family counselors. *Counselor Education and Supervision, 31,* 121–131.

Duhl, B. (1983). *From the inside out and other metaphors.* New York: Brunner/Mazel.

Duhl, B. S., & Duhl, F. J. (1981). Integrative family therapy. In A. S. Gurman & D. P. Kniskern (Eds.), *Handbook of family therapy* (pp. 483–513). New York: Brunner/Mazel.

Duhl, F. J., Kantor, D., & Duhl, B. S. (1973). Learning, space, and action in family therapy: A primer of sculpture. In D. A. Bloch (Ed.), *Techniques of family psychotherapy* (pp. 69–76) New York: Grune & Stratton.

Framo, J. L. (1996). A personal retrospective of the family therapy field: Then and now. *Journal of Marital and Family Therapy, 22,* 289–316.

Geddes, M., & Medway, J. (1977). The symbolic drawing of family life space. *Family Process, 16,* 219–228.

Gladding, S. T. (1992). *A life in a day of aging.* Unpublished manuscript.

Irwin, E., & Malloy, E. (1975). Family puppet interview. *Family Process, 14,* 179–191.

Jefferson, C. (1978). Some notes on the use of family sculpture in therapy. *Family Process, 17,* 69–76.

Kane, C. M. (1994). Family making: A Satir approach to treating the H. family. *The Family Journal, 2,* 256–258.

Keeney, B. P. (1986). Cybernetics of the absurd: A tribute to Carl Whitaker. *Journal of Strategic and Systemic Therapies, 5,* 20–28.

Keith, D. V. (1987). Intuition in family therapy: A short manual on post-modern witchcraft. *Contemporary Family Therapy, 9,* 11–22.

Keith, D. V., & Whitaker, C. A. (1982). Experiential/symbolic family therapy. In A. M. Horne & M. M. Ohlsen (Eds.), *Family counseling and therapy* (pp. 43–74). Itasca, IL: F. E. Peacock.

Kempler, W. (1968). Experiential psychotherapy with families. *Family Process, 7,* 88–89.

Kwiatkowska, H. Y. (1967). Family art therapy. *Family Process, 6,* 37–55.

Moreno, J. L., & Eleftery, D. G. (1975). An introduction to group psychodrama. In G. M. Gazda (Ed.), *Basic approaches to group psychotherapy and group counseling* (pp. 69–100). Springfield, IL: Thomas.

Napier, A. Y., & Whitaker, C. A. (1978). *The family crucible.* New York: Harper & Row.

Nerin, W. F. (1986). *Family reconstruction: Long day's journey into light.* New York: Norton.

Nichols, M. P., & Schwartz, R. C. (1995). *Family therapy: Concepts and methods* (3rd ed.). Boston: Allyn & Bacon.

Papp, P. (1976). Family choreography. In P. J. Guerin, Jr. (Ed.), *Family therapy* (pp. 465–479). New York: Gardner.

Satir, V. M. (1964). *Conjoint family therapy.* Palo Alto, CA: Science and Behavior Books.

Satir, V. M. (1972). *Peoplemaking.* Palo Alto, CA: Science and Behavior Books.

Satir, V. M. (1982). The therapist and family therapy: Process model. In A. M. Horne & M. M. Ohlsen (Eds.), *Family counseling and therapy.* Itasca, IL: F. E. Peacock.

Satir, V. (1986). A partial portrait of a family therapist in process. In H. C. Fishman & B. L. Rosman (Eds.), *Evolving models for family change: A volume in honor of Salvador Minuchin* (pp. 278–293). New York: Guilford Press.

Satir, V. M. (1988). *The new peoplemaking.* Mountain View, CA: Science and Behavior Books.

Satir, V., & Baldwin, M. (1983). *Satir step by step.* Palo Alto, CA: Science and Behavior Books.

Satir, V. M., & Bitter, J. R. (1991). The therapist and family therapy: Satir's human validation process model. In A. M. Horne & J. L. Passmore (Eds.),

Family counseling and therapy (2nd ed.) (pp. 14–45). Itasca, IL: F. E. Peacock.

Satir, V., Bitter, J. R., & Krestensen, K. K. (1988). Family reconstruction: The family within—a group experience. *Journal for Specialists in Group Work, 13,* 200–208.

Satir, V., Stachowiak, J., & Taschman, H. A. (1975). *Helping families to change.* New York: Aronson.

Sauber, S. R., L'Abate, L., & Weeks, G. R. (1985). *Family therapy: Basic concepts and terms.* Rockville, MD: Aspen.

Simon, R. (1984, November/December). Stranger in a strange land: An interview with Salvador Minuchin. *Family Therapy Networker, 8,* 20–31.

Simon, R. (1985, September/October). Take it or leave it: An interview with Carl Whitaker. *Family Therapy Networker, 9,* 27–34.

Simon, R. (1989, January/February). Reaching out to life: An interview with Virginia Satir. *Family Therapy Networker, 13,* 36–43.

Stoltz-Loike, M. (1992). Couple and family counseling. In R. L. Smith & P. Stevens-Smith (Eds.), *Family counseling and therapy* (pp. 80–108). Ann Arbor, MI: ERIC/CAPS.

Sugarman, S. (1987). Teaching symbolic-experiential family therapy: The personhood of the teacher. *Contemporary Family Therapy, 9,* 138–145.

Whitaker, C. A. (1975). Psychotherapy of the absurd: With a special emphasis on the psychotherapy of aggression. *Family Process, 14,* 1–16.

Whitaker, C. A. (1976). The hindrance of theory in clinical work. In P. J. Guerin, Jr. (Ed.), *Family therapy: Theory and practice.* New York: Gardner.

Whitaker, C. A. (1989). *Midnight musings of a family therapist.* New York: W. W. Norton.

Whitaker, C. A. (1990). 'I had to learn because I wasn't being taught.' *Contemporary Family Therapy, 12,* 181–183.

Whitaker, C. A., & Bumberry, W. M. (1988). *Dancing with the family: A symbolic-experiential approach.* New York: Brunner/Mazel.

Whitaker, C. A., & Keith, D. V. (1981). Symbolic-experiential family therapy. In A. Gurman & D. Kniskern (Eds.), *The handbook of family therapy* (pp. 187–225). New York: Brunner/Mazel.

Winter, J. (1989). *Family research project: Treatment outcomes and results.* Unpublished manuscript, the Family Institute of Virginia, Richmond.

Woods, M. D., & Martin, D. (1984). The work of Virginia Satir: Understanding her theory and technique. *American Journal of Family Therapy, 12,* 3–11.

Behavioral and Cognitive–Behavioral Family Therapies

They trade insults and accusations like children
afraid to be vulnerable and scared not to be.

Underneath all the words and bravado
is a backlog of bitter emotion
dormant so long that like dry kindling
it burst into flames when sparked.

Through the dark and heated fights
points are made that leave a mark.

In the early morning, she cries silently
into black coffee grown cold with age
while he sits behind a mahogany desk
and experiences the loneliness of depression.

Gladding, 1991

B ehaviorism is one of the oldest traditions in the helping professions. It developed from the research and writings of Ivan Pavlov, John B. Watson, and B. F. Skinner. Initially, it focused on observable behavior and concentrated on assisting individuals modify dysfunctional behaviors. Since the 1970s, the impact of *cognitions* (i.e., thoughts) have become incorporated into behaviorism, an approach known as **cognitive-behavioral therapy**.

Behavioral family therapy is a fairly recent treatment methodology that had its origins in research involving the modification of children's actions by parents (Horne, 1991). The initial work in this area was conducted at the Oregon Social Learning Center under the direction of Gerald Patterson and John Reid in the mid-1960s. It involved training parents and significant adults in a child's environment to be agents of change (Patterson, 1975; Patterson & Gullion, 1971). Treatment procedures were based on **social learning theory** (Bandura & Walters, 1963), which stressed the importance of modeling new behaviors. Techniques included "the use of buzzer boxes and M&Ms candy but quickly moved toward using basic point systems, modeling, time out, and contingent attention" (Horne, 1991, p. 467). The emphasis in this program gradually shifted toward working with families in their natural settings.

From this rather structured beginning in which observers recorded family problems on a checklist that was linear in nature (i.e., "A" caused "B"), behavioral family therapy grew to embrace a more interactional style of explaining family behavior patterns and treating family behavior problems (Falloon, 1988). A type of behavioral family therapy that is basically systemic is **functional family therapy** (Barton & Alexander, 1981; Alexander & Parsons, 1982).

Likewise, cognitive-behavioral family therapy is a fairly new treatment, although the importance of thoughts have been stressed throughout history. Cognitive-behavioral theorists postulate that "cognitions such as irrational beliefs, arbitrary inference, dichotomous reasoning, and overgeneralization can be primary factors in causing, or at least maintaining, maladaptive behaviors and psychological disorders in individuals" (Sullivan & Schwebel, 1995, p. 298). Since the 1970s a concerted effort has been made to apply cognitive-behavioral theory and procedures to couples and families (e.g., Baucom & Epstein, 1990; Beck, 1976; Ellis, 1991; Ellis, Sichel, Yeager, DiMattia, & DiGuiseppe, 1989; and Schwebel & Fine, 1994). Unfortunately, cognitive-behavioral approaches to working with families are not as fully developed as behavioral therapies, or even as advanced as cognitive-behavioral couple therapy (Ellis, 1993). Some of the leading proponents of cognitive-behavioral marital and family therapy are Aaron Beck, Albert Ellis, Nathan Epstein, and Andrew Schwebel.

This chapter examines the major forms of behavioral and cognitive-behavioral family therapy.

Major Theorists

There are many well-known behavior and cognitive-behavioral theorists. Early pioneers in this area were John B. Watson, Mary Cover Jones, and Ivan Pavlov. It was not, however, until the emergence of B. F. Skinner that behaviorism gained national prominence. Skinner was the first to use the term *behavior therapy* and "argued convincingly that behavior problems can be dealt with directly, not simply as symptoms of underlying psychic conflict" (Nichols & Schwartz, 1995, p. 322). Skinner was also the originator and a proponent of **operant conditioning**. This viewpoint is that people learn through rewards and punishments to respond behaviorally to their environments in certain ways. For instance, if a man smiles at a woman and she smiles back, he may voluntarily approach and talk with her because his initial action was reinforced. Skinner publicized his ideas on operant conditioning in such scholarly texts as *Science and Human Behavior* (1953) and in popular books such as *Walden Two* (1948).

It is on the work of Skinner, combined with that of Joseph Wolpe and Albert Bandura, that much of behavioral family therapy and cognitive-behavioral family therapy were built. Other significant contributions in this area have come from Gerald Patterson, Richard Stuart, Norman Epstein, Neil Jacobson, Walter Mischel, Robert Weiss, Ed Katkin, Gayola Margolin, Michael Crowe, Albert Ellis, Aaron Beck, David Burns, and Donald Meichenbaum. Gerald Patterson and Neil Jacobson are highlighted here as representatives of this approach.

Gerald Patterson

Gerald Patterson is often credited as being the primary theorist who began the practice of applying behavioral theory to family problems in the 1960s (Barker, 1986). His work at the Oregon Social Learning Center, especially in training parents to act as agents of change in their children's environment, led to the identification of a number of behavior problems and corrective interventions. Among the interventions utilized in helping parents and children are **primary rewards,** such as the use of candy, and innovative techniques involving modeling, point systems, time out, and contingent attention (Patterson & Brodsky, 1966; Patterson, Jones, Whittier, & Wright, 1965; Patterson, McNeal, Hawkins, & Phelps, 1967). Through their observations of parents and children in laboratories and natural environments (such as homes, neighborhoods, and schools),

Patterson and his associates have developed a *family observational coding system* to use in assessing dysfunctional behaviors.

Patterson (1975) has also been instrumental in writing **programmed workbooks for parents** to employ in helping their children, and ultimately their families, modify behaviors. Overall, Patterson is credited as playing a critical role in the extension of learning principles and techniques to family and marital problems. His practical application of social learning theory has made a major impact on family therapy. He has influenced other behaviorists to work from a systemic perspective in dealing with families.

Neil Jacobson

Neil Jacobson, like a number of prominent theorists in behavioral family therapy, began his work in the 1970s. As a graduate student in psychology at the University of North Carolina in 1972, he initially intended to be a psychoanalytically oriented clinician. However, after reading books and articles by Albert Bandura, Walter Mischel, Richard Stuart, Gerald Patterson, and Bob Weiss, and meeting some of these individuals at the conferences of the Association for the Advancement of Behavior Therapy, he changed his mind and became a behaviorist (Wood & Jacobson, 1990).

After completing his doctorate, Jacobson settled into an academic career at the University of Washington in 1979. There, as elsewhere in his life, he has developed a clinical practice based on research. His practice has helped refine his theoretical contributions to behavioral marital therapy. His graduate students have also kept him focused on theory and challenged him to refine it.

Jacobson is on the leading edge of the family therapy field. He is constantly making discoveries, for example, that Type I male batterers have lower (i.e., decelerated) heart rates during times of physical assault (Jacobson, Gottman, & Wu Shortt, 1995). Jacobson's findings are challenging marital and family therapy practitioners to be more innovative and effective in their work. For example, prior to Jacobson's research, all batterers were treated for impulse control deficiency. However, Type II batterers suffer from this deficiency; and Type I batterers do not.

Premises of Behavioral and Cognitive-Behavioral Family Therapies

Behavioral Family Therapy

In its simplest forms, behavioral family therapy is based on the theoretical foundations of behavioral therapy in general. An assumption underlying this premise is that all *behavior is learned* and that people, including families, act according to how they have previously been reinforced. Behavior is maintained by its consequences and will continue unless more rewarding consequences result from new behaviors (Patterson, 1975).

A second major principle of this approach is that maladaptive behaviors, and not underlying causes, should be the targets of change. The primary concern of behaviorists is with changing present behavior, not dealing with historical developments. Ineffective behaviors can be extinguished and replaced with new sequences of behavior patterns. To do this, continuous assessment of treatment is recommended. Tangible behavior changes in the present are the focus of behaviorally based family therapists.

A third premise behind behavioral family therapy is the belief that not everyone in the family has to be treated for change to occur. In fact, many behavioral family therapists work with only one member of a couple or family. In most reported cases involving one individual, the targeted person is the wife. The reason is that women have traditionally been more open to therapy and therapeutic interventions than men. Regardless, in the therapeutic process, behaviorists teach this person new, appropriate, and functional skills, such as **assertiveness** (i.e., asking for what one wants) and desensitization (i.e., overcoming unnecessary and debilitating anxiety associated with a particular event) (Goldiamond, 1965; Lazarus, 1968). Behavioral family therapists who are more systemic concentrate on dyadic relationships, such as a parent and child or the couple system (Gordon & Davidson, 1981; Stuart, 1980). The idea behind this procedure is that the correction of dysfunctional behaviors in key members of a family results in significant, measurable positive changes in the family as a whole.

Because of its focus on identifiable, overt behavioral changes with individuals sometimes apart from the family as a unit, the behavioral approach is not usually considered a systemic approach to working with families in the fullest sense of the term. However, behaviorism does share with systems theory an emphasis on the importance of "family rules and patterned communication processes, as well as a functional approach to outcome" (Walsh, 1982, p. 17). Furthermore, a number of behaviorally based family therapists, known as functional family therapists, operate from a systemic perspective (e.g., Barton & Alexander, 1981; Alexander & Parsons, 1982).

Regardless of its degree of systems orientation, behavioral family therapy emphasizes the major techniques within a behavioral theory approach, such as stimulus, reinforcement, shaping, and modeling. In addition, some practitioners of this approach incorporate **social exchange theory** (Thibaut & Kelley, 1959), which stresses the rewards and costs of relationships in family life according to a behavioral economy. For example, individuals stay in marital relationships because the rewards they receive are equal to or greater than the cost to them in time, effort, and resources. Otherwise, they leave. A major focus behind the idea of social exchange is mutual reciprocity, for example, pleasantness begets pleasantness.

Cognitive-Behavioral Family Therapy

Many behavioral therapists also emphasize cognitive aspects of treatment (DiGuiseppe, 1988; Epstein, Schlesinger, & Dryden, 1988; Freeman & Zaken-Greenberg, 1989). In the **cognitive-behavioral approach,** attention focuses on what family members are thinking, as well as how they are feeling and behaving. The premise behind cognitive-behavioral theory is that "the relationship-related cognitions individuals hold, shape how they think, feel, and behave in couple and family relationships." Relationship-related cognitions held by individuals concern (Sullivan & Schwebel, 1995, p. 298) assumptions about how relationships work and the roles people play in them; expectations and perceptions regarding what particular events occur in relationships, and standards about how individuals in relationships should behave and how relationships ought to work.

In cognitive-behavioral family therapy, there are health promoting relationship-related cognitions that promote growth and negative relationship-related cognitions that lead to distress and conflict. In healthy relationships, partners might believe, for example, that it takes work to build a relationship; that both partners' needs are important; and that relationships are not always going to be free of conflict. Conversely, partners in unhealthy relations might believe that they do not have to work at relationships, that one partner's needs are more important than the other's, and that good relationships are free of conflict.

In addition, therapists must deal with irrational beliefs on the part of resistant family members. Examples of such irrational beliefs (Ellis, 1985, p. 32) include:

- "I must do well at changing myself, and I'm an incompetent, hopeless client if I don't."
- "You [the therapist and others] must help me change, and you're rotten people if you don't."
- "Changing myself must occur quickly and easily, and it's horrible if it doesn't."

Types of Behavioral and Cognitive-Behavioral Family Therapies

Behaviorism (with or without a cognitive component) has more specific forms of treatment than any other form of family therapy, with the exception of strategic family therapy. The most prevalent forms of behavioral and cognitive-behavioral family therapy are behavioral parent training, behavioral and cognitive-behavioral marriage therapy and education, treatment of sexual dysfunctioning, and functional family therapy.

Behavioral Parent Training

Behavioral parent training is sometimes referred to as **parent-skills training**. In this model, the therapist serves as a social learning educator whose prime responsibility is on changing parents' responses to a child or children, both through thoughts and actions. By effecting such a change in parents, children's behavior is altered. This type of treatment is linear in nature, and therapists who utilize it are precise and direct in following a set procedure.

For example, one of the initial and main tasks of the therapist is to define a specific problem behavior. The behavior is monitored in regard to its antecedents and consequences. The parents are then trained in social learning theory (Bandura, 1969). Parent-training procedures usually include verbal and performance methods. Verbal methods involve didactic instruction as well as written materials. The aim is to influence thoughts and messages. Performance training methods may involve role playing, modeling, behavioral rehearsal, and prompting. Their focus is on improving parent/child interactions. Regardless of the form of the training, parents are asked to **chart** the problem behavior over the course of treatment. Successful efforts are rewarded through encouragement and compliments by the therapist.

Behavioral and Cognitive-Behavioral Marriage Therapies and Education

The initial efforts in behavioral marital therapy were initiated by Robert Liberman (1970) and Richard Stuart (1969). Liberman expressed his approach to couples in the language of behavioral analysis and worked with families to define specific behavioral goals. His initial efforts to help couples were based on operant conditioning and included such techniques as positive reinforcement, shaping, and modeling. Later, he and his colleagues devised a more sophisticated behavioral approach that included aspects of social learning theory and communications theory (Liberman, Wheeler, deVisser, Kuehnel, & Kuehnel, 1980). This more refined focus helped couples recognize and increase their positive interactions while eliminating negative interactions. The approach also focused on problem-solving, building communication skills, and teaching couples how to use contingency contracts in order to negotiate the resolution of persistent problems.

Stuart's early initiatives in marital therapy were described as an operant interpersonal approach. He assumed that, as in exchange theory (Thibaut & Kelley, 1959), the interactions between spouses at any one time were the most rewarding of alternative possibilities. He also believed, like Don Jackson, that successful relationships were based on a **quid pro quo** formula (i.e., something for something). To take advantage of the positive basis of relationships, Stuart proposed that couples make explicit reinforcement contracts with each other that were of a positive nature. He later refined his theory to include an eight-step model in order to accelerate positive behavioral change (Stuart, 1980).

Among the most creative of Stuart's techniques to increase consistent pleasure within marriages is one called **caring days.** In this procedure, one or both marital partners act as if they care about their spouse regardless of the other's action(s). This type of technique, which is at the heart of Stuart's approach, embodies the idea of a "positive risk." It represents a unilateral action that is not dependent on another for success. Stuart has been quite detailed in describing his behavioral theory and methods in couple treatment, as indicated by the caring days contract shown in Figure 7.1.

Overall, behavioral marital therapy typically includes four basic components (Hahlweg, Baucom, & Markman, 1988):

1. *A behavioral analysis of the couple's marital distress.* This analysis is based on interviewing, administering self-report questionnaires, and making behavioral observations.

2. *The establishment of positive reciprocity.* This type of behavior is generated through techniques such as "caring days" and contingency contracts.

3. *Communication skills training.* In this type of training, couples learn to use **"I" statements** to express their feelings. They also learn to stick to here-and-now problems, rather than dwell on the past. Furthermore, they begin to describe their spouse's specific behavior rather than apply a label to it, such as "lazy," "aloof," or "frigid." Finally, in this type of training, couples are taught how to provide positive feedback to their significant other in response to similar behavior from that person.

4. *Training in problem solving.* This component of behavioral marital therapy helps equip couples with new problem-solving skills, such as specifying what they want, negotiating for it, and making a contract.

As mentioned earlier, cognitive-behavioral approaches to working with couples are also strong. For example, Ellis uses rational emotive behavior therapy (REBT) to help couples **dispute irrational thoughts** they have about themselves, their spouses, or their marriages. In this *ABC* procedure, *A* stands for the event, *B* stands for the thought, and *C* stands for the emotion. The event might be, for example, forgetting a spouse's request to get something from the store. The other spouse might react negatively and think, for example, that "he doesn't love me anymore," which could lead to depression or other unhealthy emotions. Through disputation, the therapist could help the spouse and the couple to learn to think about events either neutrally (e.g., "He did not bring home what I requested.") or positively (e.g., "Because my spouse did not get what I requested, I can now ask for more, and I am sure he/she will be more sensitive this time.").

Other methods cognitive-behavioral family therapists use with couples are teaching them to employ rational coping statements, cognitive distraction (thinking of other than negative things), and psychoeducational methods (i.e.,

Bill	Agreements	Jocelyn
9/3 9/4 9/6 9/7 9/8 9/9	Ask how I spent the day.	9/3 9/4 9/6 9/7 9/8 9/9
9/10 9/11 9/12 9/14		9/10 9/12 9/14 9/16
9/17 9/20 9/21		9/20 9/21 9/23
9/3 9/4 9/9	Offer to get the cream or sugar for me.	9/4 9/9
9/10 9/14 9/16		9/12 9/15
9/20 9/21 9/22 9/23		9/23
9/3 9/7 9/9	Listen to "mood music" when we set the clock radio to go to sleep.	9/3 9/7 9/9
9/15		9/15
9/21 9/23		9/21 9/23
9/7 9/8	Hold my hand when we go for walks.	9/7 9/8
9/11		9/11 9/16
9/19		9/19 9/21 9/23
9/9	Put down the paper or your book and look at me when we converse.	9/4 9/6 9/7 9/8
9/14 9/16		9/10 9/13 9/14 9/16
9/23		9/18 9/20 9/21 9/22 9/24
9/4 9/7	Rub my back.	9/5 9/8
9/11 9/12 9/14 9/16		9/10 9/14 9/15
9/21 9/23		9/19
9/3 9/4 9/5 9/7 9/8	Tuck in the sheets and blankets before we go to bed.	9/6 9/9
9/11 9/16		
9/19		9/23
9/3 9/8	Call me during the day.	9/5 9/6 9/7 9/8 9/9
9/15		9/11 9/13 9/14 9/16
9/17		9/18 9/20 9/21 9/22 9/23
9/4 9/6	Offer to play short games with the children when my friends drop in for a few minutes.	9/8
9/13		9/12 9/15
		9/21
9/7	Offer to read the rough drafts of my reports and offer comments.	9/9
9/11 9/16		
9/23		9/20
9/5 9/7 9/8 9/9	Sit down with me when I have coffee even if you don't want any, just for the company.	9/7
9/11 9/14 9/17		9/10 9/13
9/18 9/21		9/23
9/7	Call my folks just to say "hello."	9/9
9/12		
9/20 9/23		9/23
9/6 9/7	Fold the laundry.	9/9
9/15		9/10 9/14 9/15
9/18 9/20 9/23		9/20
9/4 9/7 9/9	Buy me a $1 present.	9/8 9/9
9/13		9/12 9/14
9/18		9/21 9/23

Figure 7.1

Caring days agreement.

From *Helping Couples Change: A Social Learning Approach to Marital Therapy* (p. 200) by R. B. Stuart, 1980, New York: Guilford. Reprinted by permission of the publisher.

reading books, attending workshops, and listening to audio-visual material) (Ellis, 1991, 1993). The psychoeducational method, in which individuals are taught to be more aware of their relationship-related cognitions and the benefits and deficits of these thoughts, shows promise in reducing the divorce rate for participants (O'Leary & Smith, 1991). It also could have a favorable effect on couple and family units (Schwebel & Fine, 1994).

Behavioral Treatment of Sexual Dysfunctioning

The behavioral treatment of sexual dysfunctionality came of age in the United States in the late 1960s and early 1970s with the publication of Masters and Johnson's *Human Sexual Response* (1966) and *Human Sexual Inadequacy* (1970). Prior to these publications, "people with sexual dysfunctions relied primarily on folk cures or saw psychodynamically oriented therapists, who offered long-term insight-oriented treatment with questionable results" (Piercy & Sprenkle, 1986, p. 94).

Masters and Johnson (1970) were not original in all of their contributions, but from their research and clinical observations, they delineated **four phases of sexual responsiveness:** excitement, plateau, orgasm, and resolution. They also discovered the importance of learning in the remediation of sexual dysfunctioning and the importance of behavioral techniques. In their approach to the treatment of sexual dysfunctionality, techniques are tailored to specific problems. In almost all cases, however, couples are taught to relax and enjoy touching and being touched. Then, through *in vivo desensitization,* they learn how to gradually become more intimate with one another and how to feel comfortable either asking for sex or refusing it. For couples who have specific problems, specialized treatments are used. For example, in treating premature ejaculation, the **squeeze technique** (in which the woman learns to stimulate and stop the ejaculation urge in a man through physically stroking and firmly grasping his penis) is used. Other treatments, such as the **teasing technique** (in which a woman starts and stops stimulating a man) are also employed to overcome performance anxiety.

Masters and Johnson stressed the conjoint treatment of couples using a dual-sex therapy team. A basic assumption in the Masters and Johnson approach is that there is no such thing as an uninvolved partner in a relationship in which some form of sexual inadequacy exists. To tailor a treatment plan for a couple, Masters and Johnson (1966, 1970) took an extensive sexual history on each partner, a practice that is still followed. Their work from beginning to end is systemic.

In addition to Masters and Johnson, Helen Singer Kaplan (1974) developed direct behavioral treatment strategies to work with couples and combined this approach with psychoanalytic techniques. Unlike Masters and Johnson, Kaplan's approach employs an outpatient treatment practice. According to Kaplan, couple sexual dysfunctioning can result from one force or a combination of forces, for example, intrapsychic conflict (e.g., guilt, trauma, or shame), interpersonal couple conflict (e.g., marital discord, distrust), and **anxiety** (e.g., pressure to please, fear of failure).

Joseph LoPiccolo (1978) and associates have also reported success with behavioral sex therapy techniques. In analyzing the success of heterosexual couples in behavioral sex therapy, Heiman, LoPiccolo, and LoPiccolo (1981) reported that behavioral approaches had the following elements in common:

- the reduction of performance anxiety
- sex education including the use of sexual techniques
- skill training in communications
- attitude change methodologies

Overall, the behavioral treatment of sexual dysfunctioning is rich in pragmatic and specific techniques. It includes the modification of thoughts (e.g., attitudes, beliefs), as well as behaviors.

Functional Family Therapy

For functional family therapists, all behavior is adaptive and serves a function. Behaviors represent an effort by the family to meet needs in personal and interpersonal relationships. Ultimately, behaviors help family members achieve one of three interpersonal states (Alexander & Parsons, 1982):

1. *Contact/closeness (merging).* In the contact/closeness state, family members are drawn together (e.g., in their concern over the delinquent behavior of a juvenile).
2. *Distance/independence (separating).* In this state, family members learn to stay away from each other for fear of fighting.
3. *A combination of 1 and 2 (midpointing).* In this situation, family members fluctuate in their emotional reactions to each other so that individuals are both drawn toward and repelled from each other.

Functional family therapy, which is systemic, is a three stage process. In the first stage, **assessment,** "the focus is on the function that the behavioral sequences serve" (Fenell & Weinhold, 1989, p. 167). The question is, Do behavioral sequences promote closeness, create distances, or help the family achieve a task? The therapist determines this through gathering information about the family both by asking questions and by observing.

The second stage of therapy involves change. The purpose is to help the family become more functional. It is carried out by:

- clarifying relationship dynamics
- interrelating thoughts, feelings, and behaviors of family members
- interpreting the functions of current family behavior
- relabeling behavior so as to alleviate blame
- discussing how the removal of a behavior will affect the family
- shifting the treatment from one individual to the entire family

The third and final stage of functional family therapy, maintenance, focuses on educating the family and training them in skills that will be useful in dealing with future difficulties. Specific skills taught during this stage of therapy are those dealing with effective communication, team-building, and behavioral management (e.g, contracting).

Treatment Techniques

As a rule, behavioral and cognitive-behavioral family therapists use a variety of learning theory techniques to bring about change in families. Originally devised for treating individuals, these techniques are modified and applied to problems encountered by families. Among the most well known of these procedures are positive reinforcement, extinction, shaping, desensitization, contingency contracts, and cognitive/behavior modification. These techniques and others are described in the following sections. They are usually applied in combination so that family members learn individually and/or collectively how to give recognition and approval for desired behavior, instead of rewarding maladaptive actions.

"A review of behavioral-family-therapy practice reveals that a relatively small number of interventions tend to form the basis for most therapeutic plans across a broad range of settings. They include education, communication and problem-solving training, operant conditioning approaches, and contingency management" (Falloon, 1991, p. 81).

Education includes the use of didactic lectures, visual aids, books, handouts, and intimate discussions. These educational methods are intended to help family members see the rationale behind the strategies employed.

Communication and problem-solving strategies and techniques are intended to help families develop mutually enhancing social exchanges. "Instruction, modeling, and positive reinforcement (e.g., praise) are used to enhance communication skills until a level of competence has been achieved that satisfies the family and therapist" (Falloon, 1991, p. 82). Problem solving is directed at the resolution of conflict within the family.

Operant conditioning is employed mostly in parent/child relationships. "The most common approach involves teaching parents to use shaping and time out procedures to increase the desirable behavior patterns in children" (Falloon, 1991, p. 83).

Contracting is used when family interactions have reached a severe level of hostility. Contracts build in rewards for behaving in a certain manner. A **token economy** is one type of contract; but in many cases, more sophisticated ways of earning points and reinforcing appropriate behavior are used.

The following sections highlight more specific techniques used in the four behavioral and cognitive-behavior family therapy approaches. Almost all of these techniques are used frequently in various forms of behavioral and cognitive-behavioral family therapy. They have the common characteristics of being operationally definable, precise, and measurable. They are applicable to psychological and, in some cases, sexual situations. Furthermore, they foster change through having clients try new forms of acting. Overall, they are able to bring about fairly rapid and significant change in a short period of time. (Miechenbaum's self-instructional training and stress inoculation techniques are particularly suited for children.)

Classical Conditioning

Classical conditioning is the oldest form of behaviorism. In it, a stimulus that is originally neutral is paired up with another event to elicit certain emotions through association. In the case of Pavlov's dogs, the ringing of a bell was paired with the presenting of food so that the sound of the bell elicited a salutary response in the dogs. In families, classical conditioning is used to associate a person with a gratifying behavior, such as a pat on the back or a kind word. For instance, when a preschool child gets dressed, a parent might gently touch and praise him or her immediately after the task is completed. Through such a timely and rewarding interaction, the child may come to view the parent in a different and more positive way, that is, one that represents a pleasant association. Therefore, the relationship becomes more valued.

Coaching

In **coaching,** a therapist helps individuals, couples, or families make appropriate responses by giving them verbal instructions. For example, the therapist might say: "Sally, when you want John to make eye contact with you and he is looking around, gently touch him on the knee. John, that will be your signal to look directly at Sally." Just as athletes excel through coaching, individuals, couples, and families do best when they are informed about what to do and then have an opportunity to practice their new responses.

Contingency Contracting

In **contingency contracting** (see Figure 7.2) "a specific, usually written schedule or contract [describes] the terms for the trading or exchange of behaviors and reinforcers between two or more individuals" (Sauber, L'Abate, & Weeks, 1985, p. 34). One action is contingent, or dependent, on another. For example, a child and her parent may write up an agreement whereby the daughter will receive an allowance of $5.00 a week upon taking the garbage out every day after supper. The way this type of contract is assessed is known as contingency management.

Extinction

Extinction is the process by which previous **reinforcers** of an action are withdrawn so that behavior returns to its original level. For example, a child is ignored by a parent when having a temper tantrum. Similarly, a spouse may not be rewarded by his mate for saying unkind remarks. In almost all cases of extinction, it is important that a replacement behavior be positively reinforced to take the place of the behavior that is being extinguished. For example, in the case of the child or the spouse just mentioned, attention should be given to appropriate or pleasing behaviors.

Positive Reinforcement

A **positive reinforcer** is usually a material (e.g., food, money, or medals) or a social action (e.g., a smile or praise) that increases desired behaviors. For a reinforcer to be positive, the person involved must be willing to work for it. For example, children are often willing to perform certain actions when the reward is money, candy, or tokens. Adults may be prone to work for verbal or physical recognitions such as praise or smiles.

Contingency Contract
week one
(must earn 5 points for a reward)

	make bed	clean room	hang up clothes	pick up toys	set table	read a book	Goal
George	✓	✓		✓	✓	✓	Pizza
Will		✓		✓			Baseball game
Ann	✓	✓	✓	✓	✓	✓	Spend-the-night party

Figure 7.2
Contingency contract.

Quid Pro Quo

Literally translated, the Latin phrase, **quid pro quo,** means "something for something." Behavioral marital contracts are often based on quid pro quo—that is, a spouse agrees to do something as long as the other spouse does something comparable. For example, in maintaining a house, one spouse may agree to do the dishes if the other does the laundry. In a quid pro quo arrangement, everyone wins. When quid pro quo arrangements are in written form, they often take the form of contingency contracts.

Reciprocity

The concept of **reciprocity** involves "the likelihood that two people will reinforce each other at approximately equitable rates over time" (Piercy & Sprenkle, 1986, p. 76). Many marital behavior therapists view marriage as based on this principle (Stuart, 1969). When spouses are not reinforced reciprocally, one of them will often leave the relationship either emotionally or physically. For example, if a spouse feels he or she is doing most of the couple's work, such as paying the bills and keeping the house, but is not receiving adequate appreciation, he or she may stop taking care of these duties.

Shaping

The process of learning in small, gradual steps is called **shaping.** It is often referred to as "successive approximation" (Bandura, 1969). For example, during potty training, children are reinforced in small steps from "running to the potty," to "pulling down their pants," to "sitting on the potty," to "having a bowel movement in the potty." Gradually, children put all of these actions together. In a similar fashion, couples learn to say and act in routine ways that help them bond. For instance, he fixes breakfast in the morning while she takes a shower and gets dressed; then they share a meal and conversation together; then she fixes his lunch and starts the car while he gets dressed; and, finally, they leave for work together.

Systematic Desensitization

The process of **systematic desensitization** is one in which a person's dysfunctional anxiety is reduced or eliminated through pairing it with incompatible behavior, such as muscular or mental relaxation. This is a gradual procedure in which progressively higher levels of anxiety are treated one step at a time (Wolpe, 1969). This treatment is one of the main approaches to several forms of sexual disorders, such as vaginismus. It may also be used to help individuals feel less anxious about stating what they need from other members of the family. In all such instances, a hierarchy of troublesome behaviors is set up and worked through (see Figure 7.3).

Time Out

The process of **time out** involves the removal of persons (most often children) from an environment in which they have been reinforced for certain actions. Isolation, or time out, from reinforcement for a limited amount of time (approximately 5 minutes) results in the cessation of the targeted action. For example, a child who is biting his sibling during play has to sit down in a separate room and face a wall for 5 minutes each time it happens.

"Time outs can be used to shape the behaviors of normal children as well as the maladaptive behaviors of problem children. Time outs are best accompanied by a retraining program in which rewards are given when the undesirable behavior is absent for an agreed-upon period of time or if a competing new desirable behavior occurs several times a day" (Thomas, 1992, p. 288).

Charting

The procedure of **charting** involves asking a client or clients to keep an accurate record of the problematic behavior (Katkin, 1978). The idea is to get the family member to establish a **baseline** (i.e., a recording of the occurrence of targeted behaviors before an intervention is made). From this baseline, modifications can be made to reduce problem behaviors. For instance, a couple might

Targeted Behavior: Speaking to others without being anxious	
Event	*Anxiety Rating*
Speaking in public to a large audience (20 people or more)	100%
Speaking in public to a small audience, e.g., my scout troop	90%
Speaking with a group of strangers	80%
Speaking casually with someone in a public place	70%
Speaking to someone at a social event	55%
Speaking casually with someone when we are alone	40%
Speaking with my friends when I have an idea	30%
Speaking with my friends in casual conversation	15%
Speaking with my family	5%
Being alone	0%

Figure 7.3
Hierarchy of a troublesome behavior.

be asked to make a chart of the number of fights they have a day and the type of fights that occur. Similarly, a child may be asked to keep a chart of the number of fights he or she has with parents and when they occur.

Premack Principle

The **Premack Principle** is a behavioral intervention in which family members must first do less pleasant tasks before they are allowed to engage in pleasurable activities (Premack, 1965). For example, a child having problems with school work would be required to do his or her homework before going outside to play. This technique may have as a by-product closer parent/child relationships because parents serve as reinforcers for their children's task accomplishment.

Disputing Irrational Thoughts

Disputing irrational thoughts through the use of an *ABC* format (*A* stands for the event, *B* stands for the thought, and *C* stands for the emotion) was discussed previously. It is crucial to realize that in disputing—for example, with couples—the absurdity of irrational thoughts is often stressed by cognitive-behavioral family therapists with remarks such as "Where is it written that you should have all your needs filled in marriage?" (Ellis et al., 1989). It is hoped that through disputing, couples and families will develop more rational thoughts and behaviors.

Thought Stopping

The technique of **thought stopping** is used when a family member unproductively obsesses about an event or person. The therapist teaches the individual, or even in unusual cases the whole family, how to quit this repetitive and unhealthy behavior. This is done through inviting the person or persons involved to begin ruminating on a certain thought, for example, "My life is unfair." In the midst of this rumination, the therapist yells, "Stop!" This unexpected response disrupts the person's or family's thought process. Instruction is then given to those involved on how to move from an external disruption like the one they just had to an internal process. As in the case of disputation, neutral or healthy thoughts are substituted for those that have been nonproductive or unhealthy.

Self-Instructional Training

Self-instructional training is a form of self-management that focuses on people instructing themselves (Meichenbaum, 1977). It is assumed that self-instruction affects behavior and behavioral change. Thus, problems may be based on maladaptive self-statements. In self-instructional training, a self-statement can serve as a practical clue in recalling a desirable behavioral sequence, or it can interrupt automatic behaviors or cognitive thought chains and thereby encourage more adaptive coping strategies. In families, spouses can use this approach in dealing with each other; however, it is more often employed in helping impulsive children "modulate their impulsivity through deliberate and task-oriented 'self-talk'" (Schwebel & Fine, 1994, p. 26).

Modeling and Role Playing

Modeling and **role playing** can take many forms (Bandura, 1977). In certain situations, family members might be asked to "**act as if**" they were the person they wanted to be ideally. In other cases, family members might practice a number of behaviors to see which work best. Feedback and corrective action, which are a part of modeling and role playing, can be given by the therapist and/or other family members.

"Shame attack," a process within role playing, occurs when a family member does something he or she has previously dreaded (Ellis, 1991), for example, asking for an allowance. Individuals who use this technique find that when they do not get what they asked for, they are not worse off for having asked. Similarly, family members may steel themselves for what lies ahead through a **stress inoculation** (Meichenbaum, 1985). In this process, members break down potentially stressful events into manageable units that they can think about and handle through problem-solving techniques. Then the units are linked together so that the entire possible event can be envisioned and handled appropriately.

Role of the Therapist

In behavioral and cognitive-behavioral family therapies, the therapist is the expert and teacher (Schwebel & Fine, 1992). He or she helps families identify dysfunctional behaviors and then works with these families to set up behavioral and cognitive-behavioral management programs that will assist them in bringing about change. Part of the process of teaching new behaviors to families includes modeling, giving corrective feedback, and learning how to assess behavior modification.

To be effective, the therapist has to learn to play many roles and be flexible. This process has been described as the Anatomy of Intervention Model (AIM) (Alexander, 1988). AIM delineates five phases in therapy:

1. Introduction
2. Assessment

3. Motivation

4. Behavior change

5. Termination

"Each phase has different goals, central tasks, needed skills of the therapist, and therapeutic activities or techniques" (Thomas, 1992, p. 289). In addition to utilizing structural skills to achieve the goals of each phase, a therapist must also be able to exhibit relationship skills such as warmth, humor, non-blaming, and self-disclosure. From a behavioral and cognitive-behavioral perspective, the effective treatment of a family is complex.

Cognitive-behavioral family therapists, especially concentrate on modifying or changing family members' cognitions as well as their interactions (Schwebel & Fine, 1992). For instance, a negative thought by a son about his father might be: "He cares more about his work than he does me." Such a cognition might be modified to: "He cares about me, but he has to work long hours and sometimes cannot give me the type of attention I want." To make changes in thoughts and consequently behaviors, cognitive-behavioral family therapists spend more time discussing issues with family members than do strictly behavioral family therapists.

Being a behavioral or cognitive-behavioral family therapist means taking an active part in designing and implementing specific strategies to help families. Such a process can help members eliminate dysfunctional behaviors and replace them with more effective ways of relating. Behavioral and cognitive-behavioral family therapists must have persistence, patience, knowledge of learning theory, and specificity in working with family members. Therapeutic interventions require a great deal of energy and investment.

Process and Outcome

If behavioral and cognitive-behavioral family therapy is successful, family members will learn how to modify, change, or increase certain behaviors and/or cognitions in order to function more effectively. Simultaneously, they will learn how to eliminate or decrease maladaptive or undesirable behaviors, including negative thoughts. Behavioral and cognitive-behavioral family therapies stress the employment of specific techniques aimed at particularly important actions. For example, a behavioral approach used in marital therapy might concentrate on communication skills in which a couple is taught to listen, to make requests using "I" statements, to give positive feedback, to use immediate reinforcement, and to clarify through questioning the meaning of verbal and nonverbal behaviors (Stuart, 1980).

Behavioral family therapy has especially focused on increasing parenting skills, facilitating positive couple communication and interaction, and improving sexual behaviors. Cognitive-behavioral family therapy is most powerful in helping families deal with stress (Freeman & Zaken-Greenberg, 1989), addiction (Schlesinger, 1988), and adult sexual dysfunctions (Walen & Perlmutter, 1988). In practice there is often a blending of behavioral and cognitive-behavioral techniques.

By the end of treatment, couples and individuals should be able to modify their own maladaptive behaviors and/or cognitions. They should also be able to lower their anxieties about troublesome situations by using relaxation procedures, such as desensitization or thought stopping.

Unique Aspects of Behavioral and Cognitive-Behavioral Approaches

Behavioral and cognitive-behavioral family therapies, like other therapeutic approaches, have both unique and universal points. Practitioners who are considering using these approaches need to be sure they are aware of the commonalities and differences imbedded in their theory and practice. In this way, they can assure themselves and others of the best possible outcome.

Emphases

One unique characteristic of behavioral and cognitive-behavioral family therapies involves the theory behind these approaches. The behavioral and cognitive-behavioral approaches utilize learning theory, which is a well-formulated and highly researched way of working with people. Learning theory focuses on pinpointing problem behaviors and making use of behavioral and cognitive techniques, such as setting up contingency contracts, reinforcement, punishment, and extinction.

Another emphasis of behavioral and cognitive-behavioral family therapy approaches is research. The results of applying learning theory to families indicate that such a process gives parents a management tool that works at home and has a carryover effect at school. Behavioral family therapy aimed at one child's dysfunctional behavior seems to generalize in many cases so as to positively influence interactions with other children, especially siblings. Parental self-esteem and the family's ability to function seems to adequately improve as well (Gurman, Kniskern, & Pinsof, 1985).

A third aspect of these approaches involves continued evolvement. Behavioral family therapy has evolved from a focus on parent management to a focus on the family as a system (i.e., functional family therapy). In addition, behavioral family therapy has incorporated many ideas from cognitive approaches in its handling of families (Falloon, 1988). Because of their considerable flexibility, behavioral and cognitive-behavioral family therapies are able to focus on a variety of problems and concerns, from promoting changes within individuals in families to altering family interaction styles. Likewise, the procedures and processes within behavioral and cognitive-behavioral family therapies have influenced other approaches, such as the structuralists in their treatment of anorexia nervosa (Minuchin, Rosman, & Baker, 1978).

A fourth unique quality of behavioral and cognitive-behavioral family therapies is their short-term treatment. Therapists who work from these perspectives "take presenting problems seriously and examine them in their interpersonal context" (Fish, 1988, p. 15). Thus, on a more microscopic level, the therapist is able to break down the problem into definable parts and then target strategies to either teach skills or extinguish behaviors associated with difficulties.

A fifth emphasis of behavioral and cognitive-behavioral family therapies is that they reject the medical model of abnormal behavior. "Behavior therapists believe many problems result from inadequate personal, social, or work-related skills . . . [and that] inadequately skilled clients need training" (Fish, 1988, p. 15). Time is not spent on looking for biological or chemical causes of behavior or cognition, nor is time spent on examining the history of the client. Because of an immediate focus, problems can be addressed more directly and efficiently without labeling (Atwood, 1992).

Overall, "behavioral family therapy has been demonstrated to have specific benefits in the treatment of conduct disorders of childhood and adolescence" (Falloon, 1991, p. 88). It, combined with cognitive processes, is useful in the management of many adult mental disorders, such as depression. Overall, behavioral and cognitive-behavioral family therapies can be useful on a number of levels as long as they are employed as part of a comprehensive treatment plan that takes into account the uniqueness of families.

Comparison with Other Theories

Compared with other ways of working with families, behavioral and cognitive-behavioral family therapies are less systemic. The orientation of learning theory, on which these approaches are based, is to bring about linear changes in individuals or subunits of the family. Such a perspective often hinders the introduction of a complete family change process. For example, in behavior parent training, a child may be viewed as "the problem" that the therapist is "to fix." With such a view, modification of behaviors and/or cognitions that would benefit everyone in the family, such as learning to communicate more clearly, are not addressed.

Another distinction of behavioral family therapy is that some behavioral family therapists do not focus on the affective components of behavior, such as feelings. Instead, they look primarily at behaviors and secondarily at thoughts (i.e, cognitive-behaviors) (Piercy & Sprenkle, 1986). Thus, some family members who have been through this type of treatment may act properly but not feel or think differently. In such cases, the operational procedures are successful, but a price is paid in regard to helping the recipients of the services access their emotions and thoughts.

A third distinct aspect of behavioral and cognitive-behavioral family therapies compared with others is their preciseness. Some therapists who use these approaches think they need to be rigid in their application. Their lack of spontaneity and dependence on techniques may result in their losing rapport with families. In such cases, both the family and therapist end up becoming frustrated, and the therapy is not as effective as it might be otherwise (Wood & Jacobson, 1990).

A fourth aspect of behavioral and cognitive-behavioral family therapies compared with other approaches is the consideration of historical data. Although it is true that as behaviorists Masters and Johnson (1970) emphasize the importance of sexual histories, their approach is more the exception than the rule. By not attending to the past, users of behavioral and cognitive-behavioral family theory may misunderstand family patterns and dynamics. Once a symptomatic behavior is eliminated, another one may appear out of habit or tradition. For example, alcoholism may be brought under control while workaholism emerges.

A final comparable dimension of the behavioral and cognitive-behavioral perspective in family therapy is that these approaches generally stress family action over family insight. As a result, too much emphasis may be given to the employment of methods that facilitate change without insuring family members' comprehension. For instance, in a situation in which a child has been acting out, parents might learn to use behavioral techniques, such as time out; but they might not comprehend the dynamics that led to the child's misbehavior in the first place.

CASE ILLUSTRATION

THE BROWN FAMILY

Bill Brown, age 50, has reached a stalemate with his wife, Amy, age 47. They are a dual career couple and have been highly successful financially. Yet Bill is tired of being on the road three nights a week and wants to take an early retirement. Amy, who loves her in-home computer job, cannot imagine such a situation. Bill, a former football athlete, has always had plenty of energy and drive. His early retirement would mean he would be around the house more and probably interfere with her business and routine. As an only child, Amy values her space and privacy. Now that Bill, Jr., age 17, is ready to go to college, she thinks that her husband should "stick it out" for at least 4 or 5 more years for the good of the family.

Bill disagrees. He has a history of heart trouble, and his father died of a heart attack at age 62 during Bill's senior year of college. He wants to quit his job now. He believes that if he stays on much longer, he will become very unhappy and distressed. Open fights that last late into the night began about a month ago. No one in the family is saying anything constructive to anyone else. The tension is as thick as an early morning fog.

Conceptualization of Family: Behavioral and Cognitive-Behavioral Perspective

The Browns both have strong beliefs about what should occur. Yet, they lack the proper skills to negotiate and settle their dispute. Bill thinks he has worked hard and deserves a rest. He also thinks he will endanger his health by continuing in his present position. Amy thinks if he quits now, he will get in her way and, in addition, not be able to help their son through college. Neither one is reinforcing the other. The result is disruptive behavior and fights that are growing in intensity.

Process of Treatment: Behavioral and Cognitive-Behavioral Family Therapies

To help the Browns, a behavioral or cognitive-behavioral family therapist would work with the couple to set up a quid pro quo relationship. This would most likely mean drawing up a contingency contract that would describe the terms for exchanging behaviors and reinforcers. For example, if Bill is going to give up his job, he might agree to do it gradually, instead of all at once. Furthermore, regardless of the manner in which he quit his job, he would come to an agreement with Amy as to how much time per day he would spend around the house and with her. On Amy's part, she would be explicit about what time she would like to have Bill at home. Beliefs as well as wishes would be aired.

Once decisions regarding Bill's job and time together were settled, the couple would concentrate with the therapist on the extinction of negative behaviors, such as fights and irrational thoughts. For instance, they might use thought stopping or disputation to deal with the underlying cognitions that lead to their conflict. At the same time, the couple would work on the establishment of reinforcing behaviors, for example, establishing enough time alone for Amy and adequate time together for Bill. Specific rewards could be built into the contingency contract, and the contract itself could be prominently displayed on the refrigerator or some other mutually agreed upon setting.

To help the couple and the family as a whole, the therapist might need to help shape their behaviors toward one another and give them a means to disengage from negative interactions, such as the use of time out. Through all of this action, the couple and therapist would chart the behaviors displayed and refine the process of working with each other on a weekly basis.

Summary and Conclusion

Behavioral and cognitive-behavioral family therapies are relatively recent phenomena that are based on one of the most thoroughly researched approaches in the helping professions—learning theory. The origin of the theory can be traced back to the beginning of the twentieth century. It included such luminaries as Ivan Pavlov, John B. Watson, and B. F. Skinner.

Behavioral family therapy has four basic forms: behavioral parent training, behavioral marital therapy, treatment of sexual dysfunctionality, and functional family therapy. These emphases often utilize cognitive-behavioral methods. All except the last approach are linear and stress individual or dyadic relationships. Many of the interventions used in behavioral and cognitive-behavioral family therapies are the same as those employed in individual treatment. Reinforcement, shaping, modeling, role playing, thought stopping, and extinction are common. However, aspects of behavioral and cognitive-behavioral family therapies also include novel implementations such as contingency contracts, unilateral contracts, and behaviors based on the principle of quid pro quo.

In their therapeutic role, both the behaviorist and cognitive-behaviorist are the experts, teachers, and trainers. The instructions of the therapist are usually carried out by an individual, a couple, or a family, and are carefully monitored. Overall, the therapist is quite powerful and rewards positive behaviors and thoughts as often as possible. In his or her central role, the therapist helps clients learn how to reinforce themselves as well.

If all goes well during the treatment process, there are measurable results. Traditionally, this has included the emergence of overt behaviors such as parent/child interactions. In more recent times, treatment has focused on the modification of cognitive processes as well, such as the elimination of negative self-statements.

At its best, behavioral and cognitive-behavioral family therapies are concrete and readily applicable to helping parents, couples, and families change. A branch of this approach, functional family therapy, is systemic. The basic concepts on which treatment is based have been extensive and well researched. Of all the family therapies, behavioral and cognitive-behavioral family approaches are the most scientific.

On the other hand, behavioral and cognitive-behavioral family therapies, for the most part, still continue to rely too heavily on a linear and limited view of families. These approaches assume that if treatment is applied to one unit in the family and to symptoms, the other aspects of the family will change.

SUMMARY TABLE

Behavioral and Cognitive-Behavioral Family Therapies

Major Theorists
B. F. Skinner
John Watson
Richard Stuart
Norman Epstein
Neil Jacobson
Gerald Patterson
Robert Weiss
Gayola Margolin
Albert Ellis
Albert Bandura
Walter Mischel
William Masters
Virginia Johnson
Joseph Wolpe
Aaron Beck
Donald Meichenbaum
Helen Singer Kaplan
Ed Katkin

Underlying Premises
Behavior is maintained or eliminated by consequences.
Maladaptive behaviors can be unlearned or modified. Adaptive behaviors
can be learned.
Likewise, cognitions are either rational or irrational. They can be modified
and, as a result, bring about a change in couple or family behaviors and
interactions.

Role of the Therapist
The therapist uses direct and careful assessment and intervention. He or
she is a teacher and an expert, as well as a reinforcer. Presenting problems are the focus.

Unit of Treatment
In behavioral family therapy, the focus is on parent training, behavioral
marriage therapy, couple communication, and the treatment of sexual
dysfunctions. Cognitive-behavioral family therapy also emphasizes
working with those under stress in the same ways.
Dyads and individuals are seen more than families. The emphasis is on
dyadic interactions, except in functional family therapy.

Goals of Treatment

In behavioral family therapy, the emphasis is to bring about behavioral changes by modifying the antecedents or consequences of an action. Special attention is paid to modifying the consequences. Emphasis is on elimination of undesirable behavior and acceleration of positive behavior. Teaching social skills and preventing problems from reoccurring is stressed, too. Promoting competence in individuals and/or couples and fostering an understanding of the dynamics of behavior is highlighted.

In cognitive-behavioral family therapy, the focus is on modifying irrational or unproductive beliefs and the behaviors that go with them.

Therapeutic Techniques

Behaviorists and cognitive-behaviorists rely primarily on:

- Operant conditioning
- Classical conditioning
- Social learning theory
- Cognitive-behavioral strategies

Techniques include:

- Systematic desensitization
- Positive reinforcement
- Intermittent reinforcement
- Generalization
- Fading
- Extinction
- Modeling
- Reciprocity
- Punishment
- Token economies
- Quid pro quo exchanges
- Charting
- Problem-solving training
- Rational coping statements
- Reframing
- Cognitive distraction
- Psychoeducational methods

Unique Aspects of the Approach

Behavioral and cognitive-behavioral family therapies emphasize:

- straightforwardness with attention paid to observations, measurements, and use of the scientific theory
- the treatment of presenting symptoms and problems
- teaching new social skills and eliminating dysfunctional ones
- positive controls and enlightened education procedures rather than punishment

- (with regard to behaviorism) a simple and pragmatic intervention with a variety of workable techniques, such as use of contracts, or (with regard to cognitive-behaviorism) a straightforward approach that can be pragmatically employed
- research data that accompany these approaches and measure their effectiveness
- short-term treatment

Comparison with Other Theories

Many behaviorists operate from a linear perspective and work on individual rather than system concerns. The exception is functional family therapy. Cognitive-behavioral therapy, for example, REBT, is somewhat systemic, but primarily linear.

Behaviorism and cognitive-behaviorism disregard the use of historical data in the treatment of families.

Some behavioral and cognitive-behavioral procedures are mechanical and may become sterile or inefficient when used by certain practitioners.

Some critics of behavioral and cognitive-behavioral family therapies claim there is too much emphasis on action in these approaches and not enough attention to family dynamics.

Behaviorism does not focus attention on affective responses or deal with emotional problems. Cognitive-behaviorism is more attuned to affect and emotion but emphasizes that affect is dependent on thoughts.

References

Alexander, J. F. (1988). Phases of family therapy process: A framework for clinicians and researchers. In L. C. Wynne (Ed.), *The state of the art in family therapy research: Controversies and recommendations* (pp. 175–188). New York: Family Process Press.

Alexander, J., & Parsons, B. V. (1982). *Functional family therapy.* Pacific Grove, CA: Brooks/Cole.

Atwood, J. D. (1992). The field today. In J. D. Atwood (Ed.), *Family therapy: A systemic behavioral approach* (pp. 29–58). Chicago: Nelson-Hall.

Baucom, D. H., & Epstein, N. (1990). *Cognitive-behavioral marital therapy.* New York: Brunner/Mazel.

Bandura, A. (1969). *Principles of behavior modification.* New York: Holt, Rinehart, & Winston.

Bandura, A. (1977). *Social learning theory.* Englewood Cliffs, NJ: Prentice-Hall.

Bandura, A., & Walters, R. H. (1963). *Social learning and personality development.* New York: Rinehart & Winston.

Barker, P. (1986). *Basic family therapy* (2nd ed.). New York: Oxford.

Barton, C., & Alexander, J. F. (1981). Functional family therapy. In A. S. Gurman & D. P. Kniskern (Eds.), *Handbook of family therapy* (pp. 403–443). New York: Brunner/Mazel.

Beck, A. T. (1976). *Cognitive therapy and the emotional disorders.* New York: International Universities Press.

DiGuiseppe, R. (1988). A cognitive-behavioral approach to the treatment of conduct disorder children and adolescents. In N. Epstein, S. E. Schlesinger, & W. Dryden (Eds.), *Cognitive-behavioral therapy with families* (pp. 183–214). New York: Brunner/Mazel.

Ellis, A. (1985). *Overcoming resistance: Rational-emotive therapy with difficult clients*. New York: Springer.

Ellis, A. (1991). Rational-emotive family therapy. In A. M. Horne & J. L. Passmore (Eds.), *Family counseling and therapy* (2nd ed., pp. 403–434). Itasca, IL: F. E. Peacock.

Ellis, A. (1993). The rational-emotive therapy (RET) approach to marriage and family therapy. *The Family Journal, 1,* 292–307.

Ellis, A., Sichel, J. L. , Yeager, R. J., DiMattia, D. J., & DiGuiseppe, R. (1989). *Rational-emotive couple therapy*. New York: Pergamon.

Epstein, N., Schlesinger, S. E., & Dryden, W. (1988). Cognitive- behavioral family therapy: Summary and future directions. In N. Epstein, S. E. Schlesinger, & W. Dryden (Eds.), *Cognitive-behavioral therapy with families* (pp. 361–366). New York: Brunner/Mazel.

Falloon, I. R. (1988). *Handbook of behavioral family therapy*. New York: Guilford.

Falloon, I. R. H. (1991). Behavioral family therapy. In A. S. Gurman & D. P. Kniskern (Eds.), *Handbook of family therapy* (Vol. II, pp. 65–95). New York: Brunner/Mazel.

Fenell, D. L., & Weinhold, B. K. (1989). *Counseling families*. Denver, CO: Love.

Fish, J. M. (1988, July/August). Reconciling the irreconcilable. *Family Therapy Networker, 12,* 15.

Freeman, A., & Zaken-Greenberg, F. (1989). A cognitive-behavioral approach. In C. R. Figley (Ed.), *Treating stress in families* (pp. 97–121). New York: Brunner/Mazel.

Gladding, S.T. (1991). *The fight*. Unpublished manuscript.

Goldiamond, I. (1965). Self-control procedures in personal behavior problems. *Psychological Reports, 17,* 851–868.

Gordon, S. B., & Davidson, N. (1981). Behavioral parent training. In A. S. Gurman & D. P. Kniskern (Eds.), *Handbook of family therapy*. New York: Brunner/Mazel.

Gurman, A. S., Kniskern, D. P., & Pinsof, W. N. (1985). Research on the process and outcome of family therapy. In S. L. Garfield & A. E. Bergin (Eds.), *Handbook of psychotherapy and behavior change* (3rd ed., pp. 525–623). New York: Wiley.

Hahlweg, K., Baucom, D. H., & Markman, H. (1988). Recent advances in therapy and prevention. In I. R. H. Falloon (Ed.), *Handbook of behavioral family therapy*. New York: Guilford Press.

Heiman, J. R., LoPiccolo, L., & LoPiccolo, J. (1981). The treatment of sexual dysfunction. In A. S. Gurman & D. P. Kniskern (Eds.), *Handbook of family therapy*. New York: Brunner/Mazel.

Horne, A. (1991). Social learning family therapy. In A. M. Horne & J. L. Passmore (Eds.), *Family counseling and therapy* (2nd ed., pp. 463–496). Itasca, IL: F. E. Peacock.

Jacobson, N. S., Gottman, J. M., & Wu Shortt, J. (1995). The distinction between Type I and Type II batterers—Further considerations. *Journal of Family Psychology, 9,* 272–279.

Kaplan, H. S. (1974). *The new sex therapy*. New York: Quadrangle Books.

Katkin, E. S. (1978). Charting as a multipurpose treatment intervention in family therapy. *Family Process, 17,* 465–468.

Lazarus, A. A. (1968). Behavior therapy and group marriage counseling. *Journal of the American Society of Medicine and Dentistry, 15,* 49–56.

Liberman, R. P. (1970). Behavioral approaches to family and couple therapy. *American Journal of Orthopsychiatry, 40,* 106–118.

Liberman, R. P., Wheeler, E., deVisser, L. A. J. M., Kuehnel, J., & Kuehnel, T. (1980). *Handbook of marital therapy: A positive approach to helping troubled relationships*. New York: Plenum.

LoPiccolo, J. (1978). Direct treatment of sexual dysfunction. In J. LoPiccolo & L. LoPiccolo (Eds.), *Handbook of sex therapy*. New York: Plenum.

Masters, W. H., & Johnson, V. E. (1966). *Human sexual response*. Boston: Little, Brown.

Masters, W. H., & Johnson, V. E. (1970). *Human sexual inadequacy*. Boston: Little, Brown.

Meichenbaum, D. H. (1977). *Cognitive-behavior modification: An integrative approach*. New York: Plenum.

Meichenbaum, D. H. (1985). *Stress inoculation training*. New York: Pergamon.

Minuchin, S., Rosman, B. L., & Baker, L. (1978). *Psychosomatic families*. Cambridge, MA: Harvard University Press.

Nichols, M. P., & Schwartz, R. C. (1995). *Family therapy* (3rd ed.). Boston: Allyn & Bacon.

O'Leary, K. D., & Smith, D.A. (1991). Marital interactions. *Annual Review of Psychology, 42,* 191–212.

Patterson, G. R. (1975). *Families: Applications of social learning to family life.* Champaign, IL: Research Press.

Patterson, G. R., & Brodsky, A. (1966). A behavior modification programme for a child with multiple behavior problems. *Journal of Child Psychology and Psychiatry, 7,* 277–295.

Patterson, G. R., & Gullion, M. E. (1971). *Living with children: New methods for parents and teachers* (rev. ed.). Champaign, IL: Research Press.

Patterson, G. R., Jones, R., Whittier, J., & Wright, M. (1965). A behavior modification technique for a hyperactive child. *Behavior Research and Therapy, 2,* 217–226.

Patterson, G. R., McNeal, S., Hawkins, N., & Phelps, R. (1967). Reprogramming the social environment. *Journal of Child Psychology and Psychiatry, 8,* 181–195.

Piercy, F. P., & Sprenkle, D. H. (1986). *Family therapy sourcebook.* New York: Guilford Press.

Premack, D. (1965). Reinforcement theory. In D. Levine (Ed.), *Nebraska symposium on motivation.* Lincoln, NB: University of Nebraska Press.

Sauber, R. S., L'Abate, L., & Weeks, G. R. (1985). *Family therapy: Basic concepts and terms.* Rockville, MD: Aspen.

Schlesinger, S. E. (1988). Cognitive-behavioral approaches to family treatment of addiction. In N. Epstein, S. E. Schlesinger, & W. Dryden (Eds.), *Cognitive-behavioral therapy with families* (pp. 254–291). New York: Brunner/Mazel.

Schwebel, A. I., & Fine, M. A. (1992). Cognitive-behavioral family therapy. *Journal of Family Psychotherapy, 3,* 73–92.

Schwebel, A. I., & Fine, M. A. (1994). *Understanding and helping families: A cognitive behavioral approach.* Hillsdale, NJ: LEA Press.

Skinner, B. F. (1948). *Walden two.* New York: Macmillan.

Skinner, B. F. (1953). *Science and human behavior.* New York: Macmillan.

Stuart, R. B. (1969). Operant-interpersonal treatment of marital discord. *Journal of Consulting and Clinical Psychology, 33,* 675–682.

Stuart, R. B. (1980). *Helping couples change: A social learning approach to marital therapy.* New York: Guilford.

Sullivan, B. F., & Schwebel, A. I. (1995). Relationship beliefs and expectations of satisfaction in marital relationships: Implications for family practitioners. *The Family Journal, 3,* 298–305.

Thibaut, J., & Kelley, H. H. (1959). *The social psychology of groups.* New York: Wiley.

Thomas, M. B. (1992). *An introduction to marital and family therapy.* New York: Macmillan.

Walen, S., & Perlmutter, R. (1988). Cognitive-behavioral treatment of adult sexual dysfunctions from a family perspective. In N. Epstein, S. E. Schlesinger, & W. Dryden (Eds.), *Cognitive-behavioral therapy with families* (pp. 325–360). New York: Brunner/Mazel.

Walsh, F. (1982). Conceptualizations of normal family functioning. In F. Walsh (Ed.), *Normal family processes* (pp. 3–44). New York: Guilford.

Wolpe, J. (1969). *The practice of behavior therapy.* New York: Pergamon Press.

Wood, L. F., & Jacobson, N. S. (1990). Behavioral marital therapy: The training experience in retrospect. In F. W. Kaslow (Ed.), *Voices in family psychology* (Vol. 2, pp. 159–174). Newbury Park, CA: Sage.

C H A P T E R 8

Structural Family Therapy

She flips through a magazine on the blue-striped couch
sometimes entertained but often bored,
while he gulps down popcorn and televised football,
feeling occasionally excited yet often empty.

At midnight when the lights go off
and the news of the day and the games are decided,
She lays in anticipation, but without hope, of his touch
while he tackles fullbacks in his sleep
and ignores inner needs.

Alone, they together form a couple,
together, all alone, they long for a relationship.

Gladding, 1991

Structural family therapy was initially based on the experiences of Salvador Minuchin and his colleagues at the Wiltwyck School, a residential facility in New York for inner-city delinquents. The treatment was created out of necessity. Long-term, passive, and historically-based approaches to working with these families proved unsuccessful (Piercy & Sprenkle, 1986). The active and often aggressive nature of family members at the Wiltwyck School and their tendencies to blame others and react immediately meant therapists had to be powerful and quick. Minuchin soon discovered that dramatic and active interventions were necessary to be effective.

Since its conception, structural family therapy has grown in popularity and use. It was refined at the Philadelphia Child Guidance Clinic in the 1960s and 1970s. Today, its numerous practitioners are found in many mental health settings, with Philadelphia continuing to be a major center for this approach. **Structural family therapy's major thesis** is that an individual's symptoms are best understood when examined in the context of family interactional patterns. A change in the family's organization or structure must take place before symptoms can be relieved. This idea about the impact of family structure and change on the lives of individuals has continued to be influential in the current practice of many family therapists, even those outside of a structural family therapy orientation.

Major Theorists

There are several prominent theorists in structural family therapy, including Braulio Montalvo, Bernice Rosman, Harry Aponte, and Charles Fishman. The best known, however, is the founder of the theory, Salvador Minuchin.

Salvador Minuchin

In 1921, Salvador Minuchin was born in Argentina to Russian Jewish emigrants. He never felt total allegiance to Argentina, but he did learn the rituals of Latin pride and ways of defending his honor against anti-Semitic remarks (Simon, 1984). He completed a medical degree in Argentina; but in 1948, he joined the Israeli army as a doctor and spent the next 18 months in this position. In 1950, Minuchin came to the United States with the intention of studying with Bruno Bettelheim in Chicago. However, he met Nathan Ackerman in New York and chose to stay there. After another 2 year return to Israel, Minuchin returned to the United States for good. In 1954, he began studying psychoanalysis; and a few years later, he took a position as the medical director of the Wiltwyck School.

Through his experiences at Wiltwyck, Minuchin became a systems therapist and, along with Dick Auerswald and Charles King in 1959, began developing a three-stage approach to working with low socioeconomic black families. As time progressed, the Minuchin team "developed a language for describing family structure and methods for getting families to directly alter their organization" (Simon, 1984, p. 24). It was his innovative work at Wiltwyck that first gained Minuchin widespread recognition. The essence of the method used was published in *Families of the Slums* (Minuchin, Montalvo, Guerney, Rosman, & Schumer, 1967).

In 1965, Minuchin became the director of the Philadelphia Child Guidance Clinic. He transformed the clinic into a family therapy center. In the process, he gained a reputation as a tough and demanding administrator. Minuchin was always creating ideas. One of the most innovative of these was the Institute for Family Counseling, a training program for community paraprofessionals that proved to be highly effective in providing mental health services to the poor.

Minuchin worked closely at Philadelphia with Braulio Montalvo and Jay Haley, who he hired from California. "Probably Minuchin's most lauded achievement at the Clinic was his development of treatment techniques with psychosomatic families, particularly those of anorectics" (Simons, 1984, p. 24). In 1974, Minuchin published *Families and Family Therapy,* one of the most clearly written and popular books in the family therapy field. This work propelled Minuchin into widespread notoriety. In 1975, he stepped down as director of the clinic, but he remained its head of training until 1981.

Since 1981, Minuchin has studied normal families, written several plays (and books), and commented on the overall field of family therapy. In addition, he set up the Family Studies Institute in New York City. He still continues to give workshops and to train therapists from all over the world. He remains an expert on working with families from diverse cultures and settings. He is passionately committed to social justice and is involved in the foster care system in New York. Overall, even in retirement, Minuchin remains a force in the field of family therapy.

Premises of the Theory

The structural approach as a theory is quite pragmatic. Minuchin's theoretical conceptualization was influenced by the philosophy of Ortega y Gasset, which "emphasizes individuals interacting with their environment" (Walsh & McGraw, 1996, p. 42).

One of the primary premises underlying structural family therapy is that every family has a **structure**. This structure is revealed only when the family is in action. In other words, structure is an invisible set of functional demands by which family members relate to each other (Minuchin, 1974).

Structure influences families for better or worse. In some families, structure is well organized in a hierarchical pattern and members easily relate to each other. In other families, there is little structure and few arrangements are provided by which family members can easily and meaningfully interact. In both cases, developmental or situational events increase family stress, rigidity, chaos, and dysfunctionality, throwing the family into crisis (Minuchin, 1974). However, families that have an open and appropriate structure recover more quickly and function better in the long term than families without such an arrangement.

The structural approach emphasizes the family as a whole, as well as the interactions between subunits of family members. In some dysfunctional families, coalitions arise (Minuchin, Rosman, & Baker, 1978). A **coalition** is an alliance "between specific family members against a third member. A *stable coalition* is a fixed and inflexible union (such as a mother and son) that becomes a dominant part of the family's everyday functioning. A *detouring coalition* is one in which the pair hold a third family member responsible for their difficulties or conflicts with one another, thus decreasing the stress on themselves or their relationship" (Goldenberg & Goldenberg, 1996, p. 196).

Furthermore, a major thesis of structural theory is that a person's symptoms are best understood as rooted in the context of family transaction patterns. The family is seen as the client. The hope is that through structuring or restructuring the system all members of the family and the family itself will become stronger (Minuchin, 1974). Families are conceptualized from this perspective as living systems. They operate in an ever changing environment in which communication and feedback are important (Friedlander, Wildman, & Heatherington, 1991). Consequently, lasting change is dependent on altering the balance and alliances in the family so that new ways of interacting become realities.

Subsystems are another important aspect of the theory. **Subsystems** are smaller units of the system as a whole. They exist to carry out various family tasks. Without subsystems the overall family system would not function. They are best defined by the boundaries and rules connected with them. Subsystems are formed when family members join together to perform various functions. Some of these functions are temporary, such as painting a room. Others are more permanent, such as parenting a child. Of particular significance are the spousal, parental, and sibling subsystems (Minuchin & Fishman, 1981).

The *spousal subsystem* is composed of the marriage partners. In families where there are two such individuals, the way they support and nurture each other has a lot to do with how well structured the family is and how functionally it runs. Spousal subsystems work best when there is "complementarity of functions." In such circumstances, a husband and wife, for example, would operate as a team and accept their interdependency.

The *parental subsystem* is made up of those responsible for the care, protection, and socialization of children. As with the spousal subsystem, the parental subsystem is considered healthy if it does not function in a cross-generational way. A **cross-generational alliance** in a family contains members of two different generations within it. For example, if a parent and child collude to obtain certain objectives or needs, such as love or power, there is a cross-generational alliance. Parental subsystems must change as children grow. The rules that are applicable, for example, at age 8 do not work at age 18. Therefore, parents are constantly challenged to define appropriate, clear, and permeable boundaries that help family members gain access to each other without becoming fused or distanced.

The *sibling subsystem* is that unit within the family whose members are of the same generation. For example, brothers and sisters are considered to be a sibling subsystem. In some families, the sibling subsystem is composed of those born of the same parents. In other families, such as in remarried arrangements (i.e., step-families), the sibling subsystem is made up of unrelated children. Age differences may affect how well sibling subsystems function. Subsystems of siblings are often composed of those children who are relatively close to each other in age, for example, 2 or 3 years apart. They are generally closer to one another psychologically because of their opportunities to interact together. The larger the age gap between siblings, the less likely they will become allies (i.e., a subsystem).

A third major aspect of structural family therapy is the issue of boundaries. Basically, **boundaries** are the physical and psychological factors that separate people from one another and organize them. "For proper family functioning, the boundaries of subsystems must be clear" (Minuchin, 1974, p. 54). The strength of boundaries is represented in structural family mapping systems by broken, solid, and dotted lines. There are three major types of boundaries: clear (represented by a broken horizontal line, i.e., - - - - -); rigid (represented by a solid line, i.e., _____); and diffuse (represented by a separated dotted line, i.e.,. . . . .).

Clear boundaries consist of rules and habits that allow family members to enhance their communication and relationships with one another because they encourage dialogue. In families with clear boundaries, members freely exchange information and give and receive corrective feedback. For example, in such a family, only one person at a time talks. With clear boundaries, negotiation and accommodation can successfully occur in families. These processes facilitate change, but still maintain the stability of the family. Parents and children feel a sense of belonging, but nevertheless individuate. For a functional two-parent family with children, clear boundaries might be represented as shown in Figure 8.1.

Rigid boundaries are inflexible and keep people separated from each other. In families with rigid boundaries, members experience difficulty relating in an intimate way to one another, and therefore, individuals become emotionally detached or cutoff from other family members. For example, a family in which a husband and wife are detached from each other is represented in Figure 8.2.

In the case of **diffuse boundaries,** there is not enough separation between family members. In this arrangement, some family members are said to be "fused." Instead of creating independence and autonomy within individuals, as with clear boundaries, diffused boundaries encourage dependence. A two-parent family with children in which diffused boundaries exist is represented in Figure 8.3.

Other symbols are also used to show how families relate. Among the most common are:[1]

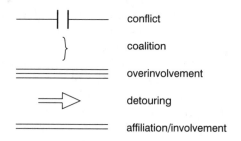

A two-parent family with children in which there is conflict and overinvolvement is represented in Figure 8.4. In such families, triangulation exists, and the relationships between the parents and children become closer as the conflict between the parents intensifies.

Another family in which a coalition between a parent and children exists is represented in Figure 8.5. In this situation, a child becomes parentified as the parents disengage from one another.

In the development of families, boundaries may change regardless of the type of family. It is crucial not to mistake normal family development and growing pains for pathological patterns (Minuchin, 1974). It is also important to realize that during the course of family life over time alignments are formed. **Alignments** are the ways family members join together or oppose one another in carrying out a family activity.

In addition to structure, subsystems, and boundaries, structural family therapy is based also on (1) roles and rules and (2) power (Figley & Nelson, 1990). In

---

[1]Source: Reprinted by permission of the publishers from *Families and Family Therapy* by Salvador Minuchin, Cambridge, MA: Harvard University Press. Copyright © 1974 by the President and Fellows of Harvard College.

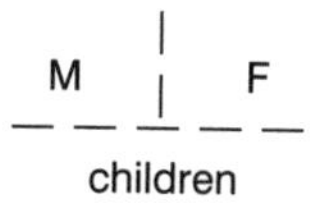

Figure 8.1
Clear boundary family.

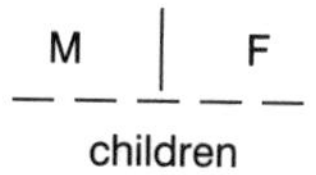

children

Figure 8.2
Detached husband/wife.

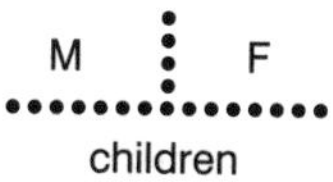

children

Figure 8.3
Diffused family boundaries.

children

Figure 8.4
Conflictual parents who
are overinvolved with their
children.

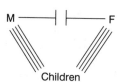

Children

Figure 8.5
Coalition between one parent
and a child to form a cross-
generational alliance.

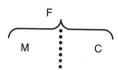

regard to *roles and rules,* families experiencing difficulties have members who
relate to each other according to certain expectations that are either outdated or
ineffective. The inefficiency of these families includes "little or no expectations
that anyone will hear or be affected by what they say [and] little or no expectation of reward for appropriate behaviors (McWhirter & McWhirter, 1989, p. 23).
For instance, the youngest member of such a family may constantly be placed in
the role of "the baby" and never be taken seriously by anyone.

Similarly, rules that the family first developed may be adhered to regardless
of the changes that have occurred in the family's life style or outside circumstances. For example, a family in which the chief wage earner is laid off may
still insist on buying clothes at expensive stores. Such a rule, when adhered to,
is to the detriment of the family as a functioning unit. Overall, rules in families
"may be explicit or implicit." More functional families generally have more
explicit rules. Regardless, rules "provide the family . . . with structure"—an
organized pattern that becomes predictable and manifests itself in repeated patterns (Friesen, 1985, p. 7).

Power is the ability to get something done. In families, power is related to
both authority and responsibility (or the one who makes and the one who carries

out the decisions). Structural family therapists observe that in dysfunctional families, power is vested in only a few members. The ability of family members to give input into the decision making process that governs the family is limited. Disenfranchised family members may either cut themselves off from the family, become enmeshed with stronger members, or battle to gain some control in an overt or covert way. The structural family therapist, after noting how power is distributed in the family, will use his or her skills to often unbalance the family and help them learn new ways of dealing with situations that are power based.

Treatment Techniques

Structural family therapy is sometimes referred to as a way of looking at families. According to Minuchin (1974), dysfunctionality results from the development of *dysfunctional sets*. "Dysfunctional sets are the family reactions, developed in response to stress, that are repeated without modification whenever there is family conflict" (Goldenberg & Goldenberg, 1996, p. 203). For example, one spouse might verbally attack the other, bringing charges and countercharges, until the fight escalates into physical violence or the couple withdraws from each other.

There are a number of procedures associated with the structural family therapy approach (Friesen, 1985; Minuchin & Fishman, 1981). These techniques are sometimes employed in a sequential manner, or they may be combined. The most frequently used structural treatment methods are highlighted in the following sections.

Joining

Joining is defined as "the process of 'coupling' that occurs between the therapist and the family, leading to the development of the therapeutic system" (Sauber, L'Abate, & Weeks, 1985, p. 95). It involves the therapist making contact with each family member. In the process, the therapist allies with family members through expressing interest in them as individuals and working with and for them (Minuchin & Fishman, 1981). In this leadership role, the therapist helps initiate the treatment process. Joining is considered one of the most important prerequisites to restructuring. It is a contextual process that is continuous. "It's particularly important to join powerful family members, as well as angry ones. Special pains must be taken to accept the point of view of the father who thinks therapy is hooey or of the angry teenager who feels like a hunted criminal. It's also important to reconnect with such people at frequent intervals, particularly as things begin to heat up" (Nichols & Schwartz, 1995, p. 229).

There are four ways of joining a family from the structural family therapy approach. The first is by **tracking.** In tracking, the therapist follows the content of the family (i.e., the facts). For instance, the therapist might say to a woman: "So as I understand this situation, you and your husband were married last May and had your first child this past March. You do not think you had enough time to establish a relationship with your spouse before you were required to start one with your baby."

During tracking, judgements are not made by the therapist (at least not overtly). Rather, information is gathered through using open-ended questions to inquire about the interests and concerns of family members. Tracking is best exemplified when the therapist gives a family feedback.

The second way of joining is through **mimesis.** In mimesis, the therapist becomes like the family "in the manner or content of their communications, for example, joking with a jovial family, or talking slowly or sparsely with a slow-talking family" (Sauber et al., 1985, p. 107). Or, if a family frequently uses road metaphors to describe what is occurring between its members, a therapist would do likewise by stating: "I want to help you find a highway you can travel that leads somewhere and that everyone enjoys."

A third way of joining is through confirmation. The process of **confirmation of a family member** involves "using a feeling word to reflect an expressed or unexpressed feeling of that family member or by a nonjudgmental description of the behavior of the individual" (Thomas, 1992, p. 327). For example, a therapist might say to a daughter who stares at the floor when addressing her father: "I sense that your looking at the floor when you talk to your father is connected with some depression you feel inside."

The final way to join with a family is by **accommodation.** In accommodation, the therapist makes personal adjustments in order to achieve a therapeutic alliance. For example, the therapist would remove his or her coat if the family came to the session in shirt sleeves (Minuchin, 1974).

Reframing

The technique of **reframing** involves changing a perception by explaining a situation from a different context. In this activity, the facts of an event do not change, but the meaning of the situation is examined from a new perspective (Sherman & Fredman, 1986). Through this process, a negative situation can sometimes be viewed in a more favorable light. This type of change is crucial to the promotion of movement in family therapy. For example, if disruptive behavior is reframed by the therapist as being "naughty" instead of "incorrigible," family members can find ways to modify their attitudes toward the "naughty" person and even help him or her make changes.

Unbalancing

Unbalancing (or allying with a subsystem) is a procedure wherein the therapist supports an individual or subsystem against the rest of the family. For instance, a therapist may sit next to a daughter who is being accused of not living up to the family's tradition. In this position, the therapist can also take up for the daughter against the family and give reasons why it is important for the daughter to create new ways of behaving. Family members, individually and as a group, are then forced to act differently with the person or subsystem. They have to expand their roles and functions. When this technique is used to support an underdog in the family system (as it usually is), a chance for change within the total hierarchical relationship is fostered (Sauber et al., 1985).

Enactment

The process of **enactment** consists of families bringing problematic behavioral sequences into treatment by showing them to the therapist in a demonstrative transaction. For example, a family that frequently argues about how they are going to spend their Saturdays is asked to have a heated argument in front of the therapist instead of waiting for the fight to occur at another time. The idea is to see how family members interact with one another and to challenge their existing pattern and rules. This method can also be used to help family members gain control over behaviors they insist are beyond their control. It puts an end to members' claims that they are helpless in controlling their actions, thoughts, and feelings. The result is that family members experience their own transactions with heightened awareness (Minuchin, 1974). In examining their roles, members often discover more functional ways of behaving.

Working with Spontaneous Interaction

Working with spontaneous interaction is similar to being a lighting expert who focuses "the spotlight of attention on some particular action" (Nichols & Schwartz, 1991, p. 467). It occurs whenever families display behaviors in a session that are disruptive or dysfunctional, such as members yelling at one another or parents withdrawing from their children. In these cases, therapists can see firsthand the dynamics within a family's interactions. On such occasions, therapists can point out the dynamics and sequencing of behaviors. The focus is on process not content. It is crucial that therapists use such occasions to help families recognize patterns of interaction and what changes they might make to bring about modification.

Boundary

A boundary is an invisible line that separates people or subsystems from each other psychologically (Minuchin, 1974). In order to function effectively, families need different types of boundaries at distinct times of stage development. For example, in times of crises, families may need more rigid boundaries in order to make sure that everyone works together as a team. "Part of the therapeutic task is to help the family define, redefine, or change the boundaries within the family. The therapist also helps the family to either strengthen or loosen boundaries, depending upon the family's situation" (Sauber et al., 1985, p. 16).

Intensity

Intensity is the structural method of changing maladaptive transactions by using strong affect, repeated intervention, or prolonged pressure. "Tone, volume, pacing, and choice of words can be used to raise the affective intensity of statements" (Nichols & Schwartz, 1995, p. 232). For example, intensity is manifested if a therapist keeps forcefully telling a family to "do something different" (Minuchin & Fishman, 1981). The persistence employed in this technique breaks down family patterns of equilibrium and challenges the family's perception of reality. Intensity works best if therapists know what they want to say and do so in a direct, unapologetic manner that is goal specific.

Restructuring

The procedure of **restructuring** is at the heart of the structural approach. In fact, the goal of this approach to family therapy is structural change. Restructuring involves changing the structure of the family. The rationale behind restructuring is to make the family more functional by altering the existing hierarchy and interaction patterns so that problems are not maintained. It is accomplished through the use of enactment, unbalancing, and boundary formation.

For instance, if a father dominates to the point where children feel intimidated, the therapist may ask the family to enact a "father-dominated scenario." As it occurs, the therapist may instruct the rest of the family members to behave in a certain way, for example, uniformly refusing to do what the father requests without getting something in return. If these instructions are carried out, the family behaves differently and change becomes possible. If change occurs, members generally feel more enfranchised and invested in the family.

Shaping Competence

In the process of **shaping competence,** structural family therapists help families and family members become more functional by highlighting positive behaviors. For example, therapists may reinforce parents who make their children behave, even if the parents succeed only momentarily in accomplishing this feat. In effect, shaping competence is a matter of therapists not acting as experts all of the time. Instead, therapists reinforce members for doing things right or making their own appropriate decisions. As a result, positive abilities are highlighted and appropriate alternative ways of working with problems are produced.

Diagnosing

One of the main tasks of structural family therapists is to "diagnose in such a way as to describe the systematic interrelationships of all family members" (Nichols & Schwartz, 1995, p. 231). This type of mapping, as shown in Figures 8.1 through 8.5, allows therapists to see what needs to be modified or changed if the family is going to improve. For example, therapists may note disruptive coalitions or triangles among family members.

Diagnosing is done early in the therapeutic process before the family can induct the therapist as a part of their system. By diagnosing interactions, therapists become proactive, instead of reactive, in promoting structural interventions.

Adding Cognitive Constructions

Although structural family therapy is primarily action oriented, it includes verbal components in the form of words to help families help themselves. The multiple aspects of the technique of **adding cognitive constructions** include advice, information, pragmatic fictions, and paradox. *Advice* and *information* are derived from experience and knowledge of families in therapy. They are used to calm down anxious family members and to reassure them about certain actions. They may occasionally include explanations about structure within the family. For example, if a family member says: "I'll bet you've never seen a family as messed up as we are," the therapist may reply: "Your family is unique in quite a few ways, but many of your concerns and behaviors are common among families I see."

Pragmatic fictions are pronouncements that help families and family members change. For instance, therapists may occasionally tell children that they are acting younger than their years. **Paradox,** on the other hand, is a confusing message meant to frustrate or confuse families and motivate them to search for alternatives. For example, a family that is resistant to instructions and change may be told not to follow the therapist's instructions and not to change. Given this permission to do as they wish, families may defy the therapist and become better, or they may explore reasons why their behaviors are as they are and make changes in the ways they interact.

Role of the Therapist

The structural family therapist is both an observer and an expert who is active in making interventions to modify and change the underlying structure of the family. To be a structural family therapist requires high energy and precise timing (Minuchin et al., 1967).

The therapist's role changes over the course of therapy (Minuchin, 1974). For example, in the first phase of treatment, the therapist joins the family and takes a leadership position. In phase two, the therapist mentally maps out the family's underlying structure. In the final phase, the therapist helps transform family structure. Thus, during treatment the therapist watches "the family 'dance' and then enters ('joins') and leaves the interactional field at will in order to transform it therapeutically" (Friedlander et al., 1991, p. 397).

The therapist uses a number of techniques to accomplish the goal of change, including "unbalancing" (e.g., siding with one member of the family), praise, challenges, direct orders, and judgments (Fishman, 1988; Minuchin & Fishman, 1981). An implicit, if not explicit, assumption is that the therapist has a "correct" interpretation of what is happening within the family and powerful tools for helping the family construct and maintain a more functional system.

In some cases, the therapist acts dramatically (if this is the only way to get the attention of the family) (Simon, 1984). For instance, the therapist may say to a withdrawn or denying family member: "Admit it, through your actions and passivity you are playing a major role in how this family operates." At other times, the therapist is low key and notices repetitive interactions, such as a young girl clinging to her mother. On such occasions, the therapist may or may not mention the actions. Regardless, the therapist works to change the structure of the family at crucial times so that family members can unite together in a healthy and productive way.

Process and Outcome

The process of change within structural family therapy is probably best described as gradual but steady. It is geared to the cultural context of the family but follows some general patterns. When successful, this approach results in symptom resolution and structural changes. Usually, significant changes occur after a few sessions because the therapist uses specific techniques to help family members interact in new ways. These techniques are often used in an overlapping manner in order to help the family to become less homeostatic. The idea is to emphasize action over insight. Family members are given "homework" (i.e., activities to do outside of the session) in addition to the work they do within their therapeutic time.

In successful treatment, the overall structure of the family is altered and reorganized. This change in structure enables family members to relate to one another in a more functional and productive manner. As a part of this process, dated and outgrown rules are replaced by those more related to the family's current realities. In addition, parents are in charge of their children, and a differentiation between distinct subsystems emerges (Piercy & Sprenkle, 1986).

Unique Aspects of Structural Family Therapy

Emphases

One strong aspect of structural family therapy is its versatility. The structural approach has proven successful in treating families experiencing difficulties with juvenile delinquents, alcoholics, and anorexics (Fishman, 1988). It is as appropriate for low-socioeconomic families as for high-income families. It can be adapted for use with minority and cross-cultural populations as well (Boyd-Franklin, 1987; Jung, 1984). In essence, structural family therapy is suitable for a wide variety of client families. It is sensitive to the effect of culture on families.

A second characteristic of this approach is its emphasis on terminology and ease of application. Basically, structural family therapy has clearly defined terms and procedures. Treatment methods and techniques are described in such a way that novice therapists can easily conceptualize what they are to do and when to do it (Minuchin & Fishman, 1981). The process is clear because of the clarity of the theory.

A third attribute of structural therapy is that it helped make family therapy as a whole acceptable to medicine in general and psychiatry in particular (Simon, 1984). As a psychiatrist, Minuchin was able to make a case with the medical community for his approach and for family therapy treatment. Without this recognition and implicit endorsement, family therapy would be more of an intellectual exercise and a mystery.

A fourth aspect of the structural approach is its emphasis on symptom removal and reorganization of the family. "Changes in family structure contribute to changes in behavior and the inner psychic processes of the members of the system" (Minuchin, 1974, p. 9). Families have a different emphasis as a result of treatment and are able to cope better. Members experience their families in new and positive ways.

A fifth dimension of structural family therapy is its pragmatic, problem-solving emphasis. Therapists are active in bringing about change (Colapinto, 1982). For example, by using reframing, a structural family therapist can help a family conceptualize a situation as being "depressive" rather than "hopeless." By seeing the difficulty in this way, the family can take steps to cope with or address depression and thereby gain greater control over themselves and their environment. In essence, structural family therapy was born out of necessity. It has not deviated from its origins.

Comparison with Other Theories

Compared with other family therapy approaches, structural family therapy is lacking in a strong theoretical foundation. The advocates of this approach have not addressed the complexity of family life to a great extent. Structural family therapy is basically action oriented, and practitioners of this treatment process deal with present interactions. The methods they have developed make this theory pragmatic but not profound in regard to examining complicated issues of family life.

A second point of comparison is based on the accusation by some clinicians that the focus of the theory lends itself to reinforcing sexism and sexual stereotypes (Simon, 1984). These critics stress that Minuchin encourages husbands to take on executive roles and wives to take on expressive roles in the family so that everyone does not suffer (Luepnitz, 1988). They contend that mothers should be encouraged and supported to become more effective. In fairness, it must be said that Minuchin developed his theory with low-income families in which husbands had little power or in which women were single parents.

A third distinction of the structural approach is that it focuses on the present. Past patterns and history are not emphasized (Minuchin, 1974). Structural family therapy basically ignores historical data. For example, structuralists mentally map the present configuration of the family rather than pay attention to the historic or developmental landmarks of the family over time.

A fourth aspect of structural family therapy is that it is sometimes hard to distinguish from strategic family therapy (Friesen, 1985; Stanton, 1981). In both approaches, there is a pragmatic emphasis on identifying and blocking present behaviors that are destructive and repetitive. There is also a focus on the process, as opposed to the content, of sessions. The therapist takes a great deal of responsibility for initiating change through such techniques as enactments or homework assignments. In both approaches, the time frame for treatment is relatively short term—less than 6 months.

A final distinction of structural family therapy is that families may not become as empowered because the therapist is active and in control of the process (Friesen, 1985). This aspect of treatment may be helpful to families who would not have taken an initiative by themselves, but for others it may hinder the speed of progress.

CASE ILLUSTRATION

THE JOHNSON FAMILY

Melinda Johnson, age 28, is the mother of four children: Will, age 12, Sally, age 8, Holly Jean, age 5, and Michael, age 2. Her common law husband, George, lives with the family on occasions but usually stays away because he fears Melinda's social worker will cut off government support if he is discovered in her apartment. Because of George's frequent absence and his financial inability to contribute to the family, Melinda and her children often go without needed food and medical care. Their apartment in "the projects" is in serious disrepair.

Melinda recently told her social worker that Will has been sneaking out late at night. She is unable to control him, and the social worker is considering removing him from the family. Melinda fears the effects of such a process and is equally distressed at the thought that Will may become part of a gang and endanger her and the younger children. Her social worker wants specific detailed information on what Will is doing. Melinda's mother, age 45, who lives nearby, is urging Melinda to "do something and do it quickly."

Conceptualization of Family: Structural Perspective
From a structural perspective, the Johnson family is unorganized and problematic. It lacks resources. Melinda does not have a supportive relationship with either George or her mother. The fact that Will is beginning to act out is indicative of this lack of a hierarchy and the effects of poverty. Power is being usurped by Will because the boundaries within the family unit are diffused. If the family structure is not strengthened soon, Will will most likely become triangulated.

Process of Treatment: Structural Family Therapy
To help the Johnsons, a structural family therapist would first join with all members of the family that come for treatment. The therapist would then urge all members of the family, including George and Melinda's mother, to attend most, if not all, sessions. The therapist would then mentally map the family after they are seated and notice who sits next to whom and the verbal interactions that take place. Then, to help the family begin to help itself, the therapist would move members around until natural subsystems within the family are grouped together, such as parents and children. With the Johnsons, the therapist would concentrate also on mimesis and match the family's feeling mood, most likely hopelessness.

After the therapist "joins" and "accommodates" the family, he or she would begin to take a leadership role in the family. First, he or she would unbalance the family by allying with the parent subsystem. By doing so, the therapist emphasizes the importance of a strong couple subsystem, that is, both Melinda and George. The therapist might then work with spontaneous interactions within the session itself. For example, if Melinda and George ask Will to sit down and he does not, the therapist might insist through the use of an intensity method of repetition and would keep trying until successful. Then, even if only momentarily, the therapist would note the success and in so doing shape competence. The therapist might also use reframing, for example, state that Melinda's mother, through her overinvolvement in pressuring her daughter to act, is "quite concerned" about her daughter and the family's well being.

In this approach, the therapist would always begin an intervention with the parent subsystem in order to clarify and emphasize boundaries. As treatment progresses each session, the therapist would seek to put less attention on Will and more on family dynamics and processes as influenced by structure. Will would lose his status as the identified patient and the family would become the treated unit. As boundaries and structure are changed, power would regress to the parent subsystem. At this time, the therapist would share with Melinda and George some pragmatic and cognitive knowledge to help them stay on top of the family situation.

Summary and Conclusion

Structural family therapy was formed out of necessity in the 1960s by Salvador Minuchin and his colleagues at the Wiltwyck School in New York. It was begun because traditional methods of treatment, especially psychoanalysis, were not effective in serving the needs of inner-city ghetto boys from low-income families, who were the primary residents of this facility. It was refined at the Philadelphia Child Guidance Clinic in the 1970s and 1980s. It continues to be a major theoretical approach to helping families change.

"Like most systems theorists, the structuralists are interested in how the components of a system interact, how balance or homeostasis is achieved, how family feedback mechanisms operate, [and] how dysfunctional communication patterns develop" (Goldenberg & Goldenberg, 1996, p. 191). A particular emphasis of the structural approach is that all families have structures that are revealed through member interactions. Some family structures are more functional than others. Families that have a hierarchy that is well organized adjust better to their environment and crises than families that are not set up in this manner. Of special interest to structural family therapists are spouse, parent, and sibling subsystems and the clearness of boundaries between them. In addition, roles, rules, and power within the family are emphasized.

A number of innovative techniques and procedures have come from structural family therapy. Among the best known and most effective are joining, reframing, unbalancing, enacting, working with spontaneous interaction, boundary formation, intensity, restructuring, shaping competence, and adding cognitive constructions. Like an artist, structural family therapists time the intensity and emphasis of their inputs. On some occasions, they "map" family interactions; on others, they intervene in dramatic fashion. This unpredictability can be a powerful feature of the approach.

If all works well, families leave structural family treatment with more functional ways by which members can interact and with clearer boundaries. Families may not have insight into their new behaviors, but they have new ways of relating. Structural family therapy is versatile in the types of families with which it can be used. It is also easily combined with other family therapy approaches, such as strategic family therapy. Critics of the approach claim it concentrates too much on surface issues and that it may be implicitly sexist. Yet, as a treatment methodology, structural family therapy remains popular.

SUMMARY TABLE

Structural Family Therapy

Major Theorists
Salvador Minuchin
Braulio Montalvo
Charles Fishman
Bernie Rosman
Harry Aponte
Duncan Stanton
Thomas Todd

Underlying Premises
Family functioning involves family structure, subsystems, and boundaries.
Overt and covert rules, hierarchies, and interpersonal accommodation must be understood and changed, if necessary, to keep the family flexible and adjusted to new situations.

Role of the Therapist
Therapists mentally "map" their families and work actively in counseling sessions. They instruct families to interact through enactments and spontaneous sequences. Therapists are like theater directors.

Unit of Treatment

The family is treated as a system or a subsystem. However, individual needs are not ignored.

Goals of Treatment

One goal of treatment is to bring problematic behaviors out in the open so therapists can observe and help change them.

Another goal is to bring about structural changes within families, such as organizational patterns, hierarchies, and sequences.

Therapeutic Techniques

Therapeutic techniques include the following:

- Joining
- Accommodating
- Restructuring
- Working with interaction (enactment, spontaneous behaviors)
- Intensifying messages
- Unbalancing
- Reframing
- Shaping competence
- Making boundaries

Unique Aspects of the Approach

Structural family therapy emphasizes the following:

- The approach was the first developed for low-socioeconomic families and is very pragmatic.
- It was one of the first developed exclusively for families.
- It was influential in getting the profession of psychiatry to respect family therapy as an approach to treatment.
- The tenets and techniques of the therapy are clearly stated by Minuchin, Fishman, Stanton, and others.
- Treatment has proven effective in working with families of addicts, eating disorders, and suicidals.
- The therapy is well researched, systemic, problem focused in the present, and relatively short term (generally less than 6 months).
- Therapists and families are active during the sessions.
- Homework is sometimes assigned in between sessions.

Comparison with Other Theories

The theory appears to be more simple than it is because treatment is focused on the present, and past patterns are not usually discussed.

Some feminists believe the theory promotes gender stereotypes by emphasizing traditional paternal roles.

The theory is not as strong in explaining family dynamics and development as the practice of this approach is in fostering change.

The therapist must be active and creative. He or she is highly influential in the change process and may inadvertently prevent maximum family interaction and employment.

Structural family theory and strategic family theory are sometimes conceptualized as one in the same, which makes it hard for some therapists to discern the unique aspects of each. The result is often a failure to appreciate the contributions of structural family therapy or to use it appropriately.

References

Boyd-Franklin, N. (1987). The contribution of family therapy models to the treatment of black families. *Psychotherapy, 24,* 621–629.

Colapinto, J. (1982). Structural family therapy. In A. M. Horne & M. M. Ohlsen (Eds.), *Family counseling and therapy* (pp. 112–140). Itasca, IL: F. E. Peacock.

Figley, C. R., & Nelson, T. S. (1990). Basic family therapy skills, II: Structural family therapy. *Journal of Marital and Family Therapy, 16,* 225–239.

Fishman, C. H. (1988). *Treating troubled adolescents: A family therapy approach.* New York: Basic Books.

Friedlander, M. L., Wildman, J., & Heatherington, L. (1991). Interpersonal control in structural and Milan systemic family therapy. *Journal of Marital and Family Therapy, 17,* 395–408.

Friesen, J. D. (1985). *Structural-strategic marriage and family therapy.* New York: Gardner.

Gladding, S. T. (1991). *Monday nights.* Unpublished manuscript.

Goldenberg, I., & Goldenberg, H. (1996). *Family therapy: An overview* (4th ed.). Pacific Grove, CA: Brooks/Cole.

Jung, M. (1984). Structural family therapy: Its application to Chinese families. *Family Process, 23,* 365–374.

Luepnitz, D. A. (1988). *The family interpreted: Feminist theory in clinical practice.* New York: Basic Books.

McWhirter, J. J., & McWhirter, E. H. (1989). Poor soil yields damaged fruit: Environmental influences. In D. Capuzzi & D. R. Gross (Eds.), *Youth at risk* (pp. 19–40). Alexandria, VA: American Association for Counseling and Development.

Minuchin, S. (1974). *Families and family therapy.* Cambridge, MA: Harvard University Press.

Minuchin, S., & Fishman, C. H. (1981). *Family therapy techniques.* Cambridge, MA: Harvard University Press.

Minuchin, S., Montalvo, B., Guerney, B. G., Rosman, B. L., Schumer, F. (1967). *Families of the slums.* New York: Basic Books.

Minuchin, S., Rosman, B., & Baker, L. (1978). *Psychomatic families: Anorexia nervosa in context.* Cambridge, MA: Harvard University Press.

Nichols, M., & Schwartz, R. (1991). *Family therapy concepts and methods* (2nd ed.). Boston: Allyn & Bacon.

Nichols, M., & Schwartz, R. (1995). *Family therapy concepts and methods* (3rd ed.). Boston: Allyn & Bacon.

Piercy, F. P., & Sprenkle, D. H. (1986). *Family therapy sourcebook.* New York: Guilford.

Sauber, S. R., L'Abate, L., & Weeks, G. R. (1985). *Family therapy: Basic concepts and terms.* Rockville, MD: Aspen.

Sherman, R., & Fredman, N. (1986). *Handbook of structural techniques in marriage and family therapy.* New York: Brunner/Mazel.

Simon, R. (1984, November-December). Stranger in a strange land: An interview with Salvador Minuchin. *Family Therapy Networker, 8,* 21–25.

Stanton, M. D. (1981). An integrated Structural/Strategic approach to family therapy. *Journal of Marital and Family Therapy, 7,* 427–439.

Thomas, M. B. (1992). *An introduction to marital and family therapy.* New York: Macmillan.

Walsh, W. M., & McGraw, J. A. (1996). *Essentials of family therapy.* Denver, CO: Love.

CHAPTER 9

Strategic and Systemic Family Therapies

After giving birth to Nathaniel
you asked for a Wendy's shake and fries.

I can still remember as if yesterday
the words that broke the silence
surrounding the miracle of new life:
"I'm hungry."

Walking from your room still dazed,
through the Sunday streets of Birmingham,
I brought you back your first request from labor.

That cold November morning is now a treasure in my mind
as are you and the child that you delivered.

Gladding, 1993

S trategic and systemic family therapies are method-oriented and brief in duration. In this chapter, the essence of these theories is examined and compared. Strategic and systemic therapies are indebted to the work of Milton Erickson, whose work influenced their founders. Erickson's goal in treatment was change. He believed in utilizing the resources of his clients and designing a "strategy for each specific problem" (Madanes, 1991, p. 396). Erickson then worked with his clients to help them become active in assisting themselves. He did so through giving them directives and indirect suggestions. He did not care if people gained insight as long as their actions produced beneficial results. "If Freud was a philosopher-priest from Vienna, Erickson was a samurai warrior from Wisconsin" (Wylie, 1990, p. 28).

Despite sharing a common heritage—both obtained ideas from Erickson and used some of the same methods (e.g., seeing families for a limited period of time)—strategic and systemic family therapies are distinct. The differences between these approaches have been articulated by theorists from:

- the Mental Research Institute (MRI) (i. e., strategic family therapists)
- the Family, or Haley-Madanes, Institute (i.e., strategic family therapists)
- the Milan Systems Group (i.e., systemic family therapists)

The MRI form of strategic family therapy is the oldest of these therapeutic approaches. It is a descendent of the Bateson communications studies group, which was conducted in Palo Alto from 1952 to 1962. Among the most active modern proponents of this approach are Paul Watzlawick and John Weakland. Other figures connected with this branch of strategic family therapy are Lynn Hoffman, Peggy Penn, and Richard Rabkin.

A second type of strategic family therapy is that articulated at the Family, or Haley-Madanes, Institute of Washington, D.C. The most noted therapists of this approach are Jay Haley and Cloe Madanes. Both Haley and Madanes have influenced other theories, theorists, and teams of researchers, including those in the MRI Palo Alto group.

The third group of theorists considered here is from Milan, Italy. The genesis of this branch of family therapy, which is usually referred to as **systemic family therapy,** was formulated by a team of practitioners whose members originally included Mara Selvini Palazzoli, Luigi Boscolo, Gianfranco Cecchin, and Guiliana Prata (Campbell, Draper, & Crutchley, 1991, p. 325). The team leader of this effort was Selvini Palazzoli. In 1967, she established the Milan Center for the Study of the Family. Previous to this landmark event, Selvini Palazzoli had devoted her life to the study and treatment of anorexia nervosa, with limited success (Selvini Palazzoli, 1974). Systemic family therapy has been characterized as **long brief therapy** because of the spacing in between sessions (usually a month) and the duration of treatment (up to a year) (Tomm, 1984).

The format of this chapter consists of discussions of the underlying principles of strategic and systemic theories as unique but related approaches. Included in this examination is a brief description of major professionals involved in formulating these theories. The primary assumptions and underpinning techniques of these positions are highlighted. The foci of therapists using these orientations are then discussed. Finally, process and outcome of these theories are described along with their unique contributions to the field of family therapy.

Strategic Family Therapies

The strategic family therapy approaches have a history that is both long and distinguished. Jay Haley (1973) coined the term *strategic therapy* to describe the work of Milton Erickson. Erickson conducted therapy by paying extreme attention to details of the symptoms his clients presented. His focus, like that of most present-day strategic therapists, was to change behavior by manipulating it and not to instill insight into those with whom he worked.

Erickson achieved his objectives in therapy by:

- accepting and emphasizing the positive (i.e., he framed all symptoms and maladaptive behaviors as helpful)
- using indirect and ambiguously worded directives
- encouraging or directing routine behaviors so that resistance is shown through change and not through normal and continuous actions (Haley, 1963)

Major Strategic Family Theorists

Strategic family therapies have many well-known practitioners, such as Paul Watzlawick, John Weakland, and Cloe Madanes. However, as a representative of these approaches, the background of Jay Haley is highlighted here.

Jay Haley

Haley influenced the Bateson group and the MRI group as a founding member of each and set up the Family Therapy (Haley-Madanes) Institute of Washington, D.C. His theoretical writings and techniques have also had a powerful impact on the Milan systems approach originated by Selvini Palazzoli.

As implied previously, Jay Haley is one of the most distinguished and controversial pioneers in the field of family therapy. He has served as an effective communicator between people and groups and has been a strong advocate of family therapy in public and professional settings. Haley's development is unique among family therapists. He learned from and with the three people who had the most influence on the evolution of family therapy: Milton Erickson, Gregory Bateson, and Salvador Minuchin.

Haley began his career with Gregory Bateson in 1952. Because he had a masters degree in communications, his chief responsibility in the research team Bateson assembled was to take a lead in diagnosing communication patterns in schizophrenic families. As a result of his work, Haley became interested in studying the hypnotherapy communication process of Milton Erickson. He learned hypnosis from Erickson in 1953 and later taught and practiced it (Simon, 1982). He incorporated much of Erickson's ideas into his own concepts about how to do therapy. Erickson supervised him as he learned to become a therapist. Basically, he adopted and modified Erickson's individual emphasis to working with families.

In 1962, after the Bateson team dissolved, Haley joined the Mental Research Institute (MRI) staff, where he worked until 1967. It was at this time that he stopped doing therapy and became primarily involved in "family research and the observation of therapy" (Simon, 1982, p. 20). He also became the first editor of the initial journal in the field of family therapy, *Family Process,* a position he held from 1962 to 1969. Haley became even more involved in supervision when he moved east to join Salvador Minuchin at the Philadelphia Child Guidance Center in 1967. With Minuchin, he organized "the **Institute for Family Counseling** (IFC), a project training people from the Philadelphia ghetto, who had no formal education beyond high school, to be family therapists" (Simon, 1982, p. 20). This process further established his prominence.

In 1974, he moved to the Washington, D.C. area to establish the Family Therapy Institute with Cloe Madanes. This institute was renamed the Haley-Madanes Institute in 1989. After this move, he published two of his most influential books, *Problem Solving Therapy* (1976) and *Leaving Home* (1980). These books spelled out the essence of strategic family therapy as Haley views it, an approach that distinguishes itself by its emphasis on power and hierarchy. Today, Haley devotes most of his time to the Haley-Madanes Institute, which is a major training center for family therapy (Simon, 1982, 1986). He is described as having the skills of a power broker and a military strategist and having made these skills "respectable therapeutic techniques" (Wylie, 1990, p. 28). Overall, Jay Haley is an experienced innovator who generates controversy and change.

Premises of Strategic Family Therapy

As a group, strategic family therapies follow Ericksonian principles. They emphasize short-term treatment, about 10 sessions. Often strategic therapies are characterized as brief therapy. The term *brief,* used in this way, is misleading. **Brief therapy** has to do more with the clarity about what needs to be changed rather than with time. "A central principle of brief therapy is that one evaluates which solutions have so far been attempted for the patient's problem" (Priebe & Pommerien, 1992, p. 433). After the evaluation, different solutions in therapy are tried. These solutions are often the opposite of what has already been attempted (Watzlawick, 1978).

For instance, if parents have begged a daughter to make good grades, treatment might focus on having the parents ask the daughter to show them how she manages to do so poorly in school. They may even instruct her to continue what she has been doing. "Brief therapists hold in common the belief that therapy must be specifically goal-directed, problem-focused, well-defined, and, first and foremost, aimed at relieving the client's presenting complaint" (Wylie, 1990, p. 29).

In general strategic family therapists concentrate on the following dimensions of family life:

- **Family rules**—the overt and covert rules families use to govern themselves, such as "you must only speak when spoken to"
- **Family homeostasis**—the tendency of the family to remain in its same pattern of functioning unless challenged to do otherwise, for example, getting up and going to bed at the same time
- **Quid pro quo**—the responsiveness of family members to treat others in the way they are treated, that is, something for something
- **Redundancy principle**—the fact that a family interacts within a limited range of repetitive behavioral sequences
- **Punctuation**—the idea that people in a transaction believe that what they say is caused by what others say
- **Symmetrical relationships** and **complementary relationships**—the fact that relationships within a family are both among equals (symmetrical) and unequals (complementary)
- **Circular causality**—the idea that one event does not "cause" another but that events are interconnected and that the factors behind a behavior, such as a kiss or a slap, are multiple.

Strategic Family Therapy Treatment Techniques

As a group, strategic family therapists are very innovative. They believe that telling people what they are doing wrong is not helpful. The same is true concerning the encouragement of catharsis (Haley, 1976). If families are going to change, alterations in the ways their members act must precede new perceptions and feelings. The number of ways to accomplish this goal are almost endless. For example, some problems can be resolved by not treating them as problems, such as not becoming overly concerned when a 2-year-old throws a temper tantrum because that is typical behavior at that age.

Each intervention in strategic therapy is tailored to the idiosyncrasies of persons and problems. The customization makes strategic therapies some of the most technique-driven of all family therapies. Among the various schools of strategic family therapy, different concepts and methods are highlighted. In general, strategic family therapists emphasize reframing, directives, paradox, ordeals, pretend, and positioning.

Reframing

Reframing involves the use of language to induce a cognitive shift within family members and alter the perception of a situation. In reframing, a different interpretation is given to a family's situation or behavior. In this process, a circumstance is given new meaning and, as a consequence, other ways of behaving are explored. Reframing does not change a situation, but "the alteration of meaning invites the possibility of change" (Piercy & Sprenkle, 1986, p. 35). For instance, "depression" may be conceptualized as "irresponsibility" or "stubbornness."

Overall, reframing helps establish rapport between the therapist and the family and breaks down resistance. Through the use of reframing, what was once seen as out of control behavior may become voluntary and open to change.

Directive

A **directive** is an instruction from a family therapist for a family to behave differently. "The directive is to strategic therapy what the interpretation is to psychoanalysis. It is the basic tool of the approach" (Madanes, 1991, p. 397). Many types of directives can be given in strategic therapy. They include nonverbal messages (e.g., silence, voice tone, and posture), direct and indirect suggestions (e.g., "go fast" or "you may not want to change too quickly"), and assigned behaviors (e.g., when you think you won't sleep, force yourself to stay up all night). The purpose of these "outside of therapy" assignments is to help people to behave differently so that they can have different subjective experiences. Directives also increase the influence of the therapist in the change process and give the therapist information on how family members react to suggested changes.

An example of a directive is to tell a family to "go slow" in working to bring about change. In this situation, their resistance to change may dissolve as they attempt to disobey the directive. On the other hand, if they follow the directive, the therapist can gain more influence in their lives.

Paradox

One of the most controversial and powerful techniques in strategic family therapy is **paradox** (Sexton & Montgomery, 1994). Although there are fine distinctions that can be made, this process is very similar to **prescribing the symptom**. It gives client families and their members permission to do something they are already doing and is intended to lower or eliminate resistance. Jay Haley (1976) is one of the best-known proponents of this technique. Paradox takes many forms, including the use of restraining, prescribing, and redefining.

1. In **restraining,** the therapist tells the client family that they are incapable of doing anything other than what they are doing. For example, a therapist might say: "In considering change, I am not sure you can do anything other than what you are presently doing."

2. In **prescribing,** family members are instructed to enact a troublesome dysfunctional behavior in front of the therapist. For instance, parents may be asked to show how they argue with their 16-year-old about when he will be allowed to get a driver's license. They are to continue the argument for about the same amount of time it usually takes and to come up with the same impasses.

3. **Redefining** is attributing positive connotations to symptomatic or troublesome actions. The idea is that symptoms have meaning for those who display them whether such meaning is logical or not. In the case of a school phobic child, the therapist might redefine her behavior as an attempt to keep her parents together in the marriage through focusing their attention on her.

(handwritten margin note: they change to also spite you)

Ordeals

Ordeals involves helping the client to give up symptoms that are more troublesome to maintain than they are worth (Haley, 1984). In this method, the therapist assigns a family or family member(s) the task of performing an ordeal in order to eliminate a symptom. The ordeal is a constructive or neutral behavior that must be performed before engaging in the undesirable behavior. For example, an ordeal might be to do exercise before the onset of depression or to give a present to a despised person or group. In essence, the ordeal is always healthy, but is not an activity that those directed to do it want to engage in. The hope is that those involved will give up the symptom in order to avoid performing the constructive behavior.

Pretend

Pretend is a more gentle and less confrontive technique than most of the other procedures used in strategic family therapy. Cloe Madanes (1981, 1984) is identified as the creator of this concept. Basically, the therapist asks family members to pretend to do a troublesome behavior, such as having a fight. The act of pretending to engage in a fight helps individuals change through experiencing control of a previously involuntary action.

Positioning

The act of **positioning** by the therapist is one that involves acceptance and exaggeration of what family members are saying (Piercy & Spenkle, 1986). If conducted properly, it helps the family see the absurdity of what they are doing. They are thereby freed to do something else. For example, if a family member states that her relationship with her father is "difficult," the therapist might respond: "No, it is hopeless" (Watzlawick, 1983).

Role of the Strategic Family Therapist

The role of strategic therapists differ among their subschools. However, those who work within this methodology share a belief in being active and flexible with their family clients. It is the therapist's responsibility in these family therapy approaches to plan strategies to resolve family problems. Therapists often proceed quickly and specifically in their focus on resolving presenting problems and virtually ignore family histories and personal diagnoses (Wylie, 1990). "They are symptom focused and behaviorally oriented" (Snider, 1992, p. 20).

"The first task of the therapist is to define a presenting problem in such a way that it can be solved" (Madanes, 1991, p. 396). Although the problem can be conceptualized in a number of ways, the therapist usually tries to define it as one that the family has voluntary control over and that involves a power struggle. In defining the problem in such a manner, the therapist sets out to help family members make changes that alter the family dynamics from a competitive stance (in which there are winners and losers) to a cooperative position (in which everyone wins) (Watzlawick, 1983).

Most strategic therapists are overtly active. For instance, Haley (1990) believes it is essential to make changes in people and families within the first three sessions. Thus, he works hard at reframing client's perceptions and presenting complaints. He also strives to come up with a unique innovative method to use in each case. He tailors his approach for each family in the same way as Milton Erickson, one of his mentors, and in the same way a surgeon would plan an operation.

Overall, strategic family therapists try to use presenting problems as ways to bring change in families by giving them tasks that are usually carried out between sessions, that is, homework. "Therapists also use structural interventions such as attempting to unbalance family systems by joining with one or more members on a conflictual point, fortifying generational boundaries, and supporting members at particular times to accomplish a specific objective" (Snider, 1992, p. 20).

Outcome and Process of Strategic Family Therapy

The goal of strategic family therapy is to resolve, remove, or ameliorate the problem the family agreed to work on (Snider, 1992). In addition, the family must learn, at least indirectly, how to address other problems in a constructive manner. Often, resolving family difficulties involves a multitude of interventions or steps. Four common procedures for ensuring a successful outcome include:

1. defining a problem clearly and concisely
2. investigating all the solutions that have previously been tried
3. defining a clear and concrete change to be achieved
4. formulating and implementing a strategy for change (Watzlawick, 1978)

Overall, the emphasis in strategic therapy (as in systemic family therapy) is on process rather than content. The methods used in bringing about change focus on breaking up vicious cycles of interaction and replacing them with virtuous cycles that highlight alternative ways of acting (Friesen, 1985).

Unique Aspects of Strategic Family Therapy

Emphases of Strategic Family Therapy

A major emphasis of strategic family therapy is its flexibility as a viable means of working with a variety of client families. This approach has been successfully used in treating families and their members who display such dysfunctional behaviors as enmeshment, eating disorders, and substance abuse (Haley, 1980; Stanton & Todd, 1982).

A second characteristic of this approach is that, with the exception of a few true believers, most therapists who use it "now concede that real change is possible at the individual and dyadic level—that the entire system need not always be involved in lower-order change" (Fish, 1988, p. 15). Because significant change can be brought about without having the entire family involved in treatment sessions, the chances of obtaining a desirable outcome are increased.

A third emphasis of strategic family therapy is its focus on innovation and creativity. As previously mentioned, strategic therapists trace their lineage to Milton Erickson, who was especially potent in devising novel ways to help his clients. Many of today's strategic family therapy practitioners, especially Cloe Madanes (1990), are a part of this tradition. For example, Madanes has devised a 16-step procedure for working with sex offenders and their victims. This approach is notable for its concreteness in obtaining clear facts, its linkage in connecting sexuality with spirituality, and its power in persuading the offender to seek forgiveness from the victim on his knees.

As a group, strategic family clinicians view the major goal of therapy as changing the perception, and hence the interaction, of families. Through their "introduction of the novel or unexpected, a frame of reference is broken and the structure of reality is rearranged" (Papp, 1984, p. 22).

A fourth quality of strategic family therapy is the way it can be employed with a number of other therapies, particularly the behavioral and structural family therapy schools of thought (Alexander & Parsons, 1982; Fish, 1988; Haley, 1976). One reason this quality is so prevalent in strategic therapy is that one of its codevelopers, Jay Haley, worked at the Philadelphia Child Guidance Clinic in a structural setting and incorporated parts of that theory into his version of strategic treatment. Another reason is that behavioral family therapy focuses on defining, clarifying, and changing specific interactional patterns in a parallel manner to the strategic approach (Fish, 1988). A final reason is that many influential therapists have a historical or personal connection with strategic therapy. Consequently, they continue to be influenced in their thoughts and actions by dialogue and debate among strategic family therapists.

Comparison of Strategic Family Therapy with Other Theories

One aspect of strategic family therapy, especially the MRI group, that set it apart from other family therapies early in its development is that it concentrates on one problem. Basically, a strategic family therapist focuses on one problem and helps families marshall their resources in dealing with an identified difficulty quickly and efficiently (Snider, 1992).

A second point of comparison is based on the accusation that strategic family therapy is too "cookbookish" and "mechanical" (Simon, 1984). This charge is the result of prescribed methods of treatment by the MRI and Jay Haley. In fairness, however, there is considerable flexibility among therapists who embrace this theory.

A third comparable quality associated with strategic family therapy is the controversial view about schizophrenia proposed by one of its leading proponents, Jay Haley. Haley, in essence, denies the existence of schizophrenia.

A fourth comparative feature of strategic family therapy involves the skill necessary to implement some of its methods. For instance, the use of paradox can be powerful in the hands of a skilled clinician, but its use can be a catastrophe if employed in a naive way (Friesen, 1985). Some strategic family therapy approaches demand considerable training of practitioners before they can be implemented properly.

A fifth comparative factor of strategic family therapy concerns time and emphasis. All subschools within this orientation restrict the number of therapeutic sessions. Although this format motivates families to work, it is limiting. For example, the seriousness or extent of problems may not be dealt with adequately (Wylie, 1992). It is hoped that by resolving one specific situation, families will learn problem-solving skills. Although this is the case for some families, it is not universal.

A final comparable quality of strategic family therapy is its lack of collaborative input from client families. Some strategic family therapy models, such as those devised by Haley, emphasize power techniques and the expertness of the therapist. All stress the creativeness of the therapist to find a solution for the family. Much like a physician, the strategic therapist who does not produce the desired results in clients usually takes the blame. This type of procedure is the antithesis of most other forms of family therapy.

A comparison between strategic and structural family therapies is shown in Figure 9.1. In some instances, the two approaches are so compatible that theorist Duncan Stanton (1981) has suggested they be integrated into a single approach. (Stanton's idea is not universally shared.) Although some professionals experience confusion over the differences between the two therapies, rules and guidelines are available to help either combine the two approaches or sequence them in a complementary manner. For example, a general rule is that when structural interventions fail, therapists should try strategic methods because these methods were developed on more highly resistant clients (Friesen, 1985).

Systemic (Milan) Family Therapy

Systemic (Milan) family therapy is sometimes confused with the overall concept of "systemic" as an approach to family therapy. *Systemic* as a general term is inclusive and encompassing. It describes a therapeutic approach with interrelated elements. Systemic family therapy, also known as the Milan approach, stresses the interconnectedness of family members while also emphasizing the importance of second-order change in families (Tomm, 1984a, b).

Major Systemic Family Theorist

Mara Selvini Palazzoli

Like many well-known therapists in the family therapy field, Mara Selvini Palazzoli was initially trained as a psychoanalyst. In her native Italy, she specialized in working with patients who had eating disorders, but she became increasingly frustrated with the results (Selvini Palazzoli, 1974). In 1967, she became the leader of a group of eight psychiatrists who were the forerunners in applying psychoanalytic ideas to working with families. Later they discovered the ideas of Bateson, Haley, Watzlawick, and others and began to modify their approach. By 1971, there was a systemic factioning of the group. Selvini Palazzoli, Boscolo, Cecchin, and Prata formed the Center for the Study of the Family in Milan, where they developed the Milan model.

The Milan team split up in 1980. Selvini Palazzoli and Prata continued to do family systems research until 1982. At that time, Selvini Palazzoli formed a new group to work with families of schizophrenics and anorectics (Selvini, 1988). Simultaneously, her conceptual ideas underwent change, and she began to describe her client families as engaged in a series of **games**. When families are engaged in games, the children and parents stabilize around disturbed behaviors in an attempt to benefit from them. To break up these games, family therapists must first meet with families and then with parents separately to give them an invariant or variant prescription (explained later in the techniques section) that is designed to produce a clear and stable boundary between generations.

Common View of the Family
- People are seen as interacting within a context that they influence and are influenced by.
- The family life cycle and developmental stages are important in the assessment of families and their members.
- Symptoms are system-maintained and maintain the system.
- The family can change its behavior if the overall context in which they live is changed.

Overlap in Therapy Process
- Treatment is viewed from a pragmatic perspective, although structural family therapy follows a more detailed plan of action in providing services than strategic family therapy.
- The emphasis is on the present, not the past.
- Repetitive and destructive patterns of behavior are focused on as targets of change.
- The emphasis of intervention is on family process not content.
- Both structural and strategic families therapies are symptom oriented.
- The family therapist is active in helping families change and often directs the process.
- Contracts for change are negotiated between the family and the therapist and are aimed at presenting problems and goals of treatment.
- Reframing is emphasized, not insight.
- Considerable effort is made by the therapist in "joining" the family and establishing rapport.
- The therapist assigns homework and tasks to be completed outside of the therapy sessions.
- The total time of treatment is relatively short, about 6 months.

Distinctions Between Strategic and Structural Family Therapies
- "Structuralists emphasize the importance of system role relationships . . . whereas strategists emphasize mainly function or process" (Fraser, 1982, p. 14). In essence, the structuralists strive to help a family member change his or her position; the strategic family therapists concentrate on breaking up or changing dysfunctional repetitive patterns.
- "Structural views are centered around negative feedback cycles and breaking homeostatic bonds, whereas strategic views focus on positive feedback cycles and interrupting vicious cycles to create virtuous ones" (Fraser, 1982, p. 14). A negative feedback loop is one that maintains homeostasis. Structural family therapists try to break the status quo through restructuring, for example, by helping the family create new rules for an adolescent because rules that worked for him or her as a child are no longer appropriate. On the other hand, strategic family therapists seek to help families do less, not more, of a particular activity, for example, arguing. In the beginning of a family's history, arguing may have resolved some issues, so arguing continued (a positive feedback loop) with the expectation that more issues would be resolved. However, the results were negative (a vicious cycle). In strategic family therapy, attention is paid to positive deviations that are adaptable (a virtuous cycle).
- "The unit of intervention in structural therapy is the entire family unit and its subunits as they function now. . . . The Strategic unit of intervention may be with a subsystem of the family system" including an individual (Fraser, 1982, p. 14).

Figure 9.1

Distinctions and Similarities in Strategic and Structural Family Therapy.

Source: Adapted from "Structural and Strategic Family Therapy: A Basis for Marriage, or Grounds for Divorce? by J. S. Fraser, 1982, *Journal of Marital and Family therapy*, 8(2), 13–22. Copyright 1982, American Association for Marriage and Family Therapy. Reprinted by permission; and "An Integrated Structural/Strategic Approach to Family Therapy" by M. D. Stanton, 1981, *Journal of Marital and Family Therapy*, 7(4), 427–439. Copyright 1981, American Association for Marriage and Family Therapy. Reprinted with permission.

Premises of Systemic (Milan) Family Theory

Systemic family therapy is premised on the idea that therapists will take a systemic (circular) view of problem maintenance and a strategic (planned) orientation to change. Symptoms serve a purpose. Individual distress, anguish, or acting out is seen as the "thermometer of family functioning" (Snider, 1992, p. 13). Aberrant behaviors by one member of the family suggest a disturbance within the entire family. Therefore, systemic therapies concentrate on the consequences of family communication patterns and conflict between competing hierarchies. They shy away from doing anything more than accepting the symptoms as described by the family or family members.

The concept of neutrality is one of the main pillars underlying the Milan family systems approach (Selvini Palazzoli, Boscolo, Cecchin, & Prata, 1980). It is referred to as **therapeutic neutrality**. It keeps the therapist from being drawn into family coalitions and disputes and gives the therapist time to assess the dynamics within the family. This type of neutrality also encourages family members to generate solutions to their own problems (Boscolo, Cecchin, Hoffman, & Penn, 1987).

Systemic (Milan) Family Therapy Treatment Techniques

Systemic (Milan) therapists have created and utilized a number of therapeutic treatment techniques. In addition to **paradox** (described earlier) are five other widely utilized techniques: hypothesizing, positive connotation, circular questioning, invariant/variant prescriptions, and rituals.

Hypothesizing

Hypothesizing is central to the Milan approach. It involves a meeting of treatment team members before the arrival of a family in order to formulate and discuss aspects of the family's situation that could be generating a symptom. During this pre-session, the team members attempt to prepare themselves for treating the family. Their belief is that they must come up with ideas about how a particular family operates, or the family will define the problem and treatment in a faulty way. Hypotheses are modified as treatment continues. Circularity throughout the family system is stressed.

Positive Connotation

A **positive connotation** is a type of reframing in which each family member's behavior is labeled as benevolent and motivated by good intentions. For example, if a mother is overinvolved with her daughter, the therapist might label her behavior as one of concern. By giving positive connotations to behaviors, therapists simultaneously reduce resistance to treatment by the family and establish rapport.

Circular Questioning

Circular questioning originated with the Milan team (Selvini Palazzoli et al., 1980). It focuses attention on family connections through framing every question so that it addresses differences in perception by family members about events or relationships. For example, each family member might be asked to state how he or she perceived the family dealing with a crisis situation. The intent is to highlight information, differences, and circular processes within the family system. It gives the family clear information while breaking down the idea of individual causes and helping family members raise questions.

Invariant/Variant Prescriptions

An **invariant prescription** involves a specific kind of ritual, and it is given to parents with children who are psychotic or anorexic in an attempt to break up the family's **dirty game** (i.e., power struggle between generations sustained by symptomatic behaviors) (Selvini Palazzoli, 1986; Simon, 1987). The invariant prescription requires parents to unite so that children can not manipulate them or stereotype them as "winners" or "losers" and thereby side with them.

The essence of this technique is that parents tell their symptomatic children that they have a secret, but they never reveal what the secret is. In addition, they record the reactions of family members to the fact that the parents have a secret. They then go out together for varying periods of time (some of them quite long) without telling their children where they are going or when they will return. This mysterious type of behavior allies parents in a new way and gives them an opportunity to observe and discuss the family's reactions. In the process, changes within the parents themselves and the family as a whole are noted. Constructive changes are preserved.

A **variant prescription** is given for the same purpose as an invariant one. The difference is that a variant prescription is tailored to a particular family and considers unique aspects of that family.

Rituals

The assignment of **rituals** is an attempt to break up dysfunctional rules in the family (Selvini Palazzoli, Cecchin, Prata, & Boscolo, 1978). In essence, rituals are specialized directives that are meant to dramatize positive aspects of problem situations (Boscolo et al., 1987). Rituals occur daily at mealtime, bedtime, and during chores. They can occur, for example, when sitting down to a meal together or when saying "goodnight" to everyone before bed. They include five components essential to family health: membership, belief expression, identity, healing, and celebration (Imber-Black, 1988, 1989). In essence, "a ritual is a type of prescription that directs the members of the family to change their behavior under certain circumstances. By changing the actions of the family members, the therapist hopes to change the cognitive map or meaning of the behavior. When prescribing a ritual, the therapist should state a specific time when the ritual is to be carried out" (Thomas, 1992, p. 411).

Effective rituals are specific in describing what is to be done, who is to do it, and how it is to be done. For example, an anorexic girl might be given the assignment of saying to her dying grandmother every night: "I love you so much that I did not want my parents to feel much pain about your impending death, so I am starving myself to cause them to worry about me." The grandmother would respond: "Thank you, but your parents are strong enough to handle my situation and still love you."

Role of the Systemic Family Therapist

In the Milan family systems approach, the therapist is both an expert and "a co-creator of the constantly evolving family system" (Friedlander, Wildman, & Heatherington, 1991, p. 397). The therapist in these roles takes a non-blaming stance, gives directives, and is neutral to the point of even avoiding the use of the verb "to be" (Boscolo et al., 1987). Thus, the Milan family systems therapist does not usually try overtly to challenge or change families. Instead, the therapist takes a paradoxical position of being a change agent who argues against change (Simon, 1987). As such, the therapist uses "circular questioning" and other indirect forms of intervention to bring about family transformation. The therapist stresses the **positive connotations** of a behavior and explains to the family how even the most troublesome symptom is "ultimately in the service of family harmony" (Simon, 1987, p. 19).

Outcome and Process of Systemic Family Therapy

When successful, systemic family therapy results in symptom resolution in a relatively short period of time (10 or less sessions). In addition, family dynamics change. The family experiences how family members are interlinked. The connection between what family members do and how the health of every member influences the others becomes evident. In addition, one member of the family stops being the focus of the family's problems, that is, the **scapegoat**. Further, nonproductive interactions and "games" change. As the family evolves and discards the **old epistemology,** or dated ideas, that do not fit their current situation, more productive and appropriate behaviors emerge (Tomm, 1984a). Perhaps most importantly, families make changes that are directed to their particular circumstance. For example, a family that was centered around eating problems can now become focused on affirmation of one another and clear communication.

In addition, if the therapy is successful, the process of growth within families continues after they formally terminate therapy. Growth continues because the family has experienced a pattern of change on which they can build; they have moved from a vicious to a virtuous cycle of interaction with renewed energy and focus.

Unique Aspects of Systemic Therapy

Emphases of Systemic Therapy

One characteristic of systemic family therapy is its flexibility in being a viable means of working with a variety of client families. This approach has been successfully used in treating families and their members who display such dysfunctional behaviors as enmeshment, eating disorders, and substance abuse (Selvini Palazzoli, 1981).

A second aspect of systemic (Milan) family therapy is that therapists work in teams to help families solve problems. With few exceptions, systemic family therapists work with some team members present with the family and others behind a one-way mirror (Simon, 1986). The team approach is monetarily expensive, but it is effective. The team concept has been borrowed and modified by a number of other schools of family therapy and has proven especially popular as a format to use in educating novice family therapists.

The team approach is especially powerful in the hands of skilled clinicians, such as Peggy Papp (1980), who has devised a form of it known as the **Greek Chorus.** In this format observers of a family treatment session (i.e., the team) may do such things as debate the merits of what a therapist is doing to bring about change. Families are helped to acknowledge and feel their ambivalence.

A third aspect of systemic therapy is its concentration on one problem over a short period of time. In so doing, systemic therapy helps families marshall their resources in dealing with an identified difficulty (Snider, 1992). Therapists who follow this approach might help a family find ways to share free time together so that members are not in competition with one another. Once that problem has been resolved, the family and therapist might spend their time and resources in more productive ways.

Comparison of Systemic Therapy with Other Theories

A major contrast of the Milan School with other theories is its "European bias toward non-intervention" (Simon, 1984, p. 28). The roots of the non-intervention approach, according to Salvador Minuchin, come from the European experience of Hitler and Nazi Germany. "In Europe, there is a great respect for people's individual boundaries" (Simon, 1984, p. 28). This same type of view is not shared world wide, and the mentality of this approach is not universal.

A second comparable quality associated with systemic family therapy is the controversial view about schizophrenia proposed by one of its leading proponents, Mara Selvini Palazzoli. It is Selvini Palazzoli's contention that "schizophrenia always begins as a child's attempt to take sides in the stalemated relationship between . . . parents" (Simon, 1987, p. 19). Although Selvini Palazzoli's view is not exactly the same as that of Jay Haley in this matter, it is interesting that Selvini Palazzoli, who was influenced by Haley, holds such a view, because Haley (as previously seen) is controversial in his position on schizophrenia.

A final comparative feature of the Milan systemic approach is that similar to strategic family therapy, there is an attempt in this treatment to tailor interventions to the specifics of a family. Therapists working as a team are responsible for creating innovative treatment plans. Like strategic and structural family therapies, systemic family therapy takes on some of the most outwardly difficult families with which to work.

CASE ILLUSTRATION

THE WILSON FAMILY

Bob and Harriet Wilson have been married for 15 years and are the parents of Rich, age 12, and Ryan, age 11. Rich is learning disabled and is in a special school. He is also physically handicapped, having been born with dislocated hips. He requires frequent medical attention from physicians and is described as "a source of worry" by his parents. He wears braces. Ryan, on the other hand, is bright, attractive, and full of energy. He loves sports and is a member of a number of youth teams, including soccer, basketball, and baseball. He seems to have little interest in his brother's condition and is quite demanding on his parents, insisting that they "take him" to games and play with him.

Bob is a painter and his work is seasonal. During the winter months, he has more time for his family and himself. He has tended to drink heavily during the winter months, but over the past 3 years, he has begun drinking heavily all year round. As a result, he misses work, gets fired from jobs, and is not paid regularly. He has lost the medical benefits he once had. Harriet is a waitress. She initially just worked during the lunch shift, but over the past year, she has begun working breakfast and dinner shifts as well. She is physically drained at the end of the day but has to do housework when she is home. She is concerned that none of the males in her life are doing well and that the family is "falling apart." She made the call for the therapy appointment.

Conceptualization of Family

The Wilsons are disengaged interpersonally and are under a lot of financial and physical stress. They are displaying a number of repetitive patterns, such as excessive drinking and overwork, that are not benefiting family members individually or the family as a whole. The children are demanding physically and psychologically. Harriet is overfunctioning; Bob is underfunctioning.

Process of Treatment

To treat the Wilsons, strategic and systemic family therapists would convey to them initially that treatment would consist of a limited number of sessions, for example, ten. The family would be asked before treatment began to define their problem/concern in a solvable format, for example, "to decrease the amount of friction, that is, the number of fights/arguments, between family members." Removal of the problem/concern would be seen as an index of change (Bodin, 1981). Regardless of what the problem/concern was, it would be accepted and seen by the therapist as serving some useful function.

In treatment, it would be ideal if the whole family could be seen. The therapist, in any of these approaches, would initiate actions and interventions and would clearly be in charge. The therapist would first gather information through such procedures as circular questioning or direct observations of nonverbal behaviors. During this process, the problem of friction would be reframed as behaviors associated with concern by family members for the well-being of the family as a whole. Attention would be focused on creating a specific approach that would help the Wilson family make needed transitions and second order change. Some of the initial interventions of strategic and systemic family therapists might go as follows:

1. In the MRI form of strategic therapy, a directive might initially be given to break up the family's homeostasis: "Spend an hour with each other doing a mutually decided activity, such as playing board games like checkers and monopoly." The rules of the game, as well as the rules of the family (e.g., how decisions are made to play games), would be discussed when the family returned for its next appointment.

2. In the Haley/Madanes form of strategic therapy, the use of pretend might be employed. This would require members of the family to pretend to care for each other in some specific way, such as giving one another imaginary gifts of traits/characteristics (e.g., bravery, assertion) or needed necessities. Thus, activity would take place in the presence of the therapist. If such an approach were not utilized, an ordeal might be employed. For example, a son might be required to give his mother money before he would be allowed to argue with her.

3. In the Milan format, the therapist along with the observation/treatment team might have the family engage in a ritual, such as eating dinner together in silence, for an extended period of time. At the conclusion of the meal, each member of the family would have to convey to the rest of the family how isolated and lonely he or she felt, and the others would simply acknowledge what they heard.

Regardless of their initial intervention, strategic and systemic family therapists would be active in sessions with this family and look for ways to bring about rapid change. With the Wilsons, a focus might be to get the parents more involved with each other and with their children. This might mean further treatment for the alcoholism and workaholism in Bob and

Harriet, respectively. It might also mean finding ways for Rich and Ryan to cooperate with each other and with their parents. Ryan, for instance, might be able to focus some of his attention on tutoring Rich academically and athletically; Rich could concentrate on encouraging and supporting Ryan in his practices and games.

Summary and Conclusion

Strategic and systemic family therapies are among the most popular approaches to working with families. They are short term, specific, positive, and appealing to families that have difficulty with organization and development. Inherent in their techniques are directives designed to change behaviors and thoughts, which are often overlooked by other therapeutic approaches (Perry, 1992).

The Mental Research Institute (MRI), following the creative genius of Milton Erickson, formulated the innovative foundation of the strategic therapy model in the 1960s. Members of this Palo Alto institute limited to ten the number of sessions they would agree to see families. They also consented to accept for treatment the problems families wished to work on, as long as they were clearly definable. Instead of trying to change families as they saw fit, these pioneers in family therapy focused on working with symptomatic behavior(s) and viewed dysfunctional behavior as having an underlying positive and beneficial basis. The MRI version of strategic family therapy has stood the test of time and is still being both refined and utilized.

The MRI therapeutic approach was later modified by Jay Haley, one of its initial participants. Haley has especially contributed to ways of working with young adults and their families who conspire to keep them from leaving home. His partner at their Washington institute, Cloe Madanes, is among the most creative therapists anywhere. Both versions of strategic family therapy have similarities and differences related to structural family therapy. They have influenced a wide variety of therapeutic approaches.

Strategic family therapy, particularly the MRI approach, was one of the influences in the original Milan, Italy, systemic family therapy treatment team. The Milan group originally concentrated on treating eating disorders, but from its study of strategic family therapy, it broadened its base.

Systemic family therapy has been both praised and criticized for its treatment procedures. Overall, some of the techniques employed in strategic and systemic family therapies—for example, hypothesizing, utilization of teams, invariant prescriptions, circular questioning, and the use of paradox—are among the most creative ever formulated. These therapeutic approaches appear to be strong and are becoming even more so. They are applauded for making necessary and sufficient changes that help families work better. However, these brief-oriented family therapies are criticized for not dealing extensively enough with family problems. Overall, strategic and systemic family therapies are well-defined, specific, and goal-directed treatments that employ a variety of techniques.

SUMMARY TABLE

Strategic and Systemic Family Therapies

Major Theorists
Strategic:
Jay Haley
Cloe Madanes
Milton Erickson
Paul Watzlawick
John Weakland
Richard Fisch
Systemic:
Mara Selvini Palazzoli
Luigi Boscolo
Gianfranco Cecchin
Guiliana Pata
Karl Tomm
Lynn Hoffman
Peggy Papp
Olga Silverstein
Peggy Penn
Richard Rabkin
Joel Bergman
Carlos Sluzki
James Coyne

Underlying Premises
People and families can change quickly.
Treatment should be simple and pragmatic.
The concentration is on changing symptomatic behaviors and rigid rules.
With hard work and the use of techniques such as enactment, ordeals, paradox, pretend, and rituals, families can change their unhealthy behaviors.

Role of the Therapist
The therapist is responsible for overcoming resistance in the family and designing strategies for solving problems that are novel. One way to

overcome resistance is to positively accept whatever problem the family brings.

The therapist is much like a physician in taking responsibility for the success of treatment.

The therapist must plan ahead and develop strategies for helping families change.

Unit of Treatment

Although these approaches can be selectively used with dyads and individuals, the family is treated as a system.

Goals of Treatment

The focus of treatment is on resolving present problems and bringing about change. Definable behavioral goals are targeted. Insight is minimized.

Therapeutic Techniques

Therapeutic techniques include the following:

- Reframing (including positive connotation)
- Using directives
- Using compliance-based and defiance-based paradox (including prescribing the symptoms)
- Using invariant and variant prescriptions (to disrupt dirty games)
- Promoting second order change
- Discouraging interpretation
- Pretending
- Using cooperative hierarchies
- Assigning ordeals
- Assigning rituals
- Utilizing teams
- Using circular questioning

Unique Aspects of the Approaches

Strategic and systemic therapies emphasize:

- seeing symptoms in a positive way
- short-term treatment (usually 10 sessions or less)
- changing present problematic behavior
- tailor-made techniques for each family
- innovative treatments
- flexible, evolving, and creative approaches (that combine easily with other theories)

Comparison with Other Theories

Historical patterns of family interaction are ignored.

The medical model, that is, expertise, is emphasized.

The use of teams, such as in the Milan approach, is featured.

The employment of paradox is widely used.

Families can change in treatment but not understand why.

Some confusion exists about the differences between strategic and structural family therapy.

References

Alexander, J., & Parsons, B. (1982). *Functional family therapy.* Pacific Grove, CA: Brooks Cole.

Bodin, A. (1981). The interactional view: Family therapy approaches to the Mental Research Institute. In A. S. Gurman & D. P. Kniskern (Eds.), *Handbook of family therapy* (Vol. I, pp. 267–309). New York: Brunner/Mazel.

Boscolo, L., Cecchin, G., Hoffman, L., & Penn, P. (1987). *Milan systemic family therapy.* New York: Basic Books.

Campbell, D., Draper, R., & Crutchley, E. (1991). The Milan systemic approach to family therapy. In A. S. Gurman & D. P. Kniskern (Eds.), *Handbook of family therapy* (Vol II, pp. 325–362). New York: Brunner/Mazel.

Fish, J. M. (1988, July/August). Reconciling the irreconcilable. *Family Therapy Networker, 12,* 15.

Fraser, J. S. (1982). Structural and strategic family therapy: A basis for marriage or grounds for divorce? *Journal of Marital and Family Therapy, 8,* 13–22.

Friedlander, M. L., Wildman, J., & Heatherington, L. (1991). Interpersonal control in structural and Milan systemic family therapy. *Journal of Marital and Family Therapy, 17,* 395–408.

Friesen, J. D. (1985). *Structural-strategic marriage and family therapy.* New York: Gardner.

Gladding, S. T. (1993). *Milestones.* Unpublished manuscript.

Haley, J. (1963). *Strategies of psychotherapy.* New York: Grune & Stratton.

Haley, J. (1973). *Uncommon therapy.* New York: Norton.

Haley, J. (1976). *Problem-solving therapy.* San Francisco: Jossey-Bass.

Haley, J. (1980). *Leaving home: The therapy of disturbed young people.* New York: McGraw-Hill.

Haley, J. (1984). *Ordeal therapy.* San Francisco, CA: Jossey Bass.

Haley, J. (1990). Interminable therapy. In J. Zeig & S. Gilligan (Eds.), *Brief therapy: Myths, methods, and metaphors.* New York: Brunner/Mazel.

Imber-Black, E. (1988). *Families and larger systems: A family therapist's guide through the labyrinth.* New York: Guilford.

Imber-Black, E. (1989, July/August). Creating rituals in therapy. *Family Therapy Networker, 13,* 39–47.

Madanes, C. (1981). *Strategic family therapy.* San Francisco: Jossey-Bass.

Madanes, C. (1984). *Behind the one-way mirror: Advances in the practice of strategic therapy.* San Francisco: Jossey-Bass.

Madanes, C. (1990). *Sex, love, and violence.* New York: Norton.

Madanes, C. (1991). Strategic family therapy. In A. S. Gurman & D. P. Kniskern (Eds.), *Handbook of family therapy* (Vol II, pp. 396–416). New York: Brunner/Mazel.

Papp, P. (1980). The Greek chorus and other techniques of paradoxical therapy. *Family Process, 19,* 45–57.

Papp, P. (1984, September/October). The creative leap. *Family Therapy Networker, 8,* 20–29.

Perry, V. (1992). *An examination of attention deficit disorders without hyperactivity: A case study from a strategic family systems perspective.* Unpublished masters research report. Wake Forest University, Winston-Salem, North Carolina.

Piercy, F. P., & Sprenkle, D. H. (1986). *Family therapy sourcebook.* New York: Guilford.

Priebe, S., & Pommerien, W. (1992). The therapeutic system as viewed by depressive inpatients and outcome: An expanded study. *Family Process, 31,* 433–439.

Selvini, M. (1988). *The work of Mara Selvini Palazzoli.* Northvale, NJ: Jason Aronson.

Selvini Palazzoli, M. (1974). *Self-starvation.* London: Human Context Books.

Selvini Palazzoli, M. (1981). *Self-starvation: From the intrapsychic to the transpersonal approach to anorexia nervosa.* New York: Aronson.

Selvini Palazzoli, M. (1986). Towards a general model of psychotic family games. *Journal of Marital and Family Therapy, 12,* 339–349.

Selvini Palazzoli, M., Boscolo, L., Cecchin, G., & Prata, G. (1980). Hypothesizing-circularity-neutrality. *Family Process, 19,* 73–85.

Selvini Palazzoli, M., Cecchin, G., Prata, G., & Boscolo, L. (1978). *Paradox and counterparadox.* New York: Jason Aronson.

Sexton, T. L., & Montgomery, D. (1994). Ethical and therapeutic acceptability: A study of paradoxical techniques. *The Family Journal, 2,* 215–228.

Simon, R. (1982, September/October). Behind the one-way mirror: An interview with Jay Haley. *Family Therapy Networker, 6,* 18–25, 28–29, 58–59.

Simon, R. (1984, November/December). Stranger in a strange land: An interview with Salvador Minuchin. *Family Therapy Networker, 8,* 20–31.

Simon, R. (1986, September/October). Behind the one-way kaleidoscope: An interview with Cloe Madanes. *Family Therapy Networker, 10,* 19–29, 64–67.

Simon, R. (1987, September/October). Good-bye paradox, hello invariant prescription: An interview with Mara Selvini Palazzoli. *Family Therapy Networker, 11,* 16–33.

Snider, M. (1992). *Process family therapy.* Boston: Allyn & Bacon.

Stanton, D., Todd, T., & Associates. (1982). *The family therapy of drug abuse and addiction.* New York: Guilford.

Thomas, M. B. (1992). *An introduction to marital and family therapy.* New York: Macmillan.

Tomm, K. M. (1984a). One perspective on the Milan approach: Part I. Overview of development, theory, and practice. *Journal of Martial and Family Therapy, 10,* 113–125.

Tomm, K. M. (1984b). One perspective on the Milan approach: Part II: Description of session format, interviewing style, and interventions. *Journal of Marital and Family Therapy, 10,* 253–271.

Watzlawick, P. (1978). *The language of change.* New York: Basic Books.

Watzlawick, P. (1983). *The situation is hopeless but not serious.* New York: W. W. Norton.

Wylie, M. S. (1990, March/April). Brief therapy on the couch. *Family Therapy Networker, 14,* 26–35, 66.

Wylie, M. S. (1992, January/February). The evolution of a revolution. *Family Therapy Networker, 16,* 17–29, 98–99.

Solution-Focused and Narrative Family Therapies

He changed
giving her small compliments at breakfast such as:
"I like the way your hair looks" or
"Nice dress."

She wondered:
"What is he doing?"
But she also knew she liked his words.

So as the days continued
she responded
and acts of kindness became more common.

He changed
She changed
They changed
And it was for the better.

Gladding, 1996

The most recent theoretical development in the field of family therapy is the creation of solution-focused and narrative family therapies. Solution-focused family therapy grew "out of the soil of strategic therapy (particularly the MRI model), and yet, it also represents a departure from that tradition" by concentrating on finding solutions instead of dealing with problems (Nichols & Schwartz, 1995, p. 444). Narrative family therapy originated in Australia and New Zealand and focuses on helping families solve difficulties by depersonalizing them and rewriting their own family stories.

The two most experienced and elegant spokespersons for solution-focused family therapy are Bill O'Hanlon and Steve deShazer, both of whom studied with Milton Erickson. The model appeared in its earliest form in the writings of Steve deShazer and his associates at their Brief Family Therapy Center in Milwaukee (deShazer, 1982, 1985, 1988, 1991). The writings and work of William O'Hanlon and his associates at the Hudson Center in Omaha, Nebraska, also are solution-focused, and are both similar to and distinct from that of deShazer (O'Hanlon & Wilk, 1987; O'Hanlon & Weiner-Davis, 1989). Present advocates of the solution-focused theoretical position include Patricia O'Hanlon Hudson (Hudson & O'Hanlon, 1991), Michele Wiener-Davis, Alan Gurman, Eve Lipchik, Scott Miller, and Simon Budman.

Michael White and David Epston (1990) formulated narrative therapy. While the focus of this approach is on engaging families in solution-oriented therapeutic processes, it is distinct from the approaches of deShazer and O'Hanlon. Difficulties are externalized and families are asked to work together as a team in developing strategies to overcome problems. Yet, just as solution-focused therapy has a Midwest origin with a worldwide application, so narrative family therapy has a Pacific Rim genesis with a global usefulness.

In this chapter, solution-focused family therapy is examined first, followed by an examination of narrative family therapy.

Solution-Focused Family Therapy

Major Theorists

Many of the major figures in solution-focused therapy originally worked with one another at the Brief Family Therapy Center in Milwaukee. Notables attached to the Center at one time or another include the husband/wife team of Steve deShazer and Insoo Berg, Michele Weiner-Davis, and Eve Lipchik. Even though Bill O'Hanlon was never a part of this group, he has been influenced by the Brief Family Therapy Center at least indirectly in his collaborative writing with Weiner-Davis. DeShazer and O'Hanlon are highlighted here.

Steve deShazer

Steve deShazer began his career by working at the Mental Research Institute in the mid-1970s. In the late 1970s, deShazer and a group of individuals in Milwaukee established the Brief Family Therapy Center. He first gained national attention as director of the Center and began to emerge and gain recognition as a major theorist in family therapy in the 1980s. Initially, deShazer was considered to be a strategic family therapist who was influenced by the work of not only Milton Erickson but also Gregory Bateson, and the staff of the Mental Research Institute (Walsh & McGraw, 1996). Yet, during that decade and into the 1990s, the writings and presentations of deShazer and Berg have become distinct from the mainstream of the strategic family therapy approach.

DeShazer (1982) identifies his theory as **brief family therapy,** and describes it as an ecosystemic approach. His approach, like that of the Milan group, employs a team whenever possible. The team, collectively known as consultants, transmits messages to the therapist at a designated break time in the session. They observe from behind a one way mirror. Thus, the family in treatment is sometimes the beneficiary of multiple inputs. As with any theory, de-Shazer has devised special terms to describe the techniques that make his approach unique.

Bill O'Hanlon

Bill O'Hanlon entered family therapy because of his interest in his own life experiences. As an adolescent, he was unhappy and shy. As a college student, he was isolated and uncomfortable in the world. He reports that he felt "like all exposed nerve—no skin—everything hurt" (Krauth, 1995, p. 24). He experimented with drugs and noticed that "the reality we all take for granted could be changed by a couple of micrograms of something introduced into one's body" (Bubenzer & West, 1993, p. 366). He also contemplated suicide, but changed his mind when a friend offered him hope by promising him a lifetime of free rent on a Nebraska farm she would inherit, if he would stay alive. That possibility changed his outlook on life and led to his interest in therapeutic work beyond repairing damage or dealing with pathology.

Later, after earning a tailor-made masters degree from Arizona State in family therapy, he went on to receive special tutelage under Milton Erickson in exchange for being Erickson's gardener. The influence of Erickson on O'Hanlon was profound and shifted his attention to focusing on solutions. O'Hanlon was also influenced by the work done at the Mental Research Institute.

In 1980, O'Hanlon set out to become a major proponent of solution-focused therapy, which he now prefers to call **possibility therapy** (Bubenzer & West,

1993; Krauth, 1995). His motivation was to shift the focus of family therapy from problems to solutions. He characterizes his approach as one that is pragmatic and full of Midwest values.

Premises of Solution-Focused Family Therapy

Solution-focused family treatment is built on the philosophy of **social construction,** that is, family therapy includes the social context, or cultural context, of a family. Because culture influences the way families view the world, the philosophy of constructivism also must be considered in working with families. **Constructivism** states that reality is not an objective entity, but a reflection of observation and experience (Maturana & Varela, 1987; Simon, Stierlin, & Wynne, 1985).

In addition, solution-focused therapy shares some of the same premises about families as the MRI strategic and Milan systemic approaches. At the foundation of this approach is the belief that dysfunctional families get "stuck" in dealing with problems (deShazer, 1985). These families basically use an unsatisfactory method to solve their difficulties, that is, they rely on patterns that do not work (Bubenzer & West, 1993). Solution-focused family therapy is aimed toward breaking such repetitive, nonproductive behavioral sets by deliberately setting up situations in which families take a more positive view of troublesome situations and actively participate in doing something different. "It is not necessary to know the cause of the complaint or even very much about the complaint itself in order to resolve it" (Cleveland & Lindsey, 1995, p. 145). Therefore, there is no need for extensive analysis.

Identifying what is a problem versus what is not a problem is a key component in the solution-focused perspective (deShazer, 1988). Exceptions to general ways of behaving and viewing situations are emphasized (O'Hanlon & Wilk, 1987). The aim is to help families unlock their set views, to be creative, and to generate novel approaches that may be applicable in a number of circumstances. It is believed that all families have resources and strengths with which to resolve complaints (Cleveland & Lindsey, 1995). The task is simply getting them to use the abilities they already have. Therefore, the focus is on solutions, not problems. To increase motivation and expectation, solution-focused family therapy, like strategic and systemic therapy, emphasizes short-term treatment, between 5 to 10 sessions.

As a theory, solution-focused family therapy does not focus on a detailed family history of problems. Such a process is believed to be unhelpful (deShazer, 1985; O'Hanlon & Weiner-Davis, 1989). A foundational belief of this approach is that causal understanding is unnecessary. To stress this point, O'Hanlon and Wilk (1987) state that every psychotherapy office should have a couch for therapists, instead of clients, because "every now and then, in the course of a session, a hypothesis might accidentally enter the therapist's head, and the best remedy for it is to lie down until it goes away" (p. 98).

Another premise of solution-focused family therapy is that families really want to change. As a way of underscoring this idea, deShazer (1984) has declared the death of resistance as a concept. Thus, when families do not follow therapists directions, they are "cooperating" by teaching therapists the best way to help them.

A final concept underlying solution-focused family therapy is that only a small amount of change is necessary. An analogy that is used to illustrate this point is that a one degree error in flying across the United States will result in a plane being considerably off course in the end (deShazer, 1985). Small amounts of change can also be reinforcing to families in helping them realize they can make progress. It boosts confidence and optimism and, in effect, creates a "ripple effect" (Spiegel & Linn, 1969).

Solution-Focused Family Therapy Treatment Techniques

Solution-focused therapy constructs solutions in collaboration with the client (Kiser, Piercy, & Lipchik, 1993). One subtle but primary treatment technique is to co-create a problem with a family. For the therapeutic process to be productive, initially, an agreement must be made as to which problem they want to solve. For example, it is crucial that a therapist and a family agree that a family's failure to discipline a child properly is the difficulty that needs to be addressed.

Another emphasis involves **second-order (qualitative) change,** or a qualitatively different way of doing something. The goal is to change the family's organization and structure. This can be done through planning interventions in accordance with the order of events within a family's life or by altering the frequency and duration of a dysfunction (O'Hanlon, 1987). For example, a family that has been having long fights at dinner might agree to finish their meal before arguing and then limit their disagreement time to 15 minutes. This type of change in the structure and length of events is likely to alter family dynamics.

A third intervention is to give the family a **compliment**. For solution-focused therapists, especially deShazer (1982), a compliment is a written message designed to praise a family for its strengths and build a "yes set" within it. A compliment consists of a positive statement with which all members of a family can agree. For example, the therapist might say: "I am impressed with your hard work to bring about change and the way all of you are discussing what needs to happen next." A compliment is always planned as a lead-in to giving a family a task or assignment.

A fourth technique is to provide the family with a **clue,** or an intervention that mirrors the usual behavior of a family. It is intended to alert a family to the idea that some behavior is likely to continue (deShazer, 1982). For example, the intervention of the therapist might be: "Don't worry about working too hard in trying to spend time together talking, because conversation is something that regularly occurs in your environment and you can do it naturally." The idea behind cluing is "to build mutual support and momentum for carrying out later interventions" (Sauber, L'Abate, & Weeks, 1985, p. 23).

A fifth treatment technique is to use interventions that have worked before and that have a universal application. These **skeleton keys** will help families unlock a variety of problems (deShazer, 1985). For instance, deShazer has refined five interventions that have been useful to him in a number of situations (deShazer, 1985; deShazer & Molnar, 1984):

1. "Between now and next time we meet, we(I) want you to observe, so that you can tell us(me) next time, what happens in your (life, marriage, family, or relationship) that you want to continue to happen" (p. 298). Such a request encourages a client family to look at the stability of the problems on which they wish to work.

2. "Do something different" (p. 300). This type of request encourages individuals and the family to explore the range of possibilities they have, rather than to continue to do what they believe is correct. For instance, deShazer gives an example of a woman who complained that her husband, a police detective, was staying out late every night with his friends. The message she received from the deShazer team was that her husband might want more mysterious behavior from her. Therefore, one night she hired a babysitter, rented a motel room, and stayed out until 5 A.M. Her husband came in at 2 A.M. Nothing was said, but her husband began staying home at night.

3. "Pay attention to what you do when you overcome the temptation or urge to . . . perform the symptom or some behavior associated with the complaint" (p. 302). This instruction helps families to realize that symptoms are under their control.

4. "A lot of people in your situation would have . . . " (p. 302). This type of statement again helps family members realize they may have options other than those they are exercising. Through such awareness, they can begin to make needed changes.

5. "Write, read, and burn your thoughts." This experience consists of writing about past times, such as times spent with an ex-spouse, and then reading and burning the writings the next day (deShazer, 1985).

Overall, solution-focused therapy interventions help the client family to view their situation differently. These interventions can also give them hope, thereby assisting clients in powerful ways (Bubenzer & West, 1993). To use the words of deShazer and Molnar (1984): "It now appears to us that the therapists' ability to see change and to help the clients to do so as well, constitutes a most potent clinical skill" (p. 304). Families become more empowered as a result of participating in solution-focused therapy.

A sixth technique is to **focus on exceptions,** that is, to look for "negative" or "positive" space (or time when a family goal may be happening) (Krauth, 1995).

For example, a family that is quarrelling a lot might be peaceful in the presence of its minister. At such times, they may agree to disagree and actually have civil conversations with one another. By examining the dynamics of the family at this time, members may learn something about how they can achieve their goals.

A seventh technique is to ask a family for a hypothetical solution to their situation. Such a process is often achieved by asking a **miracle question,** for example: "If a miracle happened tonight and you woke up tomorrow and the problem was solved, what would you do differently?" (Walter & Peller, 1993, p. 80). Such a question invites family members to suspend their present frames of reference and enter a reality that they wish to achieve. A miracle question is asked only after the therapist has gained enough background information on a family and the family itself has demonstrated its ability to respond positively to treatment and to notice exceptions to its complaints.

Role of the Solution-Focused Family Therapist

The solution-focused family therapist is a "facilitator of change, one who helps clients access the resources and strengths they already have but are not aware of or are not utilizing" (Cleveland & Lindsey, 1995, p. 145). Thus, solution-focused practitioners focus attention on complaints that families want to change and work with families in helping them gain a different perspective on a problem. In the process, language becomes important, and positive assumptions about change are constantly conveyed by the therapist. For example, the therapist might ask a "presuppositional question": "What good thing happened since our last session?" rather than "Did anything good happen since our last session?" "By selecting a specific verb tense, or implying the occurrence of a particular event, the family is led to believe that a solution will be achieved" (Gale, 1991, p. 43).

Solution-focused family therapists believe that it is important to "fit" therapeutic interventions into the context of family behavior. The fit of a solution has been particularly articulated by deShazer (1985). He contends that a solution does not have to be as complex as the presenting problem and need not include everyone in the family. He uses the metaphor of locks and keys to illustrate what he means. Locks may be complex, but opening them does not require a similar complexity of keys. In fact, several keys may fit the lock (or problem) well enough *to open the door to change.* **Skeleton keys** (i.e., standardized therapeutic techniques) can be helpful in dealing with most locks regardless of complexity.

To obtain a proper solution fit for a family, deShazer (1985) uses a team to begin **mapping** or sketching out the course of successful intervention. From the mapping experience, multiple perspectives about the family's problem are given. It is up to the family to define what they wish to achieve; the therapist then helps them define clear, specific goals that can be conceptualized concretely (deShazer, 1985; O'Hanlon & Weiner-Davis, 1989). It is through this process that families and therapists begin to create solutions, that is, desired behaviors. "Therapy is over when the agreed upon outcome has been reached" (O'Hanlon & Wilk, 1987, p. 109).

Solution-focused family therapists encourage families to make small changes and to do so rapidly (deShazer, 1985; O'Hanlon & Weiner-Davis, 1989). The therapist encourages the family to focus on changes in their behaviors, changes in their perceptions, and the recognition and use of family resources/strengths that can be brought to bear on a problematic situation (Cleveland & Lindsey, 1995).

In solution-focused family therapy, the therapist does not distinguish between short-term and long-term problems, because such a difference is irrelevant. Some problematic behaviors endure longer than others because often the right solutions have not been tried. Solution-focused therapists are always challenging families to envision a "future that has possibilities of change" (Bubenzer & West, 1993, p. 372).

Process and Outcome of Solution-Focused Family Therapy

Solution-focused family therapy concentrates on encouraging client families to seek solutions and tap internal resources. It encourages, challenges, and sets up expectations for change. The concept of pathology does not play a part in the treatment process. Rather, solution-focused therapists see client families as cooperative. They frequently commend the family on an aspect of a member's behavior, even if the behavior seems negative to the family. Solution-focused therapy takes the Ericksonian position that change is inevitable; it is only a matter of when it will happen. This type of therapy is oriented toward the future and helps client families change their focus and reframe their situations positively. By stressing that the family can change, finding incidents where the family acts differently than usual, asking optimistic questions, and reinforcing small but specific movement, solution-focused family therapy helps its families resolve difficulties and make needed changes.

Unique Aspects of Solution-Focused Family Therapy

Emphases

As a group, solution-focused family therapies concentrate on and are directed by a family's theory (i.e., their story). Before any attempt is made to help families change, their experiences are accepted. O'Hanlon compares this type of approach with the Rogerian concept of first listening attentively to how people are feeling before trying to implement change (Bubenzer & West, 1993).

A second characteristic of solution-focused therapy is that therapists assist families in defining their situations clearly, precisely, and with possibilities. "The defined problem should be achievable" (Todd, 1992, p. 174). Sometimes success is measured in the elimination of problems. Often, therapy is significant if the family changes its perception of a situation or discovers exceptions to troublesome times. Regardless, whatever the family brings to therapy is examined from a broad context. The past is not emphasized, except when it calls attention to the present.

A third emphasis is that solution-focused therapy does not focus on clinical understanding of the family situation by the family or the therapist. Rather, the focus is on change. The therapist's job is to produce change by helping the family to focus on what they see as solutions to the problems they have reported. For example, families should look at exceptions to behaviors. Therapists also produce changes in families by challenging their world view, by asking them appropriate questions, and by giving them "skeleton keys," that is, universal tasks that have the power to help families find ways to unlock their potential.

A fourth quality of solution-focused family therapy is that it is empowering and meant to assist families in assessing and utilizing their resources. Formula tasks, such as "Do something different," and awareness exercises, such as "Find times when symptoms do not occur," help families help themselves. Families "are encouraged to imagine a future without the problem(s) so that they can identify what they will be doing (solutions)" (Kok & Leskela, 1996, p. 398).

Finally, achievable goals are emphasized, such as small changes in behavior. These changes are seen as the basis for larger systemic changes. Therapists encourage and reinforce any type of family change. The idea is that once change starts, it will continue. "Solution-focused brief therapy further asserts that change is inevitable and that clients want to change" (Kok & Leskela, 1996, p. 398).

Comparison with Other Approaches

Unlike Bowen or psychoanalytic theory, virtually no attention is paid to history. Rather, perception and minimal change is the focus of solution-focused therapy. If families change their views on situations, they behave differently, or more functionally (Bubenzer & West, 1993). Likewise, if a family begins to interact differently, they begin to see their situation from a new perspective.

Like strategic and systemic family therapy, solution-focused family therapy is brief in regard to the situation focused on and the amount of time allotted to it. Structuring the sessions in a way that emphasizes the therapist's expectations regarding doing something different, encourages rapid change. Difficulties lose their potency. Sometimes this results in a one-session treatment (Bubenzer & West, 1993). Milton Erickson's influence on rapid changes is an obvious factor in all solution-focused approaches.

Therapy ends when an agreed upon behavioral goal is reached, rather than when a hypothetical therapeutic issue is discussed (O'Hanlon & Wilk, 1987). If there is no complaint or objective, there is no need for treatment. In this respect, solution-focused family therapy is similar to many forms of behavioral family therapy, as it concentrates on resolving a concrete objective.

Like systemic (Milan) family therapy, some proponents of solution-focused therapy, mainly deShazer, use a team in helping the family help itself. Therefore, the expense of treatment may be high even though there are generally fewer sessions than in some other approaches, such as psychoanalytic therapy.

Like MRI strategic therapy, solution-focused therapy aims to help client families change their thoughts or actions so that they become more satisfied with their lives. However, solution-focused therapists trust and utilize family resources more than MRI strategic therapists (Nichols & Schwartz, 1995).

CASE ILLUSTRATION

THE ROBERTS FAMILY

After 25 years of marriage and the raising of two children, Don and Kathy Roberts are contemplating a divorce. This crisis has led them to family therapy. Since the children left home 2 years ago, they have been drifting apart. Both Don, a computer analyst, and Kathy, a school superintendent, think they have little in common any more. Thus, they work long hours, take separate vacations, spend the weekends with friends or by themselves, and basically just share space in their house. The couple are saddened by the fact that their marriage is no longer vibrant, but they are proud of their children and what they accomplished while the children were young.

Conceptualization of the Family: Solution-focused Therapy
Don and Kathy are at a critical stage in their personal, professional, and couple life. They have focused on their children and activities outside the marriage to the extent that they have failed to cultivate common interests and activities. Both seem to have taken a fatalistic view that their marriage is over. Yet, by coming to therapy, they have some hope that perhaps their relationship can be saved.

There is a long history on which to build in working with this couple. Finding patterns and exceptions are real possibilities. The couple has some motivation and considerable abilities given their jobs and their past successes. A drawback to this situation is that the couple may be operating in the cognitive domain. Also, the spouses are presently detached from each other.

Process of Treatment: Solution-focused Therapy
In working with the Roberts, a solution-focused family therapist would first listen to their concerns. In this case, a lack of closeness and common interests would most likely surface. From the first session, the therapist would begin to discuss with the Roberts exceptions to their complaint, that is, times when they were close and with common interests. For example, they may have both shared a love for knowledge at the beginning of their marriage and throughout the time of raising their children.

In the deShazer model of solution-focused therapy, the therapist might take a break after listening to the complaints and exceptions. At the break, the therapist would either consult with a team of other professionals watching the session or think alone about setting up a homework assignment for the Roberts. When the therapist returned, he or she would lead off with a compliment to build a "yes set" and then give the homework assignment. In the O'Hanlon model, this structure (especially the break and the possible use of a team) would not be implemented. Instead, the therapist would focus on giving the couple a task to either make a small change or increase what they have been doing less of (i.e., make a second-order change).

In either form of solution-oriented therapy, the emphasis would be on working with the couple to do something different. In the deShazer version of this model, the couple would be asked on return appointments to check on clues (i.e., What is different this week than last?). There would also be an emphasis on scaling (i.e., ranking the concern on a scale of 1 [bad] to 10 [good]). The idea behind this method would be to get the Roberts to become increasingly aware of their improvement in therapy and to give them hope that their situation could be better. In both forms of solution-focused therapy, there would be considerable emphasis on the strengths of the Roberts, for example, their intelligence, hard-working spirit, motivation, and past success. There would also be considerable talk about change by the therapist. In the deShazer model, the miracle question might be employed to encourage more thought about change and elicit solution-focused information, if the therapeutic process did not proceed smoothly or efficiently.

The total number of sessions needed to work with the Roberts or a typical client family would be between 5 and 6. By the end of therapy, the Roberts should have made changes in their lifestyle and have skills to take with them should they drift apart again.

Narrative Family Therapy

Major Theorists

The most prominent professionals associated with narrative family therapy are Michael White (who is highlighted here), the codirector of the Dulwich Centre in Adelaide, South Australia, and David Epston, the codirector of the Family Therapy Centre in Auckland, New Zealand. Other professionals include associates of White and Epston, such as Michael Durrant.

Michael White

Michael White began his work as a family therapist in the 1970s in Australia. He was initially attracted to the work of Gregory Bateson. Along with this interest and his reading on the development of family therapy, White began to make his own interpretation of ideas that influenced the originators of family therapy theories. He has read extensively outside the field of family therapy and has drawn heavily from literary theory, anthropology, and critical theory. White finds the writings of Michele Foucault (1980, 1982, 1984), a French intellectual, particularly interesting. He has also been influenced by feminist theory (Bubenzer, West, & Boughner, 1994).

In recent years, "White has increasingly turned towards the narrative metaphor (and away from systems thinking), seeing people's problems as related to the stories they have about themselves, which in turn often reflect oppressive cultural practices" (Nichols & Schwartz, 1995, p. 462). One uniqueness about White's narrative approach, compared with others based on constructivism, is that White does not see one description of reality as better than any other. Instead, values play a role in actions, such as action against abuses of power, against neglect, against cruelty, and against injustice (White, 1993).

Premises of Narrative Family Therapy

Narrative family therapy is based on "a liberation philosophy consistent with postmodernism and social constructionism" (Becvar & Becvar, 1996, p. 282). It eschews attempts to formulate universal, generic principles. Indeed, the creators of this theory base much of their approach on the writings of Michael Foucault (1965, 1980), who asserts that human sciences (including social sciences like family therapy) generally characterize, classify, and specialize along a scale that objectifies people. As such, human sciences repress personal experiences and stories. The result is that people internalize and judge themselves in a logical and normative way that limits their options.

Thus, the narrative therapy approach distinguishes between **logico-scientific reasoning,** which is characterized by empiricism and logic, and narrative reasoning, which is characterized by stories, substories, meaningfulness, and liveliness. According to the narrative family viewpoint, "people live their lives by stories" (Kurtz & Tandy, 1995, p. 177). Therefore, the emphasis in this approach is shifted to a narrative way of conceptualizing and interpreting the world. Narrative therapy emphasizes empowering client families to develop their own unique and alternative stories about themselves in the hope that they will come up with novel options and strategies for living. By reauthoring their lives, families are enabled to change in ways not possible before (Bubenzer et al., 1994; Hodas, 1994; White, 1995).

In the process of changing their lives by changing their stories, client families are urged to **externalize problems** in order to solve them. "Externalization breaks the habitual reading and retelling of the compliant-saturated story as residing in the person" (Becvar & Becvar, 1996, p. 283). In externalization "the problem becomes a separate entity" (White & Epston, 1990, p. 38). Family members reduce their arguments about who owns a problem and ideally form a team and enter into dialogue about problem solving.

Narrative Therapy Treatment Techniques

Many narrative family treatment techniques are quite innovative. The most prevalent are highlighted here.

Externalization of the Problem

As previously implied, through **externalization,** therapists seek to separate problems from people. The result is usually (1) a decrease in unproductive conflict between persons, (2) a lessening of the sense of failure an unresolved problem has on persons, (3) an increase of cooperation among family members to problem solve and dialogue with each other, (4) an opening up of new possibilities for action, and (5) a freeing of persons to be more effective and less stressed in approaching problems (White & Epston, 1990).

In externalization, the problem is the problem. As such, it becomes objective and can be addressed in unique ways (White, 1991). In some cases, the problem can be described in such a way that it takes on a personality of its own, such as encopresis being given the name "Sneaky Poo" (White, 1989). In situations like this, all family members can relate to what is facing them.

Influence (Effect) of the Problem on the Person

The goal of asking how a problem has influenced a person is to increase the person's awareness and objectivity. This type of awareness can best be generated by the therapist asking each family member to give a detailed, no-holds-barred account of how the problem has effected them (e.g., dominated their life). A typical question in this process might be: "How has the problem influenced you and your life and your relationships?"

Influence (Effect) of the Person on the Problem

The purpose of asking family members how they have influenced a problem is twofold. First, it makes them increasingly aware of their response to a problem. Second, it helps them realize their strengths or potential in facing such a situation. In essence, this technique is the opposite of "Influence of the Problem on the Person." Again, this type of treatment breaks a fixed perception or behavior pattern and creates a new possible way to combat or stand up against a problem.

Raising Dilemmas

The effect of raising dilemmas is to get client families to examine possible aspects of a problem before the need arises. For instance, parents might be asked in relation to their misbehaving son how they would cope with "Worry" if the son's behavior became better, worsened, or remained the same. They might also be asked to consider how they would handle "Worry" if their youngest sibling began misbehaving as well.

Predicting Setbacks

Setbacks in family therapy are almost inevitable. Narrative family therapy takes the approach that setbacks are best dealt with when they are planned for or anticipated (White, 1986). By doing so, families can decide ahead of time how they will act in the face of adversity. For instance, in regard to "Worry," narrative therapists might ask a family what they would do if once they appear to have resolved their problem, "Worry" reappeared. In other words, would they give up and let "Worry" reenter their lives or would they fight back and drive "Worry" away?

Using Questions

Through the use of questions, therapists can challenge families to examine the nature of the difficulties they bring to therapy and what resources they have and can use to handle their problems. Questions can take a variety of forms but two of the most prevalent types are those that explore exceptions and those that deal with significance.

Exceptions questions are directed toward finding instances when a situation reported to be a problem was not true. For instance, if a family reports they are in chaos, an exceptions question would be aimed at finding examples of times when the family was not chaotic. The idea behind such questions is to challenge the family's view of the world and to offer them hope that their lives can be different because some change has already taken place. Most exceptions questions begin with *when* or *what*. Research on exceptions questions reveals that blaming statements decrease and positive statements increase during exceptions questions conditions (Meidonis & Bry, 1995).

Significance questions are "unique redescription questions, they search for and reveal the meanings, significance, and importance of the exceptions" (Kurtz & Tandy, 1995, p. 189). For example, a family might be asked: "Now that you are more aware of how you acted in this situation, to what do you attribute that behavior?"

Letters

Writing letters to families after therapy sessions is an important part of narrative therapy. According to Epston (1994), "words in a letter don't fade or disappear the way a conversation does. . . . A client can hold a letter in hand, reading and rereading it days, months, and years after the session" (p. 31). Thus, letters can serve as a medium for continuation of the dialogue between the therapist and family members and as a reminder of what has occurred in therapy session. For Epston, letters are case notes. Through them, he attempts to be transparent and congruent in his statements to families while they're in therapy.

Celebrations and Certificates

Celebrations and certificates are a unique and important part of narrative therapy and are used to bring closure to therapy. They serve as tangible affirmations of the defeat of a problem. They also mark the beginning of a new description of a family (White & Epston, 1990). Celebrations can and should take on a festive air, and include cakes, cookies, punch, and other goodies that signify a victory or an achievement.

Certificates can and should be tailored for the family and the situation they have faced. Certificates are best when printed and affixed with a logo. For instance, in regard to a family that has defeated "Apathy," a certificate might read: "This certificate is awarded to the Fong Family in recognition of their conquest of Apathy and its insidious affect upon their lives. Family members are commended for their persistence in the face of inertia and their ability to mobilize their energy to do something about troublesome situations rather than wait for them to go away."

Role of the Narrative Family Therapist

The narrative family therapist works in a number of ways. The therapist does not assume that symptoms serve a function for families. In fact, just the opposite is true. Problems are seen as oppressive for families. They need to be addressed and eliminated as rapidly as possible. Therefore, the narrative therapist is a questioner who works to find unique outcomes or exceptions when families experience problems. The therapist is also notable for examining the meaning of situations for families.

To help families, the therapist assists them in separating themselves from old, problem-saturated stories by constructing new stories in which they, instead of their problems, are in control. This procedure is called reauthoring (White, 1992, 1995) It involves the redefining of lives and relationships in a new narrative. Sometimes this process can be accomplished creatively such as through the use of music and verse (Hodas, 1994). At other times, it is accomplished through a series of questions and the careful use of language. Regardless, family members and families as a whole are successful when they organize to help themselves and escape the power of oppressive influences.

Process and Outcome of Narrative Family Therapy

The process of narrative family therapy is one in which families are aided in learning to value their own life experiences and stories. In therapy, families are challenged to examine exceptions to problems they bring in and to change their behaviors so that they collectively address difficulties by externalizing them. The history of a problem is not as important as making the effort to reconstruct or reauthor a story so that problems are less dominant and significant in a family's life. Questions are raised that aim toward finding exceptions to the dominant influence of problems. The externalization of the problem unites the family in attacking it and, thus, helps the family to avoid scapegoating. By marshalling family resources, expecting setbacks, and raising dilemmas, narrative family therapists help families construct new stories and meaning in their lives without falling into old and unproductive patterns of perception and behavior.

Narrative family therapy has been applied to the following problems: couple relationships, substance abuse, adolescent sexual offenders, schizophrenia, AIDS, learning disabilities, temper problems within a family, anorexia/bulimia, and grief. Most of the outcome studies on its effectiveness have been in the form of case reports.

Overall, narrative therapy is a social constructionism approach that is eclectic and uses the literary metaphors of story telling and writing. Therapeutic relationships are collaborative. It emphasizes co-creating differences, new stories, and new realities. Problems are investigated in terms of exceptions and meaning rather than causes.

Unique Aspects of Narrative Family Therapy

Emphases

Narrative family therapy emphasizes the reauthoring by families of their life stories. According to White (1992, p. 121), a key component of family therapy is a "deconstruction," which involves "procedures that subvert taken-for-granted realities and practices" and helps the client move beyond symptom-maintaining myths to create a more vital story. Family problems are externalized to increase cooperation among family members to problem solve and create new possibilities for action.

In narrative family therapy, the family is asked to look for exceptions to the difficult situations they are experiencing. The idea is to focus on solutions, which are the exceptions, rather than problems, which are the rule. Questions are used extensively.

The expectation of setbacks and the raising of dilemmas is built into narrative family therapy so that families can realize ahead of time some of the problems they might have in creating new life styles. Expecting setbacks may be especially helpful in lowering resistance to making changes.

Letters are sent to families about their progress. Celebrations are held and personalized certificates are issued when goals are achieved.

Comparison of Narrative Family Therapy with Other Theories

Both solution-focused and narrative family therapy are based on postmodern, social constructionist points of view. In these approaches, there is no normative family pattern that should be achieved. Rather, meaning, purposefulness, and health are determined by each family based on their life history and culture.

Narrative family therapy pays particular attention to the use of language. This emphasis on the importance of verbal behavior is similar to most other forms of family therapy.

Little attention is paid in narrative family therapy to the history of the concern (or complaint) brought by the family. In this regard, narrative family therapy is similar to solution-focused, strategic, systemic, and behavioral therapies in its focus on the present rather than the past. Like systemic family therapy, the origins of narrative family therapy began outside the United States. Less narrative family therapy focuses on collaborative therapeutic relationships, which is similar to solution-focused and systemic family approaches.

CASE ILLUSTRATION

THE BEARCLAW FAMILY

David Bearclaw married Claire Standback in a civil ceremony after a whirlwind courtship lasting 3 months. David, age 23, was new to city life and missed the comfort of friends and family on the reservation where he grew up. Claire, age 22, was away from her family for the first time. The couple shared a high hope for their marriage and a physical attraction for one another, but their cultural backgrounds were different as were their expectations for the relationship. David expected to be a good provider and to head the household. Claire, although not opposed to these roles, expected to have a say in the way the family functioned, especially after the birth of their daughter, Rose, now age 5, and their son, Hunter, now age 3. The trouble was that David worked construction and was often between jobs. During these times, he would insist that Claire not work and that she use the money they had saved to pay the bills and keep creditors from bothering them. David also would isolate himself from Claire during these times of unemployment and would leave home to meditate. Claire became depressed but continued going to church and nurturing her children.

Conceptualization of Family: Narrative Therapy Perspective

The 6-year-old marriage of David and Claire is stressed due to economic concerns, a lack of common strategies for problem solving, the stress of preschool children, and other external and internal pressures. The couple has had time to get to know one another, but it appears they do not. They live according to rigid and passive gender roles that do not serve them or their family well. Their lack of outside social support and their tendency to retreat from talking with each other during times of heightened stress contributes to their difficulties.

Process of Treatment: Narrative Therapy

To help the Bearclaws, narrative family therapists would first listen to their story and help them rank order the difficulties they face. In this case, financial stress would be rated number one and the therapist would then work with the Bearclaws to externalize the problem and give it a name, such as "Money." After externalizing the problem, the Bearclaws would be asked by the therapist to state how the problem had had an effect on them and how they had influenced the problem as well.

The therapist would then use questions to help the Bearclaws find times when there were exceptions to their present way of acting and how that behavior impacted on them. For instance, the therapist would compliment the Bearclaws on their ability to buy necessary items on sale and on their agreement to make and keep a budget that allowed for some savings during times of employment. The therapist would make case notes in a letter to the Bearclaws on these exceptions and their work on the troublesome problem of "Money." The therapist would raise dilemmas during treatment on aspects of "Money" the Bearclaws may not have considered and would predict setbacks in the Bearclaws solving their "Money" trouble, too.

Through all of the sessions, the narrative therapist would encourage the Bearclaws to create a new story of their lives, such as switching roles when David is out of work and letting Claire bring home "Money" by working for a temporary employment agency while David takes care of the children. In such a story, the Bearclaws could be more united and less concerned about "Money." The result should lead to a celebration and new strategies for living as a family.

Summary and Conclusion

Since the 1980s, and especially in the 1990s, the work of deShazer and O'Hanlon has brought national attention to solution-focused therapy. This approach concentrates on bringing change to a wider range of client family problems. It is short term, specific, positive, and concentrates on bringing about small changes in the process of facilitating larger ones. Both deShazer and O'Hanlon have been greatly influenced by Milton Erickson.

In the 1990s, narrative family therapy has emerged as another strong approach. Like solution-focused therapy, it is based on a postmodern, social constructionist view of the world that emphasizes the subjective nature of reality and the importance of families making their own meaning in the world by creating stories that are not problem centered. In this approach, difficulties are externalized and, like solution-focused therapies, exceptions to problems are noted and utilized to help families change their behaviors for the better.

Both solution-focused and narrative family therapies are concerned with changing present behaviors, not examining past histories. They both stress that families have untapped resources that can and should be marshalled in helping them help themselves. Likewise, these therapies are creative in innovative ways that go beyond traditional forms of family therapy, such as emphasizing that change is inevitable. Together, solution-focused and narrative family therapies represent the best of the developing, dynamic family therapy approaches that continue to develop.

SUMMARY TABLE

Solution-Focused Therapy

Major Theorists

Steve deShazer
Insoo Berg
Bill O'Hanlon
Michele Weiner-Davis
Eve Lipchik
Alan Gurman
Scott Miller
Simon Budman
Patricia O'Hanlon Hudson

Underlying Premises

Focus is on exceptions to dysfunctionality, hypothetical solutions, and small changes.
Reality is seen as a reflection of observation and experience not as objective reality.
Exceptions to patterns are highlighted.
The present is emphasized.
The family is viewed as an ally that is wanting to change.

Role of the Therapist

The solution-oriented family therapist is a facilitator who asks questions and talks change. Simple and universal solutions are emphasized by the therapist whenever possible.

Unit of Treatment

The unit of treatment is the family as a system, although solution-focused approaches can be selectively used to help dyads and individuals make changes.

Goals of Treatment

The goals of treatment are:

- to help the family to seek solutions and tap internal resources
- to help the family perceive the world differently, especially in regard to the inevitability of change and the importance of making small changes

Therapeutic Techniques

The therapeutic techniques include:

- Joining
- Listening and accepting
- Noting of patterns and exceptions
- Awareness exercises
- Compliments
- Scaling
- Clues
- Mapping
- Skeleton keys
- Hypothetical solutions, such as the "miracle question"
- Task assignments
- Emphasizing making small changes.

Unique Aspects of the Approach

Unique aspects of solution-focused therapy include:

- the acceptance of a family's situation through listening
- an emphasis on the present and clear definition of a family's situation
- the noting of exceptions to family patterns and raising of awareness (including family resources)
- a focus on small changes through completion of an assigned task or through observation within the family

Comparison with Other Theories

Unlike Bowen or psychoanalytic approaches, no attention is paid to history.

Like strategic and systemic family therapies, solution-focused therapy is brief (usually 5 to 6 sessions).

Like behavioral therapy, treatment ends when goals are achieved. However, universal solutions may be utilized in the process of fostering change.

Like systemic family therapy, a team is sometimes used in treatment (deShazer).

Like MRI strategic therapy, solution-focused therapy is aimed at helping families think and act differently.

Narrative Family Therapy

Major Theorists

Michael White

David Epston

Associates of White and Epston

Underlying Premises

Narrative therapy is based on a postmodern and social constructionist perspective that rejects classification systems based on empiricism and promotes empowering persons and families through emphasizing their stories.

Problems are seen as external to persons and families.

Problems should be attacked in a cooperative manner by families who work as teams and utilize their resources.

Role of the Therapist

The therapist views problems as oppressive to families and in need of elimination.

The therapist works to find unique outcomes, that is, exceptions, to families' problems.

The therapist uses questions and helps families create new stories where they, and not their problems, are in control.

Unit of Treatment

Narrative therapy treats family units, and sometimes subunits or individuals.

Goals of Treatment

The focus of treatment is on helping families reauthor their lives and bring about change so that they and not their problems dominate.

Therapeutic Techniques

Narrative therapy treatment techniques include:

- Externalization of the problem
- Influence (effect) of the problem on the person
- Influence (effect) of the person on the problem
- Raising dilemmas
- Predicting setbacks
- Use of questions (exceptions and significance questions)
- Letters
- Celebrations and certificates

Unique Aspects of the Approach

Families learn to value their own life experience and stories and to reauthor their lives.

Families learn to find exceptions to their regular patterns of living.

Problems are externalized and worked on cooperatively.

Expectations of setbacks and the raising of dilemmas help lower resistance.

Letters to families by their therapists are sent regarding their progress.

Celebrations by families and therapists are held when goals are reached.

Comparison with Other Theories

Narrative therapy is postmodern and based on social constructionist viewpoint like solution-focused therapy.

The theory originally developed outside of the United States, like that of systemic therapy

The emphasis of therapy is on the present as compared with the historical emphasis of Bowen and psychoanalytic approaches.

The focus of the approach is on collaborative effort of families and therapists, like strategic and solution-focused family therapies.

References

Becvar, D. S., & Becvar, R. J. (1996). *Family therapy: A systemic integration* (3rd ed.). Boston: Allyn & Bacon.

Bubenzer, D. L., & West, J. D. (1993). William Hudson O'Hanlon: On seeking possibilities and solutions in therapy. *The Family Journal, 1,* 365–379.

Bubenzer, D. L., West, J. D., & Boughner, S. R. (1994). Michael White and the narrative perspective in therapy. *The Family Journal, 2,* 71–83.

Cleveland, P. H., & Lindsey, E. W. (1995). Solution-focused family interventions. In A. C. Kilpatrick & T. P. Holland (Eds.), *Working with families* (pp. 145–160). Boston: Allyn & Bacon.

deShazer, S. (1982). *Patterns of brief family therapy.* New York: Guilford.

deShazer, S. (1984). The death of resistance. *Family Process, 23,* 11–21.

deShazer, S. (1985). *Keys to solution in brief therapy.* New York: W. W. Norton.

deShazer, S. (1988). *Clues: Investigating solutions in brief therapy.* New York: W. W. Norton.

deShazer, S. (1991). *Putting differences to work.* New York: W. W. Norton.

deShazer, S., & Molnar, A. (1984). Four useful interventions in brief family therapy. *Journal of Marital and Family Therapy, 10,* 297–304.

Epston, D. (1994). Extending the conversation. *Family Therapy Networker, 18,* 30–37, 62–63.

Foucault, M. (1965). *Madness and civilization: A history of insanity in the use of reason.* New York: Random House.

Foucault, M. (1980). *Power/knowledge: Selected interviews and other writings.* New York: Pantheon Books.

Foucault, M. (1982). The subject and power. In H. Dreyfus & P. Rabinow (Eds.), *Michael Foucault: Beyond structuralism and hermeneutics.* Chicago, IL: University of Chicago Press.

Foucault, M. (1984). Space, knowledge and power. In P. Rabinow (Ed.), *The Foucault reader.* New York: Pantheon.

Gale, J. E. (1991). *Conversion analysis of therapeutic discourse: The pursuit of a therapeutic agenda.* Norwood, NJ: Abex.

Gladding, S. T. (1996). *Small change.* Unpublished manuscript.

Hodas, G. R. (1994), Reversing narratives of failure through music and verse in therapy. *The Family Journal, 2,* 199–207.

Hudson, P. O., & O'Hanlon, W. H. (1991). *Rewriting love stories: Brief marital therapy.* New York: Norton.

Kilpatrick, A. C., & Holland, T. P. (1995). *Working with families* (pp. 175–197). Boston: Allyn & Bacon.

Kiser, D. J., Piercy, F. P., & Lipchik, E. (1993). The integration of emotion in solution-focused therapy. *Journal of Marital and Family Therapy, 19,* 233–242.

Kok, C. J., & Leskela, J. (1996). Solution-focused therapy in a psychiatric hospital. *Journal of Marital and Family Therapy, 22,* 397–406.

Krauth, L. D. (1995, December). Strength-based therapies. *Family Therapy News, 26,* 24.

Kurtz, P. D., & Tandy, C. C. (1995). Narrative family interventions. In A. C. Kilpatrick & T. P. Holland (Eds.), *Working with families* (pp. 177–197). Boston: Allyn & Bacon.

Maturana, H., & Varela, F. (1987). *The tree of knowledge.* Boston: New Science Library.

Meidonis, G. G., & Bry, B. H. (1995). Effects of therapist exceptions questions on blaming and positive statements in families with adolescent behavior problems. *Journal of Family Psychology, 9,* 451–457.

Nichols, M. P., & Schwartz, R. C. (1995). *Family therapy: Concepts and methods*. Boston: Allyn & Bacon.

O'Hanlon, W. H. (1987). *Taproots: Underlying principles of Milton Erickson's therapy and hypnosis*. New York: W. W. Norton.

O'Hanlon, W. H., & Weiner-Davis, M. (1989). *In search of solutions*: *A new direction in psychotherapy*. New York: W. W. Norton.

O'Hanlon, W. H., & Wilk, J. (1987). *Shifting contexts: The generation of effective psychotherapy*. New York: Guilford Press.

Sauber, S. R., L'Abate, L., & Weeks, G. R. (1985). *Family therapy: Basic concepts and terms*. Rockville, MD: Aspen.

Simon, F., Stierlin, H., & Wynne, L. (1985). *The language of family therapy*. New York: Family Process Press.

Spiegel, H., & Linn, L. (1969). The "ripple effect" following adjunct hypnosis in analytic psychotherapy. *American Journal of Psychiatry, 126,* 53–58.

Todd, T. (1992). Brief family therapy. In R. L. Smith & P. Stevens-Smith (Eds.), *Family counseling and therapy* (pp. 162–175). Ann Arbor, MI: ERIC/CAPS.

Walter, J., & Peller, J. (1993). Solution-focused brief therapy. *The Family Journal, 1,* 80–81.

Walsh, W. M., & McGraw, J. A. (1996). *Essentials of family therapy*. Denver: Love Publishing.

White, M. (1986). Negative explanation, restraint, and double description: A template for family therapy. *Family Process, 25,* 169–184.

White, M. (1989). *Selected papers*. Adelaide, Australia: Dulwich Center Publications.

White, M. (1991). Deconstruction and therapy. *Dulwich Center Newsletter, 3,* 21–40.

White, M. (1992). Deconstruction and therapy. In M. White & D. Epston (Eds.), *Experience, contradiction, narrative, and imagination* (pp. 109–151). Adelaide, South Australia: Dulwich Centre Publications.

White, M. (1993). The histories of the present. In S. Gilligan (Ed.), *Therapeutic conversations*. New York: W. W. Norton.

White, M. (1995). *Re-authoring lives*. Adelaide, South Australia: Dulwich Centre Publications.

White, M., & Epston, D. (1990). *Narrative means to therapeutic ends*. New York: Norton.

PART THREE

SPECIAL POPULATIONS IN FAMILY THERAPY

C H A P T E R   1 1

Working with Single-Parent Families

She talks about her unborn
as three small children noisily play
in the dusty red dirt around her cluttered yard
with hand-me-down toys
from their richer peers in Buena Vista.

Amid the chaos and bleakness,
I wonder how she survives summer's heat
or manages a smile in the face of stress
as her bills pile up like unwashed clothes
in a house without running water
and her resources dry up like shallow ponds in sunlight.

But in the silence,
as the noise of that scene fades in my mind,
at the end of a day filled with mental struggles
I hear the strength of resolve in her voice,
remember her caring eyes and toughness,
and in it all I know, though pained, she will prevail.

Gladding, 1993

The term *single-parent families* has been applied to a number of different family forms. The families covered under this designation include those created as a result of divorce, death, abandonment, unwed pregnancy, and adoption. These types of families hold in common the distinction that a sole parent is responsible for taking care of himself or herself and a child or children (Walsh, 1991). They differ in regard to dynamics. Single-parent families vary depending on the number of people within the unit, the background and resources of the members, and the stage of the individual and family life cycle at the time the unit was formed. Thus, there is no prototype of a single-parent family.

The number of single-parent families in the United States has increased sharply in recent years. Prior to 1970, about one family in ten (10%) was headed by a single parent, usually the mother (Goldenberg & Goldenberg, 1994; Seward, 1978). By 1990, however, "almost one third of the 35 million households with children in the United States" were headed by a single parent (Krauth, 1995, p. 14). This increase has affected some groups more than others (Usdansky, 1992). Figure 11.1 indicates how three major populations—whites, African Americans, and Latinos/Hispanics—have changed in regard to the number of two-parent and single-parent households.

Historically, most single-parent families have been created by the death or desertion of a spouse. In the 1950s, a new trend began: The percentage of single-parent families created by divorce started to exceed those created by death (Levitan & Conway, 1990). Further, the decision of many unmarried women to bear and raise children by themselves, which began in the 1970s, also increased the number of single-parent families—to appropriately 25% of those with dependent children. The number of births "to unmarried mothers hit a record high in 1990 of 1,165,384." Approximately "20 percent of white births, 37 percent of Hispanic births, and 67 percent of black births" were to unmarried women (Associated Press, 1993a, p. 2). This trend is not expected to significantly subside (Morrison, 1991).

This chapter examines three distinct single-parent family lifestyles (those created by divorce, death, and election to bear children alone). It also examines the dynamics underlying and affecting these types of single-parent families, as well as single-parent families in general. The common stressors and strengths associated with the single-parent family life styles are highlighted. Finally, therapeutic approaches for working with single-parent families, who experience difficulties, are discussed from selected theoretical and self-help perspectives. The role of the family therapist and expected outcomes are highlighted.

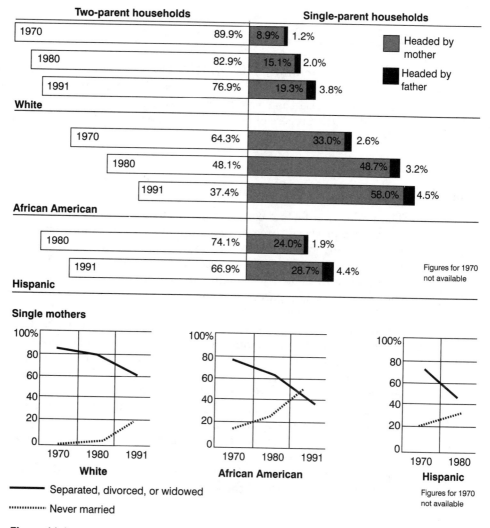

Figure 11.1

Single-parent families on the rise.

From *Counseling Today's Families* (2nd ed.) by H. Goldenberg and I. Goldenberg. Copyright © 1998, 1994, 1990 Brooks/Cole Publishing Company, Pacific Grove, CA 93950, a division of International Thomson Publishing Inc. By permission of the publisher.

Types of Single-Parent Families

Single-parent families vary greatly. Their development occurs over time, whether they are planned or unplanned. Three major types of single-parent families are those that develop as a result of divorce, death, or intentionality. Regardless, the process of becoming a single-parent family is one that has definable stages.

Single Parenthood as a Result of Divorce

The underlying factors contributing to divorce are complex. For whatever reasons, "two of every three divorces [in the United States] are now initiated by women" (Silverstein & Levant, 1996, p. 18). Regardless, when single-parent families begin as a result of divorce, there are two subunits that must be considered (except in some cases of joint custody arrangements). One subunit involves the custodial single parent and his or her interactions with the ex-spouse and children. The other subunit includes the noncustodial single parent and his or her relationships with the ex-spouse and children (Carter & McGoldrick, 1988).

Both parental/child arrangements for single-parent families of divorce have stresses and rewards. For custodial parents in such situations, stressors include rebuilding financial resources and social networks. A major benefit for successful custodial parents is a renewed sense of confidence in oneself. For the noncustodial parent in such a family, stressors include finding ways to continue to be involved with one's children as a parent and the rebuilding of social networks. When successful, noncustodial parents experience rewards. The rewards include devising creative problem-solving methods and gaining renewed self-confidence. Carter and McGoldrick (1988, p. 22) conceptualize the stages of single-parent families formed through divorce as shown in Table 11.1.

Single Parenthood as a Result of Death

In single-parent families that begin as a result of death, the stages of development have not been as specifically delineated as in those single-parent families resulting from divorce. However, it is clear that death has an overall impact on family life and that reestablishment of the family is a major task (Brown, 1988; Moody & Moody, 1991). The family's development may involve three stages, as shown in Table 11.2. The first stage is mourning. It is vital in the mourning stage for surviving family members to release both positive and negative feelings about the deceased. This type of catharsis makes it possible to move to the second stage—readjustment. The readjustment stage involves learning to do new tasks, dropping old tasks, and/or reassigning duties previously done by the

Table 11.1

Dislocations of the Family Life Cycle Requiring Additional Steps to Restabilize and Proceed Developmentally

Phase	Emotional Process of Transition Prerequisite Attitude	Developmental Issues
Divorce		
1. The decision to divorce	Acceptance of inability to resolve marital tensions sufficiently to continue relationship	Acceptance of one's own part in the failure of the marriage
2. Planning the breakup of the system	Supporting viable arrangements for all parts of the system	a. Working cooperatively on problems of custody, visitation, and finances b. Dealing with extended family about the divorce
3. Separation	a. Willingness to continue cooperative coparental relationship and joint financial support of children b. Work on resolution of attachment to spouse	a. Mourning loss of intact family b. Restructuring marital and parent-child relationships and finances; adaptation to living apart c. Realignment of relationships with extended family; staying connected with spouse's extended family
4. The divorce	More work on emotional divorce: Overcoming hurt, anger, guilt, etc.	a. Mourning loss of intact family: giving up fantasies of reunion b. Retrieval of hopes, dreams, expectations from the marriage c. Staying connected with extended families
Post divorce family		
1. Single-parent (custodial household or primary residence)	Willingness to maintain financial responsibilities, continue parental contact with ex-spouse, and support contact of children with ex-spouse and his or her family	a. Making flexible visitation arrangements with ex-spouse and spouse's family b. Rebuilding own financial resources c. Rebuilding own social network
2. Single-parent (noncustodial)	Willingness to maintain parental contact with ex-spouse and support custodial parent's relationship with children	a. Finding ways to continue effective parenting relationship with children b. Maintaining financial responsibilities to ex-spouse and children c. Rebuilding own social network

From "Overview: The Changing Family Life Cycle: A Framework for Family Therapy" by B. Carter and M. McGoldrick, in *The Changing Family Life Cycle* (2nd ed., p. 22) by B. Carter and M. McGoldrick, 1988, New York: Gardner. Reprinted by permission of publisher.

Table 11.2
Single-Parent Families Created by Death

Stage	Task	Results
Mourning	Emotional catharsis	Resolution of past relationship
Readjustment	Learning/dropping of duties	Performance of essential duties
Renewal and accomplishment	Personal and family development	Acquiring of new skills and interests

ex-spouse to other members of the family (Murdock, 1980). When this stage is completed, the family can move into a final stage—renewal and accomplishment—in which family members, and the family as a whole, can concentrate on finding and engaging in new growth opportunities. This last stage, which may or may not be achieved, results in new collective and individual identities and relationships.

Single Parenthood by Intent

The final way in which single-parent families begin involves intentionality. The actions associated with intent are (1) purposefulness in conceiving a child out of wedlock, (2) deciding to carry a child to term after accidentally becoming pregnant out of wedlock, or (3) adopting a child as a single adult. The unique aspect of this type of single-parent family is that the parent has time to prepare before the child arrives. Furthermore, it is clear to the parent in these situations that there will usually be no other support outside of the parent's resources. In these cases, single-parent families go through the stages, processes, and outcomes listed in Table 11.3.

Table 11.3
Single-Parent Families Created by Intention

Stage	Task	Result
Planning	Preparing for the arrival of the child	Marshalling of resources Mental expectation of change
Arrival	Creating a parent and child relationship	Physical and emotional bonding
Adjustment and achievement	Resolving situational and development needs	Growth of family and individual

In general, the formation of these types of single-parent families occurs over time. There is no one type of single-parent family that works best in all situations. Also, time lines must be kept flexible when considering single-parent family development. Different circumstances within each type of family require adjustment considerations that are unique. Two years after the family first develops, however, reality (as opposed to idealization) should be present in all of these types of families (Freeman, 1985).

Dynamics Underlying the Formation of Single-Parent Families

In defining how single-parent families are formed, it is vital to examine the roots from which they spring: divorce, death, and intentionality. By understanding the dynamics underlying these diverse ways of establishing single-parent families, therapists can make better decisions in formulating treatment strategies.

Dynamics of Single-Parent Families Formed Through Divorce

Numerous factors influence the decision for couples to divorce. Among the top three considerations affecting the dissolution of marriages are social, personal, and relationship issues (Bornstein & Bornstein, 1986).

On a social level, there has been a rapid pace of change in American life, especially since World War II (Levitan & Conway, 1990). Major changes include new technology, more alternatives, less stability, and the opportunity for greater frustration, fulfillment, and alienation. Women's roles have changed; and the alliance between men and their work has weakened. In addition, the mobility of society has contributed to an acceptance of options, transitions, and a new openness to mores and laws. Divorce is more acceptable today (Bumpass, 1990; Goldenberg & Goldenberg, 1994).

A second reason for not staying married involves personal issues. People marry at different levels of psychological maturity and with varied expectations. If they are immature, their decisions and actions will most likely reflect it (Bowen, 1978). There are some relationships that are doomed to failure before they begin because of the personalities of those involved. In these marriages, the individuals involved are probably best served when the relationship dissolves, especially if they seek help in becoming more autonomous and mature.

Interpersonal issues are a third variable related to divorce. Marriage and family life involve give and take interactions (i.e., a quid pro quo, or something for something). People often do not stay married when they perceive that they are giving more than they are receiving (Klagsbrun, 1985). There are ways to rectify such situations, but frequently couples do not seek help or seek it too late. The result is the splitting of a relationship.

In all of these situations, men or women who become single parents following divorce and separation deal with the following issues (Garfield, 1982):

- resolution of the loss of the marriage
- acceptance of new roles and responsibilities
- renegotiation and redefinement of relationships with family and friends
- establishment of a satisfactory arrangement with one's ex-spouse

The transition is not easy. In fact, "divorce is much more devastating than people who go into the process anticipate" (Moody, 1992, p. 171). Individuals who have ample resources in the form of psychological or financial aid/support find the difficulties less intense but still formidable. At least 10% of individuals who experience marital separation or divorce see a therapist or counselor (Sweet, Bumpass, & Call, 1988).

Dynamics of Single-Parent Families Formed Through Death

Even when death is expected, it is still a shock. This reaction is especially prevalent if a person is survived by a spouse and child(ren). "About 800,000 spouses . . . die every year" (McGoldrick, 1986, p. 30), leaving behind millions of immediate family members to mourn the loss. It is important that survivors of these deaths properly grieve. Such a process may be difficult because of the lack of mourning rituals in modern society. Yet if family members, especially widows and widowers, do not appropriately grieve for their former spouses, their chances of reestablishing themselves or establishing a healthy single-parent family are greatly lessened.

Therefore, it is crucial that family members talk to one another and others, such as neighbors, extended kin, or counselors, after the death of a spouse/parent. By doing so, they release their feelings and are enabled to see the dead person as mortal instead of superhuman. Such a perspective helps family members deal with their feelings and external demands productively and realistically.

Dynamics of Single-Parent Families Formed Through Choice

The number of people, especially women, who raise a family by themselves is large and growing. It cuts across racial, social, and economic divisions in American society (Associated Press, 1993b). Some of the reasons for this pattern are due to tradition, some to change and acceptance by society, and some to choice. Each reason is be examined here briefly.

Historical tradition is one factor that helps explain why certain groups of women have children out of wedlock. In some subcultures, a maternally-oriented society has evolved in which children have been raised by single-parent mothers. In these subcultures, there is an inclination for many young women and men to avoid marriage and to follow the pattern they grew up in, especially if they are not exposed to other role models. The socioeconomic milieu in such cases has a strong influence that can prove detrimental to the subculture and simultaneously give it a distinction and even, ironically, pride. Racism, ignorance, and socioeconomic crises also contribute to such a pattern of maternal single parenting and make it hard to break the cycle (Strong & DeVault, 1992).

Acceptance is a second reason women elect to have children out of wedlock. The upheavals in American society following World War II helped break down stigmas and taboos. The turbulence of the 1960s further eroded some traditional norms and patterns, such as ostracizing women who bore children out of wedlock. Since the 1970s there has been an increase in the number of women who have elected to have children out of wedlock (National Center for Health Statistics, 1991). In 1992, the percentage of women ages 18 to 44 giving birth outside of marriage was 24%. Most were between ages 25 and 39 and most were non-white: 56% for African American women, 33% for Hispanic women, 15% for white women, and 7% for Asian women (Erbe, 1993). "Society is not frowning on them any more" (Associated Press, 1993b, p. 2).

A final factor that has influenced the increased number of women bearing children out of wedlock is a choice. A small percentage of women who thoughtfully decide to bear and raise children by themselves are well educated; about 33% are high school graduates; and over 8% hold a managerial or professional position (Associated Press, 1993b). In addition, the number of prominent older women who thoughtfully decided to raise a baby by themselves increased in the 1980s. Two well-publicized examples are Mia Farrow and Goldie Hawn (Erbe, 1993).

In addition, the dramatization of the lives of fictitious women who choose parenthood outside of marriage as seen in movies, such as *The Big Chill,* or television programs, such as *Murphy Brown,* has been extensive. Whether one agrees or disagrees with their decisions, the fact is that more mothers over age 25 are deciding to have babies outside of marriage; "about one quarter in 1980 compared with about one third in 1988," with no slow down in the trend expected (Bray, 1993, p. 95).

Although not a complete parallel, the reasons for unmarried women choosing to adopt babies have some similarity to those who become pregnant. For instance, it is more socially acceptable for unwed women to adopt babies than it was in the past. Furthermore, because of resources and desire, many professional women are electing to adopt and raise children by themselves. Two major differences between single women who adopt and those who elect to biologically have a baby are timing and resources. Women who adopt can more precisely pick the time they wish to become a parent. Many of the women are affluent. Like other single women, they are not encumbered by the demands of a marital relationship and can therefore give more time and nurturance to their child(ren) (Groze, 1991). Overall, as a group, unmarried mothers (except for those who adopt) "tend to be younger, poorer, less educated, and more dependent on welfare" (Goldenberg & Goldenberg, 1994, p. 91).

Single-Parent Mothers and Fathers

Gender issues can have an impact on how single-parent families function. To understand the life and needs of these families, it is necessary to be aware of how they differ according to who is parentally in charge. Although single-parent families are formed in a number of different temporary and permanent ways, they are ultimately headed by either a mother or father (Hill, 1986).

Families of Single-Parent Mothers

Historically, between 85% and 90% of children in single-parent households live with their mothers (Glick, 1988; Krauth, 1995). Although this figure varies from year to year, "in 1988, more than 13 million children lived with their mothers only" (Levitan & Conway, 1990, p. 8). The percentage of children living in mother only families was approximately 22% of all children in the United States.

In regard to single-parent mothers and finances, research shows contrasts. Children whose single-parent mothers engage in full-time, paid work report "more positive self-esteem and daily affect and arousal" than those whose mothers do not engage in paid work (Duckett & Richards, 1995, p. 427). In addition, employment has been found to contribute to single mothers' health. However, because women are paid, on average, lower wages than men, these single-parent mothers and their children generally have fewer resources than most families in the United States. For instance, the median income of a married couple with children in 1990 was $41,260, as compared with a single-parent father's income of $25,211 and a single-parent mother's income of $13,092 (Ward, 1993).

Single-parent mothers who have been married may potentially collect either insurance or child support. However, "nearly 70 percent of noncustodial fathers become delinquent within a few years of child support" (Levitan & Conway, 1990, p. 18). When there is regular child support, it does not usually come without some restrictions. Noncustodial fathers who pay support often wish and have the right to be involved in decisions made regarding the welfare of their children (Melli, 1986). With unwed mothers, particularly if they are adolescents themselves, there is the difficulty of obtaining enough financial support to make ends meet. Violence and abuse are unfortunately associated with mother-only homes at the poverty level (Gelles, 1989).

In addition to limited financial assets and the drawbacks that come with them, single-parent mothers may also be pressed for time (Murdock, 1980). Often they sacrifice time in personal care activities, including sleep and rest, in order to take care of their families (Sanik & Mauldin, 1986). They also have new time demands to take care of, such as work duties or school obligations. For some there is the difficulty of dealing with a former spouse's family. These families may want to visit with the child(ren) on occasions, regardless of whether it is convenient for the custodial parent. This type of time demand may interfere with the welfare of the single-parent family as a whole, but it may especially affect the mother.

Furthermore, there is the problem of identity or establishing a different identity. Young single-parent mothers are frequently in need of care, support, and guidance. As a group, they are usually low in self-esteem, work experience, and education (Levitan & Conway, 1990). In addition to difficulties involving identity and functioning, the parent within these households frequently lacks knowledge of how to obtain medical and psychological services. On the other hand, women over 40, especially if they have mainly worked inside the home, have an extremely hard time rebuilding their lives socially, psychologically, and economically (Wallerstein, 1986). Overall, the health and well-being of households headed by single-parent mothers depends on the age and stage of the parent and her children, as well as her level of education, income, and social support. Conditions are often perilous. For example, "children raised by single-parent mothers drop out of high school twice as often as children from two-parent households, and their daughters are twice as likely to become teen mothers" (Krauth, 1995, p. 14). Yet, despite numerous difficulties, there are many mother headed single-parent families that function quite well.

Families of Single-Parent Fathers

Single-parent families headed by fathers are growing fast numerically and as a percentage of families headed by single-parents. "Between 1985 and 1989 alone, the number . . . soared from 1.3 million to 1.8 million, three times the rate of female-headed families" (Elias, 1992, 1A). If this rate continues, single-parent families headed by men may well exceed its historical 10% to 15% rate.

One advantage fathers have as single-parents is that they usually have access to over twice the financial resources of women (Elias, 1992). This monetary strength allows them flexibility in what they do with their children. It also enables them to hire more caretakers as a group than single-parent women and take much needed breaks from the duties of raising children. Thus, these parents can afford to choose when to be close to their children and be good role models for them. What they give up, however, is time with their offspring. Quality time alone seldom brings closeness to a relationship the way that a combination of qualitative and quantitative time does. In addition, children of single-parent fathers who hire domestic help to take care of them may find that their children have incorporated the help's value system into their lives.

An advantage of single-parent fathers in general is that most feel comfortable and competent as single-parents (Riseman, 1986). This characteristic seems to hold true regardless of the reason for custody or the father's financial status. However, societal norms and personal traditions dictate that men should generally place work responsibilities above parenting duties. This means single-parent fathers may be absent from their children more than single-parent mothers. Otherwise, they have to take less desirable and demanding jobs, which lessens their financial resources and stops or regresses their career advancement.

A final factor associated with single-parent families headed by fathers involves time and social life. Like single-parent mothers, single-parent fathers frequently are pressed for time and may experience exhaustion at the end of the day, with no relief from others. Socially and parentally, single-parent fathers are sometimes hindered by fatigue (Elias, 1992). The plight of Dustin Hoffman as a single-parent father in *Kramer vs. Kramer* is a good example of all the factors and dilemmas facing men who opt for such a life style.

Effects of Divorce and Death on Children

Children are affected by divorce and death, although they do not always immediately show it. The adjustment of the family and the children before such an event, experiences surrounding the event, and the resources available to children after the event are the major factors that influence the impact of these experiences.

Children of Divorce

Children whose parents divorce tend to do best if their mothers and fathers continue or resume their parenting roles, manage to put differences aside, and allow children to have a continuing relationship with both of them (Wallerstein, 1992). "Children who experience a positive relationship with their parents show fewer behavioral problems regardless of family structure" (Duckett & Richards, 1995, p. 419). Unfortunately, most children do not experience such an atmosphere. As a result, these children suffer mental and emotional anguish long after their parents divorce and may act out behaviorally.

In a 15-year follow-up of children whose parents divorced, Wallerstein (1990) found that children had vivid memories of their parents' separation. Ironically, those who were most distressed during the time of the breakup, pre-schoolers, were best adjusted as a group at the time of follow-up. Those who were adolescents during the time of divorce, were the most pained as a group at the time of follow-up, when they were young adults. They felt physically and emotionally abandoned. Overall, Wallerstein concluded that "divorce is not an event that stands alone in children's or adults' experience. It is a continuum" (1992, p. 167). For instance, children from families disrupted by divorce are less likely to do well educationally including applying, being admitted, and enrolling in more select colleges (Gose, 1996).

One of the primary tasks for society in the years ahead is to strengthen families, not by turning back the clock, but by helping children feel as socially, economically, and emotionally secure as possible. Otherwise, children who emerge from particularly conflictual divorces may become what Nurse (1996, p. 22) calls "cardboard kids . . . good surface, but nobody knows the depth, or if in fact there is any depth, or authentic self." Suggestions from Glang and Betis (1993) for helping children through the divorce process include:

- having both parents tell the children about the divorce with care and concern
- giving children advanced warning before a parent moves out
- ensuring that children do not feel they are being divorced from either parent
- explaining divorce to children in words they understand
- giving children space of their own both physically and psychologically
- helping children look forward to the visit of a noncustodial parent (which includes realizing and accepting the fact that children often wish their parents to reconcile)

Children Who Lose a Parent by Death

Children who experience death within the family, especially of a parent, express a number of emotions and behaviors depending on their age and attachment to the deceased. They may become anxious, hope for a reunion, blame themselves or others, and become overly active (Olowu, 1990). In order to cope, they need to be given accurate information on what happened and the support of the surviving parent. These children also need to go through three distinct stages of bereavement: protest, despair, and detachment.

Adolescents have some of the same reactions to the death of a parent as younger children. Support from the surviving parent and peers is generally helpful to them (Gray, 1988, 1989). In addition, their grief and response is influenced by their adjustment prior to the parent's death and their religious beliefs (Gray, 1987).

Strengths and Limitations of Single-Parent Families

Embedded within the structure of single-parent families are inherent strengths and liabilities. Sometimes these two aspects of family life are ironically the same. For example, the freedom that single-parent families have to interact with a wide variety of people can also be a detriment to them because of the resources such types of relationships demand. Despite this irony, some unique aspects of single-parent families are mainly positive or negative.

Strengths of Single-Parent Families

A strength of single-parent families as a whole is they tend to be more democratic than most family types (Wallerstein & Kelly, 1980; Weiss, 1979). An informal way of relating to each other is developed out of necessity. This aspect of family life often helps children and their parents interact in unique ways. When decisions have to be made, the needs of all parties, parent and child(ren), are usually taken into consideration.

Another strength of single-parent families relates to roles and rules. Because of limited resources, many single-parent families are flexible in regard to which members will perform what tasks. For example, in single-parent families, any member can wash dishes, sweep the floor, or work in the garden. Adjustability in regard to members' responsibilities is essential and usually occurs.

A third unique quality of single-parent families is the pace at which members go through developmental stages. In single-parent families, children often learn how to take responsibility for their actions at an early age (Wallerstein & Kelly, 1980). They also learn essential skills, such as finding a bargain or saving money, faster than most children. This behavior often endears these individuals to the parent with whom they live and gives them a certain maturity beyond their years in relating to adults.

The final area in regard to assets of single-parent families is the matter of resources. On the positive side, the children of single-parents, and the adults themselves, often are creative in locating and utilizing needed materials for their overall well-being. They learn to survive through being frugal as well as innovative. Single-parent family members realize quite realistically the value of commodities, such as money and time, that other families take for granted (Ahrons & Rodgers, 1987).

Limitations of Single-Parent Families

A limitation of single-parent families involves boundaries and roles (Glenwick & Mowrey, 1986). Troublesome areas include boundary disputes between former spouses and between children and their custodial parent or joint custody parents. Boundary issues with former spouses involve everything from visitation situations to sexuality (Goldsmith, 1982). Within single-parent families, the democratic nature of these families may blur needed boundary distinctions between a parent and child. In either of these cases, if boundaries are not clear and enforced, chaotic and confusing interactions may result and children may get out of control (Glenwick & Mowrey, 1986; Goldenberg & Goldenberg, 1994). Unfortunately, children who grow up in single-parent households often exhibit behavior problems as a result of boundary issues. They are "more than twice as likely to have emotional and behavioral problems" as those who grow up in intact families (Urschel, 1993).

Roles are likewise a problem. Although role flexibility may prove useful and valuable in helping single-parent families as a whole accomplish tasks, it may add stress and work onto select members of these families. They in turn may experience role reversal or role overload (Weiss, 1979). In fact, fatigue and burnout on the part of one or more members of the family unit is often the outcome of this type of open operating procedure.

Another limitation of single-parent families, especially when they result from divorce, is educational achievement. Children have noticeable academic difficulties during the first 18 months of their parent's divorce (Benedek & Benedek, 1979). These effects may be long lasting. For instance, children reared in single-parent families, especially boys, are likely to receive reduced schooling (Krein, 1986). "On the average, children of divorced parents are less educated than others their age and are less likely to graduate from high school than are children of similar backgrounds who grow up in intact families" (Carlson & Sperry, 1993, p. 6).

A third limitation of single-parent families is connected with identity. Many children, especially those who have been raised in a single-parent family as a result of divorce, have difficulty in establishing a clear and strong identity and in relating to others of the opposite gender. "Children of divorce leave home earlier than others, but not to form families of their own. They are far more likely than their peers to cohabit before they marry, and when they do marry, they also are more likely to divorce" (Carlson & Sperry, 1993, p. 6). They may not experience childhood to the fullest. In adulthood they may come to resent growing up so fast and may consciously or unconsciously display less personal maturity.

A fourth limitation and problem of single-parent families is poverty. As a group, single-parent families are financially less well off than other family forms. For instance, they are six times as likely to be poor when compared with nuclear families (Urschel, 1993). Part of the disparity in income is due to the disproportionate number of female headed single-parent families. Approximately 90% of these families are led by women who in general earn less comparatively than men. In addition to generally lower wages earned by women, the lack of child support has further strained the financial resources of these families. Recent data by the Center for the Study of Social Policy shows that of the single-parent families headed by a female that receive child support or alimony, 43% are white, 18% are Hispanic, and 17% are African-American (McLean, 1993). Overall, 50% of children living in single-parent households live below the poverty line (Walsh, 1991).

A final limitation of being a single-parent family relates to emotions. The psychological feelings expressed by parents and children in these families include helplessness, hopelessness, frustration, despair, guilt, depression, and ambivalence (Baruth & Burgraff, 1991; Goldsmith, 1982; Murdock, 1980). These feelings come with the awareness that one has not resolved matters with a significant other, such as a former spouse or parent. These feelings are complicated when one does not have ready access to the needed person. With time, these feelings increase and stress intensifies. They keep the person within the single-parent family "hooked" emotionally to historical times and situations. It usually takes 2 or more years for single-parent family members to resolve their plethora of emotions and to form into a functional unit (Goldenberg & Goldenberg, 1994).

Approaches for Treating Single-Parent Families

Several family therapy approaches work well with single-parent families (Westcot & Dries, 1990). All are dependent on therapists taking the time and effort to get to know the unique aspects of each family. Assessment of the unique as well as universal aspects of a single-parent family always precedes therapeutic interventions. To effectively treat single-parent families, therapists must help them work together as a team systematically.

Family Theory Approaches

Five family theories most often employed with single-parent families are (1) structural, (2) strategic, (3) solution-focused, (4) Bowen, and (5) experiential.

Structural family therapy appears to be popular because it deals with common concerns of single-parent families such as structure, boundaries, and power (Minuchin & Fishman, 1981). The interventions of structural family therapists seek to restructure or redefine family systems (Minuchin, 1974). For example, this approach is designed to put the parent in charge of the way the family functions. As such, the family moves from being a system in which there is a **parentified child** or an equalized relationship among parents and children to one in which power is vested in a custodial parent.

Strategic family therapies are utilized frequently with single-parent families because they focus on immediate problem solving in connection with a particular problem, such as acting out behavior (Westcot & Dries, 1990). The interventions of these approaches may be direct, but often they are more subtle, for example, as in reframing, the use of paradox, and prescribing symptoms. One strategic method that may be particularly effective is reframing. For instance, a reframe may be used to describe a child's behavior as "depressed" instead of "hostile." In such a case, single-parent family members can rally around the child rather than make accusations and continually argue about the child's behavior.

Solution-focused therapy may be particularly helpful to single-parent families because it helps them focus on new aspects of their lives by finding exceptions to difficult situations and doing something different (deShazer, 1991; O'Hanlon & Weiner-Davis, 1989). The emphasis on making small changes is ideally suited to the beginning developmental phase of single-parent family life in which there is much unrest and the ability to participate in therapeutic work is limited because of demands and fatigue. However, if family members perceive when they are in harmony with each other, they can then focus their energy and efforts on cultivating these exceptional times and in the process make significant and healthy changes.

Bowen family therapy is employed because of its emphasis on resolving the past and examining historical family patterns (Bowen, 1978). Through the construction of a genogram, single-parent families may come to notice and deal with the absent person or persons that have influenced them positively or negatively previously. For example, a solo parent may realize he is still trying to live up to the words of his mother who admonished him to "stay married at all costs" and "always put your children's needs before your own." In the process of constructing a genogram, such "ghosts" from the past lose their power to interfere with the family's present interactions because they are recognized as historical figures over which one has control (Goldenberg & Goldenberg, 1994).

Experiential family therapy, especially as advocated by Virginia Satir (1967), is useful for single-parent families in helping their members enact metaphorically—through sculpting and choreography—troublesome and unresolved situations. The feelings that arise in connection with these symbolic experiences often help family members work through emotions and experience affective relief from circumstances they can no longer influence or control.

Regardless of what theoretical approach is employed with single-parent families, therapists should keep in mind that a number of children and parents in these units have already formed opinions about treatment. The reason is that "children in single-parent families are twice as likely to have behavior problems and undergo professional help for these problems than are children in nuclear families" (Bray, 1993, p. 95). Therefore, although these families are in need, they may have mixed feelings—ranging from prejudice to negative expectations—about entering treatment. If complicating and detrimental factors are not addressed, families may not be helped.

Other Approaches to Working with Single-Parent Families

Several other strategies work well in helping single-parent families. These non-theory strategies are especially useful if they are employed simultaneously.

One approach is to help family members communicate clearly and frequently with each other. Clear family communication patterns are associated with the well-being of single-parent families (Hanson, 1986). A forum family therapists can use in this way is the Adlerian concept of a weekly family conference (Baruth & Burgraff, 1991). This type of meeting in which all members are present and talk about their concerns encourages families to resolve problems and plan for the future.

A second approach in working with single-parent families involves linking family members and the family as a whole to needed sources of social support. For example, **Parents Without Partners** is a national organization that helps single-parents and their children deal with the realities of single-parent family life in educational and experiential ways (Murdock, 1980). Single-parents also need the positive involvement and care of extended family and friends whenever possible (Gladow & Ray, 1986).

A third non-theory way of working with single-parent families involves assisting them in getting their financial matters resolved. As a general rule, most single-parent families have economic problems (Norton & Glick, 1986). Financial counseling through, for example, United Way agencies or volunteers can be quite beneficial for these families. Job training and educational opportunities connected with advancement also can help. Through these types of assistance, family members can best utilize their resources.

A final approach to working with single-parent families is through educational methods, especially bibliotherapy (Gladding, 1992). Bibliotherapy involves a family, literature, and the processing of the reading/writing literary experience with the therapist. A number of appropriate books written for all members of single-parent families and for the families themselves can help individuals involved realize they are not alone in what they are experiencing. For example, *This Is Me and My Single-Parent* (Evans, 1989) is a discovery type of workbook that children (ages 4 to 12) and single-parents can work on together. In addition, even a simple newsletter that provides educational information and emotional support can make a difference in the adjustment and well-being of single-parent families (Nelson, 1986).

Role of the Family Therapist

The role of family therapists in working with single-parent families parallels in some ways their role in helping other types of families. For instance, therapists must deal with issues related to boundaries, hierarchies, and engagement/detachment. However, there are both subtle and obvious differences that must be taken into consideration when treating single-parent families. These distinctions are related to the uniqueness of these families as well as their commonness with other families. As a general rule, family therapists "should not be guided by the intact family model and attempt to replicate a two-parent household" (Walsh, 1991, p. 533). Single-parent families are socially, psychologically, and economically unique.

In working with single-parent families, therapists must lay aside personal prejudices and biases. The ability to avoid making judgements and criticisms is especially difficult if therapists have not resolved their own personal problems (e.g., a divorce) that might involve the issue of single-parent family. To be effective, family therapists must deal directly with people, hierarchies, and circumstances of these families, not myths (Bray, 1993). Likewise, therapists must assist single-parent families in giving up any negative stereotypes of themselves.

A second area family therapists must address, especially with those who have become single-parents due to divorce, involves emotional volatility. "Interactional conflict between former spouses is the norm" (Walsh, 1991, p. 532). Therapists must help their clients "distinguish between emotional divorce issues and legal divorce issues and to understand that the emotional issues must be set aside at times in order to make mature and reasonable legal decisions" (Oliver, 1992, p. 41). Getting single-parents to separate their feelings from their functions is at best difficult. It requires that therapists stay focused and balanced in their interactions with family members.

A third role of family therapists in working with single-parent families is to help members and the family as a whole tap their own inner resources as well as utilize support groups (Juhnke, 1993). Many single-parent families are caught up in their problems and biased against themselves. In these situations, members become discouraged and unable to perceive successful problem-solving methods. For instance, a single-parent mother may find through treatment that she is better at achieving results with her children when she listens to them instead of yells at them. The talent to tap this resource may go unused if the family therapist does not help the parent discover and utilize it. Similarly, in assisting the family, the therapist needs to be aware of both formal and informal support groups, such as friends in the neighborhood. Through such groups, parents and children may find encouragement, relief from each other, and renewal through interacting with different people and ideas.

Process and Outcome

Single-parent families that are successful in family therapy show a variety of improvements. Four of the most important are highlighted here, with the realization that other changes may be unique to particular families.

First, as a result of therapeutic interventions, single-parent families manifest more confidence and competence in themselves (Baruth & Burgraff, 1991). Often single-parent families and their members lose self-esteem and exhibit dependence, helplessness, and hopelessness. Single-parent mothers may feel especially overloaded in performing their executive tasks as head of these families (Weltner, 1982). If treatment has been beneficial, family members rely more on themselves and extended networks of family and friends. They function with greater efficiency. They also have a better knowledge of a number of agencies or networks from which they can get the help they need. Furthermore, these families as units have a decrease in behavior problems and stress and an increase in relationship skills, especially between parent and child(ren) (Soehner, Zastowny, Hammond, & Taylor, 1988).

A second expected outcome of family treatment with single-parent families is that members within these units are helped to have clear and functional boundaries (Westcot & Dries, 1990). Single-parent families are frequently enmeshed with cross-generational alliances and nonproductive structures (Glenwick & Mowrey, 1986). When a family breaks up, the custodial parent must help himself or herself, as well as any children involved, adjust to a new hierarchy. Ideally, this type of structure allows for the interaction between the new single-parent family and others (Minuchin & Fishman, 1981). In the case of divorce, an amiable relationship between children and both former marriage partners is needed whether or not there is joint custody.

When these outcomes do not occur, children and adults are forced to operate in inappropriate ways (Juhnke, 1993). For example, when single-parent families are enmeshed, a child, usually the oldest, is often "parentified." (Minuchin, Montalvo, Guerney, Rosman, & Schumer, 1967). **Parentified children** are forced to give up their childhoods and act like adult parents even though they lack the necessary knowledge and skills. When freed from intergenerational enmeshment, the parentified child's role is no longer necessary and can be given up. If all goes well in family therapy, members of single-parent families gain a clearer perspective on their lives, the dynamics of their families, and appropriate behaviors.

A third area of improvement involves the ability to make informed decisions regarding remarriage. Research shows there is a strong tendency for single-parents to move into new marital relationships too quickly. The majority of single-parents are single for less than 5 years. Yet, remarriage is a move that "often compounds problems rather than leading to resolution" (Carlson & Sperry, 1993, p. 6). Remarriages have a higher probability of dissolving than first marriages (Levine, 1990). Counseling can help single-parents and their children examine more thoroughly the pros and cons of remarriage options. Through such a process, single parents can make better decisions, and children can work through their feelings before instead of after the marriage.

Finally, families are able to utilize resources in the community better and make use of their own resources to the fullest. Improvements are seen in financial and personal management areas. Negative feelings accumulated through past experiences begin to dissipate. And, the development of friends, the tapping of family, and the pulling together of family members within the single-parent family unit should occur.

Summary and Conclusion

Single-parent families have a life style that is both temporary and permanent. Although there have always been single-parent families, the growth in their number within the United States has increased drastically since World War II. The reasons for the quantitative rise are varied and complex but include such factors as history, choice, and detrimental circumstances, such as death or divorce. In the 1950s, divorce became the leading cause of the formation of single-parent families. It continues to be a driving force in the 1990s, along with death of a spouse and choice.

Single-parent families come in many forms. They include at least one parent who is biologically related to the child (or the children) or who has assumed such a role through adoption. Because of the structure of single-parent households, a less structured and more democratic setup is created. This type of atmosphere may promote psychological bonding but may also blur needed boundary lines and lead to some confusion and frustration. As a group, single-parent families are less affluent than other family forms, and the majority of them are headed by women.

The possibilities and problems of single-parent families are numerous. As a group, single-parent families may find it easier to relate to a variety of family types and individuals. Most of these families are flexible in their form and functionality. On the other hand, finding resources to support themselves and finding time together (or alone) to enjoy each other (or themselves) is difficult. Many single-parent families live in or close to poverty. They are often adversely affected by such environments.

Through therapeutic interventions, family therapists can help these families maximize their potential and minimize their limitations. In working with single-parent families, therapists utilize mainstream theories, such as structural, strategic, solution-focused, Bowen, and experiential family therapies. They also employ communication procedures, bibliotherapy, and linkage with relevant outside groups, such as "Parents Without Partners" and financial counselors. The role of the family therapist is to be an advocate for these families in finding resources within themselves and others. To do so, therapists must lay aside prejudices and deal with volatile emotions.

If therapy is successful, single-parent families should show a number of improvements. These improvements include more confidence and competence, better efficiency, clear and functional boundaries and structures, and better decision making ability in regard to considerations such as remarriage and finances.

SUMMARY TABLE

Single-Parent Families

The term *single-parent families* is applied to a number of different family forms such as those created by divorce, death, abandonment, unwed pregnancy, and adoption.

A common thread of single-parents is that one parent is primarily responsible for himself/herself and a child or children.

Single-parent families compose over 20% of today's families.

Historically most single-parent families have been created by death or divorce.

One reason single-parent families are increasing, however, is that many single women are choosing to bear and raise children themselves.

Types of Single-Parent Families

Single-parent families that form as a result of divorce contain both custodial and noncustodial parents. Each parent faces challenges individually and in connection with her or his child(ren).

Single-parent families that form as a result of death face the task of having all members go through the stages of mourning, readjustment, and achievement.

Single-parent families formed as a result of intentionality must deal with planning, arrival, and adjustment stages of development.

Generally, all types of single-parent families require time (about 2 years) to form into functional units.

Dynamics Underlying the Formation of Single-Parent Families

By understanding the dynamics underlying the formation of single-parent families, therapists can best help them.

Single-parent families that form as a result of divorce have spouses who have generally been influenced by rapid change, personality compatibility factors, and unequal distribution of power.

Members must deal with the loss of the marriage, new roles, redefinement of relationships, and establishment of a satisfactory arrangement with the ex-spouse or noncustodial parent.

Single-parent families formed from death of spouse must deal with shock, grief, new family reality, and internal/external demands.

Single-parent families that form as a result of intentionality must successfully combat societal pressures. Furthermore, they must justify their decision, and marshall their resources.

Single-Parent Mothers and Fathers

Families headed by single-parent mothers make up between 85% and 90% of all single-parent households. They face problems associated with finances, role overload, extended family or ex-spouse interference, and parental identity. Conditions are often perilous.

Families headed by single-parent fathers make up between 10% and 15% of all single-parent households. They are usually more affluent than those of single-parent mothers. In addition, confidence and competence in single-parent fathers is high. Negatives of these families are job/career limitations, social restrictions, and physical fatigue.

Effects of Divorce and Death on Children

Children's reactions to divorce or death in a family setting are sometimes delayed or inhibited.

Children of divorce do best if their custodial parents allow relationships with both parents to continue and put aside differences.

Regardless of adjustment, children whose parents divorce have memories of it. Their later reactions depend on their ages at the time of separation and the support they receive in working through their feelings about the divorce.

Children who face the death of a parent must deal with their grief through proper mourning and not become overanxious, blameful, or overactive. Detachment is the final stage of the grief process after bereavement and despair. Surviving parents and peer support groups are most helpful.

Strengths and Limitations of Single-Parent Families

Single-parent families often have the following strengths:

- They are more democratic.
- They have flexible roles and rules.
- The children mature and take responsibility earlier.
- They are creative in locating needed resources.

Single-parent families often have the following limitations:

- They have unclear or undefined boundaries and roles.
- They have overall limited academic achievement by children.
- The children contend with identity confusion.

- The children may have difficulty relating to the opposite gender.
- They live with poverty.
- They cope with depression and other negative emotional residue.

Approaches for Treating Single-parent families

Theories that work with single-parent families are:

- structural
- strategic
- solution-focused
- Bowen
- experiential (Satir)

In addition to theories, family therapists can utilize:

- communication methods (e.g., Adlerian family council)
- social support groups (e.g., Parents Without Partners)
- financial counseling services
- bibliotherapy

Role of the Family Therapist

The role of the family therapist includes dealing with boundaries, hierarchies, and engagement/detachment.

Family therapists must lay aside personal biases/prejudices.

Family therapists must deal with emotional volatility of the family.

Family therapists must help foster inner resources and support groups for family members.

Process and Outcome

If single-parent family therapy is successful, families should:

- manifest more competence and confidence in themselves
- have clear and functional boundaries
- make better financial and remarriage decisions
- utilize their own and community resources more fully

References

Ahrons, C. R., & Rodgers, R. H. (1987). *Divorced families: A multi- disciplinary developmental view.* New York: Norton.

Associated Press (1993a, February 26). Single mothers growing in number. *Winston-Salem (NC) Journal, 331, 2.*

Associated Press. (1993b, July 14). Study: More unwed women having babies. *Winston-Salem (NC) Journal, 331, 2.*

Baruth, L. G., & Burgraff, M. Z. (1991). Counseling single-parent families. In J. Carlson & J. Lewis (Eds.), *Family counseling: Strategies and issues* (pp. 157–173). Denver: Love.

Benedek, R., & Benedek, E. (1979). Children of divorce. Can we meet their needs? *Journal of Social Issues, 35,* 155.

Bornstein, P. H., & Bornstein, M. T. (1986). *Marital therapy: A behavioral-communications approach.* New York: Pergamon.

Bowen, M. (1978). *Family therapy in clinical practice.* New York: Jason Aronson.

Bray, J. H. (1993). Families in demographic perspective: Implications for family counseling. *The Family Journal: Counseling and Therapy for Couples and Families, 1,* 94–96.

Brown, F. H. (1988). The impact of death and serious illness on the family life cycle. In B. Carter & M. McGoldrick (Eds.), *The changing family life cycle* (2nd ed.) (pp. 457–482). New York: Brunner/Mazel.

Bumpass, L. L. (1990). What's happening to the family? Interactions between demographic and institutional change. *Demography, 27,* 483–498.

Carlson, J., & Sperry, L. (1993, January/February). The future of families: New challenges for couple and family therapy. *Family Counseling and Therapy, 1,* 1–14.

Carter, B., & McGoldrick, M. (1988). Overview: The changing family life cycle: A framework for family therapy. In *The Changing Family Life Cycle* (2nd ed., p. 22). New York: Gardner.

deShazer, S. (1991). *Putting differences to work.* New York: W. W. Norton.

Duckett, E., & Richards, M. H. (1995). Maternal employment and the quality of daily experience for young adolescents of single mothers. *Journal of Family Psychology, 9,* 418–432.

Elias, M. (1992, June 19-21). Parenting turns men's lives on end. *USA Today,* 1A, 2A.

Erbe, B. (1993, July 19). Stop surge of unwed mothers. *USA Today,* 11A.

Evans, M. (1989). *This is me and my single-parent.* New York: Brunner/Mazel.

Freeman, M. G. (1985). *The concepts of love and marriage* (film). Atlanta: Emory University.

Garfield, R. (1982). Mourning and its resolution for spouses in marital separation. In J. C. Hansen & L. Messinger (Eds.), *Therapy with remarriage families* (pp. 1–16). Rockville, MD: Aspen.

Gelles, R. J. (1989). Child abuse and violence in single-parent families: Parent absence and economic deprivation. *American Journal of Orthopsychiatry, 59,* 492–501.

Gladding, S. T. (1992). *Counseling as an art: The creative arts in counseling.* Alexandria, VA: American Counseling Association.

Gladding, S. T. (1993). *Birth and Resolve.* Unpublished manuscript.

Gladow, N. W., & Ray, M. P. (1986). The impact of informal support systems on the well being of low income single-parents. *Family Relations, 35,* 113–123.

Glang, C., & Betis, A. (1993). Helping children through the divorce process. *PsychSpeak, 13,* 1–2.

Glenwick, D. S., & Mowrey, J. D. (1986). When parent becomes peer: Loss of intergenerational boundaries in single-parent families. *Family Relations, 35,* 57–62.

Glick, P. C. (1988). The role of divorce in the changing family structure: Trends and variations. In S. A. Wolchik & P. Karoly (Eds.), *Children of divorce: Empirical perspectives on adjustment* (pp. 3–34). New York: Gardner.

Goldenberg, H., & Goldenberg, I. (1994). *Counseling today's families* (2nd ed.). Pacific Grove, CA: Brooks/Cole.

Goldsmith, J. (1982). The postdivorce family system. In F. Walsh (Ed.), *Normal family processes* (pp. 297–330). New York: Guilford.

Gose, B. (1996, July 12). Study finds children of divorced parents less likely to enroll at selective colleges. *Chronicle of Higher Education, XLII,* A35–A36.

Gray, R. E. (1987). Adolescent response to the death of a parent. *Journal of Youth and Adolescence, 16,* 511–525.

Gray, R. E. (1988). The role of school counselors with bereaved teenagers: With and without peer support. *The School Counselor, 35,* 185–193.

Gray, R. E. (1989). Adolescent's perceptions of social support after the death of a parent. *Journal of Psychosocial Oncology, 7,* 127–144.

Groze, V. (1991). Adoption and single-parents: A review. *Child Welfare, 70,* 321–332.

Hanson, S. M. (1986). Healthy single-parent families. *Family Relations, 35,* 125–132.

Hill, (1986). Life cycle stages for types of single-parent families: Of family developmental theory. *Family Relations, 35,* 19–29.

Juhnke, G. A. (1993). *Effective family counseling: Applications for school counselors.* Paper presented at the 66th annual convention of the North Carolina Counseling Association. Raleigh, NC.

Klagsbrun, F. (1985). *Married people*. New York: Bantam.

Krauth, L. D. (1995, December). Single-parent families: The risk to children. *Family Therapy News, 26*(6), 14.

Krein, S. F. (1986). Growing up in a single-parent family: The effects on education and earnings of young men. *Family Relations, 35,* 161–168.

Levine, A. (1990, January 29). The second time around: Realities of remarriage. *U.S. News and World Report,* 50–51.

Levitan, S. A., & Conway, E. A. (1990). *Families in flux*. Washington, DC: Bureau of National Affairs.

McGoldrick, M. (1986, November/December). Mourning rituals. *Family Therapy Networker, 10,* 29–30.

McLean, E. A. (1993, April 8). Who gets child support. *USA Today,* 1A.

Melli, M. S. (1986). The changing legal status of the single-parent. *Family Relations, 35,* 31–35.

Minuchin, S. (1974). *Families and family therapy*. Cambridge, MA: Harvard University Press.

Minuchin, S. , & Fishman, H. C. (1981). *Family therapy techniques*. Cambridge, MA: Harvard University Press.

Minuchin, S., Montalvo, B., Guerney, B., Rosman, B., & Schumer, F. (1967). *Families of the slums*. New York: Basic Books.

Moody, F. (1992). Divorce: Sometimes a bad notion. In O. Pocs (Ed.), *Marriage and family ⁹²/₉₃* (pp. 171–176). Guilford, CT: Dushkin.

Moody, R. A., & Moody, C. P. (1991). A family perspective: Helping children acknowledge and express grief following the death of a parent. *Death Studies, 15,* 587–602.

Morrison, P. A. (1991). *Congress and the year 2000: A demographic perspective on future issues*. Santa Monica, CA: Rand Corporation.

Murdock, C. V. (1980). *Single-parents are people too*. New York: Butterick.

National Center for Health Statistics. (1991). *Advanced report of final natality statistics, 1989* (Monthly vital statistics report). Hyattsville, MD: Public Health Service.

Nelson, P. T. (1986). Newsletters: An effective delivery mode for providing educational information and emotional support to single-parent families? *Family Relations, 35,* 183–188.

Norton, A. J., & Glick, P. C. (1986). One parent families: A social and economic profile. *Family Relations, 35,* 9–17.

Nurse, A. R. (1996, Spring). The cardboard kids. *The Family Psychologist, 13,* 22–23.

O'Hanlon, W. H., & Weiner-Davis, M. (1989). *In search of solutions: A new direction in psychotherapy*. New York: W. W. Norton.

Oliver, C. J. (1992). Legal issues facing families in transition: An overview for counselors. *New York State Journal for Counseling and Development, 7,* 41–52.

Olowu, A. A. (1990). Helping children cope with death. *Early Child Development and Care, 61,* 119–123.

Riseman, B. J. (1986). Can men "mother"? Life as a single father. *Family Relations, 35,* 95–102.

Sanik, M. M., & Mauldin, T. (1986). Single versus two parent families: A comparison of mothers' time. *Family Relations, 35,* 53–56.

Satir, V. (1967). *Conjoint family therapy*. Palo Alto, CA: Science and Behavior Books.

Seward, R. (1978). *The American family: A demographic history*. Newbury Park, CA: Sage Publications.

Silverstein, L. B., & Levant, R. F. (1996, Spring). Children need fathers not patriarchs. *The Family Psychologist, 13,* 18–19

Soehner, G., Zastowny, T., Hammond, A., & Taylor, L. (1988). The single-parent family project: A community-based, preventive program for single-parent families. *Journal of Child and Adolescent Psychiatry, 5,* 35–43.

Strong, B., & DeVault, C. (1992). *The marriage and family experience* (5th ed.). St. Paul: West Publishing.

Sweet, J. A., Bumpass, L. L., & Call, V. (1988). *The design and content of the National Survey of Families and Households* (Working paper NSFH-1). Madison, WI: University of Wisconsin, Center for Demography and Ecology.

Urschel, J. (1993, April 8). Stopping high-risk marriages. *USA Today,* 12A.

Usdansky, M. L. (1992, July 17). Wedded to the single life. *USA Today,* 8A.

Wallerstein, J. S. (1986). Women after divorce: Preliminary report from a 10-year follow up. *American Journal of Orthopsychiatry,*

Wallerstein, J. S. (1990). *Second chances*. New York: Ticknor & Fields.

Wallerstein, J. S. (1992). Children after divorce. In O. Pocs (Ed.), *Marriage and Family ⁹²/₉₃* (pp. 163–168). Guilford, CT: Dushkin.

Wallerstein, J. S., & Kelly, J. (1980). *Surviving the breakup: How children actually cope with divorce*. New York: Basic Books.

Walsh, F. (1991). Promoting healthy functioning in divorced and remarried families. In A. S. Gurman & D. P. Kniskern (Eds.), *Handbook of family therapy* (Vol. II, pp. 525–545). New York: Brunner/Mazel.

Ward, S. (1993, May 6). Median income of families with children. *USA Today,* D1.

Weiss, R. (1979). *Going it alone: The family life and social situation of the single-parent.* New York: Basic Books.

Weltner, J. S. (1982). A structural approach to the single-parent family. *Family Process, 21,* 203–210.

Westcot, M. E., & Dries, R. (1990). Has family therapy adapted to the single-parent family? *American Journal of Family Therapy, 18,* 363–372.

Working with Remarried Families

They were a trio,
a mother and young adolescents
scared and scarred.

Learning to sing songs without a bass
while opening jars and opportunities
through the strength of sheer persistence.

He became a part of them,
breaking through boundaries with clumsy actions
while exposing his feelings with caring words.

Slowly, through chaos, a family emerged
as a group, like a jazz quartet.

Through improvisation
they developed a syncopated rhythm.

In an atmosphere of hope,
came the sounds of harmony.

Gladding, 1992

Many terms are used to describe **remarried families** including *step-families, reconstituted families, recoupled families, merged families,* and *blended families.* Regardless of the terminology used, these families "consist of two adults and step-, adoptive, or foster children" (Pearson, 1993, p. 51). Although most prevalent among white Americans because of their high divorce and remarriage rate, remarried families are found among all cultural groups within the United States. They are rapidly "becoming the norm in American society" (Martin & Martin, 1992, p. xi).

Remarried families have always been a part of American family life. However, the way they are formed has changed, and their numbers have increased dramatically in recent years. For example, in the 1880s, the divorce rate for first marriages was only 7%, and the most prevalent reason for forming remarried families was due to the death or desertion of a spouse (Martin & Bumpass, 1989). These figures slowly shifted in the decades that followed. After World War II, the divorce rate in the United States began to rise rapidly. The 1960s and the 1970s saw divorce reach an unprecedented height quantitatively, with approximately 50% of all marriages ending in divorce (Levitan & Conway, 1990). These decades also marked the beginning of a large remarriage movement (Braver, Wolchik, Sandler, Sheets, Fogas, & Bay, 1993).

By the 1990s, there were over 11 million remarried families among American couples, with one million of the two million marriages in the United States each year involving at least one formerly married person. In addition, over 35 million adults had been or were stepparents by this time. Furthermore, it was estimated that "about a third of all Americans" would "remarry at least once in their lives" (Levine, 1990, p. 50).

As a result of the remarried family trend, many children began living in this type of arrangement. It has been predicted that approximately 40% of all children born in the 1980s and 1990s will have such a living arrangement before they reach the age of 18 (Glick, 1989). Indeed, the growth of remarried families is one reason that during the last half of the twentieth century the perception of what is "normal" or "common" in family life has changed.

This chapter examines the dynamics and life cycle of remarried families. These families share unique and universal qualities with other types of families. It is important to delineate and address the issues faced by these families if therapists are going to work with them effectively. By understanding the nature of remarried families, family therapists can assess areas of distinction and commonness (Hayes & Hayes, 1991). "One of the difficulties" of remarried families is that they are fairly new and "we have neither terminology to discuss" them "nor do we have research that explains the complex nature" of them (Pearson, 1993, p. 51). In addition, there is little information in the professional literature about clinically working with remarried families (Darden & Zimmerman, 1992). Thus, remarried families are a professional challenge. The issues surrounding them, however, are understandable.

Forming Remarried Families

There are many kinds and possible configurations of remarried families. Compared with "first-marriage families, the structures are more complex" (Bray, 1994, p. 67). Remarried families are most commonly formed when a person whose previous marriage ended in death, divorce, or abandonment marries either another previously married person or someone who has never been married. The result is a new combination of people, histories, issues, and interactions that are unique to that particular relationship. Unique opportunities arise from this complex joining of personalities and families. However, in this section an emphasis is placed on the most common concerns of remarried families, because they are the issues therapists deal with frequently.

Common Concerns of Remarried Families

Establishing a remarried family is a more complicated process than creating a nuclear family (Visher & Visher, 1982). Remarried families face many situational and developmental tasks that are quite different from those found in other family lifestyles. They must systemically deal with complex kinship networks, define ill-defined goals, develop patterns of interaction that assist them in being cohesive, and reach consensual goals (Bernstein & Collins, 1985; Roberts & Price, 1986). As a way of understanding remarried families and the issues they encounter, Carter and McGoldrick (1988) have formulated a table (see Table 12.1) that outlines the stages, prerequisite attitude, and developmental issues of these family forms.

Dealing with the Death of a Parent

Before the twentieth century, one out of every two adults died before age 50. "Families had to face the possibility that neither parent would survive to raise children to maturity. Not more than a third of the population had a single marriage last more than 10 years. Fifty percent of the time, children lost a parent

Table 12.1

Remarried Family Formation: A Developmental Outline

Steps	Prerequisite Attitude	Developmental Issues
1. Entering the new relationship	Recovery from loss of first marriage (adequate "emotional divorce")	Recommitment to marriage and to forming a family with readiness to deal with the complexity and ambiguity
2. Conceptualizing and planning new marriage and family	Accepting one's own fears and those of new spouse and children about remarriage and forming a stepfamily Accepting need for time and patience for adjustment to complexity and ambiguity of: 1. Multiple new roles 2. Boundaries: space, time, membership and authority 3. Affective issues: guilt, loyalty conflicts, desire for mutuality, unresolvable past hurts	a. Work on openness in the new relationships to avoid pseudo-mutuality b. Plan for maintenance of cooperative co-parental relationships with ex-spouses c. Plan to help children deal with fears, loyalty conflicts and membership in two systems d. Realignment of relationships with extended family to include new spouse and children e. Plan maintenance of connections for children with extended family of ex-spouse(s)
3. Remarriage and reconstitution of family	Final resolution of attachment to previous spouse and ideal of "intact" family; Acceptance of a different model of family with permeable boundaries	a. Restructuring family boundaries to allow for inclusion of new spouse—stepparent b. Realignment of relationships throughout subsystems to permit interweaving of several systems c. Making room for relationships of all children with biological (noncustodial) parents, grandparents, and other extended family d. Sharing memories and histories to enhance stepfamily integration

From *The Changing Family Life Cycle* (2nd ed., p. 24), edited by E. A. Carter and M. McGoldrick, 1988, New York: Gardner Press. Reprinted by permission of the publisher.

before reaching maturity" (McGoldrick, 1986, p. 30). "The fundamental uncertainty of life was much harder for families to avoid" (McGoldrick, 1986, p. 29). Life shortening events included women dying in childbirth and men dying in accidents. The result was a blending of families and kinship networks. Another consequence of such times was that families developed rituals to deal with death and move on with life (McGoldrick & Walsh, 1983).

Today, a death is denied or covered up in many families. Death often occurs in hospitals away from all family members. Funeral services usually include a closed coffin, and those who have died are often described in vague expressions (e.g., "departed" or "passed on") that fail to adequately describe the realities of death. This type of experience with death is particularly true of American families of European descent. Therefore, forming a remarried family after the death of a spouse is difficult because grief may not have been adequately expressed or processed. Furthermore, there are no established guidelines for couples and their offspring to follow in coming together. Indeed, "new roles and rules need to be worked out, relationships developed and maintained, and a working relationship created between households" (Visher & Visher, 1994, p. 208). The process differs in kind and degree from establishing such a family after a divorce (Visher & Visher, 1988).

Dealing with the Divorce of a Couple

It is estimated that approximately 50% of first marriages end in divorce (Glick & Lin, 1986; Brown, 1988). This rate has held steady since the late 1980s. However, some demographers argue that the actual divorce rate is greater than 50% (Castro-Martin & Bumpass, 1989). They estimate that if you include the couples who separate but never file for divorce, the number of first marriages that end in divorce or separation may be as high as 66% (Walker, 1990).

One phenomenon is that two thirds of divorces occur in the first 10 years of marriage. Thus, the median duration of marriage in the United States is 7 years (National Center for Health Statistics, 1988). Two prevalent times of breakup occur during the first few years of a couples' marital relationship. The first is when newlyweds are adjusting to each other and decide that the relationship they have entered is not working. The second is after the birth of a child, when the family becomes unsettled and stressful as new routines are established and disrupted because of infant needs. Although the National Center for Health Statistics reports that the ages of men and women who divorce rose slightly from 1970 to 1990 (from 35.6 to 37.3 years for men and from 32.7 to 34.8 years for women), these figures are more a reflection of later first marriages than increased marriage/family stability (Mullins, 1993).

A second factor associated with the dissolution of marriage is that most people who go through this experience eventually remarry. In fact, approximately "two thirds of divorced women and three fourths of divorced men" marry again (Bray & Hetherington, 1993, p. 3). The trend is so prevalent some "demographers have projected that by the year 2000 the stepfamily will be the predominant family structure in the United States" (Pill, 1990, p. 186).

A third phenomena associated with marriage breakup is that ethnic groups experience the consequences of this activity differently. For instance, when compared with whites, African-American couples are more likely to separate and stay separated longer before obtaining a divorce. They are also less likely to remarry once separated (Cherlin, 1992). A greater percentage of African-American children (75%), as opposed to white children (40%), will experience their parents divorce or separation by age 16 (Bumpass & Sweet, 1989).

A fourth outcome of marital dissolvement is that contact between nonresidential parents and their children declines over the years (Bray, 1994; Seltzer, 1991). Noncustodial mothers (about 10% to 15% of nonresidential parents) maintain better contact with their children than do nonresidential fathers (Furstenberg, 1990). Boys are particularly impacted in a negative way when their nonresidential fathers fail to maintain contact with them (Depner & Bray, 1993; Hetherington, 1990; Weiss, 1979). As a group, they become less competent and exhibit more behavioral problems than do children in other types of family arrangements.

Making Healthy Adjustments in Remarried Families

Making healthy adjustments in remarried families is easier to conceptualize than to achieve. It takes dedication and work. In order for remarried families to achieve a sense of harmony and stability, family members must concentrate on taking care of their own individual issues, as well as family issues (Roberts & Price, 1986). They must learn to relate productively to others with whom they now interact in a manner that connects them as a system. The two subunits that must make this systemic change are children and parents (Bray, 1993).

Transitions for Children in Remarried Families

Issues for children in making the adjustment to remarried families revolve around liabilities and benefits that result from such arrangements. Resolving issues surrounding the death of a parent takes time. It is a loss in which the normal grief period is from 6 to 36 months. Divorce for children also takes time. Divorce is a psychological death, as opposed to a physical death, of an intimate relationship. "The ways in which children perceive and respond to their parents' divorce vary by age, gender, parental conflict, pre- and postseparation, caretaking arrangements, individual resiliency characteristics, and the availability of emotional support" (Schwartz, 1992, p. 324). Liabilities for children may include losing the closeness of a previous parent relationship, losing one's ordinal position from a previous family experience (especially seniority), moving into a new house and/or neighborhood, and having to relate to stepsiblings and a stepparent (Wald, 1981; Wallerstein & Kelly, 1980).

Despite the loss of a family member, benefits for children in remarried families may be significant. For instance, children may gain a closeness with their biological parents as well as their stepparent. They may also be the recipient of increased positive attention from known and new relatives and relations. A third advantage for children in remarried families is they may find areas of common interest among their new stepsiblings and develop lasting friendships.

Finally, moving (if it occurs) may provide children in remarried families the opportunity to establish a different identity that is more congruent with who they wish to become (Kitson & Holmes, 1992; Visher & Visher, 1988).

Transitions for Parents and Stepparents in Remarried Families

Parenting and stepparenting have drawbacks and attractions associated with them. One unattractive aspect of stepparenting is uncertainty. "There are no accepted social roles for stepparents" (Bray, 1994). In the case of a new stepparent, he or she may find that their spouse and stepchildren have routines that have already been established and that are difficult to modify or break. Therefore, a previously unmarried parent may have to work especially hard to make a place for himself or herself within the family system. In the process, these individuals may alienate or create friction among the ones with whom they are trying to relate (Bray, 1993).

For previously married spouses, the difficulties of forming a remarried family involve expectations and realities. These individuals may expect their reformed family to act similarly to their previous one. The reality may be quite different and a source of consternation. In addition, previously married spouses may have unpleasant memories, or unpleasant present encounters, involving an ex-spouse. These types of situations may magnify the stress under which formerly married spouses operate in reestablishing themselves in a new family (Visher & Visher, 1985). The nature of the relationship between ex-spouses is a significant predictor of intimacy in the remarried spouses (Gold, Bubenzer, & West, 1993).

Dynamics Associated with Remarried Families

It is sometimes said that remarried families are born out of loss and hope. As previously indicated, most adults and children who form this type of union have experienced a divorce, an abandonment, or a death. They wish, as well as expect, the remarried family to be a different and better experience. A characteristic of remarried family members is that they often carry a positive fantasy with them about what family life can be like (Schulman, 1972). For the most part, adults who form a remarried family believe marriage and family life can be good. Most children who come into these relationships share a similar belief (Visher & Visher, 1982).

Before a remarriage can develop, however, previous experiences in life, especially those associated with a former family, must be resolved. Adults and children of these former unions are often in mourning and must work through their feelings before they can emotionally join a new family. The extent to which loss is resolved or hope fulfilled makes a major difference in how the people in such arrangements adjust (Pill, 1990).

Another factor that influences the dynamics of remarried families is structure. Remarried families have structural characteristics that make them unique (Galvin & Brommel, 1986; Visher & Visher, 1979). Structural distinctions of remarried families include:

- a biological parent elsewhere
- a relationship in the family between an adult (parent) and at least one child that predates the present family structure
- at least one child who is a member of more than one household
- a parent who is not legally related to at least one child
- a couple that begins other than simply as a dyad
- a complex extended family network

The structure of most remarried families initially is "a weak couple subsystem, a tightly bonded parent-child alliance, and potential 'interference'" (Martin & Martin, 1992, p. 23).

A third dynamic characterizing remarried families is that they are **binuclear,** that is, two interrelated family households that comprise one family system (Ahrons, 1979; Piercy & Sprenkle, 1986). As a remarried (REM) family form, these families have multiple subsystems that include an entourage of adults, children, and legally related persons such as cousins and stepgrandparents (Sager, Brown, Crohn, Engel, Rodstein, & Walker, 1983). They have **quasi kin** who are a "formerly married person's ex-spouse, the ex-spouse's new husband or wife, and his or her blood kin" (Ihinger-Tallman & Pasley, 1987, p. 43). These people are a part of the extended kin network of remarried spouses' families. They make communications and relations among family members difficult.

Issues within Remarried Families

Many issues arise in remarried families. Because each family is unique, the importance of these concerns varies. Among the most prominent that surface, according to Carter and McGoldrick (1988), are those that center around:

- resolving the past
- alleviating fears and concerns about stepfamily life
- establishing or reestablishing trust
- fostering a realistic attitude
- becoming emotionally/psychologically attached to others

In addition, a major issue in remarried families is finding time to consolidate the couple relationship (Pill, 1990). Research shows that children below the age of 9 accept a stepparent more readily than those above this age (Hetherington, Cox, & Cox, 1981). At the same time, young children are more physically demanding on parents than older children. They may keep the new couple from adequately bonding. Likewise the presence of older children may complicate the bonding process, because of the needs of adolescents to establish identities through interactions that can often take the form of rebellion or disruption (Schwartzberg, 1987). Less cohesion in remarried families is more common during the early years of a family's formation (Bray, 1994).

A second factor that becomes an issue in reconstituting a remarried family is that of feelings. The life circumstances surrounding the dissolution of the previous marriage and the adjustment and life experiences of present family members since that time must be worked through (McGoldrick & Carter, 1988). Romantic and negative feelings must be sorted out in a timely and appropriate way. Sometimes partners in a remarried family do not think through the feelings they bring into the relationship until after it is formed (Pill, 1990). What they expect in regard to closeness may therefore be shattered. Likewise, when members of a newly formed family are still mourning the loss of a previous relationship, they may not be adaptable or open to changes. In either of these cases, the past relationships and present realities are issues that inhibit or facilitate the adjustment and satisfaction of these families as units (Pill, 1990).

A third issue that occurs in remarried families is the integration of members into a cohesive family unit. "Cohesion and adaptability represent two pivotal dimensions of family behavior related to family function" (Pill, 1990, p. 186). In the professional literature, "stepfamilies are described as less cohesive, more problematic, and more stressful than first-marriage families" (Bray & Hetherington, 1993, p. 5). Both stepparent-child and sibling relationships are characterized as less warm and intimate than those in first-marriage families. Most members of remarried families have to work harder than those in nuclear or extended families in order to create interpersonal connectedness and rapport with other family members. The process of relating in remarried families is often troubled in stepfather-daughter interactions, especially when the arrangement involves preadolescent children (Hetherington, 1991). Many other arrangements of children and stepfathers also are bothersome (Grove & Haley, 1993; Stern, 1978; Visher & Visher, 1978). A relatively high percentage of stepchildren have behavioral problems in remarried families during the first 6 months of the new union (Bray, 1988).

On average it takes approximately 2 to 5 years for stepparents to form an in-depth relationship with stepchildren and to achieve the role of being a primary parent (Dahl, Cowgill, & Asmundsson, 1987). This 2- to 5-year forming period parallels that of the first stage of the newly married couple (DuVall, 1977). According to Visher and Visher (1986), the eight tasks listed in Figure 12.1 must be completed in order to develop a stepfamily identity.

1. Dealing with losses and changes
2. Negotiating different developmental needs
3. Establishing new traditions
4. Developing a solid couple bond
5. Forming new relationships
6. Creating a "parenting coalition"
7. Accepting continual shifts in household composition
8. Risking involvement despite little societal support

1. Dealing with losses and changes
   - Identifying/recognize losses for all individuals
   - Support expressions of sadness
   - Help children talk and not act out feelings
   - Read stepfamily books
   - Make changes gradually
   - See that everyone gets a turn
   - Inform children of plans involving them
   - Accept the insecurity of change
2. Negotiating different developmental needs
   - Take a child development and/or parenting class
   - Accept validity of the different life-cycle phases
   - Communicate individual needs clearly
   - Negotiate incompatible needs
   - Develop tolerance and flexibility
3. Establishing new traditions
   - Recognize ways are *different*, not right or wrong
   - Concentrate on important situations only
   - Stepparents take on discipline enforcement slowly
   - Use family meetings for problem solving and giving appreciation
   - Shift "givens" slowly whenever possible
   - Retain/combine appropriate rituals
   - Enrich with new creative traditions
4. Developing a solid couple bond
   - Accept couple as primary long-term relationship
   - Nourish couple relationship
   - Plan for couple "alone time"
   - Decide general household rules as a couple
   - Support one another with the children
   - Expect and accept different parent-child and stepparent-stepchild feelings
   - Work out money matters together

Figure 12.1

Tasks that must be completed to develop a stepfamily identity.

From *Stepfamily Workshop Manual* (pp. 235–236) by E. B. Visher and J. S. Visher, 1986, Baltimore, MD: Stepfamily Association of America. Reprinted by permission of the publisher.

5. Forming new relationships
   - Fill in past histories
   - Make stepparent-stepchild one-to-one time
   - Make parent-child one-to-one time
   - Parent make space for stepparent-stepchild relationship
   - Do not expect instant love and adjustment
   - Be fair to stepchildren even when caring not developed
   - Follow children's lead in what to call stepparent
   - Do fun things together

6. Creating a "parenting coalition"
   - Deal directly with parenting adults in other household
   - Keep children out of the middle of parental disagreements
   - Do not talk negatively about adults in other household
   - Control what you can and accept limitations
   - Avoid power struggles between households
   - Respect parenting skills of former spouse
   - Contribute own "specialness" to children
   - Communicate between households in most effective manner

7. Accepting continual shifts in household composition
   - Allow children to enjoy their households
   - Give children time to adjust to household transitions
   - Avoid asking children to be messengers or spies
   - Consider teenager's serious desire to change residence
   - Respect privacy (boundaries) of all households
   - Set consequences that affect own household only
   - Provide personal place for nonresident children
   - Plan special times for various household constellations

8. Risking involvement despite little societal support
   - Include stepparents in school, religious, sports activities
   - Give legal permission for stepparent to act when necessary
   - Continue stepparent-stepchild relationships after death or divorce of parent when caring has developed
   - Stepparent include self in stepchild's activities
   - Find groups supportive of stepfamilies
   - Remember that all relationships involve risk

Strengths and Limitations of Remarried Families

Remarried families come in many forms. They share some universal qualities; but also they have unique situational and developmental factors that either help or hinder them in their total functioning and interpersonal relationships.

Strengths of Remarried Families

The strengths of blended families are important to the stability and survival of these units. Sometimes they are overlooked. However, if utilized, remarried families grow stronger in both their relationships and their overall functioning.

Life Experience

One of the strongest assets of remarried family members is their life experience. For instance, sometimes a stepparent can offer a new spouse or stepchildren something that was not there before, such as a common interest or opportunity unavailable in the original family of origin (Marino, 1996). In addition, both adults and children who form blended families have survived a number of critical incidents that have usually taught them something about themselves and others (Hetherington, 1991). This life knowledge can help them understand their environments in different and potentially healthy ways. It can assist members in being empathic toward new family members, and it can influence individual and family resilience in adverse situations.

Kin and Quasi-Kin Networks

A second strength of remarried families is the kin and quasi-kin networks that they establish. Remarried couples and families are sometimes isolated and frustrated when dealing with societal events, such as father/son or mother/daughter events in community clubs, associations, or educational institutions (Martin & Martin, 1992). Through kin and quasi-kin networks, remarried family members can help one another in a variety of ways, such as offering moral support, guidance, or physical comfort.

Creativity and Innovativeness

A third positive facet of remarried families is their creativity and innovativeness. Sometimes remarried family members are able to generate new ideas, perceptions, and possibilities because they realize that what they have tried before has not worked. As in gestalt therapy, remarried families who develop these abilities are able to see and act on their perceptions of relationships involving present situations (i.e., figure) and less important present situations or those in the future (i.e., ground) (Papernow, 1993). For example, a stepmother and daughter in a remarried family might decide to throw a surprise birthday party for their husband/father, rather than doing routine shopping. By doing so, they create a memory of a shared experience that strengthens the relationship bonds between them. The result may be a synergistic flow of energy and enthusiasm that lasts a lifetime.

Appreciation and Respect for Differences

Another strength of remarried families is their ability to appreciate and respect differences in people and ways of living (Crohn, Sager, Brown, Rodstein, & Walker, 1982). Through experiencing stepparents and new siblings, children especially can benefit. For instance, they learn that mothering or fathering can take on several forms. In the process of obtaining this insight, they pick up new habits from their stepsiblings that may benefit them. Remarriage makes it possible for individuals to observe a richer variety of models for emulating than they may have typically experienced.

Making the Most of Situations

Still another strength of remarried families is their ability to make the most of situations and in the process teach other families how to have fulfilling relationships (Martin & Martin, 1992). Not all remarried families and their members learn how to cope with difficulties, such as loss, or how to promote care and open communication within a new context. However, in remarried families that develop these abilities, the insight they bring to other families in distress can be rewarding and enabling. It is a dynamic that therapists and educators must utilize whenever possible.

Limitations of Remarried Families

There also are limitations of and problems to resolve in remarried families. Some of these difficulties revolve around psychological phenomenon, such as competing for attention; and others center on physical realities, such as the fact that remarried families move three times as often as dual-parent households (Krauth, 1995).

Loss of an Important Member

One problem almost all remarried families face is the loss of an important member(s) of the former family. For example, even though a noncustodial parent may be physically absent from a household, such a person may retain a "tremendous impact," both directly and indirectly, on the remaining family members (Braver et al., 1993, p. 9). The loss of significant others is complicated when difficulties arise concerning feelings about these individuals and they are unavailable. The result is a ripple effect throughout the family. All members of the family can be affected by one individual's unresolved personal issues related to loss.

Establishment of a Hierarchy

Another significant trouble area for remarried families is the establishment of a hierarchy. Children may have difficulty in this area because they can lose status in regard to their ordinal position in the family. For example, a sibling can become the middle child instead of the oldest, and in the process lose his or her leadership role and privileges. This loss of place and power may be complicated even further if the children involved do not particularly like their new stepsiblings or stepparent (Goldenberg & Goldenberg, 1994). Because working out relationships among children takes time and is not always amiable, newly formed remarried families with children are vulnerable to disruption and volatile outbreaks of emotional, if not physical, struggle (White & Booth, 1985). Adults must give up myths and unrealistic expectations in order to rectify this potential problem area (Bray, 1994).

Boundary Difficulties

A third problem sometimes endemic to remarried families concerns boundaries. "Unlike biological families in which family membership is defined sanguinely, legally, and spatially and is characterized by explicit boundaries, the structure of a stepfamily is less clear" (Pasley, Rhoden, Visher, & Visher, 1996, p. 344). The result is that children who are a part of two families may experience *boundary ambiguity*, which results in loyalty conflicts and feelings of guilt about belonging simultaneously to two households. Overall, "boundary difficulties include issues of:

1. Membership (Who are the 'real' members of the family?)
2. Space (What space is mine? Where do I really belong?)
3. Authority (Who is really in charge? Of discipline? Of money? Of decisions? etc.)
4. Time (Who gets how much of my time and how much do I get of theirs?) (McGoldrick & Carter, 1988, pp. 406–407).

Often, stepfamily members who have boundary problems characterize their relationships as chaotic (Pill, 1990). They are unsure of who and what is involved in making their lives adaptable. To resolve issues around the confusion in boundaries, most remarried families need time, flexibility, and commitment (Ihinger-Tallman & Pasley, 1987). They must deal with issues in a straightforward manner, including those involving sexuality between unrelated siblings or parents and siblings. Members can and should discuss and negotiate how they would like their blended family to function (Fenell & Weinhold, 1996).

Resolving Feelings

The fourth problem area remarried families must address is related to feelings. In some remarried families, especially those in which members have been in denial, there are unresolved emotions. These include guilt, loyalty, and anger (McGoldrick & Carter, 1988). A typical response for some remarried family members is to suppress their emotions when they begin to recognize that such affect is related to unresolved feelings. For example, a teenage boy might deny his anger toward his stepmother especially if he still has unresolved anger toward his mother. An equally destructive way of handling these emotions is to project them onto others. For instance, some remarried family members may act in such a manner that stepsiblings or stepparents become negatively characterized or stereotyped (Marino, 1996). In such a situation, a stepmother might be seen as a "witch."

Economic Problems

Another problem remarried families encounter is economic. As a group, blended families are less affluent than other family types (except single-parent families), with only 37% having household incomes of $50,000 or more and 39% having incomes below $30,000 a year (American Demographics, 1992). The lack of money adds additional stress to family members and the family as a whole (Coleman & Ganong, 1989). In addition, many remarried families have expenses, such as child support or the cost of maintaining two residences, that other families do not have. Such families may have a difficult time making ends meet.

Working with Remarried Families

"Many stepfamilies seek therapy when emotional tensions are high, integration seems impossible, and the family is functioning in ways that increase rather than reduce stress" (Pasley et al., 1996, p. 344). Fortunately, there are a number of approaches that work in helping remarried families. These approaches range from educational to theoretical interventions (Visher & Visher, 1994; Woestendiek, 1992).

Guidance in Retaining Old Loyalties

First of all, remarried family members must be helped to recognize that they do not have to give up old loyalties in order to form new ties (Visher & Visher, 1988). Too often individuals, especially children, believe that they must not think or talk about their past lives. This type of repression is likely to lead to resentment, exclusion, isolation, and depression rather than adjustment and growth. In addition, often the new stepparent is treated like an "outsider." This situation can cause the stepparent to feel angry and frustrated, which in turn can lead to complete withdrawal or violence. The important thing is that family members learn through interaction with the therapist to be inclusive rather than exclusive. This may mean that the therapist draws instructional diagrams for the family of how they are operating and also challenges them to participate in cooperative interactive events, such as picnics or board games.

Focusing on Parental Involvement

Another way of helping remarried families is to focus on parental involvement. Stepparents need to maintain a balance in being involved with their natural children (if any), new children (if any), former spouse (where applicable), and present spouse. The more children and spouses in one's past, the harder this task is to accomplish. Therefore, before and after their wedding, stepparents should spend time discussing the impact of past relationships on new relationships (Martin & Martin, 1992). They can then work with a family therapist to overcome unresolved issues and, thus, learn to contribute to the well-being of all family members.

Providing Education

Education is one of the best ways to help remarried families to adapt, adjust, and grow. For example, remarried family members need to understand the differences between a stepfamily and a non-stepfamily system (Pasley et al., 1996). Learning what to expect and having guidelines for handling typical situations is rated high by remarried families (Visher & Visher, 1994). Stepparents are often unsure, for example, of how to discipline the other spouse's children (Woestendiek, 1992). Likewise, children brought into remarried families are frequently confused about how to relate to their new parent and stepsiblings.

A number of popular books and pamphlets are available for individuals in newly created blended families to read and discuss with members of their new family. For instance, the Family Service Association of America publishes materials that are helpful in developing effective stepparenting skills (Larson, Anderson, & Morgan, 1984). Likewise, a program has been devised for building remarried family strengths (Duncan & Brown, 1992). Numerous books that can be utilized in a bibliotherapeutic way are available for children (Pardeck & Pardeck, 1987). An example is a book authored by Richard Gardner (1971) entitled *The Boys and Girls Book About Stepfamilies*. It is a work meant to be read and responded to verbally by stepparents and children (Gardner, 1984). *This is Me and My Two Families* (Evans, 1988) is an engaging and therapeutically oriented scrapbook/journal for children ages 4 to 12 living in remarried families.

Assisting in the Creation of Family Traditions and Rituals

A fourth therapeutic way of working with remarried families is through assisting them in devising their own traditions and rituals (Coale, 1994). Rituals facilitate "developmental transitions, maintenance of stability and continuity; healing processes; and connectedness.... Healthy ritual life can also serve to buffer families from toxic effects of stress and pathology" (Giblin, 1995, p. 37).

The use of rituals has also been found to be powerful in assisting remarried families in thinking through their definition of what makes a family (Peterson, 1992; Whiteside, 1989). Traditions and rituals include ways of celebrating nodal events, such as birthdays and anniversaries. They also include mundane daily transactions, such as when to go to bed, when to get up, and who will do what chores. When these situations are worked out, new and predictable ways of interacting are established that give family members predictability and stability. Such a process allows time to have fun while allowing family members to experience security.

In addition to their celebration and enjoyment functions, rituals may facilitate:

- the forming of relationships
- the resolution of ambiguous boundaries
- the healing of loss
- the settling of hierarchy and power struggles
- the creating of beliefs
- the beginnings of changes (Coale, 1994; Roberts & Imber-Black, 1992).

For instance, by gathering all members of a new family together once a week for "game night," a stepmother may help family members learn more about each other and develop friendships. The overall impact is one that is likely to result in the building of trust and care.

Applying Structural Family Therapy

A particularly effective theoretical approach for working with remarried families is structural family therapy. The reason is that structural family therapy concentrates on setting up a clear hierarchy within the family and establishing boundaries (Minuchin, 1974). If remarried families do not structurally readjust boundaries after the new family unit is formed, the family may experience conflict that is prone to escalation in negative outcomes such as anger or abuse (Friesen, 1985).

In working from a structural perspective, it is crucial that the family be encouraged to set up an open system "with permeable boundaries between current and former spouses and their families" (Goldenberg & Goldenberg, 1990, p. 141). The reason for such an arrangement is that it facilitates coparenting relationships and prevents children from exerting a type of inappropriate power to decide important parental prerogatives such as "remarriage, custody, or visitation" (Goldenberg & Goldenberg, 1990, p. 141).

Applying Experiential Family Therapy

Another approach for helping remarried families is experiential family therapy. Some of the methods associated with the work of Virginia Satir may be especially useful (Satir, Banmen, Gerber, & Gomori, 1991). For example, sculpting and choreography may help family members see the closeness or distance of relationships and the interrelatedness of certain actions. Role playing also may assist family members to become sensitized to the real and imagined restraints that keep them in dysfunctional patterns. Such information helps them become aware of how they can break out of vicious cycles and make progress in their personal and interpersonal lives.

Doing Transgenerational Work

A final theoretical perspective that is pertinent for remarried families is transgenerational work, especially Bowen Family Therapy (Bowen, 1981; McGoldrick & Carter, 1988; Visher & Visher, 1988). In this approach, the use of a three-generational genogram helps families detect patterns that can both inform and assist them in forming a new family unit. By examining the past through a genogram, remarried families can plan for a productive future and avoid previous mistakes. This process is the same as that for other family types.

Role of the Therapist

Therapists who work with remarried families wear many hats. They must deal with a variety of dynamics and complexities that are more complicated than those found in nuclear families (Visher & Visher, 1988). For example, they must deal with issues involving separation and custody; they must be concerned with the developmental dilemmas within newly formed families (Bray & Berger, 1992); and they must concentrate on fostering a strong and healthy parental coalition (Visher & Visher, 1994). "Because stepfamily issues and needs are diverse and often emotionally charged, the ability to be active, to take charge of intensely emotional sessions, and to be flexible and resourceful in the use of different therapeutic modalities contributes to therapists' effectiveness in working with families" (Pasley et al., 1996, p. 347).

In working with remarried families in regard to separation and custody issues, children within the family system must be given special consideration. "Child clients may experience confusion, fear, and depression as they become aware that they are the focal point in a custody, visitation, or child support dispute" (Oliver, 1992, p. 41). In order to alleviate undue anxiety and distress, family therapists need to be well informed about legal processes as well as psychological ones. For example, they should be aware of legal precedence concerning custody decisions. Family therapists who are knowledgeable about such aspects of family jurisprudence can help all members of families make better decisions. They are enabled and empowered by such legal insight to work in helping the family process information on an emotional and intellectual level so that everyone in the family, including small children, understands what is happening or can happen (Oliver, 1992).

Family therapists must also work with the family in arranging predictable and mutually satisfactory arrangements between former parents and their child or children (if the family was formed as a result of divorce). The continuity and quality of children's relationships with their parents following a divorce is a major factor in determining the children's healthy development (Wallerstein, 1990). Therefore, in some cases, counseling sessions may include the noncustodial parent, as well as the reconstituted family. In these situations, family therapists must focus their attention on helping families negotiate arrangements that will benefit everyone involved.

Fostering strong and healthy parental coalitions means helping stepparents work together to nurture one another and find ways for them to work together to be effective parents. Such a task may involve the couple spending select time together, working with former spouses (if present) to be supportive of them, and finding ways for children in the new family to care for one another physically and psychologically (Visher & Visher, 1994).

Hayes and Hayes (1986) mention four more issues that must be dealt with:

1. *Family members must be encouraged to relinquish personal myths they have carried into the new family relationship.* These myths may take many forms, but often they involve seeing former relationships as idyllic and viewing other people as either saints or devils.

2. *Family members must learn effective ways of communicating with each other.* Effective communication skills used in remarried families are the same as those used in facilitating other counseling relationships. They include paying attention to verbal and nonverbal messages, the use of "I" messages, and concreteness (Meier, 1989).

3. *Family members need structured programs of parent training and reading lists of materials that are germane to their situation in the new family structure.* Material provided in this bibliotherapeutic process should include research, especially for the adults in the relationship, as well as other books or pamphlets that are more simply formatted.

4. *Family members, especially children, need a forum within the therapeutic setting in which they can mourn the loss of previous relationships and develop relationships in the reconstituted family.*

Overall, the family therapist working with remarried families must focus on external and internal factors that tend to unbalance the family system. Although family therapists dealing with traditional two-parent families concentrate on some of these same factors, the degree and complexity of the dynamics are not the same. Remarried families have more emotional, historical, and internal issues that must be settled.

To be effective, family therapists who work with remarried families must devote large amounts of energy and effort to bringing about multiple-person resolutions. They must join with members of the family in order to understand the frustrations inherent in each person's role while seeking to bring about resolutions to real and potential problems within the family system as a whole (Fennell & Weinhold, 1996). It is not an easy or simple task.

Process and Outcome

If therapy is successful with remarried families, these families come to understand themselves better as systems. This goal is often disruptive and stressful because remarried families are "an evolving family system in which each member reciprocally influences and is influenced by other family members" (Bray, 1993, p. 272). Yet, the process of better understanding the unity of the family can be achieved in several ways.

One systemic based way of helping remarried families come to terms with themselves is by supporting the new parent and sibling subunits. This type of support stresses the importance of the couple and children learning to work, play, and make mistakes together. If successful, remarried families become aware of themselves as family units composed of subsystems (Martin & Martin, 1992). They begin to gel in age and stage appropriate ways. For instance, children within remarried families may unite to ask for special privileges or a raise in their allowance. Similarly, parents may present a unified front as to behaviors that are and are not acceptable.

Effective therapy also helps family members become tolerant of and deal realistically with one another and family life events. This means that persons within reconstituted families must avoid projection and distortions. For instance, "the entrance of a new parent figure is a . . . unique experience" for children who may "displace their anger" onto this person (Walsh, 1991, p. 521). Likewise, all involved in a remarried family must give up romanticizing or idealizing those who are now outside the formal structure of the family, such as a parent who no longer lives with his or her children (Everett & Volgy, 1991).

On a developmental level, effective therapy helps family members find their place in the new family as it is now. In some remarried families, congruence between individual and family developmental issues exists, such as in remarried families with young children. In this case, both parents and children seek cohesion. On the other hand, in other remarried families, divergence between the goals of individuals and families exists, such as in a remarried family with adolescents. In this case, the new couple might be developmentally prone to closeness while the teenagers are ready to separate (Bray, 1993). When family therapy is successful, members become aware that they are in an environment in which novel roles can be explored (Martin & Martin, 1992). Such an environment is one in which family members are safe, and the overall atmosphere is one in which members can deal with their losses, gains, aspirations, and/or regrets.

A fourth dimension of process and outcome involves fostering new traditions, including those dealing with both responsibility and celebrations (Imber-Black, 1988). Many rituals in American society are inadequate as ways of terminating relationships (Everett & Volgy, 1991, p. 522). Likewise, few models are available for joining family members from different backgrounds (Imber-Black, 1988). Family therapy helps remarried families create new and lasting ways of humanizing relationships. For example, new traditions can be built around a commonly shared meal, such as dinner, in which everyone is given space and time to relate. Similarly, holiday periods can become opportunities for family members to celebrate old and new traditions.

Finally, in working with remarried families, therapists must help them develop a healthy self-concept of themselves as a family. The mass media and even some scholarly journals generally portray remarried families in a negative way. For example, Whitehead (1993) states that research has found "stepfamilies disrupt established loyalties, create new uncertainties, provoke deep anxieties, and sometimes threaten a child's physical safety as well as emotional security" (p. 71). Therefore, to do well, remarried families must first find internal strength, in order to deal with the external pressures and stereotypes that are less than healthy (or accurate).

Summary and Conclusion

Working with remarried families is a challenging process because of the multitude of variables and personalities involved. Family therapists who work with such families need to realize that remarried families have unique as well as universal characteristics. For example, remarried families have a particular life cycle of their own. They are binuclear in their structure. Many members of remarried families are dealing with loss and grief because their previous relationships ended in death, abandonment, or divorce. The expression of feelings is probably higher than in traditional nuclear families.

On the other hand, like other family forms, members of remarried families must deal with the universal aspects of parent/children and sibling relationships. Members must balance concerns so that neither the individual nor the family suffers or is ignored.

Helping remarried families means that therapists must be sensitive to their own biases and perceptions and flexible in their theoretical approaches. Structural, experiential, and transgenerational family therapies are three ways to assist these families in resolving the issues and tasks before them. The use of rituals from a strategic family therapy point of view is also an important therapeutic tool that can be employed. Remarried families need to formulate and practice new traditions in a ritualistic manner. Such behavior helps them bond and overcome physical and psychological barriers that would otherwise hinder them. Bibliotherapy and psychoeducational processes are yet other possible ways to help.

Family therapists who work with remarried families need energy and imagination in the process. They are called upon to engage family members in ways that are complex and taxing. At times therapists may need to see significant others in the family outside of those living under one roof. Just as being a successful remarried family requires negotiation skills from members, the same is demanded of family therapists. With the number of remarried families growing, it is doubtful one can be a family therapist without acquiring skills in regard to this population. Therefore, the challenge is to continuously learn about common elements special to remarried families while treating each new remarried family as a one-of-a-kind phenomenon.

SUMMARY TABLE

Working with Remarried Families

A remarried family consists of two adults and step-, adoptive, or foster children. They are most prevalent among white Americans, although they are found among all cultural groups.

Historically, remarried families have always been part of American family life, although their numbers have increased dramatically in recent years.

It is predicted that up to 40% of children born in the 1980s will spend part of their life in a remarried family.

The growth of remarried families is a major reason the perception of what is "normal" in family life has changed.

One of the problems of treating remarried families is that there is no terminology to discuss the complex dynamics within them.

Forming Remarried Families

A remarried family is most commonly formed when a person from a previous marriage remarries someone who is single or previously married. One or both of the marriage partners comes into this arrangement with children.

Prior to the 1950s, death was the most frequent reason for the ending of a marriage. Rituals helped survivors deal with death. In the 1990s, about 800,000 spouses die each year. Many do not mourn their loss appropriately.

Over one million divorces occur each year. The actual divorce rate is between 50% and 66%. About two-thirds of divorces occur in the first 10 years of marriage. Most who divorce eventually remarry. Ethnic groups experience divorce differently. After divorce, contact between a child and a noncustodial parent usually declines.

Healthy Adjustment in Remarried Families

Heathy adjustment in remarried families depends on members working on both individual and family issues.

Children must deal with real and perceived losses such as parental closeness, seniority privileges, moving, and adjustment to new stepsiblings and a stepparent.

Benefits for children in remarried families include closeness to a new adult parent figure, increased attention, new friendships, and the opportunity to establish a different identity.

Drawbacks for new stepparents include breaking into or modifying established routines, adjusting to expectations and realities, and managing the stress of different relationships.

Dynamics Associated with Remarried Families

Remarried families are born out of loss and hope.

Most children and adults who become part of a remarried family can have a good experience; but first they must resolve past experiences and modify unrealistic fantasies.

Remarried families have structures that both help and inhibit bonding and alliances. These structures are different from those of nuclear families.

Many remarried families are binuclear and involve the interrelating of two or more households.

Issues with Remarried Families

Remarried families face situational and developmental tasks that are different from those of other families. They must resolve the past, alleviate fears, deal with trust, be realistic, and become psychologically/physically attached.

The ages and stages of children and parents influence how many issues remarried families face and how they are resolved.

Integrating members into remarried families is difficult and takes at least 2 years. Some relationships, such as that between children and stepfathers, are bothersome.

Strengths and Limitations of Remarried Families

Assets remarried family members bring to each other include:

- different life experiences
- kin and quasi-kin networks
- creativity and innovativeness
- appreciation and respect for differences in living styles
- the ability to make the most of situations and model appropriate coping strategies for other families

Problems that remarried families must deal with include:

- the loss of an important member (or members) of the former family
- the establishment of a workable family hierarchy
- boundary difficulties
- unresolved emotions
- economic concerns and financial difficulties

Working with Remarried Families

To deal effectively with remarried families, therapists should:

- help families to recognize and deal appropriately with old loyalties and new ties
- help families become involved constructively with significant others, such as a former spouse or new children
- provide families with educational materials
- help families to develop their own rituals and traditions
- apply structural, strategic, Bowen, and experiential family therapy to deal with issues such as history, boundaries, structure, and feelings

Role of the Therapist

Therapists who work with remarried families wear many hats. They must help remarrieds deal with separation/custody issues rationally and psychologically.

Therapists must help remarried families to arrange predictable and mutually satisfactory interactional patterns, including relinquishing personal myths, teaching communication skills, offering parent training, and providing a forum for the airing of common and unique concerns.

Overall, family therapists must work with a variety of internal and external issues that tend to unbalance remarried families.

Process and Outcome

As a result of effective family therapy interventions, remarried families are:

- able to understand personal and systemic issues related to this arrangement
- aware of subunits within their families and more tolerant and realistic with each other

- able to find their place within these families and deal effectively with individual and family developmental issues
- able to understand the importance of integrating family members into a working system through creating unique family ways of operating and traditions
- stronger internally and able to withstand negative portrayals of remarried families in the popular press

References

Ahrons, C. R. (1979). The binuclear family: Two households, one family. *Alternative Lifestyles, 2,* 499–515.

American Demographics. (1992, July). *American households.* (Suppl. Desk Reference Series #3). Ithaca, NY: Author.

Bernstein, B. E., & Collins, S. K. (1985). Remarriage counseling: Lawyers and therapist's help with the second time around. *Family Relations, 34,* 387–391.

Bowen, M. (1981). The use of family theory in clinical practice. In J. Haley (Ed.), *Changing families.* Philadelphia: Grune & Stratton.

Braver, S. L., Wolchik, S. A., Sandler, I. N., Sheets, V. L., Fogas, B., & Bay, R. C. (1993). A longitudinal study of noncustodial parents: Parents without children. *Journal of Family Psychology, 7,* 9–23.

Bray, J. (1988). Children's development during early remarriage. In E. M. Hetherington & J. Arastek (Eds.), *The impact of divorce, single-parenting, & stepparenting on children* (pp. 279–298). Hillsdale, NJ: Lawrence Erlbaum.

Bray, J. H. (1993). Becoming a stepfamily: Developmental issues for new stepfamilies. *The Family Journal, 1,* 272–275.

Bray, J. H. (1994). What does a typical stepfamily look like? *The Family Journal, 2,* 66–69.

Bray, J. H., & Berger, S. H. (1992). Stepfamilies. In M. E. Procidano & C. B. Fisher (Eds.), *Contemporary families: A handbook for school professionals* (pp. 57–79). New York: Teachers College Press.

Bray, J. H., & Hetherington, E. M. (1993). Families in transition: Introduction and overview. *Journal of Family Psychology, 7,* 3–8.

Brown, F. H. (1988). The impact of death and serious illness on the family life cycle. In B. Carter & M. McGoldrick (Eds.), *The changing family life cycle* (2nd ed., pp. 457–482). New York: Gardner.

Bumpass, L., & Sweet, J. A. (1989). Children's experience in single-parent families: Implications of cohabitation and marital transitions. *Family Planning Perspectives, 6,* 256–260.

Carter, B., & McGoldrick, M. (1988). Overview: The changing family life cycle—A framework for family therapy. In B. Carter & M. McGoldrick (Eds.), *The changing life cycle* (2nd ed., pp. 3–28). New York: Gardner.

Castro-Martin, T., & Bumpass, L. (1989). Recent trends and differentials in marital disruption. *Demography, 26,* 37–51.

Cherlin, A. J. (1992). *Marriage, divorce, remarriage* (rev. ed.). Cambridge, MA: Harvard University Press.

Coale, H. W. (1994). Therapeutic use of rituals with stepfamilies. *The Family Journal, 2,* 2–10.

Coleman, M., & Ganong, L. H. (1989). Financial management in stepfamilies. *Lifestyles, 10,* 217–232.

Crohn, H., Sager, C. J., Brown, H., Rodstein, E., & Walker, L. (1982). A basis for understanding and treating the remarried family. In J. C. Hansen & L. Messinger (Eds.), *Therapy with remarriage families.* Rockville, MD: Aspen.

Dahl, A. S., Cowgill, K. M., & Asmundsson, R. (1987). Life in remarriage families. *Social Work, 32,* 40–44.

Darden, E. C., & Zimmerman, T. S. (1992). Blended families: A decade review, 1979-1990. *Family Therapy, 19,* 25–31.

Depner, C. E., & Bray, J. H. (Eds.) (1993). *Nonresidential parents. New vistas in family living.* Newbury Park, CA: Sage.

Duncan, S. F., & Brown, G. (1992). RENEW: A program for building remarried family strengths. *Families-in-Society, 73,* 149–158.

Duvall, E. M. (1977). *Marriage and family development* (5th ed.). Philadelphia: Lippincott.

Evans, M. (1988). *This is me and my two families.* New York: Brunner/Mazel.

Everett, C. A., & Volgy, S. S. (1991). Treating divorce in family-therapy practice. In A. S. Gurman & D. P. Kniskern (Eds.), *Handbook of family therapy* (Vol. II, pp. 508–524). New York: Brunner/Mazel.

Fenell, D. L., & Weinhold, B. K. (1996, March). Treating families with special needs. *Counseling and Human Development, 28,* 1–12.

Friesen, J. D. (1985). *Structural-strategic marriage and family therapy.* New York: Gardner.

Furstenberg, F. F. (1990). Divorce and the American family. *Annual Review of Sociology, 16,* 379–403.

Galvin, K. M., & Brommel, B. J. (1986). *Family communication: Cohesion and change* (2nd ed.). Glenview, IL: Scott, Foresman.

Gardner, R. A. (1971). *The boys and girls book about stepfamilies.* New York: Bantam.

Gardner, R. (1984). Counseling children in stepfamilies. *Elementary School Guidance and Counseling, 19,* 40–49.

Giblin, P. (1995). Identity, change, and family rituals. *The Family Journal, 3,* 37–41.

Gladding, S. T. (1992). *Blendings.* Unpublished manuscript.

Glick, P. C. (1989). Remarried families, stepfamilies, and stepchildren: A brief demographic profile. *Family Relations, 38,* 24–27.

Glick, P. C., & Lin, S. L. (1986). Recent changes in divorce and remarriage. *Journal of Marriage and the Family, 48,* 737–747.

Gold, I. M., Bubenzer, D. L., & West, J. D. (1993). Differentiation from ex-spouses and stepfamily marital intimacy. *Journal of Divorce and Remarriage, 19,* 83–95.

Goldenberg, H., & Goldenberg, I. (1990). *Counseling today's families.* Pacific Grove, CA: Brooks/Cole.

Goldenberg, H., & Goldenberg, I. (1994). *Counseling today's families* (2nd ed.). Pacific Grove, CA: Brooks/Cole.

Grove, D. R., & Haley, J. (1993). *Conversations on therapy: Popular problems and uncommon solutions.* New York: W. W. Norton.

Hayes, R. L., & Hayes, B. A. (1986). Remarriage families: Counseling parents, stepparents, and their children. *Counseling and Human Development, 18*(7), 1–8.

Hayes, R. L., & Hayes, B. A. (1991). Counseling remarried families. In G. Carlson & J. Lewis (Eds.), *Family counseling: Strategies and issues* (pp. 175–188). Denver, CO: Love Publishing.

Hetherington, E. M. (1990). Coping with family transitions: Winners, losers, and survivors. *Child Development, 60,* 1–14.

Hetherington, E. M. (1991). Families, lies and videotapes. *Journal of Research on Adolescence, 1,* 323–348.

Hetherington, E. M., Cox, M., & Cox, R. (1981). The aftermath of divorce. In E. M. Hetherington & R. D. Parke (Eds.), *Contemporary readings in child psychology* (2nd ed., pp. 99–109). New York: McGraw-Hill.

Ihinger-Tallman, M., & Pasley, K. (1987). *Remarriage.* Newbury Park, CA: Sage.

Imber-Black, E. (1988). Normative and therapeutic rituals in couple therapy. In E. Imber-Black, J. Roberts, & R. Whiting (Eds.), *Rituals in families and family therapy.* New York: W. W. Norton.

Kitson, G. C., & Holmes, W. M. (1992). *Portrait of divorce: Adjustment to marital breakdown.* New York: Guilford Press.

Krauth, L. D. (1995, December). Single parent families: The risk to children. *Family Therapy News, 26*(6), 14.

Larson, J. H., Anderson, J. O., & Morgan, A. (1984). *Effective stepparenting.* New York: Family Service Association of America.

Levine, A. (1990, January 29). The second time around: Realities of remarriage. *U. S. News & World Report,* 50–51.

Levitan, S. A., & Conway, E. A. (1990). *Families in flux.* Washington, D. C.: Bureau of National Affairs

Marino, T. W. (1996, August). Families often merge onto a highway of frustration. *Counseling Today,* 8.

Martin, D., & Martin, M. (1992). *Stepfamilies in therapy.* San Francisco, CA: Jossey-Bass.

Martin, T. C., & Bumpass, L. (1989). Recent trends and differentials in marital disruption. *Demography, 26,* 37–51.

McGoldrick, M. (1986, November/December). Mourning rituals. *Family Therapy Networker, 10,* 29–30.

McGoldrick, M., & Carter, B. (1988). Forming a remarried family. In B. Carter & M. McGoldrick (Eds.), *The changing family life cycle* (2nd ed., pp. 399–429). New York: Gardner.

McGoldrick, M., & Walsh, F. (1983). A systemic view of family history and loss. In M. Aronson (Ed.), *Group and family therapy*. New York: Brunner/Mazel.

Meier, S. T. (1989). *The elements of counseling*. Pacific Grove, CA: Brooks/Cole.

Minuchin, S. (1974). *Families and family therapy*. Cambridge, MA: Harvard University Press.

Mullins, M. E. (1993, July 14). Divorcing couples growing older. *USA Today*, D1.

National Center for Health Statistics. (1988). Births, marriages, divorces, and deaths for November 1987. *Monthly vital statistics report, 36,* 13, Washington, DC.

Oliver, C. J. (1992). Legal issues facing families in transition: An overview for counselors. *New York State Journal for Counseling and Development, 7,* 41–52.

Papernow, P. L. (1993). *Becoming a stepfamily*. San Francisco, CA: Jossey-Bass.

Pardeck, J. T., & Pardeck, J. A. (1987). Using bibliotherapy to help children cope with the changing family. *Social Work in Education, 9,* 107–116.

Pasley, K., Rhoden, L., Visher, E. B., & Visher, J. S. (1996). Successful stepfamily therapy: Clients' perspectives. *Journal of Marital and Family Therapy, 22,* 343–357.

Pearson, J. C. (1993). *Communication in the family* (2nd ed.). New York: Harper Collins.

Peterson, K. S. (1992, November 25). Traditions that put life in context. *USA Today*, D1-2.

Piercy, F. P., & Sprenkle, D. H. (1986). *Family therapy sourcebook*. New York: Guilford.

Pill, C. J. (1990). Stepfamilies: Redefining the family. *Family Relations, 39,* 186–193.

Roberts, J., & Imber-Black, E., (1992). *Rituals for our times: Celebrating, healing, and changing our lives and our relationships*. New York: Harper-Collins.

Roberts, T. W., & Price, S. J. (1986). A systems analysis of the remarriage process: Implications for the clinician. *Journal of Divorce, 9,* 1–25.

Sager, C. J., Brown, H. S., Crohn, H., Engel, T. Rodstein, E., & Walker, L. (1983). *Treating the remarried family*. New York: Brunner/Mazel.

Satir, V., Banmen, J., Gerber, J., & Gomori, M. (1991). *The Satir model: Family therapy and beyond*. New York: Science and Behavior Books.

Schulman, G. L. (1972). Myths that intrude on the adaptation of the stepfamily. *Social Casework, 53,* 131–139.

Schwartz, L. L. (1992). Children's perceptions of divorce. *American Journal of Family Therapy, 20,* 324–332.

Schwartzberg, A. Z. (1987). The adolescent in the remarriage family. *Adolescent Psychiatry, 14,* 259–270.

Seltzer, J. A. (1991). Relationships between fathers and children who live apart: The father's role after separation. *Journal of Marriage and the Family, 53,* 79–101.

Stern, P. N. (1978). Stepfather families: Integration around child discipline. *Issues in Mental Health Nursing, 1,* 50–56.

Visher, E. B., & Visher, J. S. (1978). Common problems with stepparents and their spouses. *American Journal of Orthopsychiatry, 48,* 252–262.

Visher, E. B., & Visher, J. S. (1979). *Stepfamilies: A guide to working with stepfamilies and stepchildren*. New York: Brunner/Mazel.

Visher, E. B., & Visher, J. S. (1985). Stepfamilies are different. *Journal of Family Therapy, 7,* 9–18.

Visher, E. B., & Visher, J. S. (1986). *Stepfamily workbook manual*. Baltimore, MD: Stepfamily Association of America.

Visher, E. B., & Visher, J.S. (1988). *Old loyalties; new ties: Therapeutic strategies with stepfamilies*. New York: Brunner/Mazel.

Visher, E. B., & Visher, J. S. (1994). The core ingredients in the treatment of stepfamilies. *The Family Journal, 2,* 208–214.

Visher, J. S., & Visher, E. B. (1982). Stepfamilies and stepparenting. In F. Walsh (Ed.), *Normal family processes* (pp. 331–353). New York: Guilford.

Wald, E. (1981). *The remarried family: Challenges and promise*. New York: Family Service Association of America.

Walker, L. D. (1990). Problem parents and child custody. *American Journal of Family Law, 4,* 155–168.

Wallerstein, J. S., (1990). *Second chances*. New York: Ticknor & Fields.

Wallerstein, J. S., & Kelly, J. B. (1980). *Surviving the break up: How children and parents cope with divorce*. New York: Basic Books.

Walsh, F. (1991). Promoting healthy functioning in divorced and remarried families. In A. S. Gurman & D. P. Kniskern (Eds.), *Handbook of family therapy* (Vol. II, pp. 525–545). New York: Brunner/Mazel.

Weiss, R. S. (1979). *Going it alone*. New York: Basic Books.

White, L. K., & Booth, A. (1985). The quality and stability of remarriages: The role of children. *American Sociological Review, 50,* 689–698.

Whitehead, B. D. (1993). Dan Quayle was right. *The Atlantic Monthly, 271,* 47–84.

Whiteside, M. F. (1989). Family rituals as a key to kinship connections in remarried families. *Family Relations, 38,* 34–39.

Woestendiek, J. (1992, August 15). You are not my mother. *Winston-Salem Journal,* 22–23.

CHAPTER 13

Working with Culturally Diverse Families

She works cleaning clothes and ironing sheets,
a person of color in a bland and bleached world
where there is little emotion amid the routine
as the days fade like memories into each other.

He struggles trimming hedges and mowing grass,
a solitary white man surrounded by people
whose skin is darker than his.

Sometime when discouraged she struggles
to stop her dreams from slipping away,
like the fresh steam from her always hot iron,
by giving them vividness in her mind
and calling her hopes by name.

He too concentrates on the future
amid the tedium of routine and long hours
as he images scenes of those who love him
and conjures up pictures of home.

Gladding, 1992

Distinct cultures and culturally diverse families have been a part of American society since its inception. In fact, "every family's background is multicultural. All marriages are to a degree cultural intermarriages. No two families share exactly the same cultural roots" (McGoldrick & Giordano, 1996, p. 6).

It was not until the civil rights struggles of the 1960s, however, that the majority of people in the United States began to recognize and accept cultural pluralism (Lee & Richardson, 1991). Before this time, many Americans were cut off from the mainstream of society because of racial, language, or custom differences. These barriers to accessibility resulted in many new immigrants and cultural minorities isolating themselves in order to establish a sense of community, preserve traditional values, and be protected. In most major cities, there are enclaves of Italians, Haitians, Poles, Ukrainians, Irish, Koreans, Nigerians, Vietnamese, Mexicans, and others distinct family groups who live physically and psychologically apart. This type of separation, along with the societal tradition of often ignoring or exaggerating differences, has made it hard for family therapists to understand culturally distinct families and their issues. Thus, compassionate and effective treatment has been, until recently, almost nonexistent for these families.

As the population of the United States becomes more diverse, it is essential that family therapists gain knowledge about different family types and skill in treating them. Increasingly, family therapists are "finding themselves working with families in multicultural context" (Goldberg, 1993, p. 1). Instead of looking at actions in the context of isolated individuals, therapists now see persons as a part of families and their behaviors as a part of a sociocultural context (Falicov, 1983). Put another way, therapists strive to understand individuals and families "in the context of the family's culture" and the culture at large (Gushue, 1993, p. 489).

Different culturally diverse families have much to teach each other, and therapists. For instance, situations that encompass the lifespan, from dealing with health to reacting to death, are treated differently by distinct cultural groups (Brown, 1988; McGoldrick, Preto, Hines, & Lee, 1991). Thus, in working with families, therapists must take into account how different cultures instill in family members attitudes and actions, such as social and communication patterns (Goldenberg & Goldenberg, 1993). When family therapists do not comprehend the values and characteristics of specific cultures and their families, the behaviors associated with these beliefs and traditions are likely to be undervalued, misunderstood, and/or pathologized (Billingsley, 1968; McGoldrick & Giordano, 1996).

This chapter discusses various aspects of culturally diverse families. The emphasis is on the dynamics that are common to a broad range of families. Issues involved in working from a multicultural point of view are stressed. In addition, some special aspects of conducting family therapy with African-American, Asian-American, Hispanic/Latino-American, and Native-American families are highlighted.

What Is a Culture?

To tackle the issues involved in multicultural family therapy, it is necessary to define *culture* and to distinguish it from race and ethnicity. Such a procedure helps clarify concepts and the interrelatedness of terms. It is a difficult process and one in which there is not universal agreement.

Culture can be defined in numerous ways, but it is generally considered to be "the customary beliefs, social forms, and material traits of a racial, religious, or social group" (Webster, 1989, p. 314.). "This broad definition implies that culture is a multidimensional concept that encompasses the collective realities of a group of people" (Lee, 1991, p. 11). As such, culture is made up of behaviors and traditions that have been cultivated over a long period of time. It may be a conscious aspect of a family's identity, such as taking pride in ancestry, or it may consist of unconscious practices that family members perform and never question. Both conscious and unconscious practices of culture involve seeing and being in the world through a persistence to continue to live a certain way despite information to the contrary (Watzlawick, 1976).

A culture includes diverse groups of people who may differ in regard to race, religion, or social status but who identify themselves collectively in a particular way. For instance, it is possible to speak about Jewish, Christian, Buddhist, or Muslim cultures that encompass people from a wide range of social classes. It is also appropriate to talk about specific countries and their cultures, such as Japanese, Egyptian, Kenyan, or Indian. Culture may be spoken of in regard to those who are racially in either the majority or the minority. The point is that cultures operate on many levels, that is, inclusive and exclusive, specific and general. Many cultures are open to people of various backgrounds who identify with them and act in accordance with their traditions and values. Some are closed. In a pluralistic society such as the United States, "a complex melange of cultural influences" exist that impact families and their members (Szapocznik & Kurtines, 1993).

Racial groups and *ethnicity* are not so broadly defined. A racial group is "a family, tribe, people, or nation belonging to the same stock" (Webster, 1989, p. 969). It may include an ethnic group, but "*race* is primarily a biological term"

(Lee, 1991, p. 12). Ethnic groups are "large groups of people classed according to common racial, national, tribal, linguistic, or cultural origin or background" (Webster, 1989, p. 427). Ethnic identity "is anything but homogenous" (Giordano & Carini-Giordano, 1995, p. 352). In describing ethnic groups, the term *ethnicity* is used reflecting a sociological concept (Lee, 1991). "Ethnicity . . . influences the kinds of messages that people learn . . . for example, Scandinavian patterns for expressions of intimacy may differ greatly from Italian and Greek messages" (Mason, 1991, p. 481). Therefore, ethnic family customs influence a groups' "fit" within an overall culture, just as race does.

Although race and ethnicity may be used at times synonymously to refer to people who share similar traits or characteristics, they differ when employed in their most precise form. Therefore, the term *culture* is more widely utilized when discussing a group of people with similar backgrounds, beliefs, and behaviors. The broadness of *culture* is the primary reason it is employed in this chapter as a modifier of family diversity.

Dynamics Affecting Culturally Diverse Families

Culturally diverse families are affected by the same social pressures that impact other families. These families must learn to cope with the stressors associated with money, work, children, aging, death, success, and leisure (Turner, 1993). However, the way families from different cultural backgrounds view and respond to life events differ. For instance, some general and striking characteristics of Jewish families are to marry within the group, to encourage children, to value education, and to use guilt as a way of shaping behavior; in general, Italian families place importance on expressiveness, personal connectedness, enjoyment of food and good times, and traditional sex roles (McGoldrick & Rohrbaugh, 1987). Regardless, minority culture families are effected both quantitatively and qualitatively in regard to life experiences in ways that members of majority families are not (Sue & Sue, 1990). "Certain moments in the family life cycle will represent greater crisis for one culture than for another" (Gushue, 1993, p. 489). For instance, in Irish families, "death is generally considered the most significant life cycle transition and members will go to great lengths not to miss a wake or a funeral" (McGoldrick, 1986, p. 31). On the other hand, "because of the stress on interdependence in Puerto Rican culture, the loss of a family member is experienced as an especially profound threat to the family's future and often touches off reactions of extreme anxiety" (Garcia-Preto, 1986, p. 33).

In addition, culturally diverse families who are in the minority must also contend with overt as well as covert criticism of their patterns of family interaction that may not be universally accepted (Tseng & Hsu, 1991). For example, if women are treated by certain families as inferior or subservient, these families and their culture may be taken to task by others. Likewise, a majority culture may ignore important civic or religious holidays in particular culture groups and both directly and indirectly convey to members of these groups their disinterest or disdain in them as people.

Another difficulty for culturally diverse families is appearance. Members of such families may be recognized by their distinct skin color, physical features, or dress. Therefore, they must deal with subtle and blatant prejudice and discrimination on an almost continuous basis (Ho, 1987). As a result of discrimination or hatred based on outward appearance, some families are faced with the task of nurturing and protecting each other in ways unknown to majority culture families.

A fourth dynamic that affects culturally diverse families involves their access to mental health services (Sue & Sue, 1990). The location of mental health services, their formality, and the way they advertise their services is often a turnoff for culturally diverse families. For example, Native American Indians may have to drive miles for treatment and then find that the clinic operation hours are not convenient to their life style. This kind of situation is known as an **institutional barrier**. Other institutional barriers include the use of a language not understood by minority families and the lack of culturally diverse practitioners.

A final factor influencing culturally diverse families involves economics (Arnold & Allen, 1995). To function well in society, families must include one or more persons earning wages that make it possible to live beyond a survival level. Often minority cultures are excluded from jobs or have employment opportunities limited by events in society such as the rise of technology and service industries and the shrinkage of the working class in the United States. These events have resulted in many heads of minority households being cut out of employment opportunities that paid good wages and falling into the ranks of the working poor and underclass.

Working with Culturally Diverse Families

A number of critical issues are involved in working with culturally diverse families. These issues center around attitudes, skill, and knowledge. No family therapist can be an expert on all cultures (McGoldrick et al., 1991). However, most family therapists can acquire general abilities that enable them to be effective in helping a wide variety of families. Such factors as sensitivity, experience, acceptance, ingenuity, specificity, and intervention often determine whether family therapists are successful or not.

Sensitivity
The issue of sensitivity is one with which all helping professionals must deal. If family therapists are not sensitive to the similarities and differences between themselves and the families they work with, they may make assumptions that

are incorrect and unhelpful (Boynton, 1987). Professionals who are insensitive have been described as **culturally encapsulated counselors** (Wrenn, 1962, 1985). They tend to treat everyone the same, and in so doing, make mistakes. For instance, every Hispanic/Latino family differs in regard to its makeup and the strategies members use to resolve problems. If therapists are not sensitive to this fact, they may try the same methods with all Hispanic/Latino families and get mixed results.

Experience

The issue of experience refers to that of the family therapists as well as that of the families they treat. Professionally, it may be hard for a family therapist to work with a family of a diverse background if the therapist has not had some life experiences with members of that culture. For instance, a family therapist who has been socially isolated in a white, middle-class culture may become lost when trying to help a newly immigrated Vietnamese family resolve family conflict.

Also important is the experience of specific culturally diverse families. If a family of Hispanic/Latino descent has a history of affluence and acceptance within mainstream society, a family therapist needs to recognize and respect the socioeconomic factors that influence that family. Specific cultural backgrounds are often influenced by a family's experiences in the larger society. Such families and their members often find themselves having conflicts because of their inheritance of two different cultural traditions (Ho, 1987; Sue & Sue, 1990).

Acceptance

The issue of acceptance encompasses therapists' personal and professional comfortableness with a family. If therapists cannot openly accept culturally diverse families, they are likely to display overt or covert prejudice that negatively impacts the therapeutic process. Therefore, it is of utmost importance that therapists assess their thoughts and feelings about the families that are before them. The question of racism must be raised early if the family and therapist are of different racial backgrounds (Franklin, 1993). Social, behavioral, and economic differences need to be examined also in order to assess whether the family and therapist are a good match. Models for examining therapists' values in regard to families and self have been developed by Ho (1987) (see Table 13.1).

Ingenuity

To be effective in treating culturally diverse families, therapists must use their ingenuity. There are natural help-giving networks in most cultural settings (Sue & Sue, 1990, p. 135). Effective family therapists utilize these networks and are innovative as well. Instead of trying to treat some families within the confines of an office, therapists act as a consultant to agencies and persons who can best work with certain families. For example, in the African-American community, churches and ministers have traditionally been a source of strength and help. Thus, therapists may act in conjunction with and in direct and open collaboration with these sources in treating a family in context (Boszormenyi-

Table 13.1

Cultural value preferences of middle-class white Americans and ethnic minorities: A comparative summary.

Area of Relationships	Middle-Class White Americans	Asian/Pacific Americans	American Indian, Alaskan Native	African Americans	Hispanic Americans
Man to nature/environment	Mastery over	Harmony with	Harmony with	Harmony with	Harmony with
Time orientation	Future	Past-present	Present	Present	Past-present
Relations with people	Individual	Collateral	Collateral	Collateral	Collateral
Preferred mode of activity	Doing	Doing	Being-in-becoming	Doing	Being-in-becoming
Nature of man	Good and bad	Good	Good	Good and bad	Good

From *Family Therapy with Ethnic Minorities* (p. 232) by M. K. Ho, 1987, Newbury Park, CA: Sage. Copyright © 1987 by Sage Publications, Inc. Reprinted by permission of Sage Publications, Inc.

Nagy, 1987). On the other hand, "with traditional Asian Americans, subtlety and indirectness may be called for rather than direct confrontation and interpretation" (Sue & Sue, 1990, p. 136).

Specificity

Specificity is necessary because each family is unique and must be treated differently. Family therapists must assess the strengths and weaknesses of individual families and design and implement specific procedures for each. Although Strategic Family Therapy (Haley, 1973, 1976) and Solution-Focused Therapy (deShazer, 1988) pride themselves on devising approaches that address the needs of specific families, other family therapy models also modify their goals, guidelines, and interventions, depending on the particular families they are treating. In practical terms, family therapists must realize, for example, that the needs and issues of first generation families differ from those of more acculturated families. Contrary to popular belief, as families become acculturated, they do not drop former cultural ways but instead add new ones and synthesize "both the new and the old in a creative manner" (Newlon & Arciniega, 1991, p. 202). The issue of specificity is a reminder that the application of treatment needs to be congruent with and tailored to families' experiences.

Intervention

A final aspect of being an effective counselor with culturally diverse families involves the challenge of intolerance within systems. Such a goal is accomplished when a counselor assumes the role of a systematic change agent (Lee, Armstrong, Brydges, 1996). In this type of role, a counselor tries to intervene on behalf of families in unhealthy and intolerant systems. There are two types of unhealthy systems. One involves a "passive insensitivity to diversity" (Lee et al., 1996, p. 5), that is, the plight of people outside one's culture are simply ignored. The other intolerant system is "one characterized by an active and intentional insensitivity to diversity" (Lee et al., 1996, p. 5). This latter type of system fosters active discrimination that is easier to identify. Bringing about change in either type of system takes courage, persistence, and time.

Characteristics of Culturally Diverse Families

Culturally diverse families share some characteristics in common. For example, the importance and influence of the extended family and kinship ties are almost universal in families from all cultural backgrounds (Johnson, 1995). However, all families have unique characteristics that must be considered when working with them. It is important to consider, for example, that "the definition of *family*, as well as the timing of life cycle phases and the importance of different transitions, varies depending on a family's cultural background" (Carter &

McGoldrick, 1988, p. 25). With that in mind, the following sections highlight some common aspects of four culturally diverse family groups—African Americans, Asian Americans, Hispanic/Latino Americans, and Native Americans.

African-American Families

African Americans are the "largest minority group in the United States" (Sue & Sue, 1990, p. 209). There were approximately 33.5 million African Americans in 1995, according to the Census Bureau (Associated Press, 1996). Their families are diverse in regard to background and traditions. However, they share a commonness in that many of their ancestors were brought to America as slaves and their black skin color differentiates them from the majority of people in the United States. These two characteristics have kept them "at an extreme disadvantage" in acculturating and being accepted in society (Walsh, 1982, p. 417). In addition, African-American families have had to face racism, poverty, and discrimination continuously. As a group, they have faced many socioeconomic disadvantages and a great deal of stress (Kazdin, Stolar, & Marciano, 1995). On popular television shows and in films, African Americans have been depicted as being wise and witty (e.g., *The Cosby Show*); middle-class (e.g., *Laural Avenue*); violent and unruly (e.g., *Boyz N the Hood*); and heroic (e.g., *Passenger 57*). In truth, African-American families vary, just like other types of families.

In regard to strengths, African-American families are known for being "strong" in the areas of kinship bonds. Most African-American families "are embedded in a complex kinship and social network" that includes both blood relatives and close friends (Lambie & Daniels-Mohring, 1993, p. 74). Another strength is their religious orientation and spirituality; they often utilize the resources of their clergy and churches (Richardson, 1991). Cooperation, achievement, and work orientation are other positive characteristics that describe African Americans (Hill, 1972). Finally, African Americans are "adaptable" in their family roles. Members of such families are less likely to stereotype each other into roles based on gender (Ericksen, Yancey, Ericksen, 1979).

Despite their strengths, African-American families face a number of negatives. Internally, African-American male-female relationships have "become more problematic, conflictual, and destructive" (Willis, 1990, p. 139). The reasons for this phenomenon are complex and relate to factors—such as mistrust, insecurity, unemployment, and rage—that are the conscious and unconscious legacies of slavery and a changing society. Regardless of the underlying dynamics, the result is that despite their belief in the institution of marriage, fewer African Americans marry today than at any time in history (Cherlin, 1992). Out of wedlock births account for 2 out of 3 first births to African-American women under age 35 (Ingrassia, 1993).

In addition, African-American families must deal with outside pressures, such as racism, prejudice, poverty, and discrimination (Lee, 1995). The social and economic turmoil surrounding the civil rights movement, the women's movement, and the Vietnam War changed the overall makeup of African-American families. Two of the best aspects of change that occurred in African-American families in the 1970s were financial and social upward mobility. Employment and educational opportunities, previously closed because of racial barriers, opened. Housing and social options became more available. The opposite side of the upward mobility movement was the poverty and hopelessness of the African Americans left behind, especially in inner-city ghettos. These African Americans tended to be poorer and less educated, and to have less opportunity to advance. Unemployment rose in general among African-American men from the late 1950s on because of the elimination of many working-class jobs (Gaston, 1996). The consequence was that a large economic underclass of African Americans developed. Within this class was a loosening of family ties because of the stress and strain associated with single parenting, high unemployment, and living in or near poverty level. With this phenomenon came social frustration and anger that led to an increase in violence and the incarceration of a large percentage of young black men who dropped out as potentially available marriage partners and constructive citizens (Jones, 1993).

These external factors influence the inner realities affecting family dynamics today (Franklin, 1993). Such stress within any group takes its toll on family life and individuals within these families. Boys and young men in African-American communities seem to have been especially negatively impacted.

Therapeutic Treatment of African-American Families

The concept of family therapy is new to most African-American families (Willis, 1988; Wilson & Stith, 1991). Traditionally, African Americans have relied on extended family networks to take care of their needs. Yet, many African-American families may benefit from time-specific therapy approaches that are problem-focused or multi-generational in nature (Boyd-Franklin, 1993). For example, structural, Bowen, and strategic family therapy theories have been found appropriate in working with African-American families (Boyd-Franklin, 1987). In addition, psychoeducation, especially with single parent African-American women, can be effective (Lee, 1995). However, in treating African-American families, there is "no prescriptive approach" that can be applied universally in the helping process (Newlon & Arciniega, 1991, p. 192).

To be successful, family therapists need to understand the historical and social background of African-American families in the United States. They must also appreciate the issue of trust that arises between African-American families and non-African-American family therapists (Willis, 1988). An important point for family therapists to comprehend is that many African-American families first need to perceive treatment as a form of social support that can benefit them. Then, they can more readily accept it.

Therefore, working with African-American families requires that therapists have an understanding of **multigenerational family systems** (Hines, Garcia-Preto, McGoldrick, Almeida, & Weltman, 1992). In addition, they must be sensitive to the importance of respect for elderly family members. Often family therapy is begun by African-American families because therapists have emphasized to older family members that therapy can be of value.

Therapists must assure African-American families that through the therapeutic process they can learn how to handle many of their own problems. Through "education about various issues (e.g., parental rights in educational systems) and concrete skills training," confidence and competence may be enhanced in African-American families so they can advocate on their own behalf (McGoldrick et al., 1991, p. 561). For instance, Lee (1995) describes how single African-American mothers may be empowered to effectively deal with their children and extreme environmental hardships through helping these women foster a positive culture identity in their children. In addition, these women can be assisted by helping them appreciate parenthood from an Afrocentric perspective.

Finally, in working with African-American families, therapists need to address social and institutional issues that have adversely affected African Americans. This includes working in an outreach fashion to marshall support of institutions, such as governments and churches, that can lend support to African-American families and help change policies that may have a detrimental effect on these families.

Asian-American Families

In 1996, Asian Americans constituted about 3% of the population of the United States. However, by 2010, they are expected to make up about 10% of the nation's population. Asian Americans trace their cultural heritages to countries such as China, Japan, Vietnam, Cambodia, India, Korea, the Philippines, and the Pacific islands. The background of Asian Americans is diverse, "with as many as 32 different Asian ethnic groups now identified in the U.S." (Cheng, 1996, p. 8). They differ in regard to language, history, and socioeconomic factors. Yet, Asian Americans share many cultural values, such as a respect and reverence for the elderly and the family. They also place a strong emphasis on self-discipline, order, social etiquette, and hierarchy (Hong, 1989; London & Devore, 1992).

"Traditional Asian/Pacific values governing family life have been heavily influenced by Confucian philosophy and ethics, which strongly emphasizes specific roles and proper relationships among people in those roles" (Ho, 1987, p. 25). Three main relationship roles that are stressed within the family are father/son, husband/wife, and elder/younger siblings (Keyes, 1977). In these relationships, there are feelings of obligation and shame. If a member of a family behaves improperly, the whole family loses face. Buddhist values also are prevalent in Asian-American families. These values stress harmonious living and involve "compassion, a respect for life, and moderation of behavior; self-discipline, patience, modesty, and friendliness" (Ho, 1987, p. 25).

As Asian-American families have moved into mainstream American society, they have had to contend with a number of problems that are both unique and universal to other families. For instance, like other families, Asian-American families have had to face the fact that geographically and emotionally, families are moving further apart. This is a trend in American society that places more emphasis on the individual than the family (Sue & Morishima, 1982). Unique to Asian-American family culture is the reality that "parents can no longer expect complete obedience, as families become more democratic and move away from the patriarchal system of the past" (London & Devore, 1992, p. 368). In many ways, Asian-American families and other U.S. families appear the same, but the dynamics underlying them differ substantially.

Treatment of Asian-American Families

In working with Asian-American families, therapists must take acculturation into account. First generation Asian-American families, for instance, may need assistance from family therapists in learning how to interrelate properly to other families and societal institutions. They may likewise face problems involving social isolation, adjustment difficulties to a particular location, and language barriers (Hong, 1989). The role of the therapist in such cases is primarily educational and avocational rather than remedial. It is directed toward outreach efforts (Cheng, 1996). On the other hand, many established Asian-American families need help in resolving intrafamily difficulties, such as intergenerational conflicts, role confusion, and couple relationships (McGoldrick et al., 1991). In these cases, therapists work according to universal treatment model procedures.

Like African-American families, Asian-American families seem to do best in family therapy when the focus of sessions is problem or solution oriented and when the family is empowered to help itself through its own and community resources. Most Asian-American families are reluctant to initiate family therapy; and if therapists are to be of assistance to these families, they must do the following:

- orient them and educate them to the value of therapy
- establish rapport quickly through the use of compassion and self-disclosure
- emphasize specific techniques families can use in improving their relationships and resolving their problems

Problematic to Asian-American families, and all recognizable ethnic minority families, is racism, which may disrupt their internal family dynamics as well as outside relationships (Sue & Morishima, 1982). In such situations, family therapists not only work to address societal changes but also focus with family members on assessing the values and skills within the family for dealing with prejudice and discrimination. This type of work utilizes family cultural strengths and family therapy strengths.

Overall, in working with families of Asian origin, therapists need to recognize that they may be most effective if they are knowledgeable about Asian philosophers, such as Leo Tzu and Confucius. They are also usually at their best when they seek "to create a safe and nurturing environment that mirrors a supportive and caring family and where each participant is respected, and without fear, can explore relevant problems and concerns" (Cheng, 1996, p. 8).

Hispanic/Latino-American Families

"The term ***Hispanic,*** or ***Latino,*** refers to people who were born in any of the Spanish-speaking countries of the Americas (Latin America), from Puerto Rico, or from the U.S. who trace their ancestry to either Latin America or to Hispanic people from U.S. territories that were once Spanish or Mexican" (Cohen, 1993, p. 13). Almost one in ten residents (9%) of the United States is of Hispanic/Latino origin, with a combined population of 22.4 million. "By 2010, Hispanics are projected to be the nation's largest minority, surpassing blacks" (Benedetto, 1992, 5A). Their total numbers at that time will be about 40 million people (Puente, 1993). The majority (76%) of Hispanic/Latino-American families are those whose ancestry is Mexican, Cuban, or Puerto Rican.

Considerable diversity exists among Hispanic/Latino-Americans and the families they create. Most wish to be in the mainstream of society in the United States, and a majority do not support "traditional" roles for women (Benedetto, 1992). As a group, Hispanics/Latinos also tend to be family oriented. However, differences in distinct groups of Hispanics/Latinos means that each family is unique, sharing both common and special qualities when compared with others.

As a group, Hispanic/Latino families have the following difficulties (Puente, 1993; Usdansky, 1993):

- They have a higher unemployment rate than non-Hispanic/Latinos.
- They live below the poverty line at over twice the rate of non-Hispanic/Latinos.
- They lag behind non-Hispanic/Latinos in earning high school diplomas and college degrees.

However, Hispanic/Latino families have a number of assets and strengths. For instance, as a group, they are very family oriented, with unwavering love and loyalty to their families (Ruiz, 1981; Ponce, 1995). "Family members are viewed as interdependent, and no sacrifice is seen as too great for the family" (Lambie & Daniels-Mohring, 1993, p. 73). Parents appear to be especially dedicated in Hispanic/Latino families. Children, in turn, show gratitude through submitting to family rules. In addition, the extended family plays a positive part in Hispanic/Latino families in the teaching "of such traditional values as *dignidad* (dignity), *orgullo* (pride and self-reliance), *confianza* (trust and intimacy), and *respecto* (respect)" (Johnson, 1995, p. 319).

Treatment of Hispanic/Latino Families

In working with Hispanic/Latino families, it is helpful for family therapists to develop a basic knowledge about cultural traditions before attempting to employ treatment modalities. For example, traditional rituals, such as religious festivities, *Quinceanos* (when a daughter is presented to society as a woman), engagements, weddings, and funerals, are highly valued in Hispanic/Latino culture and bring families together (Ponce, 1995, p. 7). In addition, "Hispanic/Latino individuals are interested in getting to know someone as a person rather than assessing a person based on external factors such as occupational or socioeconomic status" (Cooper & Costas, 1994, p. 32). Furthermore, as a group, Hispanic/Latinos tend to be "physically expressive, such as gesturing with their hands and face (e.g., eyes/eyebrows and mouth) while they talk" (Ponce, 1995, p. 7).

This type of cultural information can be obtained through specific academic courses as well as through direct observation and continuing education opportunities. Educational information helps therapists learn as well as, if not better than, case-by-case supervision (Inclan, 1990). Regardless of the approach family therapists employ, several unique factors must be taken into consideration when helping Hispanic/Latino families (Sue & Sue, 1990).

The first factor is external. A disproportionate number of Hispanic/Latino families live at or below the poverty level (Facundo, 1990). More than 40% of Hispanic/Latino children live in poverty, with the proportion of Puerto Rican children especially high (57%) (Usdansky, 1993). Stress related to economic factors and working conditions often contributes to intrafamily difficulties. Serving as an advocate and a resource is a crucial role family therapists sometimes need to play in helping poor Hispanic/Latino families help themselves.

Another area that family therapists need to address with Hispanic/Latino families relates to acculturation (LeVine & Padilla, 1980). As a group, Hispanics/Latinos seek to fit into the larger United States culture as rapidly as possible. However, family members may do so at different rates. For instance, school age children may become "Americanized" at a faster and easier rate than grandparents. It is older Hispanic/Latino family members who may fear the loss of their children and traditions to a new culture and who may become isolated and depressed because of rapid changes and loss (Baptiste, 1987). Therefore, in working with Hispanic/Latino families, therapists should consider how the pressure for acculturation may contribute to family turmoil, especially as it relates to family loyalty (Hines et al., 1992). Language factors, especially bilingualism, must also be explored (Sciarra & Ponterotto, 1991).

Another consideration in treating Hispanic/Latino families involves outside sources and internal beliefs. An institution that encompasses both of these helpful dimensions is the Catholic Church, especially for Mexican Americans and Puerto Ricans (Johnson, 1995). Historically, the Catholic Church has provided social, economic, and emotional support to Hispanic/Latino families when there were few other community services available.

A fourth area that needs to be addressed in Hispanic/Latino families is the length of therapy and its focus. Because Hispanic/Latino families are accustomed to being treated by physicians, they generally expect mental health services to be similar. Therefore, family therapists need to be active and employ direct and short-term theories. Two family therapy approaches that appear to be best suited for use with this population are behavioral family therapy and structural family therapy (Canino & Canino, 1982; Juarez, 1985; Ponterotto, 1987). Structural family therapy can be especially useful in addressing problems of extreme enmeshment—that is, "when several generations live in the same household, causing problems like lack of privacy, undefined boundaries in the family structures, and confusion as to who gives the discipline at home" (Ponce, 1995, p. 11).

Native-American Families

Between 1.5 and 1.8 million Native Americans live in the United States. They are an extremely diverse group belonging to 517 state-recognized tribes (321 in the lower 48 states and 196 in Alaska) (Herring, 1991). Collectively, Native American life has been built around cultures that emphasize harmony, acceptance, cooperation, sharing, and a respect for nature and family. "Family, including extended family, is of major importance, and the tribe and family to which one belongs provide significant meaning" (Newlon & Arciniega, 1991, p. 196).

Difficulties within this population vary. Because the extended family is important in most Native-American cultures, one prevalent problem is the breakup or dysfunctionality of these families (Herring, 1989). Some historical practices of the United States government have resulted in "between 25% and 55% of all Native-American children" being separated from their family-of-origin "and placed in non-Native-American foster homes, adoption homes, boarding homes, or other institutions" (Herring, 1991, pp. 39–40). Many Native Americans who have had such experiences have suffered both a confusion about their identity and a trauma about their relationships to others. Families have likewise been negatively affected.

Another problematic family concern centers on geography and culture. Many Native Americans are torn between living with their families on a reservation or trying to adjust to life in the dominant culture of the United States. Cultural connectedness with other like-minded individuals is important to Native Americans, as is a relationship with the land. Yet, there are more Native Americans living in urban areas than on reservations (U.S. Bureau of Census, 1980). Urban life is stressful and is often not conducive to maintaining good mental health. For Native-American families as a group, isolation from their roots presents multiple difficulties in terms of functionality.

A final problem of Native-American families involves substance abuse, particularly alcoholism (Hill, 1989). In some family groups, drinking is encouraged as a form of socialization (Manson, Tatum, & Dinges, 1982). The results are manifest in higher death and disorder rates. Suicide, cirrhosis of the liver, and fetal alcohol syndrome are three examples of problems within Native-American families related to alcohol.

Treatment of Native-American Families

Treating Native-American families requires sensitivity, cultural knowledge, and innovation. Outsiders, including family therapists, do not gain entrance into the family easily (Ho, 1987). To be accepted and be effective with Native Americans, therapists who treat these families should recognize that some techniques work better than others. For example, indirect forms of questioning and open-ended questions lead to responses. Direct forms of questioning and closed-ended questions do not (Tafoya, 1994). Also, there are certain symbols therapists should know and utilize. For example, the circle, is considered sacred and represents unity and reciprocal relationships (Tafoya, 1994). This symbol, and others like it, can be used metaphorically as models for relationships (Tafoya, 1989). Finally, the admission by therapists that they may make mistakes in treatment because of cultural ignorance can go a long way in establishing rapport and trust (Tafoya, 1989).

One approach for working with Native-American families is to use **home-based therapy** (Schacht, Tafoya, & Mirabla, 1989). This method requires that family therapists be with a family before attempting to help it. Thus, therapists spend more time than usual with families and may actually do chores with them before discussing troublesome areas of family life. From a pragmatic point of view, this approach does not appear to be the most efficient use of time. However, by devoting one's self to home-based therapy, essential services can be offered to families who would not receive them otherwise.

Another approach to working with Native-American families is to combine structural family therapy with traditional healing modalities. In both structuralism and traditional healing, the concepts of spontaneity, joining, and complementarity are utilized (Napoliello & Sweet, 1992). Family therapists can therefore employ concepts that transcend two cultures in order to promote change and resolution. This type of family therapy recognizes the importance of the fit between a therapeutic ideology and a family/cultural tradition (Hodges, 1989).

Finally, the "importance of visual mode should be noted—for a number of Native-American languages, the verb 'to learn' is a combination of the verbs 'to see' and 'to remember'" (Tafoya, 1994, p. 28). Therefore, concrete and active behavior, rather than insight, is stressed in traditional Native-American healing. In working with Native-American families, therapists would be wise to use therapeutic approaches that are directive but open-ended, such as those that are strategically oriented.

Approaches to Working with Culturally Diverse Families

Two main approaches are used in working with culturally diverse families. The first is the culture specific model; the second is the universal perspective model. The culture specific model emphasizes the values, beliefs, and orientation of different ethnic cultural groups (Sue, 1994). Most courses offered in higher education reflect this model. In such an approach, students memorize cultural variations among groups. Although this knowledge may be extremely valuable for therapists working with some families, it has its drawbacks. Basically, the culture specific model may become unwieldy and may lead to stereotyping in which group characteristics, instead of unique characteristics, are singled out.

The universal perspective model is more general. It assumes that counseling approaches already developed can be applied with minor changes to different cultural groups. Thus, cultural differences are recognized from a family systems perspective. This approach also attempts to "identify human processes that are similar, regardless of ethnicity or cultural backgrounds" (Sue, 1994, p. 19). The only problem is that this way of working with culturally diverse families may be too general to be of any real use to a therapist.

In essence, the task of finding one approach that is always useful in working with culturally diverse families is impossible. However, a number of general guidelines can help family therapists choose an appropriate approach for working with specific families.

A broad guideline for therapists to use in selecting an intervention strategy is to assess whether the family's difficulties are mainly internal or external. If the problems are primarily internal, such as a failure to communicate effectively, well-established theoretical approaches may be employed. On the other hand, if the concerns are external, such as racism, the therapist may need to shift to a culture specific way of helping.

Another guideline is to determine the family's degree of acculturation. Families that are more "Americanized" are generally open to a wider range of theoretical approaches than those that are new immigrants or those that are second generation.

A third guideline to use in working with culturally diverse families is to explore their knowledge of family therapy and their commitment to resolving their problems or finding solutions. If the family is unsophisticated about mental health services and pressed for time, the therapist is wise to use both educational and/or direct, brief theory driven treatments, such as behavioral family therapy, solution-focused therapy, or structural family therapy. Otherwise, a culture specific approach may be employed.

A fourth guideline for choosing an approach for culturally diverse families is to find out what has been tried and what is preferred. By determining what has been tried, therapists can devise methods that are appropriate and that overcome resistance. Preference is important to the establishment of rapport and effectiveness of treatment. "There are certain culture-preferred patterns for families to cope with problems" (Tseng & Hsu, 1991, p. 107). For instance, upwardly mobile African-American families gravitate toward dependence on extended family members during times of high stress (McAdoo, 1982). Therefore, in working with these families, therapists should include extended family members.

Role of the Therapist

For family therapists to be competent in working with culturally diverse families, they must examine their own biases and values. This examination must be conducted on both an intellectual and an emotional level (Sue & Sue, 1990). For instance, research indicates that some white therapists may minimize or avoid the impact of societal expectations on cultural minority families (Rowe, Bennett, & Atkinson, 1994). Therefore, it is crucial for these family therapists to examine their thinking and feelings in regard to families whose cultural heritage differs from theirs. In general, culturally skilled family therapists are:

- aware and sensitive to their "own cultural heritage and to valuing and respecting differences"
- "comfortable with differences that exist between themselves and their clients in terms of race and beliefs"
- "sensitive to circumstances (personal biases, stage of ethnic identity, sociopolitical influences, etc.) that may dictate referral" of a family
- knowledgeable of their own "racist attitudes, beliefs, and feelings" (Sue & Sue, 1990, pp. 167–168)

After family therapists have dealt constructively with themselves, they are then able to fulfill vital roles in working with culturally diverse families (Fenell & Weinhold, 1996). "One obvious question is how different styles of family therapy (e.g., more or less active, directive, collaborative, strategic, interpretive, etc.) intersect with the cultural or ethnic values that families bring to the therapy room. It is reasonable to expect that cultural values differentially affect family members' expectations for the therapist's behavior, their communication patterns in the session, and their perceptions of the therapeutic alliance" (Friedlander, Wildman, Heatherington, & Skowron, 1994, p. 411).

An initially important role of family therapists is to be concurrently culturally sensitive and open to themselves and to the families with whom they work (Franklin, 1993). If family therapists are not attuned and responsive to specific aspects of families, stereotyping may occur to the detriment of everyone involved (Tseng & Hsu, 1991). This lack of openness confines the topics that can be discussed and the good that can be achieved through family therapy.

A second role of family therapists is to help culturally diverse families acknowledge and deal with their thoughts and emotions. For example, many of these families suppress anger and manifest depression. Although white, Anglo-Saxon, Protestant (WASP) families are most known for the suppression of thoughts and feelings, other cultural groups, such as Asian Americans, also utilize this approach (Tseng & Hsu, 1991). It is important that where and when appropriate, cognitions and emotions are expressed and therapeutically dealt with.

A third role of family therapists is to help culturally diverse families acknowledge and celebrate their heritages. "It is essential for clinicians to consider how ethnicity intersects with the life cycle and to encourage families to take active responsibility for carrying out the rituals in their ethnic or religious group(s) to mark each phase" (Carter & McGoldrick, 1988, p. 25). By being true and loyal to their pasts, culturally diverse families can deal better with the present.

A fourth role of family therapists is to help culturally diverse families move through and adjust to family life stages in the healthiest way possible. This means helping them become aware of, accept, and function in new family life cycle roles, whether in a nuclear or extended family.

Overall, to be effective with culturally diverse families, family therapists would do well to remember the acronym **ESCAPE** (Boynton, 1987). This symbolic word stands for four major investments therapists must make: (1) **e**ngagement with families and process, (2) **s**ensitivity to **c**ulture, (3) **a**wareness of family **p**otential, and (4) knowledge of the **e**nvironment.

Process and Outcome

The process of family therapy with culturally diverse families is one that takes into consideration the uniqueness and common components of each family and culture. Process has an impact on outcome. Similarly, cultural patterns and traditions have an impact on families, and families have an influence on cultures (Tseng & Hsu, 1991).

Initial Phase of Working with Culturally Diverse Families

Working with culturally diverse families requires that the family therapist first establish rapport. This may be done in a number of ways, but it could be problematic because many "ethnic minority Americans find it difficult to trust a family therapist who represents the majority system" (Ho, 1987, p. 255). One way to broach this barrier is for family therapists to define their roles clearly and early in the initial session. By so doing, they set the stage for future relationships.

A second way to establish rapport is through office furnishings and decorations. If family therapists show they have a broad knowledge and appreciation for cultural differences, families who exemplify these characteristics will feel much more comfortable. They are also likely to be more trusting.

A third way of helping culturally diverse families is for family therapists to respect the family hierarchy (Minuchin, 1974). This means talking to the person of highest status first, usually the husband/father, and then to others in the family. Such a procedure demonstrates an appropriate personal/family interest.

A final way to help culturally diverse families become a part of the therapeutic process is for therapists to set the rules of operation (Napier & Whitaker, 1978). This type of action alleviates anxiety and gives families an indication of where therapy will lead.

Middle Phase of Working with Culturally Diverse Families

After family therapists have earned the respect, trust, and faith of culturally diverse families, they can begin to help these families deal with their problems. This middle phase of the process involves setting a mutually agreed upon focus and goal for families. Usually, this process involves families and therapists working together in a consensual manner. In this phase, therapists must be patient and help family members be as specific as possible.

A number of techniques can be employed at this time to help families reach a productive outcome, for example, stressing family values, using reframing, or even employing a therapist-helper, such as a grandparent or family friend (Ho, 1987). All of these techniques are meant to utilize resources within families for promoting change without violating their cultural heritage.

Final Phase of Working with Culturally Diverse Families

In the last phase of process and outcome, family therapists evaluate with culturally diverse families what has been achieved and what still needs to be accomplished. This phase focuses on the abilities that family members have to work in harmony with each other in accomplishing a task. It draws families closer together through formal or informal celebrations. The ways in which families made their changes is highlighted so that the model of interacting may be utilized again.

Summary and Conclusion

The multidimensional aspects of working with culturally diverse families was covered in this chapter. As the United States becomes a country of increased diversity, it is critical that family therapists become competent in helping families from many backgrounds. This does not mean that family therapists must learn specific information about all cultures, for cultures are broad-based entities. However, it does mean that therapists must be aware of where to find appropriate information and guidelines to follow in being of assistance to families that clearly differ from them.

Culturally diverse families face most of the same life situations other families encounter. The difference is that in addition to expected stress, these families often encounter barriers, such as prejudice or access to services, in resolving these dilemmas. Thus, the dynamics affecting culturally diverse families differ from those that other families face.

In working with culturally diverse families, therapists must be sensitive to their own backgrounds and those of their client families. Furthermore, they must become innovative and experienced in applying theories to specific situations. They should obtain supervision and specialized educational training when needed. Family therapists must also be accepting of themselves and others. Otherwise, culturally diverse families are labeled pathological and are not helped. Successful treatment of most culturally diverse families depends on their ability to tap nontraditional centers of help. Using extended family members or institutions, such as the church, may provide families with a sense of empowerment as well as assistance. Finally, therapists need to be guided by specificity so that they make appropriate cultural interventions.

African-American, Asian-American, Hispanic/Latino-American, and Native-American families all share common and unique concerns. In selecting approaches to employ with these families, therapists need to consider the degree of acculturation, the individual/family life stages, and the level of understanding and commitment to family therapy. The role of the therapist is to be sensitive and sensible when working with culturally diverse families. Also, family therapists need to realize that the process of assisting these types of families is a process that has a beginning, middle, and final phase in which some interventions are more appropriate than others in achieving a positive outcome. Overall, "family therapy has a great deal of promise in working with ethnic minority families, but it needs to be modified to include a comprehensive understanding of the diverse entities we call families" (Sue, 1994, p. 21).

SUMMARY TABLE

Working with Culturally Diverse Families

Culturally diverse families have always been a part of American society, but often they have been cut off physically and psychologically from mainstream society.

As American culture becomes more diverse, family therapists must learn to work with families within their cultural context.

When culture is ignored families are misunderstood or pathologized.

Definitions of Culture, Race, and Ethnicity

Culture is a broadly defined term referring to the customary beliefs, social forms, and traits of a group.

Race is more narrowly defined as primarily a biological term.

Ethnicity is a sociological concept that is used to classify people according to a common origin or background.

Dynamics Affecting Culturally Diverse Families

Culturally diverse families face the same pressures as other families, but they are affected in qualitatively and quantitatively different ways.

Certain family life cycle events have more impact on some families than others.

Unique traditions, distinctions in appearance, and access to mental health services can adversely affect culturally diverse families.

Issues in Working with Culturally Diverse Families

Family therapists cannot become experts in all cultures. Instead they must acquire more general abilities to work with culturally diverse families. The following factors determine the effectiveness of family therapists:

- Sensitivity (i.e., the ability to be open, rather than "culturally encapsulated")
- Experience (i.e., social life experience with and knowledge of specific cultural backgrounds)
- Acceptance (i.e., personal/professional comfortableness)
- Ingenuity (i.e., the willingness to try innovative methods)
- Specificity (i.e., the ability to access the strengths/weaknesses of a particular family)

Characteristics of Culturally Diverse Families

African-American Families

Commonalities among African-American families include slave history, skin color, and past discrimination treatment (i.e., racism).

Strengths associated with African-American families include kinship bonds, social networks, religion, cooperation, work orientation, and adaptability.

Weaknesses associated with African-American families include internal stresses (e.g., male-female relationships) and external pressures (e.g., discrimination, poverty, single parenting, less education, high unemployment).

The weaknesses associated with African-American families have a negative systemic impact on these families as a whole and increase prejudice.

African-American families generally benefit when treatment is time-specific, problem-focused, and multi-generational.

Structural, Bowen, and strategic family therapies are often used with African-American families; but there is no prescriptive approach.

Developing trust, understanding African-American culture (including the importance of extended families), and assuring families that therapy is useful in self-help are keys to successful treatment.

Asian-American Families

Asian-American families come from diverse cultural heritages with different languages, histories, and values.

Most of these families have reverence for the family and the elderly.

Confucian and Buddhist philosophies influence roles and relationships.

Family strengths include an emphasis on self-discipline, patience, modesty, and friendliness.

Acculturation into mainstream society is associated with problems in Asian-American families, including issues of loyalty.

Therapy with Asian-American families must take into consideration problems associated with acculturation, such an intergenerational conflict and role confusion. Racism must also be addressed.

Asian-American families usually respond best to treatment when it is problem-focused and empowering.

Family therapists do best when they orient themselves to Asian-American values, establish rapport quickly, and emphasize relationship enhancement and problem-solving therapies.

Hispanic/Latino Families

Hispanic/Latino families, the second largest minority, trace their roots to Spanish-speaking countries.

Hispanic/Latino families wish to acculturate, do not support traditional roles for women, and are family oriented.

Weaknesses associated with Hispanic/Latino families include high unemployment, poverty, and low educational attainment.

Strengths associated with Hispanic/Latino families include family loyalty and parent/child dedication.

The treatment of Hispanic/Latino families includes developing a knowledge about their culture, assessing the relationship between financial factors and intrafamily difficulties, and addressing acculturation.

Family therapists work best with Hispanic/Latino families when they are active and direct, and therapy is short-term. Structural and behavioral family therapies are usually appropriately employed.

Native-American Families

Native-American families are diverse, belonging to 517 state-recognized tribes.

Strengths of these families include an emphasis on harmony, acceptance, cooperation, sharing, and respect for nature/family.

Weaknesses include alcoholism and dysfunctional families as a result of government policies regarding the removal of children.

Successful treatment of Native-American families requires sensitivity, cultural knowledge, innovation, and use of certain symbols, for example, the circle.

Indirect questions work best with Native-American families. Home-based approaches and a variation of structural family therapy and native healing modalities have also been utilized.

General Guidelines Applicable to Culturally Diverse Families

Specific approaches for working with culturally diverse families include those that are culture specific and those that are based on a universal perspective. Other general guidelines family therapists need to master include:

- determining if difficulty is primarily internal or external
- determining the degree of a family's acculturation
- exploring a family's knowledge of family therapy and commitment to problem
- finding out what has been tried

Role of the Therapist

Family therapists must examine their own biases and values before beginning to work with culturally diverse families.

Effective family therapists are aware of their own heritage, comfortable with differences, sensitive to circumstances, and knowledgeable of feelings/attitudes.

Family therapists must be open to themselves and to families to avoid stereotyping.

Family therapists must help families acknowledge their emotions when appropriate.

Family therapists must help families celebrate their cultural heritage.

Family therapists must assist families in dealing successfully with events in the family life cycle.

Process and Outcome

Process has an impact on outcome, as culture has an influence on families.

In the initial phase of the therapy process, the therapist establishes rapport, builds trust, defines his role clearly, makes the family comfortable, shows respect for the family hierarchy, and sets the rules for operation.

In the middle phase of the therapy process, the therapist helps the family focus on goals and achievement of a productive outcome through the use of specific family therapy techniques that are mainstream and innovative.

In the final phase of the therapy process, the therapist helps the family evaluate achievements and celebrate changes.

References

Arnold, M. S., & Allen, N. P. (1995). Andrew Billingsley: The Legacy of African American families. *The Family Journal, 3,* 77–85.

Associated Press. (1996, June 11). Black population, education rise. *The State* (Columbia, SC), A3.

Baptiste, D. A. (1987). Family therapy with Spanish-heritage immigrant families in cultural transition. *Contemporary Family Therapy, 9,* 229–251.

Benedetto, R. (1992, December 16). Hispanics feeling at home. *USA Today,* 5A.

Billingsley, A. (1968). *Black families in White America.* Englewood Cliffs, NJ: Prentice Hall.

Boyd-Franklin, N. (1987). The contribution of family therapy models to the treatment of Black families. *Psychotherapy, 24,* 621–629.

Boyd-Franklin, N. (1993, July/August). Pulling out the arrows. *Family Therapy Networker, 17,* 54–56.

Boynton, G. (1987). Cross-cultural family therapy: The ESCAPE model. *American Journal of Family Therapy, 15,* 123–130.

Boszormenyi-Nagy, I. (1987). *Foundations of contextual therapy.* New York: Brunner/Mazel.

Brown, F. H. (1988). The impact of death and serious illness on the family life cycle. In B. Carter & M. McGoldrick (Eds.), *The changing family life cycle* (2nd ed., pp. 457–482). New York: Gardner.

Canino, I., & Canino, G. (1982). Cultural syntonic family for migrant Puerto Ricans. *Hospital and Community Psychiatry, 33,* 299–303.

Carter, B., & McGoldrick, M. (1988). Overview: The changing family life cycle — A framework for family therapy. In B. Carter & M. McGoldrick (Eds.), *The changing family life cycle* (2nd ed., pp. 3–28). New York: Gardner.

Cheng, W. D. (1996, Spring). Pacific perspective. *Together, 24,* 8.

Cherlin, A. (1992). *Marriage, divorce, remarriage.* Cambridge, MA: Harvard University Press.

Cohen, E. (1993, August). Who are Latinos? *Family Therapy News, 24,* 13.

Cooper, C., & Costas, L. (1994, Spring). Ethical challenges when working with Hispanic/Latino families: Personalismo. *The Family Psychologist, 10,* 32–34.

deShazer, S. (1988). *Clues: Investigating solutions in brief therapy.* New York: W. W. Norton.

Ericksen, J. A., Yancey, W. L., & Ericksen, E. P. (1979). The division of family roles. *Journal of Marriage and the Family, 41,* 301–313.

Facundo, A. (1990). Social class issues in family therapy: A case study of a Puerto Rican migrant family. *Journal of Strategic and Systemic Therapies, 9,* 14–34.

Falicov, C. J. (Ed.). (1983). *Cultural perspectives in family therapy.* Rockville, MD: Aspen.

Fenell, D. L., & Weinhold, B. K. (1996, March). Treating families with special needs. *Counseling and Human Development, 28,* 1–12.

Franklin, A. J. (1993, July/August). The invisibility syndrome. *Family Therapy Networker, 17,* 32–39.

Friedlander, M. L., Wildman, J., Heatherington, L., & Skowron, E. A. (1994). What we do and don't know about the process of family therapy. *Journal of Family Psychology, 8,* 390–416.

Garcia-Preto, N. (1986, November/December). Puerto Rican families. *Family Therapy Networker, 10,* 33–34.

Gaston, J. (1996, July 8). Roots of disunion. *Winston-Salem Journal,* D1–D2.

Giordano, J., & Carini-Giordano, M. A. (1995), Ethnic dimensions in family treatment. In R. H. Mikesell, D-D. Lusterman, & S. H. McDaniel (Eds.), *Integrating family therapy* (pp. 347–356). Washington, DC: American Psychological Association.

Gladding, S. T. (1992). *Differences in awareness.* Unpublished manuscript.

Goldberg, J. R. (1993, August). Is multicultural family therapy in sight? *Family Therapy News, 24,* 1, 7, 8, 16, 21.

Goldenberg, H., & Goldenberg, I. (1993). Multiculturalism and family systems. *Progress: Family Systems Research and Therapy, 2,* 7–12.

Gushue, G. V. (1993). Cultural-identity development and family assessment: An interactive model. *The Counseling Psychologist, 21,* 487–513.

Haley, J. (1973). *Uncommon therapy.* New York: Norton.

Haley, J. (1976). *Problem-solving therapy.* San Francisco: Jossey-Bass.

Herring, R. D. (1989). The Native American family: Dissolution by coercion. *Journal of Multicultural Counseling and Development, 17,* 4–13.

Herring, R. D. (1991). Counseling Native American youth. In C. C. Lee & B. L. Richardson (Eds.), *Multicultural issues in counseling: New approaches to diversity* (pp. 37–47). Alexandria, VA: American Counseling Association.

Hill, A. (1989). Treatment and prevention of alcoholism in the Native American family. In G. W. Lawson & A. W. Lawson (Eds.), *Alcoholism and substance abuse in special populations* (pp. 247–272). Rockville, MD: Aspen.

Hill, R. (1972). *The strengths of black families.* New York: Emerson-Hall.

Hines, P. M., Garcia-Petro, N., McGoldrick, M., Almeida, R., & Weltman, S. (1992). Intergenerational relationships across cultures. *Families in Society: The Journal of Contemporary Human Services, 73,* 323–338.

Ho, M. K. (1987). *Family therapy with ethnic minorities.* Newbury Park, CA: Sage.

Hodges, M. (1989). Culture and family therapy. *Journal of Family Therapy, 11,* 117–128.

Hong, G. K. (1989). Application of cultural and environmental issues in family therapy with immigrant Chinese Americans. *Journal of Strategic and Systemic Therapies, 8,* 14–21.

Inclan, J. (1990). Understanding Hispanic families: A curriculum outline. *Journal of Strategic and Systemic Therapies, 9,* 64–82.

Ingrassia, M. (1993, August 30). Endangered family. *Newsweek,* 17–27.

Juarez, R. (1985). Core issues in psychotherapy with Hispanic children. *Psychotherapy, 22,* 441–448.

Johnson, A. C. (1995). Resiliency mechanisms in culturally diverse families. *The Family Journal, 3,* 316–324.

Jones, C. (1993, April 12). Alone: Marriage rate for blacks is declining. *Winston-Salem Journal,* 43–44.

Kazdin, A. E., Stolar, M. J., & Marciano, P. L. (1995). Risk factors for dropping out of treatment among white and black families. *Journal of Family Psychology, 9,* 402–417.

Keyes, C. (1977). *The golden peninsula.* New York: Macmillan.

Lambie, R., & Daniels-Mohring, D. (1993). *Family systems within educational contexts.* Denver: Love Publishing.

Lee, C. C. (1991). Cultural dynamics: Their importance in multicultural counseling. In C. C. Lee & B. L. Richardson (Eds.), *Multicultural issues in counseling: New approaches to diversity* (pp. 11–17). Alexandria, VA: American Counseling Association.

Lee, C. C. (1995). Empowering the African American family: New perspectives on single parenthood. *The Family Digest, 8,* 1, 3, 11.

Lee, C.C., Armstrong, K. L., & Brydges, J. L. (1996). The challenges of a diverse society: Counseling for mutual respect and understanding. *Counseling and Human Development, 28*(5), 1–8.

Lee, C. C., & Richardson, B. L. (1991). Promise and pitfalls of multicultural counseling. In C. C. Lee & B. L. Richardson (Eds.), *Multicultural issues in counseling: New approaches to diversity* (pp. 3–9). Alexandria, VA: American Counseling Association.

LeVine, E., & Padilla, A. (1980). *Cross cultures in therapy: Pluralistic counseling for the Hispanic.* Pacific Grove, CA: Brooks/Cole.

London, H., & Devore, W. (1992). Layers of understanding: Counseling ethnic minority families. In R. L. Smith & P. Stevens-Smith (Eds.), *Family counseling and therapy* (pp. 358–371). Ann Arbor, MI: ERIC/CAPS.

Manson, S. M., Tatum, E., & Dinges, N. G. (1982). Prevention research among American Indian and Alaska Native communities: Charting further courses for theory and practice in mental health. In S. M. Manson (Ed.), *New directions in prevention among American Indian and Alaska Native Communities* (pp. 1–61). Portland, OR: Oregon Health Sciences University.

Mason, M. J. (1991). Family therapy as the emerging context for sex therapy. In A. S. Gurman & D. P. Kniskern (Eds.), *Handbook of family therapy* (Vol. II, pp. 479–507). New York: Brunner/Mazel.

McAdoo, H. P. (1982). Stress absorbing systems in black families. *Family Relations, 31,* 479–488.

McGoldrick, M. (1986, November/December). Irish families. *Family Therapy Networker, 10,* 31.

McGoldrick, M., & Rohrbaugh, M. (1987). Researching ethnic family stereotypes. *Family Process, 1,* 89–100.

McGoldrick, M., & Giordano, J. (1996). Overview: Empathy and family therapy. In M. McGoldrick, J. Giordano, & J. K. Pearce (Eds.), *Ethnicity and family therapy* (2nd ed., pp. 1–27). New York: Guilford.

McGoldrick, M., Preto, N. G., Hines, P. M., & Lee, E. (1991). Ethnicity and family therapy. In A. S. Gurman & D. P. Kniskern (Eds.), *Handbook of family therapy* (Vol. II, pp. 546–582). New York: Brunner/Mazel.

Minuchin, S. (1974). *Families and family therapy.* Cambridge, MA: Harvard University Press.

Napier, A. Y., & Whitaker, C. (1978). *The family crucible.* New York: Bantam Books.

Napoliello, A. L., & Sweet, E. S. (1992). Salvador Minuchin's structural family therapy and its application to Native Americans. *Family Therapy, 19,* 155–165.

Newlon, B. J., & Arciniega, M. (1991). Counseling minority families: An Adlerian perspective. In J. Carlson & J. Lewis (Eds.), *Family counseling: Strategies and issues* (pp. 189–223). Denver, CO: Love.

Ponce, A. (1995, Winter). The Hispanic family. *The Family Digest, 7,* 7, 11.

Ponterotto, J. G. (1987). Counseling Mexican-Americans: A multimodal approach. *Journal of Counseling and Development, 65,* 308–312.

Puente, M. (1993, July 16). Hispanics debating their 'destiny' in USA. *USA Today,* 10A.

Richardson, B. L. (1991). Utilizing the resources of the African American church: Strategies for counseling professionals. In C. C. Lee & B. L. Richardson (Eds.), *Multicultural issues in counseling: New approaches to diversity* (pp. 65–75). Alexandria, VA: American Counseling Association.

Rowe, W., Bennett, S. K., & Atkinson, D. R. (1994). White racial identity models: A critique and alternative proposal. *The Counseling Psychologist, 22,* 129–146.

Ruiz, A. (1981). Cultural and historical perspectives in counseling Hispanics. In D. W. Sue (Ed.), *Counseling the culturally different: Theory & practice* (pp. 186–215). New York: Wiley.

Sciarra, D. T., & Ponterotto, J. G. (1991). Counseling the Hispanic bilingual family: Challenges to the therapeutic process. *Psychotherapy, 28,* 473–479.

Schacht, A. J., Tafoya, N., & Mirabla, K. (1989). Home-based therapy with American Indian families. *American Indian and Alaska Native Mental Health Research, 3,* 27–42.

Sue, D. (1994, Spring). Incorporating cultural diversity in family therapy. *The Family Psychologist, 10,* 19–21.

Sue, D. W., & Sue, D. (1990). *Counseling the culturally different* (2nd ed.). New York: Wiley.

Sue, S., & Morishima, J. K. (1982). *The mental health of Asian Americans.* San Francisco: Jossey-Bass.

Szapocznik, J., & Kurtines, W. M. (1993). Family psychology and cultural diversity: Opportunities for theory, research, and application. *American Psychologist, 48,* 400–407.

Tafoya, T. (1989). Circles and cedar: Native Americans and family therapy. *Journal of Psychotherapy and the Family, 6,* 71–98.

Tafoya, T. (1994, Spring). Epistemology of native healing and family psychology. *The Family Psychologist, 10,* 28–31.

Tseng, W-S., & Hsu, J. (1991). *Culture and family.* Binghamton, NY: Haworth.

Turner, W. L. (1993, April). Identifying African-American family strengths. *Family Therapy News, 24,* 9, 14.

U. S. Bureau of the Census. (1980). *Subject Report: American Indians.* Washington, DC: Government Printing Office.

Usdansky, M. L. (1993, August 23). Census shows diversity of Hispanics in USA. *USA Today,* A1.

Walsh, F. (1982). Conceptualization of normal family functioning. In F. Walsh (Ed.), *Normal family processes* (pp. 3–44). New York: Guilford.

Watzlawick, P. (1976). *How real is real?* New York: Random House.

Webster's ninth new collegiate dictionary. (1989). Springfield, MA: Merriam-Webster.

Willis, J. T. (1988). An effective counseling model for treating the Black family. *Family Therapy, 15,* 185–194.

Willis, J. T. (1990). Some destructive elements in African-American male-female relationships. *Family Therapy, 17,* 139–147.

Wilson, L. L., & Stith, S. M. (1991). Cultural sensitive therapy with Black clients. *Journal of Multicultural Counseling and Development, 19,* 32–43.

Wrenn, C. G. (1962). The culturally-encapsulated counselor. *Harvard Educational Review, 32,* 444–449.

Wrenn, C. G. (1985). Afterward: The culturally-encapsulated counselor revisited. In P. B. Pedersen (Ed.), *Handbook of cross-cultural counseling and therapy.* Westport, CT: Greenwood Press.

P A R T F O U R

PROFESSIONAL ISSUES, RESEARCH, AND TRENDS IN FAMILY THERAPY

CHAPTER 14

Ethical, Legal, and Professional Issues in Family Therapy

As an old dog, he has survived
the marriage of his master to a Nutmeg woman,
the first clumsy steps of sandy-haired toddlers,
and the crises of moves around eastern states.

So in the gentle first light of morning
he rolls leisurely in piles of yesterday's clothes
left over from last night's baths by little boys,
an act of independence.

Then slowly, with a slight limp,
he enters his daily routine,
approaching the kitchen at the breakfast rush hour
to quietly consume spilled cereal
and dodge the congested foot traffic.

Sure of his place in a system of change
he lays down to sleep by an air vent.

A family grows around him.

Gladding, 1991

Professional issues in family therapy focus on matters pertaining to ethics, law, and identity. In the process of helping families, there is a link between the selection of treatment procedures and the consideration of professional issues (Huber, 1994). For instance, therapeutic interventions must be based on ethical and legal factors. However, professional issues generally receive less attention than therapeutic ones. Perhaps it is because these former matters are so basic. Regardless, professional matters are usually written about in more mechanical and less appealing ways than those related to treatment. Ethical guidelines, legal standards, and association bylaws are worded in a matter-of-fact, prosaic manner. They are not inviting to read and are not always clear. Yet, the codes, guidelines, and associations that make up family therapy are at the heart of the profession. It is crucial that the issues surrounding the work of family therapy be well understood by clinicians and the public.

Moreover, it is essential that family therapists be vigilant in their pursuit and knowledge regarding ethical, legal, and professional identity issues. If they are not, the result may be clinical or personal actions that are harmful though well intended. Just as the family is a system, so the field of family therapy is systemic. For family clinicians to stay healthy they, and their colleagues, must abide in harmony with ethical codes and legal statutes and practice according to the highest standards possible. In addition, they must form a strong identity as family therapists. Membership in an association that nourishes and enriches them professionally is necessary. For the sake of colleagues, and themselves, family therapists must deal with professional issues (Wendorf & Wendorf, 1992).

This chapter examines issues connected with ethics, the law, and family therapists' identities. Ignorance of these aspects of therapy can get practitioners into serious trouble and cost them time and money, or their careers.

Overview of Ethics in Families and Family Therapy

Human experience is a moral enterprise (Doherty, 1995). **Ethics** are moral principles from which individuals and social groups, such as families, determine rules for right conduct. Families and society are governed by "relationship ethics." The basis for these ethics is **equitability** or the proposition "that everyone is entitled to have his or her welfare interests considered in a way that is fair from a multilateral perspective" (Boszormenyi-Nagy, 1981, p. 160). Ironically, family therapy initially grew up in an atmosphere in which its practitioners believed that the theories and practices involved in working with families were "value free" (Krasner & Houts, 1984). The result was that ethical principles for working with families were rarely discussed by family therapists on a formal or informal basis until the mid-1960s (Grosser & Paul, 1964; Hurvitz, 1967). Even in the 1990s, ethics in family therapy is often treated lightly and in a nonsystemic manner (Wendorf & Wendorf, 1992).

Thus, it is understandable that there is a great deal of uncertainty about ethical decision making in family therapy. When faced with an ethical dilemma, especially if it is complex, many clinicians are quite sure they will be making a big mistake regardless of what path they choose (Hundert, 1987). Yet, despite this historical conflict and present reality, the domain of ethics is part and parcel of the total fabric of family treatment. It needs to be considered in a thoughtful and systemic way. Family therapists probably face more ethical conflicts than any other type of therapist (Morrison, Layton, & Newman, 1982).

Ethics and Values

Ethical decision making is based on an awareness and understanding of values. A **value** is "the ranking of an ordered set of choices from the most to the least preferable" (Spiegel, 1971, p. 53). Basically, there are four domains of values: personal, family, political/social, and ultimate. Each has an impact on the other (Thomas K. Hearn, March 23, 1993, personal communication). Family therapy, theoretically and clinically, is a profession that now acknowledges it is based on multiple sets of values (Huber, 1994). Effective therapists realize the therapeutic process is influenced by the complexity of personal values, client family values, and theoretical values. They examine their own values first. These "are influenced by a therapist's age; marital status; gender; . . . and ethnic, religious, and socio-cultural background" (Aponte, 1992, p. 273). For example, a young, single, Catholic Hispanic/Latino male family therapist from an affluent background may have values different from an older, divorced, Native American who is the parent of two adolescents and has lived in poverty most of her life. Once aware of their values and how they are different and similar to others, family therapists can then begin work with families.

Next, they look at the values of their client families. In families, it is clear to see how personal values of members or political/social values make an impact. Inherited values within the family also have an influence (McGoldrick & Gerson, 1985). In working with families, their values must be examined from a systemic point of view—that is, how family members' values affect the family as a whole. Such a perspective complicates the matter of dealing with values; but simultaneously, it puts values into a realistic framework and makes the study of them a dynamic enterprise. If therapists and their client families are far apart in regard to espoused core values, negotiations between them or a referral may be needed.

Finally, therapists explore values connected to the theories, processes, and outcomes they embrace (Giblin, 1993). In this last arena, ethical issues in family therapy are seen in relationship to which values in families need to be kept, emphasized, and reinforced and which ones should be changed (Carter, 1986). Some family therapies center on helping families remove symptoms. Others focus on establishing a new structure or boundaries. Still others concentrate on helping individuals differentiate from their families of origin or find new solutions.

Uninformed practitioners may try to deny the nature or even importance of values. Others may attempt to "use therapy as a means to campaign for the revisions [of values] they favor" (Wendorf & Wendorf, 1992, p. 316). Both approaches are filled with flaws and possible danger. In the long run, values are the driving force behind ethical behavior and the conduct of family therapy.

How Do Values Influence Ethical Practice?

Values influence ethics in the sense that as "beliefs and preferences," they "undergird the ethical decisions made by individuals and groups. In other words, all ethical issues involve values as grounds for decision making, and all values that deal with social rights and obligations inevitably surface in ethical decisions" (Doherty & Boss, 1991, p. 610).

Some therapists work from an individual therapeutic approach in the presence of the family as a group. This type of treatment raises a value and an ethical question because problems of the family in such an arrangement are not being viewed from their "context as a whole" (Fishman, 1988, p. 5). The result is that recommendations for modifications in the family's way of interacting do not consider the overall complexity of the situation. Because such an approach is limited, it is not clear whether it is of value or ethical when a more effective treatment would work better.

In practice, family therapists are "ethically bound to be honest and forthright with . . . clients, clearly informing them of their choices, [the therapist's] biases, and . . . professional judgments" (Wendorf & Wendorf, 1992, p. 317). The values that family therapists embrace directly affect their clinical practices.

Guidelines for Making Ethical Decisions

To guard against making unethical decisions, family therapists can use a number of resources, once they are aware of what values are involved. Four of the most prevalent and useful are codes of ethics, educational resources, professional consultation, and interactions with colleagues and supervisors.

Codes of Ethics

One of the strongest resources for family therapists are codes of ethics. "Ethical codes are set up not to prevent what *will* happen, but to prevent what *might* happen" (Kaplan & Culkin, 1995, p. 337). Both the American Association for Marriage and Family Therapy (AAMFT) (1991) (see Appendix A) and the International Association of Marriage and Family Counselors (IAMFC) (1993) (see Appendix B) have codes of ethics, each containing eight sections, that address issues confronting family therapists.

The AAMFT ethics code contains sections on the following topics:

1. responsibility to clients
2. confidentiality
3. professional competence and integrity
4. responsibility to students, employees, and supervisors
5. responsibility to research participants
6. responsibility to the profession
7. financial arrangements
8. advertising

In comparison, the IAMFC ethics code covers the following topics:

1. client well-being
2. confidentiality
3. competence
4. assessment
5. private practice
6. research and publications
7. supervision
8. media and public statements

Family therapists face a number of ethical dilemmas that are discussed in these codes of ethics, as well as some that are not (Green & Hansen, 1989). Many of the most common ethical concerns are those that involve treating the entire family, being current on new family therapy developments, seeing one family member without the others present, and sharing values with clients (Green & Hansen, 1986).

Unfortunately, there are few specific behavioral guidelines in codes of ethics that direct family therapists on what to do. In addition, codes of ethics are limited as a result of "excessive concreteness, some lack of consensus, and a tendency to seem simplistic" (Ryder & Hepworth, 1990, p. 128). These limitations become pronounced when ethical codes attempt to deal with complex and complicated issues such as dual relationships. Determining the best course of action from reading an ethical code is sometimes difficult for experienced, as well as for beginning, therapists. Most practitioners need to do more than read codes of ethics when they are making important decisions.

Educational Resources

A second source family therapists can utilize in making informed ethical decisions is educational material. One of the best educational resources is in the form of case histories related specifically to dilemmas in family therapy. For instance, Peggy Papp (1977) has compiled a book of full-length case studies to which family therapists can refer. In addition, and briefer in format, is the regular column in *The Family Journal: Counseling and Therapy for Couples and Families,* which features case consultations from a particular theoretical view. This material highlights a different case and theory each issue. Such educational cases need to be studied on a systematic basis. A knowledge of how family therapists made decisions in the past can be useful to current practitioners.

Case studies can also help family therapists reason through the steps needed in making ethically appropriate choices. In ethical decision making, step-by-step processes have been established (Corey, Corey, & Callanan, 1993). These processes emphasize generating a continuum of alternative actions that therapists can take for the good of the family's welfare and to meet their own professional responsibilities. Therapists then evaluate and weigh the consequences of these alternatives. From this process, they make a tentative decision, and implement that decision, after they have double-checked it with supervisors, consultants, or colleagues if they are in doubt. The final step involves documenting what has been done (Mitchell, 1991). Documenting should be based on customary practices or reputable suggested practices that are defensible ethically and legally (Wilcoxon, 1993).

Professional Consultation

A third resource for making ethical decisions is professional consultation. Professional consultation is the use of experts to enhance one's own knowledge and abilities (Kurpius & Fuqua, 1993). However, consultants vary. For instance, they can be internally or externally oriented, process- or outcome-focused, and formal or informal. However, the idea is that through their services, family therapists can gain a broader view of the principles and case histories associated with specific aspects of ethical codes. In consultation encounters, therapists become consumers of services that are aimed toward prevention, enlightenment, and change.

Interaction With Colleagues and Supervisors

A final source of support in making ethical decisions is one's colleagues and supervisors. Family therapists need to interact with their peers for many reasons, but mainly to share in the collected wisdom and opinions of these individuals when it comes to matters of ethical conduct. Peers are usually more accessible than consultants and educational materials. Furthermore, the cost of using peers, such as in peer supervision, is inexpensive or free and may actually pay psychological dividends both in knowledge and support. In addition, colleagues can often inform professionals of new trends.

Direct supervision of one's work by noncolleagues is also effective and recommended in some cases. Unlike individual supervision, family therapy supervision is systemic and includes a focus on interpersonal as well as intrapersonal issues (Gladding, Wilcoxon, Semon, & Myers, 1992). Furthermore, family therapy supervision places an emphasis on the critiquing of videotapes as well as the use of one-way mirrors for live observation and intervention (Schwartz, Liddle, & Breunlin, 1988). By using various forms of supervisory interaction—such as a supervision team behind a one-way mirror or a "bug in the ear" method (in which the therapist receives messages from a supervisor through a telephone hookup device)—family therapists are less likely to make ethical mistakes through omitting data or avoiding personal/professional issues.

Common Ethical Concerns

Some conduct in family therapy is considered unethical regardless of the experience of the professional involved. However, some practices are not as clearly defined. Common ethical concerns are examined here.

Confidentiality

Confidentiality is "the ethical duty to fulfill a contract or promise to clients that the information revealed during therapy will be protected from unauthorized disclosure" (Arthur & Swanson, 1993, p. 7). In addition to its ethical focus, confidentiality is a legal matter as well. In a 1996 U.S. Supreme Court decision (*Jaffe v. Redmond*), the high court upheld that a therapist could not be forced to testify about confidential communications in treatment settings (Seppa, 1996). However, if confidentiality is broken during treatment, it may become an ethical and/or legal nightmare. Therefore, family therapists need to take precautions ahead of time.

One of the best strategies for family therapists to initiate is to inform all family members in the initial session that the family holds the rights to confidentiality (Kaplan & Allison, 1993b). This process can be done verbally, but it is also effective to use a **professional self-disclosure statement.** This statement, which contains essential information about therapy, is signed by the family and returned to the therapist, and a copy is then given to all members of the family (see chapter 4 for an example of a professional self-disclosure statement).

By using a professional disclosure statement, family members are concretely informed about the parameters of therapy including confidentiality. In the process, they are discouraged from seeking individual sessions with therapists unless appropriate. They are also informed that they should not try to persuade therapists to keep their secrets from other family members. This approach basically reinforces a systems perspective, that is, the family is an interrelated unit and what affects one member has an impact on the entire family.

At times, family therapists may have to break confidentiality. These times are dictated by ethical and legal considerations regarding the well-being of the family (Kaplan & Allison, 1993c). In these situations, the question of **privileged communication** comes to the forefront. Privileged communication is "a client's legal right, guaranteed by statute, that confidences originating in a therapeutic relationship will be safeguarded" (Arthur & Swanson, 1993, p. 7). However, if it becomes clear during a session that, for example, a child in the family is being abused, the therapist has a legal and ethical obligation to report the abuse to an agency responsible for dealing with it, usually a department of social services. All states grant immunity from criminal or civic liability to professionals who report child abuse (Huber, 1994). Family therapists need to check their state regulations and seek advice from colleagues, professional association guidelines, supervisors, and attorneys if there is ever a question of what they should reveal professionally or legally.

Confidentiality broken through carelessness is another matter. Carelessness can involve an impropriety such as talking about a case in public. However, it can also be more innocent such as using a cellular phone to call a client or an insurance agency. Electronic communication tools (including E-mail and fax) provide no guarantee that information will be received by the person for whom it is intended without being intercepted or read by someone else (O'Malley,

1995). Such situations constitute an ethical violation, and it is possible that a civil suit will follow (Woody, 1988). Therefore, proper precautions must be used in employing electronic devices.

Gender Issues

Gender can be an important ethical issue in conducting family therapy. "Gender is not just a set of behaviors and expectations but rather a principal of social organization that structures relations, especially the power relations, between men and women" (Smith & Stevens-Smith, 1992, p. 436). The gender of the therapist and of those in the family play a part in what issues are addressed during treatment and how they are addressed (Walsh, 1993). In its initial years, family therapy was male-focused (Weiner & Boss, 1985). The result was that sometimes social and system issues involving women were ignored or glossed over (Costa & Sorenson, 1993).

Since the 1980s, gender issues have been dealt with extensively in family therapy (Hare-Mustin, 1987). The status of core inequality among individual members within the family, especially women, has been focused on (Carter, 1992). Nevertheless, the conduct of many families and that of family therapy have not changed for the most part. Males and females who did not grow up in a nonstereotyped environment tend to act and react in the same manner as their caretakers. "In the future, both men and women must continue to question the rigid stereotypical roles that society has imposed on them" (Smith & Stevens-Smith, 1992, p. 436). Not to do so has ethical implications because traditional roles have inhibited the growth, change, and healthy functioning of both genders. For example, "women are typically the ones forced to change in therapy, because they tend to be more cooperative with the therapist" (Nixon, 1993, pp. 161–162). Likewise, many men think they cannot make concessions within the family without losing face or power.

Therefore, in working with whole families, therapists must be attuned to such ethical and practical issues as:

- the balance of power between a husband and wife both financially and physically
- the rules and roles played by members of different genders and how these are rewarded
- what a shift in a family's way of operating will mean to the functionality of the family as a whole (McGoldrick, 1988)

A balance needs to be kept in perspective in regard to gender and change. Urging or implementing change in gender prescribed behaviors within a family solely because a therapist believes it is right may be quite costly to all involved (Wendorf & Wendorf, 1992). On the other hand, condoning through silence emotional abuse or intimidation that is lethal to the life and functioning of the family is irresponsible, too. Ethical and systemic considerations need to be addressed when discussing gender issues in family therapy (Bograd, 1992). This is especially true when changes in relationship patterns are being contemplated or implemented.

Sex Between a Therapist and a Family Member

One of the most important ethical taboos in professional family therapy is for a therapist to become sexually involved with a client. Unfortunately, in the history of mental health treatment, there have been blatant cases of sexual affairs between therapists and those they have treated. Movies from "Spellbound" to "The Prince of Tides" have portrayed forbidden intimacy within the confines of analysis (Ansen & Springen, 1992). In the annals of therapeutic history, two publicized cases of sexual involvement with clients are those documented between Carl Jung and a couple of the women he treated who became his mistresses, and Otto Rank who had a long love affair with one of his patients (Beck, Springen, & Foote, 1992).

Although noted practitioners in the mental health field have warned against such liaisons since the beginning, sexual relations between a therapist and client are forbidden in the code of ethics of all family therapy professional associations. Unfortunately, the practice clearly goes on even though "fewer therapists admit to indiscretions these days even in anonymous surveys" (Beck et al., 1992, p. 54).

When it is discovered that this type of conduct is probably occurring, the person receiving the news should confront the accused professional with the evidence in order to verify its truthfulness. If there is a conflict of information between the therapist and client, a written report of the incident by the client should be made. After the complaint is made, the national ethics board that governs the mental health discipline under which the person in question is a member (e.g., AAMFT, ACA, or APA) has the authority to gather evidence, to hear testimony if necessary, and, then, to make a decision.

Theoretical Techniques

Some theoretical techniques are controversial and should only be used as a last resort and with discretion. For instance, the use of conscious deceit or paradox as applied in strategic family therapy is not recommended when a straightforward approach would work just as well (Henderson, 1987; Solovey & Duncan, 1992). Similarly, the strategic stance of neutrality is of questionable ethical use when there is violence between family members. In such cases, family therapists who practice from the strategic point of view should concentrate on actively bringing the violence within the family to cessation and initiate a contract between members for nonviolence (Willbach, 1989). Only by working with the family in such a way can therapists hope to bring about stability and change. Again, legal as well as ethical factors may need to be considered in deciding on a course of action.

Multicultural Therapy Issues

A final area in which ethical issues commonly arise is in the multicultural domain. When family therapists are counseling with families whose cultural background differs from theirs, they need to carefully evaluate what is being done, what it means, and how they can operate within ethical guidelines if a behavior seems to contradict an ethical code principle. For example, family therapists generally avoid touching clients. Yet, Hispanic/Latino family members may openly touch or hug therapists, especially in greeting them (Cooper & Costas, 1994). In such circumstances, therapists need to respect cultural traditions and adjust to culturally appropriate behaviors while at the same time making sure they do not violate ethical codes regarding intimacy between therapists and families. These situations are difficult to handle, and supervision and/or consultation are recommended as ways to keep perspective and act ethically.

Addressing Unethical Behavior

By reading codes of ethics, consulting with colleagues, studying cases, and receiving supervision, family therapists can usually avoid making unethical decisions. However, at times therapists may notice unethical actions in fellow professionals. When such behavior comes to the attention of a therapist, he or she should address it. The first step in such a process is to discuss the violation directly with the professional in whom it was observed or who allegedly acted in an unethical way.

If the situation is not resolved on this level, the family therapist should report it to an appropriate professional association, such as the AAMFT or IAMFC, as well as inform licensure or certification boards regulating the practice of family counseling. When reported to such agencies, a formal investigation will take place. If found guilty, professionals under the jurisdiction of these agencies are usually admonished and expelled (Kaplan & Culkin, 1995, p. 337).

Legal Issues in Family Therapy

"Ethics and law frequently overlap" (Wilcoxon, 1993, p. 3). For instance, if a family requests that they be billed for individual counseling, rather than for the couple therapy that they are receiving, and a family therapist complies, the parties involved are not only violating sections of the AAMFT and IAMFC codes of ethics but also committing insurance fraud (Kaplan & Allison, 1993a; Stevens-Smith & Hughes, 1993). If such a complaint is raised against a therapist, it may be handled by an ethics committee, a state regulatory commission, or a court of law (Woody, 1988).

Because of the interrelatedness of family ethics and law and the prevalence of law in governing interpersonal relationships, family therapists need to be aware of legal issues affecting therapy. Family therapists are not exempt from dealing with the legal system anymore than they are exempt from being involved in ethical decision making. It is important that family therapists "be aware of legislative decisions, legal precedents, and professional practices" connected with the law (Wilcoxon, 1993, p. 3) in case they are called upon to participate in the legal system.

The Legal System

The term *legal* refers to "law or the state of being lawful"; the term *law* refers to "a body of rules recognized by a state or community as binding on its members" (Shertzer & Stone, 1980, p. 386). In contrast to popular belief, "law is not cut and dried, definite and certain, or clear and precise" (Van Hoose & Kottler, 1985, p. 44). Yet, most family therapists are not familiar with American jurisprudence in more than a superficial way. They do not realize the fluidity within the legal system. The reason is largely because the law is a specialty that requires years of study and practice for one to become proficient. However, without becoming an expert in law, family therapists must master certain aspects of the legal system is order to be effective within this domain.

Interestingly, similarities exist between the legal and therapy communities. For example, both are concerned with setting up healthy relationships between people. In addition, both handle cases that involve drama and resolution. Also, ironically, professionals in both fields are referred to sometimes as "counselors."

Yet, the differences between the legal and the therapeutic systems are greater than their areas of overlap. A few of these differences are quite noticeable. For instance, the legal system is concerned with gathering evidence based on facts; and therapy is more interested in processes and making changes.

Therefore, attorneys spend more time gathering information and concentrating on content than therapists do. Another distinction is that the legal system relies on adversity (Huber, 1994); and the therapeutic system relies on cooperation. Although some legal decisions may involve compromises, attorneys focus on "winning" cases for their clients. Therefore, lawyers engage in discrediting or disproving other evidence that contradicts their cases. For attorneys, their clients' well-being and right is based on representation that is singularly focused. Finally, although attorneys represent families as a whole in some legal cases, they do not deal with whole families when there are internal disputes. Rather, in the legal system each family member involved in a dispute is represented by a different legal counselor. In such situations, the focused outcome is on a just settlement rather than family change and resolution.

In recognition of the growing need for marriage and family therapists to have affordable, regular, and up-to-date information about managing legal risks in their practices, the American Association for Marriage and Family Therapy (AAMFT) established a Legal and Risk Management Plan in 1995 for its members. Under the plan, clinical members can receive "one free legal consultation per quarter with the AAMFT in-house attorney" (Jester, 1995, p. 6).

Types of Law

There are several types of law with which family therapists should be familiar. Some of the most important of these types of law have been defined by Huber (1994) and Huber and Baruth (1987). They are common law, statutory law, administrative (regulatory) law, case law (court decisions), and civil and criminal law.

Common Law
Common law is law derived from tradition and usage. The common law of the United States has its roots in England and the tradition of accepting customs passed down from antiquity. The idea behind common law is that all law does not need to be derived from written sources. For instance, there are common law family matters, such as common law marriages.

Statutory Law
In contrast to common law, **statutory law** consists of those laws passed by legislative bodies, such as state and national legislatures, and signed by an authorized source, such as a governor or the president. Statutory laws are only valid in the jurisdiction in which they are passed. Some states have laws, for instance, addressing marital rape, and other states do not.

Administrative (Regulatory) Law

Administrative (regulatory) law consists of specialized regulations passed by authorized government agencies that pertain to certain specialty areas. For example, laws governing the use of federal land are often made under this arrangement. Some regulations in regard to families, such as those dealing with abuse cases, may also fall in this category.

Case Law (Court Decisions)

As the name implies, **case law** is the type of law decided by decisions of courts at all levels from state to federal. Cases are decided in regard to legal statutes, but "many nuances enter the process" (Huber & Baruth, 1987, p. 86). "Even a minor change in the facts can change the decision of the court" (Huber & Baruth, 1987, p. 90). Matters pertaining to child support, for example, may be decided by case law.

Civil Law Versus Criminal Law

"**Civil law** pertains to acts offensive to individuals, **criminal law** to acts offensive to society in general" (Huber & Baruth, 1987, p. 91). Most of the law involving family therapists falls into the civil law classification (Hopkins & Anderson, 1990). One of the primary civil legal issues confronting some family therapists is divorce. Therapists who are familiar "with the legal issues facing families in transition can be effective in helping those clients make informed, rational, and realistic decisions" (Oliver, 1992, p. 41). The essential element at such times is being knowledgeable about therapeutic and legal issues.

There are some incidents in family therapy in which the issues involved are legally criminal in scope. In such cases, therapists must be aware of what their duties and responsibilities are and what roles they need to play professionally. Two examples of criminal actions within families are spouse abuse and child abuse. In both cases, family therapists have a duty to take actions that are not usually within their domains, such as reporting their knowledge to a legally responsible agency.

Legal Situations that Involve Family Therapists

There are a number of legal situations that may involve family therapists. Most of these occur on the state or local level. Some of the most common legal issues that come up in family counseling "revolve around state laws focusing on the reporting of child abuse, maltreatment, and neglect of minors" (Kaplan & Culkin, 1995, p. 337). Therefore, it behooves family therapists to become familiar with their state's legal system and even the courts and judges in their area (Stevens-Smith & Hughes, 1993). "It is difficult to uphold state laws if you don't know what they are" (Kaplan & Culkin, 1995, p. 337).

Therapists may be called upon to participate in some legal and legally related situations in the following capacities:

- expert witness
- child custody evaluator
- reporter of abuse
- court-ordered witness

Expert Witness

As an **expert witness,** family therapists are asked to give testimony in regard to probable causes and recommendations in regard to family members, such as juveniles who are acting out behaviorally. Because courts are adversarial, therapists must prepare themselves before their appearance. They must stay objective and establish their credibility through presenting their credentials and qualifications. They must speak from authoritative sources and be specific. This type of preparation can help them increase their confidence and competence.

Child-Custody Evaluator

As a **child-custody evaluator,** family therapists are asked to determine what is in the best interest of a child in custody arrangements. In these cases, "the child custody evaluator represents the children and the courts, not the parents" (Stevens-Smith & Hughes, 1993, p. 27). The evaluation of a child includes home visits, testing, and conversations with the child involved. It requires that family therapists involved have a background and experience in child development, family systems, parenting skills, psychometry, counseling, and witness testimony (Remley & Miranti, 1992).

Reporter of Abuse

As a reporter of **abuse,** family therapists must break confidentiality. In doing so, therapists are following the Child Abuse Prevention and Treatment Act of 1974, which mandates the reporting of such situations for the greater good of society. Abuse includes all forms of maltreatment whether physical, sexual, or emotional. It is recommended that family therapists advise families when they are obligated to report abuse and explain to these families how the reporting process works (Stevens-Smith & Hughes, 1993).

Court-Ordered Witness

As a **court ordered witness,** family therapists must appear before a court to testify in behalf of or against a family or family member. If given a choice, most family therapists "would prefer to refuse to testify because they see problems as being systemic and no one is to blame" (Green & Hansen, 1989, p. 156). However, in cases in which they are subpoenaed, family therapists can help themselves and the persons involved by preparing ahead of time. One way they may do this is to seek the advice of attorneys (Remley, 1991). By learning about trial procedures and role playing possible situations, family therapists come to understand courts of law as they do other systems. Thus, they are able to function more effectively.

Issues of Law in Family Therapy

Legal issues in family therapy are usually in the background, as opposed to the foreground, of a clinician's practice. Most involve matters germane to the question of **malpractice,** which is "the failure to fulfill the requisite standard of care" (Woody, 1988, p. 2). Malpractice can occur because of "omission (what should have been done, but was not done) or commission (doing something that should not have been done)" (Woody, 1988, p. 2). In both cases, negligence must be proved for a malpractice suit to be brought forward. Such an incidence may happen if the family therapist either fails to report criminal activities (*Missouri v. Beatty*) or does not inform a family or some of its members that they are in grave danger (*Tarasoff v. Regents of the University of California*).

Two other frequent situations that relate to malpractice involve advertising and record keeping. In regard to advertising, most states "place legal limits" on what family practitioners can do to advertise their skills and services (Bullis, 1993, p. 15). These limits take the form of protecting a title. Thus, only professionals who have met the necessary criteria can call themselves "licensed marriage and family therapists." Because state laws vary, family therapists need to become informed of their state's general statutes before they advertise. They must also check professional ethics codes. For instance, the AAMFT has an extensive section in their code on advertising. The AAMFT also tries to protect its members who advertise, for example, by having an outside agency contact clinical AAMFT members in an area to help them prepare their yellow pages directory advertisement.

In the matter of record keeping, clinical notes should be kept "accurately and professionally" and "separately" from any required business transactions (Hopkins & Anderson, 1990, p. 18). Accuracy encompasses the sequential and cogent nature of what was written. In maintaining accuracy, therapists should "indicate any addendum to records and sign and date such additions. All changes to diagnoses or treatment plans must be made as separate entries" (Marine, 1995, p. 11). Professionalism deals with the legibility and protection of records. "Therapists must always know where their records are and who is responsible for them. Failure to produce records reflects poorly on malpractice litigation" (Marine, 1995, p. 11). Therefore, it is advisable for family therapists to keep their records locked in filed cabinets that are then secured in locked storage areas. In general, most states require all therapists to keep client records and have stipulations as to the length of time records must be kept. "Because family therapy has a long maturation process for claims (sometimes 10, 15, or 20 years after treatment is terminated), maintaining records is a primary risk management technique" (Marine, 1995, p. 11).

Overall, family therapists can help themselves and their client families by being current on acceptable practices and codes within the family therapy field and by making referrals to other more skilled clinicians when they are beyond their level of competence (Hopkins & Anderson, 1990). Carrying professional liability insurance is a must (Bullis, 1993). Such insurance protects therapists financially from legal claims that they have mishandled family needs or members. The responsibility for legally and ethically protecting client families lies squarely on the shoulders of family therapy professionals.

Family/Divorce Mediation

Family/divorce mediation is related to legal issues in family therapy but differs in its scope and emphasis. It is the process of helping couples and families settle disputes or dissolve their marriages in a non-adversarial way. "Mediation is an increasingly utilized alternative to court action" (Huber & Baruth, 1987, p. 106). As a **family/divorce mediator,** family therapists are specially trained to function in a legally related role as an impartial, cognitive, neutral, third party to facilitate negotiation between disputing parties, often a husband and wife. The objective is to help those involved make an informed and mutually agreed upon decision that resolves differences between themselves in a practical and fair manner (Ferstenberg, 1992; Waxman & Press, 1991). "Mediation involves the resolution of conflict, not merely the cessation of it" (Huber, Mascari, & Sanders-Mascari, 1991, p. 117).

Steps involved in the mediation procedure include the mediator obtaining a brief history of the couple/family including information about children. The family members also disclose to the mediator their assets, incomes, liabilities, and goals, whenever appropriate. Furthermore, they prioritize their most important issues. Where necessary, the mediator may involve or consult with other professionals, such as accountants. However, information, ideas, and decisions are generally limited to the parties involved and the mediator.

In contrast to divorce proceedings, mediation is less time consuming, less costly, less hostile and stressful, and more productive (Ferstenberg, 1992). It protects clients and their records from public scrutiny and helps them problem solve and reconstruct their lives in a reasonable and settled manner. There is an external deadline, and mediation concludes with a negotiated written agreement. The important point that family therapists who function as mediators must remember is that they have to help the parties involved learn how to bargain and come to a fair agreement. In doing so, they function in a role quite apart from that of a family therapist, let alone an attorney.

Organizations family therapists may consult in finding out more about mediation include the Academy of Family Mediators in Lexington, MA (617) 674-2663; the Association of Family and Conciliation Courts in Madison, WI (608) 251-4001; the National Institute for Dispute Resolution in Washington, DC (202) 466-4764; and the Society for Professionals in Dispute Resolution in Washington, DC (202) 783-7277.

Professional Identification as a Family Therapist

In addition to ethical and legal questions in the practice of family therapy, there is at least one other professional issue: professional identification. A professional's educational background is usually related to his or her identification. This background also influences future professional opportunities, self-esteem, colleagues, and clinical practices. To be a member of an association and/or licensed/certified by a respectable professional group or state is important. Associations and licensure groups establish standards for their members to follow. They also offer a means for those within the public domain to address grievances or concerns related to a practitioner or the profession in general. Belonging to a professional association or being licensed helps clinicians and the public relate to one another on a higher plane and in a better way than would otherwise be possible.

There are numerous professional associations with whom family therapists affiliate. However, there are six that are the most widely recognized and respected in the field of family therapy, and they are examined here.

American Association for Marriage and Family Therapy (AAMFT)

The American Association for Marriage and Family Therapy (AAMFT) is the oldest and largest professional family therapy organization (Nichols, 1992). It was initially established in 1942 as the American Association of Marriage Counselors (AAMC). The driving force behind the forming of this group was Lester Dearborn of Boston, who organized the AAMC like a private club. Some of the most prominent names in the field of marriage counseling were charter members of the AAMC including Emily Mudd, Ernest Groves, and Abraham Stone (see chapter 3 on the Rationale and History of Family Therapy for more details on the establishment of AAMFT). From 1942 to 1967 the AAMC was "an elite interest group" that struggled in regard to both its identity and its financial stability (Nichols, 1992, p. 5).

In 1970, the AAMC became the American Association for Marriage and Family Counselors (AAMFC). At the same time, membership standards were lowered and membership (and revenue) increased. It changed its name to the American Association for Marriage and Family Therapy in 1979. After having moved its headquarters around the country, the association settled in Washington, D.C., in 1982.

In the 1990s, the AAMFT and its affiliate organizations have concentrated on accrediting educational programs that meet prescribed standards and advocating for licensure for family therapists on the state level. The AAMFT also produces videos on family therapy and publishes professional literature in this area, including the *Journal of Marital and Family Therapy* and the *Family Therapy News*. An annual convention is sponsored by the AAMFT, and it lobbies for passage of select federal legislation that is in the interest of family therapy, including the recognition of family therapists as "core" mental health providers. Overall, the AAMFT is a multifaceted, multidisciplinary professional association that is active in positively impacting the health care delivery system in the United States as it affects families.

American Family Therapy Association (AFTA)

The American Family Therapy Association (AFTA) was founded by Murray Bowen in 1977. Its stated objectives include:

- advancing theories and therapies that regard the entire family as a unit
- promoting research and professional education in family therapy and allied fields
- making information about family therapy available to practitioners in other fields of knowledge and to the public
- fostering the cooperation of all who are concerned with the medical, psychological, social, legal, and other needs of the family
- promoting the science and practice of family therapy.

There are five categories of AFTA membership: charter, clinical-teacher, research, distinguished, and foreign. Association members represent a wide variety of disciplines. Membership requirements are essentially a terminal professional degree, 5 years of post-degree clinical experience with families, and 5 years of teaching family therapy or performing significant research in the family field. The membership numbers approximately 1,000 family therapy teachers and researchers who meet once a year to share ideas and develop common interests (Kaslow, 1990).

Division 43 of the American Psychological Association: Family Psychology

Division 43 (Family Psychology) of the American Psychological Association (APA) was established in 1984 to enable psychologists who worked with families to keep their identity as psychologists (Kaslow, 1990). As a division, Family Psychology includes more than 3,000 practitioners and academicians who are concerned with the science, practice, public interest, and education of psychologists who work with families. Family psychologists are involved in premarital, marital, divorce, and remarriage counseling. They focus on family abuse and violence, pediatrics, geriatrics, and governmental policies connected with family issues.

To become a division member, a professional must hold membership in the American Psychological Association. Like the AAMFT and AFTA, the Division of Family Psychology sponsors a number of programs in which members may participate, including the annual convention of the American Psychological Association. It has established task forces and committees that members may join. A bulletin, *The Family Psychologist,* is published regularly by the division, and many Division 43 members contribute to the APA periodical *Journal of Family Psychology*.

According to L'Abate (1992), family psychology differs from family therapy in three areas. First, "family psychology is interested in the whole functionality-dysfunctionality continuum, while family therapy is mainly concerned with dysfunctionality." Second, "while family psychology focuses reductionistically on the relationship of the individual within the family, family therapy focuses holistically on the family as a whole unit or system." Third, "family psychology stresses objective evaluation and primary and secondary prevention approaches." Family therapy, on the other hand, "stresses the subjective understanding of the family and sees therapy as one type of tertiary prevention" (p. 3). Not all family therapists agree with L'Abate, and the debate about the identity of family psychology continues.

International Association of Marriage and Family Counselors (IAMFC)

The International Association of Marriage and Family Counselors (IAMFC) is a division of the American Counseling Association (ACA). It was established in 1986. IAMFC membership is interdisciplinary. The major elements common to the approximately 7,000 members include professional training in marriage and family counseling/therapy and an interest/involvement in working with couples and families directly or tangentially. Members participate in regional and national conferences sponsored by the IAMFC and the ACA. In addition, the IAMFC has developed national training standards accepted by its membership and the Council for Accreditation of Counseling and Related Educational Programs (CACREP) (Stevens-Smith, Hinkle, & Stahman, in press).

The IAMFC publishes the *IAMFC Newsletter,* which is devoted to examining current issues related to marriage and family counseling, and *The Family Jour-*

nal: Counseling and Therapy for Couples and Families, a quarterly periodical. It also produces videos and publishes books related to family therapy. In addition, the association is involved in credentialing marriage and family counselors/therapists. It is helping to upgrade ethical standards within the ACA on marriage and family counseling/therapy, but maintains its own standards as well (Lynn Miller, personal correspondence, August, 1992).

National Council on Family Relations (NCFR)

The National Council on Family Relations (NCFR) is the oldest professional association dedicated to working with families. It was established in 1939, and many of its members helped to create and support the AAMFT (Nichols, 1992). Throughout its history, the NCFR has concentrated on education. Its membership is interdisciplinary and includes family life educators, sociologists, family researchers, and family therapists.

A specialty of the NCFR is delineating information about family history, family forms and functions, and family life in a variety of settings. It publishes a variety of publications including the *Journal of Marriage and the Family* and *Family Relations.* It also sponsors annual conventions in which professionals from a wide variety of settings can exchange ideas. One of its major subspecialty groups is devoted to family therapy.

Affiliated Council for Marriage Enrichment (ACME)

One of the oldest interdisciplinary associations for marriage enrichment is the Affiliated Council for Marriage Enrichment (ACME), established in 1975. This association, like others, has gone through a number of transitions. Its constituent members are comprised of various enrichment group leaders from across the United States. It is preventative in nature and is sometimes overlooked as a resource for family therapists.

Issues in Professional Identification

As is evident from this overview of professional family therapy associations, practitioners have a wide choice as to what group or groups they align. Each association has unique aspects or foci. For instance, the Affiliated Council for Marriage Enrichment concentrates primarily on preventive services (i.e., primary intervention). On the other hand, the National Council on Family Relations is most concerned with education and training (i.e., secondary intervention). The other associations all have a concentration on therapy and the treatment of dysfunctionality (i.e., tertiary intervention). In all fairness, however, each of these associations sponsors programs and speakers that address the issues involved in prevention and education. They all like to think of themselves as holistic in their approaches, and indeed the case can be strongly made for the AAMFT, IAMFC, AFTA, and Division 43 of APA following such a comprehensive model.

Emphasis aside, considerable friction still exists among associations that are dedicated to family therapy. In all likelihood, the turf issues surrounding this uneasiness will not diminish in the foreseeable future. This aspect of family therapy is discussed further in the final chapter of this text.

Summary and Conclusion

Ethical, legal, and professional identity issues are of major importance to family therapists. Ignorance of codes, standards, and associations are no excuse for acting unethically, illegally, and/or unprofessionally.

Family and societal conduct are based on relationship ethics. Family therapy is not value free, either. When faced with a dilemma, family therapists must know their own values, the values ethical codes are based on, and the values of the families with whom they work. They can then make informed ethical decisions. Four of the most useful tools they can use in this process are codes of ethics, educational resources, professional consultation, and interaction with colleagues, including supervisors. Common ethical concerns are related to confidentiality, gender inequality, sexual relationships, and therapeutic techniques, and multicultural therapy issues.

Legal issues often overlap with ethical matters. The law and therapy share some common concerns regarding setting up relationships between people. They differ in their emphases on facts/process and adversarial/cooperative approaches. The most common type of law most family therapists are concerned with is civil law (acts offensive to individuals). However, it is important that therapists know other types of law and local/state statutes related to families. Family therapists are most likely to participate in legal situations as expert witnesses, child custody evaluators, reporters of abuse, and court-ordered witnesses. They must actively protect themselves against malpractice by adhering to commonly accepted and legal ways of handling family therapy cases. Furthermore, they must carry malpractice insurance. Family therapists may act as family mediators if they receive advanced training. Such positions involve the resolution of conflict in a non-adversarial and rational way.

In regard to identity, family therapists generally belong to one or more professional associations including AAMFT, AFTA, Family Psychology (APA), IAMFC, NCFR, and ACME. All of these groups have much to offer that can positively influence the careers of family therapists; however, they sometimes quarrel.

SUMMARY TABLE

Professional Issues in Family Therapy

Ethics, law, and identity are of major concern to family therapists.

It is crucial for family therapists to be knowledgeable of issues in ethics, law, and identity if they are to practice according to high standards and avoid serious trouble.

Overview of Ethics in Family Therapy

Families and societies are governed by relationship ethics based on the principle of equitability.

Family therapy is also governed by principles of ethics that have been codified.

Ethics are a part of the total system of family therapy.

Family therapists face more ethical conflicts than other therapists.

Ethics and Values

Ethical decision making is based on an awareness and understanding of values. A value is a choice that is more or less preferable.

Effective therapists are aware of their own values and those of the families with whom they work. Values have an impact on families and undergird ethical decisions.

Ethical dilemmas in family therapy are related to deciding which values to keep and which to discard. Emphasis of values is of concern.

Guidelines for Making Ethical Decisions

Four prevalent resources family therapists use in ethical decision making are:

- codes of ethics
- educational resources
- professional consultation
- interactions with colleagues including supervision

Both the AAMFT and the IAMFC have developed code of ethics.

Ethical codes are sometimes limited by the complexity of issues.

Educational resources include case studies and columns on family therapy ethics. Ethical decision making is a step-by-step process.

Professional consultation involves the use of experts to enhance one's knowledge and abilities.

Interactions with peers, including supervision, helps family therapists draw on the wisdom and opinions of others in a systemic manner.

Common Ethical Concerns
Among the most common ethical concerns are those involving:
- confidentiality (i.e., the revealing to others of information revealed in a therapy session)
- gender issues (e.g., inequality of men and women)
- sex between a therapist and a client
- use of some theoretical techniques (e.g., conscious deceit or neutrality)

Legal Issues in Family Therapy
Ethics and law frequently overlap, such as with cases involving intentional misdiagnosis.

Family therapists are not immune to dealing with the legal system and must be aware of legal decisions, precedents, and practices.

The Legal System
Legal refers to "law or being lawful." *Law* refers to a body of rules, made on a variety of levels such as state or federal, that are binding in certain locales and under specific situations.

The legal and therapeutic systems are similar in that they both are concerned with setting up healthy relationships and both handle cases that involve drama and resolution.

Differences between legal and therapeutic systems also exist. The legal system is concerned with gathering evidence based on facts, and the therapeutic system is more interested in process and change. In addition, the legal system relies on adversity, and the therapeutic system relies on cooperation.

Categories of Law
The most common types of law are:
- common law (i.e., law derived from tradition)
- statutory law (i.e., rules passed by legislative bodies)
- administrative law (i.e., rules made by government agencies)
- case law (i.e., court decisions)
- civil versus criminal law (i.e., offenses against individuals versus those against society in general)

Therapists who are knowledgeable about the law can help themselves and their client families.

Legal Situations Involving Family Therapists
Family therapists may be called upon to participate in some legal and legally related situations in the following capacities:
- expert witness (i.e., one who gives testimony in the form of recommendations about a family or family member)

- child custody evaluator (i.e., one who determines the best interest of a child in a custody hearing)
- reporter of abuse (i.e., one who informs members of the legal system about the maltreatment of a family member)
- court-ordered witness (i.e., one who is subpoenaed to testify in court about a family seen in treatment)

Issues of Law in Family Therapy

Malpractice is a major legal issue and can occur through omission as well as commission. In either case, negligence must be proved.

Advertising and record keeping are two other legal issues. The first involves protecting a title and representing one's skills adequately. The second focuses on keeping accurate and professional notes.

Liability insurance is a must if one is going to be legally protected as a family therapist.

Family/Divorce Mediation

Mediation is the process of helping couples/families settle disputes or dissolve relationships in a non-adversarial way.

Skills associated with mediation include abilities to be cognitive, neutral, impartial, practical, and fair minded.

Steps in the mediation process include taking a brief history of the couple/family and obtaining disclosure of assets, incomes, liabilities, and goals. Prioritizing choices is essential.

Overall, mediation is less time consuming, costly, hostile, and stressful than legal divorce proceedings. It is also more productive.

Professional Identification

A family therapist's education, background, self-perception, and opportunities are associated with professional identity.

There are six national professional associations related to family therapy. They are:

- AAMFT was established in 1942. It is the oldest and largest association devoted to family therapy. Its membership is interdisciplinary.
- AFTA was established in 1977 by Murray Bowen. It is the most focused on teaching and research.
- Family Psychology (APA) was established in the early 1980s to allow psychology practitioners who work with families to keep their identity as psychologists.
- IAMFC was established in 1986. It is the second largest family therapy association. It parallels many aspects of AAMFT but is more affiliated with counseling as a profession.
- NCFR was established in 1939, but only one group within the association is dedicated to working with families.

- ACME is an interdisciplinary association for marriage enrichment groups, like a confederation. It was established in 1975.

Despite areas of overlap, there is still competition among these groups for recognition by the public and government agencies.

References

American Association for Marriage and Family Therapy. (1991). *AAMFT Code of Ethics*. Washington, DC: Author.

Ansen, D., & Springen, K. (1992, April 13). A lot of not so happy endings. *Newsweek,* 58.

Aponte, H. J. (1992). Training the person of the therapist in structural family therapy. *Journal of Marital and Family Therapy, 18,* 269–281.

Arthur, G. L., & Swanson, C. D. (1993). *Confidentiality and privileged communication*. Alexandria, VA: American Counseling Association.

Beck, M., Springen, K., & Foote, D. (1992, April 13). Sex and psychotherapy. *Newsweek,* 52–57.

Bograd, M. (1992). Values in conflict: Challenges to family therapists' thinking. *Journal of Marital and Family Therapy, 18,* 245–256.

Boszormenyi-Nagy, I., & Ulrich, D. N. (1981). Contextual family therapy. In A. S. Gurman & D. P. Kniskern (Eds.), *Handbook of family therapy*. New York: Brunner/Mazel.

Bullis, R. K. (1993). *Law and the management of a counseling agency or private practice*. Alexandria, VA: American Counseling Association.

Carter, B. (1986). Success in family therapy. *Family Therapy Networker, 10,* 16–22.

Carter, B. (1992). Stonewalling feminism. *Family Therapy Networker, 16,* 64–69.

Cooper, C., & Costas, L. (1994, Spring). Ethical challenges when working with Hispanic/Latino families: Personalismo. *The Family Psychologist, 10,* 32–34.

Corey, G., Corey, M. S., & Callanan, P. (1993). *Issues and ethics in the helping professions* (4th ed.). Pacific Grove, CA: Brooks/Cole.

Costa, L., & Sorenson, J. (1993). Feminist family therapy: Ethical considerations for the clinician. *The Family Journal, 1,* 17–24.

Doherty, W. J. (1995). *Soul searching: Why psychotherapy must promote moral responsibility*. New York: Basic Books.

Doherty, W. J., & Boss, P. G. (1991). Values and ethics in family therapy. In A. S. Gurman & D. P. Kniskern (Eds.), *Handbook of family therapy* (Vol. II, pp. 606–637). New York: Brunner/Mazel.

Ferstenberg, R. L. (1992). Mediation versus litigation in divorce and why a litigator becomes a mediator. *American Journal of Family Therapy, 20,* 266–273.

Fishman, C. H. (1988). *Treating troubled adolescents*. New York: Basic Books.

Giblin, P. (1993). Values: Family and other. *The Family Journal: Counseling and Therapy for Couples and Families, 1,* 240–242.

Gladding, S. T. (1991). *Eli*. Unpublished manuscript.

Gladding, S. T., Wilcoxon, A. S., Semon, M. G., & Myers, P. (1992). Individual and marriage/family counseling supervision: Similarities, differences, and implications for training. *Journal of the Florida Association for Counseling and Development, 1,* 58–71.

Green, S. L., & Hansen, J. C. (1986). Ethical dilemmas in family therapy. *Journal of Marital and Family Therapy, 12,* 225–230.

Green, S. L., & Hansen, J. C. (1989). Ethical dilemmas faced by family therapists. *Journal of Marital and Family Therapy, 15,* 149–158.

Grosser, G. H., & Paul, N. L. (1964). Ethical issues in family group therapy. *American Journal of Orthopsychiatry, 34,* 875–884.

Hare-Mustin, R. T. (1987). The problem of gender in family therapy theory. *Family Process, 26,* 15–27.

Henderson, M. C. (1987). Paradoxical process and ethical consciousness. *Family Therapy, 14,* 187–193.

Hopkins, B. R., & Anderson, B. S. (1990). *The counselor and the law* (3rd ed.). Alexandria, VA: American Counseling Association.

Huber, C. H. (1994). *Ethical, legal, and professional issues in marriage and family therapy* (2nd ed.). New York: Macmillan.

Huber, C. H., & Baruth, L. G. (1987). *Ethical, legal, and professional issues in marriage and family therapy*. Columbus, OH: Merrill.

Huber, C. H., Mascari, J. B., & Sanders-Mascari, A. (1991). Family mediation. In J. Carlson & J. Lewis (Eds.), *Family counseling: Strategies and issues*. Denver, CO: Love.

Hundert, E. M. (1987). A model for ethical problem solving in medicine, with practical applications. *American Journal of Psychiatry, 144,* 839–846.

Hurvitz, N. (1967). Marital problems following psychotherapy with one spouse. *Journal of Consulting and Clinical Psychology, 31,* 38–47.

International Association of Marriage and Family Counselors. (1993). Ethical code for the International Association of Marriage and Family Counselors. *The Family Journal, 1,* 73–77.

Jester, S. (1995, December). Legal and risk management plan and *Practice Strategies* newsletter join growing list of AAMFT member benefits. *Family Therapy News, 26,* 7.

Kaplan, D., & Allison, M. (1993a). Family ethics. *The Family Journal: Counseling and Therapy for Couples and Families, 1,* 72–77.

Kaplan, D., & Allison, M. (1993b). Family ethics. *The Family Journal: Counseling and Therapy for Couples and Families, 1,* 158–159.

Kaplan, D., & Allison, M. (1993c). Family ethics. *The Family Journal: Counseling and Therapy for Couples and Families, 1,* 246–248.

Kaplan, D., & Culkin, M. (1995). Family ethics: Lessons Learned. *The Family Journal, 3,* 335–338.

Kaslow, F. (1990). *Voices in family psychology.* Newbury Park, CA: Sage.

Krasner, L., & Houts, A. C. (1984). A study of the "value" systems of behavioral scientists. *American Psychologist, 39,* 840–850.

Kurpius, D. J., & Fuqua, D. R. (1993). Fundamental issues in defining consultation. *Journal of Counseling & Development, 71,* 598–600.

L'Abate, L. (1992). Family psychology and family therapy: Comparisons and contrasts. *American Journal of Family Therapy, 20,* 3–12.

Marine, E. (1995, December). Preserving your records. *Family Therapy News, 26*(6), 11.

McGoldrick, M. (1988). Women and the family life cycle. In B. Carter & M. McGoldrick (eds.). *The changing family life cycle* (2nd ed., pp. 29–68). New York: Gardner.

McGoldrick, M., & Gerson, R. (1985). *Genograms in family assessment.* New York: Norton.

Missouri v. Beatty, 770 S. W. 2d 387 (Mo.Ct.App. 1989).

Mitchell, R. W. (1991). *Documentation in counseling records.* Alexandria: American Counseling Association.

Morrison, J., Layton, B., & Newman, J. (1982). Ethical conflict in clinical decision making: A challenge for family therapists. In J. Hansen (Ed.), *Values, ethics, legalities and the family therapists.* Rockville, MD: Aspen.

Nichols, W. C. (1992). *Fifty years of marital and family therapy.* Washington, DC: American Association for Marriage and Family Therapy.

Nixon, J. A. (1993). Gender considerations in the case of "The Jealous Husband": Strategic therapy in review. *The Family Journal: Counseling and Therapy for Couples and Families, 1,* 161–163.

Oliver, C. J. (1992). Legal issues facing families in transition: An overview for counselors. *New York State Journal for Counseling and Development, 7,* 41–52.

O'Malley, P. (1995, December). Confidentiality in the electronic age. *Family Therapy News, 26,* 9.

Papp, P. (1977). *Family therapy: Full-length case studies.* New York: Gardner.

Remley, T. P. (1991). *Preparing for court appearances.* Alexandria, VA: American Counseling Association.

Remley, T. P., Jr., & Miranti, J. (1992). Child custody evaluator: A new role for mental health counselors. *Journal of Mental Health Counseling, 13,* 334–342.

Ryder, R., & Hepworth, J. (1990). AAMFT ethical code: "Dual relationships." *Journal of Marital and Family Therapy, 16,* 127–132.

Schwartz, R. C., Liddle, H. A., & Breunlin, D. C. (1988). Muddles in live supervision. In H. A. Liddle, D. C. Breunlin, & R. C. Schwartz (Eds.), *Handbook of family therapy training* (pp. 172–182). New York: Guilford.

Seppa, N. (1996, August). Supreme court protects patient-therapist privilege. *APA Monitor, 27,* 39.

Shertzer, B., & Stone, S. (1980). *Fundamentals of counseling* (3rd ed.). Boston: Houghton Mifflin.

Solovey, A. D., & Duncan, B. L. (1992). Ethics and strategic therapy: A proposed ethical direction. *Journal of Marital and Family Therapy, 18,* 53–61.

Smith, R. L., & Stevens-Smith, P. (1992). Future projections for marriage and family counseling and therapy. In R. L. Smith & P. Stevens-Smith (Eds.), *Family counseling and therapy* (pp. 433–440). Ann Arbor, MI: ERIC/CAPS.

Spiegel, J. (1971). *Transactions: The interplay between individual, family, and society.* New York: Science House.

Stevens-Smith, P., Hinkle, J. S., & Stahman, R. F. (1993). Professional accreditation standards in marriage and family counseling and therapy. *Counselor Education & Supervision, 33,* 116–126.

Stevens-Smith, P., & Hughes, M. M. (1993). *Legal issues in marriage and family counseling.* Alexandria, VA: American Counseling Association.

Tarasoff v. Regents of the University of California, 551 P. 2d 334 (Cal. 1976).

Van Hoose, W. H., & Kottler, J. (1985). *Ethical and legal issues in counseling and psychotherapy* (2nd ed.). San Francisco: Jossey-Bass.

Walsh, W. M. (1993). Gender and strategic marital therapy. *The Family Journal: Counseling and Therapy for Couples and Families, 1,* 160–161.

Waxman, G. L., & Press, S. (1991). Mediation: Part II. Mediation in Florida. *Nova Law Review, 15,* 1212–1225.

Weiner, J. P., & Boss, P. (1985). Exploring gender bias against women: Ethics for marriage and family therapy. *Counseling and Values, 30,* 9–21.

Wendorf, D. J., & Wendorf, R. J. (1992). A systemic view of family therapy ethics. In R. L. Smith & P. Stevens-Smith (Eds.), *Family counseling and therapy* (pp. 304–320). Ann Arbor, MI: ERIC/CAPS.

Wilcoxon, S. A. (1993, March/April). Ethical issues in marital and family counseling: A framework for examining unique ethical concerns. *Family Counseling and Therapy, 1,* 1–15.

Willbach, D. (1989). Ethics and family therapy: The case management of family violence. *Journal of Marital and Family Therapy, 15,* 43–52.

Woody, R. H. (1988). *Fifty ways to avoid malpractice.* Sarasota, FL: Professional Resource Exchange.

Research and Assessment in Family Therapy

He counts the coat hooks up to 39
that line the wall from the door to his classroom.

An unrefined scientist, at the age of four,
he delights in adding up objects
that fill his world with fascination.

Gladding, 1993

R esearch and assessment are vitally interlinked with family therapy and have a long association with it. From the time the term *family therapy* was first used in the 1950s until now, there has been a focus upon assessment and healing among mental health professionals working with families (Shields, Wynne, McDaniel, & Gawinski, 1994). Indeed, "the assessment of individuals and their family relationships has been and is an evolving part of the marriage and family counseling literature" (Sporakowski, 1995, p. 60). Most of the pioneers in family therapy used procedures that were research-based to evaluate and work with families. They were in effect "researcher-clinicians" (Sprenkle & Moon, 1996, p. 3). Although some of their research was "soft" by today's standards, initially, "research came first and therapy was . . . a secondary activity" (Barker, 1986, p. 270). Many early studies of therapeutic changes in families conducted by groups, such as those led by Bateson, Wynne, and Minuchin, excelled in family therapy research and assessment (Wynne, 1983). Historically, in the world of family therapy, there has been "a synergistic interplay among research, theory, and practice" (Sprenkle & Piercy, 1984, p. 226).

It is unfortunate but, after the genesis of family therapy, many practitioners drifted away from research and assessment. This split is most dramatically seen in some influential schools of family therapy whose advocates have gained considerable prominence but whose methods have little empirical evidence to support their effectiveness (Gurman, Kniskern, & Pinsof, 1986). During the 1960s, therapists and researchers became two distinct groups, a fact that has been lamented by Jay Haley (1978), among others.

In the 1990s, both interest in family therapy and the conducting of research are growing again. Research "can be found in more places than one can keep up with" (Liddle, 1992, p. 17). In addition, research by family therapists now includes a multitude of methods such as "surveys, personal interviews, observational studies, and content analysis of historical documents" (Bird & Sporakowski, 1992, p. x). The increase in the volume of family therapy research, and its more sophisticated procedures, is adding to the power and credibility of family therapy. The number of professionals who identify themselves as research/practitioners is on the rise (Sprenkle & Moon, 1996).

Likewise, the assessment of families is making a comeback. **Assessment** focuses on dimensions of particular families and usually includes the administration of formal or informal tests or evaluation instrument(s) along with behavioral observations. Assessment focuses on the normal functioning of a unit, a family; research concentrates on the changes or lack thereof when therapeutic interventions are made.

Assessment is dependent on having "a theoretical model of how families function and of the ways in which their functioning may go awry" (Barker, 1986, p. 77). It is crucial to make assessments about families before taking therapeutic initiatives. Sometimes this type of information is easily obtained, but often it is not. The field of family assessment is less developed and more complex than that of individual evaluation (Drummond, 1992; Snyder, Cavell, Heffer, & Mangrum, 1995). Ways of conducting assessment are covered in this chapter, and some of the most common assessment instruments are described. First, however, the most prominent features of family research are considered.

The Importance of Research in Family Therapy

Research is important in family therapy for many reasons, but three of the most important involve accountability, practicality, and uniqueness.

In regard to accountability, research studies provide family therapists with the means to prove they are not "witch doctors, snake oil peddlers, or overachieving do-gooders" (Hubble, 1993, p. 14). Research results are a necessary element in the increasing respectability of family therapy.

On the level of practicality, research also has a payoff. Although research studies sometimes do not yield immediate applicability, they do have "an influence on clinical practice" in the long run (Hubble, 1993, p. 15). Therefore, it is critical that practitioners as well as statisticians become familiar with family therapy research methods and outcomes.

Finally, in regard to uniqueness, it is through research that the field of family therapy establishes its common bond and point of departure with other mental health counseling approaches. In the process of gaining knowledge about treatment methods and approaches, the profession of family therapy establishes itself as a type of entity that can make claims for its theories, practices, and clinicians (Schwartz & Breunlin, 1983). Thus, research is a vital link in the claim that family therapy should and does stand on its own as a type of specialized treatment (Piercy & Sprinkle, 1986).

Research Findings in Family Therapy

Research on the effectiveness of family therapy is connected to research on the overall effectiveness of all types of psychotherapies. In general, most individuals improve when they receive therapy of any kind, especially when compared with a control group left on their own to resolve problems (Hubble, 1993). Comprehensive reviews of family therapy research indicates specifically that:

1. The improvement rate in family therapy is similar to the improvement rate in individual therapy.
2. The deterioration rate in family therapy is likewise similar to the deterioration rate in individual therapy.
3. "Deterioration may occur because:

    a. The therapist has poor interpersonal skills.
    b. The therapist moves too quickly into sensitive topic areas and does not handle the situation well.
    c. The therapist allows family conflict to become exacerbated without moderating therapeutic intervention.
    d. The therapist does not provide adequate structure in the early stages of therapy.
    e. The therapist does not support family members" (Fenell & Weinhold, 1992, p. 333).

4. Family therapy is as effective as individual counseling for personal problems or family conflict.
5. Brief therapy of 20 sessions or less is as effective as long-term therapy.
6. Participation of fathers in family therapy is much more likely to bring about positive results than family therapy without them.
7. Relationship skills of family therapists are crucial in producing positive outcomes.
8. Less severe forms of mental/psychological distress are more likely to be successfully treated than those that are severe.
9. Psychosomatic problems can be treated successfully with a modified version of structural family therapy.
10. The type of family, its background, and present interactional style relate to the success or failure of family therapy.

Some of the most promising research in the area of family therapy has been conducted by Jose Szapocznik and his associates at the Spanish Family Guidance Center in Miami (Letich, 1993). This clinically based research has concentrated on Hispanic/Latino-American families but has general implications. Among the contributions made by Szapocznik are:

- the development of the Strategic Family Systems Rating (SFSR), a research tool that objectively measures and evaluates family functioning on six dimensions—structure, resonance, developmental stage, identified patienthood, flexibility, and conflict resolution (Szapocznik, Rio, Hervis, Kurtines, Faraci, & Mitrani, 1991)

- the creation of One-Person Family Therapy (OPFT), in which strategic family therapy is offered to any person who comes to therapy in order to help that person make changes in the family system (Szapocznik, Kurtines, Foote, Perez-Vidal, & Hervis, 1990)

- a comparison of outcome in boys and their families of the efficacy of individual, psychodynamic, child therapy versus family therapy (a landmark study in supporting the family therapy concept of **complementarity,** i.e., if one person gets better without changing the family structure, the rest of the family gets worse (Szapocznik et al., 1989)

Szapocznik's research demonstrates a commitment to rigor and control with an orientation to practical use. His work represents the best of clinician research. It is often idealized but seldom emulated by those within the field of family therapy (Schwartz & Breunlin, 1983).

Two Types of Family Therapy Research

There are two types of family therapy research: qualitative and quantitative. **Qualitative research** is still in its infancy. It is rooted in the traditions of anthropology and sociology (Moon, Dillon, & Sprenkle, 1990). Most qualitative research is characterized by:

- open-ended, discovery-oriented questions that are holistic
- small samples carefully chosen to "fit research goals (criterion-based selection)" or to "help elaborate developing theory (theoretical selection)" (p. 369)
- participant-observer researchers who are subjectively explicit
- visual or verbal data reporting rather than numerical data reporting
- data analysis occurring simultaneously with data collection
- "analytic induction and constant comparison" (p. 369) by researchers who try to discern patterns in analyzing results of time/labor intense investigations
- results that "take the form of theoretical assertions, discovered theory, or categorical systems (taxonomies)" (p. 369)
- reports that are well written, often as books, but with no standardized form

- reliability and validity based on journalistic reflections, thick descriptions of data, audits, comparison analysis, and "participant critiques of research reports" (p. 369)

Qualitative research, at its best, is found in extended interviews and autobiographies. A good example of a qualitative research study is the interview study of ten couples with children in which both partners worked outside the home (Hochschild, 1989). In this research, written as a book, couples were asked about who did what work around the house as well as information about their backgrounds. Patterns were then detected and commented upon. The advantages of qualitative research over quantitative research include a more integrated and holistic view of client families and greater interaction between researcher/clinicians and client families. Qualitative research also increases the flexibility of therapists to meet the needs of families (Hood & Johnson, 1991).

Quantitative research grew out of the scientific traditions of physics, chemistry, and biology, and is the way most research is reported. Quantitative research is characterized by an emphasis on closed-ended questions, such as "Does a certain variable, such as working outside the home, have an impact on a family's happiness?" To answer this type of question, quantitative research utilizes large sample sizes to gather information. Objective researchers then focus on gathering data in a precise form frequently using standardized instruments. Usually, the data from such studies is reported in a statistical format, such as averages of specific test scores. After the data is collected, it is analyzed and deductive conclusions are made based on the data analysis. The results tend to "prove" or "disprove" theories and assertions that formed the basis for the research in the first place.

A final report is then written in a standard and prosaic form. In it a description of what was done and how it was done is included. The report highlights characteristics of the population used; the reliability and validity of the instruments employed; and the process, conclusions, and recommendations for further research (Gay, 1996; Goldman, 1990).

Quantitative research is one reason that family therapy is seen as a science as well as an art. By using quantitative methods, researchers are careful to define what they are doing and to record their results in a precise and scholarly manner. When they present their findings, quantitative researchers are likely to be able to focus on interventions that made a difference overall in their treatment. One example of an empirical study is the investigation of systemic and nonsystemic diagnostic processes by McGuirk, Friedlander, and Blocher (1987) in which they found that "systemic clinicians, in contrast with . . . nonsystemic ones, identified as relevant a greater number of different subsystems, more triads, and fewer monads" (p. 69).

Whether family therapy researchers choose qualitative or quantitative research methods, they must deal with complexities that are usually quite complicated. Family therapy is premised on a systemic perspective that emphasizes **circular causality** (i.e., *A* and *B* affect each other) rather than linear thinking that stresses cause and effect (e.g., *A* caused *B*). Thus, the emphasis in treatment and research is on the interaction of family members with each other (West, 1988). Difficulties stemming from this model present themselves in many forms. Questions related to one's choice of **research design,** sampling, instrumentation, and procedure are critical. Theoretical and statistical choices are also important in regard to researching the process and outcome of family therapy.

Difficulties in Family Therapy Research

There are many difficulties associated with rigorously researching the effectiveness of family therapy. These include, but are not limited to, the complexity of relationships within families. In the study of family relationships, the question is, "What within the family is the focus of attention?" For example, family therapy research can concentrate on the **identified patient (IP),** the marriage, the total family system, cross-generational relationships, and so forth (Gurman & Kniskern, 1981). The problems connected with studying families are further complicated by environmental factors. Are families studied within their environments or in a laboratory setting? Furthermore, the time commitment needed to study the effects of family therapy is great, and the number of personnel who must be devoted to gathering and analyzing data is difficult as well as expensive to sustain over time.

Assuming that the questions of focus and environment can be controlled, it then becomes important to focus attention on another pertinent aspect of research—its design.

Design

The way research is designed ultimately effects the results (Gay, 1996). Poorly designed studies yield worthless results; well-designed studies produce reports worth reading. In considering the design of a research study, investigators must make sure the design fits the families to be studied and that it is efficient (Miller, 1986).

Overall, there are five categories of research design: exploratory, descriptive, developmental, experimental, and correlational. In exploratory research a qualitative approach is often taken because issues are still being defined. Therefore, many exploratory research designs consist of interviews between researchers and families. In descriptive research, the design is set up to describe specific variables, for example, subpopulations within the United States.

Developmental research designs focus on studying changes over time. The most characteristic of this type of design is a longitudinal study, although some cross-sectional studies are developmental in nature, too. A study focusing on the effects within families in which a member had AIDS is an example of a longitudinal study. Experimental research designs are those that adhere to classic "hard science" methodologies, such as an hypothesis and dependent/independent variables. In an experimental research design, at least one variable is manipulated.

Finally, in correlational research designs, the degree of association or relatedness between two variables is calculated. This type of research is usually *ex post facto* (after the fact) rather than *a priori* (before the fact). With correlational research, unlike experimental research, it is difficult to state in any precise way what factors were most influential and with whom. A correlational study might be one that examined the number of divorces in marriages of children of divorce.

Sampling

Because it is virtually impossible to study all families within a community, the **sample** that one chooses becomes extremely important. When conducted properly, a randomly chosen sample of families is representative of an entire group of families. "There is no substitute for randomly assigning families to treatment conditions. Without random assignment, group differences are uninterpretable; the study is not worth conducting" (Jacobson, 1985, p. 154).

In a random assignment sampling procedure, every family has an equal chance of being selected. The families that are chosen are by the luck of the draw, such as assigning each family a number and blindly pulling numbers out of a hat to set up a control and experimental group. The results of such studies are generalizable to the selected population of families as a whole.

When a sample is not chosen wisely, bias and/or misinformation results. Such has been the case with a large number of family studies (Gurman et al., 1986). There are several creative ways to collect samples of families. Two of the most frequently used are those based on probability and those based on nonprobability. "Probability samples are drawn from a known population in such a way that it is possible to calculate the likelihood . . . of each case being included in the sample" (Miller, 1986, p. 70). In this method, it is also possible to estimate the margin of error between the sample data and the entire population. Ways of conducting probability sampling include conducting:

- a simple random sample, in which each family within a population has an equal chance of being selected
- a systematic random sample, in which the first family to be studied is selected at random, and then every *n*th family is automatically included
- a stratified sampling, in which random samples are drawn from different strata or groups of a population, such as families headed by women and families headed by men

Nonprobability samples are the opposite of probability samples. They may be used "when representativeness of a whole population is not as important as the information itself or when probability sampling is not feasible" (Nelson, 1996, p. 454). Despite a reluctance to use nonprobability samples, they "have an important place in marriage and family research" (Miller, 1986, p. 70). This is especially true in studies that "are more exploratory and qualitative, hypothesis generating rather than hypothesis testing" (Miller, 1986, p. 71). Ways of collecting nonprobability samples are through:

- convenience (i.e., using local families or those known by the researcher)
- snowballing (i.e., asking participating families to refer other families)
- purposiveness (i.e., choosing families because they are thought by the researcher to be representative of the study population)

Instrumentation

The type of instrument used in a study has an influence on what is reported as outcome. For instance, a self-report instrument yields a different result than a behaviorally based observation report. Self-reports have an advantage in family therapy research in they can be distributed to a large number of families at a relatively low cost. Their scoring is also objective, and this makes it relatively easy to establish external validity (i.e., generalization) (Copeland & White, 1991). In addition, self-report instruments can "provide family members an opportunity to systemically understand what the other members' concerns are" and "to self-disclose through paper and pencil rather than their usual method, which has failed" (Brock & Barnard, 1988, p. 41). On the other hand, self-reports are questionable in regard to construct validity (i.e., measuring what they report to measure).

More open-ended or behaviorally based instruments have an advantage in that they focus on specific actions that can be observed in the present. They also allow researchers an opportunity to establish a baseline by which future interactions can be measured (Miller, 1986). This type of data is more complete than self-reports. However, it is more complicated to obtain. "Direct observational assessment is characterized by the use of coders, raters, or judges, who usually are not participants in the interpersonal system being studied and whose task is to unitize and assign meaning to some aspects of the family therapy process (Alexander, Newell, Robbins, & Truner, 1995, p. 355).

The weaknesses of open-ended and behaviorally based instruments include interrater reliability (i.e., raters may not always agree on what they saw) and other types of bias that may slip into the reports that are made (Copeland & White, 1991). Direct observation of families can also be very expensive and time consuming (L'Abate & Bagarozzi, 1993). One attempt to resolve this problem has been to videotape families and have more than one observer evaluate their actions (Lewis, Beavers, Gossett, & Phillips, 1976).

Procedure

Procedure involves how families are studied. It can take numerous forms. It should be remembered, however, that research procedures and paradigms are not neutral but instead reflect the **epistemology** (i.e., the world view) of the investigator (Colapinto, 1979). For instance, researchers who are interested in proving the effectiveness of a theory or method generally concentrate on outcome research, that is, what is achieved as a result of a therapeutic intervention. In this type of research, families are exposed to a task or condition, and a measure is made of the impact (i.e., the reaction) (Beavers, 1985). On the other hand, researchers who wish to examine "the 'how' and the 'why' of effective or noneffective therapy" concentrate on doing process research (Diamond & Dickey, 1993, p. 23). Process research is time consuming and labor intensive (Liddle, 1992). However, the results are often enlightening and clinically meaningful. They can inform practitioners of what treatments under what conditions and with what types of clients are most effective. Furthermore, process research "can assess the systemic and contextual processes that characterize family therapy" (Diamond & Dickey, 1993, p. 24).

Theory

Theory is a basis for research. Well-designed research is based on questions that have usually arisen from a theory. Investigators conduct their inquiries to prove or disprove specific theoretical hypotheses, such as the importance of establishing permeable boundaries in family functioning. In using theory as a basis for conducting studies, researchers should pick a strong and relatively simple, clear theory that is logically connected (Shields, 1986). Most family therapy is based on general systems theory. This theory has made specific inquiry into how families change (Reiss, 1988). Some theoretical research, such as that on addicts and their families by Stanton, Todd, and Associates (1983), has been successful because of the careful way it was set up. However, in numerous cases, the questions that have been asked and the answers that have been derived have been insignificant or even harmful.

An example of a group of detrimental inquiries not carefully based on general systems theory is found in some research studies on African-American families that employ "a deficit theoretical underpinning" (Turner, 1993, p. 9). In these studies, the focus is on African-American childhood aggression, within-race violence, household father absence, family disruption, and social/health problems. This type of approach assumes that African-American families can and should be compared with "ideal families" or families from other cultural groups. It "overlooks the political realities that individuals and families are affected by race, economic status, and cultural values" (Turner, 1993, p. 9). Research of this nature fails to view whatever family form or family group being studied as "embedded in larger social systems" (Turner, 1993, p. 9).

Statistics

Researchers can be excellent methodologists but weak statisticians. Likewise, statisticians may not be able to design research studies in a scientific manner. Regardless, when research results are reported in a statistical manner, they need to be clinically relevant and readable to practitioners as well as scientists (Gay, 1996). One way to do this is to use descriptive statistics as a supplement to other statistical procedures. "By reporting the proportion of clients who improve to a clinically significant degree, the data from family therapy outcome research will be much more useful to family therapists than it will if researchers limit their reports to group means and statistical significance tests" (Jacobson, 1985, p. 151).

In general, statistics can show that a family is improved under the following circumstances:

- "if the posttherapy status places" the family "outside the distribution of dysfunctional clients (or families) and/or within the limits of a functional distribution of clients"
- "if the amount of change during the course of therapy exceeds expectations" (Jacobson, 1988, p. 141)

Problems in reporting statistics are related to whether the sample they were based on was skewed or normally distributed.

Validity/Reliability

The term *validity* "is the extent to which a measuring instrument measures what it was intended to measure" (Miller, 1986, p. 58). There are three main measures of validity:

- content, which is aimed at actually tapping into representative beliefs or behaviors
- criterion, which is the degree to which what is measured actually relates to life experience
- construct, which is the degree to which a measured performance matches a theoretical expectation

Reliability refers to the consistency or dependency of a measure. Another way to conceptualize reliability is that it truly measures the differences between families. Perfect reliability is expressed as a correlational coefficient of 1.00, which is seldom achieved. "Measures can be reliable but not valid, but they cannot be valid unless they are reliable" (Miller, 1986, p. 59).

Family therapy research must have strong degrees of validity and reliability in order to be considered substantial. Consumers of research need to focus on the validity and reliability of outcomes in studies as they evaluate results.

The Importance of Assessing Families

An assessment procedure is any method "used to measure characteristics of people, programs, or objects" (American Educational Research Association, American Psychological Association, & National Council on Measurement in Education, 1985, p. 89). As such, assessment is a vital part of family therapy. Through assessment, therapists gain information that helps them understand and respond to the families with whom they are working. For example, in assessment, therapists gain insight into a family's structure (i.e., roles, boundaries); control (i.e., power, flexibility); emotions/needs (i.e., affective expression, affective themes); culture (i.e., social position, cultural heritage); and development (stage of life) (Fisher, 1976).

"In the past, the DSM (Diagnostic and Statistical Manual) series have given little attention to marital and family diagnostic categories, approaching them simply with the 'V' codes. The V code section for the fourth edition of the DSM (DSM-IV; American Psychiatric Association, 1994) brings slightly more focus on relational problems, such as parent-child, sibling, and partner relationships and physical and sexual abuse" (Sporakowski, 1995, p. 61). Regardless, if family therapists are to plan proper treatments for families, they need to diagnose when possible so that a plan of action can be developed and followed. Assessment is a vital link in this process.

In addition, assessment and the resulting assessment knowledge can help families and their members clarify goals and gain a sense of perspective (Hood & Johnson, 1991). As opposed to testing, which is usually a task in which people are asked to do their maximum best, assessment evaluates typical performances, behaviors, or qualities. It is broader than any one test measure. In brief, one main reason for assessment is that it assists therapists and families in understanding themselves better on global and specific levels.

Another reason for assessment relates to accountability with third-party providers. These providers require documentation of services, such as record keeping, in order for practitioners to receive payment for treatment. It is the belief of some experts in the family therapy field that "in the future, practitioners who are able to evaluate their interventive endeavors by using reliable and valid measures of change and established research procedures will be more likely to receive third-party payments" (L'Abate & Bagarozzi, 1993, p. xi). Family therapy is moving to become more scientific and precise. Family clinicians who wish to improve their skills and serve the public are increasingly likely to rely on assessment instruments. Such reliance is a matter of survival and responsibility.

Dimensions of Assessing Families

Most assessment with families is based on a **systemic approach**. This approach "requires that one utilize the transactions between individuals, rather than the characteristics of each given individual, as primary data. Even when, for one reason or another, attention is focused on one person, his/her behavior is analyzed in terms of its power to affect and shape the behavior of other members of the system and in terms of the variables of the ecosystem that may have affected it" (Sluzko, 1978, p. 366). Therefore, when questions are asked in therapy sessions, they focus on transactions and relationships more than demographic data. For instance, they might include inquiries such as "When John gets angry, Mary, what do you do?" or "Carole, how do you react when the other children leave you out of their activities?"

Fishman (1988) states there are four aspects of assessment for therapists to consider: "contemporary developmental pressures on the family, history, structure, and process" (p. 14). "The four-dimensional model should give therapists, like cubist painters, a kaleidoscopic view of their subject. It allows therapists to look at a moving system from different perspectives. It also takes into consideration therapists' positions in the process as they move in and out of the system, sometimes as neutral observers, other times as involved protagonists who support a particular family member or suddenly realize the family's control. This emphasis on processes and therapists' active place in them is what helps define family therapy as a therapy of experience.

Methods Used in Assessing Families

"Assessment techniques available" to family therapists "are many and varied" (Sporakowski, 1995, p. 61). Both informal and formal methods are used in the assessment of families. Informal methods include observational data related to either natural or game-playing situations that may or may not be quantified. Formal methods are usually field-tested instruments, some of which are based on a theoretical foundation and some of which are not (L'Abate & Bagarozzi, 1993).

Informal Methods of Assessing Families

One of the best informal methods of assessing a family is through using the Family Assessment Form (Piercy, McKeon, & Laird, 1983). This form is succinct. Yet, it provides family therapists of all theoretical orientations a means for fine tuning their approach with a particular family. As can be seen from examining the family assessment form in Figure 15.1, therapists can gain a lot of knowledge in a relatively short amount of time. They can then tailor clarification questions and possible interventions accordingly.

Another way to informally assess families is through direct observation. In contrast to individual counseling, family therapy "offers the unique opportunity to observe directly the problematic interpersonal exchanges of clients and to contrast these with subjective appraisals of these events" (Snyder et al., 1995, pp. 163–164). Even though this process is complex because of the number of individuals in some sessions and possible expressions of hostility, it is an invaluable tool for picking up information that other instruments cannot provide.

Formal Methods of Assessing Families

There are over 1000 assessment instruments available to family therapists (Touliatos, Perlmutter, & Straus, 1990). They cover areas as diverse as intimacy, power, parenthood, and adjustment. "Instruments can enrich the practitioner's and the clients' assessment and treatment process when used in combination" (Thomas, 1995, p. 285). Although this text examines some of the best-known and refined family and marital tests, clinicians need to consult reference works and abstracts for specific measures pertinent to their situations.

It is important to note that with all assessment instruments, scales used in family therapy must be employed judiciously. Furthermore, these instruments should be scrutinized in regard to the variables being measured, the scales and subscales being reported, the ease or difficulty of scoring directions and interpretation of test results, and the evidence available about validity and reliability (Sprenkle & Piercy, 1984).

Despite availability of an increasing number of family therapy measurement devices, clinicians are reticent to use them. The reasons for this reticence include the fact that using assessment instruments removes family therapists from the cutting edge of innovative practice (Shields et al., 1994). In addition, many practitioners lack adequate training in family assessment instruments (Thomas & Olson, 1993). Therefore, family therapists who tend to employ measuring devices in their practices most often use individually focused assessment instruments, such as the MMPI-2 and the Myers-Briggs Type Indicator (Boughner, Bubenzer, Hayes, & West, 1993). Table 15.1 examines some conceptual issues and formal assessment techniques across family system levels.

Family Name _____ (Age)_____

Father _____ (___) Mother _____ (___)

Occupation _____ Occupation _____

Years Married _____

Children: _____(___) _____(___) _____(___)

_____(___) _____(___) _____(___)

Blended Family Relationships (Number of marriages, children by other marriages, etc.)

_____

_____

Referral Source _____

1. Presenting Problem/Change Desired (from each person's perspective)

2. Repetitive Nonproductive Behavioral Sequences (attempted solutions, attempts to maintain homeostatic balance)

3. Family Structure (family map; enmeshment, isolation or individuation, chaos, rigidity or flexibility; power structure; generational boundaries; spousal relationships, alliances, roles played, intrusions, etc.)

4. Communication and Interaction Styles (direct, clear, indirect, confused, vague, double binding, affective, cognitive, positive, supported, negative, aggressive, etc.)

5. Hypotheses Regarding Symptom Maintenance (how might the symptom serve a function)

6. Family Life Stages (courtship, early marriage, child bearing, child rearing, parents of teenagers, launching, middle years, retirement, etc.)

7. Pertinent Family-of-Origin Information (positive or negative influence from past generations)

8. External Sources of Stress and Support (relationships outside immediate family: community, work, friends, relatives)

9. Family Strengths

10. Significant Physical Conditions/Medication

11. Other Information (previous treatment, test results, etc.)

12. Therapeutic Goals:

13. Proposed Therapeutic Interventions (means for reaching goals)

_____   _____
Counselor's Signature   Date

Figure 15.1

Family assessment form.

From "A Family Assessment Process for Community Mental Health Clinics" by F. P. Piercy, D. McKeon, and R. A. Laird, 1983, *AMHCA Journal, 5*(3), pp. 94–104. Reprinted by permission of the publisher.

Table 15.1

Model Conceptual Issues and Formal Assessment Techniques Across Family System Levels

Modal conceptual issues	Formal assessment techniques
Individual	
How may cognitive style or abilities influence family members' response to therapy or each other?	Short-form Wechsler administrations (Silverstein, 1990)
	Peabody Picture Vocabulary Test–Revised (Dunn & Dunn, 1981)
	Attributional Style Questionnaire (Peterson & Villanova, 1988)
	Children's Attributional Style Questionnaire (Fielstein et al., 1985)
What dimensions of individual emotional or behavioral functioning influence family interaction? Which of these, if any, warrant separate treatment? Which reflect strengths?	Minnesota Multiphasic Personality Inventory–2 (Butcher, Dahlstrom, Graham, Tellegen, & Kaemmer, 1989)
	Millon Clinical Multiaxial Inventory–II (Millon, 1987)
	NEO Personality Inventory–Revised (Costa & McCrae, 1992)
	Schedule for Affective Disorders and Schizophrenia (Endicott & Spitzer, 1978)
How should current issues be viewed from a developmental perspective?	Child Behavior Checklist (Achenbach & Edelbrock, 1983)
	Personality Inventory for Children (Wirt, Lachar, Klinedinst, & Seat, 1984)
	Kiddie-Schedule for Affective Disorders and Schizophrenia (Puig-Antich & Chambers, 1978)
Dyad	
What are the sources and levels of distress or satisfaction in the marriage? In the parent-child relationships?	Marital Satisfaction Inventory (Snyder, 1981)
	Sexual Functioning Inventory (Derogatis, 1975)
	Parenting Stress Index (Abidin, 1986)
What patterns of communication typify these relationships?	Marital Interaction Coding System–Global (Weiss & Toiman, 1990)
	Rapid Couples Interaction Scoring System (Krokoff, Gottman, & Hass, 1989)
	Parent–Adolescent Interaction Coding System (Robin & Weiss, 1980)
How consistent and functional are relationship expectations? How do members view each other's behavior or motives?	Relationship Brief Inventory (Edelson & Epstein, 1982)
	Relationship Attribution Measure (Fincham & Bradbury, 1992)
	Child's Report of Parental Behavior Inventory (Burger & Armentrout, 1971)

From "Marital and Family Assessment: A Multifaceted, Multilevel Approach" by D. K. Snyder, T. A. Cavell, R. W. Heffer, & L. F. Mangrum, in *Integrating Family Therapy* (pp. 163–182), edited by R. H. Mikesell, D. D. Lusterman, & S. H. McDaniel, 1995, Washington, DC: American Psychological Association. Reprinted by permission of the publisher.

Modal conceptual issues	Formal assessment techniques
Nuclear family	
How close do family members feel to each other? How effective is the family in responding to daily challenges and crises?	Family Environment Scale (Moos & Moos, 1986)
	Children's Version–Family Environment Scale (Pino, Simons, & Slawinowski, 1984)
	Family Assessment Measure–III (Skinner, Steinhauer, & Santa-Barbera, 1984)
	Family Adaptability and Cohesion Evaluation Scales III (Olson, Portner, & Lavee, 1985)
How is the family organized along dimensions of affect, authority, and control? What strategies do family members use to influence each other?	Child-Rearing Practices Report (Block, Block, & Morrison, 1981)
	Family Behavior Interview (Robin & Foster, 1989)
	Family Interaction Coding System (Reid, 1978)
Extended system	
To what extent do relationships with extended family, friends, or co-workers serve as sources of support or stress?	Genogram (McGoldrick & Gerson, 1985)
	Interpersonal Support Evaluation List (Cohen, Mermelstein, Kamarck, & Hoberman, 1985)
	Survey of Children's Social Support (Dubow & Ullman, 1989)
	My Family and Friends (Reid, Landesman, Treder, & Jaccard, 1989)
How do family members vary in their sources of external stress or support? How are these shared in the marriage or nuclear family?	
Community and culture	
What community resources are available to this family? Are these resources used? How does the community contribute to this family's distress or survival?	Mothers' Activities Checklist (Kelley & Carper, 1988)
	Community Interaction Checklist (Wahler, 1980)
	Eco-Map (Hartman, 1979)
To what extent do family members identify with a particular ethnic heritage?	Behavioral Acculturation Scale (Szapocznik, Kurtines, & Fernandez, 1980)

Family Therapy Scales

To make an informed decision on what assessment instrument(s) would serve their clients best, therapists must conceptually clarify the areas in which they need to obtain information. A brief description of some of the most widely used assessment devices in family therapy follows.

Family-of-Origin Scale (FOS)

The family-of-origin scale was developed to measure self-perceived healthiness in one's family of origin (Hovestadt, Anderson, Piercy, Cochran, & Fine, 1985). The scale is based on a five-point Likert format and contains 40 questions. Outcome scores can range from 40 to 200, with higher scores indicative of better overall family health. The test-retest reliability coefficient has been reported to be .97 for undergraduates on whom the scale was normed.

> Two subscales of the FOS reflect 10 core constructs of family healthiness, principally derived from Lewis, Beavers, Gossett, and Phillips (1976). The Autonomy subscale emphasizes characteristics of healthiness such as clarity of expression, personal responsibility, respect for other family members, and openness to others within and outside the family system. The Intimacy subscale emphasizes characteristics such as expression of feelings, emotional warmth, conflict resolution without undue stress, sensitivity to other family members, and trust (Wilcoxon, Walker, & Hovestadt, 1989, p. 226-227).

The Personal Authority in the Family System Questionnaire (PAFS)

The PAFS is a self-report questionnaire based on the theoretical work of family systems theorists, such as Bowen, Boszormenyi-Nagy, and Williamson. It assesses relationships in three generational families. It contains 132 items, all of which are scored on a five-point Likert scale. There are five subscales that measure intergenerational themes such as dependence/independence, intergenerational triangles, intergenerational intimidation, personal authority, and intergenerational fusion/individuation (Bray, Williamson, & Malone, 1984).

Reliability measures range from a test-retest low of .55 to an internal consistency of .95. Construct and concurrent validity are both solid. Overall, "the PAFS describes an individual's current interaction with his or her family of origin" (West, 1988, p. 176).

PREPARE/ENRICH

The PREPARE/ENRICH inventories are part of a package of material developed for couples striving to become more aware of or to nourish their relationships (Fredman & Sherman, 1987). PREPARE is designated for engaged couples; ENRICH is for already married couples. Both scales are composed of a 125-item inventory that is designed to identify relationship strengths and weaknesses in 10 specific areas of couple/family life. These areas are (1) personality issues, (2) communication, (3) conflict resolution, (4) financial management, (5) leisure activities, (6) sexual relationship, (7) children and marriage, (8) family and friends, (9) egalitarian roles, and (10) religious orientation (Olson, Fournier, & Druckman, 1987). Each scale also measures idealistic distortion; although PRE-PARE alone gets a reading on realistic expectations, and ENRICH alone obtains a score on marital satisfaction.

An individual score for each person on every scale is generated, and areas of agreement and disagreement are duly noted. PREPARE and ENRICH both have strong reliability and validity scores in most areas. Both also have been found to have some predictive uses. For example, in a 3-year follow-up of couples who took the PREPARE scale, scores were better than 80% accurate in predicting marital happiness versus separation/divorce (Flowers & Olson, 1986).

Family Adaptability and Cohesion Evaluation Scale III (FACES III)

FACES is similar to PREPARE/ENRICH in that it is based on the circumplex model of family functioning (i.e., adaptability and cohesion) (Olsen, McCubbin, Barnes, Larsen, Muxen, & Wilson, 1985). This instrument has undergone considerable refinement since it was introduced in 1979. Basically, it can be taken twice in order to derive ideal and perceived descriptions of a family. The discrepancy between these two outcome scores "provides a measure of family satisfaction with current levels of adaptability and cohesion" (West, 1988, p. 173). Reliability and validity are within acceptable limits.

Family Inventory of Life Events and Changes (FILE)

The purpose of FILE is to "investigate the impact of life stresses on family well-being" (L'Abate & Bagarozzi, 1993, p. 176). As emphasized in this text, families undergo many transitions that affect them for better or worse. Sometimes stress events "pileup" on families and have negative consequences. FILE, as a 71-item self-report instrument, examines the normative and non-normative events that have been experienced by families during a year, including financial, intra-family, work, legal, loss, illness, marital, moving, and pregnancy/childbearing (McCubbin, Thompson, Pirner, & McCubbin, 1988). By gathering this information, therapists are more aware of where to address their interventions. Reliability and validity of FILE is high.

Family Environment Scale (FES)

The FES is "a 90-item, true-false, self-report questionnaire with 10 subscales designed to measure the social and environmental characteristics of a family" (Fredman & Sherman, 1987, p. 82). It is divided into 10 subscales that come under three major categories: (1) Relationship (i.e., cohesion, expressiveness, and conflict subscales); (2) Personal Growth (i.e., independence, achievement orientation, intellectual-cultural orientation, active-recreational orientation, and moral-religious emphasis subscales); and (3) System Maintenance (i.e., organization and control subscales).

"The FES can be used to describe and compare family social environments, contrast parent and child perceptions, and examine actual and preferred family milieus" (Moos & Moos, 1986, p. 11). It is "probably the most widely accepted measure of the family climate" and "among the first" objectively scored methods of family assessment to be developed (Oliver, Handal, Enos, & May, 1988, p. 470). One of the reasons for the popularity of the FES is that it comprehensively addresses all aspects of family environment. It has a Real Form (which measures families' actual perceptions), an Ideal Form (which measures families' perceptions of how they would like their family to be), and an Expectations Form (which measures what people expect their families to be like).

Family Assessment Device (FAD)

The FAD is based on the McMaster Model of Family Functioning (Epstein, Baldwin, & Bishop, 1983). The McMaster model examines six dimensions of family functioning: (1) problem solving, (2) communication, (3) roles, (4) affective responsiveness, (5) affective involvement, and (6) behavior control. The FAD attempts to measure these dimensions plus the family's overall health and pathology. This 240-item questionnaire has been criticized in regard to its formulation and validity/reliability (L'Abate & Bagarozzi, 1993). Nevertheless, the model it is based on has intrinsically heuristic qualities.

Family Strengths

Family Strengths is a brief, 12-item inventory that is appropriate for adults and adolescents (Olson, Larson, & McCubbin, 1985). It is scored on a five-point Likert index and is aimed at identifying how happy families resemble one another. The inventory was initially based on the family strength work of Stinnet (1981); but the final version of the test is less comprehensive, measuring only family pride and family accord. Reliability for the total scale is reported at .83.

Family Coping Strategies Scale (F-COPES)

The F-COPES is a measure of internal and external family coping strategies (McCubbin, Larsen, & Olsen, 1982). Internal strategies include reframing and passive appraisal; external strategies are those connected with acquiring social support, seeking spiritual support, and mobilizing the family to seek and accept help. Reliability of the instrument is in the .60 range.

Marital Therapy Scales

Marital and couple assessment is aimed at obtaining information in a fast and efficient manner so that therapists can concentrate on particularly difficult relationship areas. Some of the earliest assessment instruments in the marital and family therapy areas were initially developed for this purpose. Those instruments described here are among the most widely used.

Locke-Wallace Marital Adjustment Test (MAT)

The MAT is one of the oldest and most widely used tests of marital satisfaction. It consist of 15 items that are of a self-report nature. It can be completed in about 10 minutes and is scored by a therapist. This inventory has been successfully modified for use with premarital couples. It has been reported to have a reliability of .90 (Locke & Wallace, 1959). Furthermore, the MAT is the standard by which other marriage adjustment inventories correlate their results (Fredman & Sherman, 1987). The main drawback to the MAT is that a few of its items are now considered out of date.

Bienvenu Marital Communication Inventory (MCI)

The MCI is a 46-item, self-administered questionnaire concerning the perceived quality of marital communication. Each question is graded on a 0- to 4-point scale, with a range of scores from 0 to 138. Higher scores are indicative of better perceived couple communication patterns. The split-half reliability is .93 (Bienvenu, 1970). This instrument is used in both marital and premarital counseling and can be interpreted as a measure of perceptions concerning the quality of communication (Schumm, 1983). Only a seventh-grade reading ability is required.

Dyadic Adjustment Scale (DAS)

This 32-item instrument is a self-report, pencil and paper questionnaire of marital satisfaction (Spanier, 1976). The DAS possesses good reliability and discriminant validity. It yields an overall score as well as a number of factor scores. The usual cutoff point between distressed and nondistressed couples is 100, with higher scores indicating a better relationship (Floyd & Markman, 1983). The range of scores for the DAS is from 0 to 151. The reliability of this instrument is high (.96). Validity is also quite good (Fredman & Sherman, 1987).

Marital Coping Questionnaire (MCQ)

The MCQ is an 18-item, self-report questionnaire in which respondents indicate how frequently they engage in each of a set of coping efforts (Fleishman, 1984; Menaghan, 1982; Pearlin & Schooler, 1978). The six most reliable coping factors are "(1) seeking advice (e.g., ask the advice of relatives about getting along in marriage); (2) emotional discharge (e.g., yell or shout to let off steam); (3) positive comparison (e.g., how would you compare your marriage to that of most other people like yourself—better, the same, less good); (4) negotiation (e.g., try to find a fair compromise in marital problems); (5) resignation (e.g., just keep hurt feelings to yourself); (6) selective ignoring (e.g., try to ignore difficulties by looking only at good things)" (Sabourin, Laporte, & Wright, 1990, pp. 91-92).

Primary Communication Inventory (PCI)

The PCI is a 25-item, self-report, questionnaire, with a 5-point scale designed to measure a couple's verbal and nonverbal communication (Locke, Sabagh, & Thomas, 1956). It is one of the oldest and most frequently used marriage therapy indexes and has been the subject of several significant research studies (L'Abate & Bagarozzi, 1993). It distinguishes satisfied and dissatisfied couples from each other, but has some problems in regard to validity.

Marital Satisfaction Inventory (MSI)

The MSI is a 280-item, true-false questionnaire that has been compared with the MMPI because of both its length and number of scales (i.e., 11 scales). The inventory has a test-retest reliability on average of .89 for each subscale. The MSI also distinguishes between distressed and nondistressed couples (Snyder, 1981; Snyder & Regts, 1982). Overall, the MSI is a well-constructed inventory that is strong in regard to its research and clinical application.

Marital Instability Scale (MIS)

The MIS is a paper and pencil instrument designed to assess marital instability among intact couples (Booth & Edwards, 1983). It has a 20- and a 5-question form, both of which are scored from 0 (never) to 3 (now). Higher scores are more indicative of marital instability. Both reliability and validity factors are high, with the shorter form of the scale being less reliable.

Dyadic Trust Scale (DTS)

The DTS is an eight-item, pencil and paper questionnaire that takes less than 3 minutes to take. Its focus is on trust between marriage partners rather than trust in general (Larzelere & Huston, 1980). It has high internal consistency reliability (.93), good face validity, and correlates well with scales of love and self-disclosure. The main drawback to this instrument is that its initial sample size was limited and, in norming the test, all participants were volunteers (Fredman & Sherman, 1987).

Marital Problem-Solving Scale (MPSS)

The MPSS is a nine-item, seven-point Likert scale that measures problem-solving ability (Baugh, Avery, & Sheets-Haworth, 1982). It has strong internal consistency (.95) and test-retest reliability (.86). Validity is also good. An interesting aspect about the MPSS is that it "has demonstrated concurrent validity with behavioral coding assessments, enabling one to say that it is just as good as the time-consuming and expensive methods of behavior coding" (L'Abate & Bagarozzi, 1993, p. 145).

Summary and Conclusion

Family research and assessment efforts have a long history. They began with the genesis of the field and have continued to the present. Research is the backbone of family therapy, because through it family therapists can prove what they do is beneficial, unique, and practical. Fortunately, family therapy research indicates that treating families is at least equal to that of working with individuals. Particularly encouraging are findings that show the importance of therapists' relationship skills and the critical nature of having certain members of families, such as fathers, participate in treatment. From these data, clinician/researchers, such as Jose Szapocznik, have advanced the field of family therapy even further through innovative research projects.

In examining family therapy research, it must be remembered that there are many difficulties associated with it because of the systemic nature of family therapy. Among problematic areas are those that involve whether to conduct qualitative or quantitative research. The design of the research, along with sampling procedures and choosing instruments, are also important. Equally crucial are considerations involving whether procedures should focus on process or outcome results, the statistical methods, if any, to employ, and the theoretical base on which to center the study. As the field of family therapy grows, there will be an increased effort to incorporate research methods and findings into training/educational programs, along with renewed attention on the importance of research to practice (Liddle, 1992).

Like research, assessment is based on systemic theory and has been highlighted more in recent years. Assessment may take "many forms depending on the theory, practice, clients, and personal, professional development of the counselor" (Sporakowski, 1995, p. 63). There are a number of family assessment approaches, from those that consider limited data to those that encompass a broad perspective. Informal as well as formal methods of assessment are available. Formal methods, although well researched, have still not been as utilized by family therapists as some popular, more individualized assessment tools, such as the Myers-Briggs Type Indicator and the MMPI-2. Nevertheless, there is an abundance of assessment instruments that will most likely grow in use and usefulness in the future.

Overall, research and assessment are a vital part of the practice of family therapy. It is essential that clinicians keep current with advancements and related research. Otherwise, they will be handicapped in the treatment of their client families, and all will suffer as a result.

SUMMARY TABLE

Research and Assessment in Family Therapy

Research and assessment has a long association with family therapy that dates back to the 1950s and pioneers in the field such as Bateson, Wynne, and Minuchin.

During the 1960s, therapists and researchers became two distinct groups.

In the 1990s, research in family therapy is growing again.

Assessment, which focuses on a family unit rather than a group of families, is also growing.

Good assessment instruments are based on theoretical models.

Importance of Research in Family Therapy

Research is important in family therapy as a result of accountability, practicality, and uniqueness. Research results help family therapy gain respect.

Clinicians gain from research studies in the long run. Research also helps family therapists claim their area as a specialization.

Research Findings in Family Therapy

Family therapy is as effective as other psychotherapies, according to research.

Deterioration in family therapy is related to poor skills and timing on the therapist's part.

Brief family therapy (20 sessions or less) is as effective as long-term family therapy.

Participation by the father in family therapy makes it more likely to have a positive outcome.

Less severe family problems are most successfully treated.

Some family therapies are more suited to certain types of problems than others.

The research of Jose Szapocznik is a good example of how research results can have practical application.

Two Types of Family Therapy Research

Qualitative and quantitative research methods are often used in measuring the impact of family therapy.

Qualitative research is characterized by its open-endedness. It uses small samples, with the participant/observer/researcher gathering and analyzing data simultaneously in a narrative manner.

Quantitative research is characterized by its closed-ended questions, large sample sizes, objective data reporting, and numerical data analysis after the data is collected. Its conclusions are deductive, written in a prosaic form, with reference to standard measures of validity and reliability. It seeks to prove or disprove a theory or hypothesis.

Whether one chooses qualitative or quantitative research methods, studying families is complicated, especially if a systems model is followed.

Difficulties in Family Therapy Research

Difficulties in family therapy research are associated with:

- where to focus (e.g., on the marriage, the identified patient, etc.)
- what environment to use (natural or laboratory)
- what research design to use (exploratory, descriptive, developmental, experimental, or correlational)
- sampling (random or nonprobable)
- instrumentation (self-report or behavioral open-ended)

- procedure (outcome or process based)
- theory (simple, clear, and systemic or not)
- statistics (descriptive and clinically relevant or not)
- validity (content, criterion, and construct)
- reliability (i.e., the consistency/dependability of a measure)

The Importance of Assessing Families

Assessment is the evaluation of families in particular cases with specific instruments. It is usually clinically relevant in regard to a family in treatment.

Assessment is related to diagnosis and, consequently, to treatment plans and outcomes.

Assessment is the basis for accountability with third-party providers.

For therapists, assessing families is necessary for survival as well as a matter of being responsible.

Dimensions of Assessing Families

Most assessment is conducted on a systematic level.

Dimensions of assessment are those related to:

- pressures on the family
- family history
- family structure
- family process

Assessment is a continuous process.

Methods Used in Assessing Families

Both informal and formal methods are used in assessment.

Informal methods include family assessment forms.

Formal methods include the over 1000 assessment instruments available to family therapists.

Family therapy scales used by clinicians include:

- Family-of-Origin Scale (FOS)
- Personal Authority in the Family System Questionnaire (PAFS)
- PREPARE/ENRICH
- Family Adaptability and Cohesion Evaluation Scale III (FACES III)
- Family Inventory of Life Events and Change (FILE)
- Family Environment Scale (FES)
- Family Assessment Device (FAD)
- Family Strengths
- Family Coping Strategies Scale (F-COPES)

Marital therapy scales used by clinicians include:

- Locke-Wallace Marital Adjustment Test (MAT)
- Bienvenu Marital Communication Inventory (MCI)

- Dyadic Adjustment Scale (DAS)
- Marital Coping Questionnaire (MCQ)
- Primary Communication Inventory (PCI)
- Marital Satisfaction Inventory (MSI)
- Marital Instability Scale (MIS)
- Dyadic Trust Scale (DTS)
- Marital Problem-Solving Scale (MPSS)

References

Alexander, J. F., Newell, R. M., Robbins, M. S., & Turner, C. W. (1995). Observational coding in family therapy process research. *Journal of Family Psychology, 9,* 355–365.

American Educational Research Association, American Psychological Association, & National Council on Measurement in Education (1985). *Standards for educational and psychological testing.* Washington, DC: American Psychological Association.

American Psychiatric Association. (1994). *Diagnostic and statistical manual of mental disorders* (4th ed.). Washington, DC: Author.

Barker, P. (1986). *Basic family therapy* (2nd ed.). New York: Oxford University Press.

Baugh, C. W., Avery, A. W., & Sheets-Haworth, K. L. (1982). Marital Problem Solving Scale: A measure to assess relationship conflict negotiation ability. *Family Therapy, 9,* 43–51.

Beavers, R. (1985). *Successful marriage.* New York: Norton.

Bienvenu, M. J. (1970). Measurement of marital communication. *The Family Coordinator, 19,* 26–31.

Bird, G. W., & Sporakowski, M. J. (1992). The study of marriage and the family. In G. Bird & M. J. Sporakowski (Eds.), *Taking sides* (pp. x–xv). Guilford, CT: Dushkin.

Booth, A., & Edwards, J. (1983). Measuring marital instability. *Journal of Marriage and the Family, 45,* 387–393.

Boughner, S., Bubenzer, D. L., Hayes, S., & West, J. (1993). *Use of standardized assessment instruments by marital and family practitioners.* Atlanta: American Counseling Association annual convention.

Bray, J. H., Williamson, D. S., & Malone, P. E. (1984). Personal Authority in the Family System: Development of a questionnaire to measure personal authority in intergenerational family processes. *Journal of Marital and Family Therapy, 10,* 167–178.

Brock, G. W., & Barnard, C. P. (1988). *Procedures in family therapy.* Boston: Allyn & Bacon.

Colapinto, J. (1979). The relative value of empirical evidence. *Family Process, 18,* 427–441.

Copeland, A. P., & White, K. M. (1991). *Studying families.* Newbury Park, CA: Sage.

Diamond, G., & Dickey, M. (1993, Spring). Process research: Its history, intent and findings. *The Family Psychologist, 9,* 23–25.

Drummond, R. J. (1992). *Appraisal procedures for counselors and helping professionals* (2nd ed.). New York: Macmillan.

Epstein, N. B., Baldwin, L. M., & Bishop, D. S. (1983). The McMaster Family Assessment Device. *Journal of Marital and Family Therapy, 9,* 171–180.

Fenell, D. L., & Weinhold, B. K. (1992). Research in marriage and family therapy. In R. L. Smith & P. Stevens-Smith (Eds.), *Family counseling and therapy* (pp. 331–337). Ann Arbor, MI: ERIC/CAPS.

Fisher, L. (1976). Dimensions of family assessment: A critical review. *Journal of Marriage and Family Counseling, 2,* 367–382.

Fishman, C, H. (1988). *Treating troubled adolescents.* New York: Basic Books.

Fleishman, J. A. (1984). Personality characteristics and coping patterns. *Journal of Health and Social Behavior, 25,* 229–244.

Flowers, B., & Olson, D. (1986). Predicting marital success with PREPARE: A predictive validity study. *Journal of Marital and Family Therapy, 12,* 403–413.

Floyd, F. J., & Markman, H. J. (1983). Observational biases in spouse interaction: Toward a cognitive/behavioral model of marriage. *Journal of Consulting and Clinical Psychology, 51,* 450–457.

Fredman, N., & Sherman, R. (1987). *Handbook of measurements for marriage and family therapy.* New York: Brunner/Mazel.

Gay, L. R. (1996). *Educational research* (5th ed.). Englewood Cliffs, NJ: Prentice Hall.

Gladding, S. T. (1993). *Nathaniel's entrance.* Unpublished poem.

Goldman, L. (1990). Qualitative assessment. *The Counseling Psychologist, 18,* 205–213.

Gurman, A. S., & Kniskern, D. P. (1981). Family therapy outcome research: Knowns and unknowns. In A. S. Gurman & D. P. Kniskern (Eds.), *Handbook of family therapy.* New York: Brunner/Mazel.

Gurman, A. S., Kniskern, D. P., & Pinsof, W. M. (1986). Research on the process and outcome of marital and family therapy. In S. L. Garfield & A. E. Bergin (Eds.), *Handbook of psychotherapy and behavioral change* (3rd ed., pp. 565–624). New York: Wiley.

Haley, J. (1978). Ideas which handicap therapists. In M. M. Berger (Ed.), *Beyond the double bind.* New York: Brunner/Mazel.

Hochschild, A. (1989). *The second shift: Working parents and the revolution at home.* New York: Viking.

Hood, A. B., & Johnson, R. W. (1991). *Assessment in counseling.* Alexandria, VA: American Counseling Association.

Hovestadt, A. J., Anderson, W. T., Piercy, F. P., Cochran, S. W., & Fine, M. (1985). A family of origin scale. *Journal of Marital and Family Therapy, 11,* 287–297.

Hubble, M. A. (1993, Spring). Therapy research: The bonfire of the uncertainties. *The Family Psychologist, 9,* 14–16.

Jacobson, N. S. (1985). Family therapy outcome research: Potential pitfalls and prospects. *Journal of Marital and Family Therapy, 11,* 149–158.

Jacobson, N. S. (1988). Guidelines for the design of family therapy outcome research. In L. C. Wynne (Ed.), *The state of the art in family therapy research* (pp. 139–155). New York: Family Process Press.

L'Abate, L., & Bagarozzi, D. A. (1993). *Sourcebook of marriage and family evaluation.* New York: Brunner/Mazel.

Larzelere, R., & Huston, T. (1980). The Dyadic Trust Scale: Toward understanding interpersonal trust in close relationships. *Journal of Marriage and the Family, 43,* 595–604.

Letich, L. (1993, September/October). A clinician's researcher. *Family Therapy Networker, 17,* 77–82.

Lewis, J. M., Beavers, W. R., Gossett, J. T., & Phillips, V. A. (1976). *No single thread.* New York: Brunner/Mazel.

Liddle, H. A. (1992, October). Assessing research productivity and impact. *Family Therapy News, 23,* 17, 29.

Locke, H. J., Sabagh, G., & Thomas, M. (1956). Correlates of primary communication and empathy. *Research Studies of the State College of Washington, 24,* 116–124.

Locke, H., & Wallace, K. (1959). Short marital adjustment and prediction tests: The reliability and validity. *Marriage and Family Living, 21,* 251–255.

McCubbin, H. I., Larsen, A., & Olson, D. H. (1982). F-COPES: Family coping strategies. In D. H. Olson, H. I. McCubbin, H. Barnes, A. Larsen, M. Maxen, & M. Wilson (Eds.), *Family inventories: Inventories used in a national survey of families across the family life cycle* (pp. 101–120). St Paul: University of Minnesota.

McCubbin, H. I., Thompson, A. I., Pirner, P. A., & McCubbin, M. A. (1988). *Family types and strengths: A life cycle and ecological perspective.* Edina, MN: Burgess.

McGuirk, J. G., Friedlander, M. L., & Blocher, D. H. (1987). Systemic and nonsystemic diagnostic processes: An empirical comparison. *Journal of Marital and Family Therapy, 13,* 69–76.

Menaghan, E. (1982). Measuring coping effectiveness: A panel analysis of marital problems and coping efforts. *Journal of Health and Social Behavior, 23,* 220–234.

Miller, B. C. (1986). *Family research methods.* Beverly Hills, CA: Sage.

Moon, S. M., Dillon, D. R., & Sprenkle, D. H. (1990). Family therapy and qualitative research. *Journal of Marital and Family Therapy, 16,* 357–374.

Moos, R. H., & Moos, B. S. (1986). *The family environment scale manual* (rev. ed.). Palo Alto, CA: Consulting Psychologists Press.

Nelson, T. S. (1996). Survey research in marriage and family therapy. In D. H. Sprenkle & S. M. Moon (Eds.), *Research methods in family therapy* (pp. 447–468). New York: Guilford.

Oliver, J. M., Handal, P. J., Enos, D. M., & May, M. J. (1988). Factor structure of the family environment scale: Factors based on items and subscales. *Educational and Psychological Measurement, 48,* 469–477.

Olson, D. H., Fournier, D. G., & Druckman, J. M. (1987). *Counselor's manual for PREPARE/ENRICH* (rev. ed.). Minneapolis, MN: PREPARE/ENRICH Inc.

Olson, D. H., Larsen, A. S., & McCubbin, H. I. (1985). Family Strengths. In D. Olson, H. McCubbin, H. Barnes, A. Larsen, M. Muxen, & M. Wilson (Eds.), *Family inventories* (rev. ed.). St Paul, MN: University of Minnesota.

Olson, D. H., McCubbin, H. I., Barnes, H., Larsen, A., Muxen, M., & Wilson, M. (1985). *Family inventories: Inventories used in a national survey of families across the family life cycle.* St Paul, MN: Family Social Science, University of Minnesota.

Pearlin, L. T., & Schooler, C. (1978). The structure of coping. *Journal of Health and Social Behavior, 19,* 2–21.

Piercy, F. P., McKeon, D., & Laird, R. A. (1983). A family assessment process for community mental health clinics. *AMHCA Journal, 5,* 94–104.

Piercy, F. P., & Sprenkle, D. H. (1986). *Family therapy handbook.* New York: Guilford.

Reiss, D. (1988). Theoretical versus tactical inferences. In L. C. Wynne (Ed.), *The state of the art in family therapy research* (pp. 33–46). New York: Family Process Press.

Sabourin, S., Laporte, L., & Wright, J. (1990). Problem solving self-appraisal and coping efforts in distressed and nondistressed couples. *Journal of Marital and Family Therapy, 16,* 89–97.

Schumm, W. R. (1983). Theory and measurement in marital communication training programs. *Family Relations, 32,* 3–11.

Schwartz, R. C., & Breunlin, D. (1983). Research: Why clinicians should bother with it. *Family Therapy Networker, 7,* 22–27, 57–59.

Shields, C. G. (1986). Critiquing the new epistemologies: Toward minimum requirements for a scientific theory of family therapy. *Journal of Marital and Family Therapy, 12,* 359–372.

Shields, G., Wynne, L. C., McDaniel, S. H., & Gawinski, B. A. (1994). The marginalization of family therapy: An historical and continuing problem. *Journal of Marital and Family Therapy, 20,* 117–138.

Sluzko, C. E. (1978). Marital therapy from a systems theory perspective. In T. J. Paolino & B. C. McCrady (Eds.), *Marriage and Marital Therapy.* New York: Brunner/Mazel.

Snyder, D. K. (1981). *Marital Satisfaction Inventory manual.* Los Angeles: Western Psychological Services.

Snyder, D. K., & Regts, J. M. (1982). Factor scales for assessing marital disharmony and disaffection. *Journal of Consulting and Clinical Psychology, 50,* 736–743.

Snyder, D. K., Cavell, T. A., Heffer, R. W., & Mangrum, L. F. (1995). Marital and family assessment: A multifaceted, multilevel approach. In R. H. Mikesell, D-D. Lusterman, & S. H. McDaniel (Eds.), *Integrating family therapy* (pp. 163–182). Washington, DC: American Psychological Association.

Spanier, G. B. (1976). Measuring dyadic adjustment: New scales for assessing the quality of marriage and similar dyads. *Journal of Marriage and the Family, 38,* 15–28.

Sporakowski, M. J. (1995). Assessment and diagnosis in marriage and family counseling. *Journal of Counseling & Development, 74,* 60–64.

Sprenkle, D. H., & Moon, S. M. (1996). Toward pluralism in family therapy research. In D. H. Sprenkle & S. M. Moon (Eds.), *Research methods in family therapy* (pp. 3–19). New York: Guilford.

Sprenkle, D. H., & Piercy, F. P. (1984). Research in family therapy: A graduate level course. *Journal of Marital and Family Therapy, 10,* 225–240.

Stanton, M. D., Todd, T. C., & Associates (1982). *The family therapy of drug abuse and addiction.* New York: Gardner Press.

Stinnet, N. (1981). In search of strong families. In N. Stinnet, B. Chesser, & J. DeFrain (Eds.), *Building family strengths: Blueprints for action.* Lincoln, NE: University of Nebraska Press.

Szapocznik, J., Kurtines, W., Perez-Vidal, A., Hervis, O., & Foote, F. (1990). One person family therapy. In R. A. Wells & V. A. Gianetti (Eds.), *Handbook of brief psychotherapies* (pp. 493–510). New York: Plenum.

Szapocznik, J., Rio, A., Hervis, O., Kurtines, W., Faraci, A. M., & Mitrani, V. (1991). Assessing change in family functioning as a result of treatment: The structural family systems rating scale (SFSR). *Journal of Marital and Family Therapy, 17,* 295–310.

Szapocznik, J., Rio, A., Murray, E., Cohen, R., Scopetta, M., Rivas-Vasquez, A., Hervis, O., Posada, V., & Kurtines, W. (1989). Structural family therapy versus psychodynamic child therapy for problematic Hispanic boys. *Journal of Consulting and Clinical Psychology, 57,* 571–578.

Thomas, V. (1995). The clinical report: Integrating family assessment instruments into family counseling practice. *The Family Journal, 3,* 284–297.

Thomas, V., & Olson, D. H. (1993). Problem families and the Circumplex Model: Observational assessment using the Clinical Rating Scale (CRS). *Journal of Marital and Family Therapy, 19,* 159–175.

Touliatos, J., Perlmutter, B. F., & Straus, M. A. (Eds.) (1990). *Handbook of family measurement techniques.* Newbury Park, CA: Sage.

Turner, W. L. (1993, April). Identifying African-American family strengths. *Family Therapy News, 24,* 9, 14.

West, J. D. (1988). Marriage and family therapy assessment. *Counselor Education and Supervision, 28,* 169–180.

Wilcoxon, S. A., Walker, M. R., & Hovestadt, A. J. (1989). Counselor effectiveness and family-of-origin experiences: A significant relationship? *Counseling and Values, 33,* 225–229.

Wynne, L. C. (1983). Family research and family therapy: A reunion? *Journal of Marital and Family Therapy, 9,* 113–117.

Current Trends in Family Therapy

As a child of five he played in leaves
his father raked on autumn days,
safe in the knowledge that the yard was home
and that dinner would be served at sunset.

Now middle-aged he examines fences,
where from within his own children frolic
in the deep shadowed light of dusk,
Aware that strong boundaries help create bonds
that extend time and memory beyond the present.

Gladding, *1992*

amily life is constantly changing, and what is considered functional and healthy in one era is not necessarily seen the same way later (Cherlin & Furstenberg, 1987). For instance, in the 1890s, there was widespread agreement among white, middle-class Americans within urban centers in the United States that a healthy and functional family was patriarchal (Footlick, 1990). Fathers were bread winners and rule makers; mothers were bread makers and caregivers. This type of picture is still attractive to many people, but realistically there are, and always have been, various forms of functional families. What were once considered nontraditional family forms (e.g., single-parent, dual-worker, and remarried), now outnumber nuclear families (Ahrons & Rodgers, 1989). In all probability, families will become even more diversified in the future (Walz, 1991).

With variety in family form has come an increased awareness of family problems and the issues that face family therapists (Popenoe, 1993). For example, "if current divorce rates continue, about two out of three marriages that begin this year will not survive as long as both spouses live. The proportion of American adults who are married is decreasing, the share of out-of-wedlock births has soared, and most children under age 18 will spend part of their childhood living with only one parent" (Glenn, 1992, p. 30). Being a family therapist today is more challenging than ever before. "The families of today—postmodern families—are characterized by diversity, not only diversity of structure but also diversity along class, ethnic, culture, and gender lines" (Ahrons, 1992, p. 3). This last chapter focuses on what family therapists can expect in the future and some ways they can constructively address changes within families, therapeutic treatment, and society.

Predictions About Family Therapy

There have been numerous predictions about the future of family therapy. Some hypotheses about the development of the field are based on more accurate information than others. Among the best predictors are two experienced practitioners in the field: Gurman and Kniskern (1992). These clinicians picture the following changes in the practice of family therapy:

1. The practice of family therapy will be more strongly influenced by insurance reimbursement policies than in the past. This means that treatments will be briefer, entail clearly defined and specific goals, and be more oriented toward psychoeducation.

2. The practice of family therapy will be more integrated and less theory driven than before. Books that specialize in outlines and procedures instead of theory, such as Sherman and Fredman's (1986) *Handbook of Structured Techniques in Marriage & Family Therapy*, are one indication of the evolvement of this trend. Other indications are professional journal articles, such as Kuehl's (1996) attempt to connect intergenerational approaches with solution-focused and narrative family therapies through the use of genograms.

3. The practice of family therapy will be more geared toward the treatment of certain psychiatric disorders. For example, some adolescent conduct disorders have been found to respond best to family therapy. Consequently, family therapy is the preferred method for working with such problematic behavior.

4. The practice of family therapy will pay more attention to the therapist/patient/family relationship. The reason for this increased emphasis is that families have the potential to help heal those that have been hurt. By demonstrating greater understanding, concern, warmth, and empathy, family therapists can help families implement positive changes.

5. The practice of family therapy will be more influenced by research-based treatments. Family therapists will become similar to physicians in offering clinical services based on empirical data instead of what they intuitively suspect will work. Neil Jacobson's startling discovery that severe wife abusers' heart rates dropped instead of rose during arguments is an example of important data that will have clinical implications for years to come (Peterson & Painter, 1993).

New Family Therapy Approaches

As with other therapeutic approaches, there continues to be development of new methods and techniques in family therapy. For instance, Cloe Madanes (1990) has formulated an approach for the forgiveness of male sex abusers by their victims. This procedure takes the form of a ritual and requires the remorseful seeking of forgiveness by the perpetrator. It has proven effective from all reports thus far. It is one example of the type of creativity that continues to emerge in the family therapy field, especially from practitioners such as

Madanes (West & Bubenzer, 1993). Other theorists have also created different ways of working with families.

Along with the work in specific theories is an increased emphasis on the **new epistemology**—the idea that the cybernetic approach of Bateson (1972, 1979) and others must be incorporated in its truest sense into family therapy. Among other things, the new epistemology emphasizes **second-order cybernetics**—the cybernetics of cybernetics—which stresses the impact of the family therapist's inclusion and participation in family systems (Keeney, 1983). On its most basic level, second-order cybernetics emphasizes positive feedback in system transformation. It extends first-order cybernetics foci beyond the homeostatic and adaptive properties of family systems in general. The new epistemology also concentrates on the importance of family belief systems in treatment and on **ontology** (i.e., a view of the world) that stresses the circularity and autonomy of systems (in contrast to linear causality). Whether sociopolitical conservative thought will allow the new epistemology to emerge to its fullest and how this evolution might occur are yet to be determined (MacKinnon & Miller, 1987).

Related to these developments in theory and emphasis is the "Basic Family Therapy Skills Project," which was established in 1987 and has focused on determining, defining, and testing "the skills essential for beginning family therapists to master for effective therapy practice" (Figley & Nelson, 1990, p. 225). There have been four basic family therapy skills research reports thus far. In these reports, structural, strategic, brief, and transgenerational family therapies have been examined from the perspective of distinctive and generic skills critical for beginning therapists (Nelson, Heilbrun, & Figley, 1993). The identified skills generated from this project will continue to be researched and refined in future years as educators, practitioners, and researchers seek to determine what therapeutic interventions are most important and when.

Dealing with Different Types of Families

Prior to the 1980s, family therapy, with some notable exceptions, concentrated on working with traditional, middle-class families. Since that time, however, it has become evident that the future of the profession of family therapy is dependent on the ability and flexibility of professionals to work with a wide variety of families. Some of the most prevalent family forms that are important in the future of family therapy are discussed here.

Ethnic Families

Past research has indicated that distinct and relatively small-sized ethnic family groups are often misunderstood by majority cultures. This misunderstanding is associated with cultural prejudices, flaws in collecting data about minorities, stereotyping, and unrecognized economic differences (Hampson, Beavers, & Hulgus, 1990). Bias is unfortunate because it perpetuates myths that may cause harm. Ethnic families need to be seen in regard to their strengths and liabilities both collectively and individually.

One trend of the future is to study ethnic families from the perspective of their competencies, social class, and observed family styles (Billingsley, 1992; Hampson et al., 1990). This type of approach makes it more likely that significant differences and similarities of families from various ethnic backgrounds will be reported accurately and fairly.

Dual-Career Families

Dual-career families are those in which both marital partners are engaged in work that is developmental in sequence and to which they have a high commitment (Rapoport & Rapoport, 1969, 1971; Stoltz-Loike, 1992). Over "50% of married couples in the United States are pursuing careers," and the likelihood is that their numbers will continue to increase (Chiappone, 1992, p. 368). The reasons for this trend are complex, but they are related to the large number of women in the work force, economic pressures, and the tendency for professionals to marry other professionals.

"Balancing the dual-career and family life can lead to conflict and create a considerable source of stress" (Thomas, 1990, p. 174). Such a situation is likely if one or both members of the couple are inflexible in redefining traditional sex roles related to their careers and family obligations. In the past, men have reported that their career interests interfered with their fathering roles; women have stated that parenting interfered with their career roles (Gilbert, 1985; Nicola, 1980). Learning new skills, staying flexible, and continually assessing and revising work and family life are necessary if dual-career couples are to thrive.

In the future, the life stages and life styles of dual-career couples will be studied more closely (Schnittger & Bird, 1990). Because there are multiple variables in family life that affect the quality of life of these couples, their coping strategies over time will be examined. In addition, the career and personal patterns of men and women who enter into these relationships will become a target of analysis.

Single-Parent Families

Single-parent families will continue to be a challenge for family therapists unless the divorce rate in the United States wanes. Over 17% of all family households in the United States in 1992 were headed by single women, and 4.5% of all households were headed by single men (Albert, 1993). By the year

2000, it is estimated that approximately 50% of all children under age 18 will spend some time growing up in a single-parent household (Casto & Bumpass, 1989). For some groups, such as African-American children, the figure is even higher (Harris, 1992). These families are often some of the most economically and relationally disadvantaged. About 87% of single-parent families are headed by women (Krauth, 1995). However, there is a trend for an increasing number of men to seek and gain custody of their children (Bumpass & Sweet, 1989; Elias, 1992).

The challenge for family therapy professionals is how to best serve these families. In the 1960s, innovators such as Salvador Minuchin developed creative approaches for working with low-income, dysfunctional families, many of them headed by single parents. Minuchin viewed family structure as the primary part of the family needing to change. He found that single-parent families who were able to establish a hierarchical structure could eliminate some of their chaos. However, structure alone is not sufficient. To help these families form healthy and productive life styles, family therapists need to assist them in marshaling resources within their communities. The theoretical work of Nagy, which emphasized community connectedness, is probably one of the most functional and least utilized theories to date available for working with single-parent families (Boszormenyi-Nagy, 1987).

Childless Families

Many couples consciously decide not to have a child (or children). For others, childlessness is a result of chance (such as marrying late) or biology (infertility). For couples born between 1946 and 1955 (the initial wave of the baby-boomers), "nearly one in five is childless. For college educated women in their 40s, the rate is one in four" (Shulins, 1992, p. 14). This significant rate of childlessness is expected to continue for women born in the 1960s. It is not an all-time high, but it is equal to the childless rate of "women born around World War I who matured during the depression" (Usdansky, 1993b, 8A).

Childless couples, especially women, face pressures in regard to electing to be childless. Women are sometimes stigmatized and made to feel out of place in social gatherings. Extended family relationships are sometimes strained, especially when siblings of the childless couple have children. Childless couples may also have difficulty in mourning the children they never had or in coming to terms with the choices they made not to have children.

In any of these situations, family therapists may need to involve other family members related to the couple. They may need to emphasize the opportunities available to childless couples and the advantages of this state, such as having less stress, more discretionary income, and greater options to serve in the community. The acronym **DINKS** (double income no kids) is one that family therapists will increasingly encounter.

Remarried Families

By the year 2000, **remarried families** (along with first marrieds and single-parent families) are predicted to be one of three main types of families that "will dominate the lives of most Americans" (Cherlin & Furstenberg, 1987, p. 215). Reasons for the growth of this type of family are associated with the fact that approximately three out of every four people who divorce eventually remarry. As discussed previously, remarried families are quite complex in regard to relationships. Family therapists of the future need to be prepared to deal with the multifaceted nature of these families and equipped with ways to help individuals in them bridge physical and psychological gaps in relating to each other.

Gay/Lesbian Families

Before the Stonewall riots in 1969, "gay communities, much less gay and lesbian families, did not exist in the way they do today, except in isolated and invisible pockets" (Patten, 1992, p. 10). However, since the 1970s, same-sex couples have become increasingly prevalent in the United States. It is estimated that between 1% to 10% of the population of the United States is homosexual. A number of gays and lesbians are choosing to live as families. "The 1990 Census counted . . . 69,200 lesbian couples and 88,200 gay male couples—well below 1% of American households and far fewer than the number of people actually thought to live with homosexual partners" (Usdansky, 1993a, p. 8A). Census data suggests that partners of gays and lesbians are better educated than those of heterosexuals. Furthermore, gay couples have higher incomes than heterosexual couples; and lesbian couples approach the average income of heterosexual couples.

The high education and income levels contribute to the varied lifestyles of gay/lesbian couples. The families they create range in composition from those including a significant other to those composed of a number of people. Some of these families have children from previous marriages; others, especially lesbian couples, conceive children through biological means. Almost all gay/lesbian couples face some form of discrimination and prejudice in the communities in which they live, which tend to be large cities (May, 1994; Usdansky, 1993a).

Most family therapists face a challenge when dealing with these partners. The first challenge they face is sorting out their feelings in regard to homosexuality (May, 1994). Some therapists are homophobic; others are opposed to homosexuality on religious or philosophical grounds. In these and other similar cases, therapists do not work well with gay and lesbian couples and need to refer them to other professionals. A second challenge is dealing with the diversity of gay and lesbian cultures (Snead, 1993). Treatment that may be appropriate in one case may not be appropriate in another.

A third challenge is understanding gay and lesbian families. These families have traditionally had "fluid boundaries and flexible composition" (Patten,

1992, p. 34). Finally, family therapists face the challenge of helping these families relate positively to the heterosexual families from which most came, to the communities in which they live, and to themselves as homosexuals. The process is a two-way street; and in working with gay and lesbian families, therapists often have to work with society at large and its institutions (May, 1994). All of these processes take time, support, and creativity.

Aging Families

The American family is aging in proportion to the population of the United States. It is estimated that "by the year 2020, the typical family will consist of at least four generations" (Goldberg, 1992, p. 1). Furthermore, by the year 2040, nearly a quarter of the population of the United States will be 65 years of age and older. Yet, the study of aging families is a new frontier that "still lacks identifiable landmarks and road maps" (Goldberg, 1992, p. 1).

What we do know is that with increased age, families become concerned with different personal, family, and societal issues. For instance, on an individual level, there is more emphasis on one's health (Melville, 1992). This focus spills over into family and institutional relationships as well. In addition to health, aging families are involved with the launching or relaunching of their young adult children. The crisis of launching or relaunching can be acute, as it was in 1991 when 31% of unmarried adults between the ages of 25 and 29 were living with their parents (Usdansky, 1992). Financial and social arrangements are affected when young adults continue to live in their parents' homes.

Other factors associated with aging families include increased stress and rewards as elderly relatives move into their children's homes (Montalvo & Thompson, 1988). In these situations, couples and families sometimes have to change their household and community routines in order to take care of their parents. This type of situation can increase tension, anger, joy, guilt, gratitude, and grief among all involved. It is an uneven experience that fluctuates in its rewards and restrictions. It is a process that family therapists must become familiar with if they are to help aging families and their members cope with a significant period in the family life span.

The literature is still sparse in regard to aging and family therapy (Van Amburg, Barber, & Zimmerman, 1996). Issues facing aging families, other than those already mentioned, include transition to retirement, widowhood, sexual dysfunction, dealing with adult children, and long-lived marriages.

Singles

The proportion of single adults in the United States (i.e., those 18 years and over) is rising, according to the U.S. Census Bureau. Approximately 5% to 10% of the total population in the United States in the 1990s is composed of never-married adults, a level last reached in the 1940s. For instance, in 1991 approximately 64% of women and 80% of men ages 20 to 24 were unmarried (Usdansky, 1992). That compares to a 1970 figure for these two groups of 36% and 55%, respectively. Never marrieds, together with a large number of divorced and widowed persons, make singles a significant part of the adult population in the United States (approximately one third of all people over age 18).

With an increase in singlehood, life styles within society are changing with a greater emphasis on individual events. Societal institutions that have been bastions for family sponsored activities, such as churches, are being reshaped to be more accommodating to singles. The field of family therapy must change by necessity in response to the steady rise of singles. For instance, the importance of treating the individual from a family systems perspective will take on increased importance (Nichols, 1987).

Multigenerational Families

The number of **multigenerational families** grew from 1.3 million in 1980 to 2.4 million in 1991. These are households that include "a child, a parent, and a grandparent, according to the U.S. Bureau of the Census definition" (Ames, Lewis, Kandell, Rosenberg, & Chideya, 1992, p. 52). Common before World War II, multigenerational families decreased from that time until the 1980s. All indications are that the number of multigenerational families will continue to grow in number in the upcoming decades.

Two factors are influencing the increase in the number of these families. The first has to do with economics. When the economy is in recession, such as in the early 1990s, young people cannot find work and often come back to live with their family of origin. The second factor involves medicine. The aging population of the United States is living longer because of advances in medicine. Individuals, especially those past their mid-70s, often cannot keep up a house by themselves and, consequently, move in with their children.

The advantages of multigenerational families are many. Different generations get to interact and enjoy each other more directly. There are often more people to do the work. The stress of cleaning or taking care of children is sometimes lessened. However, the disadvantages of this type of arrangement can be considerable. For instance, there may be increased stress on the parent subunit to take care of children and grandparents. There can also be new financial and psychological difficulties as the parent subunit has to take care of more people with the same amount of money and is simultaneously squeezed to provide adequate living space.

Homeless Families

Among the homeless population, approximately 43% are families with children (U.S. Conference of Mayors, 1993). Working with these families presents special challenges for government agencies and family therapists. Policy makers often treat homeless families as a homogeneous group (Anderson & Koblinsky, 1995). When treatment of families is based on such a principle, family members may be forced to split up in order to receive shelter and other needed services. Such a split may discourage parents from taking care of their children and may estrange these families from social support networks.

To address the needs of homeless families, Huber (1995a) suggests that family therapists focus on changing environmental forces as well as family problems. Such an approach has a community and change agent emphasis that requires therapists to take on a variety of roles, including that of consultant, outreach worker, ombudsperson, and facilitator of indigenous support systems.

Welfare of Children/Child Abuse

With life style changes in the form and behavior of American families, there has been increased concern over the welfare and well-being of children (Popenoe, 1993). The issue of "family values," which is often discussed in political elections, is but one example of the prevalence of this concern. Children face a number of problems in American families. Among them are "delinquency and crime (including an alarming juvenile homicide rate), drug and alcohol abuse, suicide, depression, eating disorders, and the growing number of children in poverty" (Popenoe, 1993, p. A48).

Child abuse is also a major concern. The effects of trauma resulting from abuse is often lifelong. One of the most insidious forms of child abuse is sexual abuse. "It is generally believed that sexual abuse of all children is significantly underreported, with sexual abuse of boys being reported least" (Tomes, 1996, p. 55). In sexual abuse situations, "most abuse of boys is done by perpetrators outside the family; girls' abuse is predominantly intrafamilial" (Hutchins, 1995a, p. 21). Almost one in three girls is sexually abused by age 18; about one in six boys is sexually abused by age 16 (Tomes, 1996).

Child abuse has become prominent news, from notorious cases to lesser-known court trials (Shapiro, 1993). There is even a National Committee for Prevention of Child Abuse, which addresses this problem. When family therapists encounter child abuse cases of any type, they "should not attempt to take the focus off the abuser, as this approach serves only to lead family members and community service agencies to believe that the therapist is excusing the violent acts" (Fenell & Weinhold, 1996, p. 5). However, the therapist should concentrate on (1) assisting the abuser in learning how to delay acting impulsively and (2) helping the abuser and the abused family members to recognize and select alternatives other than violence. Motivation for achieving these goals is greatest immediately following abusive behavior, when the family is in crisis and the abuser is usually feeling badly about what has happened.

Spouse Abuse and Domestic Violence

Increasing attention is being given to spouse abuse and domestic violence in the United States. Although some men are the victims of abuse and violence by their mates, the large majority of those assaulted each year are women. About 13% of all murders involve husbands killing their wives, and at least 1.6 million wives are severely beaten by their husbands each year (Gottman et al., 1995). Even premarital rates of physical violence are high—about 36% (McLaughlin, Leonard, & Senchak, 1992). Family therapists will become increasingly involved in addressing spouse abuse and domestic violence in the future.

Alcohol and Substance Abuse

Early in its history, family therapy addressed the problem of alcohol and substance abuse as a family systems problem. The documentation of the effectiveness of family therapy forms of treatment for drug abuse and addiction was particularly well demonstrated in the structural/strategic emphasis of Stanton, Todd, and Associates (1982). The meticulous work of these researchers underscored the importance of family dynamics in such situations, and the crucial nature of involving the entire family in treatment.

Alcohol and substance abuse treatment using family therapy continues to be emphasized. Approximately one in eleven Americans suffers from severe addictive problems, and "one third of all American families are affected by alcohol problems" (Daw, 1995, p. 19). In addition, domestic abuse occurs in 50% to 70% of alcoholic relationships, according to a 1996 Harvard Families and Addiction Program study.

Todd and Stanton recommend models for treatment and prevention, especially regarding alcohol-affected families. Treatment should initially address drinking—to get it stopped. This may mean getting inpatient detoxification, enrolling appropriate family members in Alcoholics Anonymous or AlAnon, and mobilizing support networks. Effective therapy may also take a Bowen approach using genograms to promote an understanding of how patterns developed and have been maintained. Behavioral therapies have produced good results, too. Prevention, especially in regard to teen alcohol abuse, may take the form of "giving kids accurate information about alcohol use in an objective way; presenting information through a 'teen-respected' source; helping kids say yes to life, not just no to drugs; parent networking; setting strict rules about drinking with kids and continued pressure to 'take back the communities'" (Daw, 1995, p. 19).

Organizations Associated with Family Therapy

Before the 1980s, the four major associations dealing with issues connected with family therapy were the American Association for Marriage and Family Therapy (AAMFT), the American Family Therapy Association (AFTA), the Affiliated Council for Marriage Enrichment (ACME), and the National Council on Family Relations (NCFR). Of the four, the AAMFT was dominant in regard to membership and influence.

However, in the 1980s, two new family therapy associations were established that will probably challenge the AAMFT for dominance in the future. The first was Division 43 (of Family Psychology), which was established within the American Psychological Association (APA) in 1984. The second fledgling group established in 1986 was the International Association for Marriage and Family Counseling (IAMFC). The IAMFC has been connected with the American Counseling Association (ACA) from its beginning.

At present there is a struggle going on to determine which group or groups will dominate the field of family therapy. The AAMFT claims an historical right to this position, but family psychology and IAMFC also have legitimate claims and followings. In addition, there are physicians who wish to "corral" family therapy into a medical specialty. It will be interesting to watch what happens in the last half of the 1990s and beyond. As with other professions, political circumstances influence dominance.

Education of Family Therapists

The educational programs of family therapists are conducted in collaboration with learned societies and associations. The formal process of education is overseen by representatives from a number of associations, such as the Commission on Accreditation for Marriage and Family Therapy Education (COAMFTE) or the Council on Accreditation of Counseling and Related Educational Programs (CACREP).

Table 16.1

An example of coursework areas required for a master's degree in AAMFT-accredited and CACREP-accredited programs

CACREP CURRICULUM	AAMFT CURRICULUM
Human Growth & Development	Introduction Family/Child Dev.
Social and Cultural Foundations	Marital & Family Systems
Helping Relationships	Intro. Family/Child Development
Groups	Dysfunctions in Marriage/Family
Lifestyle & Career Development	Advanced Child Development
Appraisal/Assessment	Assessment in Marital/Family
Research and Evaluation	Research Methods Child/Family
Professional Orientation	Professional Issues Family
Theoretical Foundation MFT	Theories of MFT
Techniques/Treatment MFT	Marriage/Family Pre-practicum
Clinical Practicum/Internship	Clinical Practicum
Substance Abuse Treatment	Human Sexual Behavior
Human Sexuality	Thesis
Electives	Electives

From "The Training of Marriage and Family Counselors/Therapists: A 'Systemic' Controversy among Disciplines" by Michael Baltimore, 1993, *Alabama Counseling Association Journal, 19*, 40. Reprinted by permission.

In recent years the curriculums for graduating master's degree family therapists have been similar in accredited AAMFT and CACREP programs. Table 16.1 shows the required coursework areas for these two programs in 1993.

There are numerous problems associated with current educational programs in family therapy. For example, among professional association groups, there is considerable in-fighting for recognition that one method of educating family therapists is superior to others. This type of "turfism" is sometimes conducted in a blind fashion, with some professional groups refusing to recognize other similar groups. If family therapy is to be a core provider of health care services, this bickering and belittling must stop (Baltimore, 1993).

A second serious weakness in family therapy education programs as they are presently structured is that "they tend to ignore issues that are controversial and difficult to teach" (Smith & Stevens-Smith, 1992, p. 438). In the future, areas that arouse emotion in regard to therapeutic content and process need to be examined. For example, divorce, substance abuse, homelessness, teen pregnancies, extramarital affairs, and the impact of AIDS on family life are but a handful of these subjects. They may require specialized courses or they may be explored in different regular course offerings. Regardless, they cannot be scanned over or left out.

Licensure of Family Therapists

In 1996, 37 states regulated the practice of marriage and family therapy. That number continues to grow. Unfortunately, almost all states define the practice of marriage and family therapy differently, even though a state license verifies the abilities of a clinician to address family mental health problems. In addition, becoming licensed or certified as a family therapist in one state does not guarantee recognition of that license or certification by another state. However, in the early 1990s, a movement was started to control the professional recognition of the practice of marriage and family therapy. Gaining uniformity of requirements for licensure and recognition of licensure across state lines is a growing trend.

The Personhood of Family Therapists

As education programs for family therapists become competitive and licensure standards rigorous, the personhood of family therapists grows in its importance. "The methods and techniques of therapy are never wholly separate from the qualities of the person applying them" (Nichols & Schwartz, 1995, p. 535-536). Not everyone who is bright, articulate, and attuned to systems theory and the process of change should enter the profession of family therapy. Indeed, individuals who have had negative family of origin experiences may find that they cannot deal successfully with or do not wish to work with dysfunctional families (Bowen, 1978). Persons who treat difficult families must often engage in a considerable amount of therapy on an individual and family level (Wilcoxon, Walker, & Hovestadt, 1989).

Major stressors for family therapists include increased depression from listening to a client family's problem, less time for one's own family because of work demands, unrealistic expectations of one's own family, and psychological distancing from one's family because of professional status (Duncan & Duerden, 1990; Wetchler & Piercy, 1986). However, enhancers for family therapists include an increased ability to solve one's own family problems, an acceptance of one's part in contributing to family dysfunctionality, a deeper appreciation of one's own family, and a greater ability and desire to communicate effectively (Duncan & Duerden, 1990; Wetchler & Piercy, 1986). Being a family therapist is clearly a multifaceted process.

Overall, a family therapist "should be a healer: a human being concerned with engaging other human beings therapeutically, around areas and issues that cause them pain, while always retaining great respect for their values, areas of strength, and esthetic preferences" (Minuchin & Fishman, 1981, p. 1). To achieve the role of a healer requires dedication, awareness, and stable mental health. It is the exceptional person who can achieve this balance. Those who are best suited in nature to be helpers of families most often have artistic qualities, that is, they are intuitive and feeling in regard to interpersonal relationships (Brammer, 1993). It is these individuals who some educators recommend for training in the field of family therapy. Regardless, more attention is now being placed on the personhood of the therapist (Aponte, 1992; Satir, 1987).

Research in Family Therapy

Family therapy has become increasingly sophisticated in its research. For example, John Gottman (1994) has undertaken a truly imposing research project in his attempt to understand the longitudinal course of marriages. In his work, he has reduced social psychophysiological observations of marital interactions to a numbered coding of positives and negatives.

Yet, despite researchers such as Gottman, there are many questions surrounding research on families and "the effectiveness of family therapy" (Smith & Stevens-Smith, 1992, p. 435). As Lyman Wynne (1986) pointed out, there is a need for replication studies. Too often family researchers have concentrated on innovation rather than reliability. Frequently, clinicians have disregarded the work of other researchers and, at the same time, have refused to engage in the process themselves (Schwartz & Breunlin, 1983). In addition, there is a tendency to separate family therapy from other mainstream mental health professions. Further, there has been a prevalence among family therapists to be more political than empirical in emphasizing the virtues of family therapy (Liddle, 1991). In truth, despite impressive gains in recent years in regard to research methods and results, there is still much that needs to be done in this area.

Fortunately, some needed changes in research have begun to take place. For one thing, more emphasis is now placed on connecting process and outcome in family therapy research (Liddle, 1991). In the future, family therapy research needs to concentrate on emphasizing the clinical practice-researcher link (Smith & Stevens-Smith, 1992). It also needs to accurately report data, and make the translation of research findings into practical ways of working with dysfunctional families (Liddle, 1991). Because these issues are being addressed in the professional literature, a trend toward strengthening the research in family therapy is emerging.

Computers in Family Therapy

Although a computer will never take over the job of a family therapist, computers can be used as adjuncts in the therapeutic process. For instance, Betts (1993a) reports that a software package known as *Family Origins* (Parsons Technology, One Parsons Drive, Hiawatha Iowa 52233) can help practitioners organize details of a family's history in a concise manner and thereby facilitate the practitioner's intervention with the family. Likewise, a software piece named *B.A.B.Y.* (Software Marketing Corporation, 602-893-3377) can be utilized in working with expectant parents in discussing health information and special cases related to childbirth (Betts, 1993c).

In the 1990s, more computer software packages that teach and aid students and clinicians in understanding the theory and practice of family therapy can be expected. Many of them will be like the already marketed software program known as *Brief Therapy Coach* developed by Gary Schultheis and Bill O'Hanlon, which can be a "tool for teaching the practice of brief therapy as well as a reference for practitioners" (Betts, 1993b, p. 29). It may even be possible through computer technology in the future to have families work on resolving presenting difficulties by employing computer programs. For example, computer-generated genograms are already a part of some therapists' work with families in regard to issues surrounding their families of origin (Gerson, 1984).

In addition to computer software to assist in the therapeutic process, computers will continue to help family therapists streamline their business practices. Examples of effective and flexible billing or practice management packages include *Psychotherapy Office Planner* (1-800-787-3194), *ShrinkRapt* (1-800-448-6899), *The Therapist* (1-800-895-3344), *Touched* (1-800-588-6824), and *The Psychotherapy Practice Manager* (1-800-895-1618) (Parks, 1995).

"Office personnel may need to be trained to think preventively about possible violations of confidentiality that may occur with a computer system" (O'Malley, 1995, p. 9). This type of protection would include placing the computer in a discrete position so that only office staff can view it. Family therapists who use computers to type progress notes must also take care with computer access and display. Furthermore, client notes and records that are typed on computer discs must be protected in the same way as hard copy notes.

Feminist Theory and Gender Issues in Family Therapy

Since the late 1970s, feminist theory and gender issues have influenced the field of family therapy. In fact, the feminist critique of family therapy has been one of the most powerful trends in the field in the past decade (Fenell & Weinhold, 1996). The Women's Project in Family Therapy (Walters, Carter, Papp, & Silverstein, 1988) has been a major undertaking of feminist theorists. These researchers and practitioners have sought to emphasize the absence of gender in the formation of systems theory. Yet, the impact of addressing feminist and gender issues in family therapy has been uneven. For instance, "feminist family therapists are still fighting many of the battles that began in the 1970s" (Smith & Stevens-Smith, 1992, p. 436). In addition, feminist and gender issues have sometimes been misunderstood. For example, the term *feminist* has often been viewed as aligning the therapist with one gender. Similarly, the word *gender* has sometimes been construed as another term for *sex role stereotypes*.

As an approach, **feminist family therapy** "is an attitude, a lens, a body of ideas about gender hierarchy and its impact rather than a specific model of therapy or a grab bag of clinical techniques. Feminists recognize the overriding importance of the power structure in any human system" (Carter, 1992, p. 66) (see Table 16.2). The influence of this perspective seems to be spreading. Part of the reason is the realization that what feminists have said has a truthfulness to it that cannot be ignored. A second reason is the increased numbers of women entering the profession of marriage and family therapy. Many of these women realize the need to "include women's voices and experiences" within the family therapy field in order to gain a richer and more evenly balanced perspective on family life and to discern what changes are needed in families (Carter, 1992, p. 69).

In the future, it may be more productive for family therapy to concentrate on examining "gender-sensitive issues in therapy" rather than feminine or masculine issues (Smith & Stevens-Smith, 1992). In such an approach, differences in genders may be recognized in a less emotionally or politically volatile way. In such a climate, changes for men and women within the family and society may be voiced with a greater likelihood that people from all walks of life may work for healthier changes. Thus, talents and unique assets of males and females may be highlighted individually as well as within a family system. Likewise, commonalities and differences in males and females may be featured so that they work together and separately for families and their members (Berg, 1991). Training models that place gender at the heart of educating family therapists have been and will continue to be developed (e.g., Storm, 1991).

Table 16.2
Characteristics of Gender-Sensitive Family Therapy

Nonsexist counseling	Empowerment/feminist/ gender-aware counseling
Does not reinforce stereotyped gender roles.	Helps clients recognize the impact of social, cultural, and political factors on their lives.
Encourages clients to consider a wide range of choices, especially in regard to careers.	Helps clients transcend limitations resulting from gender stereotyping.
Avoids allowing gender stereotypes to affect diagnoses.	Recognizes the degree to which individual behaviors may reflect internalization of harmful social standards.
Avoids use of sexist assessment instruments.	Includes gender-role analysis as a component of assessment.
Treats male and female clients equally.	Helps clients develop and integrate traits that are culturally defined as "masculine" and "feminine."
Avoids misuse of power in the counseling relationship.	Develops collaborative counselor-client relationships.

Source: Judith Lewis.

Managed Health Care

Managed health care began to emerge in the 1980s when businesses saw a predominantly fee-for-service health care system characterized by overutilization and little accountability. In 1992, General Motors, for example, "spent more on employee health care than it did on steel" (Hutchins, 1995b, p. 15). Thus, to reduce overall health care costs to their companies, businesses have contracted with managed care organizations. In 1995, approximately 60% of Americans (i.e., 108 million) enrolled in health care programs were covered by a managed care contract.

The issue of managed health care is of increasing importance to family therapists. It continues to have a deep impact on private practitioners and agency clinicians in regard to the number of practitioners available to see families and the compensation they receive for their services (Adams, 1987). For example, "between 1989 and 1992, 30% of private sector mental health treatment providers went out of business" (Hutchins, 1995b, p. 15). Fees for family therapy also plummeted, in some cases reaching lows of $35 a session.

Managed mental health care (MMHC) involves a service delivery system that is driven more by costs than by client needs. Limits are placed "on the amount and type of services, by monitoring services intensely, and by changing the nature of services (Foos, Ottens, & Hill, 1991, p. 332). One common component of MMHC is called the utilization review (UR). "UR entails the practitioner submitting a written justification for treatment along with a comprehensive treatment plan. The justification and plan are reviewed by a utilization reviewer, who, if the plan is approved, typically allocates a specific number of sessions; further sessions are subject to reapplication and approval by the reviewer. Only under these conditions can claims be reimbursed" (Huber, 1995b, p. 42). Another emerging managed care method of cutting cost is the capitated contract "in which providers . . . agree to provide treatment for a population for a per person per year fee. In essence, providers become their own case managers" (Hutchins, 1996, p. 7).

The most prevalent managed care organizations are preferred provider organizations (PPOs) and health maintenance organizations (HMOs) (Levitan & Conway, 1990). With government as well as private interest in the health care field growing, family therapy is becoming a part of the system, but with significant difficulty. There continues to be an especially high demand in managed health care for brief family therapy approaches. The emphasis in such an approach is "to work more productively" (Hawley, 1993, p. 64). Solution-focused and strategic forms of family therapy seem especially well suited for managed health care programs. Regardless, "in a managed care setting, providers must be able to draft a treatment plan, follow it, and provide documentation that it is being followed and, most importantly, that treatment is effective" (Hutchins, 1995b, p. 15).

Family Therapy and AIDS

Up until 1981, "few Americans had heard the term *acquired immunodeficiency syndrome* (AIDS)" (Bradley & Ostrovsky, 1992, p. 405). Fewer yet understood its meaning or the impact it would have on them and their families. In the 1990s, all has changed. The number of AIDS cases is epidemic. It is a "'paranoid's delight' because it has generated so many theories about its causation and transmission" (Bruhn, 1989, p. 455).

In truth, AIDS affects persons of all ages and stages within the life cycle. It is increasing most rapidly in children (most of whom are infected by their mothers during the prenatal period); but it is also becoming more prevalent in the heterosexual community (Bradley & Ostrovsky, 1992). In addition to individuals infected by this disease, families of these persons are impacted. They face problems connected not only with fear and stigma but also with loss and grief.

In helping AIDS families, therapists need to keep in mind a family's level of stress, coping resources, and stage in the family life cycle. In the future, more professional literature and resources will be dedicated to family therapists who are working with AIDS families.

Marriage and Family Enrichment

The idea of **marriage and family enrichment** is based on the concept that couples and families stay healthy or get healthier by actively participating in certain activities, usually in connection with other couples (Mace & Mace, 1977). There are over two dozen enrichment organizations in the United States on a national level, and the material in this field has mushroomed (Mace, 1987). Marriage and family enrichment is a third way of helping couples/families outside of the approaches of education as information-giving and family therapy (Mace, 1987).

Recommended ways to achieve health in families include involvement in couple and family retreats, interactive cooperative activities, and family councils. Research shows that enrichment, as opposed to therapy, can be helpful to couples and families who are not in distress. However, enrichment experiences, especially those involving marriage encounter weekends, can be quite disruptive and damaging to distressed couples and can lead to further deterioration of their relationships (Doherty, Lester, & Leigh, 1986). Care must be exercised in selecting couples and families to participate in these programs.

A part of marriage and family enrichment involves self- and couple help. This type of help is often in the form of couples and family members participating in structured exercises that theoretically and practically bring them closer together through sharing information and experiences (Calvo, 1975; Guerney, 1977). For instance, couples may learn to give and receive nonverbal and verbal messages and reflect on positive times in their life together. They may also be able to give and receive feedback on important relationship topics such as sexuality, finance, parenting, and household chores (Johnson, Fortman, & Brems, 1993).

Use of Family Therapy Methods in Other Helping Arenas

The use of family therapy techniques in other human relations areas is not surprising given that many family therapists are cross-disciplinary in background and interests. However, it is noteworthy to observe how many family therapy tools are being borrowed for use in other specialties. For instance, the field of medicine has traditionally traced illness in families; but many physicians are now more observant of significant events within families and their impact on the well-being of members and the family as a whole. The impact of death on other behaviors and the development of various symptoms within family members is now better understood and appreciated (Paul & Paul, 1982).

Professionals in the field of career development have also come to understand and appreciate family dynamics more. For example, the interconnection between family systems and birth order from an Adlerian and Bowen perspective has been articulated by Bradley and Mims (1992). These practitioners have their clients construct genograms as part of the career counseling process. Then, they examine family relationships in regard to the Bowen perspective of looking at boundaries, myths, roles, and rules. Finally, they inquire about client birth order and sibling relations. These exercises help clients understand about their career choices and family influences. An appreciation for these factors is a complementary process.

In the future, family therapy theory, techniques, and professionals will interface with a number of other systems. Future family therapists "will be expected to work with macrosystems" (Smith & Stevens-Smith, 1992, p. 439). Thus, they will need to expand their skills and knowledge about which intervention strategies work best in which areas.

Summary and Conclusion

Like most professional fields, family therapy is changing. It is "moving out of its adolescence and into adulthood" (Nichols & Schwartz, 1995, p. 536-537). Some of the changes associated with this growth are unsettling, but most of them are productive. Crucial issues in the upcoming years involve those connected with licensure, theory, training, influence, and research. Demographic shifts in the population of the United States in regard to age, singleness, divorce, childlessness, disease, and cultural diversity mean that family therapists in the future will need to be more sensitive, skilled, and flexible in their outlooks and practices.

This chapter examined major types of families in the United States and the outlook for their growth and development. The place of theory, and even the types of theoretical models employed, will be influenced by the health or dysfunctionality of these family forms as well as the growth and development of theoretical ideas. In addition, this chapter covered trends in the education of future family therapists and emphasized that individuals who devote their lives to this profession must not only learn scholarly content involved in the process of working with families but also resolve their own personal and family concerns. Such an emphasis on the health of the therapist as well as the family is consistent with a systemic and a gender-sensitive approach to treatment.

The impact of technology and research was also discussed in this chapter. It is virtually impossible for family therapists to be efficient and productive without relying on these modern tools of society. In fact, family therapists who try to work in isolation from research or technology may find themselves not only frustrated but also dated. In addition to working on remediation issues, this chapter emphasized that family therapy methods are also applicable to larger systems such as those involving schools and communities. Furthermore, family therapists need to become more aware of and skilled in the use of enrichment for families and couples.

In summary, the field of family therapy is changing. Informed and motivated family therapists will change with it. The future is both predictable and a result of chance. Family therapists who are well grounded in the history, theory, practice, and process of the profession will most likely respond positively to whatever the future brings. In doing so, they will position themselves and the clinical domain of family therapy to address common and controversial issues in exciting, innovative, and pragmatically healthy ways.

SUMMARY TABLE

Current Trends in Family Therapy

Various forms of functional families have always existed.

Families are continuing to become more diversified.

Because of current trends in families and in therapy, being a family therapist will be a challenge in the future.

Predictions About Family Therapy

Among the changes seen in the future of family therapy are those related to:

- insurance reimbursement policies (including those for brief therapy)
- more integrated models of treatment
- practice geared toward certain psychiatric disorders
- greater attention paid to therapist/family relationships
- more research based treatment

New Family Therapy Approaches

Cloe Madanes and other creative family therapists continue to develop new approaches to working with families.

The new epistemology, which involves second-order cybernetics, emphasizes positive feedback in system transformation.

The Basic Family Therapy Skills Project focuses on determining, defining, and testing the skills necessary for novice therapists to master, generically and specifically.

Dealing with Different Types of Families

Among the most prevalent family forms for therapists to work with in the future are:

- ethnic minority families, especially from a cultural perspective
- dual-career families, especially in regard to stress, conflict, and pressure

- single parent families, especially in regard to form, structure, and context
- childless families, especially in regard to societal pressure
- remarried families, especially in terms of relationship complexity
- gay/lesbian families, especially as this family style emerges in many diverse forms
- aging families, especially as the number of such families grows along with related problems of health and relationships
- singles, especially as the percentage of singles rises and options for these individuals increase
- multigenerational families, especially in regard to economic, medical, and interpersonal issues
- homeless families, especially concerning public policies and family needs

Welfare of Children/Child Abuse

The welfare of children is of growing concern in American society.

In the future, family therapists will be expected to advocate more for children's rights and to make appropriate interventions in child abuse cases.

Spouse Abuse and Domestic Violence

Violence against spouses, primarily women, is growing.

Family therapists will continue to become more involved in such cases.

Alcohol and Substance Abuse

Substance abuse is a family systems problem.

Family therapy is effective in treating alcohol and substance abuse.

Prevention, as well as treatment, will be stressed in the future.

Organizations Associated with Family Therapy

In the 1980s, two new family therapy associations were established: The Division of Family Psychology was formed in APA and the International Association for Marriage and Family Counseling was formed in ACA.

These two groups will continue to struggle for dominance with more established groups such as the AAMFT, AFTA, NCFR, and ACME.

Education of Family Therapists

Accrediting agency approvals, such as those given by COAMFTE and CACREP, will be even more important in the future.

In-fighting as well as controversial and difficult issues must be addressed if the profession is to grow.

Licensure of Family Therapists

Most states now license or certify family therapists. The number will continue to grow.

Problems in regard to uniformity and verification of abilities are future issues to be addressed.

The Personhood of Family Therapists

The personhood of family therapists grows in importance as education programs become competitive and licensure standards become rigorous.

Major stressors and enhancers for family therapists continue to be highlighted and evaluated in regard to one's readiness to practice in the profession.

Research in Family Therapy

Family therapy research is becoming increasingly sophisticated.

Empirical data is crucial to the future of treating families. The practitioner/research model needs to be highlighted.

Computers in Family Therapy

A number of computer programs have already been developed for therapists to use in teaching or treating families.

Computer assisted learning and treatment will continue to evolve for most family therapy theories.

Feminist Theory and Gender Issues in Family Therapy

Gender issues and feminist theory have sensitized and polarized the field of family therapy. These viewpoints offer a different perspective than that originally developed in the field.

Gender-sensitive issues will continue to be important.

Managed Health Care

Managed health care in the form of PPOs and HMOs is likely to increase in the future and severely impact fee-for-service operations, such as private practice.

Briefer forms of family therapy will be more in demand as managed health care becomes more pervasive.

Family Therapy and AIDS

AIDS affects persons of all ages and stages in family life.

Considerations for treating families with an AIDS member will grow in the future.

Marriage and Family Enrichment

The number of associations and demand for marriage/family enrichment is expanding.

Various forms of enrichment exercises are available and becoming more important in regard to use.

Use of Family Therapy Models in Other Helping Areas
Family therapy models are being employed in medicine, career development, and other specialty areas.

In the future, family therapy models will be applied to macro, as well as micro, systems.

References

Adams, J. (1987). A brave new world for private practice? *Family Therapy Networker, 11,* 18–25.

Ahrons, C. R. (1992, October). 21st-Century families: Meeting the challenges of change. *Family Therapy News, 23,* 3, 16.

Ahrons, C., & Rodgers, R. (1989). *Divorced families: Meeting the challenges of divorce and remarriage.* New York: W. W. Norton.

Albert, J. L. (1993, August 27). The changing American family. *USA Today,* 10A.

Ames, K., Lewis, S., Kandell, P., Rosenberg, D., & Chideya, F. (1992, September 14). Cheaper by the dozen. *Newsweek,* 52–53.

Anderson, E. A., & Koblinsky, S. A. (1995). Homeless policy: The need to speak to families. *Family Relations, 44,* 13–18.

Aponte, H. J. (1992). Training the person of the therapist in structural family therapy. *Journal of Marital and Family Therapy, 18,* 269–281.

Baltimore, M. (1993). The training of marriage and family counselors/therapists: A 'systemic' controversy among disciplines. *Alabama Counseling Association Journal, 19,* 34–44.

Bateson, G. (1972). *Steps to an ecology of mind.* New York: Ballantine.

Bateson, G. (1979). *Mind and nature: A necessary unity.* New York: E. P. Dutton.

Berg, I. K. (1991). Letter to the editor. *Journal of Marital and Family Therapy, 17,* 311–312.

Betts, E. (1993a, Spring). Computers in family psychology. *The Family Psychologist, 9,* 33.

Betts, E. (1993b, Summer). Computers in family psychology. *The Family Psychologist, 9,* 29, 10.

Betts, E. (1993c, Fall). Computers in family psychology. *The Family Psychologist, 9,* 30–31.

Billingsley, A. (1992). *Climbing Jacob's ladder: The enduring legacy of African American families.* New York: Simon & Schuster.

Boszormenyi-Nagy, I. (1987). *Foundations of contextual therapy.* New York: Brunner/Mazel.

Bowen, M. L. (1978). *Family therapy in clinical practice.* New York: Jason Aronson.

Bradley, L. J., & Ostrovsky, M. A. (1992). The AIDS family: An emerging issue. In. R. L. Smith & P. Stevens-Smith (Eds.), *Family counseling and therapy* (pp. 405–429). Ann Arbor, MI: ERIC/CAPS.

Bradley, R. W., & Mims, G. A. (1992). Using family systems and birth order dynamics as the basis for a college career decision-making course. *Journal of Counseling and Development, 70,* 445–448.

Brammer, L. M. (1993). *The helping relationship: Process and skills* (5th ed.). Boston: Allyn & Bacon.

Bruhn, J. G. (1989). Counseling persons with a fear of AIDS. *Journal of Counseling and Development, 67,* 455–457.

Bumpass, L. L., & Sweet, J. A. (1989). Children's experience in single-parent families: Implications of cohabilitation and marital transitions. *Family Planning Perspectives, 21,* 256–260.

Calvo, G. (1975). *Marriage encounter: Official national manual.* St. Paul, MN: Marriage Encounter, Inc.

Carter, B. (1992, January/February). Stonewalling feminism. *Family Therapy Networker, 16,* 64–69.

Casto, M. T., & Bumpass, L. L. (1989). Recent trends in marital disruption. *Demography, 26,* 37–51.

Cherlin, A., & Furstenberg, F. F. (1987). The American family in the year 2000. In O. Pocs & R. H. Walsh (Eds.), *Marriage and Family 87/88* (pp. 215–220). Guilford, CT: Dushkin.

Chiappone, J. M. (1992). The career developmental professional of the 1990s: A training model. In H. D. Lea & Z. B. Leibowitz (Eds.), *Adult career development* (2nd ed., pp. 364–379). Alexandria, VA: National Career Development Association.

Daw, J. L. (1995, December). Alcohol problems across the generations. *Family Therapy News, 26,* 19.

Doherty, W. J., Lester, M. E., & Leigh, G. (1986). Marriage encounter weekends: Couples who win and couples who lose. *Journal of Marital and Family Therapy, 12,* 49–61.

Duncan, S. F., & Duerden, D. S. (1990). Stressors and enhancers in the marital/family life of the family professional. *Family Relations, 39,* 211–215.

Elias, M. (1992, June 19–21). Parenting turns men's lives on end. *USA Today,* 1A, 2A.

Fenell, D. L., & Weinhold, B. K. (1996, March). Treating families with special needs. *Counseling and Human Development, 28,* 1–12.

Figley, C. R., & Nelson, T. S. (1990). Basic family therapy skills II: Structural family therapy. *Journal of Marital and Family Therapy, 16,* 225–239.

Footlick, J. K. (1990, Winter/Spring). What happened to the family? *Newsweek,* 15–20.

Foos, J. A., Ottens, A. J., & Hill, L. K. (1991). Managed mental health: A primer for counselors. *Journal of Counseling and Development, 69,* 332–336.

Gerson, R. (1984). *The family recorder: Computer-generated genograms.* Atlanta: Humanware Software, 61 8th St., 30327.

Gilbert, L. A. (1985). *Men in dual-career families: Current realities and future prospects.* Hillsdale, NJ: Lawrence Erlbaum Associates.

Gladding, S. T. (1992). *Past Presence.* Unpublished manuscript.

Glenn, N. D. (1992, June). What does family mean? *American Demographics, 14,* 30–37.

Goldberg, J. R. (1992, August). The new frontier: Marriage and family therapy with aging families. *Family Therapy News, 23,* 1, 14, 21.

Gottman, J. M. (1994). *What predicts divorce? The relationship between marital processes and marital outcomes.* Hillsdale, NJ: Erlbaum.

Gottman, J. M., Jacobson, N. S., Rushe, R. H., Wu Shortt, J., Babcock, J., La Tallade, J. J., & Waltz, J. (1995). The relationship between heart rate reactivity, emotionally aggressive behavior, and general violence in batterers. *Journal of Family Psychology, 9,* 227–248.

Guerney, B. (1977). *Relationship enhancement.* San Francisco, CA: Jossey-Bass.

Gurman, A. S., & Kniskern, D. P. (1992). The future of marital and family therapy. *Psychotherapy, 29,* 65–71.

Hampson, R. B., Beavers, W. R., & Hulgus, Y. (1990). Cross-ethnic family differences: Interactional assessment of white, black, and Mexican-American families. *Journal of Marital and Family Therapy, 16,* 307–319.

Harris, F. (1992, June 17). Black fathers: Finding families. *USA Today,* 13A.

Hawley, E. (1993, September/October). Managed care. *Family Therapy Networker, 17,* 64–67.

Huber, C. H. (1995a). Community family counseling. *The Family Journal, 3,* 331–334.

Huber, C. H. (1995b). Counselor responsibility within managed mental health care. *The Family Journal, 3,* 42–44.

Hutchins, J. (1995a, December). Barrett calls for MFT mediation for false memory families. *Family Therapy News, 26,* 21.

Hutchins, J. (1995b, December). Industry downsizing, increased provider risk, and niche marketing are trends, say experts. *Family Therapy News, 26,* 15.

Hutchins, J. (1996, April). Beyond office sharing: Starting a group practice. *Family Therapy News, 27,* 7, 22.

Johnson, M. E., Fortman, J. B., & Brems, C. (1993). *Between two people: Exercises toward intimacy.* Alexandria, VA: American Counseling Association.

Keeney, B. (1983). *The aesthetics of change.* New York: Guilford.

Krauth, L. D. (1995, December). Single parent families: The risk to children. *Family Therapy News, 26*(6), 14.

Kuehl, B. P. (1996). The use of genograms with solution-based and narrative therapies. *The Family Journal, 4,* 5–11.

Levitan, S. A., & Conway, E. A. (1990). *Families in flux.* Washington, DC: Bureau of National Affairs.

Liddle, H. A. (1991). Empirical values and the culture of family therapy. *Journal of Marital and Family Therapy, 17,* 327–348.

McLaughlin, I. G., Leonard, K. E., & Senchak, M. (1992). Prevalence and distribution of premarital aggression among couples applying for a marriage license. *Journal of Family Violence, 7,* 309–319.

Mace, D, (1987). Three ways of helping married couples. *Journal of Marital and Family Therapy, 13,* 179–186.

Mace, D., & Mace, V. (1977). *How to have a happy marriage: A step-by-step guide to an enriched relationship.* Nashville, TN: Abingdon.

MacKinnon, L. K., & Miller, D. (1987). The new epistemology and the Milan approach: Feminist and sociopolitical considerations. *Journal of Marital and Family Therapy, 13,* 139–155.

Madanes, C. (1990). *Sex, love, and violence.* New York: Norton.

May, K. M. (1994, Winter). Gay and lesbian families. *The Family Digest, 7,* 1, 3.

Melville, K. (1992). *The health care crisis: Containing costs, expanding coverage.* Dubuque, IA: Kendall/Hunt Publishing Co.

Minuchin, S., & Fishman, H. (1981). *Family therapy techniques.* Cambridge, MA: Harvard University Press.

Montalvo, B., & Thompson, R. F. (1988, July/August). Conflicts in the caregiving family. *Family Therapy Networker, 12,* 30–35.

Nelson, T. S., Heilbrun, G., & Figley, C. R. (1993). Basic family therapy skills, IV: Transgenerational theories of family therapy. *Journal of Marital and Family Therapy, 19,* 253–266.

Nichols, M. (1987, March/April). The individual in the system. *Family Therapy Networker, 11,* 32–38, 85.

Nichols, M. P., & Schwartz, R. C. (1995). *Family therapy: Concepts and methods* (3rd ed.). Boston: Allyn & Bacon.

Nicola, J. S. (1980). *Career and family roles of dual-career couples: Women in academia and their husbands.* Ann Arbor, MI: University Microfilms International.

O'Malley, P. (1995, December). Confidentiality in the electronic age. *Family Therapy News, 26,* 8.

Parks, B. (1995, December). Automating your practice. *Family Therapy News, 26,* 9–10, 13.

Patten, J. (1992, October). Gay and lesbian families. *Family Therapy News, 23,* 10, 34.

Paul, N. L., & Paul, B. B. (1982). Death and changes in sexual behavior. In F. Walsh (Ed.), *Normal family processes* (pp. 229–250). New York: Guilford.

Peterson, K. S., & Painter, K. (1993, August 27). New findings on vicious wife beaters. *USA Today,* D4.

Popenoe, D. (1993, April 14). Scholars should worry about the disintegration of the American family. *Chronicle of Higher Education, XXXIX,* A48.

Rapoport, R., & Rapoport, R. N. (1969). The dual-career family. *Human Relations, 22,* 3–30.

Rapoport, R., & Rapoport, R. N. (1971). *Dual-career families.* Middlesex, England: Penguin.

Satir, V. (1987). The therapist story. *Journal of Psychotherapy and the Family, 3,* 17–25.

Schnittger, M. H., & Bird, G. W. (1990). Coping among dual-career men and women across the family life cycle. *Family Relations, 39,* 199–205.

Shapiro, L. (1993, April 19). Rush to judgment. *Newsweek,* 54–60.

Sherman, R., & Fredman, N. (1986). *Handbook of structured techniques in marriage and family therapy.* New York: Brunner/Mazel.

Shulins, N. (1992, June 27). Baby-boomers are waking up to childlessness. *Winston-Salem Journal, 14,* 17.

Schwartz, R. C., & Breunlin, D. (1983, July/August). Why clinicians should bother with research. *Family Therapy Networker, 7,* 22–27, 57–59.

Smith, R. L., & Stevens-Smith, P. (1992). Future projections for marriage and family counseling and therapy. In R. L. Smith & P. Stevens-Smith (Eds.), *Family counseling and therapy* (pp. 435–440). Ann Arbor, MI: ERIC/CAPS.

Snead, E. (1993, July 13). Lesbians in the limelight. *USA Today,* D1, D2.

Stanton, M. D., Todd, T. C., & Associates. (1982). *The family therapy of drug abuse and addiction.* New York: Guilford.

Stoltz-Loike, M. (1992). *Dual-career couples.* Alexandria, VA: American Counseling Association.

Storm, C. L. (1991). Placing gender at the heart of MFT masters programs: Teaching a gender sensitive systemic view. *Journal of Marital and Family Therapy, 17,* 45–52.

Thomas, V. G. (1990). Determinants of global life happiness and marital happiness in dual-career black couples. *Family Relations, 39,* 174–178.

Tomes, H. (1996, August). Are we in denial about child abuse? *APA Monitor, 27,* 55.

U. S. Conference of Mayors. (1993). *A status report on hunger and homelessness in America's cities: A 26-city survey.* Washington, DC: Author.

Usdansky, M. L. (1992, July 17). Wedded to the single life. *USA Today,* 8A.

Usdansky, M. L. (1993a, April 12). Gay couples, by the numbers. *USA Today,* 8A.

Usdansky, M. L. (1993b, July 14). Many women in 30s won't have kids. *USA Today,* 8A.

Van Amburg, S. M., Barber, C. E., & Zimmerman, T. S. (1996). Aging and family therapy: Prevalence of aging issues and later family life concerns in marital and family therapy literature (1986-1993). *Journal of Marital and Family Therapy, 22,* 195–203.

Walters, M., Carter, B., Papp, P., & Silverstein, O. (1988). *The invisible web.* New York: Guilford.

Walz, G. R. (1991). Nine trends which will affect the future of the United States. In G. R. Walz, G. M. Gazda, & B. Shertzer (Eds.), *Counseling futures* (pp. 61–70). Ann Arbor, MI: ERIC/CAPS.

West, J. D., & Bubenzer, D. L. (1993). Cloe Madanes: Reflections on family therapy. *The Family Journal, 1,* 98–106.

Wetchler, J. L., & Piercy, F. P. (1986). The marital/family life of the family therapist: Stressors and enhancers. *American Journal of Family Therapy, 14,* 99–108.

Wilcoxon, S. A., Walker, M. R., & Hovestadt, A. J. (1989). Counselor effectiveness and family-of-origin experiences: A significant relationship? *Counseling and Values, 33,* 225–229.

Wynne, L. C. (1986). Search and research: Inquiry as a mission for the AFTA. *American Family Therapy Association Newsletter, 23,* 6–7.

A P P E N D I X   A

AAMFT Code of Ethics

This Code is published by:
American Association for Marriage and Family Therapy
1133 15th Street NW
Suite 300
Washington, DC 20005-2710
202 / 452-0109
The Board of Directors of the American Association for Marriage and Family Therapy (AAMFT) hereby promulgates, pursuant to Article 2, Section 2.013 of the Association's Bylaws, the Revised AAMFT Code of Ethics, effective August 1, 1991.

The AAMFT Code of Ethics is binding on Members of AAMFT in all membership categories, AAMFT Approved Supervisors, and applicants for membership and the

Approved Supervisor designation (hereafter, AAMFT Member).

If an AAMFT Member resigns in anticipation of, or during the course of, an ethics investigation, the Ethics Committee will complete its investigation. Any publication of action taken by the Association will include the fact that the Member attempted to resign during the investigation.

Marriage and family therapists are strongly encouraged to report alleged unethical behavior of colleagues to appropriate professional associations and state regulatory bodies.

1. Responsibility to Clients

Marriage and family therapists advance the welfare of families and individuals. They respect the rights of those persons seeking their assistance, and make reasonable efforts to ensure that their services are used appropriately.

1.1 Marriage and family therapists do not discriminate against or refuse professional service to anyone on the basis of race, gender, religion, national origin, or sexual orientation.

1.2 Marriage and family therapists are aware of their influential position with respect to clients, and they avoid exploiting the trust and dependency of such persons. Therapists, therefore, make every effort to avoid dual relationships with clients that could impair professional judgment or increase the risk of exploitation. When a dual relationship cannot be avoided, therapists take appropriate professional precautions to ensure judgment is not impaired and no exploitation occurs. Examples of such dual relationships include, but are not limited to, business or close personal relationships with clients. Sexual intimacy with clients is prohibited. Sexual intimacy with former clients for two years following the termination of therapy is prohibited.

1.3   Marriage and family therapists do not use their professional relationships with clients to further their own interests.

1.4   Marriage and family therapists respect the right of clients to make decisions and help them to understand the consequences of these decisions. Therapists clearly advise a client that a decision on marital status is the responsibility of the client.

1.5   Marriage and family therapists continue therapeutic relationships only so long as it is reasonably clear that clients are benefiting from the relationship.

1.6   Marriage and family therapists assist persons in obtaining other therapeutic services if the therapist is unable or unwilling, for appropriate reasons, to provide professional help.

1.7   Marriage and family therapists do not abandon or neglect clients in treatment without making reasonable arrangements for the continuation of such treatment.

1.8   Marriage and family therapists obtain written informed consent from clients before videotaping, audiorecording, or permitting third party observation.

2. Confidentiality

Marriage and family therapists have unique confidentiality concerns because the client in a therapeutic relationship may be more than one person. Therapists respect and guard confidences of each individual client.

2.1   Marriage and family therapists may not disclose client confidences except: (a) as mandated by law; (b) to prevent a clear and immediate danger to a person or persons; (c) where the therapist is a defendant in a civil, criminal, or disciplinary action arising from the therapy (in which case client confidences may be disclosed only in the course of that action); or (d) if there is a waiver previously obtained in writing, and then such information may be revealed only in accordance with the terms of the waiver. In circumstances where more than one person in a family receives therapy, each such family member who is legally competent to execute a waiver must agree to the waiver required by subparagraph (d). Without such a waiver from each family member legally competent to execute a waiver, a therapist cannot disclose information received from any family member.

2.2   Marriage and family therapists use client and/or clinical materials in teaching, writing, and public presentations only if a written waiver has been obtained in accordance with Subprinciple 2.1(d), or when appropriate steps have been taken to protect client identity and confidentiality.

2.3   Marriage and family therapists store or dispose of client records in ways that maintain confidentiality.

3. Professional Competence and Integrity

Marriage and family therapists maintain high standards of professional competence and integrity.

3.1   Marriage and family therapists are in violation of this Code and subject to termination of membership or other appropriate action if they: (a) are convicted of any felony; (b) are convicted of a misdemeanor related to their qualifications or functions; (c) engage in conduct which could lead to conviction of a felony, or a misdemeanor related to their qualifications or functions; (d) are expelled from or disciplined by other professional organizations; (e) have their licenses or certificates suspended or revoked or are otherwise disciplined by regulatory bodies; (f) are no longer competent to practice marriage and family therapy because they are impaired due to physical or mental causes or the abuse of alcohol or other substances; or (g) fail to cooperate with the Association at any point from the inception of an ethical complaint through the completion of all proceedings regarding that complaint.

3.2 Marriage and family therapists seek appropriate professional assistance for their personal problems or conflicts that may impair work performance or clinical judgment.

3.3 Marriage and family therapists, as teachers, supervisors, and researchers, are dedicated to high standards of scholarship and present accurate information.

3.4 Marriage and family therapists remain abreast of new developments in family therapy knowledge and practice through educational activities.

3.5 Marriage and family therapists do not engage in sexual or other harassment or exploitation of clients, students, trainees, supervisees, employees, colleagues, research subjects, or actual or potential witnesses or complainants in investigations and ethical proceedings.

3.6 Marriage and family therapists do not diagnose, treat, or advise on problems outside the recognized boundaries of their competence.

3.7 Marriage and family therapists make efforts to prevent the distortion or misuse of their clinical and research findings.

3.8 Marriage and family therapists, because of their ability to influence and alter the lives of others, exercise special care when making public their professional recommen-

dations and opinions through testimony or other public statements.

4. Responsibility to Students, Employees, and Supervisees

Marriage and family therapists do not exploit the trust and dependency of students, employees, and supervisees.

4.1 Marriage and family therapists are aware of their influential position with respect to students, employees, and supervisees, and they avoid exploiting the trust and dependency of such persons. Therapists, therefore, make every effort to avoid dual relationships that could impair professional judgment or increase the risk of exploitation. When a dual relationship cannot be avoided, therapists take appropriate professional precautions to ensure judgment is not impaired and no exploitation occurs. Examples of such dual relationships include, but are not limited to, business or close personal relationships with students, employees, or supervisees. Provision of therapy to students, employees, or supervisees is prohibited. Sexual intimacy with students or supervisees is prohibited.

4.2 Marriage and family therapists do not permit students, employees, or supervisees to perform or to hold themselves out as competent to perform professional services beyond their training, level of experience, and competence.

4.3 Marriage and family therapists do not disclose supervisee confidences except: (a) as mandated by law; (b) to prevent a clear and immediate danger to a person or persons; (c) where the therapist is a defendant in a civil, criminal, or disciplinary action arising from the supervision (in which case supervisee confidences may be disclosed only in the course of that action); (d) in educational or training settings where there are multiple supervisors, and then only to other professional colleagues who share responsibility for the training of the supervisee; or (e) if there is a waiver previously obtained in writing, and then such information may be revealed only in accordance with the terms of the waiver.

5. Responsibility to Research Participants

Investigators respect the dignity and protect the welfare of participants in research and are aware of federal and state laws and regulations and professional standards governing the conduct of research.

5.1   Investigators are responsible for making careful examinations of ethical acceptability in planning studies. To the extent that services to research participants may be compromised by participation in research, investigators seek the ethical advice of qualified professionals not directly involved in the investigation and observe safeguards to protect the rights of research participants.

5.2   Investigators requesting participants' involvement in research inform them of all aspects of the research that might reasonably be expected to influence willingness to participate. Investigators are especially sensitive to the possibility of diminished consent when participants are also receiving clinical services, have impairments which limit understanding and/or communication, or when participants are children.

5.3   Investigators respect participants' freedom to decline participation in or to withdraw from a research study at any time. This obligation requires special thought and consideration when investigators or other members of the research team are in positions of authority or influence over participants. Marriage and family therapists, therefore, make every effort to avoid dual relationships with research participants that could impair professional judgment or increase the risk of exploitation.

5.4   Information obtained about a research participant during the course of an investigation is confidential unless there is a waiver previously obtained in writing. When the possibility exists that others, including family members, may obtain access to such information, this possibility, together with the plan for protecting confidentiality, is explained as part of the procedure for obtaining informed consent.

6. Responsibility to the Profession

Marriage and family therapists respect the rights and responsibilities of professional colleagues and participate in activities which advance the goals of the profession.

6.1   Marriage and family therapists remain accountable to the standards of the profession when acting as members or employees of organizations.

6.2   Marriage and family therapists assign publication credit to those who have contributed to a publication in proportion to their contributions and in accordance with customary professional publication practices.

6.3   Marriage and family therapists who are the authors of books or other materials that are published or distributed cite persons to whom credit for original ideas is due.

6.4   Marriage and family therapists who are the authors of books or other materials published or distributed by an organization take reasonable precautions to ensure that the organization promotes and advertises the materials accurately and factually.

6.5   Marriage and family therapists participate in activities that contribute to a better community and society, including devoting a portion of their professional activity to services for which there is little or no financial return.

6.6   Marriage and family therapists are concerned with developing laws and regulations pertaining to marriage and family therapy that serve the public interest, and with altering such laws and regulations that are not in the public interest.

6.7   Marriage and family therapists encourage public participation in the design and delivery of professional services and in the regulation of practitioners.

7. Financial Arrangements

Marriage and family therapists make financial arrangements with clients, third party payors, and supervisees that are reasonably understandable and conform to accepted professional practices.

7.1 Marriage and family therapists do not offer or accept payment for referrals.

7.2 Marriage and family therapists do not charge excessive fees for services.

7.3 Marriage and family therapists disclose their fees to clients and supervisees at the beginning of services.

7.4 Marriage and family therapists represent facts truthfully to clients, third party payors, and supervisees regarding services rendered.

8. Advertising

Marriage and family therapists engage in appropriate informational activities, including those that enable laypersons to choose professional services on an informed basis.

General Advertising

8.1 Marriage and family therapists accurately represent their competence, education, training, and experience relevant to their practice of marriage and family therapy.

8.2 Marriage and family therapists assure that advertisements and publications in any media (such as directories, announcements, business cards, newspapers, radio, television, and facsimiles) convey information that is necessary for the public to make an appropriate selection of professional services. Information could include: (a) office information, such as name, address, telephone number, credit card acceptability, fees, languages spoken, and office hours; (b) appropriate degrees, state licensure and/or certification, and AAMFT Clinical Member status; and (c)

description of practice. (For requirements for advertising under the AAMFT name, logo, and/or the abbreviated initials, AAMFT, see Subprinciple 8.15, below).

8.3 Marriage and family therapists do not use a name which could mislead the public concerning the identity, responsibility, source, and status of those practicing under that name and do not hold themselves out as being partners or associates of a firm if they are not.

8.4 Marriage and family therapists do not use any professional identification (such as a business card, office sign, letterhead, or telephone or association directory listing) if it includes a statement or claim that is false, fraudulent, misleading, or deceptive. A statement is false, fraudulent, misleading, or deceptive if it (a) contains a material misrepresentation of fact; (b) fails to state any material fact necessary to make the statement, in light of all circumstances, not misleading; or (c) is intended to or is likely to create an unjustified expectation.

8.5 Marriage and family therapists correct, wherever possible, false, misleading, or inaccurate information and representations made by others concerning the therapist's qualifications, services, or products.

8.6 Marriage and family therapists make certain that the qualifications of persons in their employ are represented in a manner that is not false, misleading, or deceptive.

8.7 Marriage and family therapists may represent themselves as specializing within a limited area of marriage and family therapy, but only if they have the education and supervised experience in settings which meet recognized professional standards to practice in that specialty area.

Advertising Using AAMFT Designations

8.8 The AAMFT designations of Clinical Member, Approved Supervisor, and Fellow may be used in public information or advertising materials only by persons holding such designations. Persons holding such designations may, for example, advertise in the following manner:

• *Jane Doe, Ph.D., a Clinical Member of the American Association for Marriage and Family Therapy.*

Alternately, the advertisement could read:

Jane Doe, Ph.D., AAMFT Clinical Member.

• *John Doe, Ph.D., an Approved Supervisor of the American Association for Marriage and Family Therapy.*

Alternately, the advertisement could read:

John Doe, Ph.D., AAMFT Approved Supervisor.

• *Jane Doe, Ph.D., a Fellow of the American Association for Marriage and Family Therapy.*

Alternately, the advertisement could read:

Jane Doe, Ph.D., AAMFT Fellow.

More than one designation may be used if held by the AAMFT Member.

8.9   Marriage and family therapists who hold the AAMFT Approved Supervisor or the Fellow designation may not represent the designation as an advanced clinical status.

8.10   Student, Associate, and Affiliate Members may not use their AAMFT membership status in public information or advertising materials. Such listings on professional resumes are not considered advertisements.

8.11   Persons applying for AAMFT membership may not list their application status on any resume or advertisement.

8.12   In conjunction with their AAMFT membership, marriage and family therapists

claim as evidence of educational qualifications only those degrees (a) from regionally accredited institutions or (b) from institutions recognized by states which license or certify marriage and family therapists, but only if such state regulation is recognized by AAMFT.

8.13   Marriage and family therapists may not use the initials, AAMFT, following their name in the manner of an academic degree.

8.14   Marriage and family therapists may not use the AAMFT name, logo, and/or the abbreviated initials, AAMFT, or make any other such representation which would imply that they speak for or represent the Association. The Association is the sole owner of its name, logo, and the abbreviated initials, AAMFT. Its committees and divisions, operating as such, may use the name, logo, and/or the abbreviated initials, AAMFT, in accordance with AAMFT policies.

8.15   Authorized advertisements of Clinical Members under the AAMFT name, logo, and/or the abbreviated initials, AAMFT, may include the following: the Clinical Member's name, degree, license or certificate held when required by state law, name of business, address, and telephone number. If a business is listed, it must follow, not precede the Clinical Member's name. Such listings may not include AAMFT offices held by the Clinical Member, nor any specializations, since such a listing under the AAMFT name, logo, and/or abbreviated initials, AAMFT, would imply that this specialization has been credentialed by AAMFT.

8.16   Marriage and family therapists use their membership in AAMFT only in connection with their clinical and professional activities.

8.17   Only AAMFT divisions and programs accredited by the AAMFT Commission on Accreditation for Marriage and Family Therapy Education, not businesses nor organizations, may use any AAMFT-related designation or affiliation in public information or advertising materials, and then only in accordance with AAMFT policies.

8.18   Programs accredited by the AAMFT Commission on Accreditation for Marriage and Family Therapy Education may not use the AAMFT name, logo, and/or the abbreviated initials, AAMFT. Instead, they may have printed on their stationery and other appropriate materials a statement such as:

The (name of program) *of the* (name of institution) *is accredited by the AAMFT Commission on Accreditation for Marriage and Family Therapy Education.*

8.19   Programs not accredited by the AAMFT Commission on Accreditation for Marriage and Family Therapy Education may not use the AAMFT name, logo, and/or the abbreviated initials, AAMFT. They may not state in printed program materials, program advertisements, and student advisement that their courses and training opportunities are accepted by AAMFT to meet AAMFT membership requirements.

A P P E N D I X B

Ethical Code for the International Association of Marriage and Family Counselors

Preamble

The IAMFC (The International Association of Marriage and Family Counselors) is an organization dedicated to advancing the practice, training, and research of marriage and family counselors. Members may specialize in areas such as: premarital counseling, intergenerational counseling, separation and divorce counseling, relocation counseling, custody assessment and implementation, single parenting, stepfamilies, nontraditional family and marriage life-styles, healthy and dysfunctional family systems, multicultural marriage and family concerns, displaced and homeless families, interfaith and interracial families, and dual career couples. In conducting their professional activities, members commit themselves to protect and advocate for the healthy growth and development of the family as a whole, even as they conscientiously recognize the integrity and diversity of each family and family member's unique needs, situations, sta-

Reprinted from *The Family Journal*, Vol. 1, January 1993, pp. 73–77. © ACA. Reprinted with permissions. No further reproduction authorized without written permission of the American Counseling Association.

tus, and member's unique needs, situations, status, and condition. The IAMFC member recognizes that the relationship between the provider and consumer of services is characterized as an egalitarian process emphasizing co-participation, co-equality, co-authority, co-responsibility, and client empowerment.

This code of ethics promulgates a framework for ethical practice by IAMFC members and is divided into eight sections: client well-being, confidentiality, competence, assessment, private practice, research and publications, supervision, and media and public statements. The ideas presented within these eight areas are meant to supplement the ethical standards of the American Counseling Association (ACA), formerly the American Association for Counseling and Development (AACD), and all members should know and keep to the standards of our parent organization. Although an ethical code cannot anticipate every possible situation or dilemma, the IAMFC ethical guidelines can aid members in ensuring the welfare and dignity of the couples and families they have contact with, as well as assisting in the implementation of the Hippocratic mandate for healers: Do no harm.

Section I: Client Well-Being

A.   Members demonstrate a caring, empathetic, respectful, fair, and active concern for family well-being. They promote client safety, security, and place-of-belonging in family, community, and society. Due to the risk involved, members should not use intrusive interventions without a sound theoretical rationale and having thoroughly thought through the potential ramifications to the family and its members.

B.   Members recognize that each family is unique. They respect the diversity of personal attributes and do not stereotype or force families into prescribed attitudes, roles, or behaviors.

C.   Members respect the autonomy of the families that they work with. They do not make decisions that rightfully belong to family members.

D.   Members respect cultural diversity. They do not discriminate on the bases of race, sex, disability, religion, age, sexual orientation, cultural background, national origin, marital status, or political affiliation.

E.   Members strive for an egalitarian relationship with clients by openly and conscientiously sharing information, opinions, perceptions, processes of decision making, strategies of problem solving, and understanding of human behavior.

F.   Members pursue a just relationship that acknowledges, respects, and informs clients of their rights, obligations, and expectations as a consumer of services, as well as the rights, obligations, and expectations of the provider(s) of services. Members inform clients (in writing if feasible) about the goals and purpose of the counseling, the qualifications of the counselor(s), the scope and limits of confidentiality, potential risks and benefits associated with the counseling process and with specific counseling techniques, reasonable expectations for the outcomes and dura-

tion of counseling, costs of services, and appropriate alternatives to counseling.

G.   Members strive for a humanistic relationship that assists clients to develop a philosophy of meaning, purpose, and direction of life and living that promotes a positive regard of self, of family, of different and diverse others, and of the importance of humane concern for the community, nation, and the world at large.

H.   Members promote primary prevention. They pursue the development of clients' cognitive, moral, social, emotional, spiritual, physical, educational, and career needs, as well as parenting, marriage, and family living skills, in order to prevent future problems.

I.   Members have an obligation to determine and inform all persons involved who their primary client is—i.e., is the counselor's primary obligation to the individual, the family, a third party, or an institution? When there is a conflict of interest between the needs of the client and counselor's employing institution, the member works to clarify his or her commitment to all parties. Members recognize that the acceptance of employment implies that they are in agreement with the agency's policies and practices, and so monitor their place of employment to make sure that the environment is conducive to the positive growth and development of clients. If, after utilizing appropriate institutional channels for change, the member finds that the agency is not working toward the well-being of clients, the member has an obligation to terminate his or her institutional affiliation.

J.   Members do not harass, exploit, coerce, engage in dual relationships, or have sexual contact with any current or former client or family member to whom they have provided professional services.

K.   Members have an obligation to withdraw from a counseling relationship if the continuation of services is not in the best interest of the client or would result in a violation of ethical standards. If a client feels that the counseling relationship is no longer productive, the member has an obligation to assist in finding alternative services.

L.   Members maintain accurate and up-to-date records. They make all file information available to clients unless the sharing of such information would be damaging to the status, goals, growth, or development of the client.

M.   Members have the responsibility to confront unethical behavior conducted by other counselors. The first step should be to discuss the violation directly with the counselor. If the problem continues, the member should first use procedures established by the employing institution and then those of the IAMFC. Members may wish to also contact any appropriate licensure or certification board. Members may contact the IAMFC executive director, president, executive board members, or chair of the ethics committee at any time for consultation on remedying ethical violations.

Section II: Confidentiality

A.   Clients have the right to expect that information shared with the counselor will not be disclosed to others and, in the absence of any law to the contrary, the communications between clients and marriage and family counselors should be viewed as privileged. The fact that a contact was made with a counselor is to be considered just as confidential as the information shared during that contact. Information obtained from a client can only be disclosed to a third party under the following conditions.

1. The client consents to disclosure by a signed waiver. The client must fully understand the nature of the disclosure (i.e., give informed consent), and only information described in the waiver may be disclosed. If more than one person is receiving counseling, each individual who

is legally competent to execute a waiver must sign.

2. The client has placed him- or herself or someone else in clear imminent danger.

3. The law mandates disclosure.

4. The counselor is a defendant in a civil, criminal, or disciplinary action arising from professional activity.

5. The counselor needs to discuss a case for consultation or education purposes. These discussions should not reveal the identity of the client or any other unnecessary aspects of the case and should only be done with fellow counseling professionals who subscribe to the IAMFC ethical code. The consulting professional counselor has an obligation to keep all shared information confidential.

B.   All clients must be informed of the nature and limitations of confidentiality. They must also be informed of who may have access to their counseling records, as well as any information that may be released to other agencies or professionals for insurance reimbursement. These disclosures should be made both orally and in writing, whenever feasible.

C.   All client records should be stored in a way that ensures confidentiality. Written records should be kept in a locked drawer or cabinet and computerized record systems should use appropriate passwords and safeguards to prevent unauthorized entry.

D.   Clients must be informed if sessions are to be recorded on audio- or videotape and sign a consent form for doing so. When more than one person is receiving counseling, all persons who are legally competent must give informed consent in writing for the recording.

E.   Unless alternate arrangements have been agreed upon by all participants, statements made by a family member to the counselor during an individual counseling or consultation contact are to be treated as confidential and are not disclosed to other family members without the individual's permission. If a client's refusal to share information from individual contacts interferes with the agreed upon goals of counseling, the counselor may have to terminate treatment and refer the clients to another counselor.

Section III: Competence

A.   Members have the responsibility to develop and maintain basic skills in marriage and family counseling through graduate work, supervision, and peer review. An outline of these skills is provided by the Council for Accreditation of Counseling and Related Educational Programs (CACREP) *Environmental and Specialty Standards for Marriage and Family Counseling/Therapy*. The minimal level of training shall be considered a master's degree in a helping profession.

B.   Members recognize the need for keeping current with new developments in the field of marriage and family counseling. They pursue continuing education in forms such as books, journals, classes, workshops, conferences, and conventions.

C.   Members accurately represent their education, areas of expertise, training, and experience.

D.   Members do not attempt to diagnose or treat problems beyond the scope of their abilities and training.

E.   Members do not undertake any professional activity in which their personal problems might adversely affect their performance. Instead, they focus their energies on obtaining appropriate professional assistance to help them resolve the problem.

F.   Members do not engage in actions that violate the moral or legal standards of their community.

Section IV: Assessment

A.   Members utilize assessment procedures to promote the best interests and well-being of the client in clarifying concerns, establishing treatment goals, evaluating therapeutic progress, and promoting objective decision making.

B.   Clients have the right to know the results, interpretation, and conclusions drawn from assessment interviews and instruments, as well as how this information will be used.

C.   Members utilize assessment methods that are reliable, valid, and germane to the goals of the client. When using computer-assisted scoring, members obtain empirical evidence for the reliability of the methods and procedures used.

D.   Members do not use inventories and tests that have outdated test items or normative data.

E.   Members do not use assessment methods that are outside the scope of their qualifications, training, or statutory limitations. Members using tests or inventories have a thorough understanding of measurement concepts.

F.   Members read the manual before using a published instrument. They become knowledgeable about the purpose of the instrument and relevant psychometric and normative data.

G.   Members conducting custody evaluations recognize the potential impact that their reports can have on family members. As such, they are committed to a thorough assessment of both parents. Therefore, custody recommendations should not be made on the basis of information from only one parent. Members only use instruments that have demonstrated validity in custody evaluations and do not make recommendations based solely on test and inventory scores.

H.   Members strive to maintain the guidelines in the *Standards for Educational and Psychological Testing,* written in collaboration by the American Educational Research Association, American Psychological Association, and National Council on Measurement in Evaluation, as well as the *Code of Fair Testing Practices,* published by the Joint Committee on Testing Practices.

Section V: Private Practice

A. Members assist the profession and community by facilitating, whenever feasible, the availability of counseling services in private settings.

B. Due to the independent nature of their work, members in private practice recognize that they have a special obligation to act ethically and responsibly, keep up to date through continuing education, arrange consultation and supervision, and practice within the scope of their training and applicable laws.

C. Members in private practice provide a portion of their services at little or no cost as a service to the community. They also provide referral services for clients who will not be seen pro bono and who are unable to afford private services.

D. Members only enter into partnerships in which each member adheres to the ethical standards of their profession.

E. Members should not charge a fee for offering or accepting referrals.

Section VI: Research and Publications

A. Members shall be fully responsible for their choice of research topics and the methods used for investigation, analysis, and reporting. They must be particularly careful that findings do not appear misleading, that the research is planned to allow for the inclusion of alternative hypotheses, and that provision is made for discussion of the limitations of the study.

B. Members safeguard the privacy of their research participants. Data about an individual participant are not released unless the individual is informed about the exact nature of the information to be released and gives written permission for doing so.

C. Members safeguard the safety of their research participants. Members receive approval from, and follow guidelines of, any institutional research committee. Prospective participants are informed, in writing, about any potential danger associated with a study and are notified that they can withdraw at any time.

D. Members make their original data available to other researchers.

E. Members only take credit for research in which they make a substantial contribution, and give credit to all such contributors. Authors are listed from greatest to least amount of contribution.

F. Members do not plagiarize. Ideas or data that did not originate with the author(s) and are not common knowledge are clearly credited to the original source.

G. Members are aware of their obligation to be a role model for graduate students and other future researchers and so act in accordance with the highest standards possible while engaged in research.

Section VII: Supervision

A. Members who provide supervision acquire and maintain skills pertaining to the supervision process. They are able to demonstrate for supervisees the application of counseling theory and process to client issues. Supervisors are knowledgeable about different methods and conceptual approaches to supervision.

B. Members who provide supervision respect the inherent imbalance of power in the supervisory relationship. They do not use their potentially influential positions to exploit students, supervisees, or employees. Supervisors do not ask supervisees to engage in behaviors not directly related to the supervision process, and they clearly separate supervision and evaluation. Supervisors also avoid dual relationships that might impair their professional judgement or increase the possibility of exploitation. Sexual intimacy with students or supervisees is prohibited.

C.   Members who provide supervision are responsible for both the promotion of supervisee learning and development and the advancement of marriage and family counseling. Supervisors recruit students into professional organizations, educate students about professional ethics and standards, provide service to professional organizations, strive to educate new professionals, and work to improve professional practices.

D.   Members who provide supervision have the responsibility to inform students of the specific expectations surrounding skill building, knowledge acquisition, and the development of competencies. Members also provide ongoing and timely feedback to their supervisees.

E.   Members who provide supervision are responsible for protecting the rights and well-being of their supervisees' clients. They monitor their supervisees' counseling on an ongoing basis, and create procedures to protect the confidentiality of clients whose sessions have been electronically recorded.

F.   Members who provide supervision strive to reach and maintain the guidelines provided in the *Standards for Counseling Supervisors* published by the ACA Governing Council (cf. *Journal of Counseling & Development*, 1990, Vol. 69, pp. 30—32).

G.   Members who are counselor educators encourage their programs to reach and maintain the guidelines provided in the CACREP *Environmental and Specialty Standards for Marriage and Family Counseling/Therapy*.

Section VIII: Media and Public Statements

A.   Members accurately and objectively represent their professional qualifications, skills, and functions to the public. Membership in a professional organization is not to be used to suggest competency.

B.   Members have the responsibility to provide information to the public that enhances marriage and family life. Such statements should be based on sound, scientifically acceptable theories, techniques, and approaches. Due to the inability to complete a comprehensive assessment, and provide follow-up, members should not give specific advice to an individual through the media.

C.   The announcement or advertisement of professional services should focus on objective information that allows the client to make an informed decision. Providing information such as highest relevant academic degree earned, licenses or certifications, office hours, types of services offered, fee structure, and languages spoken can help clients decide whether the advertised services are appropriate for their needs. Members advertising a specialty within marriage and family counseling should provide evidence of training, education, and/or supervision in the area of specialization. Advertisements about workshops or seminars should contain a description of the audience for which the program is intended. Due to their subjective nature, statements either from clients or from the counselor about the uniqueness, effectiveness, or efficiency of services should be avoided. Announcements and advertisements should never contain false, misleading, or fraudulent statements.

D.   Members promoting psychology tapes, books, or other products for commercial sale make every effort to ensure that announcements and advertisements are presented in a professional and factual manner.

Reader's Note: Mary Allison, R. P. Ascano, Edward Beck, Stuart Bonnington, Joseph Hannon, David Kaplan (chair), Patrick McGrath, Judith Palais, Martin Ritchie, and Judy Ritterman are members of the IAMFC ethics committee who formulated the IAMFC code of ethics.

Glossary

absurdity statements that are half-truths and even silly if followed out to conclusion. Whitaker and symbolic-experiential family therapists often work with families by using absurdities.

abuse all forms of maltreatment within a family, whether physical, sexual, or emotional.

accommodation a process of joining in which the therapist makes personal adjustments in order to achieve a therapeutic alliance with a family.

adding cognitive constructions the verbal component of structural family therapy, which consists of advice, information, pragmatic fictions, and paradox.

administrative (regulatory) law specialized regulations that pertain to certain specialty areas that are passed by authorized government agencies, e.g., laws governing the use of federal land.

alignments the ways family members join together or oppose one another in carrying out a family activity.

anxiety mental and physical nervousness associated with pressure to please and fear of failure.

assertiveness asking for what one wants in a timely and appropriate manner.

assessment the administration of formal or informal tests or evaluation instrument(s) along with behavioral observations.

Avanta Network an association that carries on the interdisciplinary work of training therapists in Satir's methods.

baseline a recording of the occurrence of targeted behaviors before an intervention is made.

battle for initiative the struggle to get a family to become motivated to make needed changes.

battle for structure the struggle to establish the parameters under which family therapy is conducted.

behavioral family therapy an approach to treating families that focuses on dealing with behaviors directly in order to produce change. *See also* **cognitive-behavioral family therapy.**

binuclear family a term that describes two interrelated family households that comprise one family system, such as a remarried family.

blamer according to Satir, a person who attempts to place blame on others and not take responsibility for what is happening.

boundaries the physical and psychological factors that separate people from one another and organize them.

brief therapy an approach to working with families that has to do more with the clarity about what needs to be changed rather than time. A central principle of brief therapy is that one evaluates which solutions have so far been attempted and then tries new and different solutions to the family's problem, often the opposite of what has already been attempted.

caring days part of a behavioral marital procedure in which one or both marital partners act as if they care about their spouse regardless of the other's action(s). This technique embodies the idea of a "positive risk"—a unilateral action not dependent on another for success.

case law (court decisions) the type of law decided by decisions of courts at all levels from state to federal.

centrifugal literally, directed away from a center. It describes how people move away from their family (i.e., family disengagement).

centripetal literally, directed toward a center. It describes a tendency to move toward family closeness.

charting a procedure that involves asking clients to keep an accurate record of problematic behaviors. The idea is to get family members to establish a baseline from which interventions can be made and to show clients how the changes they are making work.

child custody evaluator a family therapist who acts on behalf of a court to determine what is in the best interest of a child in a custody arrangement.

choreography a process in which family members are asked to symbolically enact a pattern or a sequence in their relationship to one another. Choreography is similar to mime or a silent movie.

circular causality the idea that actions are a part of a causal chain, each influencing and being influenced by the other.

circular questioning a Milan technique of asking questions that focus attention on family connections and highlight differences among family members. Every question is framed so that it addresses differences in perception about events or relationships by various family members.

civil law that part of the law that pertains to acts offensive to individuals. Law involving family therapists mostly pertains to civil law—for example, divorce.

classical conditioning the oldest form of behaviorism, in which a stimulus that is originally neutral is paired up with another event to elicit certain emotions through association.

clear boundaries rules and habits that allow and encourage dialogue and thus help family members to enhance their communication and relationships with one another.

clue an intervention in deShazer's brief therapy approach that mirrors the usual behavior of a family. It is intended to alert a family to the idea that some of their present behavior will continue.

coaching a technique by which a therapist helps individuals, couples, or families make appropriate responses by giving them verbal instructions.

coalition an alliance between specific family members against a third member. *See also* **detouring coalition; stable coalition.**

cognitive-behavioral family therapy an approach to working with families that takes into account the impact of cognitions (i.e., thoughts) and behaviors families have incorporated into their lives.

common law law derived from tradition and usage.

communication stance an experiential family therapy procedure of Satir's in which family members are asked to exaggerate the physical positions of their perspective roles in order to help them "level." *See also* **leveling.**

communications theory an approach to working with families that focuses on clarifying verbal and nonverbal transactions among family members. Much communication theory work is incorporated in experiential and strategic family therapy.

complementarity the degree of harmony in the meshing of family roles.

complementary relationship relationships based on family member roles or characteristics that are specifically different from each other (e.g., dominant versus submissive, logical versus emotional). If a member fails to fulfill his or her role, such as be a decision maker or a nurturer, other members of the family are adversely affected.

compliment a written message used in brief family therapy designed to praise a family for its strengths and build a "yes set" within it. A compliment consists of a positive statement with which all members of a family can agree.

computer or **rational analyzer** according to Satir, a person who interacts only on a cognitive or intellectual level.

confidentiality the ethical duty to fulfill a contract or promise to clients that the information revealed during therapy will be protected from unauthorized disclosure.

confirmation of a family member a process that involves using a feeling word to reflect an expressed or unexpressed feeling of that family member or using a nonjudgmental description of the behavior of the individual.

confrontation a procedure through which the therapist points out to families how their behaviors contradict or conflict with their expressed wishes.

conjoint therapy the involvement of two or more members of a family in therapy together at the same time.

conjoint couple therapy (dual therapy) a form of therapy devised by Whitaker.

conjoint family drawing a procedure in which families are initially given the instruction: "Draw a picture as you see yourself as a family." Each member of the family makes such a drawing and then shares through discussion the perceptions that emerge.

constructivism a philosophy that states reality is a reflection of observation and experience, not an objective entity.

contingency contracting a procedure in which a specific, usually written, schedule or contract describes the terms for the trading or exchange of behaviors and reinforcers between two or more individuals. One action is contingent, or dependent, on another.

contract a formal agreement, often in writing, about what and when behavioral changes will be made. It is used when family interactions have reached a level of severe hostility. It contains built-in rewards for behaving in a certain manner.

court ordered witness the role a family therapist assumes when he or she must appear before a court to testify in behalf of or against a family or family member.

criminal law that part of the law that deals with acts offensive to society in general.

cross-generational alliance (coalition) an inappropriate family alliance that contains members of two different generations within it, for example, a parent and child collusion.

culturally encapsulated counselors professional therapists who treat everyone the same and, in so doing, ignore important differences.

culture the customary beliefs, social forms, and material traits of a racial, religious, or social group.

cybernetics a type of systemic interrelatedness governed by rules, sequences, and feedback. The term was introduced as a concept to family therapy by Gregory Bateson. *See also* **new epistemology.**

detouring coalition a coalition in which a pair holds a third family member responsible for their difficulties or conflicts with one another.

detriangulation the process of being in contact with others and, yet, emotionally separate.

developmental crises times of change in the life span, often accompanied by turmoil and new opportunity.

differentiation (of self) a level of maturity reached by an individual who can separate his or her rational and emotional selves. Differentiation is the opposite of fusion.

diffuse boundaries arrangements that do not allow enough separation between family members, resulting in some members becoming fused and dependent on other members.

DINKS an acronym meaning *double income, no kids.*

directive an instruction from a family therapist for a family to behave differently. A directive is to strategic therapy what the interpretation is to psychoanalysis—that is, the basic tool of the approach.

disengaged the state of being psychologically isolated from other family members.

disputing irrational thoughts a cognitive-behavioral strategy in which irrational beliefs about an event are challenged.

distancing the isolated separateness of family members from each other, either physically or psychologically.

distractor according to Satir, a person who relates by saying and doing irrelevant things.

double-bind the theory that states that two seemingly contradictory messages may exist at the same time on different levels and lead to confusion, if not schizophrenic behavior, on the part of an individual who cannot comment on or escape from the relationship in which this is occurring.

dual-career families those in which both marital partners are engaged in work that is developmental in sequence and to which they have a high commitment.

dual therapy (conjoint couple therapy) a form of therapy devised by Whitaker.

emotionally cut off a Bowen concept used to describe a family in which the members avoid each other, either physically or psychologically, because of an unresolved emotional attachment.

emotional deadness a condition that exists when individuals in families either are not aware of or suppress their emotions.

emotionally overinvolved *See* **fusion.**

empty nest a term that describes couples who have launched their children and are without childrearing responsibilities.

enactments the actions of families that show problematic behavioral sequences to therapists, for example, having an argument instead of talking about one.

enmeshment loss of autonomy due to overinvolvement of family members with each other, either physically or psychologically.

epistemology the study of knowledge.

equitability the proposition that everyone is entitled to have his or her welfare interests considered in a way that is fair from a multilateral perspective. Equitability is the basis for relationship ethics.

ESCAPE an acronym that stands for four major investments therapists must make: (1) **e**ngagement with families and process, (2) **s**ensitivity to **c**ulture, (3) **a**wareness of families' **p**otential, and (4) knowledge of the **e**nvironment.

ethics the moral principles from which individuals and social groups, such as families, determine rules for right conduct. Families and society are governed by relationship ethics.

experiential symbolic family therapy the approach to working with families created by Carl Whitaker.

expert witness the role assumed by a family therapist who is asked to give testimony in regard to the probable causes of certain negative behaviors and to make recommendations in regard to a family member (e.g., an uncontrollable juvenile) displaying these behaviors.

externalizing problems a method of treatment devised by White and Epston in which the problem becomes a separate entity outside of the family. Such a process helps families reduce their arguments about who owns the problem, form teams, and enter into dialogue about solving the problem.

extinction the process by which previous reinforcers of an action are withdrawn so that behavior returns to its original level. It involves the elimination of behavior.

family "a group of two or more persons related by birth, marriage, or adoption and residing together in a household" (*Statistical Abstracts of the United States*, 1991, p. 5).

family development and environmental fit a concept that states that some environments are conducive to helping families develop and resolve crises, and others are not.

family group therapy a treatment approach that conceptualizes family members as strangers in a group. Members become known to each other in stages similar to those found in groups.

family homeostasis the tendency of the family to remain in its same pattern of functioning and resist change unless challenged or forced to do otherwise.

family of origin the family a person was born or adopted into.

family life cycle developmental trends within the family over time.

family life fact chronology a tool employed in family reconstruction in which the "star" creates a listing of all significant events in his or her life and that of the extended family having an impact on the people in the family.

family map a visual representation of the structure of three generations of the "star's" family, with adjectives to describe each family member's personality.

family/divorce mediation the process of helping couples and families settle disputes or dissolve their marriages in a non-adversarial way.

family reconstruction a therapeutic innovation developed by Satir to help family members discover dysfunctional patterns in their lives stemming from their families of origin.

family rules the overt and covert rules families use to govern themselves, such as "you must only speak when spoken to."

feedback the reinsertion of results of past performances back into a system. Negative feedback maintains the system within limits; positive feedback signals a need to modify the system.

feminist family therapy an attitude and body of ideas, but not clinical techniques, concerning gender hierarchy and its impact on conducting family therapy. Feminists recognize the overriding importance of the power structure in any human system.

first-order change the process whereby a family that is unable to adjust to new circumstances often repetitiously tries the same solutions or intensifies nonproductive behaviors, thus assuring that the basic organization of the family does not change.

focus on exceptions a technique utilized by brief family therapists to help families realize that their symptoms are not always present and that they have some power in what they are presently doing to make changes.

four phases of sexual responsiveness excitement, plateau, orgasm, and resolution.

frame a perception or opinion that organizes one's interactions.

functional family therapy a type of behavioral family therapy that is basically systemic.

fusion the merging of intellectual and emotional functions together so that an individual does not have a clear sense of self and others. Fusion is the opposite of differentiation.

games a Milan concept that stresses how children and parents stabilize around disturbed behaviors in an attempt to benefit from them.

general systems theory *see* **systems theory.**

genogram a visual representation of a person's family tree depicted in geometric figures, lines, and words; originated by Bowen.

going home again a Bowen technique in which the family therapist instructs the individual or family members with whom he or she is working to return home in order to better get to know the family in which they grew up. By using this type of information, individuals can differentiate themselves more clearly.

good enough mother a mother who lets an infant feel loved and cared for and thereby helps the infant develop trust and a true sense of self.

Greek Chorus the observers/consultants of a family treatment session (i.e., the team) as they debate the merits of what a therapist is doing to bring about change. They send messages about the process to the therapist and family. Through this process, the family is helped to acknowledge and feel their ambivalence.

guide a family therapist who helps the star or explorer, during family reconstruction, chart a chronological account of family events that include significant events in the paternal and maternal families, and the family of origin.

health an interactive process associated with positive relationships and outcomes.

Hispanic or Latino a person born in any of the Spanish-speaking countries of the Americas (Latin America), Puerto Rico, or the United States who traces his or her ancestry to either Latin America or to Hispanic people from U.S. territories that were once Spanish or Mexican.

historical time the era in which people live. Historical times consist of forces that affect and shape humanity at a particular point in time, such as during an economic depression or a war.

home-based therapy a method of treatment that requires family therapists to spend time with families before attempting to help them.

homeostasis the tendency to resist change and keep things as they are, in a state of equilibrium.

horizontal stressors stressful events related to the present, some of which are developmental, such as life cycle transitions, and others of which are unpredictable, such as accidents.

hypothesizing a technique central to the Milan approach that involves a meeting of the treatment team before the arrival of a family in order to formulate and discuss aspects of the family's situation that may be generating a symptom. Through hypothesizing, team members prepare themselves for treating the family.

"I" statements statements that express feelings in a personal and responsible way that encourages others to express their opinions.

identified patient (IP) a family member who carries the family's symptoms.

individual time the span of life between one's birth and death. Notable individual achievements are often highlighted in this perspective, for example, when recognized as "teacher of the year."

Institute for Family Counseling an early intervention program at the Philadelphia Child Guidance Center for community paraprofessionals that proved to be highly effective in providing mental health services to the poor.

institutional barrier any hardship that minority populations must endure to receive mental health services, such as the inconvenient location of a clinic, the use of a language not spoken by one's family, and the lack of diversified practitioners.

intensity the structural method of changing maladaptive transactions by having the therapist use strong affect, repeated intervention, or prolonged pressure with a family.

interlocking pathology a term created by Ackerman to explain how families and certain of their members stay dysfunctional. In an interlocking pathology there is an unconscious process that takes place between family members that keeps them together.

invariant/variant prescription a specific kind of ritual given to parents with children who are psychotic or anorexic in an attempt to break up the family's **dirty game** (i.e., power struggle between generations sustained by symptomatic behaviors). An *invariant prescription* requires parents to unite so that children cannot manipulate them as "winners" or "losers" and thereby side with them. A *variant prescription* is given for the same purpose as an invariant one. The difference is that a variant prescription is tailored to a particular family and considers unique aspects of that family.

invisible loyalties unconscious commitments that grown children make to help their families of origin, especially their parents.

joining the process of "coupling" that occurs between the therapist and the family, leading to the development of the therapeutic system. A therapist meets, greets, and forms a bond with family members during the first session in a rapid but relaxed and authentic way and makes the family comfortable through social exchange with each member.

joint family scribble an experiential family therapy technique in which family members individually make a brief scribble. Then, the whole family incorporates their scribbles collectively into a unified picture.

law a body of rules recognized by a state or community as binding on its members.

legal the law or the state of being lawful.

leveling "congruent communication" in which straight, genuine, and real expression of one's feelings and wishes are made in an appropriate context.

linear causality the concept of cause and effect—that is, forces being seen as moving in one direction, with each action causing another. Linear causality can be seen in, for example, the firing of a gun.

logico scientific reasoning a way of thinking characterized by empiricism and logic.

long brief therapy another name for systemic family therapy. *Long brief therapy* refers to the length of time between sessions (usually a month) and the duration of treatment (up to a year).

malpractice the failure to fulfill the requisite standard of care either because of omission (what should have been done, but was not done) or commission (doing something that should not have been done). In either case, negligence must be proved.

managed health care a wide range of techniques and structures that are connected with obtaining and paying for medical care, including therapy. The most common are preferred provider organizations (PPOs) and health maintenance organizations (HMOs).

mapping in brief therapy, the sketching out of a course of successful intervention; in structural family therapy, a mental process of envisioning how the family is organized.

marital schism overt marital conflict that is pathological.

marital skew a dysfunctional marriage in which one partner dominates the other.

marriage and family enrichment the concept that couples and families stay healthy or get healthier by actively participating in certain activities, usually in connection with other couples.

metacommunication the implied message within a message, typically conveyed nonverbally.

mimesis a way of joining in which the therapist becomes like the family in the manner or content of their communications—for example, when a therapist jokes with a jovial family.

miracle question a brief therapy technique in which a therapist poses a question such as, "If a miracle happened tonight and you woke up tomorrow and the problem was solved, what would you do differently?"

modeling observational learning.

multigenerational families households that include a child, a parent, and a grandparent.

multigenerational transmission process the passing on from generation to generation in families of coping strategies and patterns of coping with stress. In poorly differentiated persons, problems may result, including schizophrenia.

mystification the actions taken by some families to mask what is going on between family members, usually in the form of giving conflicting and contradictory explanations of events.

new epistemology the idea that the general systems approach of Bateson, sometimes referred to as cybernetics, must be incorporated in its truest sense into family therapy with an emphasis on "second-order cybernetics" (i.e., the cybernetics of cybernetics). Basically, such a view stresses the impact of the family therapist's inclusion and participation in family systems.

nonevent the nonmaterialization of an expected occurrence (e.g., the failure of a couple to have children).

nuclear family a core unit of husband, wife, and their children.

object relations theory a psychoanalytic way of explaining relationships across generations. According to this theory, human beings have a fundamental motivation to seek objects (i.e., people) in relationships, starting at birth.

object a significant other (e.g., a mother) with whom children form an interactional, emotional bond.

old epistemology   dated ideas that no longer fit a current situation.

old old   that group of individuals aged 75 to 84.

oldest old   that group of individuals aged 85 and over.

ontology   a view or perception of the world.

operant conditioning   a tenet of Skinner's behavioral theory that people learn, through rewards and punishments, how to respond to their environments.

ordeal   a technique in which a therapist assigns a family or family member(s) the task of performing a specific activity (i.e., an ordeal) any time the family or individuals involved display a symptom they are trying to eliminate. The ordeal is a constructive or neutral behavior (e.g., doing exercise), but disagreeable to the person directed to engage in it.

organism   a form of life composed of mutually dependent parts and processes standing in mutual interaction.

paradox   a form of treatment in which therapists give families permission to do what they were going to do anyway, thereby lowering family resistance to therapy and increasing the likelihood of change.

parallel relationships   relationships in which both complementary and symmetrical exchanges occur as appropriate.

parentified child   a child who is forced to give up childhood and act like a parent, even though lacking the knowledge and skills to do so.

parent-skills training   a behavioral model in which the therapist serves as a social learning educator whose prime responsibility is to change parents' responses to a child or children.

Parents Without Partners   a national organization that helps single parents and their children deal with the realities of single-parent family life in educational and experiential ways.

placater   according to Satir, a person who avoids conflict at the cost of his or her integrity.

positioning   acceptance and exaggeration by the therapist of what family members are saying. If conducted properly, it helps the family see the absurdity in what they are doing.

positive connotation   a type of reframing in which each family member's behavior is labeled as benevolent and motivated by good intentions.

positive reinforcer   a material (e.g., food, money, or medals) or a social action (e.g., a smile or praise) that individuals are willing to work for.

possibility therapy   another name for Bill O'Hanlon's solution-focused family therapy.

power   the ability to get something done. In families, power is related to both *authority* (the decision maker) and *responsibility* (the one who carries out the decision).

Premack principle   a behavioral intervention in which family members must first do less pleasant tasks before they are allowed to engage in pleasurable activities.

prescribing   a technique in which family members are instructed to enact a troublesome dysfunctional behavior in front of the therapist and to work it out past the point where they usually get stuck.

prescribing the symptom   a type of paradox in which family members are asked to continue doing as they have done. This technique makes families either admit they have control over a symptom or give it up.

pretend technique   a technique originated by Cloe Madanes in which the therapist asks family members to pretend to enact a troublesome behavior, such as having a fight. Through this procedure, individuals transform an involuntary action into one that is under their control.

primary rewards reinforcers that people will naturally work for, such as food.

privileged communication a client's legal right, guaranteed by statute, that confidences originating in a therapeutic relationship will be safeguarded.

process how information is handled in a family or in therapy.

professional self-disclosure statement a statement given to the family by the therapist that outlines treatment conditions related to who will be involved, what will be discussed, the length and frequency of sessions, and fees.

programmed workbooks for parents instrumental behavioral books parents may employ to help their children, and ultimately their families, modify behaviors.

pseudo-individuation/pseudo self a pretend self. This concept involves an attempt by young people who lack an identity and basic coping skills to act as if they had both.

pseudomutuality the facade of family harmony that many dysfunctional families display.

qualitative research research that is characterized by an emphasis on open-ended questions and the use of extended interviews with small numbers of individuals/families. Results are written up in an autobiographical form. This research is often used in theory building.

quantitative research research that is characterized by an emphasis on closed-ended questions and the use of large sample sizes to gather information. Data is gathered in a precise form, frequently using standardized instruments, and reported in a statistical format. Analyzed and deductive conclusions are made that

tend to "prove" or "disprove" theories and assertions.

quasi kin a formerly married person's ex-spouse, the ex-spouse's new husband or wife, and his or her blood kin.

quid pro quo literally, something for something.

reciprocity the likelihood that two people will reinforce each other at approximately equitable rates over time. Many marital behavior therapists view marriage as based on this principle.

redefining attributing positive connotations to symptomatic or troublesome actions. The idea is that symptoms have meaning for those who display them, whether such meaning is logical or not. Redefining is one way of lowering resistance.

redundancy principle the fact that a family interacts within a limited range of repetitive behavioral sequences.

reframing a process in which a perception is changed by explaining a situation from a different context. Reframing is the art of attributing different meaning to behavior.

reinforcer a consequence of an action that increases its likelihood of occurring again.

reliability the consistency or dependency of a measure.

remarried families families that consist of two adults and step-, adoptive, or foster children. Sometimes, they are referred to as *stepfamilies, reconstituted families, recoupled families, merged families,* and *blended families.*

research design the way a research study is set up. Five commonly used categories are (1) exploratory, (2) descriptive, (3) developmental, (4) experimental, and (5) correlational.

resistance anything a family does to oppose or impair progress in family therapy.

restraining telling the client family that they are incapable of doing anything other than what they are doing. The intent is to get them to show they can behave differently.

restructuring changing the structure of the family. The rationale behind restructuring is to make the family more functional by altering the existing hierarchy and interaction patterns.

rigid boundaries inflexible rules and habits that keep family members separated from each other.

rituals specialized types of directives that are meant to dramatize significant and positive family relationships or aspects of problem situations.

role playing procedures in which family members are asked to "act as if" they were the persons they ideally wanted to be. Members practice a number of behaviors to see which work best. Feedback is given and corrective actions are taken.

sample a limited number of families representative of an entire group of families.

sandwich generation couples who have adolescents and their aging parents to take care of and are squeezed psychologically and physically.

scapegoat a family member the family designates as the cause of its difficulties (i.e., the identified patient).

schism the division of the family into two antagonistic and competing groups.

sculpting an experiential family therapy technique in which family members are molded during the session into positions symbolizing their actual relationships to each other as seen by one or more members of the family.

second-order change a qualitatively different way of doing something; a basic change in function and/or structure.

second-order cybernetics the cybernetics of cybernetics, which stresses the impact of the family therapist's inclusion and participation in family systems.

shaping the process of learning in small gradual steps; often referred to as successive approximation.

shaping competence the procedure in which structural family therapists help families and family members become more functional by highlighting positive behaviors.

single-parent family families that include at least one parent who is biologically related to a child (or children) or who has assumed such a role through adoption. This parent is primarily alone in being responsible for taking care of self and a child (or children). Such families are created as a result of divorce, death, abandonment, unwed pregnancy, and adoption.

skeleton keys in deShazer's brief therapy approach, those interventions that have worked before and that have a universal application.

skew *see* **marital skew.**

social construction a philosophy based on the principle that family therapy includes the social context, or cultural context, of a family.

social exchange theory an approach that stresses the rewards and costs of relationships in family life according to a behavioral economy.

social learning theory a theory that stresses the importance of modeling and learning through observation as a primary way of acquiring new behaviors.

social time time characterized by landmark social events such as marriage, parenthood, and retirement. Family milestones are a central focus in social time.

societal regression the deterioration or decline of a society struggling against too many toxic forces (e.g., overpopulation and economic decline) countering the tendency to achieve differentiation.

splitting   viewing object representations as either all good or all bad. The result is a projection of good and bad qualities onto persons within one's environment. Through splitting, people are able to control their anxiety and even the objects (i.e., persons) within their environment by making them predictable.

squeeze technique   an approach used in sexual therapy in which a woman learns to stimulate and stop the ejaculation urge in a man through physically stroking and firmly grasping his penis.

stable coalition   a fixed and inflexible union (such as that of a mother and son) that becomes a dominant part of a family's everyday functioning.

"star" or "explorer"   a central character in family reconstruction who maps his or her family of origin in visually representative ways.

statutory law   that group of laws passed by legislative bodies, such as state and national legislatures, and signed by an authorized source, such as a governor or the president.

strategic therapy   a term coined by Jay Haley to describe the therapeutic work of Milton Erickson in which extreme attention was paid to details of client symptoms and the focus was to change behavior by manipulating it and not instilling insight.

stress inoculation   a process in which family members break down potentially stressful events into manageable units that they can think about and handle through problem-solving techniques. Units are then linked together so that possible events can be envisioned and handled appropriately.

structure   an invisible set of functional demands by which family members relate to each other.

structural family therapy's major thesis   a thesis stating that an individual's symptoms are best understood when examined in the context of family interactional patterns. A change in the family's organization or structure must take place before symptoms can be relieved.

subsystems   smaller units of the system as a whole, usually composed of members in a family who because of age or function are logically grouped together, such as parents. They exist to carry out various family tasks.

symbolic drawing of family life space   a projective technique in which the therapist draws a large circle and instructs family members to include within the circle everything that represents the family and to place outside of the circle those people and institutions not a part of the family. After this series of drawings, the family is asked to symbolically arrange themselves, through drawing, within a large circle, according to how they relate to one another.

symmetrical relationship   a relationship in which each partner tries to gain competence in doing necessary or needed tasks. Members within these units are versatile. For example, either a man or a woman can work outside the home or care for children.

system   a set of elements standing in interaction. Each element in the system is affected by whatever happens to any other element. Thus, the system is only as strong as its weakest part. Likewise, the system is greater than the sum of its parts.

systematic desensitization   a process in which a person's dysfunctional anxiety is reduced or eliminated through pairing it with incompatible behavior, such as muscular or mental relaxation. This procedure is gradual, with anxiety treated one step at a time.

systemic family therapy an approach, sometimes known as the Milan approach, that stresses the interconnectedness of family members as well as the importance of second-order change in families.

systems theory a theory, sometimes known as *general systems theory,* that focuses on the interconnectedness of elements within all living organisms, including the family. It is based on the work of Ludwig von Bertalanffy.

teasing technique a sexual therapy approach in which a woman learns how to start and stop sexually stimulating a man.

therapeutic neutrality accepting and nonjudgmental behavior by family therapists that keeps them from being drawn into family coalitions and disputes and gives them time to assess the dynamics within the family. Neutrality also encourages family members to generate solutions to their own concerns.

thought stopping a cognitive-behavioral technique in which family members are taught how to stop unproductive obsession about an event or person through overt and mental procedures.

time out a process that involves the removal of persons (most often children) from an environment in which they have been reinforced for certain actions. Isolation, or time out, from reinforcement for a limited amount of time (approximately 5 minutes) results in the cessation of the targeted behavior.

token economy a type of contract for earning points and reinforcing appropriate behavior, most often employed with children.

tracking a way of joining in which the therapist follows the content of the family (i.e., the facts).

transference the projection onto a therapist of feelings, attitudes, or desires.

triadic questioning asking a third family member how two other members of the family relate.

triangle the basic building block of any emotional system and the smallest stable relationship system in a family.

triangulating projecting interpersonal dyadic difficulties onto a third person or object (i.e., a scapegoat).

unbalancing therapeutically allying with a subsystem. In this procedure, the therapist supports an individual or subsystem against the rest of the family.

undifferentiated family ego mass according to Bowen, an emotional "stuck togetherness," or fusion, within a family.

validity the extent to which an instrument measures what it was intended to.

values the ranking of an ordered set of choices from the most to the least preferable. Basically, there are four domains of values: personal, family, political/social, and ultimate. Each has an impact on the other. Ethics is based on values.

variant prescription see **invariant/ variant prescription.**

verbalizing presuppositions an experiential technique in which a therapist helps a family take the first step toward change by talking of the hope that the family has.

vertical stressors events dealing with family patterns, myths, secrets, and legacies. These are stressors that are historical and that families inherit from previous generations.

wheel or circle of influence that circle of individuals who have been important to the star or explorer through family reconstruction.

young old that group of individuals aged 65 to 74.

Subject Index

Name Index